THE GUINNESS
WHO'S WHO OF
FOLK
MUSIC

General Editor: Colin Larkin

GUINNESS PUBLISHING

Dedicated to Sandy Denny

FIRST PUBLISHED IN 1993 BY
GUINNESS PUBLISHING LTD
33 LONDON ROAD, ENFIELD, MIDDLESEX EN2 6DJ, ENGLAND

GUINNESS IS A REGISTERED TRADEMARK OF GUINNESS PUBLISHING LTD

BRITISH LIBRARY CATALOGUING-IN-PUBLICATION DATA
A CATALOGUE RECORD FOR THIS BOOK IS AVAILABLE FROM THE BRITISH LIBRARY

ISBN 0-85112-741-X

CONCEIVED, DESIGNED, EDITED AND PRODUCED BY
SQUARE ONE BOOKS LTD
IRON BRIDGE HOUSE, 3 BRIDGE APPROACH, CHALK FARM, LONDON NW1 8BD
EDITOR AND DESIGNER: COLIN LARKIN
EDITORIAL AND PRODUCTION: SUSAN PIPE AND JOHN MARTLAND
SPECIAL THANKS: RICK CHRISTIAN, ALEX OGG, SIMON JONES, LYNDON NOON,
MICHAEL HUGHES AND FRANK WARREN
LOGO CONCEPT: DARREN PERRY

IMAGE SET BY L & S COMMUNICATIONS LTD

PRINTED AND BOUND IN GREAT BRITAIN BY THE BATH PRESS

EDITORS NOTE

The Guinness Who's Who Of Folk Music forms a part of the multi-volume Guinness Encyclopedia Of Popular Music. A further 16 specialist single volumes are planned in the near future.

Already available:
The Guinness Who's Who Of Indie And New Wave Music.
The Guinness Who's Who Of Heavy Metal,
The Guinness Who's Who Of Fifties Music.
The Guinness Who's Who Of Sixties Music.
The Guinness Who's Who Of Seventies Music.
The Guinness Who's Who Of Jazz.
The Guinness Who's Who Of Country Music.
The Guinness Who's Who Of Blues.
The Guinness Who's Who Of Soul.

To the casual observer, the folk genre is probably the most misunderstood of all forms of 20th Century popular music. As the century progressed, urban American folk blues came into its own as the blues. Country music developed in the 30s, and as I write it is the largest dollar grossing area of popular music. Both blues and country now stand on their own. So where does this leave the genre that gave birth to them? What remains of American folk is not merely Cajun and Bluegrass, mixed with the Carter Family, Pete Seeger, the Weavers, Woody Guthrie and the New Christy Minstrels. The passive growth of the post-war peace movement and civil rights in the 50s gave way to an explosion in the 60s as people became angry and indignant. Bob Dylan became the leading popular voice and together with artists such as Joan Baez and Tom Paxton they in turn spearheaded a generation of singer songwriters, performing folk-based music.
In Britain the folk movement was seen as a small cult of oddballs. The clichéd perception that folkies were either communist sympathizers or community groups gathering together round their local maypole singing 'derry derry down-o', has taken many years to live down. During the 50s skiffle briefly came and went. Only one giant emerged; Lonnie Donegan, who took American folk into the UK charts with regular and embarrassing ease. Dylan was also a major figure in the growth of British folk. Both Alex Campbell and Ewan MacColl, although vital to the movement, needed the impetus that the likes of Dylan and Baez inspired. Bert Jansch, John Renbourne, Dave Swarbrick and Martin Carthy became sought after in the clubs. Younger upstarts such as Davey Graham.John Martyn and Ralph McTell joined the throng.
However, it was left to one band to redefine the perception of what folk was, what it could include and where it would go. The pivotal Fairport Convention honed American folk/rock (Byrds, Dylan and Joni Mitchell) and sailed into uncharted waters with albums such as Unhalfbricking and Liege And Lief. One ex-Fairport member is Richard Thompson, who has since become one of the leading contemporary songwriters of his generation in addition to his place as a guitar hero.
Whilst we cannot ignore other important artists such as Pentangle, the Incredible String Band and Steeleye Span, it is the Fairports that are saluted. More than 25 years on since their debut, the folk movement is stronger than ever. Thanks are largely due to magazines such as Folk Roots who have helped in altering the perception of of the finger in the ear/real ale folkie. It's editor Ian A. Anderson shared the stage with many of the previous acts as a musician, and he is better qualified than most to help position folk and roots music into a broader and more international package. The Guinness Who's Who Of Folk Music will follow this healthy cosmopolitan direction in future editions. For now we have attempted to include artists that convey the flavour of the folk movement from Britain and America. Any selection is subjective but I hope the reader can see why the occasional inclusion of names such as the Lovin' Spoonful, the Band, the Pogues and the Men They Couldn't Hang is necessary. Powerful and committed artists such as Dick Gaughan stand shoulder to shoulder with the

Seekers, as the Tansads share space with Judy Collins. In selecting entries for this single volume we have attempted to include as many artists as space would allow. Further suggestions and additions for the next edition will be considered by writing to the editor.

In the preparation of this work contributions were received from Peter Doggett, Brian Hogg, Colin Larkin, Spencer Leigh, John Martland, Johnny Rogan, Jeff Tamarkin, Hugh T. Wilson, Tony Burke, Alan Clayson, Dave Laing, Dave McAleer, Alex Ogg, Steve Smith and John Tobler.

Special thanks go to our specialist contributors: Rick Christian, himself a performing folk artist, researched and worked on the majority of the entries. Valuable last minute help arrived in the shape of Simon Jones. The book is all the better for his suggestions and late entries. He enlisted Lyndon Noon and Michael Hughes at short notice. Finally to Frank Warren who supplied the final entry, a subject close to his heart, Cajun and Zydeco.

Photographic acknowledgements: To Tony Gale of Pictorial Press Ltd, London, who has an amazing photographic archive of many original items. He supplied over half of the material. The remaining photographs were supplied by Lynda Morrison, after frantic phone calls to the omnipresent father to us all, John Tobler. Thanks to him also for reminding me just how good John Prine is.

Eternal thanks to John Martland who joined us at a late stage and had to work on a subject that was far removed from Frank Sinatra. And finally to the cool, calm and sickeningly correct Susan Pipe for putting it all together.

Colin Larkin, July 1993

A

Abrahams, Doris

b. New York, USA. This singer/songwriter was influenced by both Bob Dylan and Pete Seeger. She visited the Greenwich Village clubs, both to play and watch performers such as Richie Havens and Dave Van Ronk. Although she started out playing a style of folk and country, this quickly evolved into a mixture of blues, ragtime and country, sprinkled with her own compositions. During the early 70s, Abrahams had a vocal backing group, called the Sleazettes, made up of Ellie Greenberg and Maria Muldaur, and they performed at the Philadelphia Folk Festival in 1972. Abrahams continued to play the college circuit and the folk clubs of her native north east, occasionally backed by Larry Packer (fiddle), Fred Holman (bass), Allen Friedman (guitar), and with Ellie Greenberg supplying the vocals.
Album: *Labor Of Love* (1976).

Accrington, Stanley

b. Mike Bray, 7 August 1951, Wyken, Coventry, Warwickshire, England. Despite having written songs throughout the 70s, Accrington did not perform in public until August 1979, at a folk club in Stalybridge, Lancashire. There followed a build up of folk club and other bookings, through the 80s. Stanley completed two short tours of the USA in 1987 and 1988, and played the Hong Kong festival in 1988. With the advent of more radio appearances and the attendant work rate, Accrington, (who was the last station master at Rochdale station), gave up his job on the railways to commit himself fully to a musical career. His songs, although amusing, often have a message, but he has written a number of non-humorous songs, such as the excellent 'Lesley', a protest song written about Sellafield Nuclear Power Station. 'The Last Train Has Gone', was a nostalgic look at the demise of the railways. Using a variety of props in his live act, Stanley has built a solid reputation on the folk scene. He is a humorous and hard working comedian, and a serious songwriter who cares deeply about people and social issues.
Albums: *Sick As A Parrot* (1981), *Over The Ball* (1982), *Offside Trap* (1983), *Game Of Two Halves* (1984), *Cynical Foul* (1986), *Yellow Card* (1988), *Just Another Game* (1989), *90 Minutes-Live* (1990), *Home Banker* (1991). Compilation: *Slow Action Replay* (1985).
Further reading: *Book Of Anagrams*, 1990.

Adams, Derroll

b. Derroll Lewis Thompson, 1925, Portland, Oregon, USA. This singer-songwriter played guitar, harmonica and banjo. Adams has had a number of his songs covered by other artists, including Joan Baez. 'Portland Town' is one such number. Adams' natural father had been a vaudeville juggler, and like him, enjoyed telling stories. While only 16 years old, he lied about his age, and joined the army in 1942, but was given a discharge a few months later. Within the year, he had joined the coast guard. Upon leaving, he settled on a number of projects, including enrolling at art school. He heard Josh White at a concert, and continued to be hooked on the records he listened to, by artists such as Pete Seeger, Woody Guthrie and Cisco Houston. Adopting the banjo as his instrument, Adams performed at meetings for Henry Wallace, of the Progressive Party. Following a variety of jobs, including being a truck driver for Max Factor, and a number of marriages, Derroll was 'discovered' and sang at concerts with an organization called World Folk Artists, which also represented Odetta and Guy Carawan. Adams played banjo on the soundtrack of the western *Durango* in 1957. Not long afterwards 'Portland Town' was written, a brief vignette of birth, life and death. Adams was invited, by 'Ramblin' Jack Elliott and his wife, to come to England and for a while was sharing accommodation with Lionel Bart and Alex Campbell. After recording for Topic Records, Adams and the Elliotts travelled to Europe and sang in the streets. They actually recorded in Milan, but shortly afterwards split up. Adams, having moved back to Paris, married for the fourth time, moved to Belgium, and gave up playing professionally, in order to help with his wife's exclusive decorating business. He had become disillusioned with playing to drunken audiences, and on a number of occasions, smashed his banjo in anger and frustration. Subsequently, his business and marriage failed. The fact that other performers were singing his songs meant that people were hearing of Derroll Adams, many for the first time, and this enabled him to play folk clubs. Adams was quite condemning of the attitude of folk 'purists', saying that he did not believe that a 500-year-old song should necessarily be sung in its original form. He was also banned by a number of folk clubs because of his swearing on stage. A 65th birthday tribute, featured artists such as Allan Taylor, Wizz Jones, various former members of Pentangle, Happy Traum, and former colleague Elliott.
Albums: with Jack Elliott *The Rambling Boys* (1957), *Portland Town* (c.50s), with Elliott *Roll On Buddy* (1957), *Feelin' Fine* (c.70s), *Songs Of The Banjoman* (1984), *Derroll Adams' 65th Birthday Concert* (1991).

Albion Country Band

This volatile traditional folk ensemble was founded in April 1972 by defecting Steeleye Span bassist Ashley Hutchings (b. 26 January 1945, Southgate, Middlesex, England). Royston Wood (b. 1935; vocals), Sue Draheim (b. August, 1949, Oakland, California, USA; fiddle) and Steve Ashley (guitar) completed the new venture alongside Simon Nicol (b. 13 October 1950, Muswell Hill, London, England; guitar) and Dave Mattacks (b. 13 March 1948, Edgware, Middlesex, England; drums), two of Hutchings former colleagues from Fairport Convention. This early line-up disintegrated six months after its inception and a caretaker unit, which included Richard Thompson, fulfilled all outstanding obligations. Hutchings, Nicol and new drummer Roger Swallow then pieced together a second Country Band with folk acolytes, Martin Carthy, Sue Harris and John Kirkpatrick, but this innovative sextet was also doomed to a premature demise. Their lone album, *Battle Of The Field*, was withheld until 1976 and only issued following public demand. Hutchings, Nicol and Mattacks were reunited in the Etchingham Steam Band, a part-time outfit formed to support folksinger Shirley Collins. The group subsequently evolved into the Albion Dance Band, a large-scale, highly flexible unit which recorded a series of collections evocative of 'merrie England' and enjoyed considerable acclaim for their contributions to several theatrical productions.

The group entered the 80s as the Albion Band and although musicians continued to arrive and depart with alarming regularity, Ashley Hutchings has remained at the helm, ensuring their dogged individuality.

Albums: as the Albion Country Band *Battle Of The Sun* (1976), as the Albion Dance Band *The Prospect Before Us* (1977), as the Albion Band *Rise Up Like The Sun* (1978), *Lark Rise To Candleford* (1983), *Light Shining* (1984), *Shuffle Off* (1984), *Under The Rose* (1984), *A Christmas Present* (1988), *Battle Of The Field* (1989), *Give Me A Saddle And I'll Trade You A Car* (1989).

Almanac Singers

This influential folk group was formed in 1940 by Pete Seeger, Lee Hayes and Millard Lampell. Taking their name from 'The Farmer's Almanac', the trio recorded a debut album prior to the arrival of a fourth member, Woody Guthrie, in June 1941. Two further collections financed a trip across the USA, during which the new line-up performed in factories and union halls. Hays and Lampell temporarily dropped out of the group on reaching Los Angeles but Seeger and Guthrie worked their way back to New York. Here they established the first of several Almanac Houses which served as co-operatives for committed local singers. Among those drawn into the circle were Cisco Houston, Sis Cunningham and Butch Hawes. The Almanac Singers officially broke up in 1942 when several members joined the armed forces. Guthrie worked in the short-lived Headline Singers with Leadbelly, Brownie McGhee and Sonny Terry before forging a prolific solo career, while Seeger and Hayes would later form the highly successful Weavers.

Albums: *Talking Union* (c.40s), *Sod Buster Ballads* (c.40s), *The Soil And The Sea* (c.40s) and *Dear Mr. President* (c.40s).

Altan

This Irish traditional group, in the mould of De Danann, has achieved popularity on its own merits. The line-up of Frankie Kennedy (b. 30 September 1955, Belfast, Northern Ireland; flute), Mairéad Ni Mhaonaigh (b. 26 July 1959, Donegal, Eire; vocals/fiddle), Ciarán Curran (b. 14 June 1955, Enniskillen, Co. Fermanagh, Northern Ireland; bouzouki), Dáithi Sproule (b. 23 May 1950, Co. Derry, Northern Ireland; guitar/vocals), and Ciarán Tourish (b. 27 May 1967, Buncrana, Co. Donegal, Eire; fiddle), has built a strong following both in Britain, and in the USA, where they first toured in 1988. The group was formed in 1987, after the release of *Altan*. At that point the group was ostensibly Frankie and Mairéad, who were married in 1981, but the others were playing on the recording and a more permanent arrangement was made. Their repertoire comes largely from Co. Donegal, and due to the area's historical links with Scotland, the music has absorbed influences from both Irish and Scottish sources. Two other members of the group, who appear occasionally, are Paul O'Shaughnessy (b. 9 June 1961, Dublin, Eire; fiddle), and Mark Kelly (b. 15 March 1961, Dublin, Eire; guitar). Altan now regularly tour the USA and Europe, and have made frequent festival appearances.

Albums: *Altan* (1987), *Horse With A Heart* (1989), *The Red Crow* (1990), *Harvest Storm* (1992).

Amazing Blondel

Formed in 1969 by John Gladwin (vocals/guitar/woodwind) and Terry Wincott (vocals/guitar/percussion), former members of Lincolnshire rock group, Methuselah. The duo completed their debut album with the assistance of session guitarist 'Big' Jim Sullivan, before switching labels from Bell Records to Island. Edward Baird (guitar/lute) joined the group in April 1970 as they honed a peculiarly English direction, embracing the music of the Elizabethan and Tudor periods. *Evensong* and *Fantasia Lindum* reflected this interest, although the trio also acquired an unsavoury reputation for a stage act that offset their scholarly music with 'off-colour' jokes. Gladwin left the group following the release of *England 72*, and the 'Amazing' prefix was then dropped from their name. Wincott and Baird continued to record throughout the 70s, augmented by a series of well-known musicians including Steve Winwood, Mick Ralphs and several members of Free, a group that had proved instrumental in introducing Blondel to Island. William Murray (drums) and Mick Feat (guitar) joined the duo for *Mulgrave Street*, their first release for DJM Records, but the unit's popularity withered in the wake of this rockier perspective. Wincott was the sole remaining original member to appear on *Live In Tokyo*, after which Blondel was dissolved.

Albums: *The Amazing Blondel And A Few Faces* (1970), *Evensong* (1970), *Fantasia Lindum* (1971), *England 72* (1972), *Blondel* (1973), *Mulgrave Street* (1974), *Inspiration* (1975), *Bad Dreams* (1976), *Live In Tokyo* (1977). Compilation: *Mulgrave Street/Inspiration* (c.70s).

Amazing Mr. Smith

b. Derek Smith, 1 April 1948, Croydon, Surrey, England. This humorous performer began playing folk clubs, accompanying himself on guitar. He then joined a series of folk groups during the 60s, until joining Wild Oats in 1970. He compensated for his weak voice by singing silly songs and using elaborate props in his stage act, such as performing with his head inside a bird-cage! After dubbing himself the Amazing Mr. Smith, he secured wider bookings. Still playing folk clubs, he also performs at theatres, arts centres and on the alternative cabaret circuit. Smith has made appearances on UK television's *Game For A Laugh* and Chris Tarrant's *Prove It*. He also released his first video, *The Atmosphere Without The Smoke,* in 1991. He remains a very popular and highly original club and festival act.

Albums: *Two Very Similar Views Of Mr. Smith* (1981), *Normal Service Will Be Resumed As Soon As Possible (*1983).

Andersen, Eric

b. 14 February 1943, Pittsburgh, Pennsylvania, USA. Anderson arrived in New York in 1964 and was quickly absorbed into the Greenwich Village folk circle. His debut album, *Today Is The Highway*, was released the following year, but it was a second collection, *'Bout Changes And Things*, which established the artist's reputation as an incisive songwriter. This particular collection featured 'Violets Of Dawn' and 'Thirsty Boots', compositions which were recorded by several artists including the Blues Project and Judy Collins. Andersen embraced folk-rock in an unconventional way when an electric backing was added to this second album and issued as *'Bout Changes And Things Take 2*. He formed a publishing company and published the *Eric Anderson Songbook* to considerable success. Later releases, including *More*

Eric Andersen (centre)

Alistair Anderson

Hits From Tin Can Alley and *Avalanche* showed a gift for both melody and inventiveness, facets the singer maintained on his 70s recordings. His romanticism was best heard on *Blue River*, an under-rated 1973 collection, but subsequent releases are of equal merit.

Selected albums: *Today Is The Highway* (1965), *'Bout Changes And Things* (1966) *'Bout Changes And Things Take 2* (1967), *More Hits From Tin Can Alley* (1968), *A Country Dream* (1968), *Avalanche* (1969), *Eric Andersen* (1970), *Blue River* (1973), *Be True To You* (1975), *Sweet Surprise* (c.70s), *The Best Songs* (1977), *Stage* (c.70s). Compilation: *Best Of Eric Andersen* (1988).

Anderson, Alistair

b. 18 March 1948, Wallsend, Tyne and Wear, England, and regarded by many as the country's finest squeezebox player. Anderson also plays concertina and Northumbrian pipes, and is a fine interpreter of traditional dance tunes of England, Ireland and Scotland. He has produced a number of fine albums and many critics rate *Steel Skies* as his finest recording. He has appeared on other records, most notably with the High Level Ranters, for whom he was a member during the 60s and 70s. The other members of the group were Tom Gilfellon (b. Durham, England; guitar), Johnny Handle (b. John Alan Pandrich, 15 March 1935, Wallsend On Tyne, Newcastle, England; accordion/piano/vocals), and Colin Ross (fiddle). It was with the High Level Ranters that Anderson visited the USA in 1971. He also toured America in 1974, appearing at both the Philadelphia and Fox Hollow folk festivals. In addition to organizing concertina workshops, and performing in a solo capacity, Anderson formed Syncopace which made its recording debut in 1991 with *Syncopace*. In addition to Anderson, the line-up features Penny Callow (cello), Ian Carr (guitar), Martin Dunn (flute/whistle/piccolo) and Chuck Fleming (fiddle/mandolin).

Albums: *Alistair Anderson Plays English Concertina* (1972), *High Level* (1972), *A Mile To Ride* (1973), *Concertina Workshop* (1974), *Traditional Tunes* (1977), *Corby Crag* (1978), *Dookin' For Apples* (1979), *Steel Skies* (1981), *The Grand Chain* (1987), *Syncopace* (1991). With the High Level Ranters: *Northumberland Forever* (1968), *The Lads Of Northumbria* (1969), *Keep Your Feet Still, Geordie Hinnie* (1970), *High Level* (c.70s), *A Mile To Ride* (c.70s), *A Miner's Life* (c.70s).

Anderson, Ian A.

b. 26 July 1947, Weston-Super-Mare, Somerset, England. Anderson specialized in the bottleneck and slide style of guitar playing. Having dabbled in a local R&B band while still at school, he started playing in a number of folk and blues clubs in the Bristol area between 1966 and 1968. About the same time, he recorded a number of EPs for Saydisc, as part of the trio Anderson, Jones, Jackson. He provided two tracks on the *Blues Like Showers* compilation album, which received attention from BBC disc jockeys John Peel and Mike Raven. As a result of the 1968 blues boom, Anderson started touring nationally, along with other acoustic blues players such as Mike Cooper and Jo Ann Kelly. He recorded *The Inverted World* with Mike Cooper for his own Matchbox label. Shortly after, he formed Ian Anderson's Country Blues Band, releasing the much neglected classic *Stereo Death Breakdown* for Liberty. From then, until 1973, Anderson worked mainly solo, still releasing albums, and including mostly self-composed material. From 1970, with the release of *Royal York Crescent*, on his own Village Thing label, he started to use the name Ian A. Anderson to avoid confusion with the leader of Jethro Tull. In 1973, Anderson formed Hot Vultures with his then wife Maggie Holland. From then on they phased out most of his previous self-written works, in favour of concentrating on an original English approach to American blues/old-time/traditional/R&B material. As Hot Vultures, they toured Britain, Europe and the USA from 1973-80, releasing three albums in the process. By the time of *Up The Line*, (on Plant Life Records), Anderson and Holland had begun to work with musicians more involved in English country dance music. Thus was born the English Country Blues Band, which included Rod Stradling (melodeon), and either Sue Harris (hammer dulcimer/oboe), or Chris Coe (hammer dulcimer). The group eventually gained John Maxwell (drums). A side project developed from this, namely Tiger Moth, an electric dance band, which had added Jon Moore (guitar) to the line-up. Tiger Moth gradually took precedence over the former set up, until disbanding in 1990. Prior to this, in 1982, Anderson had founded Rogue Records. The same year, he founded the Farnham Folk Day, now an annual one-day festival. Despite the break-up, Tiger Moth do play occasionally for one-off events and recording projects with other musicians, this time with their feet planted firmly in the roots music camp, as Orchestre Super Moth. In addition, Ian has presented series for various radio stations; from 1988 he has presented the BBC World Service series now called *Folk Routes*, whilst on London's Jazz FM he now presents a weekly World Music show *World Routes*. After editorial work for the largely regional *Southern Rag* magazine, he set up and edits the national publication *Folk Roots* which specializes in roots/folk/world music. *Folk Roots* is

Harvey Andrews

now the clear leader in its field and has done much to change people's perception of 'folk' music. Through the magazine Anderson has given a platform to Ethnic music, World music and Blues and has demonstrated their common linkage.

Albums: *Book Of Changes* (1969), *Royal York Crescent* (1970), *A Vulture Is Not A Bird You Can Trust* (1971), *Singer Sleeps On As Blaze Rages* (1972), with Mike Cooper *The Inverted World* (1968), *The Continuous Preaching Blues* (1984). Ian Anderson's Country Blues Band: *Stereo Death Breakdown* (1969). Hot Vultures: *Carrion On* (1975), *The East Street Shakes* (1977), *Up The Line* (1979). Compilation: *Vulturama* (1983). English Country Blues Band: *No Rules* (1982), *Home And Deranged* (1984), *Unruly* (1993). Tiger Moth: *Tiger Moth* (1984), *Howling Moth* (1988), Orchestre Super Moth: *The World At Sixes And Sevens* (1989).

Anderson, Pinkney (Pink)

b. 12 February 1900, Laurens, South Carolina, USA, d. 12 October 1974, Spartanburg, South Carolina, USA. For much of his life, Anderson was Spartanburg's most famous songster and medicine show huckster. He was 10 when he first learned to play the guitar in open tuning from Joe Wicks. He also earned money as a buck dancer on the streets of Laurens. In 1917 he joined 'Doctor' W.R. Kerr's medicine show, learning every facet of the calling and staying, with Peg Leg Sam as his straight man, until it ceased in 1945. When not on the road, he partnered Simmie Dooley, a blind guitarist from whom he learned to tune his guitar and play chords. In 1928 the pair recorded four titles for Columbia in Atlanta. One of the songs, 'Every Day In In The Week', also featured on a May 1950 session, recorded while Anderson was performing at the State Fair in Charlottesville, and released in conjunction with titles by another Laurens musician, Blind Gary Davis. Anderson continued to work the medicine shows, teaming up with Baby Tate, until heart trouble forced his retirement in 1957. In 1961 he recorded three albums for Bluesville, each with a theme, blues, medicine show songs and folk ballads. Gradually deteriorating health prevented him from working. An album project for Trix, begun in 1970 was never realised. Selected albums: *Carolina Blues Man* (1962), *Medicine Show Man* (1962), *Ballad And Folksinger* (1963).

Andrews, Harvey

b. 7 May 1943, Birmingham, England. Harvey has been a singer since childhood, and discovered American folk music at college. He first sang at the Jug O' Punch Folk Club, run by the Ian Campbell Folk Group, in 1964, and later became a resident performer. Andrews' first professional gig was at Stratford-upon-Avon Folk Club in 1964. The following year Andrews became the first person to record a Paul Simon song. He sang 'A Most Peculiar Man' for an EP on Transatlantic that he recorded with Martin Carthy. Andrews left his teaching job in 1968, and collaborated with a number of other writers on topical, romantic and social protest songs. The early 70s saw a breakthrough with appearances at the Cambridge Folk Festival in 1970 and 1971, followed by the release of *Writer Of Songs* in 1972, on Cube Records. The album contained the highly-acclaimed 'The Soldier', and the contrastingly beautiful, 'Boothferry Bridge'. *Writer Of Songs* was also notable for the wide range of musicians involved on the recording. Ralph McTell, Cozy Powell, and Rick Wakeman were among the credits. Other singers, such as Mary Hopkin, Christy Moore and Colin Scott started to record Harvey Andrews songs. In 1973, Andrews appeared, at the Queen Elizabeth Hall, London and, the same year, went on national and European tours with Focus. For a time, during the mid-to-late 70s, Andrews was performing and recording with guitarist Graham Cooper, with whom he recorded *Fantasies From A Corner Seat*. In 1975, Andrews featured on the BBC television series *The Camera And The Song*. In 1980, he started a period of extended convalescence following a serious car accident. Andrews started Beeswing Records in 1982. In 1985, he sang the theme tune to the television series *Golden Pennies*. *Someday* featured Pete Wingfield and included Andrews' tribute to Tony Hancock 'Mr. Homburg Hat', and 'Song For Phil Ochs'. Andrews remains important in an era when the singer-songwriter genre has undergone many changes and has recorded beautiful melodies around often telling lyrics, such as 'First You Lose The Rhyming', and 'Cheeky Young Lad' from *PG*. *25...Years On The Road* was released to celebrate his 25 year career as a professional performer, but instead of the usual re-packaging of old songs, Andrews re-recorded some of the most popular numbers from his live repertoire featuring just vocal and guitar.

Albums: *Faces And Places* (1970), *Writer Of Songs* (1972), *Friends Of Mine* (1973), with Graham Cooper *Fantasies From A Corner Seat* (1975), *Someday* (1976), *Margarita* (1980), live *Brand New Day* (1980), *Old Mother Earth* (1986), *PG* (1988), *25...Years On The Road* (1989).

Ar Braz, Dan

Breton guitarist, Ar Braz learned his trade alongside Alan Stivell in the high flying days of 70s electric folk, on albums such as *From Celtic Roots* (1974). He

joined an abortive Fairport Convention in 1976 - his photograph appeared on *Gottle O'Geer*, even though he didn't. Moving to Brittany, he recorded a series of acclaimed albums for the French label Hexagone. Although his band had its roots in folk music, they switched to a rock style on their cover of Lennon and McCartney's 'Rain'. By 1985, Ar Braz had switched to a Celtic guitar style for *Music For The Silences To Come*, a beautiful, mellow, folk mood album. Although based in Brittany, he tours England every year. Recent albums, gently electrified, have been recorded at Dave Pegg's Woodworm studio, Oxford. Ar Braz plays frequently at Fairport's Cropredy reunions.
Albums: *Douar Nevez Terre Nouvelle* (1977), *Allez Dire A La Ville* (1978), *The Earth's Lament* (1979), *Acoustic* (1983), *Music For The Silences To Come* (1985), *Septembre Bleu* (1988), *Songs* (1990), *Borders Of Salt* (1991).

Ar Log

This Welsh group, whose name means 'On Hire', have achieved considerable popularity outside their own borders. The group was formed in 1976, initially as a 'scratch' band to play at the Lorient Festival in France. The current line-up comprises Gwyndaf Roberts (b. 1 February 1954, Bangor, Gwynedd, Wales; knee harp/clarsach harp/bass/vocals), Dafydd Roberts (b. 6 December 1956, Aberystwyth, Dyfed, Wales; triple harp/flutes/vocals), Geraint Glynne Davies (b. 10 August 1953, Llanrwst, Colwyn Bay, Gwynedd, Wales; guitar/vocals), Stephen Rees (b. 20 February 1963, Rhydaman, Carmarthen, Dyfed, Wales; accordion/violin/whistles/keyboards/vocals), and Iolo Jones (b. 12 February 1955, Plymouth, Devon, England; violin/ vocals). Jones, one of the founder members, actually left the group in 1978, and re-joined them in 1984. Ar Log have toured the UK, Europe and both North and South America. The group were invited to perform during the Papal Mass at Cardiff in 1982, and in 1985, made their first trip to South America. The group's 1982 release *Meillionen* (The Clover), was an album of dance tunes. In 1985, Ar Log, along with many Welsh folk and rock artists, recorded a single 'Dwylo Dros Y Mor' along the lines of Band Aid. They made a return trip to South America, in 1987, and toured Chile, Peru, Ecuador, and Colombia. They have achieved world status, by putting Welsh folk music on the international map.
Albums: *Ar Log* (1978), *Ar Log ii* (1981), *Celtic Folk Festival* (1981), *Ar Log iii* (1982), with Dafydd Iwan *Rhwng Hwyl A Thaith* (1982), *Meillionen* (1982), with Dafydd Iwan *Yma O Hyd* (1983), *Ar Log iv* (1984), *Ar Log v* (1988).

Armstrong, Frankie

b. 13 January 1941, Workington, Cumbria, England. Armstrong possesses one of the strongest interpretive voices on the folk circuit. She began singing during the British folk revival of the early 60s, and later joined the Ceilidh Singers, a skiffle group. In 1965, Armstrong sang, at the Edinburgh Festival 'Poets In Public', with John Betjeman, Stevie Smith and Ted Hughes. She first recorded with A.L. Lloyd, Ewan MacColl, Peggy Seeger and the Critics Group during the 1965-66 period, and released her first all-women's record, *Female Frolic* in 1968. The album included Peggy Seeger and Sandra Kerr. Despite working regularly in clubs and at festivals, she continued in her profession as a social/youth worker. Many of her songs reflect this background, and cover a wide variety of social issues, on subjects such as nuclear disarmament and women's rights. Indeed, she has sung at campaigns for many of these issues since the 60s. Armstrong has appeared in both the USA and Canada regularly since 1973, and has visited Europe on a regular basis. From 1975, she started to set up voice workshops, 'for singers and non-singers alike'. These have widened into International Workshop Festivals, in Britain, Ireland and Australia. At the same time, during the mid-to late 70s, Armstrong sang with a number of experimental folk/jazz fusion groups, such as the Mike Westbrook Band, Henry Cow, and Talisker. In 1985, she decided to give up her career in social work, in order to concentrate on singing and teaching voice. Armstrong still regularly gives concerts, at home and in Europe, North America and Australia, in addition to her involvement in community arts and theatre workshops. She also occasionally performs with Leon Rosselson and Roy Bailey, having spent six years working with them in the past as a regular trio. Armstrong has written numerous pieces for journals and books, and an autobiography is currently planned for publication in 1992. *Lovely On The Water*, on Topic, was her first solo release, and was a contrast to *Let No One Deceive You*, recorded with Dave Van Ronk, which contained some classic Brecht/Weill songs, including 'Mack The Knife'.
Albums: with A.L. Lloyd and Anne Briggs *The Bird And The Bush* (1966), with various artists *Female Frolic* (70s), *Lovely On The Water* (1972), *Out Of Love, Hope And Suffering* (1974), *Frankie Armstrong* (1975), *Songs And Ballads* (1975), *And The Music Plays So Grand* (70s), folk/jazz suite by Ken Hyder *Land Of Stone* (70s), *My Song Is My Own* (70s), with Dave Van Ronk *Let No One Deceive You - Songs Of Bertholt Brecht* (70s), *I Heard A Woman Singing* (70s), *And The Music Plays* (1981), *Nuclear Power* (1981), with Brian Pearson & Blowzabella *Tam Lin* (80s),

Ways Of Seeing (80s).
Further reading: *My Song Is My Own*, Kathy Henderson and Sandra Kerr.

Ashley, Steve

b. 9 March 1946, London, England. Ashley started playing in an art college blues band and singing in folk clubs. During the late 60s he took up songwriting while in the duo Tinderbox, with guitarist Dave Monday. In 1971, with a growing reputation as a singer-songwriter with an English traditional style, Ashley became one of the founder members of the Albion Country Band. Shortly afterwards, he was signed to Island Records, with his own band Ragged Robin. The following year he released his first solo album *Stroll On*; which *Folk Review* magazine awarded the title of Contemporary Folk Album of the Year. His second solo release, *Speedy Return*, was followed by an American deal with Motown, and a tour of the USA and Canada. Ashley also toured Europe, both solo and with his own band, until releasing *Family Album* with Fairport Convention members Dave Pegg, Bruce Rowland, and Simon Nicol. This line-up, together with fiddle player Chris Leslie, performed the 'Family Show' based around the album. In 1981, Steve made *Demo Tapes*, an anti-nuclear album for CND, and recorded a single with Monsignor Bruce Kent and Lord Noel-Baker. 1989 saw the re-release of *Stroll On*. His sixth album, *Mysterious Ways*, was released on Lighthouse Records, and again featured his own Steve Ashley Band with Dik Cadbury (b.

Richard Cadbury, 12 June 1950, Selly Oak, Birmingham, England; bass, ex-Decameron and Steve Hackett), Al Fenn (b. Alastair Fenn, 9 March 1947, Chingford, Essex, England; lead guitar, ex-Decameron and Magna Carta), Chris Leslie (b. 15 December 1956, Oxford, England; fiddle, also with Whippersnapper), Alleyn Menzies (drums), Steve Harper (trumpet), and Jim Sallis (trumpet). This line-up played at all the major UK folk festivals, including Glastonbury, Cambridge, and Cropredy. In 1991, Ashley wrote the music for the Anglia Television documentary *Ballad Of The Ten Rod Plot*.
Albums: *Stroll On* (1974), *Speedy Return* (1975), *Demo Tapes* (1981), *Family Album* (1983), *More Demo Tapes* (1985), *Mysterious Ways* (1990). Compilations: various artists *Electric Muse* (1975), various artists *All Through The Year* (1991).

Au Go-Go Singers

Evolving from New York group, the New Choctawquins, this nine-piece vocal ensemble came together in Greenwich Village in 1964. Heavily influenced by the New Christy Minstrels and other commercialized folk aggregations of the period, the Au Go-Go Singers sang in an off-Broadway musical, toured the southern states and recorded one album before fragmenting in 1965. Among their alumni were Stephen Stills and Richie Furay who formed the hit group Buffalo Springfield the following year.
Album: *They Call Us The Au Go-Go Singers* (1964).

Steve Ashley

Cliff Aungier

Auldridge, Mike

This highly respected dobro player has performed on a number of bluegrass and country albums, mostly with the Seldom Scene. Auldridge is the nephew of Ellsworth T. Cozzens, the Hawaiian steel guitarist who played on several Jimmie Rodgers records. Having started playing guitar at the age of 12, Auldridge progressed to banjo within a short space of time, and was almost 20 when he played dobro for the first time. In 1969, Auldridge joined Emerson and Waldron, but with Bill Emerson leaving to join the Country Gentlemen, Auldridge continued performing with Cliff Waldron, from Jolo, West Virginia. The act grew to become the New Shades Of Grass, a six-piece outfit. Waldron planned to tour extensively, not a popular move in the eyes of Auldridge, who left with group member Ben Eldridge. With John Duffey Eldridge (banjo), Tom Gray (bass), John Starling (guitar/vocals) they formed the Seldom Scene. They have made a number of fine bluegrass recordings and Auldridge continues to do session work for other artists.
Albums: *Dobro* (1974), *Mike Auldridge* (1976), *Blues And Bluegrass* (1977), *An Old Dog* (1978), with Jeff Newman *Slidin' Smoke* (1979), *Eight String Swing* (1988), *Mike Auldrige And Old Dog* (1989), Auldridge, Reid And Coleman *High Time* (1990).

Aungier, Cliff

b. 9 April 1941, Croydon, Surrey, England. It was while watching a television documentary about Big Bill Broonzy, that Aungier was inspired to buy his first guitar. Before that he played trumpet for the Air Training Cadets, and aspired to be a pilot in the Royal Air Force. From his early influences, and having seen Broonzy playing, Aungier soon adapted his own style. He began playing the obligatory floor spots in folk clubs, when Bert Jansch, John Renbourn and Alexis Korner were on the circuit. Later, with Gerry Lockran and Royd Rivers, Aungier started a folk and blues club at the Half Moon in Putney, London. Throughout his career, Aungier has toured with acts such as Yes, Elkie Brooks, Ralph McTell, Pentangle, Joan Armatrading and Fairport Convention. *Wanderin'* was produced by Jimmy Page and featured the work of harmonica player Royd Rivers. Aungier recorded an album for Polydor in 1968, and another for RCA in 1969, neither of which were released. He did, however, receive a silver disc for his cover of Tim Hardin's 'The Lady Came From Baltimore'. Gradually, with the media hype machine in full swing, Aungier lost faith with the way his music was being presented and left the scene for a while. Disillusioned at the lack of control over his own work, he spent much of his time performing in Belgium and Holland, with only the occasional appearance in the UK. Later, with no contractual obligations to hinder him, Aungier recorded *Full Moon*, with a line-up that included Paul Millns (vocals/piano), Micky Moody (guitar), Nigel Portman-Smith (bass), Nic Pentelow (saxophone) and Chris Hunt (drums). The album featured a diversity of material, from 'You Win Again' by Hank Williams to Elton John's and Bernie Taupin's 'I Need You To Turn To'. Aungier also performs with his own Full Moon Band on occasion. In addition, he has been busy presenting a weekly folk and blues radio series for a regional network and also *The Rhythm And The Blues* for the British Forces Broadcasting Service (BFBS).
Albums: *Wanderin'* (1965), *Alex Campbell And Friends* (1967), *The Lady Came From Baltimore* (1969), *Dungeon Folk* (1971), *Full Moon* (1984), *Breathing Space* (1991).

Axton, Hoyt

b. 23 March 1938, Duncan, Oklahoma, USA. The son of Mae Axton (who wrote Elvis Presley's first hit, 'Heartbreak Hotel'). Hoyt began as a folk singer on the west coast. In 1962, he signed for Horizon Records for his first album, *The Balladeer*, which featured future Byrds leader Jim McGuinn on guitar. As the 60s unfolded, Axton expanded his repertoire to include blues and country, while also establishing himself as a songwriter of considerable talent. His first hit as a composer was the Kingston Trio's 'Greenback Dollar' and later in the decade he wrote Steppenwolf's famous drug song, 'The Pusher'. The victim of cocaine addiction for many years, he still managed to record a prolific number of albums, though it was as a composer that he enjoyed commercial success. Two major hits in the 70s, courtesy of Three Dog Night ('Joy To The World') and Ringo Starr ('No No Song') supplemented his income, while also maintaining his standing as a recording artist. Having overcome his drug dependency at the end of the decade, he appeared in the film *The Black Stallion*, formed his own record label Jeremiah, and continued touring on a regional basis. In 1991 he made an attempt to re-enter the recording market with the critically acclaimed *Spin Of The Wheel*.
Selected albums: *The Balladeer* (1962), *Thunder 'n' Lightnin'* (1963), *Saturday's Child* (1963), *Hoyt Axton Explodes* (1964), *Greenback Dollar* (1964), *Hoyt Axton Sings Bessie Smith* (1964), *My Way* (1964), *Mr Greenback Dollar Man* (1965), *My Griffin Is Gone* (1969), *Joy To The World* (1971), *Country Anthem* (1971), *Less Than A Song* (1973), *Life Machine* (1974), *Southbound* (1975), *Fearless* (1976), *Road Songs* (1977), *Snowblind Friend* (1977), *Free*

Sailin' (1978), *A Rusty Old Halo* (1979), *Where Did The Money Go* (1980), *Everybody's Going On The Road* (1982), *Spin Of The Wheel* (1991).

Aztec Two-Step

This folk-influenced duo, comprising Neal Shulman (vocals/guitar) and Rex Fowler (guitar/vocals), made its recording debut on the Elektra label in 1972. *Aztec Two-Step* showcased their informal style and featured admirable support from several exemplary associates, including Spanky McFarlane, John Seiter (both ex-Spanky And Our Gang), John Sebastian, Doug Dillard and Jerry Yester, the latter of whom also produced the set. Shulman and Fowler moved to RCA Records for their subsequent releases which, while accomplished, featured a less interesting supporting cast and lacked the charm of that first set.
Albums: *Aztec Two-Step* (1972), *Second Step* (1975), *Two's Company* (1976), *Adjoining Suites* (1977), *See It Was Like This...* (1989).

B

Baez, Joan

b. 9 January 1941, Staten Island, New York, USA. The often used cliché; the queen of folk to Bob Dylan's king, Joan's sweeping soprano is one of popular music's most distinctive voices. An impressive appearance at the 1959 Newport Folk Festival followed the singer's early performances throughout the Boston/New England club scene and established Baez as a vibrant interpreter of traditional material. Joan's first four albums featured ballads drawn from American and British sources, but as the civil rights campaign intensified, so the artist became increasingly identified with the protest movement. Her reading of 'We Shall Overcome', first released on *In Concert/Part 2*, achieved an anthem-like quality. This album also featured Dylan's, 'Don't Think Twice, It's All Right' and Baez then took the emergent singer on tour and their well-documented romance blossomed. Over the years she would interpret many of his songs, several of which, including 'Farewell Angelina' and 'Love Is Just A Four Letter Word', Dylan would not officially record. In the 60s she founded the Institute for the Study Of Nonviolence. Baez also

featured early work by other contemporary writers, including Phil Ochs, brother-in-law Richard Farina, Tim Hardin and Donovan, and by the late 60s was composing her own material. The period was also marked by the singer's increasing commitment to non-violence and she was jailed on two occasions for participation in anti-war rallies. In 1968 Baez married David Harris, a peace activist who was later imprisoned for several years for draft resistance. The couple were divorced in 1972.
Although a version of the Band song, 'The Night They Drove Old Dixie Down', gave Joan a hit single in 1971, she found it hard to maintain a consistent commercial profile. Her devotion to politics continued as before and a 1973 release, *Where Are You Now My Son*, included recordings the singer made in North Vietnam. A 1975 collection, *Diamonds And Rust*, brought a measure of mainstream success. The title track remains her own strongest song. The story of her relationship with Dylan, it presaged their reunion, after ten years apart, in the legendary Rolling Thunder Revue. That in turn inspired her one entirely self-penned album, *Gulf Winds*, in which her songwriting continued to develop, often in new and unexpected directions. In 1989, she released an album celebrating 30 years of performing - *Speaking Of Dreams*, which found her duetting with her old friends Paul Simon and Jackson Browne and, surprisingly, with the Gypsy Kings in a rumba-flamenco cover of 'My Way'. However, Joan has preferred to concentrate her energies on humanitarian work rather than recording. In 1979 she founded Humanitas International, a rapid-response human rights group who first persuaded the US President Carter to send the Seventh Fleet to rescue Boat People. She has received numerous awards and honourary doctorates for her work. In the 80s and 90s baez continued to divide her time between social activism and singing. She found a new audience among the young socially aware Europeans - 'The Children Of The Eighties', as she dubbed them in song. She retains a deserved respect for her early, highly influential releases. At the end of 1992 *Play Me Backwards* was released to universal acclaim, this smooth rock album put Baez very much in the same bracket as Mary-Chapin Carpenter. Baez sounded confident flirting with rock and country.
Albums: *Joan Baez* (1960), *Joan Baez 2* (1961), *Joan Baez In Concert* (1962), *Joan Baez In Concert/Part 2* (1963), *Joan Baez 5* (1964), *Farewell Angelina* (1965), *Noel* (1966), *Joan* (1967), *Baptism* (1968), *Any Day Now* (1968), *David's Album* (1969), *Joan Baez In Italy* (1969), *24 July 1970 all Arena Civica di Milano* (1970), *One Day At A Time* (1970), *Blessed Are* (1971), *Carry It On* (1971), *Sacco And Vanzetti*

Joan Baez

(1971), *Come From The Shadows* (1972), *Where Are You Now My Son* (1973), *Gracias A La Vida (Here's To Life)* (1974), *Diamonds And Rust* (1975), *Live In Japan* (1975), *From Every Stage* (1976), *Gulf Winds* (1976), *Blowing Away* (1977), *Honest Lullaby* (1979), *European Tour* (1981), *Live Europe 83* (1983), *Very Early Joan* (1983), *Recently* (1988), *Diamonds And Rust In The Bullring* (1989), *Speaking Of Dreams* (1989), *Play Me Backwards* (1992). Compilations: *The First Ten Years* (1970), *The Ballad Book* (1972) *The Contemporary Ballad Book* (1974), *The Love Song Album* (1975), *The Best Of Joan Baez* (1977), *Spotlight On Joan Baez* (1980).

Further reading: *Daybreak - An Intimate Journal*, Joan Baez. *And A Voice To Sing With - A Memoir*, Joan Baez.

Bailey, Roy

b. 20 October 1935, London, England. Bailey has established a solid reputation during his years on the folk circuit. He had always led a hectic life, combining the demands of a full-time Dean of Faculty at Sheffield Polytechnic, and touring the UK and the world. Bailey was formerly one of the Three City Four with Leon Rosselson and Martin Carthy. The recordings made with Leon Rosselson were highly acclaimed. *That's Not The Way It's Got To Be* was named as one of the best folk albums of 1975, at the Montreux Festival, in Switzerland, while *Love Loneliness And Laundry* was album of the year in *Melody Maker* and *Folk Review*. 1979 saw *If I Knew Who The Enemy Was* cited as album of the

year again by *Melody Maker*. Always committed to songs about struggle and oppression, *Leaves From A Tree* included songs from both the personal political and global viewpoint. He is part of a group called the Political Song Network, started in 1986, with Sandra Kerr and Leon Rosselson. In 1988, Roy suffered a heart attack, and discovered it was irreparable congested heart failure (Famine œdema). He has now retired from academic life, and in January 1989, was elected Fellow of the Royal Society of Arts. In addition to his many recordings, Bailey has also contributed to a number of compilation albums with other performers, in particular *Nuclear Power? No Thanks* in 1981, *Songs For Peace* in 1983, and *Bullets And Guitars* in 1985. *Why Does It Have To Be Me?*, an album of children's songs, was recorded with Val Bailey, John Kirkpatrick and Sue Harris. Roy still tours, but less frenetically now.

Albums: with the Three City Four *Smoke And Dust Where The Heart Should Have Been* (1966), with Val Bailey and Leon Rosselson *Oats And Beans And Kangaroos* (1967), with Val Bailey *Cobweb Of Dreams* (1967), *Roy Bailey* (1971), with Rosselson *That's Not The Way It's Got To Be* (1975), *New Bell Wake* (1976), with Rosselson *Love, Loneliness And Laundry* (1979), with Rosselson *If I Knew Who The Enemy Was* (1979), *Hard Times* (1982), *Freedom Peacefully* (1988), *Leaves From A Tree* (1988), *Why Does It Have To Be Me?* (1989), *Never Leave A Story Unsung* (1991).

Bain, Aly

b. 15 May 1946, Lerwick, Shetland, Scotland. Bain is held in high regard for his style of Shetland fiddle playing. He began playing at the age of 11, learning his craft from Tom Anderson. Aly played locally while earning his living as a joiner. He joined the Boys Of The Lough in 1988, and, in addition to pursuing his own career, has since guested on albums by others including Richard Thompson. During the latter half of the 70s, Aly recorded two albums for Topic with Tom Anderson, *The Silver Bow* and *Shetland Folk Fiddling Vol.2*. He has since been heavily in demand for television work, presenting *Down Home*, which featured a wide range of performers from the related worlds of folk music. The series looked at the spread of fiddle music from Scotland and Ireland, to large parts of North America. *Aly Bain* features not only Shetland fiddle tunes, but also tunes from France, Canada, America and Ireland. *Aly Meets The Cajuns* saw Bain travel to Louisiana to look at cajun music and lifestyle, while *Push The Boat Out* was filmed during Glasgow's Mayfest. The series, shown on BBC television in 1991, was set aboard a floating venue during Glasgow's reign, in 1990, as European City Of Culture. There followed, in 1991, *The Shetland Set*, a series for BBC television from the Shetland Folk Festival of May 1991. With such a busy schedule, Bain's long overdue follow-up solo release is due to be recorded in 1992. He also has a book about growing up in the Shetlands planned.
Albums: *Aly Bain-Mike Whelans* (1971), with Tom Anderson *The Silver Bow* (1976), with Anderson *Shetland Folk Fiddling Vol.2* (1978), *Aly Bain* (1985), *Down Home Vol.1* (1986), *Down Home Vol.2* (1986), *Aly Meets The Cajuns* (1988), *Lonely Bird* (1992).

Baker, Duck

b. Richard Royal Baker IV, 1949, Washington, DC, USA, and brought up in Florida and Richmond, Virginia. Baker has said that the nickname Duck was given to him while still a boy. He is a guitar player of incredible ability, who has not garnered the same degree of popularity as others such as Leo Kottke and Stefan Grossman with whom he has played. His styles range from blues, ragtime, celtic tunes and original compositions, making him difficult to categorize. From 1978-87, he regularly toured throughout Europe He has also appeared on the same billing for a variety of artists including the Ink Spots, the Count Basie Orchestra and Tom Paxton. In addition to his many solo recordings, Duck has made numerous instructional albums for guitar playing, as part of the Stefan Grossman Guitar Workshop. Baker also played the score for the film *Feeling Good, Feeling Proud*. In 1991, he teamed up with Molly Andrews (b. 1956,

Bluefield, West Virginia, USA; vocals/autoharp/dulcimer/banjo/guitar), and toured the USA, England, Scotland and Norway.
Selected Albums: *The King Of Bongo Bong* (1977), *When You Wore A Tulip* (1978), *The Art Of Fingerstyle* (1979), *The Kid On The Mountain* (1980), *There's Something For Everyone In America* (1980), *Under Your Heart* (1985), *You Can't Take The Country Out Of The Boy* (80s), *Both Sides* (80s), *The Salutation* (80s), with John James *Descriptive Guitar Instrumentals* (80s), with Stefan Grossman *Thunder On The Run* (80s), with Eugene Chadbourne *Guitar Trios* (80s).

Baker, Etta

b. 1913, Caldwell County, North Carolina, USA. From a black family that was proficient in blues, pop, hymns, rags, ballads, dance music and, through intermarriage, white country music, Etta Reid learned guitar, banjo, fiddle and piano, playing alongside her father, Boone Reid, and her elder sister Cora. She married 1936, when her husband, though himself a pianist, discouraged public performance. She was recorded in 1956, and her fluent, raggy guitar became something of a cult among urban folk revivalists, particularly on 'One Dime Blues'. (Her father and Cora's husband Lacey Phillips were also recorded, on banjo, in 1956.) Etta took up her career only after her husband had died. Baker resumed public performances and showed that she was still a magnificent guitarist and banjo player.
Albums: *Instrumental Music Of The Southern Appalachians* (1956), *Music From The Hills Of Caldwell County* (70s), *One Dime Blues* (1991).

Band

When the Band emerged in 1968 with *Music From Big Pink*, they were already a seasoned and cohesive unit. Four of the group, Robbie Robertson (b. Jaime Robbie Robertson, 5 July 1943, Toronto, Ontario, Canada; guitar/vocals), Richard Manuel (b. 3 April 1943, Stratford, Canada, d. 7 March 1986; piano/drums/vocals), Garth Hudson (b. Eric Hudson, 2 August 1937, London, Ontario, Canada; organ) and Rick Danko (b. 9 December 1943, Simcoe, Canada; bass/vocals), had embraced rock 'n' roll during its first flush of success. One by one they joined the Hawks, a backing group fashioned by rockabilly singer Ronnie Hawkins, which included Levon Helm (b. Mark Levon Helm, 26 May 1942, Marvell, Arkansas, USA; drums/vocals). A minor figure in America, by the late 50s Hawkins had moved to Toronto where he pursued a career largely shaped around rabble-house cover versions. 'Bo Diddley' (1963) was a major hit in Canada, but the musicians flexed their independence during sessions for the subsequent *Mojo Man*, recording 'She's 19' and 'Farther Up The Road' with Helm taking the vocal. The quintet left Hawkins later that year and criss-crossed America's small town bars, performing for 'pimps, whores, rounders and flakeouts', as Hudson later recalled! Billed as the Canadian Squires or Levon And The Hawks, they developed a loud, brash repertoire, drawn from R&B, soul and gospel styles, while the rural life they encountered left a trail of impressions and images. The group completed a single, 'Leave Me Alone', under the former appellation, before settling in New York where 'Go Go Liza Jane' and 'The Stones I Throw' were recorded as Levon And The Hawks.

The quintet enjoyed the approbation of the city's famed Red Bird label. Robertson, Helm and Hudson supported blues singer John Hammond Jnr. on his debut single, 'I Wish You Would' (1964), while Levon's pacey composition, 'You Cheated, You Lied', was recorded by the Shangri-Las. The trio maintained their link with Hammond on the latter's fiery *So Many Roads* (1965), through which they were introduced to Bob Dylan. In August 1965 Robertson and Helm accompanied the singer for his Forest Hills concert and although the drummer reneged on further involvement, within months the remaining Hawks were at the fulcrum of Dylan's most impassioned music. They supported him on his 'electric' 1966 world tour and followed him to his Woodstock retreat where, reunited with Helm, they recorded the famous *Basement Tapes* whose lyrical, pastoral performances anticipated the style the quintet would soon adopt. *Music From Big Pink* restated traditional American music in an environment of acid-rock and psychedelia. Natural in the face of technocratic artifice, its woven, wailing harmonies suggested the fervour of sanctified soul, while the instrumental pulse drew inspiration from carnivals, country and R&B. The Band's deceptive simplicity was their very strength, binding lyrics of historical and biblical metaphor to sinuous, memorable melodies. The set included three Dylan songs, but is best recalled for 'The Weight' which, if lyrically obtuse, was the subject of several cover versions, notably from Jackie DeShannon, Aretha Franklin, Diana Ross (with the Supremes and the Temptations) and Spooky Tooth. *The Band* confirmed the quintet's unique qualities. Robertson had emerged as their principle songwriter, yet the panoramic view remained intact, and by invoking Americana past and present, the group reflected the pastoral desires of a restless generation. It contained several telling compositions - 'Across The Great Divide', 'The Unfaithful Servant' and 'The Night They Drove Old Dixie Down' - as well as 'Rag Mama Rag', an ebullient UK Top 20 hit. The Band then resumed touring, the perils of which were chronicled on *Stage Fright*. By openly embracing contemporary concerns, the quintet lacked their erstwhile perspective, but in 'The Rumour' they created one of the era's most telling portraits. Yet the group's once seamless sound had grown increasingly formal, a dilemma increased on *Cahoots*. Melodramatic rather than emotional, the set offered few highlights, although Van Morrison's cameo on '4% Pantomime' suggested a *bonhomie* distinctly absent elsewhere. It was followed by a warm in-concert set, *Rock Of Ages*, arranged by Allan Toussaint, and *Moondog Matinee*, a wonderful selection of favourite oldies. It served as a spotlight for Richard Manuel, whose emotional, haunting voice wrought new meaning from 'Share Your Love', 'The Great Pretender' and 'A Change Is Gonna Come'.

In 1974 the Band backed Bob Dylan on his acclaimed *Planet Waves* album and undertook the extensive tour documented on *Before The Flood*. The experience inspired a renewed creativity and *Northern Lights Southern Cross*, their strongest set since *The Band*, included 'Arcadian Driftwood', one of Robertson's most evocative compositions. However, the individual members had decided to dissolve the group and their partnership was sundered the following year with a gala performance at San Francisco's Winterland ballroom. The event, *The Last Waltz*, featured many guest contributions, including those by Dylan, Eric Clapton, Muddy Waters, Van Morrison, Neil Young, Joni Mitchell and Paul Butterfield, and was the subject of Martin Scorsese's film of the same name and a commemorative triple album. The Band also completed their contractual obligations with *Islands*, a somewhat tepid set notable only for 'Knockin' Lost John', which featured a rare lead vocal from Robertson. Levon Helm then pursued a dual career as a performer and actor, Rick Danko recorded an intermittently interesting solo album, while Hudson saved his talent for session appearances. Robbie Robertson scored soundtracks to several more Scorsese films, but kept a relatively low profile, refusing to join the ill-fated Band reunions of 1984 and 1985. A third tour ended in tragedy when, on 7 March 1986, Richard Manuel hanged himself in a motel room. His death inspired 'Fallen Angel' on Robertson's outstanding 'comeback' album, but despite the presence of Hudson and Danko elsewhere on the record, the guitarist refused to join his colleagues when they regrouped again in 1991.

Albums: *Music From Big Pink* (1968), *The Band* (1969), *Stage Fright* (1970), *Cahoots* (1971), *Rock Of Ages* (1972), *Moondog Matinee* (1973), *Northern Lights - Southern Cross* (1975), *Islands* (1977), with various artists *The Last Waltz* (1977). Compilations: *The Best Of The Band* (1976), *Anthology Volume 1* (1978), *Anthology Volume 2* (1980), *To Kingdom Come* (1989).

Barely Works

This eclectic folk group was assembled in 1988 by former Boothill Foot-Tappers singer and banjoist Chris Thompson (b. 19 March 1957, Ashford, Middlesex, England), together with Richard Avison (b. 9 July 1958, Rothbury, Northumberland, England; trombone/vocals - ex-Happy End and Dead Can Dance), Sarah Allen (b. 22 July 1964, Tiverton, Devon, England; accordion/tin whistle/flutes - ex-Happy End and Di's New Outfit), Alison Jones (b. 6 April 1965, Sketty, Swansea, West Glamorgan, Wales; violin/vocals - ex-Di's New Outfit), Keith Moore (tuba - also a member of poet John Hegley's Popticians), Mat Fox (b. 8 November 1956; hammer dulcimer/percussion/vocals) and former Redskins drummer Paul Hookham, later replaced in 1990 by Tim Walmsley (b. 29 March 1956, Paddington, London, England - also ex-Happy End). This strange mixture of personalities signed to the radical world-music label, Cooking Vinyl and emerged from the UK folk club circuit in the late 80s and early 90s. Their performances boasted an broad range of traditional ('Byker Hill') and original material, mostly from Thompson and Allen as well as tackling the works of such artists as Captain Beefheart ('Tropical Hot Dog Nite'). The Barely Works have managed to break away from the constrictive pigeon-hole of an 'English Folk Group' and crossed over to the rock-club circuit where their virtuosity has proven them more than capable of moving a rock audience. Mat Fox left the group in early 1992 and Keith Moore was replaced by Alice Kinloch.
Albums: *The Beat Beat* (1990), *Don't Mind Walking* (1991), *Shimmer* (1992), *Glow* (1992).

Barker, Les

b. 30 January 1947, Manchester, England. Barker is a self-styled humourist and writer who has produced a large number of books of poetry and monologues. Most of his recorded works show the same humorous insight. Before turning professional, he worked as an accountant and has been writing and performing since 1975. Barker was a familiar sight at folk clubs and festivals accompanied by his dog Mrs. Ackroyd, which was renowned for snapping at members of the audience. After Mrs Ackroyd died Barker continued performing on the folk circuit. Barker's first book appeared in 1976, and others followed on an average of two per year. As its title suggests, *Dogologues* is an album of

Barker's monologues, many of which appear in his books. Various monologues are now veritable standards, in particular 'Cosmo The Fairly Accurate Knife Thrower' and 'Jason And The Arguments'. *The Stones Of Callanish* was a departure from the Barker norm, in that it was a folk opera with words by Les set to Scottish traditional music. Barker was supported on the album by June Tabor, Rod Paterson and a number of other performers including Lesley Davies and Chris Harvey who also appear with Barker in the somewhat fluid Mrs Ackroyd Band. The follow up *Oranges And Lemmings* saw a return to the humorous side with tracks such as 'Hard Cheese Of Old England' and 'Jehovah's Witness At The Door'. Tabor again appeared on the album along with Bernard Wrigley and Martin Carthy.
Albums: *The Mrs Ackroyd Rock 'n' Roll Show* (1985), *Dogologues* (1986), *Earwigo* (1988), *The Stones Of Callanish* (1989), with the Mrs Ackroyd Band *Oranges And Lemmings* (1990).
Further reading: *Her Master's Boo, Mrs Ackroyd's Diary, Paws For Thought, Mrs Ack Royds Again, Morocco And Things, Songs For Swinging Tails, Dog Ends, Something To Sniff At, Upper Cruft, Fetlar, English Book Of Penguin Folk Songs, Doggerel, Illegal Annual, Medlock Delta Blues Vols 1 & 2, Hound Of Music, The Beagle Has Landed, Extra Terrierestrial, Werneth Willie Ackroyd, Dog Byte, Viva A Spaniel, Dog Gone, Corgi And Bess, A Quite Short Goat And A Pink Dalmation, Royders Of The Lost Ack, I Camel, I Saw, I Conker, Dog Only Nose, Fidofax, King Charles Spaniel, Pup Yours, Reign Of Terrier, Al Satians To Crewe, Get A Dog And Barker Yourself.*

Barker, Sally

b. 19 September 1959, Barrow upon Soar, Leicestershire, England. One of the newer generation of folk performers, Barker has a strong blues-based voice which she accompanies on guitar. Her Influences are wide and varied, and include Bessie Smith, John Martyn and Aretha Franklin. She worked as half of a duo called Sally And Chris, with bass player Chris Watson performing folk-blues in pubs and clubs in the midlands. Later the duo went on to support Steeleye Span, Gordon Giltrap and Roy Harper. After a brief foray into radio and television, Barker moved to London in May 1986 and continued to work as a soloist. In 1987, she won the National Songsearch Competition and began touring in a support capacity to acts such as Fairport Convention, Taj Mahal and Roy Harper. Her first album was well received and contained cover versions of songs that had previously featured in her live act. The second release was an illustration of the on-going development of her maturing musical potential, and

Sally Barker

in 1990, she supported both Bob Dylan and Robert Plant in Germany. In December of the same year, she formed a group called the Poozies, playing a mixture of cajun, folk, blues and country. The line-up featured harpist Mary McMaster and Patsy Seddon from Sileas, Jenny Gardner (fiddle) and Karen Tweed (accordion). She continues to work both the folk clubs and festivals, but it is evident that her appeal actually goes far beyond the boundaries of the folk music category.

Albums: *In The Spotlight* (1988), *This Rhythm Is Mine* (1990), *Beating The Drum* (1992).

Battlefield Band

From their beginnings in 1972, there have been many personnel changes in the Battlefield Band. The most stable line-up consisted of multi instrumentalist, vocalist Brian McNeill (b. 6 April 1950, Falkirk, Scotland, founder member Alan Reid (b. 2 May 1950, Glasgow, Scotland; keyboards, vocals), Dougie Pincock (b. 7 July 1961, Glasgow, Scotland; pipes, flute, saxophone, percussion), and from 1984, Alistair Russell (b. 15 February 1951, Newcastle, England; guitar/vocals). Their self-penned material is strong on social commentary. Other members that have figured in the line-up include Jim Barnes (guitar), Sylvia Barnes (dulcimer, bodhran), Jenny Clarke (vocals, guitar), John Gahagan (concertina), Jamie McMenemy (guitar, mandolin, vocals), Pat Kilbride (guitar and vocals), Duncan McGillivray (pipes), Ged Foley (guitar, mandolin, vocals), Jim Thompson, Sandra Long, Eddie Morgan and Ricky Starrs. Two new additions to the band are Iain MacDonald (b. 28 July 1960, Inverness, Scotland; pipes/flute/whistle). MacDonald replaced Pincock, who left as he no longer wished to travel so much. MacDonald was formerly with the group Ossian, which he joined in 1981. Following Brian McNeill's decision to concentrate on his writing, and his own solo career, he was replaced by John McCusker (b. 15 May 1973, Scotland; fiddle, piano, whistle, accordion, cittern, mandolin, ex-Parcel O'Rogues). Despite McCusker's youth, there is no doubt of his ability to fit in with the current line-up. The band are particularly popular in the USA but have travelled world-wide. The Battlefield Band retain the Celtic traditions in their sound, but successfully augment it with deft use of Reid's keyboard. Their live version of the classic 'Six Days On The Road' features a lead break on bagpipes and is indicative of the the wide range of style within the group.

Albums: *Battlefield Band* (1976), *Battlefield Band 2* (1977), *At The Front* (1978), *Stand Easy* (1979), *Preview* (1980), *Home Is Where The Van Is* (1980), *Sidetracks* (1981), *There's A Buzz* (1982), *Anthem For The Common Man* (1984), *On The Rise* (1986),

Battlefield Band

Music In Trust 1 (1986, television soundtrack), *Celtic Hotel* (1987), *Music In Trust 2* (1988), *Home Ground* (1989), *New Spring* (1991). Compilations: *The Story So Far* (1982), *After Hours* (1987). Solo albums: Brian McNeill *Monksgate* (1979), *Unstrung Hero* (1985), *The Busker And The Devils Only Daughter* (1990).

Beeching, Jenny

b. 19 September 1950, Romford, Essex, England. Beeching came from a musical background. Her grandmother had been a member of the children's theatre, Casey's Court, with Charlie Chaplin. After attending dance classes as a child and learning to play guitar, Beeching began singing in folk clubs, often performing songs by Bob Dylan and Joan Baez. She obtained her first paid gig in 1966, as part of a traditional duo called the Lorelei, with Christina Williamson. A spell of solo work followed until 1968, when she joined forces with traditional singer Dave Cooper, and played dates throughout England. By 1971, Beeching had started writing songs, and went solo once more, until teaming up with Tony Cliff (piano/guitar), after which she added jazz and blues to her repertoire, as well as learning to play the banjo. At this time she was also busking and teaching folk guitar in secondary schools. *A Right Song And Dance*, her first release, coincided with Jenny taking the plunge into a full-time musical career. In 1984, Beeching teamed up with former Zumzeaux member Chris Haigh (b. 17 August 1957, Huddersfield, West Yorkshire, England; fiddle), and formed the Hotline. The two toured worldwide in 1985, playing dates in Hong Kong, Australia, and the USA. *Hotline From London* was recorded and released in Yugoslavia. Since then, Jenny has concentrated on studying for her BA in Anthropology and Geography, and doing an individual thesis entitled 'Buskers: Good For Nothing Or Good For Business', on the use of buskers in shopping malls as a tourist attraction.
Albums: *A Right Song And Dance* (1978), *No More Sad Goodbyes* (1982), with Chris Haigh *Hotline From London* (1986).

Belafonte, Harry

b. Harold George Belafonte, 1 March 1927, New York, USA. In recent years, the former 'King Of Calypso' has become better known for his work with UNICEF and his enterprise with USA For Africa. Prior to that, Belafonte had an extraordinarily varied life. His early career was spent as an actor, until he had time to demonstrate his silky smooth and gently relaxing singing voice. He appeared as Joe in Oscar Hammerstein's *Carmen Jones*; an adaptation of *Carmen* by Bizet, and in 1956 he was snapped up by RCA Victor. Belafonte was then at the forefront of the calypso craze which was a perfect vehicle for his happy-go-lucky folk songs. Early hits included 'Jamaica Farewell', 'Mary's Boy Child' and the classic transatlantic hit 'Banana Boat Song' with its unforgettable refrain; 'Day-oh, dayyy-oh, daylight come and me wanna go home'. *Calypso* became the first ever album to sell a million copies, and spent 31 weeks at the top of the US charts. Belafonte continued throughout the 50s with incredible success. He was able to cross over into many markets appealing to pop, folk, jazz as well as the with ethnic population with whom he became closely associated, particularly during the civil rights movement. He appeared in many films including *Island In The Sun*, singing the title song and *Odds Against Tomorrow*. His success as an album artist was considerable; between 1956 and 1962 he was hardly ever absent from the album chart. *Belafonte At Carnegie Hall* spent over three years in the charts, and similar success befell *Belafonte Returns To Carnegie Hall*, featuring Miriam Makeba, the Chad Mitchell Trio and Odetta with the memorable recording of 'There's A Hole In My Bucket'. Throughout the 60s Belafonte was an ambassador of human rights and a most articulate speaker at rallies and on television. His appeal as a concert hall attraction was immense, no less than seven of his albums were recorded in concert. Although his appearances in the best-sellers had stopped by the 70s he remained an active performer, recording artist and continued to appear on film, although in lightweight movies like *Buck And The Preacher* and *Uptown Saturday Night*. In the mid-80s he was a leading light in the USA For Africa appeal and sang on 'We Are The World'. His sterling work continued into the 90s with UNICEF. Belafonte was one of the few black artists who broke down barriers of class and race and should be counted with Martin Luther King as a major figure in achieving equal rights for blacks in America, although he did it through popular music in a less obvious way.
Albums: *Mark Twain And Other Folk Favorites* (1955), *Belafonte* (1956), *Calypso* (1956), *An Evening With Belafonte* (1957), *Belafonte Sings Of The Caribbean* (1957), *Belafonte Sings The Blues* (1958), *Love Is A Gentle Thing* (1959), *Porgy And Bess* (1959), *Belafonte At Carnegie Hall* (1959), *My Lord What A Mornin'* (1960), *Belafonte Returns To Carnegie Hall* (1960), *Jump Up Calypso* (1961), *The Midnight Special* (1962), *The Many Moods Of Belafonte* (1962), *To Wish You A Merry Christmas* (1962), *Streets I Have Walked* (1963), *Belafonte At The Greek Theatre* (1964), *Ballads Blues And Boasters* (1964), *An Evening With Belafonte/Makeba* (1965), *An Evening With Belafonte/Mouskouri* (1966), *In My Quiet Room* (1966), *Calypso In Brass* (1967),

Belafonte On Campus (1967), *Homeward Bound* (1970), *Turn The World Around* (1977), *Loving You Is Where I Belong* (1981), *Paradise In Gazankulu* (1988). Compilations: *Collection - Castle Collector Series* (1987), *Banana Boat Song* (1988), *All Time Greatest Hits* (1989), *The Very Best Of* (1992).

Bellamy, Peter

b. Peter Franklyn Bellamy, 8 September 1944, Bournemouth, Dorset, England, d. 24 September 1991. After leaving art school in 1964, Bellamy formed the highly influential and innovative Young Tradition in 1965, with Royston Wood and Heather Wood. The trio specialized in a cappella arrangements of traditional English folk songs Bellamy was influenced early on by traditional Norfolk singers Harry Cox and Sam Larner, and revivalists such as Ewan MacColl and A.L. Lloyd. The Copper Family were also a great influence on the Young Tradition's arrangements. They disbanded in 1969, and Peter commenced his solo career later that same year. In 1970, Bellamy began a series of recordings of his own arrangements of the poems of Rudyard Kipling. As a result of the series, he was elected to the vice-presidency of the Kipling Society. In 1977, he released *The Transports*, a self-composed Ballad Opera, featuring the talents of Martin Carthy, Nic Jones, June Tabor, Cyril Tawney, A.L. Lloyd and the Watersons among others. It was judged as Folk Album of the Year by *Melody Maker*. Bellamy's career was halted for a couple of years during the 80s, after throat problems caused him to curtail his singing. He toured the USA and Canada regularly, and occasionally accompanied himself on guitar or concertina, but usually sang unaccompanied. His high vocals were unmistakable. Sadly, despite his obvious talent, Bellamy was not well known outside the mainstream of the hardcore folk music world. In 1991, with work on the horizon, and *Songs An' Rummy Conjurin' Tricks* released, Bellamy committed suicide, leaving a void that is unlikely to be filled easily.
Albums: with the Young Tradition *The Young Tradition* (1966), with the Young Tradition *So Cheerfully Round* (1967), with the Young Tradition *Chicken On A Raft* (1968), *Mainly Norfolk* (1968), *Fair England's Shore* (1968), with the Young Tradition *Galleries* (1969), *The Fox Jumps Over The Parson's Gate* (1969), *Oak Ash And Thorn* (1970), *Won't You Go My Way?* (1971), *Merlin's Isle Of Gramarye* (1972), *Barrack Room Ballads* (1974), *Peter Bellamy* (1974), *Tell It Like It Was* (1975), *The Transports* (1977), *Both Sides Then* (1979), *Keep On Kipling* (1982), *Fair Annie* (1983), *Second Wind* (1983), *Rudyard Kipling Made Exceedingly Good Songs* (1989), *Soldiers Three* (1990), *Songs An'*

Rummy Conjurin' Tricks (1991).

Benbow, Steve

b. 29 November 1931, London, England. Benbow first became attracted to folk music during his teenage years, his first job at 16 was playing guitar at a concert party in Glasgow. Between 1950-55, Benbow served in the army as an interpreter. His ability with languages has enabled him to speak French, Italian, Arabic, Greek and Mauritian Creole. On his return to Britain, he started accompanying other singers until branching out on his own in 1957. UK television broadcasts followed, with *Guitar Club* in 1957, and continued with *Saturday Skiffle Club*, and *Easy Beat* As a result, Steve gained his own television programme in Scotland, *Plectrum*, in which he demonstrated his guitar style by playing and singing. His recording debut, in 1957, was on the 77 record label, but he was soon signed by EMI. On *Steve Benbow Sings*, he is accompanied, on a number of tracks, by Jimmie MacGregor on mandolin and guitar. *I Travel The World*, is, as the title suggests, a collection of largely traditional songs from around the world. In addition to Steve's folk career, he was also known in C&W circles. For a time he worked with the Steve Benbow Folk Four which included Jimmie MacGregor in the line-up. In the early 60s, Steve presented his own show *Have Guitar Will Travel*, on Radio Luxembourg, the only folk singer to be given a show on the station. In 1963, Benbow was also involved in stage show *Spike Milligan Meets Steve Benbow*, at the old Lyric Theatre. This led to a television series with Milligan, called *Muses With Milligan*, in 1964. Steve also wrote a regular column on folk music for *Melody Maker* during the 60s. The column was occasionally tongue-in-cheek towards many of the hypocritical attitudes pervading the folk scene. With changing trends, Benbow found himself working less on the folk circuit, and although many of his recordings are now deleted, his name is still referred to with affection on the scene. He still plays occasionally, but rarely in folk music circles.
Albums: *Steve Benbow Sings English Folk Songs* (1957), *Steve Benbow Sings American Folk Songs* (1957), *Sinful Songs* (1958), *Steve Benbow's Folk Four* (1959), *Mixed Bag* (1959), *A Jug Of Punch* (1960), *Steve Benbow Sings The Hermit And The Mole Catcher And Other Songs* (1960), *A Pinch Of Salt* (1960), *Rocket Along* (1960), *Ballad Of Little Musgrave* (1961), *Steve Benbow Sings Admiral Benbow* (1962), *I Travel The World* (1963), *Steve Benbow Tells About This That And The Other* (1964), *Irish Songs* (double 1965), *Journey Into The Sun* (1965), *Song Of Ireland* (1966), *Of Situations And Predicaments* (1967), *Little Drummer Boy* (1970), *Next Time Round* (1970), *Little*

Red Donkey (1970), *Sings Irish Songs* (1971), with Denny Wright *Friendly Folk* (1971), *Sings Irish And Other Songs* (1977).

Bikel, Theodore

b. 2 May 1924, Vienna, Austria. Bikel was a stage and screen actor as well as a folk singer. He arrived in the USA, having visited Palestine and London. He starred in the film *The African Queen* in 1951. His Jewish background enabled him to build up a comprehensive repertoire of Eastern European, Russian and Yiddish songs. His first album for Elektra, was the appropriately titled *Folk Songs From Just About Everywhere*. Bikel appeared at the 1960 Newport Folk Festival, and in over a dozen films including *My Fair Lady* in 1964, and Frank Zappa's *200 Motels* in 1971. During the early 60s Theodore had his own radio show, *At Home With Theodore Bikel*. Bikel also co-starred with Mary Martin in the Broadway production of *The Sound Of Music* in 1954. Additionally, he appeared in films such as *The Pride And The Passion*, in 1957, and *The Russians Are Coming*, in 1966. In his film roles, Bikel was able to play a variety of nationalities. Later albums appeared on Reprise. In 1977, Bikel was appointed by President Jimmy Carter, to the National Council For The Arts.
Albums: *Folk Songs From Just About Everywhere* (1959), *Bravo Bikel* (1959), *Folk Songs Of Israel* (1960), *Actor's Holiday* (60s), *From Bondage To Freedom* (1961), *On Tour* (1963), *Folksingers Choice* (1964), *Yiddish Theater And Folk Songs* (60s), *Harvest Of Israeli Folk Songs* (60s), *Jewish Folk Songs* (60s), *Songs Of The Russian Gypsy* (60s), *New Day* (1969), *Silent No More* (1972), *Song Of Songs* (70s). Compilations: *Best Of Theodore Bikel* (1962).

Bisiker And Romanov

Mick Bisiker (b. 3 July 1958, Redhill, Surrey, England; guitar/vocals), and Al Romanov (b. Ralph Allin, 29 February 1964, Halesowen, Birmingham, England; fiddle), began working as a duo in the summer of 1987. Trained on classical guitar and piano, Bisiker had started singing in folk clubs during the late 70s, and ran the university folk club in Birmingham for three years until 1983. From playing in a duo, Cogglers Awl, with Roger Huckle (guitar), they then added Clair Davenport (flute), and John Davis (bass), and formed Falstaff, which produced an independent release in 1982. Bisiker and Romanov were well received when they started to play regularly at festivals and in clubs on the folk circuit, and the attendant release of *Bisiker And Romanov*, on Fellside, was equally appreciated. The album won the Music Retailers Association Award, in 1988, for the best folk album of the year. Eventually, the two parted, as

Romanov wished to pursue a classical music path, and now fronts a trio. Bisiker continues in a solo capacity, having gone full-time into music in 1990.
Album: *Bisiker And Romanov* (1988). Solo album: Mick Bisiker *Home Again* (1991).

Black Velvet Band

This young, Irish folk and rock influenced band, led by the singer, songwriter and guitarist, Kieran Kennedy, released *When Justice Came*, in 1989. A mixture of the traditional and contemporary, it was produced by Pete Anderson (who also worked with Michelle Shocked). The songs dealt with rural and arcane imagery, and contained reminders of Hothouse Flowers and the Waterboys. The subsequent extensive world tour was followed by a brief hiatus whilst Maria Doyle (vocals) was working on the film, *The Commitments*. The second album, *King of Myself*, took a more personal, darker direction lyrically, with a stark, electric sound.
Albums: *When Justice Came* (1989), *King Of Myself* (1992).

Black, Mary

b. 23 May 1955, Dublin, Ireland. Mary is a member of the Black Family, who all have musical backgrounds, and with whom she has recorded and performed. Her father was a fiddle player and her mother a singer. Mary's early days were spent singing in the folk clubs of Dublin, but with *Mary Black* reaching number 4 in the Irish charts in 1983, it was obvious that she was destined for bigger things. In addition, she was awarded the Irish Independent Arts Award for Music for the album. Shortly after this, Black joined De Dannan, recording two albums with them, *Song For Ireland* and *Anthem*, before leaving the group in 1986. Although not credited, Mary did provide some backing vocals and production work for The Black's *Family Favourites* in 1984. Mary still maintained her solo career while with De Dannan, and teamed up with producer Declan Sinnott for *Without The Fanfare*, featuring mostly contemporary songs, which subsequently went gold. In 1987 and 1988, Mary was voted Best Female Artist in the Irish Rock Music Awards Poll. *No Frontiers*, apart from being one of Ireland's best-selling albums in 1989, also reached the Top 20 of the New Adult Contemporary charts in the USA, in 1990. The album also had a great deal of success in Japan, resulting in Black's first Japanese tour in December 1990. Although in the eyes of some critics, more recent works have seen Mary tagged as 'middle of the road' she defies straight categorization, still retaining an honest feel for her traditional background. Nevertheless, she also remains a fine interpreter of more contemporary works. Mary also sang with Emmylou Harris and Dolores Keane, in Nashville, in the television series *Bringing It All Back Home* and with Van Morrison on *Celtic Heartbeat*. In April 1991, Black returned from an American tour in order to finish *Babes In The Wood*, released in July the same year. The album went straight to number 1 in the Irish charts, staying there for five weeks. 1991 saw a concerted effort to capitalize on her success and reach a wider audience, with tours of England and another of Japan. Until *Babes In The Wood*, her albums, all on Dara, had not previously had a full distribution in Britain. Her latest album *The Holy Ground* was released in June 1993 and went platinum in Ireland on the day of release.

Albums: *Mary Black* (1983), *Collected* (1984), *Without The Fanfare* (1985), with the Black Family *The Black Family* (1986), *By The Time It Gets Dark* (1987), with the Black Family *Time For Touching Home* (1989), *No Frontiers* (1989), *Babes In The Wood* (1991). Compilation: *The Best Of Mary Black* (1991), *The Collection* (1992), *The Holy Ground* (1993).

Block, Rory

American blues singer and guitarist, raised in New York. Her father played classical violin, but at the age of 10, Block started learning to play folk music on the guitar. She later became involved in the burgeoning Greenwich Village Folk scene. It was as a teenager that she first heard the blues, and it was during this timee that she played with such names as Rev. Gary Davis, and Mississippi John Hurt. From then on she was hooked. Meeting up with Stefan Grossman, when she was 13, further encouraged her interest in the music. It was to be some 10 years before she took up playing again, having bowed out to bring up a family. In 1975, she recorded tracks for the small Blue Goose label, for an album entitled *Rory Block (I'm In Love)*. This album was re-released, in 1989, and re-mixed minus two tracks from the original recordings, but including an extra song, 'Blues Again', discovered on the original master tapes. Her first release for Rounder records, *High Heeled Blues*, was co-produced with John Sebastian. She continued in the same vein of recording, and performing, traditional blues and country blues material alongside her own compositions. The recording of *I've Got A Rock In My Sock* included such luminaries as Taj Mahal, and David Bromberg. In 1986, her 19-year-old son, Thiele, was killed in a car accident. The subsequent tribute album from Rory, *House Of Hearts*, contained 10 tracks, and all but one were Block originals. *Turning Point*, despite having a bigger production sound overall, did not detract from her earlier blues influences. Her track record speaks for itself, with her earlier apprehension that a white girl

from New York might not sound authentic singing the blues, remaining quite unfounded.

Albums: *Rory Block* (1975), *High Heeled Blues* (1981), *Blue Horizon* (1983), *Rhinestones And Steel Strings* (1983), *I've Got A Rock In My Sock* (1986), *House Of Hearts* (1987), *Turning Point* (1989), *Mama's Blues* (1991), *Ain't I A Woman* (1992). Compilations: *Best Blues And Originals* (1987).

Blowzabella

Essentially a UK folk dance band, formed in 1978, which achieved a deal of success both on the live music circuit, and on record. The group were almost as well-known for the frequent changes of personnel as their music. In 1987, sole remaining founder member John Swayne (b. Jonathan Rock Phipps Swayne, 26 June 1940, Hereford, England; alto and soprano saxophones/bagpipes) left, and Jo Fraser (b. Jo-Anne Rachel Newmarch Fraser, 4 December 1960, St. Albans, Hertfordshire, England; saxophone/vocals/whistles), joined. In 1989, Jo changed her name to Freya, owing to there being an Equity member of the same name. The rest of the group were Paul James (b. 4 April 1957, Southampton, Hampshire, England; bagpipes/soprano saxophone/percussion), Nigel Eaton (b. 3 January 1966, Lyndhurst, Hampshire, England; hurdy gurdy), Ian Luff (b. 4 January 1956, Brighton, Sussex, England; cittern/bass guitar), Dave Roberts (melodeon/darabuka) and Dave Shepherd (fiddle). Shepherd had joined the group in 1982, having previously played with folk-rock band Dr. Cosgill's Delight, alongside James. Luff joined in 1985. Blowzabella toured Brazil for the British Council in 1987, playing a large number of concerts, and *Pingha Frenzy* emerged from over 50 hours of taped sessions. *A Richer Dust* came from the music the band had written for the 500th Anniversary of the Battle of Stoke Field. A concert featuring the piece was performed on 18 June 1987. Freya, by 1989, was also pursuing a career outside Blowzabella, notably touring with Kathryn Locke (b. 30 May 1961, Upminster, Essex, England; 'cello). Shepherd left to get married and moved to live in Germany, and Andy Cutting (b. 18 March 1969, West Harrow, Middlesex, England; melodeon) joined in 1989. Cutting had previously filled in on odd dates when Shepherd was unavailable, so was no stranger to the music. Later that same year, Swayne re-joined the band. The group's repertoire included a wealth of dance material from northern Europe and France. Although considered a dance band, Blowzabella gave many concerts in such places as Ghana, Nigeria, Sierra Leone, Europe and Brazil. They played a 'farewell tour' in 1990 as it had become uneconomical to stay together and tour. The

Blowzabella

various members have become involved in their own projects and continue to perform.

Albums: *Blowzabella* (1982), *Blowzabella In Colour* (1983), *Bobbityshooty* (1984), *Tam Lin* (1984), *The Blowzabella Wall Of Sound* (1986), *The B To A Of Blowzabella* (1987), *Pingha Frenzy* (1988), *Vanilla* (1990).

Blue, David

b. Stuart David Cohen, 18 February 1941, Providence, Rhode Island, USA, d. 1982, USA. Having left the US Army, Cohen arrived in Greenwich Village in 1960, hoping to pursue an acting career, but was drawn instead into the nascent folk circle. He joined a generation of younger performers - Eric Anderson, Phil Ochs, Dave Van Ronk and Tom Paxton - who rose to prominence in Bob Dylan's wake. Blue was signed to the influential Elektra label in 1965 and released the *Singer/Songwriter Project* album - a joint collaboration with Richard Farina, Bruce Murdoch and Patrick Sky. Although Blue's first full-scale collection in 1966 bore an obvious debt to the folk-rock style of *Highway 61 Revisited*, a rudimentary charm was evident on several selections, notably 'Grand Hotel' and 'I'd Like To Know'. Several acts recorded the singer's compositions, but subsequent recordings with a group, American Patrol, were never issued and it was two years before a second album appeared. *These 23 Days In December* showcased a more mellow performer, best exemplified in the introspective reworking of 'Grand Hotel', before a further release recorded in Nashville, *Me, S. David Cohen*, embraced country styles. A further hiatus ended in 1972 when Blue was signed to David Geffen's emergent Asylum label, and his first album for the company, *Stories*, was the artist's bleakest, most introspective selection. Subsequent releases included the Graham Nash-produced *Nice Baby And The Angel* and *Com'n Back For More*, but although his song, 'Outlaw Man', was covered by the Eagles, David was unable to make a significant commercial breakthrough. During this period, he appeared alongside his old Greenwich Village friend, Bob Dylan in the Rolling Thunder Revue which toured North America. Blue resumed acting later in the decade and made memorable film appearances in Neil Young's *Human Highway* and Wim Wenders's *An American Friend*. His acerbic wit was one of the highlights of Dylan's *Renaldo And Clara* movie, but this underrated artist died in 1982 while jogging in Washington Square Park.

Albums: *Singer/Songwriter Project* (1965), *David Blue* (1966), *These 23 Days In December* (1968), *Me, S. David Cohen* (1970), *Stories* (1972), *Nice Baby And The Angel* (1973), *Com'n Back For More* (1975), *Cupid's Arrow* (1976).

Bob Delyn

This Welsh folk group, led by the harpist and poet Tym Moris, started out by busking, and then attempted to promote their own regional music in a contemporary way. In 1990, their *Sgwarnogod Bach Bob* was cheerful and fresh, and, on the 'Bob Dolig' EP, they played festive Christmas folk tunes in an improvised free music fashion. *Gedon* was full of good ideas and Breton influences, both eccentric and brilliant. Bob Delyn has shown much promise, and much is expected of them in the future.
Albums: *Swarnogod Bach Bob* (1990), *Gedon* (1992).

Boggs, Dock

b. Moran Lee Boggs, 7 February 1898, Norton, Virginia, USA, d. 1971. Boggs was known for his unusual banjo style which he learned from a black musician in Virginia. The technique involved a lower tuning of the banjo. Despite Boggs' interest in music, his devoutly religious wife frowned on him showing any real interest in music, so he continued playing as a hobby. Boggs had recorded briefly for Brunswick in 1927. He spent more than 40 years as a miner and turned again to music once he had retired. At the same time, there was growing demand for him to play at festivals and clubs. Boggs was 'discovered' by Mike Seeger on a field-collecting expedition at a time when Boggs had not played the banjo for some 25 years. He recorded mainly traditional and sentimental songs such as 'Pretty Polly' and 'Loving Nancy'. Between 1963 and 1966, Boggs recorded two albums for Folkways and one for Asch.
Compilations: *Dock Boggs, Vol.1/2 & Vols. 3/4* (c.1980).

Bogle, Eric

b. 1950, Peebles, Scotland, and now resident in Australia after emigrating in 1969. Bogle's musical career started at the age of 16 when he played in a pop group in his home town of Peebles. As a singer/songwriter, he became a household name after 1976, when his song 'And The Band Played Waltzing Matilda' achieved success and was covered and recorded by many artists. The song was written after Bogle had watched the annual Anzac Day parade of Australian ex-soldiers who had survived the Gallipolli campaign in World War I. After an indifferent response to the song initially, Bogle actually dropped it from his live set. It re-emerged after gaining third place in a song competition in Brisbane, Australia. The result almost caused a near riot as many believed he should have won. The attendant publicity helped put the song in the Australian charts. Another of his well-known songs 'Green Fields Of France', was frequently played in the folk clubs by many aspiring performers. *Now*

I'm Easy includes 'No Man's Land', another memorable Bogle composition.
Albums: *Now I'm Easy* (1980), *Scraps Of Paper* (1981), *Down Under* (1982), *In Person* (1982), *Pure* (1982), *Plain And Simple* (1983), *When The Wind Blows* (1985), *In Concert* (1986), *Singing The Spirit Home* (1987), *Something Of Value* (1988), *Voices In The Wilderness* (1991). Compilations: *The Eric Bogle Songbook* (1990).

Boiled In Lead

Formed in 1983 in Minneapolis, USA, the members describe themselves as a 'Celto-deltic-surf-world 'n' reel band'. The original line-up, consisting of Drew Miller (bass), Jane Dauphin (guitar, vocals), Dave Stenshoel (fiddle), and Mitch Griffin (drums), played Celtic folk songs in a punk and garage rock style. Todd Menton (guitar, vocals) had joined the group by the tiime they recorded *Hotheads*, which was released on their own Atomic Theory label, and voted one of the best Celtic albums of the year. By 1988, Dauphin and Griffith had departed, and world music had superseded folk in the band's repertoire. Robin Anders (drums and percussion) was recruited in an attempt to bring more acoustic elements into the arrangements, but the rock factor remained more extreme. The band toured the UK frequently, and signed with the British Cooking Vinyl label, for which they recorded two new wave world sets, including the well-received, *From The Ladle To The Grave*. More recently in the USA they released *Old Lead*, which consisted of their first two albums, plus some studio out-takes. Despite continual personnel changes, Boiled In Lead is one of the more novel units in roots music, and, as long as Miller remains as its leader, the band is capable of producing a wide range of astounding musical sounds from a variety of sources.
Albums: *Boiled In Lead* (1984), *Hotheads* (1986), *From The Ladle To The Grave* (1989), *Orb* (1990). Compilation: *Old Lead* (1991).

Bok, Gordon

b. 31 October 1939, Pennsylvania, USA. Bok's parents had a collection of folk music, and his brothers and sisters all sang and played. Teaching himself to play guitar, at the age of nine, Bok was giving concerts from the age of 15, and eventually took up performing, essentially as a hobby, while working as a sailor. Spending much of the early 60s in Philadelphia, he met others playing folk music. Inspired by his nautical interests and background, Gordon produced a large number of works related to the sea. His first release, *Gordon Bok*, appeared on Verve/Folkways Records, but subsequent recordings were released on Folk Legacy. As a

Peter Bond

sailor, and first mate, he was involved in fitting and repairing the Clearwater Sloop, which journeyed the Hudson River on an environmental ticket. As a performer Bok was appearing in concerts with artists such as Pete Seeger. Gordon has travelled widely to appear at folk clubs and festivals in the USA, Canada, England and Scotland. He made his first trip to England in 1975, and occasionally tours with Dave Goulder. In addition to his many albums, Bok has also produced a number of choral works, and written poetry. A book of his poetry, *If I Had Your Wings*, included wood engravings by Ed Porter. In 1986, Gordon formed Timberhead, his own label and company, whose first release was *Cold As A Dog And The Wind North East*. This is a collection of spoken ballads and monologues written by Ruth Moore. Bok currently spends around five months of the year on the road, and the rest of the time writing.

Albums: *Gordon Bok* (1965), *A Tune For November* (1970), *Peter Kagan And The Wind* (1971), *Seal Djiril's Hymn* (1972), *Bay Of Fundy* (1975), with Ann Mayo Muir and Ed Trickett *Turning Toward The Morning* (1975), with Muir and Trickett *The Ways Of Man* (1978), *Another Land Made Of Water* (1979), with Muir and Trickett *A Water Over Stone* (1980), *Jeremy Brown And Jeanie Teal* (1981), *Rogue's Gallery Of Songs For The 12-String* (1983), with Muir and Trickett *All Shall Be Well Again* (1983), with Muir and Trickett *Fashioned In The Clay* (1985), *Cold As A Dog and The Wind North East* (1986), with Muir and Trickett *Minneapolis Concert* (1987), *Gordon Bok, Ann Mayo Muir And Ed Trickett-Live* (1988), *Ensemble* (1988), *The Play Of The Lady Odivere* (1989), with Muir and Trickett *And So Will We Yet* (1990), *Return To The Land* (1991). Compilations: *Clear Away In The Morning* (1983).

Further reading: *If I Had Your Wings*, Gordon Bok, *Time And The Flying Snow-Songs Of Gordon Bok*, Gordon Bok.

Bolton, Polly

An extremely talented vocalist who rose through the Coventry acoustic band Dando Shaft, before joining Bert Jansch, and then finally giving up music at the end of the 70s. She left to become a market gardener - using her degree in botany. A revival gig with her old partner, Kevin Dempsey, impressed Ashley Hutchings, and she became involved in several of his projects: The Albion Dance Band's *I Got New Shoes* (1987) (she sang the female part in the tangled love of 'By Gloucester Docks I Sat Down And Wept'), and the live, *As You Like It*, by The Hutchings Allstars. She subsequently worked as a session singer, before releasing her own album in 1989. With John

Shepherd (keyboards) and Steve Dunachie (fiddle), she formed The Polly Bolton Band. Their musical plan, a mixture of traditional songs in an almost baroque, pastoral setting, was effectively displayed on *Songs From A Cold, Open Field*, on which Bolton adopts some jazz phrasing. She is at last receiving the recognition she deserves, and is one of the most in-demand singers on the folk scene.

Albums: *No Going Back* (1989), *Woodbine & Ivy* (1990), *Songs From A Cold, Open Field* (1993).

Bond, Peter

b. 16 December 1945, Stockton-On-Tees, County Durham, England. Singer/songwriter who enjoyed most of his success in the late 70s and early 80s. Bond started playing in folk clubs in 1974, and became well-known on the domestic circuit, and occasionally toured abroad. His guitar and harmonica playing were augmented by his playing clarinet on *A Duck On His Head*. After 10 years of playing and recording, Bond decided to concentrate on other projects, and gave up performing in 1985. He currently teaches guitar full-time and composes and performs for BBC Radio Schools programmes.

Albums: *It's All Right For Some* (1977), *See Me Up, See Me Down* (1979), with Tim Laycock and Bill Caddick *A Duck On His Head* (1979), *Awkward Age* (1983).

Bookbinder, Roy

b. 5 October 1941, New York City, New York, USA. Bookbinder began playing guitar in the early 60s and was initially inspired by Dave Van Ronk. He met Rev. Gary Davis in 1968, ostensibly for guitar lessons, but was travelling with him within a month. Davis regarded Bookbinder as one of his best students. Towards the end of the 60s he recorded for a Blue Goose Records anthology, and in 1970 he made his first full album for Adelphi, dedicated to Pink Anderson, whom Bookbinder brought back into the public eye. The album was extremely well-received, with most reviewers commenting on the honesty and individuality of his country blues interpretations. He continues to tour and record (currently for Rounder Records), playing what his press releases call 'old time country and hillbilly blues'.

Albums: *Travellin' Man* (1971), *Bookeroo* (1988), *The Hillbilly Blues Cats* (1992).

Boothill Foot-Tappers

Formed in 1982 by Chris Thompson (b. 19 March 1957, Ashford, Middlesex, England; banjo/vocals) and Kevin Walsh (guitar/vocals), the Boothill's full line-up was completed by Wendy May (b. Wendy May Billingsley; vocals), Slim (b. Clive Pain; accordion/piano), Marnie Stephenson (washboard/vocals), Merrill Heatley (vocals) and her brother Danny (drums). As part of an emerging 'country cow-punk' movement in the UK during the mid-80s (along with such acts as Helen And The Horns and Yip Yip Coyote), the Boothill Foot-Tappers proved to be the most adept at the genre and certainly one of the best live performers. They scored a minor UK hit on the Go! Discs/Chrysalis label with 'Get Your Feet Out Of My Shoes' in July 1984. Slim, who had been enjoying a parallel career as part of the Blubbery Hellbellies, left the group in 1983 before the recording of the Boothill's debut album and was replaced by Simon Edwards (melodeon) - although he occasionally re-joined the group for live performances. The group folded at the end of 1985 after touring to promote the album which failed to set the charts alight. After briefly working with B.J. Cole and Bob Loveday in the Rivals and later with the Devils In Disguise, Chris Thompson went on to form the Barely Works. Wendy May decided to concentrate on the running of the successful disco club 'Locomotion' at the Town And Country Club in Kentish Town, London.

Album: *Ain't That Far From Boothill* (1985).

Bothy Band

Formed in 1975, this Irish folk-rock group featured Donal Lunny (synthesizer/dulcimer), who had formerly been with Planxty, Michael O'Domhnaill (guitar/vocals), Triona Ni Domhnaill (clarinet/harpsichord), Paddyn Glackin (fiddle), and Matt Molloy (b. Ballaghaderreen, Co. Roscommon, Eire; flute/whistle). Tommy Peoples (fiddle) and Paddy Keenan (pipes), had also played in the group during its relatively short lifespan, which lasted till only 1979. Despite their traditional background, and playing largely traditional tunes, the group, in comparison to the Chieftains, pursued more of a rock orientated style, akin to Planxty. After five albums the individual members went their separate ways. Triona Ni Domhnaill moved to North Carolina, USA, forming Touchstone, while her brother Michael, along with fiddle player Kevin Burke, based themselves in Portland, Oregon, where they released albums from their own studio, as well as appearing on numerous recordings by other artists. After the break up of the Bothy Band, Planxty reformed.

Albums: *1975* (1975), *Old Hag You Have Killed Me* (1976), *The Bothy Band* (1976), *Out Of The Wind Into The Sun* (1977), *After Hours-Live In Paris* (1978) Compilation: *The Best Of The Bothy Band* (1980).

Boyle, Maggie

b. Margaret Boyle, 24 December 1956, Battersea, London, England. Boyle came from a traditional Irish background, and was brought up in the London Irish community. She was taught to play and sing by her father, Paddy Boyle (b. Co. Donegal, Ireland), and helped by Oliver Mulligan, a singer from Co. Monaghan. Boyle first performed in public at the age of 11, singing and playing in Irish clubs, and concerts. She gave a number of performances played with her brothers Paul (fiddle), and Kevin (banjo/guitar), as the 'Boyle Family'. Maggie started working professionally in 1984, as on-stage singer/musician for a folk ballet, *Sgt. Early's Dream*, choreographed by the Ballet Rambert. Her husband, Steve Tilston, also played in the production, and once the ballet ceased touring, around 1986, Boyle and Tilston started working in folk clubs. *Reaching Out*, on Run River Records, was released a year later, and included a version of Robin Williamson's 'October Song', and a combination of traditional and contemporary material. Brothers Kevin and Paul both featured on the recording, as did Bert Jansch. The album was well received by the folk media. At about the same time, she and Tilston were approached by John Renbourn to form the group Ship Of Fools, with Tony Roberts (flute/Northumbrian pipes/clarinet/recorder/saxophone). The group toured the USA, Italy and England, and released *Ship Of Fools*, also on Run River. Maggie performed and arranged the music for another ballet, 'In The Eye Of The Storm', for the Gothenburg Ballet. This was based on the novel by Jennifer Johnston, *Fool's Sanctuary*. The ballet, choreographed by Eileen Jones, was premiered in Gothenburg in 1990. Boyle also performed the earlier work, 'Sgt. Early's Dream', with the Chieftains in Cincinnati, USA, in May 1991. She continues to play the folk club circuit throughout Britain.

Albums: *Reaching Out* (1987), with Ship Of Fools *Ship Of Fools* (1988), with Steve Tilston *Of Moor & Mesa* (1992).

Boys Of The Lough

This Irish-Scottish group formed in 1967 and were well known for their arrangements of Celtic music. The original line-up of Robin Morton (b. 24 December 1939, Portadown, Northern Ireland; vocals/concertina/bodhran), Cathal McConnell (b. 8 June 1944, Enniskillen, County Fermanagh, Northern Ireland; flute/vocals/whistle), and Tommy Gunn (b. Derrylin, County Fermanagh, Northern Ireland; fiddle/bones/vocals) adopted the name Boys Of The Lough during a recording session for a television programme. After a tour of Scotland and England, Gunn left the trio, leaving McConnell and Morton to continue as a duo. In 1988, at the Aberdeen Folk Festival, they

Boys Of The Lough

performed with another duo, Aly Bain and Mike Whelans. This became the new line-up of the group. Dick Gaughan then replaced Whelans, in 1972, and in this guise appeared at the Cambridge Folk Festival, the same year, to considerable acclaim. In 1973, Gaughan left to pursue a solo career. He was in turn replaced by Dave Richardson (b. 20 August 1948, Corbridge, Northumberland, England; guitar, mandolin, cittern, concertina, tenor banjo, hammer dulcimer), for the group's upcoming American tour. The group then toured regularly for the next few years, on both sides of the Atlantic. In 1979, Morton left, to be replaced by Tich Richardson, brother of Dave, on guitar. This line-up toured worldwide into the 80s, but in September 1984, Tich was killed in a car accident. In February 1985 Christy O'Leary (b. 7 June 1955, Rathcoole, Co. Dublin, Eire; uillean pipes/vocals) joined, followed by John Coakley (b. 30 July 1951, Cork, Eire; guitar, piano). From this point, the Irish music in their act took a greater precedence. In February 1988, they celebrated their 21st Anniversary with a concert at New York's Carnegie Hall which was released as an album the following year on the Sage Arts label. Despite the personnel changes, they have retained their popularity, and the standard of musicianship has remained consistently high. The group continue to tour the USA regularly, with the various individual members undertaking their own projects concurrently. In Bain's case this has involved much

television work, including *Down Home* in 1985, *Aly Bain And Friends* in 1989, and *Push The Boat Out* in 1991. Morton, meanwhile, went on to head Temple Records in Edinburgh.
Albums: *The Boys Of The Lough* (1973), *Second Album* (1973), *Recorded Live* (1975), *Lochaber No More* (1975), *The Piper's Broken Finger* (1976), *Good Friends-Good Music* (1977), *Wish You Were Here* (1978), *Regrouped* (1980), *In The Tradition* (1981), *Open Road* (1983), *Far, Far From Home* (1986), *Welcoming Paddy Home* (1986), *Farewell And Remember Me* (1987), *Sweet Rural Shade* (1988), *Live At Carnegie Hall* (1989). Solo albums: Robin Morton and Cathal McConnell *An Irish Jubilee* (1969); Cathal McConnell *On Lough Erne's 'Shore* (1978); Aly Bain *Aly Bain-Mike Whelans* (1971), *Aly Bain* (1985), *Down Home Vol.1* (1985), *Down Home Vol.2* (1985), *Aly Bain Meets The Cajuns* (1988). Compilations: *Gaelic Folk, Vol.1* (1978), *Gaelic Folk, Vol.2* (1978).

Brady, Paul

b. 19 May 1947, Strabane, Co. Tyrone, Northern Ireland. A member of an R&B group, the Kult, while a student in Dublin, Brady later embraced folk music with the Johnstons. Renowned as a commercial attraction, the group enjoyed a minor success with a version of Joni Mitchell's 'Both Sides Now'. Brady subsequently joined Planxty, a much-respected traditional unit, where the multi-instrumentalist forged an empathy with fellow

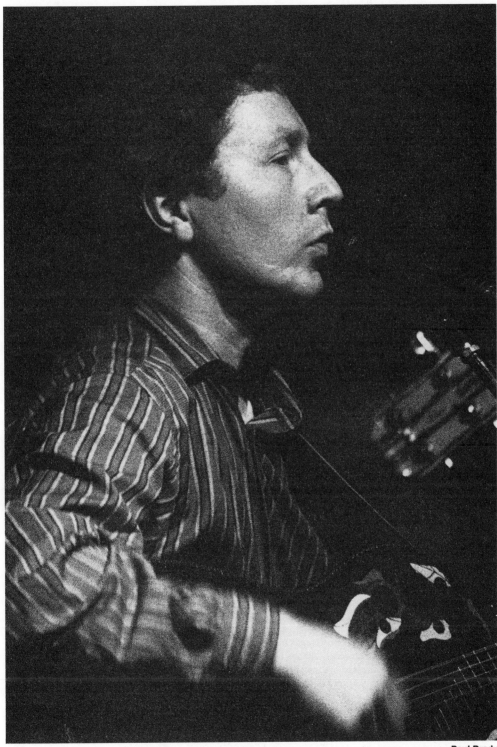

Paul Brady

member Andy Irvine. *Andy Irvine/Paul Brady* prefaced Brady's solo career which began with the much-lauded *Welcome Here Kind Stranger* in 1978. The singer abandoned folk in 1981 with *Hard Station*, which included the Irish chart-topping single, 'Crazy Dreams'. The song was then covered by Roger Chapman and Dave Edmunds while a further inclusion, 'Night Hunting Time', was later recorded by Santana. *True For You* followed a prolific period where Brady toured supporting Dire Straits and Eric Clapton, winning the approbation of their audiences. Bob Dylan and U2's Bono also professed admiration for the artist's talents while Tina Turner's versions of 'Steel Claw' and 'Paradise Is Here' cemented Brady's reputation as a songwriter. He collaborated with Mark Knopfler on the soundtrack to *Cal*, before completing a strong live album, *Full Moon*. Subsequent releases show the flowering of a mature and crafted talent, reminiscent of Van Morrison. *Trick Or Treat* was recorded under the aegis of former Steely Dan producer, Gary Katz. Bonnie Raitt, an admirer of Brady's work, gave his career a significant boost by including two of his songs on her outstanding 1991 album including the title track 'Luck Of The Draw'. It is hoped that Brady's work will receive major recognition in the future as he is clearly an important songwriter.
Albums: *Andy Irvine/Paul Brady* (1976), with Tommy Peoples *The High Part Of The Road* (1976), *Welcome Here Kind Stranger* (1978), *Hard Station* (1981), *True For You* (1983), *Full Moon* (1984), *Back To The Centre* (1986), with Matt Molloy and Tommy Peoples *Molloy, Brady, Peoples* (1986), *Primitive Dance* (1987), *Paradise Is Here* (1989), *Trick Or Treat* (1991).

Brand, Oscar

b. 7 February 1920, Winnipeg, Manitoba, Canada. This well-known folk satirist and former student of psychiatry, started something of a revival in the 40s because of his WNYC folk music radio show *The Folksong Festival*, which was first broadcast on 10 December 1945. As a performer, Brand, who played guitar and banjo, was known for songs such as 'Charlotte The Harlot', 'Blinded By Turds', 'Seven Old Ladies Locked In A Lavatory' and 'The Money Rolls In'. Despite its popularity, satire was not a new phenomenon, as his *Election Songs Of The United States* contained some numbers dating back to the 1800s. Eventually the radio show became simply *Folksong Festival* and featured a number of emerging talents in the folk field. Names such as Pete Seeger, Burl Ives, Judy Collins, Odetta, Phil Ochs and countless others, have all passed through. Such has been the success of the show that it is still broadcast weekly. During the 60s, Oscar hosted *Let's Sing Out*, a Canadian television show which, apart from including Gordon Lightfoot and Judy Collins on occasion, also featured a number of other artists and performers, blacklisted in the USA during the McCarthy era. During this period, Brand had refused to testify before the House Un-American Activities Committee. Brand has recorded over 60 albums, and in his time has acted and written books. He has recorded for Elektra, MCA, ABC, Folkways, Riverside and Impulse, written songs for Harry Belafonte and Ella Fitzgerald among others, and has appeared in films and on television.
Albums: *Noah's Ark* (1947), *Songs Inane Only* (1948), *American Drinking Songs* (1948), *Absolute Nonsense* (1948), with Jean Ritchie *Riddle Me This* (1949), *Give 'im The Hook* (1949), *Bawdy Songs And Backroom Ballads, Vol. 1* (1949), *Backroom Ballads* (1949), *Bawdy Songs And Backroom Ballads, Vol. 2* (1949), *Songs And Poems Of The Sea* (1949), *Children's Concert* (1949), with Ritchie *Courting Songs* (1949), *G.I (US Army Songs)* (1949), *Bawdy Songs And Backroom Ballads, Vol. 3* (1950), *Come To The Party* (1950), *Bawdy Songs And Backroom Ballads, Vol. 4* (1951), *Bring A Song Johnny* (1951), *Bawdy Songs And Backroom Ballads, Vol. 5* (1952), *Bawdy Sea Songs* (1952), *An Oscar Brand Songbag* (1952), with Pete Seeger *Everybody Sing* (1953), *Rollicking Sea Songs* (1954), *Bawdy Hootenanny* (1955), *Bawdy College Songs* (1955), *Bawdy Singalong* (1956), *The Wild Blue Yonder* (1956), with the Tarriers *Folksongs For Fun* (1956), *Bawdy Western Songs* (1957), *Sports Car Songs* (1957), *Every Inch A Sailor* (1958), *Up In The Air* (1959), *Out Of The Blue* (1960), *Tell It To The Marines* (1961), *Cough (Soldier songs)* (1962), *Presidential Election Songs* (1962), *Oscar Brand Sings For Adults* (1962), *Folk Festival* (1963), *For Doctors Only* (1963), *Boating Songs* (1964), *Morality* (1964), with Ritchie *Town Hall Concert* (1966), *Celebrate* (1968), *Pie In The Sky* (1969), with Ritchie *Shivaree* (1969), *Laughing America* (1970), *Celebrate America* (1971, 13 cassette set), *Politics And Elections, Vols. 1-3* (1974), *On Campus (Canadian Songs)* (1974), with Kate Smith *The Americans* (1976), with Ed Begley *Paul Bunyan* (1977), *Singing Holidays* (1978), *Billy The Kid* (1979), *First Thanksgiving* (1980), *Trick Or Treat* (1981), *Singing Is Believing* (1982), *My Christmas Is Best* (1983), *Happy Birthday* (1985), *American Dreamer* (1985), *100 Proof* (1987), *Brand X* (1987), *We All Sing 1* (1987), *Songs For Tadpoles* (1988), *We All Sing 2* (1988), *Hop, Jump, And Sing With Oscar Brand* (1988), *MacDougal And Bleecker* (1990), *Let's Have A Party* (1991), *Welcome To America* (1991). Compilations: *Best Of Bawdy Songs* (1965), *The Best Of Oscar Brand* (1975), *The Best Of The Worst* (1989).

Further reading: *The Ballad Mongers-Rise Of The Modern Folk Song*, Oscar Brand.

Brass Monkey

This short-lived group, formed in 1981, comprised John Kirkpatrick (anglo-concertina, melodeon, accordion, vocals), Roger Williams (b. 30 July 1954, Cottingham, Yorkshire, England; trombone), Howard Evans (b. 29 February 1944, Chard, Somerset, England; trumpet, flugelhorn), Martin Brinsford (b. 17 August 1944, Gloucester, England; saxophone, mouth organ, percussion) and Martin Carthy (guitar, mandolin, vocals). Brinsford had earlier been a member of the Old Swan Band. Meanwhile, another band, Home Service, still included Kirkpatrick, Evans and Williams as members. Williams was replaced in 1984 by Richard Cheetham (b. 29 January 1957, Ashton-under-Lyne, Manchester, England; trombone). The group provided something of an eyebrow-raiser when their combination of traditional folk instruments were played alongside brass instruments. The combination of folk stalwarts Carthy and Kirkpatrick and classically-trained brass musicians produced the highly acclaimed *Brass Monkey*. The group appeared on the Loudon Wainwright release *More Love Songs* in 1986, but with the various members of the band having so many other commitments, they went their separate ways the following year.

Albums: *Brass Monkey* (1983), *See How It Runs* (1986).

Brett, Paul

A former guitarist with Elmer Gantry's Velvet Opera, Brett left that particular group to join Fire, a cultishly popular combo which featured Dave Lambert, a future member of the Strawbs. Fire's original bassist, Dick Dufall and drummer, Bob Voice, then broke off to join Brett in his own group, Paul Brett Sage. This respected musician recorded prolifically throughout the 70s, honing a tasteful yet accomplished style. A 1974 collection, *Clocks*, is arguably his best remembered album, but as the decade progressed so his work became increasingly less exciting.

Albums: *Paul Brett Sage* (1970), *Jubilation Foundry* (1971), *Schizophrenia* (1972), *Paul Brett* (1973), *Clocks* (1974), *Phoenix Future* (1975), *Earthbirth* (1977), *Interlife* (1978), *Eclipse* (1979), *Guitar Trek* (1980), *Romantic Guitar* (1980).

Briggs, Anne

b. Anne Patricia Briggs, 29 September 1944, Toton, Nottinghamshire, England. Briggs started singing publicly in 1962, when aged 17. She has been credited by many as a major influence on the singing styles and techniques of singers such as June Tabor and Maddy Prior. It was only in 1990, after Fellside Records issued a compilation, *Classic Anne*

Brass Monkey

Briggs, that her daughter even knew that Briggs had sung in folk clubs some 20 years earlier. The issue of the album has re-created interest in her singing. Her first recording was an EP *The Hazards Of Love*, which won praise from A.L. Lloyd. Briggs claims Isla Cameron to be a major influence in her early years. The album *The Bird In The Bush*, a collaboration with Lloyd, was a conceptual piece exploring erotica in English folk song. The recording included the singing of Frankie Armstrong. It was not until 1971 that her first solo album was released by Topic Records. She retains a quality that is timeless, given the content of her material.

Albums: with Bert Lloyd *The Bird In The Bush* (1966), *Anne Briggs* (1971), *Classic Anne Briggs* (1990).

Brimstone, Derek

b. 29 August 1932, Islington, London, England. Having taken up classical guitar during the 50s Derek drifted into the folk scene, and was almost 30 years old before he sang professionally for the first time. There followed a three year period of 'floor spots' in folk clubs all over London, culminating in a residency in a Luton club. Appearing at the first Cambridge Folk Festival in 1965, Brimstone was subsequently featured in *Melody Maker*. His style of blues and ragtime, played on guitar, and occasionally banjo and piano, interspersed with touches of humour, has continued to prove popular with audiences. Southern Music have published two of his tutors; *Easy Pickings 5-String Banjo* (1967), and *Clawpicking Guitar Made Easy* (1968). After 25 years on the road he has reduced his live performances and only occasionally tours.

Albums: *Fire And Brimstone* (1967), *Very Good Time* (1972), *Shuffleboat River Farewell* (1974), *There Was This Bloke* (1975), *Derek Brimstones' Cheapo Album* (1984).

Bromberg, David

b. 19 September 1945, Philadelphia, Pennsylvania, USA. Bromberg was a session musician who later recorded a series of albums under his own name. Proficient on guitar (primarily acoustic), violin, mandolin and banjo, Bromberg's music took in elements of folk, blues, bluegrass, rock, comedy and lengthy narrative stories often stuck in between choruses. His career began in New York's Greenwich Village in the 60s, where he performed on sessions for diverse artists such as Jay And The Americans, Rick Derringer, Blood, Sweat And Tears, Jerry Jeff Walker, Chubby Checker and Bob Dylan - he performed on the latter's *Self Portrait* and *New Morning* albums in 1970 and 1971. He signed a recording contract with Columbia Records and released a self-titled album in 1971. His next two albums, *Demon In Disguise* and *Wanted Dead Or Alive*, included guest appearances by members of the Grateful Dead. *Midnight On The Water* featured appearances including Emmylou Harris, Linda Ronstadt, Dr. John, Jesse Ed Davis, Bonnie Raitt and Ricky Skaggs. In 1976 Bromberg signed to Fantasy Records and released a further five albums, including the live *How Late'll Ya Play 'Til?* In 1977 he appeared with other acoustic musicians, including Vassar Clements and D.J. Fontana, on the critically acclaimed albums *Hillbilly Jazz*. Bromberg gave up performing and recording throughout much of the 80s and undertook making and repairing violins and other instruments. He occasionally performed one-off gigs, including an annual appearance at New York club the Bottom Line. In 1990, Bromberg resurfaced on Rounder Records with a new album, *Sideman Serenade*. Never a large commercial success, Bromberg retains a devoted following into the 90s, despite his relaxed work schedule.

Albums: *David Bromberg* (1971), *Demons In Disguise* (1972), *Wanted Dead Or Alive* (1974), *Midnight On The Water* (1975), *How Late'll Ya Play 'Til?* (1976), *Reckless Abandon* (1977), *Bandit In A Bathing Suit* (1978), *My Own House* (1978), *You Should See The Rest Of The Band* (1980), *Sideman Serenade* (1990). Compilations: (various artists) *Hillbilly Jazz, Vol. 1* (1977), *Hillbilly Jazz, Vol. 2* (1977).

Bruce, Ian

b. 21 January 1956, Rutherglen, Glasgow, Scotland. Singer/songwriter Bruce began an early career singing in folk clubs with his brother Fraser (b. Andrew Fraser Bruce, 13 January 1947, Fulham, London, England). They recorded three albums together before Ian gradually moved into solo work. A brief sojourn with a group called Scotland Yard, which included Marilyn Middleton Pollock and Sandy Stanage, resulted in *Wishing For Friday*, which was never released. Bruce's first real acceptance as a songwriter came with the release of *Too Far From She*, with special interest being shown in the title track. He was signed to Fellside records for *Blodwen's Dream* - Fellside's first CD release. This album contained Graham Miles' excellent 'My Eldorado', and the equally fine self-penned title track. Bruce has toured the USA, Germany and Ireland, and in addition to solo work, also performs with fellow songwriter Ian Walker, the group Blue Rooster with Dez Walters (formerly of Country Dawn), and Ian Murray.

Albums: with Fraser Bruce *Mrs. Bruce's Boys Vol.1* (1980), *Veil Of The Ages* (1982), *Mrs. Bruce's Boys Vol. 2* (1985); *Too Far From She* (1988), *Blodwen's Dream* (1990), *Out Of Office* (1992).

Buckwheat Zydeco

Buckwheat Zydeco

b. Stanley Dural, 1947, Lafayette, Louisiana, USA. Dural started his musical career playing piano and organ in local bands around southeast Louisiana. As Buckwheat Zydeco emerged as one of the leaders of zydeco music, the accordion-led dance music of southern Louisiana's French-speaking Creoles, in the late 80s and early 90s. Dural, taking the nickname 'Buckwheat', worked with R&B singers Joe Tex, Barbara Lynn and Clarence 'Gatemouth' Brown during the 60s. Following a period playing keyboards in Clifton Chenier's band, he took up accordion and moved to the indigenous sound of zydeco. He formed his own funk band, the Hitchhikers, in the 70s, followed by the Ils Sont Partis Band in 1979. That outfit recorded eight albums for Blues Unlimited, Black Top and Rounder Records before accordionist Dural formed Buckwheat Zydeco. Signed to Island Records in 1987, the group had recorded three albums for the label by 1990, the latter produced by David Hidalgo of Los Lobos.

Albums: *One For The Road* (1979), *100% Fortified Zydeco* (1985), *Buckwheat Zydeco* (1986), *Waitin' For My Ya Ya* (1987), *On A Night Like This* (1987), *Taking It Home* (1988), *Turning Point* (1988), *Buckwheat Zydeco And The Ils Sont Partis Band* (1988), *Where There's Smoke There's Fire* (1990).

Buirski, Felicity

This former model, remembered as a 'page 3 pin-up girl', started her musical career at the age of 30 in England. Having been editor of a Kent newspaper when she was 18, Buirski took up modelling two years later. Later, in the 70s, she started the arts magazine *Avant Garde*. She had a musical background with a virtuoso pianist father and a mother who was a concert hall singer. Buirski claims that a chance meeting with Leonard Cohen, inspired her to take up the guitar again at the comparatively late age of 26. In 1979, she appeared in the film *The Bitch* with Joan Collins. Cohen's influence is apparent on Felicity's first album, on Run Riner Records, and was well-received by some of the folk media. It also received the award for the best folk album in the *Which CD* Hi-Fi Music Awards for 1989. Buirski played support to Eric Andersen in 1990 in the USA, but has done relatively little live work in the UK.

Album: *Repairs And Alterations* (1988).

Bully Wee Band

The original line-up consisted of founder members John Yardley (b. 7 January 1946, Dunfermline, Fife, Scotland; vocals/guitar/bodhran) and Jim Yardley (b. 23 October 1944, Dunfermline, Fife, Scotland; vocals/guitar/mandolin), together with

Bully Wee Band

Frank Simon (b. Boyle, Co. Roscommon, Eire; guitar, whistles, vocals), Ian Cutler (b. 22 December 1953, London, England) a classically trained violinist, joined in 1975, augmenting his ability by playing viola and keyboards. Colin Reece (b. 28 September 1947, London, England; vocals, guitar), rejoined in 1979, having left the group in 1974. Fergus Feely (b. July 1953, Dundalk, Eire; cello-mandolin,, vocals), joined the others in 1976. That same year Simon left. The band played contemporary and traditional songs and tunes in a rock-based format. Following the release of *Enchanted Lady*, the group toured Europe during early 1977. *The Madmen Of Gotham* (featuring Cutler, Reece, Feely and Jim Yardley) included six traditional songs showing that the band had not lost their feel for their origins. Later, in 1981, they were joined by Martin Allcock (b. 5 January 1957, Manchester, England; guitar, bass, bouzouki, mandolin, keyboards), who left, in 1983, to form a duo with Feely. Allcock subsequently joined Fairport Convention in 1985 and later became a member of Jethro Tull, in addition to doing much session work. Feely went on to join the Steve Ashley Band, then worked with the San Franciscan cajun band Le Rue for a time. Cutler and Reece produced *Face To Face* in 1982 the following year, Reece went solo, releasing one album, *Well Kept Secrets*, in 1985. Following a support tour with Elkie Brooks, Reece moved into the cabaret field, backing comedian Jim Davidson. Jim Yardley went on to play in a solo capacity in Norway, while Cutler continues to follow a folk direction playing in ceilidh bands and Albion Morris.
Albums: *Bully Wee* (1975), *Enchanted Lady* (1976), *Silvermines* (1978), *The Madmen Of Gotham* (1980). Solo albums: Colin Reece *Well Kept Secrets* (1985); Colin Reece and Ian Cutler *Face To Face* (1982).

Burland, Dave

b. 12 July 1941, Barnsley, South Yorkshire, England. A respected, and long established performer, Burland has a wide repertoire of material ranging from traditional and contemporary, including songs that often are not classified as 'folk'. Having turned professional in 1968, Burland has continued to perform and record, at folk festivals, in clubs, and has toured much of Europe, Hong Kong and Australia during his career. His first release, *A Dalesman's Litany*, an album of traditional songs, was voted *Melody Maker* Folk Album Of The Year in 1971. There followed the equally well-received *Dave Burland*, again on Trailer. *Songs And Buttered Haycocks*, featured songs by writers such as Richard Thompson, David Ackles and Mike Waterson of the Watersons. In 1978, Burland joined the folk rock band Hedgehog Pie, the combination of

guitars, flute, uillean pipes, cittern and piccolo, resulting in the release of *Just Act Normal*. This was to be the group's last album, before splitting up in 1981. During this time, Burland released *Songs Of Ewan MacColl*, which again showed his ability to interpret different styles of writing. After the split, Dave, again solo, put out *You Can't Fool The Fat Man*, which displayed his wide taste in quality songs. The album featured songs from the pens of diverse names such as Randy Newman and Cyril Tawney. Dave's other commitments included hosting folk shows on BBC and independent local radio, as well as organizing folk festivals in Leeds, with Andy Kershaw. *Rollin'*, an album of modern material, was released on the Moonraker label, and since then Burland has been touring and performing at festivals and clubs. He has also appeared as session player on albums by Mike Harding, and Nic Jones among others. *Willin'* was a live recording, and included some of Dave's earlier material alongside previously unrecorded works. He has recently released an album of Richard Thompson songs, *His Master's Choice*, and in 1992 joined the Lost Nation Band with Sara Grey and Roger Wilson.
Albums: *A Dalesman's Litany* (1971), *Dave Burland* (1972), *Songs And Buttered Haycocks* (1975), *Songs Of Ewan MacColl* (1978), with Hedgehog Pie *Just Act Normal* (1978), *You Can't Fool The Fat Man* (1978), *Rollin'* (1983), *Willin'* (1989), *His Master's Choice* (1992).

Bushwackers

Bush-rock is perhaps the only style of music which might be considered unique to Australia, unlike almost all other Australian music which is directly influenced by or even imitative of USA and UK trends. The style is a mixture of traditional Irish and Australian ballads, traditional folk dance music played on the usual rock musical instruments, with the addition of fiddle and accordion. The major proponents of this genre were the Bushwackers, themselves originally an all-acoustic band formed in 1971 playing folk dances and singing typical Australian 'bush' ballads and poems. The Bushwackers principal members comprised Dobe Newton (vocals, lagaphone), Jan Wozitsky (banjo, harmonica/vocals), Tommy Emmanuel (guitar) and Louis McManus (guitar, fiddle, mandolin). By the mid-70s the band had electrified and started playing the pubs, where they attracted the attention of the rock world, particularly with the album *Faces In The Street*, but the crossover took some years to complete. The Bushwackers toured the UK and continental Europe for several extended spells, and were popular with crowds at the summertime folk festivals. The band has at various times attracted regular rock players as members, such as Peter

Dave Burland

Farndon (bass, Pretenders) and Freddie Strauks (drums, Skyhooks) as well as some of Australia's finest folk musicians. The band also published three books of their songs and dance tunes, which sold in large quantities. By the mid-80s the band had eased back to a part-time concern, but still managed to retain a small, loyal following.

Albums: *Shearer's Dream* (1974), *And The Band Played Waltzing Matilda* (1976), *Murrumbidgee, Bushfire, The Dance Album* (1980), *Faces In The Street* (1981), *Down There For Dancing* (1982), *Warrigul Morning* (1988), *Beneath The Southern Cross* (1989), *Shoalhaven Man* (1989).

C

Caddick, Bill

b. 27 June 1944, Hurst Hill, Wolverhampton, England. Singer-songwriter and guitarist Caddick gained his first exposure to folk music while at college in Coventry. Occasionally he appeared with Mike Billington. Caddick performed at the Bromyard Folk Festival in 1972 and met Magic Lantern, a group using shadow puppets and music. Having duly impressed them with his songs he was asked to join. He later left, on New Years Day in 1975, in order to pursue a solo career, but until 1976 was out of action with throat and back problems. In 1980, Bill joined Home Service, playing guitar and dobro, as well as providing vocals. He left in 1985, unhappy with the lack of live work the group were doing. Moving back to Wolverhampton, Caddick was combining solo work with playing in a blues band. He then took a break from music and worked part-time in a psychiatric hospital until early in 1990. Caddick then moved back to London and started writing again, shortly after forming Urban Legend. He had originally intended to join Zumzeaux, but the group disbanded. *Urban Legend* was produced by Andrew Cronshaw, and featured former Zumzeaux musicians Neil Vaandrager (fiddle) and Bernard O'Neill (double bass).

Albums: *Rough Music* (1976), *Sunny Memories* (1977), *Reasons Briefly Set Down* (1979), with Peter Bond and Tim Laycock *A Duck On His Head* (1979), *The Wild West Show* (1986), *Urban Legend* (1991).

Cajun And Zydeco

Cajun music, together with its near cousin Zydeco, is indigenous to the south east of the USA, where it flourishes in parts of Louisiana and Texas bordering the gulf coast. The two musical styles have both developed out of the folk music brought to the area by French settlers who made the long and arduous trek from eastern Canada at the end of the 18th century. The music reflects the multiplicity of influences the region has been exposed to, from Creole, Spanish, German, Anglo-American, Irish, Scottish, African, Caribbean and native American Indian forms of music and customs. At the same time, it has developed in a manner removed from the everyday consensus of American lifestyle, and the preservation of the cajun culture through relative geographical and social isolation has played no small part in shaping that very same culture.

These French immigrants were forced to leave their north eastern communities (Acadie or Acadia, what is now Nova Scotia and its environs) by the British, who, in 1755, invited them to sign an oath of allegiance to the Crown and renounce their Catholicism; an offer they in turn declined. Travelling down the east coast of north America over many years, when large numbers of them perished, they finally settled in a largely inhospitable and swampy area where they were left alone to get on with their lives. They have expanded over the two centuries into a region that now comprises south and south west Louisiana and east Texas.

From 'Acadian' comes the phonetic abbreviation 'Cajun'. To this day, a large part of the community has retained the French language, although its survival had been threatened during the local oil boom years of the 50s, and a tide of American nationalism. There are almost a million cajuns in that community today, with a revived sense of pride and purpose, and they naturally exert a dominant influence on everyday life in their towns and rural communities. Most of the towns and the people retain their French names, as do virtually all of the songs and instrumental tune titles. Although some of the song lyrics have been translated into English (especially for illustrative purposes in the booklets that accompany recordings, for educational use, in songbooks, etc) they are still universally sung in the local dialect of French, Cajun French, which Europeans will find quite different to those that they remember from school.

The fiddle was the dominant melodic instrument until the arrival (from Germany) of the accordion in the second half of the 19th century. This strident, tough, bellows driven reed instrument gradually took over the lead, and partially relegated the fiddle to rhythmic and harmonic back up, until the guitar liberated the fiddle from this more secondary role.

Bill Caddick

Although accordions were imported from Germany until World War II, during that war the factories were bombed. Local resources had to be employed to create these basically simple, diatonic, ten button, single row instruments, and there are today three or four dozen Louisiana-based makers of specialised cajun accordions, who supply the many keen amateur and professional players in the state and throughout the world.

Today the standard line-up for cajun bands is accordion, fiddle and guitar, plus any number of additions: percussion, commonly triangle or 'T-fer or 'tit fer (little iron), occasionally rub-board or other percussion instruments, acoustic upright or electric bass, drums, additional fiddles and guitars. The steel guitar was featured prominently in many of the older string bands, and there are still bands who omit the accordion.

The music itself is a fertile mix of dance-based tunes and songs, the dominant forms being two steps and waltzes, although there are also cajun blues, one steps, and a smattering of more recognisable European forms. Although much of the music and lyrics reflect the cajuns' rough treatment and oppression over the years, the songs and tunes have a joyful, yearning, soaring quality to them, and are easily identified by those hearing them for the first time - a fact that has certainly helped to establish the music's popularity outside of its natural environment. The rhythmic urge of (good) cajun music compels audiences to dance, and dance is its primary function in the rural communities of Louisiana.

There is a plethora of recorded cajun music available, although the avid fan will soon discover that there are far more recorded tracks than tunes or songs. A limited folk tradition will, of course, always lead to a 'stock' repertoire. Part of the fascination of this, as with many other forms of traditional music, is discerning just where one has heard a particular number before, cloaked as they tend to be in individual styling and ornamentation, secluded by title changes and widely differing spellings, or masked by time or decidedly inferior sound quality. The discovery of a wonderful new (or old) treatment of a particular favourite is a joy in itself.

The earliest extant recordings originate from the 20s, the best known of these early artists is Joe Falcon. The 20s and 30s seem to have seen an important stage in the development of cajun music this century, when the influences of swing and string bands were incorporated into the traditional framework: bands became larger, steel guitars featured, country influences were taken on board. The Hackberry Ramblers are a band with a history of over 60 years of performing together, and clearly demonstrate this amalgam of styles on their recordings, whether they are this year's release, or catalogue survivors from 1963 or even the 30s. The Balfa Brothers, sadly extinct following Dewey Balfa's recent death, were another outfit that had performed for several decades.

The next golden age of cajun was the 50s, when the purest form of the modern sound was established. The almost blind Iry Le Jeune, who was tragically knocked over and killed by a motor car whilst still in his 20s (while his musicians were changing a tyre on their car), was a major influence on modern day musicians, as were Lawrence Walker and Nathan Abshire, both performing and recording during this period. Austin Pitre started playing the accordion in the late 30s, but his recording heyday came between 20 and 30 years later, as did Aldus Roger. During 60s and 70's many rural players were working consistently, but with little recognition (just as with blues musicians at other times).

A further revival of the music has been taking place over recent years, with many younger players taking up the reins on behalf of their (in some cases partly forgotten or neglected) heritage. Of these Steve Riley And The Mamou Playboys best represent where the music is at today, somehow looking backwards and forwards at the same time. Along the way, many distinguished musicians have recorded brilliant examples of cajun music in progress, the most innovative in recent years include Michael Doucet and Beausoleil, Wayne Toups, Joel Sonnier and Bruce Daigrepont. Those adhering to a more traditional line, but still put out excellent music, include DL Menard, Eddie Le Jeune, Mark Savoy and countless others.

The dividing line between the twin developments of cajun and zydeco is a combination of race and location. Cajun music tends, for the most part, to be performed by white musicians in largely rural communities, although a number of black musicians have performed predominantly cajun music, (Amede Ardoin, Canray or Bois Sec Fontenot). Zydeco was primarily located in black (and more urban) communities, although several white cajun musicians have taken its rhythmic influences, and some play more or less straight Zydeco.

The derivation of the term Zydeco is thought to be Les Haricots Sont Pas Sale, (trans. the beans are not salted, 'Les Haricots' > 'Zarico' > 'Zydeco'). Zydeco music was, as mentioned, a more urban form of musical expression, issuing mostly from the townships and suburbs of Louisiana, although now much in evidence in town and country. It has certainly evolved out of the cajun repertoire, and in many cases has a direct and identifiable link, with many bands performing both types of music in their set, but a more dominant African background is in force throughout Zydeco. Always performed with percussion, usually drums and rub-board (frottoir), more often utilising electric instruments (certainly electric guitar and bass) and incorporating more syncopated rhythms, zydeco is basically the local black musical style. Accordion still leads, but more usually multi-rowed button accordions or the fully chromatic piano variety, although recently many zydeco players are reverting to the 'simple', single row instrument. The songs often tend to be bilingual (even within the same song!), with lyrics alternating quite happily and very appositely between French and English.

Older zydeco tended to be very rhythmic and excitingly rough sounding, whereas much of the modern music is smoother, incorporating large slices of blues and soul and some elements of funk. Clifton Chenier, who died recently, was known as the 'King Of The Piano Accordion' and his recordings are definitely worth investigating, as are those of Queen Ida, who has visited Britain on several occasions. Rocking Dopsie is another worthy zydeco performer to have toured Britain. Boozoo Chavis plays a rural zydeco sound, and John Delafose's Eunice Playboys combine the older styles with more progressive elements, as was witnessed by their barnstorming tours of the UK in both 1992 and 1993. The band contains many family members, and during their lengthy sets they swap instruments on numerous occasions. Of the newer breed of Zydeco, Nathan And The Cha Cha's repay a listening, and Joe Walker is the possessor of a silkily soulful and wonderfully emotive voice, a testimony no doubt to the lean years when zydeco was not popular and he eked a living by turning to gospel music.

Cajun is undoubtedly the more popular form of the two forms of music in Britain, with Zydeco a more distant second, probably for two major reasons. The rhythmic differences leave those dancers who have mastered only the cajun dance style a bit perplexed when faced with a more syncopated beat, and secondly, the British bands have tended to concentrate on cajun as opposed to zydeco. The level of popularity that cajun music has reached in Britain (and some of Europe) is quite astounding, so much so, that the first British CD compilation of cajun and zydeco music has just been released. This features bands from America, France and Britain who have played the London venue the Weavers, which promotes a weekly cajun night with local or visiting British bands plus whoever is touring from abroad. In addition, there are several professional British bands playing exclusively cajun music, and a range of cajun music clubs operating (usually monthly) in such unlikely sources of exotica as

Bradford, Derby, Manchester and Southampton. Cajun dance, or a form of it, is sweeping the land and most of these clubs teach the dancing as part of the evening's entertainment. There are also several music festivals each year in Britain which are dedicated exclusively to cajun music, and cajun cuisine has reached a high profile in purely gastronomic terms, as well as being a feature at some of these functions.

The first band in Britain to play predominantly cajun and zydeco were (and still are) Derby's R Cajun And The Zydeco Brothers. They are fronted by energetic accordion player, Chris Hall, who also runs an agency specialising in cajun and zydeco. He organizes tours for bands from Louisiana, runs the successful Swamp Club in Derby twice a month, publishes the Cajun Users Manual, sells cajun and zydeco records by mail order, and has just completed the first ever series of cajun radio programmes for BBC Radio 2. R Cajun, as they are more popularly known, have been in existence for nearly 14 years, and they were followed by several British outfits in the mid 80s including London's the Crayfish Five and the Deaf Heights Cajun Aces from Edinburgh. The former have made a success of offering Swamp Pop tunes laced with the more traditionally cajun material. Following these bands, and the efforts of a few country, blues or rock musicians who dabbled with cajun and zydeco styles such as the Balham Alligators, the Electric Bluebirds and he Poorboys, came a whole host of authentic sounding and acoustic based British units, many of whom had visited Louisiana and studied the music at first hand. Of these, the Flatville Aces, the Bluebird Cajun Band and the Bearcat Cajun Playboys are excellent surviving bands who regularly play cajun music up and down the country, in Ireland and in Europe, for their livings. There are also another 20 or 30 groups performing a form of cajun or zydeco as the major part of their repertoire. In addition, many artists from the worlds of rock, folk, country have experimented with cajun or zydeco styles and incorporated elements into their own songs, be it Bob Geldof with his band Vegetarians Of Love in Britain, or Mary Chapin Carpenter's Christmas 1992 UK and US hit 'Down At The Twist And Shout'.

All of this is a far cry from the days when only the occasional cajun track was played on radio by the likes of Andy Kershaw. *Aly Bain Meets The Cajuns* was yet to be filmed (let alone broadcast on British television) and the music received virtually no other airplay, *The Big Easy* and other American films featuring cajun and zydeco music had not penetrated, and the land was not teeming with cajun bands, cajun tours, cajun festivals, cajun dance workshops, cajun food and cajun and zydeco entries in books about music.

Selected albums: for cajun music *Get Weaving Volume 2: The Cajun And Zydeco Compilation. Floyd's Cajun Fais-Do-Do. Another Saturday Night. Louisiana Cajun Special Volumes 1 & 2. Louisiana Cajun Music* (several volumes), *J'ai Tai Au Bal Volumes 1 & 2.*

For Zydeco music: *Zydeco Party!, Zydeco: Louisiana Creole Music, Zydeco Blues And Boogie, Zydeco Champs, Zydeco Shoot Out, Zydeco Live Volumes 1 & 2.*

Cajun, R., And The Zydeco Brothers

R. Cajun were formed in 1979 by Chris Hall, a former member of Shufflin' Sam and a keen enthusiast of Cajun music. The original line-up was Chris Hall (b. 2 July 1952, Sheffield, Yorkshire, England; accordion/vocals), Tony Dark (fiddle), Alf Billington (guitar/vocals), and Veronica Matthews (triangle). The following year, Trevor Hopkins (bass) joined the line-up, but was soon replaced by Beeds (b. 13 October 1947, Derby, Derbyshire, England; guitar/harmonica). The line-up, which started to make some impact on the folk circuit in 1982, consisted of Hall, Billington, John Squire (fiddle/guitar/mandolin), who joined that year, as did Beeds, and Jan Hall (b. 17 January 1953, Sheffield, Yorkshire, England; triangle/percussion). *Bayou Rhythms* included the Zydeco Brothers, Graham Jones (bass) and Neil 'Freddy' Hopwood (b. 23 April 1947, Lichfield, Staffordshire, England; drums). Hopwood had formerly been a member of Dr. Strangely Strange, and the Sutherland Brothers bands. The album contained some infectious pieces such as 'Cajun Two-Step', and 'Bayou Pom Pom Special', as well as standards such as 'Jambalaya' and 'Deportees', and quickly established them as a popular group at festivals. In 1984, Dave Blant (b. 27 November 1949, Burton Upon Trent, Staffordshire, England; bass/vocals) joined, replacing Graham Jones. Having previously left the group, Tony Dark re-joined them in 1986, in turn replacing John Squire. The same year, Clive Harvey (b. 27 November 1945, Watford, Hertfordshire, England; guitar/vocals), was added. It was this line-up that recorded *Pig Sticking In Arcadia*. Three years later, Dark again left the group, to be replaced by Derek Richardson (fiddle), then Dave 'Mitch' Proctor (b. 8 December 1952, Heanor, Derbyshire, England; fiddle) joined in 1990, replacing Richardson. Despite the various personnel changes, the overall sound of the group has remained remarkably constant. Their blend of cajun and zydeco, apart from being unusual, has added to the band's original sound and style. They are currently playing festivals, both at home and abroad, where they are equally popular.

Albums: *Bayou Rhythms* (1984), *Pig Sticking In Arcadia* (1987), *Out Of The Swamp* (1990), *No Known Cure* (1993).

Calennig

One of the principal members of the folk band Calennig, Mick Tems (b. 3 January 1950, Clapton, London, England; melodeon/synthesizer), had earlier worked with Mike James, and Peter Davies in a group called Swansea Jack, in the 70s. In 1977, Tems had released a solo offering, *Gowerton Fair*, on the Sweet Folk All label and later teamed up with Patricia Smith (b. 3 April 1952, Church Village, Glamorgan, Wales; concertina, spoons) and began working as a duo, which eventually became known as Calennig. From their earlier recordings on the Greenwich Village label, they moved on to the Welsh-based Sain Cyf. Calennig also grew to become a five-piece outfit, known as the Calennig Big Band, which included, in addition to Mick and Pat, Peter Davies (oboe, recorders, bagpipes, bombarde), Mike Kennedy (bass), and Derek Smith (guitar). Mick and Pat have recorded in a solo capacity, as well as various permutations of the line-up. As the Calennig Big Band, they regularly play Welsh dances and tunes. In 1991, Calennig were working on two projects, a suite of new and traditional Welsh music called *Fffordd Y Brynian*, and settings of the work of Welsh poet Harri Webb.

Albums: Mick Tems solo *Gowerton Fair* (1977); as Calennig: Tems and Smith *Songs And Tunes From Wales* (1980), *You Can Take A White Horse Anywhere* (1983); Tems, Smith and Kennedy *Dyddiau Gwynion Ionawr (Snowy Days In January)* (1985); Tems, Smith, Kennedy and Davies *Dwr Glan* (1990). Compilations: *Plant Mewn Angen* (1988), *Essence Of The European Tradition* (1991).

Campbell, Alex

b. 1923 (or 1928), d. 1987. Campbell, nicknamed 'Big Daddy', and 'Le Cowboy d'Ecosse' in Europe, learned his trade by busking in London and Paris. Although he was not a 'technical' folk singer, he sang from experience and with feeling. He built up a strong European following, and consequently worked extensively in Scandinavia and Germany. One of his early songs, 'Been On The Road Too Long', is regarded by many as a classic. Campbell is believed to have recorded over 100 albums. *Goodbye Booze* included the Eric Bogle song 'And The Band Played Waltzing Matilda'. 1976's *No Regrets* included the Tom Rush-composed title track and also Allan Taylor's 'Old Joe'. Campbell was renowned for his drinking habits which contributed to his death in 1987. *Alex Campbell And His Friends* included Sandy Denny, Cliff Aungier

Alex Campbell

and Johnny Silvo, while some of his other recordings were used for guitar tuition.

Albums: *Chansons Populaires Des Etats-Unis* (1958), *Chansons Populaires Des Etats-Unis 2* (1958), *Bahama's Songs* (1958), *La Contrescarpe* (1958), *American's Square Dance* (1959), *Let's Sing While We Work And Play* (1960), *Songs And Stories Of The West* (1960), *Let's Listen And Sing To American Folksongs* (1960), *Let's Visit Great Britain* (1960), *Way Out West With Alex Campbell* (1963), *Best Loved Songs Of Bonnie Scotland* (1963), *Alex Campbell Sings Folk* (1964), *The 'Waag' International* (1964), *My Old Gibson Guitar* (1964), *Alex Campbell* (1964), *Alex Campbell In Copenhagen* (1965), *Yours Aye, Alex* (1966), *Alex Campbell And His Friends* (1966), *Way Out West* (1967), *Alex Campbell At The Tivoli Gardens* (1967), *Alex Campbell Live* (1968), *The Scottish Breakaway* (1968), *Alex Campbell Sampler* (1969), *Folk Session* (1970), *This Is Alex Campbell 1* (1971), *This Is Alex Campbell 2* (1971), *Life Is Just That Way* (1972), *Alex Campbell At His Best* (1973), *Big Daddy Of Folk Music* (1976), *Goodbye Booze* (1976), *No Regrets* (1976), *Traditional Ballads Of Scotland* (1977), *Dt Er Godt At Se Dig* (1979), *Live And Studio* (1979), *CRM* (1979). Compilation: *With The Greatest Respect* (1987).

Campbell, Ian, Folk Group

This highly respected British folk group were formed in Birmingham, West Midlands in 1956 and were originally called the Clarion Skiffle Group. With his parents, Campbell had moved from his home town of Aberdeen, Scotland to Birmingham in 1946. The original line-up was Ian Campbell (b. 10 June 1933, Aberdeen, Scotland; guitar/vocals), his sister Lorna Campbell (b. 1939, Aberdeen, Scotland; vocals), Dave Phillips (guitar) and Gordon McCulloch (banjo). In 1958, they became the Ian Campbell Folk Group. McCulloch departed in 1959 and was replaced by John Dunkerley (b. 1942; banjo/guitar/accordion) who remained until 1976. In 1960, Dave Swarbrick (b. 5 April 1941, London, England; fiddle/mandola) joined, remaining until 1966. Issued in 1962, it is notable that *Ceilidh At The Crown* was the first ever live folk club recording to be released. In 1963, the group were signed to Transatlantic Records and Brian Clark (guitar/vocals) joined the line-up as a replacement for Phillips. Clark also became a long term member, staying until 1978.

By now Ian had taken a place at university as a mature student, but the group still had bookings to honour, so Ian and Lorna recruited various session players including Aiden Ford (b. 1960; banjo/mandola), and Colin Tommis (b. 1960; guitar) who stayed for 18 months, touring Scandinavia. In 1984, Neil Cox (guitar) was added,

and the group were booked by former bass player Mansell Davies to play dates in Canada. Cox then left, and the group of Ian, Lorna, Neil, and Aiden played occasionally for special dates. An album recorded in Denmark in 1977 has never been released because there was no group to promote it. The sessions included Luke Kelly of the Dubliners, Dave Swarbrick and Martin Carthy. Many of Ian Campbell's songs are often thought of as traditional, but those such as 'The Sun Is Burning' have been covered by countless others, including Simon And Garfunkel.

During the early 60s, the group had appeared on television programmes such as the *Hootenanny Show*, *Barn Dance* and *Hullabaloo*. In addition, they regularly played to full houses in concert at venues such as the Royal Albert Hall, and the Royal Festival Hall in London. In 1964, they were invited to perform at the Newport Folk Festival in the USA. In 1965, they became the first group outside of the USA to record a Bob Dylan song. Their version of 'The Times They Are A-Changin'' reached the UK Top 50 in March 1965. The group added bass player Mansell Davies in 1966, but he emigrated to Canada three years later. He later became an organizer of the big Canadian festivals such as Calgary. After Swarbrick's departure in 1966, the group worked with George Watts (flute), who appeared on only two albums: *New Impressions* and *The Ian Campbell Folk Group* which was recorded in Czechoslovakia. Unfortunately, due to the prevailing political climate of the time, with the Russians marching into Czechoslovakia, the record was never released outside the country, and the group did not receive royalties. Watts left in 1968, but a year earlier the group took on bassist Dave Pegg, who remained with them for three years until joining Fairport Convention. In 1969, Andy Smith (banjo/mandolin/guitar/fiddle) joined, leaving in 1971. That same year, Mike Hadley (bass) joined the ever changing line-up, leaving in 1974. *Adam's Rib* was a suite of 12 songs written by Ian for his sister Lorna. The songs dealt with the different crises points in a woman's life. John Dunkerley left the group, owing to ill health, in 1976, and died the following year from Hodgkinson's Disease, aged just 34. During this same period, Brian and Lorna were divorced, and the group folded in 1978.

Albums: *Ceilidh At The Crown* (1962), *Songs Of Protest* (1962), *This Is The Ian Campbell Folk Group* (1963), *The Ian Campbell Folk Four* (1964), *Across The Hills* (1964), *Coaldust Ballads* (1965), *The Ian Campbell Folk Group* (1965), *The Singing Campbells* (1965), *Contemporary Campbells* (1966), *New Impressions Of The Ian Campbell Folk Group* (1967), *Circle Game* (1968), *The Cock Doth Craw* (1968), Ian Campbell and John Dunkerley *Tam O'Shanter*

Ian Campbell Folk Group

(1968), *Ian Campbell-With The Ian Campbell Folk Group And Dave Swarbrick* (1969), *The Ian Campbell Folk Group and Dave Swarbrick* (1969), *The Sun Is Burning* (1970), *Something To Sing About* (1972), *The Ian Campbell Folk Group Live* (1974), *Adam's Rib* (1976). Compilations: *The Ian Campbell Folk Group Sampler Volume.1* (1969), *The Ian Campbell Folk Group Sampler Volume.2* (1969).

Capercaillie

The line-up of this traditional Scottish group consists of Karen Matheson (b. 11 February 1963, Oban, Argyll, Scotland; vocals), Marc Duff (b. 8 September 1963, Ontario, Canada; bodhran/whistles), Manus Lunny (b. 8 February 1962, Dublin, Eire; bouzouki/vocals), Charlie McKerron (b. 14 June 1960, London, England; fiddle), John Saich (b. 22 May 1960, Irvine, Scotland; bass/vocals/guitar), and Donald Shaw (b. 6 May 1967, Ketton, Leicestershire, England; keyboards/accordion/vocals). Formed in 1984 at Oban High School in Scotland, initially to play for local dances, the band have now built a strong reputation for their treatment of traditional and Gaelic music from the West Highlands of Scotland. Strong musicianship, featuring Manus Lunny, who is equally well known for his work with Andy M. Stewart, and the haunting vocals of Karen Matheson, have established the group wherever they have performed. Having toured the Middle-East, South America, and the USA between 1984 and 1990, the band's appeal would seem to be widening, moving beyond the restrictions of the folk music market. In 1988, the group were commissioned to compose and record the music for *The Blood Is Strong*, the television series about the history of the Gaelic Scots. The resultant success of both series and music led to the soundtrack being released, and within six months it had been awarded a platinum disc for sales in Scotland. In 1990, Capercaillie signed to Survival Records and, as evidence of their widening appeal, the single from *Delirium*, 'Coisich a Ruin' (Walk My Beloved), a traditional Gaelic work song, achieved daytime airplay on BBC's Radio 1. Touring and promoting *Delirium*, Capercaillie were on the bill at Loch Lomond, Scotland, in the summer of 1991, the venue for a 40,000 strong concert by Runrig.
Albums: *Cascade* (1984), *Crosswinds* (1987), *The Blood Is Strong* (1988), *Sidewaulk* (1989), *Delirium* (1991), *Get Out* (1992).

Capstick, Tony

A Sheffield-born folk singer and comic songwriter, Capstick was one of a spate of 'folk comedians' who emerged on the UK folk scene during the 70s. Among the others were Fred Wedlock, Mike Harding, Richard Digance and most successfully Jasper Carrott and Billy Connolly. Capstick first recorded for the Newcastle-based Rubber Records. After he provided tracks for a comedy compilation, *There Was This Bloke* (with Harding, Derek Brimstone and Bill Barclay), his first solo album had an accompaniment from folk-rock band Hedgehog Pie and was an eclectic mixture of skiffle ('Goodnight Irene'), Bob Dylan ('To Ramona') and creditable versions of traditional songs such as 'The Foggy Dew' and 'Arthur McBride'. Capstick came to national prominence when he recorded a parody of a popular television commercial for Hovis bread. 'Capstick Comes Home', with accompaniment by the Carlton Main And Frickley Colliery Band, was a surprise Top 10 hit in 1981 on the small Dingles label. Chrysalis released the album of the same name which included German and Chinese versions of the hit song, but neither that nor a seasonal follow-up, 'Christams Cracker' were successful. Capstick remains active as a local performer and radio personality in South Yorkshire.
Albums: *His Round* (1972), *Punch And Judy Man* (1974), *Capstick Comes Home* (1981), *Tony Capstick Does A Turn* (1982).

Carawan, Guy

b. July 1927, Los Angeles, California, USA. Carawan plays guitar, banjo and hammer dulcimer, sings songs of protest and freedom and is a published author. Guy started listening to folk music when he was 21 years old, inspired by artists such as Woody Guthrie, Pete Seeger and Burl Ives. After leaving college with a degree in Sociology, he travelled to New York, and stayed for the next few years with Ramblin' Jack Elliott, Eric Darling and Frank Hamilton. Carawan developed his knowledge of the folk music of the deep South by touring North Carolina and Tennessee in the company of Hamilton and Elliott. He first caught the attention of the British folk scene during his world tour in 1958. That same year, he recorded *America At Play*, with Peggy Seeger, an album largely made up of songs collected by Alan and John Lomax and Cecil Sharp. Both Guy and his wife Candie Carawan have recorded and performed together at rallies and in concert. The EP *Guy Carawan*, was released in 1960, though recorded in 1957, and included 'Boll Weevil' and 'Ain't No More Cane On The Brazos'. Guy and Candie are also music directors of the Highlander Research & Education Centre, New Market, Tennessee, USA. The centre has a long history of supporting and supplying music in situations of social and political struggle. *Come All You Coal Miners* was a documentary work, produced by Guy, and featured performers such as Hazel Dickens, Sarah Gunning,

George Tucker and Nimrod Workman. *Green Rocky Road* included songs and tunes from the Appalachians and the British Isles, and highlighted Carawan's versatility on the variety of instruments. Both he and Candie have produced a number of documentary albums based on experiences in the South and Appalachia. Carawan continues to tour, still taking music to the people.

Albums: *Guy Carawan - His Banjo And Guitar* (1957), *Mountain Songs And Banjo Tunes* (1958), with Peggy Seeger *America At Play-Folk Songs From The Southern Appalachian Mountains* (1958), *Nashville Sit-In Story* (1960), *Freedom In The Air: Albany, Georgia* (1963), *We Shall Overcome - Songs Of The Freedom Movement* (1963), *Cumberland Moonshiner Hamper McBee* (1965), *Story Of Greenwood Mississippi* (1965), *Sea Island Folk Festival: Moving Star Hall Sungers* (1966), *Been In The Storm So Long (Spirituals, Shouts, Folk Tales And Children's Songs Of Johns Island, South Carolina)* (1967), *Come All You Coal Miners* (1974), *The Telling Takes Me Home* (mid-70s), with Candie Carawan *Sitting On Top Of The World* (1975), *China: Music From The People's Republic* (1976), *George Tucker, Kentucky Coal Miner* (1976), *Earl Gilmore: From The Depths Of My Soul* (1977), *Green Rocky Road* (1977), *Jubilee* (1979), *Birmingham, Alabama - Mass Meeting* (1980), *Sing For Freedom - Southwide Workshop* (1980), *Songs Of Struggle And Celebration* (1982), *My Rhinoceros And Other Friends* (1984), *They'll Never Keep Us Down (Women From The Appalachian Coalfields)* (1984), *High On A Mountain* (1984), with Evan Carawan *Hammer Dulcimer* (1985), *The Land Knows You're There* (1986), with Candie Carawan *Tree Of Life/Arbol De La Vida* (1990). Compilations: *Sing For Freedom* (1990), *Been In The Storm So Long* (1990).

Further reading: *Ain't You Got A Right To The Tree Of Life?*, Guy and Candie Carawan. *Voices From The Mountains*, Guy and Candie Carawan. *Sing For Freedom*, Guy and Candie Carawan.

Carter Family

The Carter Family have become known as country music's first family and are responsible for several songs such as 'The Wildwood Flower' and 'Keep On The Sunny Side' becoming country standards. The original three members of the Carter Family were Alvin Pleasant (A.P.) Delaney Carter (b. 15 April 1891, Maces Springs, Scott County, Virginia, USA), d. 7 November 1960, his wife Sara Dougherty (Carter) (b. 21 July 1898, Flat Woods, Coeburn, Wise County, Virginia, USA, d. 8 January 1979) and Sara's cousin, Maybelle Addington (Carter) (b. 10 May 1909, Copper Creek, Nickelsville, Scott County, Virginia, USA, d. 23 October 1978). A.P, also known as 'Doc'

Carter began to play the fiddle as a boy and learned many old time songs from his mother. His father had been a fiddler but gave it up through religious beliefs when he married. As a young man, A.P. sang in a quartet with two uncles and his eldest sister in the local church. Initially, he worked on the railroad in Indiana but became homesick for his Clinch Mountain home in Virginia and in 1911, returned to his native area. He became interested in writing songs and found work travelling, selling fruit trees. One day in his travels, he met Sara, who legend says was playing the autoharp and singing 'Engine 143' and on 18 June 1915, they married. Sara had learned to play banjo, guitar and autoharp and, as a child, was regularly singing with Madge and Maybelle Addington and other friends in her local area. They made their home in Maces Springs where A.P. worked on varying jobs, including farming and gardening and began to appear singing and playing together at local church socials and other functions.

They auditioned for Brunswick, singing such songs as 'Log Cabin By The Sea' but when the record company suggested to A.P. that, performing as Fiddlin' Doc, he only record square dance fiddle songs, he flatly refused because he felt it was against his mother and father's strong religious beliefs. After her marriage in 1926 to A.P.'s brother Ezra J. Carter, Maybelle (Addington) joined with her relatives and the trio began to entertain locally. Like her new sister-in-law, Maybelle was equally competent on guitar, banjo and autoharp and was to become the main instrumentalist of the trio, as she developed her immediately identifiable style of picking out the melody on the bass strings and strumming a backing on the treble. (Maybelle may well have been influenced by black guitarist Leslie Riddles, who often accompanied A.P. when he went on his searching-for-songs trips). Sara, often playing chords on the autoharp, usually sang lead vocals, with A.P. providing bass and Maybelle alto harmonies. (Sara also yodelled on some of their recordings although this was probably more because of the instruction of the record company's producer than from her own free choice).

The Carter Family sound was something totally new. Vocals previously in the early folk and hillbilly music were usually of secondary importance to the instrumental work whereas the trio, with their simple harmonies, used their instruments to provide a musical accompaniment that never took precedent over their vocal work. In July 1927, their local newspaper informed that Ralph Peer of Victor Records was to audition local artists in Bristol, Tennessee. In spite of the fact that Sara had three children (the youngest only seven-months-old) and that Maybelle was seven months pregnant with her first, they travelled the 25 miles to Bristol, where on 1 August, they made their first recordings. They recorded six tracks. Peer was impressed and the records proved sufficient sellers for Victor to give them a recording contract. Between 1928 and 1935, they recorded a many tracks for Victor, including the original versions of many of their classics such as 'Keep On The Sunny Side', 'Wildwood Flower', 'I'm Thinking Tonight Of My Blue Eyes', 'Homestead On The Farm' (aka 'I Wonder How The Old Folks Are At Home'), 'Jimmie Brown The Newsboy' and 'Wabash Cannonball'.

By the end of the 20s, the Carter Family were a very well known act. In 1931 in Louisville, Kentucky, they met and recorded with Jimmie Rodgers. It was at this session that Rodgers made his only valid duet recordings with a female vocalist when he recorded 'Why There's A Tear In My Eye' and 'The Wonderful City' with Sara Carter. (The latter song also being the only sacred number that Rodgers ever recorded). Combined recordings made at this time between the two acts comprised 'Jimmie Rodgers Visits The Carter Family' and 'The Carter Family And Jimmie Rodgers In Texas'. The former consisted of duets by Sara and Maybelle on 'My Clinch Mountain Home' and 'Little Darling Pal Of Mine' with Jimmie Rodgers and A.P both joining on a quartet version of 'Hot Time In The Old Town Tonight'. The latter featured Jimmie Rodgers with a solo version of 'Yodelling Cowboy' and Sara joining in with the vocal and yodel on 'T for Texas'. Both also included some talking by the two acts. The Carter Family managed to record, even though the families at times had moved apart. In 1929, A.P. relocated to Detroit to find work and at one time, Maybelle moved to Washington, DC. In 1932, Sara and A.P separated; they divorced a few years later, but the trio continued to record and perform together. (Later in 1939, Sara married A.P's cousin, Coy Bayes). In 1935 they left Victor and moved to ARC, where they re-recorded some of their popular earlier songs, though often using different arrangements, as well as recording new numbers. They signed to Decca in 1936 and later recorded for Columbia (formerly ARC). Their hitherto reluctance to perform outside of Virginia, Tennessee and North Carolina ended in 1938, when they accepted the opportunity to work on the powerful Border Radio stations XERA, XEG and XENT on the Mexican/Texas border at Del Rio and San Antonio. Here the Carter's children began to make appearances with the family; first, Sara's daughter Janette and Maybelle's daughter Anita, followed soon after by her sisters Helen and June.

Apart from their normal studio recordings, they recorded radio transcription discs at this time, which were used on various stations and helped to increase the Family's popularity. They remained in Texas until 1941, when they relocated to WBT Charlotte, North Carolina. In 14 October 1941, after rejoining Victor, the trio made their final recordings together; in 1943, while still at WBT, Sara decided to retire and the original Carter Family broke up. During their career, they recorded almost three hundred songs, never once varying from their traditional sound. A.P. claimed to have written many of them and the arguments still persist as to just how many were his own compositions and how many were traditional numbers that he had learned as a boy or found on his many song-searching trips. Sara Carter was undeniably a vocalist of great talent and could easily have become a successful solo artist. Maybelle Carter, apart from her instrumental abilities, was also a fine vocalist. A.P, who possessed a deep bass voice, was a very nervous man who suffered with palsy for many years. Some people believe this accounted for the tremolo on his voice at times and for the fact that he was often either late with his vocal, or failed to sing at all.

The influence of the Carter Family can be seen in the work of a great many artists and their songs have been recorded by the likes of Johnny Cash, Louvin Brothers, Emmylou Harris, Mac Wiseman, Flatt And Scruggs, Bill Monroe and Stonewall Jackson. They recorded the 'Wabash Cannonball' seven years before Roy Acuff began to sing it; this and many other Carter songs have become standards and have been recorded by many artists. Many of their numbers were beautifully descriptive of their native State, such as 'Mid The Green Fields Of Virginia', 'My Clinch Mountain Home' and 'My Little Home In Tennessee'. Several of Woody Guthrie's best known songs used Carter Family tunes including 'This Land Is Your Land' ('When The World's On Fire') and 'Reuben James' ('Wildwood Flower'). He also regularly performed 'It Takes A Worried Man', which the Carters sang as 'Worried Man Blues'. Other folk artists influenced by their music include Joan Baez, who recorded many of their songs such as 'Little Darling Pal Of Mine' and 'Will The Circle Be Unbroken'. After the break up of the original trio, Maybelle and her three daughters began to perform on the *Old Dominion Barn Dance* on WRVA Richmond. They appeared as Mother Maybelle and The Carter Sisters and were a popular act between 1943 and 1948. After spells at WNOX Knoxville and KWTO Springfield, they moved to WSM Nashville and joined the *Grand Ole Opry* in 1950, taking with them a young guitarist called Chet Atkins. During the 50s, Helen and Anita left to marry and pursue their own careers and June became a solo act. Maybelle remained a featured star of the *Opry* until 1967, when she was rejoined by Helen and Anita. In 1961, Maybelle even recorded an album of Carter Family songs with Flatt And Scruggs and in 1963, she appeared at the Newport Folk Festival. After June married singer Johnny Cash in 1968, Maybelle, Helen and Anita became regular members of the *Johnny Cash Show*. They had begun to make appearances with Cash the previous year. A.P retired to Maces Springs, where he opened a country store and lived with his daughter Gladys. Sara and her husband moved to Angel's Camp, California, where she withdrew from active participation in the music scene.

In 1952, seemingly at the request of her ex-husband, she was persuaded to record once more. Between 1952 and 1956, the A.P. Carter Family consisting of Sara, A.P. and their son and daughter Joe and Janette recorded almost 100 tracks for Acme Records. These included a 1956 recording made with Mrs. Jimmie Rodgers, which consisted of talk and a version of 'In The Sweet Bye And Bye'. Although these recordings never matched the work of the original trio, they did maintain traditional standards, whereas Maybelle and her daughters moved to a more modern country sound. In 1953, A.P. opened his 'Summer Park', in his beloved Clinch Mountains, near the home of Joe and Janette and held concerts, which featured such artists as the Stanley Brothers. A.P. Carter died at his home in Maces Springs on 7 November 1960. After A.P's death record companies began to release their material on album for the first time. In 1967 Sara was persuaded to appear with Maybelle at the Newport Folk Festival; the same year she and Maybelle, with Joe Carter taking his late father's bass part, recorded their classic *An Historic Reunion* album, which included their rather nostalgic 'Happiest Days Of All'. It was recorded in Nashville. The trio surprised the recording engineers by recording 12 tracks in just over four hours - an unusual event. It was the first time the two had recorded together for 25 years. (In 1991, Bear Family reissued these recordings, plus a version of 'No More Goodbyes' that had not been released by Columbia, on a compact disc that also contained a reissue of Mother Maybelle's 1966 album, *A Living Legend* and a further previously unissued recording of her instrumental 'Mama's Irish Jig'.)

In 1970, Sara and Maybelle were both present when the Original Carter Family became the first group ever to be elected to the *Country Music Hall Of Fame*. Their plaque included the words 'They are regarded by many as the epitome of country greatness and originators of a much copied style'. Maybelle Carter, a most respected member of the country music world, continued to perform until her death in Nashville on 23 October 1978. Sara Carter died in Lodi, California, after a long illness, on 8 January 1979. The Carter Family influenced other groups to repeat their sound notably the Phipps Family of Kentucky, who among their many albums recorded tributes to the Carters such as *Echoes Of The Carter Family* and *Most Requested Sacred Songs Of The Carter Family*. Further afield the Canadian Romaniuk Family also showed their ability to repeat the Carter Family sound with albums such as *Country Carter Style*.

Albums by the Original Carter Family: *The Famous Carter Family* (1961), *Great Original Recordings By The Carter Family* (1962), *The Original And Great Carter Family* (1962), *The Carter Family (Original Recordings)* (1963), *'Mid The Green Fields Of Virginia* (1963), *A Collection of Favorites (Folk, Country, Blues And Scared Songs)* (1963), *Keep On The Sunny Side* (1964), *Home Among The Hills* (1965), *More Favorites By The Carter Family* (1965), *Great Sacred Songs* (1966), *The Country Album* (1967), *Country Sounds Of The Original Carter Family* (1967), *Lonesome Pine Special* (1971), *More Golden Gems From The Original Carter Family* (1972), *The Carter Family On Border Radio* (1972), *My Old Cottage Home* (1973), *The Happiest Days Of All* (1974), *Famous Country Music Makers* (1974, UK release), *The Original Carter Family From 1936 Radio Transcripts* (1975), *Country's First Family* (1976), *Legendary Performers* (1978), *Carter Family In Texas Volumes 1 to 7* (late 70s), *Clinch Mountain Treasures* (1992). Albums by the A.P. Carter Family: *All Time Favorites* (mid-50s), *In Memory Of A.P. Carter (Keep On The Sunny Side)* (early 60s), *A.P. Carter's Clinch Mountain Ballads* (1970), *Their Last Recording (The Original A.P.Carter Family)* (1970). Albums by Sara and Maybelle Carter: *An Historic Reunion* (1967). Albums by Mother Maybelle with Anita, Helen and June: *The Carter Family Country Favorites* (mid-60s), *Travellin' Minstrel Band* (1972).

Further reading: *The Carter Family*, John Atkins, Bob Coltman, Alec Davidson, Kip Lornell.

Carthy, Martin

b. 21 May 1940, Hatfield, Hertfordshire, England. Carthy began his career as an actor but in 1959 became a skiffle guitarist and singer with the Thameside Four. He made his first solo recording on the collection *Hootenanny In London* (1963), singing 'Your Baby 'As Gone Down The Plug Hole', later revived by Cream. By now, Carthy was recognised as a virtuoso folk guitarist and was resident at London's top folk club the Troubadour. There, he taught songs to visiting Americans including Bob Dylan and Paul Simon who adapted 'Lord Franklin' and 'Scarborough Fair' for their

Martin Carthy

own records. With Leon Rosselson, Carthy recorded as the Three City Four before making his first solo album for Fontana. On *Byker Hill* there was equal billing for violinist Dave Swarbrick, with whom Carthy was touring the folk clubs. From 1969-72, he was a member of the folk-rock band Steeleye Span with whom he first played electric guitar. Carthy later joined the more traditional vocal group the Watersons which also included his wife Norma Waterson. In the 80s he toured and recorded with Brass Monkey, a band formed by John Kirkpatrick and Sue Harris. Carthy also took part in concept albums by the Albion Country Band (1972) and in the Transports the 'folk opera' created by Peter Bellamy. Essentially, though, Carthy is at his best as a soloist or in partnership with Swarbrick with whom he toured again in 1989 and recorded the live *Life And Limb*.

Albums: *Martin Carthy* (1965), *Second Album* (1966), *Byker Hill* (1967), *But Two Came By* (1968), *Prince Heathen* (1969), *Landfall* (1971), *Sweet Wivelsfield* (1974), *Shearwater* (1975), *Crown Of Horn* (1976), *Because It's There* (1979), *Out Of The Cut* (1982), *Right Of Passage* (1989), *Life And Limb* (1990), with Dave Swarbrick *Skin & Bone* (1992). Compilation: *This Is Martin Carthy* (1972).

Castleman, Owen

b. Farm Branch, Texas, USA. He moved to Los Angeles in his teens and was a regular at Randy Sparks' Ledbetters folk club, as was John Denver. Castleman's first taste of success came under the pseudonym Boomer Clarke. Together with Travis Lewis, now better known as top country act Michael Martin Murphey, they became the Colgems recording duo, the Lewis And Clarke Expedition. After the Monkees, the duo were the label's main act in 1967 and managed a US Top 100 single with 'I Feel Good (I Feel Bad)', one of their four singles for the label. In the early 70s Castleman, a many faceted singer who was not afraid to try something new, recorded on GRT and Capitol. His biggest success came in 1975 with 'Judy Mae', a song about a young man, his young step-mother and his father's early death in the minor-chord tradition of 'Ode To Billie Joe'. In a similar controversial vein, his later records included 'Hot Day In The South' a tale of a son unsuspectingly spending time in a motel with his long lost mother! In 1977 he produced the transatlantic hit 'Telephone Man' by Meri Wilson and in the late 70s he briefly attempted a 50s rock 'n' roll style aimed at the UK market. An in-demand session man, he based himself in Nashville and became involved in country music, having some minor success as a writer with acts like Baxter, Baxter & Baxter.

Chandler, Len

b. 27 May 1935, Akron, Ohio, USA. Chandler was a popular figure during the 50s and 60s folk revival period. From playing piano, at the age of nine, he moved on to playing the oboe at school, and performing in the University Orchestra in Akron. Owing to the vagaries of the McCarthy era, Chandler's exposure to folk music was limited, although, via a professor at college, he heard artists such as Josh White, Leadbelly, and Bessie Smith, for the first time. Chandler later won a competition for Advanced Orchestral Instrumentalist, which utilised two folk songs in the process, and later on he performed them with the New Jersey Symphony Orchestra. After working as a lift attendant, and a counsellor for neglected children, Len started hearing people like Dave Van Ronk, and as a result learned more folk material. Failing to get a teaching certificate, Chandler was invited to play at the Gaslight, in New Haven, Connecticut. As a result of this, he was offered work performing in Detroit. For a while he was resident performer at the Gaslight. Towards the 60s, the poetry side of the venue gave way to the growing folk music trend, with Tom Paxton, and Peter Paul And Mary turning up to play. By now, Chandler was performing further afield, including Canada. During the early 60s, he became involved in the civil rights movement and played at conferences alongside Tom Paxton and Phil Ochs. Chandler wrote songs regularly, three a day, for *Credibility Gap*, a show on the Californian radio station KRLA, and then for the *Newsical Muse Show* on KCET. Founding the Alternative Chorus-Songwriters Showcase, in 1971, new and emerging talent was allowed a voice. Chandler has recorded for a number of labels, as well as having poetry published.

Chapman, Michael

b. 24 January 1941, Leeds, Yorkshire, England. A former teacher of art and photography, Chapman emerged from the relative obscurity of Britain's folk club circuit with his 1968 debut, *Rainmaker*. This exceptional release, which contrasted excellent acoustic performances with a handful of rock-based pieces, revealed a gifted songwriter/guitarist and established his lachrymose delivery. *Fully Qualified Survivor*, the artist's next collection, reached the Top 50 in the UK charts in March 1970, and included the emotional 'Postcards Of Scarborough' which remains his best-known work. Among the featured musicians was guitarist Mick Ronson, whose impressive contributions led to his subsequent collaborations with David Bowie. Chapman meanwhile continued to forge his mildly eccentric path, and following the release of his fourth album, *Wrecked Again*, toured the USA with

Michael Chapman

long-time associate Rick Kemp. However, their partnership was dissolved upon their return when the bassist joined Steeleye Span. In 1973 Chapman switched record labels from Harvest to Deram, but releases there failed to maintain his early promise. The collapse of Criminal Records, the company responsible for several late 70s' recordings, was a further blow, but Michael maintained his popularity through live appearances. Chapman's work as a solo artist from the late 70s and early 80s was admirably captured on *Almost Alone*, which included new performances of 'Kodak Ghosts', 'Northern Lights' and 'Dogs Got More Sense'. A brief reunion with Kemp in the during latter part of this period resulted in the single, 'All Day, All Night'/'Geordie's Down The Road' (1983). Later work has seen him sign to the Coda label, performing 'New Age' music (a tag that Chapman reportedly despises), enabling him to demonstrate these exemplary guitar skills. In August 1991, the guitarist was reported to have suffered a heart attack from which he has shown signs of recovering.

Albums: *Rainmaker* (1968), *Fully Qualified Survivor* (1969), *Window* (1971), *Wrecked Again* (1972), *Millstone Grit* (1973), *Deal Gone Down* (1974), *Pleasures Of The Street* (1975), *Savage Amusement* (1976), *The Man Who Hated Mornings* (1977), *Lived Here* (1977), *Playing Guitar The Easy Way* (1978, guitar tutor), *Life On The Ceiling* (1978), *Looking For Eleven* (1980), *Almost Alone* (1981), with Rick Kemp *Original Owners* (1987), *Heartbeat* (1987), *Navigation* (1991), *Fully Qualified Survivor* (1993). Compilations: *Lady On The Rocks* (1974), *Michael Chapman Lived Here From 1968-72* (1977), *The Best Of (1968 - 1972)* (1988).

Chapman, Tracy

b. 1964, Cleveland, Ohio, USA. During Nelson Mandela's satellite-linked 70th birthday concert at Wembley Stadium, London in 1988, this guitar-playing singer-songwriter got her big break when, owing to headliner Stevie Wonder's enforced walk-out, her spot was extended. She won the hearts of enough viewers world-wide for her debut album, *Tracy Chapman* to climb to number 3 in the British album chart within days, and become an international success. Following the Mandela show, album sales shot past the 3 million mark. 'Fast Car' became a UK Top 5 hit and the track 'Talkin' 'Bout A Revolution' became a concert favourite. She was, however, neither a second Joan Armatrading nor the overnight sensation many thought her to be. The daughter of estranged but well-heeled parents, she had attended a Connecticut school before attending the University of Massachusetts, where she became the toast of the campus folk club. Contracted by SBK Publishing,

her first album had the advantage of the sympathetic production of David Kershenbaum who had worked previously with Joan Baez and Richie Havens. Next, she acquired a most suitable manager in Elliot Roberts - who also had Neil Young on his books - and a deal with the similarly apposite Elektra Records. She appeared with Peter Gabriel, Sting and other artists for a world-wide tour in aid of Amnesty International. Afterwords, she lost momentum. Although the impact of her second album, *Crossroads* was not insubstantial, its title track single was only a minor hit. Nevertheless, a fall from this lesser prominence has not been as rapid as her rise in 1988 to a qualified international stardom. Albums: *Tracy Chapman* (1988), *Crossroads* (1989), *Matters Of The Heart* (1992).

Chatmon, Sam

b. 10 January 1897, Bolton, Mississippi, USA, d. 2 February 1983, Hollandale, Mississippi, USA. Guitarist Sam Chatmon was one of the many children of ex-slave fiddler Henderson Chatmon, all of whom were musicians. Besides Sam, Lonnie (as the fiddling half of the Mississippi Sheiks), Bo (as Bo Carter) and pianist Harry all made recordings in the 30s In addition Sam's own son, Singing' Sam, is a bass guitarist. Sam Snr.'s 1936 recordings with Lonnie, as the Chatmon Brothers are, not surprisingly, similar to those of the Mississippi Sheiks, who were the one black string band to become major stars on record. When white interest in the blues was aroused in the 60s, Sam proved to be the only member of the family to have survived with his musical faculties intact, and came out of almost 20 years of musical retirement to perform for the new audience until his death. A strong, somewhat inflexible vocalist, and a fluent, though rather anonymous, pattern picker, Chatmon in his later career played mostly blues, emphasizing the risqué when he was not covering the recorded hits of others. Perhaps more interesting than this side of his repertoire were the minstrel and popular songs of his youth like 'I Get The Blues When It Rains' and 'Turnip Greens'. He claimed, with some plausibility, to have composed 'Cross Cut Saw', twice made famous by Tommy McClennan and later by Albert King.

Albums: *The Mississippi Sheik* (1970), *The New Mississippi Sheiks* (1972), *Hollandale Blues* (1977), *Sam Chatmon's Advice* (1979), *Mississippi String Bands* (1989).

Chenier, Clifton

b. 25 June 1925, Opelousas, Louisiana, USA, d. 12 December 1987. This singer, guitarist, accordion and harmonica player is regarded by many as the 'King' of zydeco music. Chenier was given lessons

Sam Chatmon

on the accordion by his father, and started performing at dances. He also had the advantage of being able to sing in French patois, English and Creole. In 1945, Chenier was working as a cane cutter in New Iberia. In 1946, he followed his older brother, Cleveland, to Lake Charles. He absorbed a wealth of tunes from musicians such as Zozo Reynolds, Izeb Laza, and Sidney Babineaux, who, despite their talent, had not recorded. The following year, Chenier travelled to Port Arthur, along with his wife Margaret, where he worked for the Gulf and Texaco oil refineries until 1954. Still playing music at weekends, Chenier was discovered by J.R. Fulbright, who recorded Clifton at radio station KAOK, and issued records of these and subsequent sessions. In 1955, 'Ay Tee Tee' became his best selling record, and he became established as a R&B guitarist. By 1956, having toured with R&B bands, he had turned to music full-time. In 1958, Chenier moved to Houston, Texas, and from this base played all over the south. Although ostensibly a cajun musician, he had also absorbed zydeco, and R&B styles influenced by Lowell Fulson. Chenier's first ventures into recording, saw his name mistakenly spelt, Cliston. During the 60s, Chenier, played one concert in San Francisco. Chenier recorded for a number of notable labels, including, Argo and Arhoolie, in a bid to reach a wider audience. 'Squeeze Box Boogie' became a hit in Jamaica in the 50s. The style of music he played is now termed 'World Music', but was by no means widely heard before the 60s. In later life, apart from suffering from diabetes, he had part of his right foot removed due to a kidney infection in 1979. Although this prevented him from touring as frequently, his influence was already established. *Sings The Blues* was compiled from material previously released on the Prophecy and Home Cooking labels. His son C.J. Chenier carries on the tradition into a third generation of the family.

Albums: *Louisiana Blues And Zydeco* (1965), *Black Snake Blues* (1966), with Lightnin' Hopkins, Mance Lipscomb *Blues Festival* (1966), *Bon Ton Roulet* (1967), *King Of The Bayous* (1970), *Bayou Blues* (1970), *Live At A French Creole Dance* (1972), *Out West* (1974), *Bad Luck And Trouble* (1975), *Bogalusa Boogie* (1975), *In New Orleans* (1979), *Frenchin' The Boogie* (1979), *Red Hot Louisiana Band* (mid-70s), *Boogie 'N' Zydeco* (1980), *Live At The 1982 San Francisco Blues Festival* (1982), *I'm Here* (1982), with Rob Bernard *Boogie In Black And White* (mid-80s), *Live At St. Mark's* (late 80s, CD release), *The King Of Zydeco, Live At Montreux* (late 80s, CD release), *Playboy* (1992). Compilations: *Classic Clifton* (1980), *Sixty Minutes With The King Of Zydeco* (1986), *Sings The Blues* (1987).

Chieftains

Chieftains

The original Chieftains line-up - Paddy Moloney (b. 1938, Donnycarney, Dublin, Eire; uilleann pipes/tin whistle), Sean Potts (b. 1930; tin whistle/bodhran), Michael Tubridy (b. 1935; flute/concertina/whistle) and Martin Fay (b. 1936; fiddle) - met in the late 50s as members of Ceolteoiri Chaulann, a folk orchestra led by by Sean O'Raida. The quartet's first album on the Claddagh label, *Chieftains 1*, released in 1964, introduced their skilled interpretations of traditional Celtic tunes. However the group chose to remain semi-professional, and further recordings were sporadic. Despite their low-key approach, the Chieftains became established as leading exponents of Irish music. Newcomers Sean Keane (b. 1946; fiddle/whistle), Peadar Mercier (b. 1914; bodhran/bones) and Derek Bell (b. 1935; harp/dulcimer/oboe) augmented the line-up which, by *Chieftains 4*, had become a popular attraction in Britain. The group then became a full-time venture and began an association with folk entrepreneur Jo Lustig. *Chieftains 5* marked their debut with a major outlet, Island Records, and the unit was feted by rock aristocrats Mick Jagger, Eric Clapton and Emmylou Harris. They were featured on Mike Oldfield's *Ommadawn* album and contributed to the soundtrack of Stanley Kubrick's film, *Barry Lyndon* (1975). In 1976 Mercier was replaced by Kevin Conneff (b. Dublin, Eire) and later in 1979, former Bothy Band and Planxty member Matt Molloy (b. Ballaghaderreen, Co. Roscommon, Eire; flute) joined the ranks. Moloney's skilled arrangements allowed the group to retain its freshness despite the many changes in personnel. During the 80s the group continued their enchanting direction and provided two further film soundtracks plus collaborations with the popular classical flute player, James Galway. However this period is better marked by *Irish Heartbeat*, their superb 1988 collaboration with singer Van Morrison.

Albums: *Chieftains 1* (1964), *Chieftains 2* (1969), *Chieftains 3* (1971), *Chieftains 4* (1973), *Chieftains 5* (1975), *Women Of Ireland* (1976), *Bonaparte's Retreat* (1976), *Chieftains Live* (1977), *Chieftains 7* (1977), *Chieftains 8* (1978), *Vol. 9* (1979), *Boil The Breakfast Early* (1980), *Chieftains 10* (1981), *The Chieftains In China* (1984), *Ballad Of The Irish Horse* (1985), *Celtic Wedding* (1987), with James Galway *The Chieftains In Ireland* (1987), *Year Of The French* (1988), with Van Morrison *Irish Heartbeat* (1988), *A Chieftains Celebration* (1989), *The Celtic Connection - James Galway And The Chieftains* (1990), *Bells Of Dublin* (1991), *An Irish Evening* (1992), *Another Country* (1992), with the Belfast Harp Orchestra *The Celtic Harp* (1993). Compilation: *Chieftains Collection* (1989). Sean Keane, Matt Molloy And Liam O'Flynn *The Fire Aflame* (1993).

Christmas, Keith

b. 13 October 1946, Wivenhoe, Essex, England. A popular figure on the British folk circuit, Christmas emerged with a rock-oriented style on his 1969 debut, *Stimulus*. Reminiscent, in places, of Al Stewart, the album featured support from Mighty Baby as well as Southern Comfort's pedal-steel guitarist, Gordon Huntley. *Fable Of The Wings* and *Pigmy* continued this direction, during which time Christmas toured as support act for many of the top bands of the day, including: the Who, Ten Years After, King Crimson and Roxy Music. A brief liaison as vocalist with the Esperanto Rock Orchestra led to an appearance on their 1974 album, *Danse Macabre*. That same year, a return to solo work produced *Brighter Day*, which was recorded on Emerson, Lake And Palmer's Manticore label. This release offered a tougher perspective than previous albums while *Stories From A Human Zoo*, recorded in Los Angeles, featured assistance from several stellar American musicians, including Steve Cropper and Donald 'Duck' Dunn. However, Christmas was unable to transform his obvious potential into commercial success, and subsequently spent the last years of the 70s performing low-key dates in London and at summer festivals. Disenchanted with the music business, he retired from the scene in 1981 only to re-emerge in the late 80s with a fresh outlook, playing on the folk club circuit performing solo and occasionally with a backing band.
Albums: *Stimulus* (1969), *Fable Of The Wings* (1970), *Pigmy* (1971), *Brighter Day* (1974), *Stories From The Human Zoo* (1976), *Dead Line Blues* (1991), *Weatherman One* (1992).

Clan McPeake

This family from Belfast, Northern Ireland, were at one time, the sole exponents of the uillean pipes in the north. Particularly influential in the 50s and 60s, they were unable or unwilling to cross over into the more lucrative commercial market. The McPeakes still perform and play at folk clubs and festivals. The original trio of Francis McPeake (b. 4 May 1885, Belfast, Northern Ireland; uillean pipes, d. 17 March 1971), Francis McPeake II (b. 20 January 1917, Belfast, Northern Ireland; uillean pipes, d. 7 July 1986), and James McPeake (b. 9 August 1936, Belfast, Northern Ireland; harp), took Irish folk music to Russia in 1959, and won the Welsh International Eisteddfod in 1958, 1960 and 1962. During this time, they released *The McPeake Family Of Belfast* on Prestige Records in the USA. In 1962, the three were joined by Francis McPeake III (b. 30 April 1942, Belfast, Northern Ireland; uillean pipes), Kathleen McPeake, daughter of Francis II, (b. 18 June 1946, Belfast, Northern

Ireland; harp), and cousin Tommy McCrudden (b. 16 April 1930, Belfast, Northern Ireland; bass). That same year, *The McPeake Family* was released on Topic, featuring all six members of the same family. After only three more releases, on Fontana and DTS Records, the group broke up in late 1967. They once again reverted to a trio, this time consisting of Francis I, Francis III, and Kathleen. Kathleen left to get married in 1968, and three years later, Francis I died. After a long break, it was left to Kathleen to reform the group, following the death of her father, Francis II, in 1986. Re-naming themselves Clan McPeake, the group now consisted of Kathleen (harp), her sons John McIlduff (b. 21 October 1968, Belfast, Northern Ireland; uillean pipes), and Francis McIlduff (b. 28 April 1971, Belfast, Northern Ireland; pipes), nephew William McKee (b. 23 December 1963, Belfast, Northern Ireland; bodhran), and family friend Kiven Dorris (b. 2 March 1967, Belfast, Northern Ireland; bouzouki). As Clan McPeake, they are again working the folk club and festival circuit, keeping alive the traditional music of the north as the family has always done.
Albums: *The McPeake Family Of Belfast* (1961), *The McPeake Family* (1962), *Irish Traditional Folk Songs And Music* (1962), *McPeake Family* (1964), *Irish Folk* (1964), *Welcome Home* (1965), *Welcome Home* (1965), *At Home With The McPeake Family* (1965), *Ducks Of Magherlin* (1965), *Pleasant And Delightful* (1967), *Irish To Be Sure* (1975), *Clan McPeake* (1991).

Clancy Brothers And Tommy Makem

Although born in Carrick on Suir, Eire, Tom (b. 1923, d. 7 November 1990, Cork, Eire), Paddy (b. 1923) and Liam (b. 1936) were among the founders of the New York folk revival during the 50s. From a musical family, Tom and Paddy emigrated to the USA to become actors. Paddy was soon assisting the Folkways and Elektra labels in recording Irish material and in 1956 he set up his own small label, Tradition. This released material by Josh White and Odetta. By now, the younger brother Liam had also moved to America, and was song-collecting in the Appalachian mountains. He encouraged whistle player Tommy Makem (b. 1932, Keady, Co. Armagh, Northern Ireland) to move to New York. In the late 50s, the quartet began to perform, in clubs and at hootenannies, eventually recording collections of Irish material in 1959. Among them were many, including 'Jug Of Punch' and 'The Leaving Of Liverpool', that became widely sung in folk clubs on both sides of the Atlantic. The Clancys attracted a large following with their boisterous approach and gained national prominence through an appearance on the Ed

Sullivan television show. The group recorded frequently for Columbia throughout the 60s. Their sister, Peg Clancy Power made a solo album of Irish songs in the late 60s. Makem left to follow a solo career in 1969, later recording with producer Donal Lunny for Polydor in Ireland. The Clancys continued to make occasional appearances, notably their annual St. Patrick's Day concerts in New York. Louis Killen, a traditional singer from north-east England joined for a 1973 record of *Greatest Hits* on Vanguard. There were other albums for Warner Brothers in the 70s and the original group re-formed for a 1984 concert and album. Although Tom Clancy died in November 1990, the remaining brothers continued to perform together occasionally in the early 90s.

Selected albums: *The Rising Of The Moon* (1959), *Come Fill Your Glass With Us* (1959), *The Boys Won't Leave The Girls Alone* (1962), *In Person At Carnegie Hall* (1964), *Isn't It Grand Boys* (1966), *The Irish Uprising* (1966), *Freedom's Son's* (1967), *Home Boys Home* (1968), *Bold Fenian Men* (1969), *Greatest Hits* (1973), *Seriously Speaking* (1975), *Every Day* (1976), *Reunion* (1984), *In Concert* (1992). Tommy Makem solo: *In The Dark Green Woods* (1974), *Ever The Winds* (1975), *Tommy Makem And Liam Clancy* (1976).

Clannad

This group, from Gweedore in Co. Donegal, Eire have successfully crossed the bridge between folk and rock. The line-up consists of Maire Brennan (b. Marie Ni Bhroanain, 4 August 1952, Dublin, Eire; harp, vocals), Pol Brennan (guitar, vocals, percussion, flute), Ciaran Brennan (guitar, bass, vocals, keyboards), Padraig Duggan (guitar, vocal, mandolin) and Noel Duggan (guitar, vocals). They formed in 1970, playing at Leo's Tavern, run by Leo Brennan, a former showband musician, and father of the Brennan group members of Clannad. The word Clannad means 'family' in Gaelic, and the group formed initially to play folk festivals in Ireland. At the time the line-up consisted of three of the Brennan children, and two of their uncles. The group's first successes came in Germany where they toured in 1975. Clannad initially caught the attention of the wider public in the UK when they recorded the theme tune for television's *Harry's Game* in 1982. The single reached number 5 in the UK charts, and received an Ivor Novello Award. In 1984 they recorded the soundtrack to television's *Robin Of Sherwood* and reached the Top 50 in May the same year. The following year the song received a British Academy Award for best soundtrack. Further chart success followed with the 1986 UK Top 20 hit 'In A Lifetime', on which Maire duetted with Bono from U2. From their early days when despite establishing themselves into the rock mainstream, Clannad have always retained the Celtic quality in the music. Maire's sister, Enya, left the group in 1982 having joined in 1979 and pursued a successful solo career. Clannad meanwhile have not lost contact with their folk audience and continue to perform at such events as the Cambridge Folk Festival.

Albums: *Clannad* (1973), *Clannad 2* (1974), *Dulaman* (1976), *Clannad In Concert* (1978), *Crann Ull* (1980), *Fuaim* (1982), *Magical Ring* (1983), *Legend* (1984), *Macalla* (1985), *Ring Of Gold* (1986), *Sirius* (1987), *Atlantic Realm* (1989), with narration by Tom Conti *The Angel And The Soldier Boy* (1989), *Anam* (1990), *Banba* (1993). Compilations: *Clannad: The Collection* (1988), *Pastpresent* (1989).

Clark, Guy

b. 6 November 1941, Rockport, Texas, USA. Clark has achieved considerably more fame as a songwriter than as a performer, although he is revered by his nucleus of fans internationally. Brought up in the small hamlet of Monahans, Texas, Clark worked in television during the 60s, and later as a photographer - his work appeared on albums released by the Texan-based International Artists Records. He briefly performed in folk trio with Kay K.T. Oslin, and began writing songs for a living, moving to Los Angeles, which he eventually loathed, but which inspired one of his biggest songs, 'LA Freeway', a US Top 100 hit for Jerry Jeff Walker. Clark then wrote songs like his classic 'Desperados Waiting For A Train' which was covered by acts as diverse as Tom Rush and Mallard (the group formed by ex-members of Captain Beefheart's Magic Band) and the brilliant train song, 'Texas 1947', by Johnny Cash.

His first album, *Old No. 1*, was released in 1975, and included 'Freeway', 'Desperados' and '1947', as well as several more songs of similarly high quality, like 'Let It Roll'. Despite intemperate and well deserved critical acclaim, it failed to reach the charts on either side of the Atlantic. One of the finest singer/songwriter albums of its era, it continued to sell as a reissue during the 80s. Clark's 1976 follow-up album, *Texas Cooking*, was no more successful, although it again contained classic songs like 'The Last Gunfighter Ballad' and the contagious 'Virginia's Real'. Among those who contributed to these albums simply because they enjoyed Clark's music were Emmylou Harris, Rodney Crowell, Steve Earle, Jerry Jeff Walker, Hoyt Axton and Waylon Jennings.

By 1978, Clark had moved labels to Warner Brothers, which released *Guy Clark*, which included four songs from outside writers, among them Rodney Crowell's 'Viola', 'American Dream' and Townes Van Zandt's 'Don't You Take It Too Bad', while the harmonizing friends this time included Don Everly, Gordon Payne (of the Crickets) and K.T. Oslin. A three year gap then ensued before 1981's *The South Coast Of Texas*, which was produced by Rodney Crowell. Clark wrote two of the songs with Crowell, 'The Partner Nobody Chose' (a US country Top 40 single) and 'She's Crazy For Leavin'', while the album also included 'Heartbroke', later covered by Ricky Skaggs. 1983 brought *Better Days*, again produced by Crowell, which included vintage classics like 'The Randall Knife' and 'The Carpenter', as well as another US country chart single, 'Homegrown Tomatoes' and Van Zandt's amusing 'No Deal', but Clark was still unable to penetrate the commercial barriers which had long been predicted by critics and his fellow musicians. He began to work as a solo troubadour, after various unsuccessful attempts to perform live with backing musicians. At this point he developed the intimate show which he brought to Europe several times during the latter half of the 80s. This resulted in his return to recording with *Old Friends*, appearing on U2's label, Mother Records. The usual array of 'heavy friends' were on hand, including Harris, Crowell, Rosanne Cash and Vince Gill, but only two of the 10 tracks were solely written by Clark. Among the contributions were Joe Ely's 'The Indian Cowboy', Van Zandt's 'To Live Is To Fly' and a song co-written by Clark with his wife Susanna, and with Richard Leigh (who had written the massive hit, 'Don't It Make My Brown Eyes Blue', for Crystal Gayle). Even with the implied patronage of U2, at the time one of the biggest acts in the world, Clark enjoyed little more success than he had previously experienced.

It would be sad if Guy Clark were to remain merely a cult figure, as he is without doubt one of the most original musical talents of the last 30 years from Texas. He has been freely acknowledged as a significant influence on the Texan performers, such as Lyle Lovett, on whose debut album Clark wrote a dedication.

Albums: *Old No. 1* (1975), *Texas Cookin'* (1976), *Guy Clark* (1978), *The South Coast Of Texas* (1981), *Better Days* (1983), *Old Friends* (1989), *Boats To Build* (1992).

Clifton, Bill

b. William August Marburg, 5 April 1931, Riderwood, Maryland, USA. Clifton sang and played guitar, autoharp and fiddle. He became interested in the music of the Carter Family during the 40s, having been introduced to country music through visiting the tenant farmers on his father's estate. Bill subsequently made his first records for the Stinson label in 1952. By 1954 he was performing with his Dixie Mountain Boys and recording for Blue Ridge. During the 50s Clifton compiled 150 old-time folk and gospel songs and had them privately printed. He was essentially able to bridge the gap between urban folk and bluegrass, reaching both sets of audiences on an international level. In 1961, Clifton recorded 22 Carter Family songs for Starday, and later came to Britain and set up tours for Bill Monroe, the New Lost City Ramblers and the Stanley Brothers. He had been playing bluegrass and old-time country music for 11 years before arriving in England in 1963. He led a 'missionary' role, as the music was new to English ears, and by 1966 he was playing regularly and hosting a BBC radio show called *Cellar Full Of Folk*. Clifton toured throughout Europe during the 60s, and recorded a programme of old-time music for Radio Moscow in 1966. By the following year, Clifton and his family travelled to the Philippines, where he joined the Peace Corps. Later, during the 70s, he went on to New Zealand, and formed the Hamilton County Bluegrass Band. Along with Red Rector (d. 1991) and Don Stover, Clifton formed the First Generation with whom he toured the USA and Europe in 1978. Clifton has since toured Japan, the USA and Europe. He is as well known for his work arranging tours and appearances of bluegrass performers, as he is for his recordings.

Albums: with the Dixie Mountain Boys *Mountain Folk Songs* (1960), *The Bluegrass Sound Of Bill Clifton And The Dixie Mountain Boys* (1962), *Carter Family Memorial Album* (1962), with the Dixie Mountain Boys *Soldier, Sing Me A Song* (1963), with other artists *Bluegrass Spectacular* (1963), with the Dixie Mountain Boys *Fire On The Strings* (1963), with the Dixie Mountain Boys *Code Of The Mountains* (1964), with various artists *Greatest Country Fiddlers Of Our Time* (1964), with the Dixie Mountain Boys *Mountain Bluegrass Songs* (1964), *Wanderin'* (1965), with the Dixie Mountain Boys *Bluegrass In The American Tradition* (1965), *Mountain Ramblings* (1967), *Walking In My Sleep* (1969), with the Hamilton County Bluegrass Band *Two Shades Of Bluegrass* (1970), *Bill Clifton Meets The Country Gentlemen* (1971), *Happy Days* (1971), with Hedy West *Getting The Folk Out Of The Country* (1972), with the Dixie Mountain Boys *Blue Ridge Mountain Blues* (1973), with the Dixie Mountain Boys *Blue Ridge Mountain Bluegrass* (1974), *Going Back To Dixie* (1975), *Come By The Hills* (1975), with Paul Clayton, Johnny Clark and Carl Boehm *A Bluegrass Session 1952* (1975), with Red Rector *Another Happy Day* (1976), *Bill Clifton and Rector In Europe* (1976), with Rector *Are You From Dixie?* (1977), *Clifton And Company* (1977), *The Autoharp Centennial Celebration* (1981), *Beatle Crazy* (1983),

Where The Rainbow Finds Its End (1991).

Cockburn, Bruce

b. 1945 Ottawa, Canada. This singer-songwriter has long been heralded as Canada's best-kept secret. His numerous early albums (nine from 1970 to 1979) were influenced by a strong devotional feel, tied to their author's Christian beliefs. However, after his breakthrough single 'Wondering Where The Lions Are' (from *Dancing In The Dragon's Jaw*), his lyrical gaze had turned to the body politic. Cockburn had travelled prolifically throughout several continents, and this had opened his mind to a different strata of subjects: 'I always go around with my notebook open in my mind'. His experiences abroad would become the core of his work, particularly *World Of Wonders*. One song, 'They Call It Democracy', would be turned down by MTV, until the accompanying video removed the names of several high profile corporate concerns. More recent work has embraced environmental concerns; from the destruction of the rain forests ('If A Tree Falls'), to the Chernobyl nuclear disaster ('Radium Rain'). A prolific writer, Cockburn now lives in Toronto, a divorcee who enjoys horse riding and the company of his teenage daughter. He is enormously popular in his homeland yet his brand of AOR rock remains a cult item elsewhere.
Selected albums: *Bruce Cockburn* (1970), *Further Adventures Of* (c.70s), *In The Falling Dark* (c.70s), *Inner City Front* (c.70s), *Salt Sun And Time* (c.70s), *Dancing In The Dragon's Jaw* (1979), *Night Vision* (1973), *Sunwheel Dance* (c.80s), *Rumours Of Glory* (1980), *Humans* (1980), *Stealing Fire* (1984), *High Winds White Sky* (1985), *Circles In The Stream* (1985), *Joy Will Find A Way* (c.80s), *World Of Wonders* (1986), *Waiting For A Miracle* (singles collection)(1987), *Trouble With Normal* (1989), *Big Circumstance* (1989), *Live* (1990).

Coe, Pete

b. 24 March 1946, Northwich, Cheshire, England; melodeon/bouzouki/dulcimer/banjo. Coe is known equally well for his work and recorded output with former partner Chris Coe, with whom he has now split. Pete was a part-time folk club organizer in Cheltenham and Birmingham from 1965-71, after which he formed a duo with Chris, who played Hammer Dulcimer. The duo turned professional in 1971. Work with the folk puppet and theatre group Magic Lantern followed and this included a collaboration with songwriter Bill Caddick. The Coe duo also combined forces with Roger Watson (tuba), Helen Watson (piano), Suzie Adams (banjo) and John Adams (trombone) to form Muckram Wakes. They also joined Ian

Wordsworth (percussion) to form the New Victory Band in 1978. With Nic Jones and Tony Rose, Pete and Chris formed Bandoggs, releasing one album on the now defunct Leader label. In 1985, with the release of *It's A Mean Old Scene*, Pete's first solo album, on his own Backshift label, Pete formed the group Red Shift, with Paul Roberts (b. Paul Edward Westran Roberts, 21 May 1949, Stockport, Cheshire, England; fiddle), George Faux (b. 1 September 1955, Liverpool, England; viola/fiddle/guitar/mandolin/vocals), John Adams and Colin Wood. Occasionally working with the band, Coe still performs solo and from 1988-90 completed three major US tours. *A Right Song And Dance*, his second solo release followed the same path of both traditional and contemporary songs and dance music. In addition to all this, Pete calls dances with the band Hookes Law, which includes in its line-up Adams and Coe. Apart from playing festivals and clubs, Coe also tours schools as part of an education package. A number of Coe's songs have been recorded by artists such as June Tabor, the Chieftains and Leon Rosselson. Some have almost become folk 'standards', in particular 'Marching Down Through Rochester' and 'The Wizard Of Alderley Edge'. In 1991, he licensed, and relaunched *Songsmith* magazine, a cassette and booklet featuring songs by established and new songwriters.
Albums: as Pete And Chris Coe *Open The Door And Let Us In* (1971), *Out Of Season Out Of Rhyme* (1976), *Game Of All Fours* (1978); with the New Victory Band *One More Dance And Then.* (1978); with Bandoggs *Bandoggs* (1978), *Greatest Pub Band In All The Land* (1979), *Live In The Leather Bottle* (1979); solo *It's A Mean Old Scene* (1985), *A Right Song And Dance* (1989); with Red Shift *Back In The Red* (1987).

Collins, Judy

b. 1 May 1939, Seattle, Washington, USA. One of the leading female singers to emerge from America's folk revival in the early 60s, Judy Collins was originally trained as a classical pianist. Having discovered traditional music while a teenager, she began singing in the clubs of Central City and Denver, before embarking on a full-time career with engagements at Chicago's Gate Of Horn and New York's famed Gerde's. Signed to Elektra Records in 1961, Collins' early releases emphasized her traditional repertoire. However, by the release of *Judy Collins #3*, her clear, virginal soprano was tackling more contemporary material. This pivotal selection, which included Bob Dylan's 'Farewell', was arranged by future Byrds' guitarist Jim (Roger) McGuinn. *Judy Collins' Fifth Album* was the artist's last purely folk collection. Compositions by Dylan,

Judy Collins

Richard Farina, Eric Anderson and Gordon Lightfoot had gained the ascendancy, but Collins henceforth combined such talent with songs culled from theatre's bohemian fringes. *In My Life* embraced Jacques Brel, Bertolt Brecht, Kurt Weill and the then-unknown Leonard Cohen; on *Wildflower* she introduced Joni Mitchell and in the process enjoyed a popular hit with 'Both Sides Now'. These releases were also marked by Joshua Rifkin's studied string arrangements, which also became a feature of the singer's work. Collins' 1968 release, *Who Knows Where The Time Goes* is arguably her finest work. A peerless backing group, including Stephen Stills and Van Dyke Parks, added sympathetic support to her interpretations, while her relationship with the former resulted in his renowned composition, 'Suite: Judy Blue Eyes'. The singer's next release, *Whales And Nightingales*, was equally impressive, and included the million-selling single, 'Amazing Grace'. However, its sculpted arrangements were reminiscent of earlier work and although Collins' own compositions were meritorious, she was never a prolific writer. Her reliance on outside material grew increasingly problematic as the era of classic songwriters drew to a close and the artist looked to outside interests. She remained committed to the political causes born out of the 60s protest movement and fashioned a new career by co-producing *Antonia: Portrait Of A Woman*, a film documentary about her former teacher which was nominated for an Academy Award. Collins did secure another international hit in 1975 with a version of Stephen Sondheim's 'Send In The Clowns'. Although subsequent recordings lack her former perception, and indeed have grown increasingly infrequent, she remains a gifted interpreter.

Albums: *A Maid Of Constant Sorrow* (1961), *The Golden Apples Of The Sun* (1962), *Judy Collins #3* (1964), *The Judy Collins Concert* (1964), *Judy Collins' Fifth Album* (1965), *In My Life* (1966), *Wildflowers* (1967), *Who Knows Where The Time Goes* (1968), *Whales And Nightingales* (1970), *Living* (1971), *True Stories And Other Dreams* (1973), *Judith* (1975), *Bread And Roses* (1976), *Hard Times For Lovers* (1979), *Running For My Life* (1980), *Time Of Our Lives* (1982), *Home Again* (1984), *Trust Your Heart* (1987), *Fires Of Eden* (1990). Compilation: *Recollections* (1969), *Colours Of The Day: The Best Of Judy Collins* (1972), *So Early In The Spring, The First 15 Years* (1977), *Most Beautiful Songs Of Judy Collins* (1979), *Amazing Grace* (1985).

Further reading: *Trust Your Heart: An Autobiography*, Judy Collins.

Collins, Shirley And Dolly

Shirley Elizabeth Collins (b. 5 July 1935, Hastings, East Sussex, England) and Dolly Collins (b. 6 March 1933, Hastings, East Sussex, England). Shirley Collins was established as a leading English folksinger following her discovery by a BBC researcher. She accompanied archivist Alan Lomax on a tour of southern American states before making her recording debut in 1959 with *False True Lovers*, issued on Folkways Records. In 1964 she completed *Folk Roots, New Routes* with guitarist Davey Graham, an ambitious album which challenged the then-rigid boundaries of British folk music. Shirley's first solo album, *The Power Of The True Love Knot*, was a sumptuous evocation of medieval England. This enthralling collection featured sister Dolly's sympathetic arrangements and atmospheric flute organ. The Collins' were then signed to the nascent Harvest label for whom they recorded two excellent albums which maintained the atmosphere of their earlier collection. The songs ranged from those by Robert Burns to Robin Williamson, while the presence of David Munrow's Early Music Consort gave *Anthems In Eden* an authoritative air. The sisters continued to work together but Shirley was increasingly drawn into the Albion Country Band circle following her marriage to bassist Ashley Hutchings. The group, an offshoot of the Steeleye Span/Young Tradition axis, provided the backing on Shirley's *No Roses* and she continued to sing with related projects the Etchingham Steam Band and the Albion Dance Band. Her divorce from Hutchings precluded further involvement and the singer retired from music for several years following a third collaboration with her sister. Shirley Collins returned to performing during the late 80s.

Albums: as Shirley And Dolly Collins *Sweet Primroses* (1967), *The Power Of The True Love Knot* (1968), *Anthems In Eden* (1969), *Love, Death And The Lady* (1970), *For As Many As Will* (1974); Shirley Collins, Davey Graham *Folk Roots, New Routes* (1964); Shirley Collins solo *Sweet England* (1959), *False True Lovers* (1959), *No Roses* (1971), *Adieu To Old England* (1974), *Amaranth* (1976, combines one side of newly recorded material with the 'Anthems In Eden' suite from the above 1969 release). Compilations: *A Favourite Garland* (1974), *Fountain Of Snow* (1992).

Collinson, Lee

b. 15 January 1965, Dorking, Surrey, England. This aspiring guitar player and singer, with a talent belying his age, has gained a growing reputation for quality songs. Coupled with this, is his ability to switch from both contemporary and traditional folk, to 50s style and blues and jazz. Collinson started out by playing in rock band Cloud Nine, the duo, Richard III and then another rock band,

Typically Max. In 1987, Collinson embarked upon a solo career, and was twice a finalist in BBC Radio's *Folk On Two,* Young Tradition Award. The subsequent broadcast, and a chance meeting with Spiv Records at a folk festival, resulted in his debut release, *Limbo.* The album was well received in the folk media, and received a good deal of airplay. One folk magazine, *Scansfolk,* voting the work British Folk Album of 1991. Collinson contributed slide-guitar to Hancock's track 'Purple Pas de Deux', on the Hokey Pokey release *The Circle Dance* in 1990. Apart from playing the whole of the British Isles, Channel Islands, and Shetland Isles, Lee has since toured with Keith Hancock in Holland and Germany.
Album: *Limbo* (1990).

Cooper, Mike

b. c.1940. A strong singer and guitarist based for many years in Reading, Berkshire, England, Cooper was one of the leading lights of the country blues movement in Britain in the 60s. He also ran a popular folk/blues club in Reading and was one of the instigators of the Matchbox label, for which he recorded. Between 1968 and 1974 he appeared on the Pye, Dawn, and Fresh Air labels, and he also contributed his guitar work to records by Ian A. Anderson (now editor of *Folk Roots*), John Dummer, Stefan Grossman, and Heron. However, by the end of the 60s he was moving away from the blues towards a wider 'world music' approach and he appears very rarely in England these days, although he did team up with Anderson again in the mid-80s.
Selected albums: *Oh Really* (1969), *Trout Steel* (1970), with Ian A. Anderson *The Continuous Preaching Blues* (1986).

Cooper, Pete

b. 18 November 1951, Gnosall, Staffordshire, England. Cooper's fiddle playing has been acclaimed by many notable folk musicians, a number of whom he has worked with. Having started playing violin at the age of nine, he went on to learn classical music during his teenage years. He then switched to studying English at Oxford University, from where he graduated in 1973. Reverting to music, Cooper then went on to study old-time fiddle in West Virginia, shortly after teaming up with acclaimed dulcimer player Holly Tannen. Releasing *Frosty Morning,* the two then toured extensively, in the USA, Europe, and Britain. From 1983, Cooper started working with Peta Webb, recording *The Heart Is True* three years later. The two played clubs and festivals throughout the UK. Never one to sit still for long, Cooper then formed Fiddling From Scratch, in 1985, recording

All Around The World which included Tannen on two tracks, and issuing a booklet of the tunes contained therein. He has continued to study and teach traditional fiddle playing styles, and runs workshops as well as teaching. Cooper then formed Vivando!, which included former Zumzeaux fiddle player and vocalist, Neti Vaandrager (b. 21 August 1957, Rotterdam, Netherlands), Kathryn Locke (cello), and Geoff Coombs (mandola/mandolin). Together, the group play a variety of styles, encompassing Mexican and Bulgarian tunes, as well as American, and original material. Although not prolific, Cooper has nevertheless gained an admirable reputation for his work.
Albums: with Holly Tannen *Frosty Morning* (1979), with Peta Webb *The Heart Is True* (1986), *All Around The World* (1990).

Copper Family

This well-known and established family of traditional unaccompanied singers and song collectors hail from Rottingdean, Sussex, England. The family have been singing for over five generations, with songs written down by Jim Copper (1882-1954). His son Bob now has the books of songs. The family comprises Bob Copper (b. Robert James Copper, 6 January 1915, Rottingdean, Sussex, England), cousin Ron (b. Ronald Walter Copper, 1912, d. 7 January 1978), Bob's son John (b. John James Copper, 4 June 1949) and Bob's daughter Jill (b. Jill Susan Copper, 24 January 1945). The Copper family are held in high esteem for their part singing, which influenced a number of other well-known folk acts, in particular the Young Tradition and the Watersons. Bob and his father had broadcast for the BBC, on radio, as early as 1951, and together with John and Ron, performed at the Royal Albert Hall, London, at the International Folk Festival. After Jim's death, in 1954, they continued as a duo well into the 60s when Jill and John joined them. When Ron passed away, in 1978, the trio performed regularly, until even the grandchildren became involved. Bob's book, *A Song For Every Season,* won the Robert Pitman Literary Prize in 1971. Bob left the scene for a number of years while looking after his wife until her death in 1984.
Albums: Bob And Ron *English Shepherd And Farming Songs* (60s), *Traditional Songs From Rottingdean* (1964), *Two Brethren* (1975); Bob *Sweet Rose In June* (1977); with Bob, Rob and Jim *Twankydillo* (1975); with Ron, Bob, John and Jill *A Song For Every Season* (1971, 4 album set). Compilations: *Coppersongs A Living Tradition* (1988). Further reading: *A Song For Every Season-A Hundred Years Of A Sussex Farming Family,* Bob Copper. *Early To Rise-A Sussex Boyhood,* Bob Copper. *Songs*

And Southern Breezes-Country Folk And Country Ways, Bob Copper.

Coppin, Johnny

b. 5 July 1946, Woodford, Essex, England. Guitar and keyboard player Coppin has, for most of his life, lived in Gloucestershire, a county that has influenced his songwriting. He was formerly a member of the folk-rock group Decameron, which played contemporary songs mainly composed by Coppin and fellow member Dave Bell. Coppin went solo when the group split in 1976. He soon established himself as a songwriter of quality, releasing his first solo album in 1978. He has also recorded two albums with a strong Cotswold theme, by setting to music the poems of a number of Gloucestershire writers of note, including John Drinkwater, Frank Mansell, Laurie Lee and others. A third album on a similar theme, *Edge Of Day*, was released in 1989. This was both a tribute to, and a collaboration with, the writer Laurie Lee. Coppin is continually touring, having played all over the world, and has been featured on television in connection with his work, as well as many radio appearances. Coppin's fine clear voice has appeal beyond the boundaries of a folk audience.
Albums: *Roll On Dreamer* (1978), *No Going Back* (1980), *Get Lucky* (1982), *Forest And Vale And High Blue Hill* (1983), *Line Of Blue* (1985), *English Morning* (1987), *Edge Of Day* (1989), with the band of the 1st Battalion Gloucestershire Regiment *The Glorious Glosters* (1989), *Songs On Lonely Roads* (1990), *West Country Christmas* (1990).

Cordelia's Dad

Riding on the crest of the early 90s resurgence of American folk rock, which included We Saw The Wolf, The Drovers, and Bedlam Rovers, Cordelia's Dad apply a thrash and grunge style to folk songs with spectacular results. Pete Irvine (drums), Tom King (guitar) and Tim Eriksen (bass, vocals) go straight to traditional sources for their material, and, although their debut was British biased, the splendid *How Can I Sleep?* looked to Appalachian/New England music for inspiration. Eriksen's vocal is high folk which makes the resulting clash of styles all the more adventurous and exciting.
Albums: *Cordelia's Dad* (1989), *How Can I Sleep?* (1992).

Corries

One of Scotland's most popular and enduring British folk acts, the Corries rose to prominence during the mid-60s when founder member Bill Smith (guitar, vocals) was joined by Ronnie Brown (guitar, vocals) and Roy Williamson (guitar, vocals,

concertina, harmonica, bodhran, kazoo, mandolin). Initially known as the Corrie Folk Trio, their early releases for the Waverley label also featured singer Paddie Bell, who then embarked on a solo career. The group's early repertoire consisted of largely traditional material, but Williamson soon began writing songs fashioned in this style. His haunting composition, 'Flower Of Scotland', has since been adopted as Scotland's unofficial national anthem and this skilled craftsman also built many exotic instruments by hand. *Bonnet, Belt And Sword* in 1967 marked Smith's departure and Williamson and Brown truncated the group's name to that of the Corries. Their 1969 release, *The Corries In Concert*, became a best-seller, judiciously combining folk standards ('Sally Free And Easy' and 'Will You Go Lassie Go'/'Wild Mountain Thyme') with humorous material ('Granny's In The Cellar'), a combination maintained throughout the duo's career. Although undeniably popular with home-based audiences and Scots-in-exile, this has tended to undermine the Corries' exceptional talents both as musicians and curators of Caledonian heritage. Their unashamed espousal of Scottish Nationalism suggested a parochial image, while the duo affirmed their independence by founding the Pan Audio studio and label. The Corries hosted national television shows and their popularity was undiminished at the time of Williamson's premature death on 12 August 1990 following a long battle with cancer. Brown then announced the end of the group, vowing to continue the efforts to win official status for 'Flower Of Scotland' as a fitting tribute to his much-respected partner.
Selected albums: as the Corrie Folk Trio with Paddie Bell *The Promise Of The Day* (1965), as the Corrie Folk Trio *Those Wild Corries* (1966), as the Corries *Bonnet, Belt And Sword* (1967), *Kishmul's Galley* (1968), *The Corries In Concert* (1969), *Scottish Love Songs* (1970), *Strings And Things* (1971), *Sound The Pilbroch* (1972), *A Little Of What You Fancy* (1973), *Live At The Royal Lyceum Theatre Edinburgh* (1976), *The Corries Live Volume 1* (1977), *The Corries Live Volume 2* (1977), *The Corries Live Volume 3* (1977), *Peat Fire Flame* (1978), *A Man's A Man* (1980), *The Corries* (1986), *Legends Of Scotland* (1986), *Barrett's Privateers* (1987). Compilations: as the Corrie Folk Trio with Paddie Bell *The Corrie Folk Trio* (1966), *In Retrospect* (1970); as the Corries *These Are The Corries* (1974), *These Are The Corries Volume 2* (1974), *Cam' Ye By Atholl* (1974), *The Very Best Of The Corries* (1976), *Spotlight On The Corries* (1977), *16 Scottish Favourites* (1979), *Best Of The Corries* (1987), *The Compact Collection* (1988).

Cosmotheka

Brothers Dave Sealey (b. 20 February 1946,

Redditch, Worcestershire, England) and Al Sealey (b. Alan Sealey, 18 May 1940, Redditch, Worcestershire, England), formed their modern day 'music hall act' in 1971, making their debut at a folk club in Stratford-upon-Avon. Both had previously sung, Al singing with a Midlands-based folk group, while Dave had released a number of singles in his own right. The stage name, Cosmotheka, was taken from an old time 'hall' located in Paddington, London. During the mid-70s, the pair were invited to appear on *Saturday Night At The Mill*, on BBC television, with Sandy Powell. This in turn led to a number of appearances on BBC's lunch-time show *Pebble Mill At One*. It also resulted in them being given their first radio series, on BBC Radio 4, and their own mini-series *A Postcard From Cosmotheka*. They have since guested on numerous television shows where their verbal dexterity and a wealth of *double entendres* proved popular. They have produced a number of albums recalling the heyday of the music hall, keeping alive the songs of singers such as Harry Champion. The duo have appeared at folk festivals, arts festivals and arts centres throughout the British Isles, and overseas. In addition to their music hall show, 'These Are The Days', Dave and Al have written and performed *The Black Sheep Of The Family*, a show chronicling the life and songs of singer Fred Barnes. The show was debuted at the Purcell Room, on London's South Bank and has since been presented on national radio. For BBC Radio 2, Dave and Al wrote and performed *Wot A Mouth*, a 'definitive life story' of singer Harry Champion. Yet another diversion from their usual act is the tribute to variety artists of the 30s and 40s, called *In The Box*. The pair continue to promote and praise the history of the music hall and have plans to present a show charting the rise of ragtime from its beginnings through to its absorption into the popular music culture.
Albums: *A Little Bit Off The Top* (1974), *Wines And Spirits* (1977), *A Good Turn Out* (1981), *Cosmotheka* (1986), *Keep Smiling Through* (1989).

Cotten, Elizabeth 'Libba'

b. 1893, USA, and raised in Chapel Hill, North Carolina, d. 29 July 1987. Cotten had wanted a guitar from a very early age. As a result, she saved enough to buy a $3.75 Stella Demonstrator guitar. Without recourse to formal lessons, she taught herself to play in her now eccentric style using just two fingers. To complicate matters, she played a guitar strung for a right-handed player, but played it upside down, as she was left-handed. 'Freight Train' was written by Cotten when she was still just 12 years old. Being so young, and coming from a God-fearing family, she was told that it was her duty to serve the Lord and so put aside the guitar until the late 40s. Married at 15, she was later divorced and moved to Washington, D.C. to look for work. She worked as a domestic in Maryland for Ruth Crawford Seeger, the wife of ethnomusicologist Charles Seeger. One day she played 'Freight Train' in the house to Mike and Peggy Seeger. Despite the fact that Cotten had written the song many years earlier, it was not until 1957, and after numerous court cases, that she secured the copyright to the song. Her blues rag and traditional style became familiar. Her second album was recorded and edited by Mike Seeger. In 1972, Cotten received the Burl Ives Award for her role in folk music. She appeared at a number of east coast folk festivals, such as Newport and Philadelphia, and on the west coast at the UCLA festival. This was in addition to playing occasional coffee houses and concerts. In 1975 she was a guest performer at the Kennedy Centre in Washington on a programme of native American music. 'Freight Train' recorded by Chas McDevitt and Nancy Whiskey, reached number 5 in the UK charts in 1957, but was less successful in the USA where it only reached the Top 40. Cotten received a Grammy award for her third, and final, album *Elizabeth Cotten Live*, and continued performing until just a few months before her death on 29 July 1987, in Syracuse, New York, USA.
Selected albums: *Elizabeth Cotten* (1957), *Elizabeth Cotten Volume 2: Shake Sugaree* (1965), *Elizabeth Cotten Volume 3: When I'm Gone* (1965), *Elizabeth Cotten Live* (1984).

Cousins, Dave

At the forefront of the British folk-rock scene, fronting the Strawbs in the 70s, Cousins was never afraid to experiment musically, often with startling results. His early influences included Leadbelly and Muddy Waters. Visits to Cecil Sharp House in the late 50s, led him to develop a flat picking guitar technique in the style of Jack Elliot. In the early 60s he played in South London folk clubs, and switched to banjo after hearing Peggy Seeger and Earl Scruggs. These influences led him to form Britain's first bluegrass band in 1967. The Strawberry Hill Boys featured Cousins, and, in later days, the folk legend, Sandy Denny. An album was recorded, but was issued later as *Sandy & the Strawbs*, after the group had changed its name, and acheived enormous success in the early 70s. A session with producer Gus Dudgeon led to a contract with A&M, and the shortening of the band's name although by this time Denny had left. In 1969, their self-titled first album was hailed as a 'masterpiece of contemporary folk music', and featured two of Cousins' best known songs, 'The Man Who Called

Jim Couza (right)

Himself Jesus', and the 22 verse epic, 'The Battle'. A year later, *Dragonfly*, produced by Tony Visconti, was less successful, and led to radical changes in personnel and direction. Keyboard virtuoso Rick Wakeman joined the Strawbs in 1970, and, before his departure in the following year, had steered the band towards a quasi-classical style that peaked with the best-selling *Grave New World* (1972). Internal disagreements plagued the band throughout its career, and Cousins briefly quit in the early 70s, releasing the folky *Two Weeks Last Summer* in 1971. Re-formed, he led the group through a commercially satisfying period which included the UK chart hits, 'Lay Down' (1972), and the politically-charged 'Part Of The Union' (1973). A highlight of the later albums included the title cut from *Hero And Heroine*, with its blistering fiddle runs, but in the late 70s they neglected their British roots. On US tours, Cousins' idiosyncratic vocal delivery lacked mass appeal, and they eventually disbanded after *Deadlines* in 1978. Cousins resurfaced in 1979 with the folk-tinged *Old School Songs* solo album, before concentrating on commercial radio in Devon. The Strawbs still play together occasionally at folk festivals, and have recently recorded an album for the Canadian market where they retain some popularity.
Selected albums: *Sandy Denny & The Strawbs* (1967), *Strawbs* (1969), *Just A Collection Of Antiques And Curios* (1970), *From The Witchwood* (1971), *Grave New World* (1972), *Two Weeks Last Summer* (1972), *Bursting At The Seams* (1973), *Deadlines* (1978), *Old School Songs* (1979).

Couza, Jim

b. 27 April 1945, New Bedford, Massachusetts, USA. A highly respected player of the hammer dulcimer, Couza was already 21 years old before he started playing guitar, learning tunes and songs from the piano at home. The first song he learned was 'The Circle Game' by Joni Mitchell, which had then been recorded by Tom Rush. Couza gained experience playing at the coffee house of the 1st Unitarian Church in New Bedford. He heard his first hammer dulcimer at an international music festival in Foxhollow, USA. He played and was influenced by Celtic material. Couza was around when the Young Tradition played their first tour of the USA in 1968-69. He saw them perform at the Tri-Works, New Bedford. Jim met Ray Fisher, of the Fisher family, and Howard Glasser, who has one of the largest collections of British folk music in the USA. Couza came to Britain for the first time on 1 December 1981, for two months, half of which was spent recording his first album, *Brightest And Best*, and the rest on a somewhat shortened tour of UK folk clubs. He went back to the USA in February 1982, but swiftly returned three months later, and has lived in the UK since then. Regularly working the festivals and clubs in the UK and the USA, his projects include recording with the D'Urbeville Ramblers, which includes Dave Hatfield and Pete Stanley.

Albums: *Brightest And Best* (1981), *Angels Hovering Round* (1982), *Friends And Neighbours* (1984), *The Enchanted Valley* (1984), *Jubilee* (1989), *Out Of The Shadowland* (1991), *Welcome To The Fair* (1992), with the D'Uberville Ramblers *Appalachian Beach Party* (1993).

Cronshaw, Andrew

b. 18 April 1949, Lytham St. Annes, Lancashire, England. Cronshaw undertook his debut performances at Edinburgh University, where he gained a degree in psychology, and where he was involved in running the University Folksong Society. He gave up singing in favour of playing guitar, tin whistle, zither, and later, the concertina and dulcimer. *A Is For Andrew, Z Is For Zither*, released on Transatlantic's Xtra subsidiary, showcased his potential. Turning his busy hand to production, Cronshaw produced the single 'Casey's Last Ride'/'Nostradamus' by Suzie Adams, and later albums by June Tabor (*Abyssinians* and *Aqaba*) and the second release by Tabor and Maddy Prior as Silly Sisters, *No More To The Dance*. Cronshaw went on to produce *The Wild West Show* by Bill Caddick, and *Wolf At Your Door* by Zumzeaux. During this time, Cronshaw continued to record for a variety of labels, producing music that could be defined as a cross between new age and folk. Although concentrating latterly on production and writing, he also writes regular articles for *Folk Roots* and a number of other UK magazines. In 1991, Cronshaw made two tours of selected village churches in England, under the banner of the 'Splendid Venues Tour', partly in an attempt to get people out of thinking of folk music as only being performed in the dingy backrooms of public houses. He has performed for many years, with a host of 'names' from the folk scene, in duos and groups, including Ric Sanders, Martin Simpson, and June Tabor, as well as undertaking solo performances.

Albums: *A Is For Andrew, Z Is For Zither* (1974), *Earthed In Cloud Valley* (1977), *Wade In The Flood* (1978), *The Great Dark Water* (1982), *Till The Beasts Returning* (1988). Compilation: *The Andrew Cronshaw CD* (1989).

Cumberland Three

This short-lived US attraction was formed in 1960 at the behest of Roulette Records, who were anxious to find a group similar to the Kingston Trio. Folk duo John and Monty, John Stewart (b. San Diego, California, USA) and John Montgomery, were joined by bassist Gil Robbins to form the new act. The Cumberland Three remained together for 18 months, but although their debut album, *Folk Scene USA*, showed promise, two successive sets were less rewarding. Mike Settle, later of the New Christy Minstrels, augmented the trio in concert, but the group broke up when Robbins left in the summer of 1961. He subsequently joined the Highwaymen, while Stewart, already an accomplished songwriter, replaced Dave Guard in the aforementioned Kingston Trio.

Albums: *Folk Scene USA* (1960), *Civil War Almanac - Volume 1 (Yankees)* (1960), *Civil War Almanac - Volume 2 (Rebels)* (1960).

Cunningham, Agnes 'Sis'

b. 1909, Blaine County, Oklahoma, USA. After leaving school, Cunningham went to college, and later took up teaching. It was later, when she started teaching at the Commonwealth Labor College, in Arkansas, that she started writing songs and singing. She taught music, in 1937, at a socialist school in North Carolina, and upon her return home, became organizer for the Southern Tenant Farmers Union. In 1939, Agnes worked with the Red Dust Players, presenting topical sketches and songs to sharecroppers and for the Oil Workers Union. In 1941, she married Gordon Friesen and subsequently moved to New York. 'Sis' soon became involved with the Almanac Singers, with whom she occasionally sang and played accordion at union. From 1941-42, Friesen and Cunningham lived with Woody Guthrie, Lee Hays, Pete Seeger and Millard Lampell in Almanac House, in Greenwich Village. The married couple regularly composed new songs to fit old tunes, just to make them more topical. After the Almanac Singers ceased performing as such, 'Sis' worked with Sonny Terry and Brownie McGhee, or with Guthrie and Cisco Houston, calling themselves the Almanacs. Along with her husband Friesen, Pete and Toshi Seeger, and Gil Turner, she founded *Broadside* magazine, the first issue of which appeared in February 1962. One feather in its cap was providing the first publication of a Bob Dylan song, 'Talking John Birch Paranoid Blues'. The magazine provided a platform for new songwriters in the folk field.

Cunningham, Phil And Johnny

The Cunningham brothers represent the pinnacle of Scots fiddle/accordion music. In their early days, Johnny Cunningham co-founded the group, Silly Wizard, and was joined by his brother, Phil, although he was under-age. Subsequently, as a duo, they released *Against The Storm*, and promoted it by

Andrew Cronshaw (right) and Ric Sanders

playing local gigs. In 1981, Johnny recorded the solo, *Thoughts From Another World*, before moving to the USA for a time. Phil Cunningham worked as a record producer, after experimenting with synthesisers, contributed to the Relativity albums. He also collaborated with his ex-Silly Wizard partner, Andy Stewart, and Manus Lunny on *Fire In The Glen* (1986). In 1990, he released the characteristic *Palamino Waltz*, and has since been actively engaged in production for several Scots bands, notably Wolfstone.

Selected albums: Phil & Johnny Cunningham *Against The Storm* (1980), Phil Cunningham *Palamino Waltz* (1990), Johnny Cunningham *Thoughts From Another World* (1981).

D

Dab Hand

Formed in 1983, by Tom McConville (b. 6 November 1950, Newcastle-upon-Tyne, England; violin/vocals), and Tom Napper (b. England; banjo/cittern/vocals), and Jez Lowe (b. 14 July 1955, County Durham, England; guitar/vocals/cittern/banjo/dulcimer/harmonica), Dab Hand played a combination of Scots, Shetland and Northumbrian music and traditional dance. Despite capturing the imagination of many on the British folk scene, the group were short-lived, with Lowe leaving in 1984 to pursue a solo career. His place was taken by Gordon Tyrrall (b. Skipton, Yorkshire, England; guitar/vocals). With the departure of McConville, in 1987, Napper and Tyrrall continued for a while as a duo, until Tyrrall also went back to performing in a solo capacity.

Album: *High Rock And Low Glen* (1987).

Dando Shaft

Formed in Coventry, England, in 1968, at a time when hippy culture was in full swing, the original members of the group were Kevin Dempsey (guitar), Martin Jenkins (violin), Dave Cooper (vocals, guitar), Roger Bullen (bass), and Ted Kay (percussion). After moving to London, the unit received a boost with the inclusion of Polly Bolton. In the early 70s the albums *Dando Shaft* and *Lantaloon* included such titles as 'The Harp Lady I Bombed' and 'The Magnetic Beggar', testifying to

Dando Shaft's own particular brand of humour. During 1972 the band tried to become a rock group, but this caused dissention, and Dempsey and Bolton left to form a duo, eventually moving to the USA. Subsequently, Jenkins went on to Hedgehog Pie who recorded for Rubber records of Newcastle Upon Tyne. When Rubber decided to record Jenkins and Dave Cooper, the addition of Dempsey, Bolton and Kay made it into a Dando Shaft reunion. During the late 80s Jenkins and Dempsey reunited in Whippersnapper, and performed the odd Dando song. In 1989 an Italian promoter caused the group to re-form for a week's worth of what they described as 'funky' concerts. At around the same time, archive label See For Miles issued a revival compilation. A live disc of their continental performances. will be issued.

Albums: *An Evening With Dando Shaft* (1970), *Dando Shaft* (1971), *Lantaloon* (1972), *Kingdom* (1977). Compilation: *Reaping The Harvest* (1990).

Darling, Erik

b. 25 September 1933, Baltimore, Maryland, USA. An accomplished songwriter/guitarist/banjo player, Darling initially found success as a member of the Tarriers, whose hootenanny version of 'The Banana Boat Song' was a USA pop hit in 1956 (made famous by Harry Belafonte). Darling subsequently replaced Pete Seeger in the Weavers but left to pursue a solo career four years later. Erik also formed the Rooftop Singers, with Bill Svanoe and Lynne Taylor. Infatuated with a song he had discovered, Darling added a resonant 12-string guitar to its restructured arrangement and emerged with an international success, 'Walk Right In'. This energetic performance reached number 1 in the USA and number 10 in the UK in 1963, but the group was unable, and unwilling, to sustain its momentum and following several personnel changes, split up in 1967.

Darling had meanwhile continued his individual path, recording solo albums for Elektra and Vanguard, and appearing as a sessionman on countless folk selections. He later formed a songwriting partnership with Patricia Street, the final female lead in his erstwhile group, and they performed and recorded together throughout the 70s. A respected musician, Erik Darling's contribution to the development of traditional American folk should not be under-emphasized.

Albums: *Erik Darling* (c.60s), *True Religion* (c.60s) and *Train Time* (c.60s). With the Rooftop Singers *Walk Right In!* (c.60s), *Good Time* (c.60s), *Rainy River* (c.60s). With Patricia Street as Darling And Street *The Possible Dream* (1975).

Davenport, Bob

b. 31 May 1932, Gateshead, Tyne And Wear, England. Although more often known as the front man in Bob Davenport And The Rakes, both with and without the group, Davenport, enjoyed a great deal of popularity and earned a high degree of respect during the British folk revival. *Down The Long Road* included an unaccompanied version of the classic 'Whiskey In The Jar'. The Rakes formed in 1956, essentially as a dance band, but managed to combine both this role with that of backing Davenport. To many, both acts were an inseparable whole. The Rakes, then just Michael Plunkett (fiddle/whistle), and Reg Hall (melodeon), met Davenport in the Queen's Arms, Camden Town, London, in 1956. Paul Gross (fiddle), joined the Rakes later on. After earlier doing his National Service with the Royal Air Force, Davenport first sang in public in 1956, at the Bedford Arms, Camden Town, and, in 1959, won the Collet's Folk Music Contest, as the best amateur performer in London. A strong and versatile vocalist Bob has recorded with numerous singers, on radio and television. Bob was also the first person to get the late Peter Bellamy to perform in a folk club. In the early 60s, at the Singers club in Soho, London, Bellamy joined in the session on whistle. Bob appeared at the 1963 Newport Folk Festival in the USA, alongside such luminaries as Joan Baez, Phil Ochs, Bob Dylan and Tom Paxton. *The Iron Muse* was presented as a 'panorama of Industrial Folk Song', and was arranged by A.L. Lloyd. *Farewell Nancy*, released on Topic, was a recording of sea songs and shanties, and included Louis Killen, and Cyril Tawney, in addition to Davenport himself. The EP, *Folksound Of Britain*, released in 1965 on HMV, featured songs from Northumbria and the West Country, and included Bob Davenport and the Rakes. Bob took a long break from the scene during the 80s, but has again started singing in clubs. The *Will's Barn* release featured Davenport along with the Watersons, and the Copper Family, while *From The Humber To The Tweed* was in part a celebration of Whitby Folk Festival's 25th Anniversary.

Albums: *Wor Geordie* (1962), with others *The Iron Muse* (1963), with others *Farewell Nancy* (1964), *Northumbrian Minstrelsy* (1964), *Bob Davenport And The Rakes* (1965), *Bob Davenport* (1971), *Bob Davenport And The Marsden Rattlers* (1971), *Pal Of My Cradle Days* (1974), *Down The Long Road* (1975), *Postcards Home* (1977), *With The Rakes* (1977), *The Good Old Way-British Folk Music Today* (1980), with others *Will's Barn* (1990), with others *From The Humber To The Tweed* (1991). The Rakes: *The Rakes* (1976).

Davis, Gary, 'Blind' Rev.

b. 30 April 1896, Laurens, South Carolina, USA, d. 5 May 1972, Hammonton, New Jersey, USA. This highly accomplished guitarist was self-taught from the age of six. Partially blind from an early age, he lost his sight during his late twenties. During the Depression years, he worked as a street singer in North Carolina, playing a formidable repertoire of spirituals, rags, marches and square dance tunes. In 1933, he was ordained a Baptist minister and continued to tour as a gospel preacher. During the mid-30s, he recorded some spiritual and blues songs for ARC. After moving to New York in 1940, he achieved some fame on the folk circuit and subsequently recorded for a number of labels, including Stinson, Riverside, Prestige-Bluesville and Folkways. *Harlem Street Singer*, released in 1960, was an impressive work, which emphasized his importance to a new generation of listeners. Davis taught guitar and greatly inspired Stefan Grossman. Among Davis's devotees were Bob Dylan, Taj Mahal, Ry Cooder and Donovan. Davis visited the UK in 1964, and returned as a soloist on several other occasions. He appeared at many music festivals, including Newport in 1968, and was the subject of two television documentaries in 1967 and 1970. He also appeared in the film *Black Roots*. His importance in the history of black rural music cannot be overestimated.

Compiliaton: *Pure Religion And Bad Company* (1991).

Davis, Meg

b. 28 January 1953, Cincinnati, Ohio, USA. Davis is a performer of traditional Irish and Scottish music, and her own original fantasy music. She began writing and recording music at the age of 14 and later played the coffee houses of her home town. It was not until she was 18 that Davis started touring. From 1970-80, she specialized in 12-string guitar, performing for a time with the bluegrass band Vernon McIntyre and the Appalachian Grass, as well as appearing onstage with such names as Bill Monroe, Tom Paxton, and Doc Watson. Meg won the Best New Songwriter of 1978 award in Los Angeles, which was presented by Peter Yarrow of Peter, Paul And Mary. The following year saw her first release *Captain Jack And The Mermaid*, accompanied by Malcolm Dalglish on hammer dulcimer. Davis moved to Washington, DC in 1979 to concentrate on traditional Irish music, and performed there until 1985, appearing in concert, at different times, with Tommy Makem, Alan Stivell, James Keane and Joe Burke, in addition to many others. While in the USA, she worked as part of the Joe Burke Trio, and regularly toured the UK. Meg also performs at science fiction conventions, both in the USA and the UK. Some of her fantasy work is based on the writings of Lewis Carroll, as in *The Music Of Wonderland*. Despite her strong interest in traditional music, *The Claddagh Walk* was her first album of traditional Irish and Scottish music.

Albums: *Captain Jack And The Mermaid* (1979), *Dream Of Light Horses* (1982), *Swing The Cat* (1985), *The Music Of Wonderland* (1987), *Meg Davis Live* (1989), *The Claddagh Walk* (1990), *By The Sword* (1991).

Dawson, Jim

b. 27 June 1946, Miami, Oklahoma, USA. Dawson moved to Littleton, Colorado at an early age, and lived there until 1964. After teaching himself to play piano and guitar, he played in a high school group, then joined the navy. Dawson's first two albums were recorded on Kama Sutra, but he signed with RCA in 1974, releasing *Jim Dawson*. For this recording, he had worked with producers Terry Cashman and Tommy West, known for their work with Jim Croce. Although not a true folk performer in the strictest sense of the word, his work is difficult to put into one genre.

Albums: *Songman* (1971), *You'll Never Be Lonely With Me* (1972), *Jim Dawson* (1974), *Elephants In The Rain* (1975). Compilations: *Essential Jim Dawson* (1974).

De Dannan

Formed in Eire during the 70s, this group have amalgamated contemporary and traditional folk music With a line-up of Alec Finn (guitar, bouzouki), Frankie Gavin (fiddle, flute, whistle), Dolores Keane (b. Caherlistrane, Co. Galway, Ireland; vocals), Johnny 'Ringo' McDonagh (bodhran, percussion), and Jackie Daly (melodeon), they produced a highly original sound. Original singer Maura McConnell, left to pursue a solo career, with her replacement, Mary Black, doing likewise in 1986. Keane, who took over, has since gone on to record and perform in a solo capacity. At one time, they were joined by cellist Caroline Lavelle. The current line-up - Gavin, Finn, Aiden Coffey (accordion), Colm Murphy (bodhran), and Eleanor Shanley (vocals) - still retain the distinctive sound for which the group is known. Even after 15 years, with the various changes in personnel, De Dannan have still retained the quality that distinguishes them from a number of other groups, that have inevitably followed in their wake. Even when Charlie Piggot, Maura O'Connell and Jackie Daly left, at one point leaving just Finn, McDonagh and Gavin, many would have given up; instead they took on Mary Black and Martin O'Connor and produced *Song For Ireland*. The group is still popular in concert, and tour regularly, both at home and overseas.

Decameron

Albums: *De Dannan* (1975), *Selected Jigs Reels And Songs* (1977), *The Mist Covered Mountain* (1980), *Star Spangled Molly* (1981), *Song For Ireland* (1983), *Anthem* (1985), *Ballroom* (1987), *A Jacket Of Batteries* (1989), *1/2 Set In Harlem* (1991). Compilations: *Best Of De Dannan* (c.80s). Frankie Gavin: *Frankie Goes To Town* (1991).

Decameron

Formed in 1968, this group comprised Dave Bell (guitar/percussion/vocals), and Johnny Coppin (b. 5 July 1946, Woodford, Essex, England; guitar/piano/vocals). The line-up grew, in September 1969, when they added Al Fenn (guitar/mandolin/vocals), and further still with the addition of Geoff March (cello/violin/vocals), in December 1969; Dik Cadbury (bass/guitar/violin/vocals) in July 1973; and finally Bob Critchley (drums/vocals), in September 1975. From 1971-74, the group were signed to the Fingamigig agency, which was then run by Jasper Carrott and John Starkey. Based in Cheltenham, Gloucester, Decameron performed contemporary folk-rock material, much of which was composed by Bell and Coppin. The group released three singles on as many labels: 'Stoats Grope' in 1973, on Vertigo; 'Breakdown Of The Song' in 1974, on Mooncrest; and 'Dancing' in 1976, on Transatlantic. Two other singles, both on Transatlantic, were released by the band, under the name of the Magnificent Mercury Brothers, in which guise they sang 60s doo-wop style. The singles were 'New Girl In School' in 1975, and a version of the classic 'Why Do Fools Fall In Love', in 1976. Neither single achieved any great commercial success, and the group split, Coppin going on to pursue a solo career.

Albums: *Say Hello To The Band* (1973), *Mammoth Special* (1974), *Third Light* (1975), *Beyond The Light* (1975), *Tomorrows Pantomime* (1976).

Deighton Family

This seven-piece family group featuring Dave Deighton (vocals, guitar, melodeon, fiddle, harmonica), his wife Josie (b. Indonesia; guitar, bodhran), and their children Kathleen (fiddle), Arthur (guitar, mandolin), Angelina (boogie), Maya (whistle, flute), and Rosalie (fiddle, mandolin, percussion, vocals). Their music has been described as 'South Yorkshire/Indonesian/Dutch/Cajun folk pop'. *Acoustic Music To Suit Most Occasions* received good reviews when released, with the group appearing at folk festivals all over the UK. However, since the initial interest has died down, and despite the follow-up *Mama Was Right*, the novelty impact would appear to have waned. Nevertheless, the group successfully toured the USA and Canada in 1990, where their albums had been popular.

Albums: *Acoustic Music To Suit Most Occasions* (1988), *Mama Was Right* (1990), *Rolling Home* (1991).

Dement, Iris

A singer/songwriter from the rural regions of Arkansas, Dement made her initial impact on the music scene in 1992. Her early influences included gospel, Loretta Lynn and Johnny Cash, but she was 25 years of age before she began to write her own songs. Surrounded by accomplished players such as Al Perkins and Jerry Douglas, her debut album, *Infamous Angel*, was an acclaimed, acoustically-based country folk set, that mixed her homespun vocals and charming lyrics to great effect. An original talent, her rave notices resulted in a recording contract with Warner Brotherss. in 1993. Great things are expected in the future.

Albums *Infamous Angel* (1992).

Denny, Sandy

b. Alexandra Elene Maclean Denny, 6 January 1947, Wimbledon, London, England, d. 21 April 1978, London, England. A former student at Kingston Art College where her contemporaries included John Renbourn and Jimmy Page, Sandy Denny forged her early reputation in such famous London folk clubs as Les Cousins, Bunjies and the Scots Hoose. Renowned for an eclectic repertoire, she featured material by Tom Paxton and her then boyfriend Jackson C. Frank as well as traditional English songs. Work from this early period was captured on two 1967 albums, *Sandy And Johnny* (with Johnny Silvo) and *Alex Campbell & His Friends*.

The following year the singer spent six months as a member of the Strawbs. Their lone album together was not released until 1973, but this melodic work contained several haunting Denny vocals and includes the original version of her famed composition, 'Who Knows Where The Time Goes'. In May 1968 Sandy joined Fairport Convention with whom she completed three excellent albums. Many of her finest performances date from this period, but when the group vowed to pursue a purist path at the expense of original material, the singer left to form Fotheringay. This accomplished quintet recorded a solitary album before internal pressures pulled it apart, but Sandy's contributions, notably 'The Sea', 'Nothing More' and 'The Pond And The Stream', rank among her finest work.

Denny's debut album, *North Star Grassman And The Ravens*, was issued in 1971. It contained several excellent songs, including 'Late November' and the

Deighton Family

expansive 'John The Gun', as well as sterling contributions from the renowned guitarist Richard Thompson, who would appear on all of the singer's releases. *Sandy* was another memorable collection, notable for the haunting 'It'll Take A Long Time' and a sympathetic version of Richard Farina's 'Quiet Joys Of Brotherhood', a staple of the early Fairport's set. Together, these albums confirmed Sandy as a major talent and a composer of accomplished, poignant songs.

Like An Old Fashioned Waltz, which included the gorgeous 'Solo', closed this particular period. Sandy married Trevor Lucas, her partner in Fotheringay, who was now a member of Fairport Convention. Despite her dislike of touring, she rejoined the group in 1974. A live set and the crafted *Rising For The Moon* followed, but Denny and Lucas then left in December 1975. A period of domesticity ensued before the singer completed *Rendezvous*, a charming selection which rekindled an interest in performing. Plans were made to record a new set in America, but following a fall down the staircase at a friend's house Sandy died from a cerebral haemorrhage on 21 April 1978. She is recalled as one of Britain's finest singer/songwriters and for work which has grown in stature over the years. Her effortless and smooth vocal delivery still sets the standard for many of today's female folk-based singers.

Albums: *The North Star Grassman And The Ravens* (1971), *Sandy* (1972), *Like An Old Fashioned Waltz* (1973), *Rendezvous* (1977). Compilations: *The Original Sandy Denny* (1984), *Who Knows Where The Time Goes* (1986), *The Best Of Sandy Denny* (1987). Further reading: *Meet On The Ledge*, Patrick Humphries.

Denver, John

b. Henry John Deutschendorf Jnr., 31 December 1943, Roswell, New Mexico, USA. One of America's most popular performers during the 70s, Denver's rise to fame began when he was 'discovered' in a Los Angeles night club. He initially joined the Back Porch Majority, a nursery group for the renowned New Christy Minstrels but, tiring of his role there, left for the Chad Mitchell Trio where he forged a reputation as a talented songwriter.

With the departure of the last original member, the Mitchell Trio became known as Denver, Boise and Johnson, but their brief life-span ended when John embarked on a solo career in 1969. One of his compositions, 'Leaving On A Jet Plane', provided an international hit for Peter, Paul And Mary, and this evocative song was the highlight of Denver's debut album, *Rhymes And Reasons*. Subsequent releases, *Take Me To Tomorrow* and *Whose Garden Was This*, garnered some attention, but it was not

until the release of *Poems, Prayers And Promises* that the singer enjoyed popular acclaim when one of its tracks, 'Take Me Home, Country Roads', broached the US Top 3 and became a UK Top 20 hit for Olivia Newton-John in 1973. The song's undemanding homeliness established a light, almost naive style, consolidated on the albums *Aerie* and *Rocky Mountain High*. 'I'd Rather Be A Cowboy' (1973) and 'Sunshine On My Shoulders' (1974) were both gold singles, while a third million-seller, 'Annie's Song', secured Denver's international status when it topped the UK charts that same year and subsequently became an MOR standard, as well as earning the classical flautist James Galway a UK number 3 hit in 1978. Further US chart success came in 1975 with two number 1 hits, 'Thank God I'm A Country Boy' and 'I'm Sorry'. Denver's status as an all-round entertainer was enhanced by many television spectaculars, including *Rocky Mountain Christmas*, and further gold-record awards for *An Evening With John Denver* and *Windsong*, ensuring that 1975 was the artist's most successful year to date.

He continued to enjoy a high profile throughout the rest of the decade and forged a concurrent acting career with his role in the film comedy *Oh, God* with George Burns. In 1981 his songwriting talent attracted the attention of yet another classically trained artist, when opera singer Placido Domingo duetted with Denver on 'Perhaps Love'. However, although Denver became an unofficial musical ambassador with tours to Russia and China, his recording became less prolific as increasingly he devoted time to charitable work and ecological interests. Despite the attacks by music critics, who have deemed his work as bland and saccharine, Denver's cute, simplistic approach has nonetheless achieved a mass popularity which is the envy of many artists.

Albums: *Rhymes & Reasons* (1969), *Take Me To Tomorrow* (1970), *Whose Garden Was This* (1970), *Poems, Prayers And Promises* (1971), *Aerie* (1971), *Rocky Mountain High* (1972), *Farewell Andromeda* (1973), *Back Home Again* (1974), *An Evening With John Denver* (1975), *Windsong* (1975), *Rocky Mountain Christmas* (1975), *Live In London* (1976), *Spirit* (1976), *I Want To Live* (1977), *Live At The Sydney Opera House* (1978), *John Denver* (1979), with the Muppets *A Christmas Together* (1979), *Autograph* (1980), *Some Days Are Diamonds* (1981), with Placido Domingo *Perhaps Love* (1981), *Seasons Of The Heart* (1982), *It's About Time* (1983), *Dreamland Express* (1985), *One World* (1986), *Higher Ground* (1988), *Stonehaven Sunrise* (1989), *The Flower That Shattered The Stone* (1990), *Earth Songs* (1990), *Different Directions* (1992). Compilations: *The Best Of John Denver* (1974), *The Best Of John Denver*

Volume 2 (1977), *The John Denver Collection* (1984), *Greatest Hits Volume 3* (1985).
Further reading: *The Man And His Music*, Leonore Fleischer. *Rocky Mountain Wonderboy*, James M. Martin.

Denver, Karl

b. Angus McKenzie, 16 December 1934, Glasgow, Scotland. Denver, a former merchant seaman, was aged 23 before he began a career in show business. During his travels the singer accumulated a love of contrasting folk forms and his repertoire consisted of traditional material from the Middle East, Africa and China. Denver's flexible voice spanned several octaves and his unusual inflections brought much contemporary comment. The artist enjoyed four UK Top 10 hits during 1961/62, including 'Marcheta' and 'Wimoweh', the latter reaching number 4. Denver continued to enjoy minor chart success over the next two years, but he progressively turned to cabaret work. The singer has been based in Manchester for many years, which in part explains 'Lazyitis (One Armed Boxer)', his 1989 collaboration with the city's neo-psychedelic favourites, the Happy Mondays.
Albums: *Karl Denver* (1962), *Wimoweh* (early-60s), *Karl Denver At The Yew Tree* (early-60s), *With Love* (early-60s), *Karl Denver* (1970).

Dillard, Doug And Rodney

Brothers, Doug (banjo) and Rodney (guitar), were the founders of the pioneering bluegrass outfit, The Dillards. In 1968, Doug left after six reasonably successful years, and joined the Gram Parsons-era Byrds for a few months, before Parsons himself departed. This association led to the formation of the ground-breaking Dillard & Clark Expedition, with ex-Bryd, Gene Clark, and Bernie Leadon (later with The Eagles), Michael Clarke (another former Byrd) and fiddle champion, Byron Berline. Their two albums for A&M, *The Fantastic Expedition Of Dillard & Clark* (1968) and *Through The Morning, Through The Night*, produced an unusual, but highly successful blend of bluegrass and southern soul, but internal disputes caused the group to disband soon afterwards. Doug Dillard released several disjointed solo albums in the 70s, and occasionally recorded with his brother Rodney and longtime friend John Hartford. Together, they cut the promising *Dillard Hartford Dillard* in 1975, a bluegrass-folk hybrid that mixed some good picking with lighthearted tunes. Subsequently, Doug Dillard fronted his own band with vocalist Ginger Boatwright, and playing the U.S. festival circuit with The Dillards. Never a prolific writer, he nevertheless contributed several memorable 'character' songs to The Dillards repertoire, such as

'Dooley' and 'Ebo Walker'. After The Dillards split in the early 80s, he spent a couple of years with country music star Earl Scrugg's band. In 1985 Flying Fish released the misleadingly titled *Rodney Dillard At Silver Dollar City*, a low budget recording that featured Rodney on two tracks. In the early 90s, Rodney followed the excellent *Let It Fly*, by the re-formed Dillards, with his own *Let The Rough Side Drag*, a mixture of bluegrass and folk.
Selected albums: *Backporch Bluegrass* (1962), *The Fantastic Expedition Of Dillard & Clark* (1968), *Copper Fields* (1969), *Dillard Hartford Dillard* (1975), *Let It Fly* (c.90s), Rodney Dillard *Let The Rough Side Drag* (c.90s).

Dillards

Brothers Rodney (b. 18 May 1942, East St. Louis, Illinois, USA; guitar/vocals) and Doug Dillard (b. 6 March 1937, East St. Louis, Illinois, USA; banjo/vocals) formed this seminal bluegrass group in Salem, Missouri, USA. Roy Dean Webb (b. 28 March 1937, Independence, Missouri, USA; mandolin/vocals) and former radio announcer Mitch Jayne (b. 7 May 1930, Hammond, Indiana, USA; bass) completed the original line-up which, having enjoyed popularity throughout their home state, travelled to Los Angeles in 1962 where they secured a recording deal with the renowned Elektra label. *Back Porch Bluegrass* and *The Dillards Live! Almost!* established the unit as one of America's leading traditional acts, although purists denigrated a sometimes irreverent attitude. *Pickin' & Fiddlin'*, a collaboration with violinist Byron Berline, was recorded to placate such criticism. The Dillards shared management with the Byrds and, whereas their distinctive harmonies proved influential to the latter group's development, the former act then began embracing a pop-based perspective. Dewey Martin (b. 30 September 1942, Chesterville, Ontario, Canada), later of Buffalo Springfield, added drums on a folk-rock demo which in turn led to a brace of singles recorded for the Capitol label. Doug Dillard was unhappy with this new direction and left to form a duo with ex-Byrd Gene Clark. Herb Peterson joined the Dillards in 1968 and, having resigned with Elektra, the reshaped quartet completed two exceptional country-rock sets, *Wheatstraw Suite* and *Copperfields*. The newcomer was in turn replaced by Billy Rae Latham for *Roots And Branches*, on which the unit's transformation to full-scale electric instruments was complete. A full-time drummer, Paul York, was now featured in the line-up, but further changes were wrought when founder member Jayne dropped out following *Tribute To The American Duck*. Rodney Dillard has since remained at the helm of a capricious act, which by the end of the

70s, returned to the traditional music circuit through the auspices of the respected Flying Fish label. He was also reunited with his prodigal brother in Dillard-Hartford-Dillard, an occasional sideline, which also featured multi-instrumentalist John Hartford. Doug Dillard fronted his own his own band for a time with vocalist Ginger Boatwright. Never a prolific writer, he nevertheless contributed several memorable 'character' songs to the Dillards' repertoire, such as 'Dooley' and 'Ebo Walker'. In the early 80s he spent a couple of years with country music star, Earl Scruggs's band. Rodney Dillard released his own mixture of bluegrass and folk, *Let The Rough Side Drag*, in the early 90s.

Albums: *Back Porch Bluegrass* (1963), *The Dillards Live! Almost!* (1964), *Pickin' & Fiddlin'* (1965), *Wheatstraw Suite* (1969), *Copperfields* (1970), *Roots And Branches* (1972), *Tribute To The American Duck* (1973), *The Dillards Versus The Incredible LA Time Machine* (1977), *Mountain Rock* (1978), *Decade Waltz* (1979), *Homecoming & Family Reunion* (1979), *Let It Fly* (1991). Compilations: *Country Tracks* (1974), *I'll Fly Away* (1988). Rodney Dillard *Let The Rough Side Drag (c.90s)*.

Doherty, Denny

b. 19 November 1941, Halifax, Nova Scotia, Canada. Doherty established his reputation as a member of the Halifax Three, a clean-cut folk act modelled on the Kingston Trio. In 1964 he formed the Mugwumps with 'Mama' Cass Elliott, before opting for the New Journeymen, a group including John Phillips and Michelle Phillips. The seeds were thus sewn for the Mamas And The Papas, a highly popular mid-60s folk-rock attraction, of which Doherty's confident voice was an integral part. The quartet was disbanded in 1968 and Denny subsequently embarked on a solo career. *What'cha Gonna Do*, an unpretentious, country-influenced set, was not a commercial success, and thus its follow-up, *Waiting For A Song*, gained only limited exposure. The artist did complete several singles for the Paramount, Columbia and Playboy labels, but achieved a higher profile following his role in Phillips' musical *Man On The Moon*. By 1978 Doherty had returned to Halifax where he hosted a television variety show, but the following year agreed to join a reconstituted Mamas And The Papas. He remained in the line-up until the late 80s when, tired of touring, Doherty gave up his place to long-time associate Scott McKenzie.

Albums: *What'cha Gonna Do* (1971), *Waiting For A Song* (1974).

Donahue, Jerry

b. 24 Setember 1946, Manhattan, New York, USA.

This stylish guitarist arrived in Britain in 1961, aiming to further his academic education. He was, however, attracted to music, garnering plaudits in Poet And The One Man Band prior to joining Fotheringay, the short-lived but innovative unit formed by Sandy Denny. Donahue continued his exemplary work with Head Hands And Feet, but is better recalled for a spell with Fairport Convention. He remained with this renowned folk-rock group between 1972 and 1976, contributing to three of their late-period albums before opting for a career as a session musician. This did not, however, preclude solo recordings and the guitarist's recent album releases show him exploring 'new age' styles. Like Richard Thompson, Donahue is a guitarist's guitar player whose dexterity transends commercial opportunity.

Selected albums: *Telecasting* (1986), *Meetings* (1988), *Neck Of The Wood* (1992).

Donegan, Lonnie

b. Anthony Donegan, 29 April 1931, Glasgow, Scotland. Donegan as 'The King Of Skiffle' became a more homogeneous UK equivalent to Elvis Presley than Tommy Steele. Steeped in traditional jazz and its by-products, he was a guitarist in a skiffle band before a spell in the army found him drumming in the Wolverines Jazz Band. After his discharge, he played banjo with Ken Colyer and then Chris Barber. With his very stage forename a tribute to a black bluesman, both units allowed him to sing a couple of blues-tinged American folk tunes as a 'skiffle' break. His version of Leadbelly's 'Rock Island Line', issued from Barber's *New Orleans Joys* in 1954 as a single after months in the domestic hit parade, was also a US hit. Donegan's music inspired thousands of teenagers to form amateur skiffle combos, with friends playing broomstick tea chest bass, washboards and other instruments fashioned from household implements. The Beatles, playing initially as the Quarrymen, were a foremost example of an act traceable to such roots.

With his own group, Donegan was a prominent figure in skiffle throughout its 1957 prime; he possessed an energetic whine far removed from the gentle plumminess of other native pop vocalists. Donegan could dazzle with his virtuosity on 12-string acoustic guitar and his string of familiar songs have rarely been surpassed: 'Don't You Rock Me Daddy-O', 'Putting On The Style' ('putting on the agony, putting on the style'), 'Bring A Little Water Sylvie', 'Grand Coulee Dam', 'Does Your Chewing Gum Lose Its Flavour On The Bedpost Over Night' and 'Jimmy Brown The Newsboy', were but a few of Donegan's gems. He arguably made the traditional song 'Cumberland Gap' his own (his first UK number 1) and 1959's 'Battle Of New Orleans' was the finest-ever reading. He delved deeper into Americana to embrace bluegrass, spirituals, Cajun and even Appalachian music, the formal opposite of jazz. However, when the skiffle boom diminished, he broadened his appeal - to much purist criticism - with olde tyme music hall/pub singalong favourites, and a more pronounced comedy element. His final chart-topper was with the uproarious 'My Old Man's A Dustman', which sensationally entered the UK charts at number 1 in 1960. The hit was an adaptation of the ribald Liverpool folk ditty, 'My Old Man's A Fireman On The Elder-Dempster Line'. He followed it with further comedy numbers including 'Lively' in 1960. Two years later, Donegan's Top 20 run ended as it had started, with a Leadbelly number ('Pick A Bale Of Cotton'). However, between 1956 and 1962 he had numbered 34 hits.

He finished the 60s with huge sales of two mid-price *Golden Age Of Donegan* volumes, supplementing his earnings in cabaret and occasional spots on BBC television's *The Good Old Days*. The most interesting diversion of the next decade was Adam Faith's production of *Putting On The Style*. Here, at Paul McCartney's suggestion, Donegan re-made old smashes backed by an extraordinary glut of artists who were lifelong fans, including; Rory Gallagher, Ringo Starr, Leo Sayer, Zoot Money, Albert Lee, Gary Brooker, Brian May, Nicky Hopkins, Elton John and Ron Wood. While this album brushed 1978's UK album list, a 1982 single, 'Spread A Little Happiness', was also a minor success - and, as exemplified by the Traveling Wilburys 'skiffle for the 90s', the impact of Donegan's earliest chart entries continues to exert its influence on pop music. Although no longer enjoying the best of health, Donegan continues to entertain. He has long been an influential legend and clearly the man who was British skiffle music.

Selected albums: *Showcase* (1956), *Lonnie* (1958), *Tops With Lonnie* (1959), *Lonnie Rides Again* (1959), *More Tops With Lonnie* (1960), *Sings Hallelujah* (1962), *The Lonnie Donegan Folk Album* (1965), *Golden Hour Of Donegan Vol 1 & 2* (c.60s), *Lonniepops-Lonnie Donegan Today* (1970), *Lonnie Donegan Meets Leineman* (1974), *Lonnie Donegan* (1975), *Lonnie Donegan Meets Leineman-Country Roads* (1976), *Putting On The Style* (1977), *Sundown* (1978), *Jubilee Concert* (1981), *Greatest Hits: Lonnie Donegan* (1983), *Rare And Unissued Gems* (1985), *Rock Island Line* (1985), *The Hit Singles Collection* (1987), *The Best Of Lonnie Donegan* (1989), *The Collection: Lonnie Donegan* (1989), *Putting On The Styles* 3 CD set (1992).

Donovan

b. Donovan Leitch, 10 May 1946, Glasgow, Scotland. Uncomfortably labelled 'Britain's answer to Bob Dylan' the young troubadour did not fit in well with the folk establishment. Instead, it was the pioneering UK television show *Ready Steady Go* that adopted Donovan, and from then on success was assured. His first single 'Catch The Wind' launched a career that lasted through the 60s with numerous hits, developing as fashions changed. The expressive 'Colours' and 'Turquoise' continued his hit folk image, although hints of other influences began to creep into his music. Donovan's finest work, however, was as ambassador of 'flower power' with memorable singles like 'Sunshine Superman' and 'Mellow Yellow'. His subtle drug references endeared him to the hippie movement, although some critics felt his stance was just a bit fey and insipid. He enjoyed several hits with light material such as the calypso influenced 'There Is A Mountain' and 'Jennifer Juniper' (written for Jenny Boyd during a much publicized sojourn with the guru, Maharishi Mahesh Yogi). Donovan's drug/fairy tale imagery reached its apotheosis on the Lewis Carroll influenced 'Hurdy Gurdy Man'. As the 60s closed, however, he fell from commercial grace. Undeterred, Donovan found greater success in the USA; indeed, many of his later records were first issued in America and some gained no UK release. His collaboration with Jeff Beck on 'Goo Goo Barabajagal (Love Is Hot)' showed a more gutsy approach, while a number of the tracks on the boxed set *A Gift From A Flower To A Garden* displayed a jazzier feel. He had previously flirted with jazz on his b-sides, notably the excellent 'Sunny Goodge Street' and 'Preachin' Love'. *Cosmic Wheels* in 1973 was an artistic success; it sold well and contained his witty 'Intergalactic Laxative'. In anticipation of continued success, *Essence To Essence* was a bitter disappointment, and thereafter Donovan ceased to be a major concert attraction.

In 1990 the Happy Mondays bought him back into favour by praising his work and invited him to tour with them in 1991. Their irreverent tribute 'Donovan' underlined this new-found favouritism. Shortly before this, he was back on television as part of a humorous remake of 'Jennifer Juniper' with UK comedians Trevor and Simon. A new album was released and a flood of reissues arrived; for the moment at least the cognoscenti decreed that Donovan was 'okay' again. He undertook a major UK tour in 1992. *Troubadour*, a CD box set was issued in 1992 covering the vital material from his career.

Albums: *What's Bin Did And What's Bin Hid* (1965), *Catch The Wind* (1965), *Fairytale* (1965), *Sunshine Superman* (1966), *Mellow Yellow* (1967),

Wear Your Love Like Heaven (1967), For Little Ones (1967), A Gift From A Flower To A Garden (1967), Donovan In Concert (1968), Hurdy Gurdy Man (1968), Barabajagal (1969), Open Road (1970), HMS Donovan (1971), Brother Sun, Sister Moon (1972, film soundtrack), Colours (1972), The Pied Piper (1973, film soundtrack), Cosmic Wheels (1973), Essence To Essence (1973), 7-Tease (1974), Slow Down World (1976), Donovan (1977), Neutronica (1981), Love Is The Only Feeling (1981), Lady Of The Stars (1984). Selected compilations: Universal Soldier (1967), The Golden Hour Of Donovan (1971), The Donovan File (1977), Spotlight On Donovan (1981), Greatest Hits And More (1989), The EP Collection (1990), Donovan Rising (1990), 25 Years In Concert (1991), Troubadour (CD box set)(1992).

Doonan Family Band

A lively Newcastle Upon Tyne/Irish family group, with main members, John 'Da' Doonan (flute), Kevin Doonan (fiddle) and Mick Doonan (pipes). The trio are regularly augmented by Phil Murray (bass), and Stu Luckley (guitar, vocals), as well as a troupe of Irish step dancers. An excellent festival act, the high percentage of ex-Hedgehog Pie and Jack The Lad members ensures that their sets, though acoustic, have far more energy than some of the 'electric' bands. They frequently feature traditional arrangements of material by Buddy Holly and the Beatles, amongst others.
Album: Fenwick's Window (1992).

Dr. Strangely Strange

This Irish folk group - Ivan Pawle (vocals/bass), Tim Booth (vocals/guitar) and Tim Goulding (vocals/keyboards) - made its recording debut in 1969. Although Kip Of The Serenes betrayed an obvious debt to the Incredible String Band (both groups were produced by Joe Boyd), the album nonetheless offered a whimsical charm. The trio then embraced a rock-based style on Heavy Petting, despite the assistance of traditional musicians Andy Irvine and Johnny Moynahan. Guitarist Gary Moore guested on four of the tracks including the catchy yet subtly humorous 'I Gave My Love An Apple', but this electric album lacked the purpose of its predecessor. Dr. Strangely Strange disbanded in 1971 following their appearance on Mike Heron's all-star solo album, Smiling Men With Reputations.
Albums: Kip Of The Serenes (1969), Heavy Petting (1970).

Drake, Nick

b. 19 June 1948, Burma, d. 25 November 1974. Born into an upper middle-class background, Drake was raised in Tanworth-in-Arden, near Birmingham. Recordings made at his parents' home in 1967 revealed a blossoming talent, indebted to Bert Jansch and John Renbourn, yet clearly a songwriter in his own right. He enrolled at Fitzwilliam College in Cambridge, and during this spell met future associate Robert Kirby. Drake also made several live appearances and was discovered at one such performance by Fairport Convention bassist, Ashley Hutchings, who introduced the folksinger to their producer Joe Boyd. A series of demos were then completed, part of which surfaced on the posthumous release Time Of No Reply, before Drake began work on his debut album.
Five Leaves Left was a mature, melodic collection which invoked the mood of Van Morrison's Astral Weeks or Tim Buckley's Happy Sad. Drake's languid, almost unemotional intonation contrasted the warmth of his musical accompaniment, in particular Robert Kirby's temperate string sections. Contributions from Richard Thompson (guitar) and Danny Thompson (bass) were equally crucial, adding texture to a set of quite remarkable compositions. By contrast Bryter Layter was altogether more worldly, and featured support from emphatic, rather than intuitive, musicians. Lyn Dobson (flute) and Ray Warleigh (saxophone) provided a jazz-based perspective to parts of a selection which successfully married the artist's private and public aspirations. Indisputably Drake's most commercial album, the singer was reportedly stunned when it failed to reap due reward and the departure of Boyd for America accentuated his growing misgivings. A bout of severe depression followed, but late in 1971 Nick resumed recording with the harrowing Pink Moon. Completed in two days, its stark, almost desolate atmosphere made for uncomfortable listening, yet beneath its loneliness lay a poignant beauty. Two songs, 'Parasite' and 'Place To Be' dated from 1969, while 'Things Behind The Sun' had once been considered for Bryter Layter. These inclusions suggested that Drake now found composing difficult; and it was 1974 before he re-entered a studio. Four tracks were completed, of which 'Black Eyed Dog', itself a metaphor for death, seemed a portent of things to come. On 25 November 1974, Nick Drake was found dead in his bedroom. Although the coroner's verdict was suicide, relatives and acquaintances feel that his overdose of a prescribed drug was accidental. Interest in this ill-fated performer has increased over the years and his catalogue contains some of the era's most accomplished music. Drake is now seen as a hugely influential artist.
Albums: Five Leaves Left (1969), Bryter Layter (1970), Pink Moon (1972), Time Of No Reply (1986 - early recordings and demos). Compilations: Fruit Tree (1979 - triple album box-set, reissued with

Time Of No Reply in 1986), *Heaven In A Wild Flower* (1985).

Dransfields

Brothers Robin (b. Harrogate, Yorkshire, England; guitar, banjo, vocals), and Barry Dransfield (b. Harrogate, Yorkshire, England; fiddle, guitar, mandolin, gimbri, cello, vocals), were well-known and liked during the 70s. They both started singing and playing in 1962, when they were members of a Leeds-based bluegrass band, the Crimple Mountain Boys. The group only lasted for three years, at the end of which Robin and Barry decided to concentrate on British music. Barry turned professional in 1966, having been a civil servant. Robin, on the other hand, waited until 1969 before 'taking the plunge', having performed in clubs while holding down a teaching position. They appeared at London's Royal Albert Hall Festival in 1971 and, in addition to Barry's fiddle tunes, contributed four tracks to the ensuing album, including 'Who's The Fool Now', and 'The Waters Of Tyne'. The brothers made their first broadcast on BBC radio's *Folk On Friday*. On *Bowin' And Scrapin'*, Barry played a bowed Appalachian dulcimer. *The Fiddler's Dream* included Brian Harrison.
Albums: *Rout Of The Blues* (1970), *Lord Of All I Behold* (1971), various artists *The Royal Albert Hall Festival* (1971), *The Fiddler's Dream* (1976), *Popular To Contrary Belief* (1977). Solo albums: Barry Dransfield *Barry Dransfield* (1972), *Bowin' And Scrapin'* (1978); Robin Dransfield *Tidewave* (1980).

Driftwood, Jimmy

b. James Morris, 20 June 1907, Mountain View, Arkansas, USA. His name first came to prominence as a result of the Johnny Horton recording of Driftwood's song, 'The Battle Of New Orleans' in 1959. The single made the top of both the USA pop and country charts, but only the Top 20 in the UK. Lonnie Donegan reached number 2 in the UK with the song in the same year. Driftwood himself had recorded a version of the song the previous year for RCA Victor. With a strong musical heritage Driftwood learned to play guitar, banjo and fiddle while still young. Picking up old songs from his grandparents, and other members of his family, he later travelled about collecting and recording songs. While still performing at folk festivals, Jimmy continued to teach during the 40s. With the 50s, came the growing folk boom, and he found himself reaching a wider audience. RCA signed him to record *Newly Discovered Early American Folk Songs*, which included the aforementioned 'Battle Of New Orleans'. While the song's popularity grew, Driftwood was working for the *Grand Ole Opry*,

but left in order to work on a project to establish a cultural centre at his home in Mountain View. The aim was to preserve the Ozark Mountain peoples' heritage. Having later joined the Rackensack Folklore Society, he travelled the USA, talking at universities to pass on the importance of such a project. The first Arkansas Folk Festival, held in 1963, was successful and, in 1973, the cultural centre was established. One performer at such events organized by the Rackensack Folklore Society was Glenn Ohrlin.
Selected albums: *Newly Discovered Early American Folk Songs* (1958), *The Wilderness Road* (c.60s), *A Lesson In Folk Music* (c.60s), *Songs Of Billie Yank And Johnny Reb* (1961), Compilations: *Famous Country Music Makers* (c.70s), *Americana* (1991).

Dubliners

This Dublin, Eire band featured Barry MacKenna (b. 16 December 1939), Luke Kelly (b. 16 November 1939), ex-draughtsman John Sheahan (b. 19 May 1939), Ciaran Bourke and former teacher Ronnie Drew. They formed in 1962, in the back of O'Donoghues' bar in Merron Row, Dublin and were originally named the Ronnie Drew Group. The members were known faces in the city's post-skiffle folk haunts before pooling their assorted singing and fretboard skills in 1962. They played several theatre bars, made several albums for Transatlantic and gained a strong following on the Irish folk circuit. After an introduction by Dominic Behan, they were signed by manager Phil Solomon and placed on his label, Major Minor. Throughout their collective career, each member pursued outside projects - among them Kelly's stints as an actor and MacKenna's 'The Great Comic Genius', a solo single issued after the Irishmen transferred from Transatlantic to the Major Minor label in 1966. During this time they received incessant plugging on the Radio Caroline pirate radio station. Bigoted folk purists were unable to regard them with the same respect as the similarly motivated Clancy Brothers And Tommy Makem after the Dubliners were seen on *Top Of The Pops* promoting 1967's censored 'Seven Drunken Nights' and, next, 'Black Velvet Band'. 'Never Wed An Old Man' was only a minor hit but high placings for *A Drop Of The Hard Stuff* and three of its successors in the album list were a firm foundation for the outfit's present standing as a thoroughly diverting international concert attraction. A brain haemorrhage forced Bourke's retirement in 1974, and Drew's return to the ranks (after a brief replacement by Jim McCann) was delayed by injuries sustained in a road accident. Nevertheless, Drew's trademark vocal - 'like coke being crushed under a door' - was heard on the group's 25th anniversary single, 'The Irish Rover', a merger with the Pogues that signalled another sojourn in the Top 10.

Selected albums: *A Drop Of The Hard Stuff* (1967), *Best Of The Dubliners* (1967), *More Of The Hard Stuff* (1967), *Drinkin' And Courtin'* (1968), *Very Best Of The Dubliners* (1975), *Dubliners In Concert* (1982), *The Dubliners 25 Years Celebration* (1987), *20 Greatest Hits: Dubliners* (1989), *20 Original Greatest Hits* (1988), *20 Original Greatest Hits Vol. 2* (1989), *The Dubliners Ireland* (1992), *Thirty Years A-Greying* (1992), *The Original Dubliners* (1993).

Duncan, Lesley

This UK-born singer and songwriter became popular in the commercial side of the folk music field. Although starting out as a songwriter, and married to record producer Jimmy Horowitz, she became better known for her work as a session singer, especially during the 70s. It was Elton John's version of her composition 'Love Song', on his album *Tumbleweed Connection*, that inspired her to record *Sing Children Sing*. Her own albums suffered from a lack of commercial success, which was at odds with her popularity as a backing singer on a host of albums by acts as diverse as Long John Baldry, Tim Hardin, Donovan, the Alan Parson's Project, Pink Floyd, on *Dark Side Of The Moon*, and even Bunk Dogger. After her two releases on CBS, she left the label, and subsequent releases were on GM Records. Her reluctance to perform live did not help to raise her public profile. Apart from providing backing vocals for an album by Exiled, in 1980, her name has sadly been missing from sleeve note credits.

Albums: *Sing Children Sing* (1971), *Earth Mother* (1972), *Everything Changes* (1974), *Moonbathing* (1975), *Maybe It's Lost* (1977).

Dylan, Bob

b. Robert Allen Zimmerman, 24 May 1941, Duluth, Minnesota, USA. Unquestionably one of the most influential figures in the history of popular music, Dylan effectively began his musical career after dropping out of the University of Minnesota in 1960. He soon assimilated a mass of musical and literary influences, ranging from the rock 'n' roll of Little Richard and Elvis Presley to the talking blues of Woody Guthrie, the melancholy lyricism of Hank Williams, the irreverential howling of the beat poets and the startling imagery of the French symbolists. Adopting the persona of the folk troubadour, he moved from Minneapolis to New York in January 1961 and appeared at various coffee houses in Greenwich Village. After playing harmonica on albums by Harry Belafonte and Carolyn Hester, he was auditioned by producer

John Hammond and signed to Columbia Records. In March 1962, *Bob Dylan* was released. A stunning debut, it neatly encapsulated his recent influences, with songs inspired or borrowed from Village folkies Ric Von Schmidt and Dave Van Ronk, plus the poignant blues of Blind Lemon Jefferson and, significantly, two Dylan compositions: the delightfully satiric 'Talkin' New York Blues' and the reverential tribute 'Song To Woody'.

By the end of the year Dylan recorded his debut single 'Mixed Up Confusion', an electric rocker which was rapidly withdrawn for fear of conflicting with his image as the young messiah of folk. Meanwhile, Dylan was hailed by his contemporaries as a civil rights activist and began penning songs such as 'Blowin' In The Wind', later an international hit for Peter, Paul And Mary. The trio were managed by Dylan's great mentor, Albert Grossman, whose forceful entrepreneurial proprietorship protected the performer from unwanted business or personal influences.

The Freewheelin' Bob Dylan, marked the emergence of Dylan the poet in such songs as the apocalyptic 'A Hard Rain's A-Gonna Fall' and the bitter finger-pointing 'Masters Of War'. The cover of the album portrayed the singer arm-in-arm with lover Suze Rotolo, who would soon be replaced in the performer's affections by Joan Baez. The Queen of Folk avidly promoted Dylan, whose prolific output continued with *The Times They Are A-Changin'*. A notably mature work, the album displayed many facets of Dylan's writing talent, not least his ability to transform downtrodden figures like Hattie Carroll or Hollis Brown into universal symbols of tragic injustice. While the title track and 'When The Ship Comes In' ushered in a new mood of optimism, it was not insignificant that the 'rapidly fading' old order was swept aside in similes and images taken from the Old Testament. Nor were the closing lines of the final track 'Restless Farewell' to be ignored: 'I'll bid farewell and not give a damn'.

Dylan's farewell to the agitprop of the Greenwich Village folk movement was voiced most forcibly on 'My Back Pages' from his 1964 album, *Another Side Of Bob Dylan*. The chorus, 'I was so much older then, I'm younger than that now', suggested that the black and white certainties previously espoused by the singer on such songs as 'Masters Of War' required more delicate shading. 'Chimes Of Freedom', despite its title, was no mere rallying cry, but a song steeped in dense imagery that signalled a new direction. Other tracks such as 'All I Really Want To Do' and 'Motorpsycho Nightmare' stressed Dylan's humour and wordplay, while the closing tracks, 'I Don't Believe You', 'Ballad In Plain D' and 'It Ain't Me Babe', were powerful

Bob Dylan and Joan Baez

outpourings of disillusionment and insouciant vindictiveness in the wake of a broken relationship. The change in Dylan's attitude and art were mirrored by the mini-revolution taking place on the popular music front. On a visit to Britain in 1964, Dylan first fully appreciated the originality of the Beatles, and responded to the irresistible rise of the new beat groups. In July 1964, the Animals topped the UK charts with an electric version of 'House Of The Rising Sun', a track which they had learned from Dylan's own reading of the song, included on his first album. During that same period the fledgling Byrds were rehearsing at World Pacific Studios under the auspices of producer Jim Dickson, who was encouraging them to electrify an as yet unreleased Dylan tune, 'Mr Tambourine Man'. These folk rock experiments had a profound effect on the composer who, during the next three years, would produce a trilogy of albums, whose marriage of lyrical sophistication and musical punch represents the finest sustained body of work in rock music history.

Bringing It All Back Home (1965) coincided with the rise of Dylan to the status of a popular culture hero. The first side of the album contained some of his most impressive early rock workouts with 'Subterranean Homesick Blues' and 'Maggie's Farm', while the primarily acoustic side two featured four of his greatest songs: 'Mr Tambourine Man', 'Gates Of Eden', 'It's Alright Ma (I'm Only Bleeding)' and 'It's All Over Now, Baby Blue'. He was now not only an albums artist, but also a frequent visitor to the pop charts with four Top 20 hits in 1965 alone, including the six minute 'Like A Rolling Stone', a track often cited as the best single ever made. Dylan even looked the consummate rock star with his dark glasses, sharply mod-ish clothes, enigmatic persona and brooding arrogance. The film of his 1965 UK tour, *Don't Look Back*, captured the essence of Dylan's charismatic charm, while disguising none of his petulance or impatience. For the next 12 months he needed all his egotistical strength to survive the brickbats of the more regressive elements of his old audience, who responded to his electric music with ill-disguised contempt. After a stormy reception at the 1965 Newport Folk Festival, Dylan set off on a world tour backed by the Band (then known as the Hawks). This virtually unknown Canadian outfit proved the perfect complement for Dylan's rock experimentation. His stage performances were immensely powerful and daringly uncompromising, often taking the form of a war of attrition between the performer and his audience. The celebrated 1966 UK tour, which saw a disgruntled spectator scream 'Judas!' from the rear of the auditorium while hecklers catcalled in conflicting celebration,

epitomized the folk-rock schism.

Dylan's reply to his critics was in the quality of his recorded output. *Highway 61 Revisited* fused the cut and thrust R&B of 'From A Buick 6' and 'Tombstone Blues' with the satiric bite of 'Ballad Of A Thin Man' and the surreal imagery of 'Desolation Row'. Less than one year later, the double album *Blonde On Blonde* completed this remarkable phase in Dylan's career with a flourishing assortment of songs ranging from intense speculations on personal relationships ('Just Like A Woman', 'One Of Us Must Know'), to the hip wordplay of 'Stuck Inside Of Mobile With The Memphis Blues Again', the dry wit of 'Rainy Day Women Nos. 12 & 35' and 'Leopard Skin Pillbox Hat', and the philosophical speculations of 'Visions Of Johanna'. Uniquely for a pop LP of its period, the album included an entire side devoted to one song, the epic 'Sad Eyed Lady Of The Lowlands', inspired by Dylan's wife Sara Lowndes, whom he had married only months before.

The punishing schedule that Dylan had undertaken during 1966 was abruptly curtailed on 29 July following a motorcycle accident near his home in Woodstock. For the next two years he disappeared from the public eye amid exaggerated rumours that he was disfigured, brain damaged or perhaps dead. In fact, Dylan was far from creatively inactive during this long hiatus, but spent much time recording privately at his home with members of the Band. Freed from the pressure of live commitments and recording schedules, Dylan explored an impressive array of different musical styles from country and blues to cajun and folk. The tone and theme of the material was equally diverse, embracing on the one hand surreal comedy ('Please Mrs Henry', 'Open The Door Homer', 'Quinn The Eskimo' and 'Million Dollar Bash'), yet also displaying soul-searchingly introspective musings on guilt and redemption ('Tears Of Rage', 'I Shall Be Released' and 'Too Much Of Nothing'). It remains uncertain how many songs were completed during this period, although hours of tapes were recorded in the basement of Big Pink, a house in West Saugerties rented by the Band. A double album selection of this material was belatedly released in 1975 as *The Basement Tapes*.

The death of Woody Guthrie in late 1967 brought Dylan out of his self-imposed retreat to appear in a tribute concert early the following year. His re-emergence coincided with the firing of his long term manager Albert Grossman and the release of *John Wesley Harding*, a stark but brilliant work, which challenged and effectively reversed the pseudo-poeticism and psychedelic excesses prevalent in rock during the previous year. Moving away from the convoluted imagery that had characterized his previous work, Dylan chose sharp aphorisms and used quasi-allegorical figures such as John Wesley Hardin, St. Augustine and Tom Paine to express his search for fulfilment. Biblical phraseology dominated the album, most notably in the richly symbolic 'All Along The Watchtower' and 'Ballad Of Frankie Lee And Judas Priest'. Not for the first time, Dylan ended the album with a hint of his future direction in 'I'll Be Your Baby Tonight'. A seemingly unambiguous love song, it suggested a new Dylan, content, demon free and uncharacteristically mellow.

The transition was completed on *Nashville Skyline*, released in April 1969. This unlikely excursion into country music, complete with a Johnny Cash duet on a surprisingly effective reworking of 'Girl From The North Country', revealed the full extent of Dylan's diversity. For those who had previously complained about his unorthodox vocal style or lack of melodic content, there was some serious revision underway. Remarkably, the singer's voice had deepened, almost beyond recognition, and his crooning sounded assured and attractive. More importantly, on songs such as 'Lay Lady Lay' and 'I Threw It All Away' he showed a melodic skill, previously suspected but never fully revealed in such an accessible form. The ultimate achievement of *Nashville Skyline*, however, was its capacity to bring both Dylan's canon and the burgeoning country rock scene, to a wider audience. While the cream of the 60s counter culture assembled near Dylan's home for the Woodstock festival, the singer, in common with the Beatles and the Rolling Stones, declined to appear. Instead, he chose another festival in the unlikely setting of the Isle Of Wight, England. With close-cropped hair, a beard and wearing a baggy white suit, the singer played a short set in a relaxed manner. The concert anticipated Dylan's next move, arguably his most bizarre yet.

Self Portrait may have been a double set but it hardly compared with *Blonde On Blonde*. The album consisted of a hotch potch of old songs like 'She Belongs To Me' and 'Like A Rolling Stone' played live in desultory fashion, some curious covers of Richard Rodgers and Lorenz Hart's 'Blue Moon' and Simon And Garfunkel's 'The Boxer', and even a couple of instrumentals. Within such an uninspiring context, the compensatory charm of 'Copper Kettle' and 'Days Of 49' seemed almost negligible. As a deliberate attempt at demystifying his guru status the album could be seen as a perverse success for it garnered a wealth of critical abuse. Greil Marcus began his review in *Rolling Stone* with: 'What is this shit?' On another level *Self Portrait* resembled nothing less than an official bootleg and may well have reflected Dylan's periodic antipathy

towards the public dissemination of his privately recorded moments which had begun with the release a few months earlier of the first bootleg record, Great White Wonder.

The uneven and uncomplicated *New Morning*, released in October 1970, was of sufficient quality to prompt cries of celebration from some reviewers, including Ralph J. Gleason who stated in *Rolling Stone*: 'We've got Dylan back again'. Others perceived the work as a retreat into the cosiness of family life or a further rejection of his former status. The belated appearance of his novel *Tarantula* in 1971 served as a reminder of the verbal dexterity of his mid-60s work and fulfilled an almost nostalgic function. For a time, Dylan himself seemed to conjure the ghosts of his past, re-entering the political arena with the anthemic protest 'George Jackson', and appearing at George Harrison's benefit concert for the starving in Bangladesh. In contrast to his recent work he sang stirring versions of 'Mr Tambourine Man', 'Blowin' In The Wind' and 'A Hard Rain's A-Gonna Fall'. Thereafter, however, he maintained a peculiarly low profile while critics dissected his past work and pondered on the passing of a musical legend. Dylan, meanwhile, was working with director Sam Peckinpah on the film *Pat Garrett And Billy The Kid*, in which he played Billy's sidekick, Alias. The soundtrack album contained an evocative hit single 'Knockin' On Heaven's Door', the singer's first chart entry in almost two years.

With the termination of his CBS contract imminent, Dylan surprised many industry observers by signing an albums deal with David Geffen's label Asylum. Columbia responded with petulant indignation by releasing *Dylan*, a compilation containing several lamentable 1970 outtakes including the maestro's amusing version of Elvis Presley's 'A Fool Such As I' and Joni Mitchell's 'Big Yellow Taxi'. At a time when Dylan's critical reputation needed a boost, it was a sad nadir. However, 1974 saw Dylan return to the centre stage with a blistering series of concerts across America which attracted his best coverage in years. A studio album, *Planet Waves*, re-established his standing, primarily thanks to two versions of the classic 'Forever Young', plus 'Dirge' and 'Wedding Song', two of his most passionately intense outpourings. The live double, *Before The Flood*, released five months later, was almost equally well received and by the autumn CBS had re-signed the artist. Dylan immediately began work on *Blood On The Tracks*, his most sustained album since the mid-60s. It contained some scorching narratives ('Tangled Up In Blue', 'Lily, Rosemary And The Jack Of Hearts'), fascinatingly ambiguous love songs ('If You See Her Say Hello', 'Shelter From The

Storm') and a seething epic 'Idiot Wind', whose savage imagery and accusingly triumphant tone recalled the genius of 'Like A Rolling Stone'.

By the winter of 1975, Dylan was back on the road playing small clubs with the Rolling Thunder Revue, an eclectic ensemble, which included along its spiralling route Roger McGuinn, Arlo Guthrie, Joan Baez, Mick Ronson, Ronee Blakley, Joni Mitchell and Allen Ginsberg. In January 1976, the new album *Desire* opened with 'Hurricane', a punchy paean to the imprisoned boxer Ruben Carter, and ended with 'Sara', an urgent plea to a wife who would shortly commence divorce proceedings. With the assistance of co-writer Jacques Levy, Dylan penned an evocative travelogue of drama from the streets of Brooklyn to the pyramids of Egypt, taking in Mozambique, Durango and Black Diamond Bay along the way. The music was equally colourful thanks to the hauntingly expressive violin work of Scarlet Rivera and the wailing background vocals of Emmylou Harris and Ronee Blakley.

A second tour with Rolling Thunder commenced in April 1976, but the recorded results, *Hard Rain*, failed to capture the eccentric charm of the revue. Dylan's next project, the four hour movie *Renaldo And Clara*, seemed baffling, uncoordinated and indulgent, to some, though others hailed it as a work of sprawling genius. Dylan also appeared on film in Martin Scorsese's celebrated documentary of the Band's musical farewell, *The Last Waltz*. 1978 saw Dylan undertaking an extensive world tour, which coincided with *Street-Legal*, an interesting set ranging in mood from the brooding 'Senor (Tales Of Yankee Power)' to the plaintive pleading of 'Baby Stop Crying' and the curiously celebratory 'Changing Of The Guard'.

Dylan ended the decade on a dramatic note by converting to Christianity. Entering the studio in May 1979, he worked with producer Jerry Wexler and Dire Straits' Mark Knopfler on his 'born again' album *Slow Train Coming*. A subsequent concert tour was notable for Dylan's staunch refusal to play his old songs. Some of the old radicals in his audience voiced the same cries of disillusioned bewilderment or outrage that the Greenwich Village folkies had uttered when Dylan went electric in 1965, but, once again, the quality of the material was undeniable. 'Precious Angel' was a stirring statement of faith and, in common with the other songs in his repertoire, eschewed bland, beatific platitudes in favour of challenging comments on man's shortcomings. 'Gotta Serve Somebody' and 'When You Gonna Wake up' were brilliantly rhetorical putdowns, which showed Dylan taking on the non-believers with the same voice in which he had castigated the subjects of

'Positively 4th Street' and 'Like A Rolling Stone'. This was Dylan at his acerbic best.

The sharpness of Dylan's tongue was less evident on *Saved* (1980), which was the closest he ever reached to recording a pure gospel album. The underrated *Shot Of Love* (1981) had a delightfully refreshing 'back-to-basics' production and the minimalist feel suited Dylan's new material. Among the tracks was an elegiac tribute to the controversial comedian Lenny Bruce, a seemingly inappropriate secular subject, whose presence clearly indicated that Dylan's fundamentalism was far less pronounced than the majority of his followers assumed. His impatience with atheistic intolerance was still effectively voiced in the sarcastic 'Property Of Jesus', but by the time of the next release of the next album, *Infidels*, political concerns seemed uppermost in the artist's mind. A slicker production, the album saw Dylan tackling the state of trade unions and American nationalism rather than concerning himself with spiritual redemption.

Although no longer billed as the spokesperson of his generation, Dylan's contribution to popular music was emphasized in the five album retrospective *Biograph*, released in 1985. That same year the anti-climactic *Empire Burlesque* appeared, much of its contents wrapped in predictably arranged backing vocals, which gave a bland uniformity to much of the material. The capacity of Dylan to confound his audience with periodic disappointment had been evident since *Self Portrait* and even earlier in certain faltering live performances, but such fallibility had never been seen on such a global scale as the closing of Live Aid concert in July 1985. Backed by a ragged Ron Wood and Keith Richard's, Dylan stumbled through a short acoustic set which was almost inexplicably lacklustre. His reputation was further dented by a critically panned movie, *Hearts Of Fire*, and a poorly received album, *Knocked Out Loaded*. Despite a collaboration with songwriter Carol Bayer Sager and a welcome return to the narrative form, courtesy of the 11-minute 'Brownsville Girl', co-written with the playwright Sam Shepard, the album found few champions. Dylan nevertheless continued to tour, appearing at benefits for Farm Aid and Sun City and even turning up at a poetry festival in Moscow. While critics bemoaned the recent quality of his studio output, Dylanologists pointed to a wealth of material languishing in the vaults which testified to his continued greatness.

Down In The Groove (1988) settled none of the arguments, being mainly composed of old blues songs and personal favourites. Its spontaneity was appealing, its timing perhaps unfortunate. Further evidence of Dylan's love of improvisation was heard on *The Traveling Wilburys- Volume One*, on which he collaborated with Jeff Lynne, Tom Petty, George Harrison and Roy Orbison.

Throughout the late 80s, Dylan continued to tour, appearing with both Tom Petty And The Heartbreakers and the Grateful Dead. Some concerts were deemed inspired, others mediocre. Yet, there was no doubting the importance of Dylan's live work in the context of his art. More than any other performer he had used the stage as a means of redefining his work and was now well known for twisting his lyrics into new unfamiliar metres, or changing the meaning of lines or entire songs through stress or intonation. Songs such as 'It Ain't Me Babe' or 'It's All Over Now, Baby Blue' could thus be presented as testaments of celebration, apathy, disillusionment or plain disgust, depending upon Dylan's unpredictable and often eccentric inflexions. The inherent ambiguity in his best material was brilliantly evinced via live performances and added a new dimension to his work.

It was not until the end of the decade that the experiments and aberration of recent years crystallized into a universally accepted work of excellence. *Oh Mercy* (1989) brought back the musical and lyrical 'mystery' to Dylan's work that always separated him from his lesser songwriting contemporaries. The production by Daniel Lanois brought a shadowy resonance to the proceedings which perfectly complemented the air of sinister inevitability that permeated 'Man In A Long Black Coat'. The Old Testament imagery could again be found on 'Ring Them Bells' and 'Shooting Star', but Dylan was no longer dealing in cast iron certainties. 'What Was It You Wanted' seemed strangely quizzical, while the beautiful 'Most Of The Time' presented a series of positive statements undermined by the qualifications implicit in its title ('I can survive and I can endure and I don't even think about her . . . most of the time').

If *Oh Mercy* showed an underlying quest motif, then this was even more evident in his live performances, particularly the amusingly nicknamed 'Never Ending Tour' on which Dylan embarked in 1988 with a back-to-basics three-piece band, initially inspired by guitarist G.E. Smith. *Under The Red Sky* found few friendly critics when released, although time has healed what could have merely been anger at him not delivering another *Oh Mercy*, and the album is now seen as good, if not great. Dylan's punishingly exhaustive, almost obsessional touring schedule, compounded by radical alterations in his set on a nightly basis has resulted in live work of magnificent stature as well as prompting unanswerable questions about his motivations which in themselves enhance the mystique that he has sustained over 30 years as a performing artist. In addition to the glut of books published to celebrate Dylan's 50th birthday, CBS/Legacy released *The Bootleg Series, Vols 1-3, Rare And Unreleased 1961-1991* - an outstanding boxed set of his entire career composed entirely of previously unreleased tracks and alternate versions. If there ever had been any serious doubters about Dylan's achievements, this collection made amends in spectacular fashion. The following year Dylan returned to his acoustic roots and released *Good As I Been To You*. In observing the differences between this and *Bob Dylan* 30 years previous, the listener will experience a hard world-weary voice together with acoustic guitar playing as fresh and good as Dylan has ever played.

Albums: *Bob Dylan* (1962), *The Freewheelin' Bob Dylan* (1963), *The Times They Are A-Changin'* (1964), *Another Side Of Bob Dylan* (1964), *Bringing It All Back Home* (1965), *Highway 61 Revisited* (1965), *Blonde On Blonde* (1966), *John Wesley Harding* (1968), *Nashville Skyline* (1969), *Self Portrait* (1970), *New Morning* (1970), *Dylan* (1973), *Planet Waves* (1974), *Before The Flood* (1974), *Blood On The Tracks* (1975), *The Basement Tapes* (1975), *Desire* (1976), *Hard Rain* (1976), *Street-Legal* (1978), *Slow Train Coming* (1979), *At Budokan* (1979), *Saved* (1980), *Shot Of Love* (1981), *Infidels* (1983), *Real Live* (1984), *Empire Burlesque* (1985), *Knocked Out Loaded* (1986), *Down In The Groove* (1988), *Dylan And The Dead* (1989), *Oh Mercy* (1989), *Under The Red Sky* (1990), *Good As I Been To You* (1992). Various compilations have also been issued, *More Bob Dylan Greatest Hits* (1972) and *Biograph* (1985) contained some new material, while *The Bootleg Series, Vols 1-3, Rare And Unreleased 1961-1991* (1991) consisted entirely of unreleased performances.

Selected further reading: *Tarantula*, Bob Dylan. *Writings And Drawings*, Bob Dylan. *Bob Dylan*, Anthony Scaduto. *Song And Dance Man*, Michael Gray. *A Retrospective*, Craig McGregor. *On The Road With Bob Dylan*, Larry Sloman. *No Direction Home*, Robert Shelton. *Complete Lyrics*, Bob Dylan. *All Across The Telegraph - A Bob Dylan Handbook*, ed. Michael Gray and John Bauldie. *Wanted Man - In Search Of Bob Dylan*, ed. John Bauldie. *Performing Artist*, Paul Williams. *A Dylan Companion*, ed. Liz Thomson. *Oh No! Not Another Bob Dylan Book*, Patrick Humphries and John Bauldie.

E

Eclection

Formed in London in 1967, Eclection took their name from the contrasting backgrounds of its original line-up. Although Mike Rosen (guitar), Kerilee Male (vocals), Georg Hultgren (bass) and Gerry Conway (drums) were not well-known figures, guitarist Trevor Lucas had established himself on the folk circuit following his arrival from Australia. The quintet used his undoubted talent to forge an imaginative folk/rock style which showed influences from both British and American sources. Kerilee Male left the group in October 1968, following the release of Eclection's debut album. Her replacement was Dorris Henderson, a black American singer who had previously recorded two folk-influenced collections with guitarist John Renbourn. A further change occurred when John 'Poli' Palmer succeeded Mike Rosen, but the group was sadly unable to fulfil its obvious potential. In October 1969 Palmer left to join Family, and Eclection simply folded. Lucas and Conway soon resurfaced in Fotheringay, while Hultgren later changed his surname to Kajanus and found fame with the pop group Sailor. In the 70s Henderson attempted to revive Eclection with different musicians, but she was largely unsuccessful.
Album: *Eclection* (1968).

Electropathics

Formed in 1979, as the Electropathic Battery Band, this ensemble played concerts and appeared at dances as essentially a music hall band, presenting a show in costume. The original line-up was Alan Rawlinson (b. 8 May 1955, Scholes, Leeds, Yorkshire, England; trombone, trumpet, cornet, flute, sousaphone, vocals), John Gregson (guitar, vocals), John Lewis (clarinet, banjo, mandolin, saxophone, vocals), Moira Hanvey (vocals, whistles), Dave Hanvey (melodeon, vocals), Nick Tamblin (mouth organ, glockenspiel, percussion, vocals, caller), and Maggie Andrew (percussion). The group went through a number of personnel changes, with the departure of Dave and Moira Hanvey, and Nick Tamblin in 1984. Jackie Rawlinson (b. 26 May 1965, Wilmslow, Cheshire, England; fiddle, vocals), joined in 1985 with Maggie Andrew leaving the line-up in 1986. The line-up for *(Batteries Not Included)* comprised original members Alan Rawlinson and John Gregson, plus Pierce Butler (drums, percussion, vocals), who left at the end of 1987, Jackie Rawlinson, Howard Jones (hammer dulcimer, melodeon, anglo-concertina, guitar, vocals) who had joined in 1984, as well as Keith Hancock (b. 28 October 1953, Audenshaw, Lancashire, England;

Eclection

Mike Elliott

melodeon, hammer dulcimer, vocals). More changes occurred with the addition of Dave Manley (b. 20 February 1957, Warwickshire, England; flute, saxophone, vocals), and Tim Veitch (b. 29 May 1962; cello, vocals) who both joined in 1988, while Hancock left the same year to pursue a solo career. Tim Kenney (b. 15 August 1960; guitar, vocals) joined early in 1989. The most recent addition, Chris Bartram (b. 25 December 1946, Yorkshire, England; percussion, vocals), joined in 1991. The group, having changed its name to the Electropathics, and with Alan Rawlinson the only surviving original member, is still popular at festivals and dance events nationwide. Since Hancock's departure however, and although working regularly, the band seems to have maintained a lower profile in the music media.
Album: *(Batteries Not Included)* (1987).

Ellington, Marc

This 70s singer and songwriter failed to achieve any great commercial success, despite recording with a number of highly respected musicians, including Richard Thompson and Simon Nicol. *Marc Time* followed more of a country direction, and for this Ellington was joined by steel guitarist and dobro player B.J. Cole. Ellington was also engaged in much session work and provided back-up on albums by Fairport Convention and Matthew's Southern Comfort.
Albums: *Marc Ellington* (1969), *Rains/Reins Of Change* (1971), *A Question Of Roads* (1972), *Restoration* (1972), *Marc Time* (1975).

Elliott, Mike

b. 17 July 1946, Sunderland, England. A former teacher, Elliott started performing in a trio called the Northern Front. He then went on to teach drama, a talent that became useful in his performing career. Unable to do both, Elliott became a full-time performer in 1974. He has toured the USA on numerous occasions, in addition to the Middle East. More of a comedian than a folk performer, Elliott nevertheless learned his craft, like Billy Connolly and Jasper Carrott, by performing and singing traditional songs in folk clubs, in addition to using his own, highly original, comic material. His talent was recognized by Tyne Tees television, who, in 1981, made a series of six half-hour programmes starring Elliott. The series was promptly banned due to a reluctance to broadcast some of the material. Later, Channel 4 television transmitted another series of shows, *At Last...It's Mike Elliott*, although it was by and large the same material that Elliott had used for the former, banned, series. A one-hour television special entitled *Meet Mike Elliott* was also broadcast. Elliott later had a single released, 'Makin' Me Happy/Talkin' Crap', on Rubber Records, but this too was promptly banned because of the use of the word 'shit'. A man of obvious talent, Elliott has played at the Cambridge Folk Festival and toured with Lindisfarne and Jack The Lad. He is also credited as being the first British professional artist to appear in China, beating Wham! by two days!
Albums: *Out Of The Brown* (1975), *At Last It's Mike Elliott* (1984).

Elliott, Ramblin' Jack

b. Elliott Charles Adnopoz, 1 August 1931, Brooklyn, New York, USA. The son of an eminent doctor, Elliott forsook his middle-class upbringing as a teenager to join a travelling rodeo. Embarrassed by his family name, he dubbed himself Buck Elliott, before adopting the less-mannered first name, Jack. In 1949 he met and befriended Woody Guthrie who in turn became his mentor and prime influence. Elliott travelled and sang with Guthrie whenever possible, before emerging as a talent in his own right. He spent a portion of the 50s in Europe, introducing America's folk heritage to a new and eager audience. By the early 60s he had resettled in New York where he became an inspirational figure to a new generation of performers, including Bob Dylan. *Jack Elliott Sings The Songs Of Woody Guthrie* was the artist's first American album. This self-explanatory set was succeeded by *Ramblin' Jack Elliott*, in which he shook off the imitator tag by embracing a diverse selection of material, including songs drawn from the American tradition, the Scottish music-hall and Ray Charles. Further releases included *Jack Elliott*, which featured Dylan playing harmonica under the pseudonym, Tedham Porterhouse, and *Young Brigham* in 1968, which offered songs by Tim Hardin and the Rolling Stones as well as an adventurous use of dobros, autoharps, fiddles and tablas. The singer also guested on albums by Tom Rush, Phil Ochs and Johnny Cash. In 1975 Elliott was joined by Dylan during an appearance at the New York, Greenwich Village club, The Other End, and he then became a natural choice for Dylan's nostalgic, carnival tour, the Rolling Thunder Revue. Elliot later continued his erratic, but intriguing, path and an excellent 1984 release, *Kerouac's Last Dream*, shows his power undiminished.
Albums: *Jack Elliott Sings The Songs Of Woody Guthrie* (1960), *Ramblin' Jack Elliott* (1961), *Jack Elliott* (1964), *Ramblin' Cowboy* (mid-60s), *Young Brigham* (1968), *Jack Elliott Sings Guthrie And Rogers* (1976), *Kerouac's Last Dream* (1984). Compilations: *Talking Dust Bowl - The Best Of Ramblin' Jack Elliott* (1989), *Hard Travelin'* (1990)

Ramblin' Jack Elliott

English, Logan

Born and raised in Kentucky, USA, English was exposed to traditional music at an early age. He was drawn into the folk and coffee house circuit of the 50s following a brief spell as an actor, and became a regular performer on the east and west coast clubs circuit Several successful appearances at New York's Town and Carnegie Halls pre-dated the Greenwich Village boom of the early 60s. Sceptical of the newer generation of singers, English continued to work with traditional material and was subsequently surpassed by those embracing more contemporary forms. He remained a fixture on the folk scene, albeit in a lessened role, but despite enjoying the respect of his peers, commercial success proved elusive.
Album: *American Folk Ballads* (1962).

Ennis, Seamus

b. 1912, Dublin, Eire, d. 1982. Ennis played whistle and uileann pipes as well as singing in both English and Gaelic. His father played fiddle, flute and war-pipes. Ennis spent four years at college before leaving in 1938, and worked for five years at Three Candles Press. Four years later, in 1942, he joined the Irish Folklore Commission as a collector, travelling around Ireland, and some of the Gaelic areas in Scotland. He moved on, in 1947, to work for Radio Eireann, and later, in 1951, the BBC. Ennis made a number of recordings, in 78 rpm format, for the BBC during the late 40s. He had

earlier recorded a number of 78s for the Irish Gael-Linn label, in the Gaelic derivation of his name, Seosamh OhEanaigh. It was at the BBC that Ennis worked with folk collector Peter Kennedy, and they were involved in a weekly BBC series *As I Roved Out*. Ennis also released an EP, *The Ace And Deuce Of Piping*, in 1960. The posthumously released *Seamus Ennis - Master Of The Uileann Pipes*, was produced, recorded and engineered by Patrick Sky. The session was recorded in Dublin, at Liam O'Flynn's flat. In the case of *Forty Years Of Irish Piping,* the album is described as having been 'constructed' by Patrick Sky. *Our Musical Heritage,* produced by RTE, was a three- album boxed set. The concept was based on a series of programmes presented by Sean O'Riada in 1962, on Radio Eireann. Ennis, regarded by many to be a leading authority on traditional music in Ireland.
Albums: *The Bonny Bunch Of Roses* (1959), *Seamus Ennis* (1969), *The Pure Drop* (1973), *Forty Years Of Irish Piping* (1974), *The Wandering Minstrel* (1974), *Music At The Gate* (1975), *The Fox Chase* (1977), *The King Of Ireland's Son* (1977), with others *Our Musical Heritage* (1981), *Seamus Ennis - Master Of The Uileann Pipes* (1985).

Even Dozen Jug Band

Formed in 1963 by Peter Siegel and Stefan Grossman. Renowned in their respective fields, namely bluegrass and blues, the two musicians brought several colleagues into the line-up to create

a mutually satisfying style once punningly referred to as 'jug-grass'. *The Even Dozen Jug Band*, released in January 1964, was their sole recorded legacy, but the ensemble is better recalled as an important meeting point for several influential figures. Grossman and Siegel aside, the line-up also included John Benson, better known as John Sebastian, Maria D'Amato (later Maria Muldaur), Steve Katz, a future member of the Blues Project and Blood Sweat And Tears, and Joshua Rifkin, who subsequently acquired fame for his interpretations of Scott Joplin's piano rags. It should be noted, however, that not all of these artists appear on all of the songs. The Jug Band's brief tenure ended in disagreement between those who wished to maintain the group's 'fun' status and those who wished to assume a more professional approach. The split allowed the above individuals to pursue a more independent path.
Album: *The Even Dozen Jug Band* (1964).

F

Fahey, John

b. 28 February 1939. Fahey grew up in Takoma Park, Maryland, USA and learned to play country-style guitar in the footsteps of Hank Williams and Eddie Arnold at the age of 13, inspired by the recordings of Blind Willie Johnson, and other blues greats. He toured during his teens with Henry Vestine (later of Canned Heat), in addition to gaining a BA in Philosophy and Religion. Fahey's style is based on an original folk blues theme, encompassing blues, jazz, country and gospel music, and at times incorporating classical pieces, although he still retains an almost traditional edge in his arrangements. His 12-string work often features open tunings. He has now become an influence to other American acoustic guitarists. Having set up his own Takoma Records label, with a $300 loan, he released *The Transfiguration Of Blind Joe Death*. This perplexing album subsequently became a cult record during the late 60s. It was a record to be seen with rather than actually play. He later signed with Vanguard Records, in 1967, and released virtually one album a year until quitting the company. Later still, after a brief sojourn with Reprise Records, he was dropped due to

insufficient sales. Fahey was also quick to spot other talent and was the first to record Leo Kottke. His work was heard in the film *Zabriskie Point*, but generally his influence is greater than his own success. Having come through drug problems, Fahey retains a cult following. His recorded output is prolific and he continues to perform, although only occasionally. He wrote a thesis on Charlie Patton which has been published.
Selected albums: *The Transfiguration Of Blind Joe Death* (1959), *Guitar* (c.60s), *John Fahey i* (1966), *Days Are Gone By* (1967), *Requia* (1967), *John Fahey ii* (1968), *The Yellow Princess* (1969), *The Voice Of The Turtle* (1968), *Death Chants And Breakdowns* (1968), *The New Possibility: Christmas Album* (c.60s), *Of Rivers And Religion* (1972), *After The Ball* (1973), *Fare Forward Voyagers* (1974), *Old Fashioned Love* (1975), *Yes Jesus Loves You* (1980), *John Fahey Visits Washington, D.C.* (1980), *Live In Tasmania* (1981), *Let Go* (1984), *Rain Forests, Oceans And Other Themes* (1985), *Old Girlfriends And Other Horrible Memories* (1992). Compilations: *The Best Of John Fahey 1959-1977* (1977), *The Essential John Fahey* (1979).

Fairport Convention

The unchallenged inventors of British folk-rock have struggled through tragedy and changes, retaining the name that now represents not so much who is in the band, but what it stands for. The original group of 1967 comprised Iain Matthews (b. Ian Matthews MacDonald, 16 June 1946, Scunthorpe, Lincolnshire, England; vocals), Judy Dyble (b. 13 February 1949, London, England; vocals), Ashley 'Tyger' Hutchings (b. 26 January 1945, Muswell Hill, London, England; bass), Richard Thompson (b. 3 April 1949, London, England; guitar/vocals), Simon Nicol (b. 13 October 1950, Muswell Hill, London, England; guitar/vocals) and Martin Lamble (b. 28 August 1949, St. Johns Wood, London, England, d. 12 May 1969; drums). The band originally came to the attention of the London 'underground' club scene by sounding like a cross between the Jefferson Airplane and the Byrds. As an accessible alternative they immediately took to people's hearts. American producer Joe Boyd signed them and they released the charming 'If I Had A Ribbon Bow'. On their self-titled debut they introduced the then little-known Canadian songwriter Joni Mitchell to a wider audience. The album was a cult favourite, but like the single, it sold poorly. Judy Dyble departed and was replaced by former Strawbs vocalist, Sandy Denny (b. Alexandra Denny, 6 January 1948, Wimbledon, London, England, d. 21 April 1978). Denny brought a traditional folk-feel to their work which began to appear on the

John Fahey

superlative *What We Did On Our Holidays*. This varied collection contained some of their finest songs: Denny's version of 'She Moved Through The Fair', her own 'Fotheringay', Matthews' lilting 'Book Song', the superb 'I'll Keep It With Mine' and Thompson's masterpiece 'Meet On The Ledge'. This joyous album was bound together by exemplary musicianship, of particular note was the guitar of the shy and wiry Thompson. Matthews left soon after its release, unhappy with the traditional direction the band were pursuing. Following the album's critical acclaim and a modest showing in the charts, they experienced tragedy a few months later when their Transit van crashed, killing Martin Lamble and their friend and noted dressmaker Jeannie Franklyn. *Unhalfbricking* was released and, although not as strong as the former, it contained two excellent readings of Bob Dylan songs, 'Percy's Song' and 'Si Tu Dois Partir' (If You Gotta Go, Go Now). Sandy contributed two songs, 'Autopsy' and the definitive, and beautiful, 'Who Knows Where The Time Goes'. More significantly, *Unhalfbricking* featured guest musician, Dave Swarbrick, on fiddle and mandolin. The album charted, as did the second Dylan number; by now the band had opened the door for future bands like Steeleye Span, by creating a climate that allowed traditional music to be played in a rock context. The songs that went on their next album were premièred on John Peel's BBC radio show *Top Gear*. An excited Peel stated that their performance would 'sail them into uncharted waters'; his judgement proved correct. The live-set

was astonishing - they played jigs and reels, and completed all 27 verses of the traditional 'Tam Lin', featuring Swarbrick, now a full-time member, plus the debut of new drummer, Dave Mattacks (b. March 1948, Edgeware, Middlesex, England). The subsequent album *Liege And Lief* was a milestone; they had created British folk-rock in spectacular style. This, however, created problems within the band and Hutchings left to form Steeleye Span and Sandy departed to form Fotheringay with ex-Eclection and future husband Trevor Lucas. Undeterred, the band recruited Dave Pegg on bass and Swarbrick became more prominent both as lead vocalist and as an outstanding fiddle player. From their communal home in Hertfordshire they wrote much of the next two album's material although Thompson left before the release of *Ángel Delight*. They made the *Guinness Book Of Records* in 1970 with the longest-ever title 'Sir B. McKenzies's Daughter's Lament For The 77th Mounted Lancer's Retreat From The Straits Of Loch Knombe, In The Year Of Our Lord 1727, On The Occasion Of The Announcement Of Her Marriage To The Laird Of Kinleakie'. *Full House* was the first all-male Fairport album and was instrumentally strong with extended tracks like 'Sloth' becoming standards. The concept album *Babbacombe Lee,* although critically welcomed, failed to sell and Simon Nicol left to form the Albion Band with Ashley Hutchings. Swarbrick struggled on, battling against hearing problems. With such comings and goings of personnel it was difficult to document the exact changes. The lack of any animosity from ex-

Fairport Convention

members contributed to the family atmosphere, although by this time record sales were dwindling. Sandy Denny rejoined, as did Dave Mattacks (twice), but by the end of the 70s the name was put to rest. The family tree specialist Pete Frame has documented their incredible array of line-ups. Their swan-song was at Cropredy in Oxfordshire in 1979. Since then an annual reunion has taken place and is now a major event on the folk calendar. The band have no idea which ex-members will turn up! They have continued to release albums, making the swan-song a sham. With Swarbrick's departure, his position was taken by Ric Sanders in 1985 who rapidly quietened his dissenters by stamping his own personality on the fiddler's role. Some of the recent collections have been quite superb, including *Gladys Leap*, with Simon Nicol back on lead vocals, and the instrumental *Expletive Delighted*. With the release in 1990 of *The Five Seasons*, the group had established the longest lasting line-up in their history. The Fairports are now as much a part of the folk music tradition as the music itself.

Albums: *Fairport Convention* (1968), *What We Did On Our Holidays* (1969), *Unhalfbricking* (1969), *Liege And Lief* (1969), *Full House* (1970), *Angel Delight* (1971), *Babbacombe Lee* (1971), *Rosie* (1973), *Nine* (1973), *Live Convention (A Moveable Feast)* (1974), *Rising For The Moon* (1975), *Gottle O'Geer* (1976), *Live At The LA Troubadour* (1977), *A Bonny Bunch Of Roses* (1977), *Tipplers Tales* (1978), *Farewell, Farewell* (1979), *Moat On The Ledge* (1981), *Gladys Leap* (1985), *Expletive Delighted* (1986), *House Full* (1986), *Heyday: The BBC Radio Sessions 1968-9* (1987), *'In Real Time' - Live '87* (1988), *Red And Gold* (1988), *Five Seasons* (1990). Compilations: *History Of Fairport Convention* (1972), *The Best Of Fairport Convention* (1988), *The Woodworm Years* (1992).

Further reading: *Meet On The Ledge*, Patrick Humphries.

Famous Potatoes

The Famous Potatoes are a group that describe their sound as 'Soil Music'. The group comprises Keith Baxter (b. 19 October 1957, Rochford, Essex, England; banjo, trombone, washboard, zobstick), Richard Baxter (b. 13 August 1959, Westcliff-on-Sea, Essex, England; vocals, melodeon, saxophone, harmonica), Nigel Blackaby (b. 27 November 1958, Rochford, Essex, England; bass/vocals), Paul Collier (b. 12 February 1959, Rochford, Essex, England; drum, vocals), Melanie Johnson (b. 2 February 1961, Swindon, Wiltshire, England; recorder, clarinet, vocals), Paul 'Prof' McDowell (b. 30 September 1958, Rochford, Essex, England; accordion, vocals), Tony Littman (b. 17 July 1951, Westcliff-on-Sea, Essex, England; guitar), and Charlie Skelton (b. 8 February 1963, Enfield,

Middlesex, England; fiddle). Littman and Skelton replaced former members Nick Pynn (fiddle, mandolin, mandocello, banjo, viola), and Richard 'Rikki' Reynolds (guitar) who left the group. Pynn joined the reformed Cockney Rebel with Steve Harley. The 'Potatoes' style encompasses cajun, skiffle, hillbilly, gospel, western swing and, apart from concerts, they also play barn dances, and have appeared regularly at the Greenbelt Christian Arts festivals. Having formed in 1979 as the Folk Pistols to play barn dances, original members Johnson, McDowell, and the Baxter brothers have stayed with the band while Blackaby and Collier joined in 1982. As the Folk Pistols they released two albums in cassette format, *Get Your Skates On* (1981), and *Twist With Ken* (1982). Soon after this the new name was adopted. *It Was Good For My Old Mother* attracted a lot of interest on release, not least in their home territory in Essex. *The Sound Of The Ground* included the Hank Williams's classic 'I Saw The Light'.

Albums: *Dig* (1983), *It Was Good For My Old Mother* (1985), *The Sound Of The Ground* (1986), *Born In A Barn* (1989).

Farina, Mimi

b. Mimi Baez, 30 April 1945, New York, USA. The younger sister of folksinger Joan Baez, Mimi was pursuing a solo career when she met and married Richard Farina. The couple began performing together in 1964 and completed two exceptional albums, *Celebrations For A Grey Day* and *Reflections In A Crystal Wind* before Richard was killed in a motorcycle accident on 30 April 1966. Two years later Mimi helped compile the commemorative *Memories*, as well as *Long Time Coming And A Long Time Gone*, a collection of her husband's lyrics, poetry and short stories. Unsure of direction, Mimi later joined the Committee, a satirical theatre group, where she worked as an improvisational actor before returning to singing. Having forged a short-lived partnership with Tom Jans, which resulted in one low-key album, she resumed her solo career. Mimi later founded Bread And Roses, an organization which brought live music into convalescent homes, psychiatric wards and drug rehabilitation centres.

Albums: with Richard Farina *Celebrations For A Grey Day* (1965), *Reflections In A Crystal Wind* (1965), *Memories* (1967); with Tom Jans *Mimi Farina And Tom Jans* (1971). Compilation: *The Best Of Mimi And Richard Farina* (1970).

Farina, Richard

b. 1937, Brooklyn, New York, USA, d. 30 April 1966. A songwriter, novelist and political activist, Farina was drawn into folk music following his marriage to singer Carolyn Hester. Their ill-starred relationship ended in 1961 when, following a European tour, Richard decided to remain 'in exile' to work on his first novel *Been Down So Long It Looks Like Up To Me*. It was during this time that Farina's first recordings were made. *Dick Farina & Eric Von Schmidt*, the product of a two-day session in the cellar of London's Dobell's Jazz Shop, also featured an impromptu appearance by Bob Dylan, masquerading under his celebrated pseudonym, Blind Boy Grunt. Richard returned to America in 1963 where he married Mimi Baez, the sister of folksinger Joan Baez. The couple began performing together and were latterly signed to the prestigious Vanguard label. Their two superb albums were released in 1965, the first of which, *Celebration For A Grey Day*, included Richard's classic song, 'Pack Up Your Sorrows'. *Been Down So Long* was published in 1966, but its author was killed in a motorbike crash during a celebratory party. Farina's death robbed a generation of an excellent writer and gifted musician.

Albums: *Dick Farina & Eric Von Schmidt* (1964); with Mimi Farina: *Celebration For A Grey Day* (1965), *Reflections In A Crystal Wind* (1965). Compilation: *Memories* (1968, previously unreleased performances with two masters Richard produced for Joan Baez).

Faryar, Cyrus

b. Teheran, Iran. Faryar left his home country in 1939 and having spent several years domiciled in England, subsequently settled in Hawaii. Here he ran Honolulu's Greensleeves coffeehouse, prior to becoming a founder member of folk act the Whiskeyhill Singers. Faryar later formed the Lexington Trio which, with the addition of Jerry Yester, evolved in the Modern Folk Quartet. This influential act was dissolved in 1966, following which Cyrus guested on several albums, notably by the Stone Poneys and 'Mama' Cass Elliot. He narrated *The Zodiac Cosmic Sounds*, a popular astrologically-inspired collection issued by Elektra in 1967, and the same label was responsible for Faryar's solo albums. These adeptly blended folk and singer/songwriter styles, while the artist's sonorous voice, redolent of Fred Neil, added depth to already captivating compositions. Cyrus then retired from active performing and returned to Hawaii. However, he resumed his musical career in 1987 upon joining the reformed MFQ.

Albums: *Cyrus* (1972), *Islands* (1973).

Fat City

Fat City formed in Washington, DC, USA and included in their line-up the husband and wife team, Bill Danoff (b. 7 May 1946, Springfield,

Massachusetts, USA; guitar/vocals) and Taffy Danoff (b. Kathleen Nivert, 24 October 1944, Washington, DC, USA; vocals), plus Jim Parker (guitar/vocals). With their cheerful, summery vocals they released two albums, enlisting as guest musicians such notable artists as Bob James, Eric Weissberg, Artie Traum and Hubert Laws. After failing to achieve the predicted success, Fat City's ultimate demise led to the Danoff's forming a duo as Bill and Taffy which, in turn, led to the Starland Vocal Band and national fame. After the demise of Starland, the duo resurrected Fat City and, despite their marital split, they were still to be found performing together in the Washington, DC area during the 80s.

Albums: *Reincarnation* (1969), *Welcome To Fat City* (1971), *Blue Band* (1991), *Blue Band* (1991); as Bill And Taffy *Pass It On* (1973), *Aces* (1974).

Felix, Julie

b. 14 June 1938, Santa Barbara, California, USA. Felix arrived in the UK during the early 60s at a time when several US folksingers, including Paul Simon and Jackson C. Frank, had also relocated to London. Her early recordings revealed a commercial, rather than innovative talent, a fact emphasized by weekly appearances on television's *The Frost Report* (1967/68). She followed the liberal tradition of Tom Paxton or Pete Seeger, rather than that of the radical left, although was an early champion of the folk-styled singer/songwriter movement, notably Leonard Cohen and was proclaimed as 'Britain's Leading Lady of Folk'. Her humanitarian beliefs had however been put to practical use by the singer's tour of the African states of Kenya and Uganda, working for the Christian Aid and Freedom From Hunger charities. Felix enjoyed two successful British television series in her own right, *Once More With Felix* (1969/70) and *The Julie Felix Show* (1971), and scored a UK Top 20 hit in 1970 with a version of 'El Condor Pasa', produced by Mickie Most. The singer's 'wholesome' image was tarred by a conviction for possession of marijuana, but she continued a prolific recording career, albeit to less publicity, into the 80s, as well as performing for Women's Rights, Green and environmental benefits, and founding Britain's first 'New Age Folk Club'.

Albums: *Julie Felix* (1964), *2nd Album* (1965), *3rd Album* (1966), *Julie Felix Sings Dylan And Guthrie* (1966), *Changes* (1966), *Julie Felix In Concert* (1967), *Flowers* (1968), *This World Goes Round And Round* (1969), *Going To The Zoo* (1970), *Clotho's Web* (1971), *Lightning* (1974), *London Palladium* (1974), *Hota Chocolata* (1977), *Blowing In The Wind* (1982), *Bright Shadows* (1989). Compilations: *The World Of Julie Felix* (1969), *The World Of Julie Felix Volume 2* (1970), *The Most Collection* (1972), *This Is Julie Felix* (1970), *This Is Julie Felix Volume 2* (1974), *Amazing Grace* (1987).

Julie Felix

Figgy Duff

This group from Newfoundland comprises Pamela Morgan (vocals/guitar/whistle/keyboards), Dave Panting (vocals/mandolin/guitar), Geoff Butler (accordion/whistle), Derek Pelley (bass/vocal) and Noel Dinn (multi-instrumentalist). Mixing Celtic and Gaelic influences, the group essentially followed the folk rock path. Mixing traditional and contemporary tunes and songs, *Figgy Duff*, released in 1980 in the USA, was not released until 1982 in Europe. Although the follow-up, *After The Tempest*, received more attention and attracted good reviews, it still failed to give the group a higher profile.

Albums: *Figgy Duff* (1980), *After The Tempest* (1984).

Findask

This early 70s Scottish duo featured Willie Lindsay (b. 24 January 1952, Glasgow, Scotland; vocals/guitar/flute/whistles/harmonica), and Stuart Campbell (b. 16 March 1951, Glasgow, Scotland; cittern/bouzouki/guitar/mandolin/vocals). The two met at the University of Strathclyde, and started playing occasionally, leading to them playing support at festivals and concerts to groups such as Fairport Convention - who played the university and college circuit at the time. Interest shown in *Near Enough, Far Enough*, led them to release *Between The White Lines* on Temple Records. This album also included all original material performed in a traditional framework. Still performing, they released *Waiting For A Miracle*, but Campbell fell seriously ill, suffering from pernicious anaemia and for a long time was unable to work. As a result, Findask now perform only occasionally.

Albums: *Near Enough, Far Enough* (1983), *Between The White Lines* (1984), *Waiting For A Miracle* (1987).

Fisher, Cilla, And Artie Trezise

Cilla Fisher (b. 26 September 1952, Glasgow, Scotland) is the youngest of the Fisher family from Scotland. She sang on radio at the age of nine, and performed with other members of her family, Ray and Archie Fisher included. Artie Trezise (b. 3 April 1947, St. Andrews, Scotland) sang with various folk groups including the Great Fife Road Show. *Cilla And Artie*, released on Topic, was voted *Melody Maker* Folk Album of the year in 1979. *Balcanquhal* includes Allan Barty on fiddle and Cilla's brother Archie. Standards such as 'Jock Stewart' are included on the album. They underwent a transformation to children's entertainers and changed their name to the Singing Kettle, following the release of an album of the same title on their own label, Kettle Records. As a result, Cilla and Artie, along with multi-instrumentalist Gary Coupland, have been touring larger venues throughout the UK. In addition to a number of children's albums, they have been performing educational work in schools, and have made four series for BBC Television. Aside from the new musical policy, Cilla continues to tour with members of her family, and has toured the USA with her sibling Ray.

Albums: *Cilla Fisher And Artie Trezise* (1976), *Balcanquhal* (1977), *For Foul Day And Fair* (1977), *Cilla And Artie* (1979), *Songs Of The Fishing* (1989), *Reaching Out* (1990). As the Singing Kettle: *Singing Kettle 1* (1981), *Singing Kettle 2* (1984), *Scotch Broth* (1987), *Singing Kettle 3* (1988), *Singing Kettle 4* (1990), *The Big Green Planet* (1991).

Five Hand Reel

This Scottish electric folk rock group formed in 1975, and often compared with the JSD Band. Five Hand Reel included Dick Gaughan (b. Richard Peter Gaughan, 17 May 1948, Glasgow, Scotland; vocals/guitar), Chuck Fleming (fiddle), who soon left to be replaced by Bobby Eaglesham (vocals/fiddle/guitar/bouzouki), Tom Hickland (keyboards/violin/vocals), Barry Lyons (multi-instrumentalist, ex-Trees and Mr. Fox) and Dave Tulloch (drums/French horn/harmonica/vocals). Their material encompassed Irish and Scottish traditional music, with original contributions from the band. Gaughan left to pursue a solo career and was replaced by Sam Bracken (vocals/guitar, ex-Therapy) in 1978. The excellent fiddle player Fleming, known for his own recordings, as well as his work with performers such as Johnny Handle, joined Syncopace, the group formed by Alistair Anderson in 1991.

Albums: *Five Hand Reel* (1976), *For A' That* (1977), *Earl O' Moray* (1978), *Bunch Of Fives* (1979), *Nothing But The Best* (1980).

Fivepenny Piece

Originally known as the Wednesday Folks, this group from Lancashire, England was formed in 1967. They largely performed songs tinged with their native Lancashire humour. The original line-up of Lynda Meeks (b. 3 August 1941, Stalybridge, Cheshire, England; vocals), her brother John Meeks (b. 24 March 1937, Stalybridge, Cheshire, England; vocals/guitar), Eddie Crotty (b. 24 February 1942, Stalybridge, Cheshire, England; guitar), Colin Radcliffe (b. 19 January 1934, Ashton-under-Lyne, Lancashire, England; guitar/harmonica) and his brother George Radcliffe (b. 9 August 1937, Ashton-under-Lyne, Lancashire; bass/trombone). As the Wednesday Folks, they won the television talent show *New Faces* in 1968, but changed their name to the Fivepenny Piece in 1969. The group

Cilla Fisher And Artie Trezise

were featured on the BBC television series *That's Life* during the late 70s, and recorded almost a dozen shows. Despite being offered work all over the world, the group declined as they all had regular day jobs. In 1981, John Meeks left the line-up to be replaced by Trevor Chance (b. 1 March 1942, Gilsland, Cumbria, England; guitar/vocals). This was at the time that the group had its own series, *The Fivepenny Piece Show,* on BBC television. On records, Phil Barlow (drums), augmented the line-up. Many of the group's songs were self-composed, by Colin and George, but they trod the path between traditional folk and commercial acceptance and consequently did not gain sufficient appeal from either camp. However, *Makin' Tracks* made the UK Top 40 early in 1973, while *King Cotton* gained a Top 10 placing in 1976. In addition, the group achieved silver discs, in 1976, for *Songs We Like To Sing* and *The Fivepenny Piece On Stage.* When Lynda Meeks left, she was replaced by Andrea Mullen, formerly with the Caravelles, but the group broke up in 1985. Eventually, Chance went into artist management, and Colin became a full-time landscape painter.

Albums: *The Fivepenny Piece* (1972), *Makin' Tracks* (1973), *Songs We Like To Sing* (1973), *On Stage* (1974), *Wish You Were Here* (1975), *The Fivepenny Piece On Stage Again* (1977), *King Cotton* (1976), *On Stage Again* (1977), *Telling Tales* (1977), *Both Sides Of Fivepenny Piece* (1978), with various artists *Lanky Spoken Here* (1978), *Life Is A Game Of Chance* (1979), *Peddlers Of Songs* (1979), *An Evening With The Fivepenny Piece* (1980), *The Fivepenny Piece Live At The Coliseum* (1980). Compilations: *The Very Best Of Fivepenny Piece* (1980), *This Is Fivepenny Piece* (1980), *Lancashire, My Lancashire* (1980), *The Fivepenny Piece* (1991).

Flatt And Scruggs

Lester Flatt (b. 28 June 1914, Overton County, Tennessee, USA; guitar) and Earl Scruggs (b. 1924, Cleveland County, North Carolina, USA; banjo). These influential musicians began working together in December 1945 as members of Bill Monroe's Bluegrass Boys. In February 1948 they left to form the Foggy Mountain Boys with Jim Shumate (fiddle), Howard Watts aka Cedric Rainwater (bass fiddle) - both ex-Bill Monroe - and, latterly, Mac Wiseman (tenor vocals/guitar). They became an established feature of Virginia's WCYB radio station and undertook recording sessions for the Mercury label before embarking on a prolonged tour of the south. Here they forged a more powerful, ebullient sound than was associated with their chosen genre and in November 1950 Flatt and Scruggs joined Columbia/CBS Records, with whom they remained throughout their career

together. Three years later they signed a sponsorship deal with Martha White Mills which engendered a regular show on Nashville's WSM and favoured slots on their patron's television shows. Josh Graves (dobro) was then added to the line-up which in turn evolved a less frenetic sound and reduced the emphasis on Scruggs' banjo playing. Appearances on the nationally-syndicated *Folk Sound USA* brought the group's modern bluegrass sound to a much wider audience, while their stature was further enhanced by an appearance at the 1960 Newport Folk Festival. Flatt and Scruggs were then adopted by the college circuit where they were seen as antecedents to a new generation of acts, including the Kentucky Colonels, the Hillmen and the Dillards. The Foggy Mountain Boys performed the theme song, 'The Ballad Of Jed Clampett', to the popular *Beverly Hillbillies* television show in the early 60s while their enduring instrumental, 'Foggy Mountain Breakdown', was heavily featured in the film *Bonnie And Clyde.* Bluegrass students opined that this version lacked the sparkle of earlier arrangements and declared the group lacked its erstwhile vitality. By 1968 Earl Scruggs' sons, Randy and Gary, had been brought into the line-up, but the banjoist nonetheless grew dissatisfied with the constraints of a purely bluegrass setting. The partnership was dissolved the following year. While Flatt formed a new act, the Nashville Grass, his former partner added further members of his family to found the Earl Scruggs Revue.

Compilations: *Foggy Mountain Breakdown* (1975), *The Golden Era 1950-1955* (1977), *Foggy Mountain Banjo* (1978), *1959 - 1963* (1992).

Fleck, Bela

b. c.1953, New York City, New York, USA. Fleck has been credited with expanding the parameters of the banjo by combining traditional bluegrass with jazz and classical music, similar to what David Grisman did with the mandolin. Inspired by the song 'Duelling Banjos' in the film *Deliverance,* Fleck took up the banjo at the age of 14. He moved to Kentucky in his early 20s to start the bluegrass group Spectrum. In 1981 he relocated to Nashville, joining the influential New Grass Revival, with whom he stayed for eight years. In 1989 he formed the Flecktones with Howard Levy (keyboards/harmonica), Victor Wooten (bass) and Roy Wooten (drumitar - a guitar wired to electric drums). The group's debut album for Warner Brothers sold over 50,000 copies and reached the Top 20 on the *Billboard* jazz charts.

Albums: *Natural Bridge, Crossing The Tracks, Inroads* (1980), with the New Grass Revival *Deviation* (1984), *Bela Fleck And The Flecktones* (1990), *Flight*

Of the Cosmic Hippo (1992), *UFO TOFU* (1993).

Flowers And Frolics

This UK group specialized in English country dance music and music-hall songs. Flowers And Frolics were formed in 1974, but at the time the group had no official name so were credited as the Graham Smith Band, for a gig announced in *Melody Maker*. Their monicker was taken from the name of original member Graham Smith (b. Melbourne, Australia). Smith left to return to Australia before the group recorded its first album. The line-up on *Bees On Horseback* was Mike Bettison (b. 3 June 1951, Chiswick, London, England; melodeon), Roger Digby (b. 19 April 1949, Colchester, Essex, England; concertina), Bob King (b. 27 March 1952, Eastbourne, Sussex, England; banjo), Dan Quinn (b. 11 October 1949, Grimsby, South Humberside, England; melodeon), Ted Stevens (b. 27 September 1952, Redruth, Cornwall, England; percussion), and Alex West (b. 8 November 1954, England; brass/bass). By the time of *Sold Out*, King and West had been replaced by Trevor Bennett (b. 4 August 1945, Grantham, Lincolnshire, England; trombones/flugelhorn/helicon), Rob Gifford (b. 1 March 1955, Wanstead, London, England; percussion), and Nick Havell (b. Nicholas George Havell, 7 January 1951, Stratford, London, England; bass trombone). The group achieved a good deal of popularity on the folk circuit, not least for keeping many traditional dances alive. Playing a variety of jigs, hornpipes, polkas and waltzes, they performed at festivals all over Britain, and were in demand at ceilidhs and barn dances alike. Only two albums were recorded before the group split up in February 1985, having decided they had done enough. That same year, Quinn, Havell, Bennett and Gifford formed the dance band Gas Mark 5, supplemented by Chris Taylor from the Oyster Band. Quinn then left this line-up in November 1989, but continued to play on the folk circuit. Stevens is a member of the Old Hat Band, while King plays with jazz and rock bands. Bettison is a member of the Fabulous Salami Brothers, while West has left the folk scene.

Albums: *Bees On Horseback* (1977), *Sold Out* (1984).

Fogelberg, Dan

b. 13 August 1951, Peoria, Illinois, USA. Having learned piano from the age of 14, Fogelberg moved to guitar and songwriting. Leaving the University of Illinois in 1971 he relocated to California and started playing on the folk circuit, at one point touring with Van Morrison. A move to Nashville brought him to the attention of producer Norbert Putnam. Fogelberg released *Home Free* for Columbia shortly afterwards. This was a very relaxed album, notable for the backing musicians involved, including Roger McGuinn, Jackson Browne, Joe Walsh and Buffy Sainte-Marie. Despite the calibre of the other players, the album was not a success, and Fogelberg, having been dropped by Columbia, returned to session work. Producer Irv Azoff, who was managing Joe Walsh, signed Fogelberg and secured a deal with Epic. Putnam was involved in subsequent recordings by Fogelberg. In 1974, Fogelberg moved to Colorado, and a year later released *Souvenirs*. This was a more positive album, and Walsh's production was evident. From here on, Fogelberg played the majority of the instruments on record, enabling him to keep tight control of the recordings, but inevitably it took longer to finish the projects. Playing support to the Eagles in 1975 helped to establish Fogelberg. However, in 1977, due to appear with the Eagles at Wembley, he failed to show on-stage, and it was later claimed that he had remained at home to complete recording work on *Netherlands*. Whatever the reason, the album achieved some recognition, but Fogelberg has enjoyed better chart success in the USA than in the UK. In 1980, 'Longer' reached number 2 in the US singles charts, while in the UK it did not even reach the Top 50. Two other singles, 'Same Auld Lang Syne' and 'Leader Of The Band', both from *The Innocent Age*, achieved Top 10 places in the USA. The excellent *High Country Snows* saw a return to his bluegrass influences and was in marked contrast to the harder-edged *Exiles* which followed. From plaintive ballads to rock material, Fogelberg is a versatile writer and musician who continues to produce credible records and command a loyal cult following.

Albums: *Home Free* (1973), *Souvenirs* (1975), *Captured Angel* (1975), *Netherlands* (1977), with Tim Weisberg *Twin Sons Of Different Mothers* (1978), *Phoenix* (1980), *The Innocent Age* (1981), *Windows And Walls* (1984), *High Country Snows* (1985), *Exiles* (1987), *The Wild Places* (1990), *Dan Fogelberg Live - Greetings From The West* (1991). Compilation: *Greatest Hits* (1985).

Folkways Records

Founded in New York, USA in 1948 by Moe Asch and Marion Distler, Folkways has grown from informal origins to become the embodiment of America's divergent traditions. Initial releases included square dance tunes, Cuban music and jazz, but the venture was primarily devoted to folk styles. Recordings by Leadbelly established the label nationally and his prodigious output - over 900 songs were committed to tape - included several now recognized as standards, notably 'Goodnight Irene', 'Midnight Special', 'Cottonfields' and 'Rock

Island Line'. Folkways also recorded Woody Guthrie, Cisco Houston and Pete Seeger; the latter completed over 60 albums for the label, and embraced the urban folk revival of the late 50s and early 60s with releases by Dave Van Ronk, Len Chandler, Paul Clayton, Logan English and the New Lost City Ramblers. Asch also established several subsidiary outlets, including RBF and Broadside, the latter of which evolved out of a mimeographed publication devoted to the topical song. Bob Dylan, Phil Ochs and Eric Anderson were among those contributing to attendant albums. However, Folkways was not solely confined to folk and its ever-increasing catalogue included language instruction, science, spoken word and documentary material, of which *We Shall Overcome*, an audio-verite recording of the 1963 civil rights march on Washington, was particularly impressive. In 1965, Asch founded Verve/Folkways, in an effort to secure national distribution for selected repackages from his extensive library. New recordings, by Tim Hardin, the Blues Magoos and Blues Project, were also undertaken but the label's title was altered to Verve/Forecast in 1967 as electic styles prevailed over acoustic. Excellent albums by, among others, Richie Havens, Janis Ian, Odetta and James Cotton ensued, but the venture folded when parent company MGM incurred financial difficulties. Asch continued to maintain the original Folkways which, by retaining its small-scale origins, has avoided the trappings of commercialization. Between 1,500 and 2,000 titles remain in circulation at all times and the company's peerless position within America was recognized in 1988 with *Folkways: A Vision Shared*, a star-studded recording undertaken to celebrate the label's 40th anniversary. Bruce Springsteen, U2, Brian Wilson, Little Richard, Taj Mahal, Emmylou Harris and Bob Dylan were among those gathering to pay tribute through interpretations of compositions by Leadbelly and Guthrie.

Forbert, Steve

b. 1955, Meridien, Mississippi, USA. Forbert played guitar and harmonica in local rock bands before moving to New York in 1976. There he busked at Grand Central Station before making his first recordings in 1977 for Nemperor and was briefly heralded as 'the new (Bob) Dylan' because of the tough poetry of his lyrics. Forbert's biggest commercial success came when he had a Top 20 hit with 'Romeo's Tune' (1979). After four albums his contract was terminated. For most of the 80s, Forbert was based in Nashville, songwriting and playing concerts around the South with a touring group including Danny Counts (bass), Paul Errico (keyboards) and Bobby Lloyd Hicks (drums). His

1988 album for Geffen had Garry Tallent from Bruce Springsteen's E Street Band as producer. Nils Lofgren was a guest musician. After a four-year gap, Forbert returned with the highly-praised *The American In Me*, produced by Pete Anderson.
Albums: *Alive On Arrival* (1979), *Jackrabbit Slim* (1979), *Little Stevie Orbit* (1980), *Steve Forbert* (1982), *Streets Of This Town* (1988), *The American In Me* (1992).

Forest

Originally known as the Foresters Of Walesby, this Birmingham group consisted of brothers Martin and Hadrian Welham (guitars/vocals) and Derek Allensby (mandolin/pipes/harmonium). Formed in 1968, they enjoyed the patronage of pioneering disc jockey John Peel, who introduced the trio to the influential Blackhill agency and penned the liner notes to their debut album. *Forest* revealed a brand of underground, 'hippie folk', popularized by the Incredible String Band and Dr. Strangely Strange, but the set failed to reap a similar commercial success. *Full Circle*, a more professional, accomplished collection, also failed to rise above cult status and Forest split up soon after its release.
Albums: *Forest* (1969), *Full Circle* (1970).

Foster, Chris

b. 23 April 1948, Yeovil, Somerset, England. This singer and guitarist first started playing in public in 1964 at local folk clubs. His influences at the time ranged from Cyril Tawney, to Davey Graham, Big Bill Broonzy and Louis Killen. Foster included in his live performances both traditional material and songs by contemporary writers. While still at college, Foster played support on the 1971 Reverend Gary Davis tour of the UK. The following year, he left art school, and went into music in a full-time capacity, until the mid-80s. After experiencing moderate success on the folk circuit, but feeling he was getting nowhere, Foster bowed out of the scene and, apart from occasional bookings, did little musically for three years. From about 1988, Foster was playing bass in a blues band, and then, in 1991, he re-emerged to start playing in folk clubs again. *Layers* featured the fiddle of Nic Jones, while *All Things In Common* included the Bill Caddick's much covered 'Unicorns'. *Fylde Acoustic* was so named because all the artists performing on the album played Fylde instruments. The artists included Gordon Giltrap and Martin Carthy.
Albums: *Layers* (1977), with various artists *Fylde Acoustic* (1977), *All Things In Common* (1979), with various artists *Nuclear Power No Thanks!* (1981).

Fotheringay

The folk rock group Fotheringay was formed in

1970 by singer Sandy Denny upon her departure from Fairport Convention, and drew its name from one of her compositions for that group. Trevor Lucas (guitar/vocals), Gerry Conway (drums - both ex-Eclection), Jerry Donahue (guitar) and Pat Donaldson (bass; both ex-Poet And The One Man Band) completed the line-up responsible for the quintet's lone album. This impressive, folk-based set included several superior Denny originals, notably 'Nothing More', 'The Sea' and 'The Pond And The Stream', as well as meticulous readings of Gordon Lightfoot's 'The Way I Feel' and Bob Dylan's 'Too Much Of Nothing'. Although criticized contemporaneously as constrained, *Fotheringay* is now rightly viewed as a confident, accomplished work. However, the album failed to match commercial expectations and pressures on Denny to undertake a solo career - she was voted Britain's number 1 singer in *Melody Maker*'s 1970 poll - increased. Fotheringay was disbanded in 1971 during sessions for a projected second set. Some of its songs surfaced on the vocalist's debut album, *The Northstar Grassman* and whereas Donaldson and Conway began session work, Lucas and Donahue resurfaced in Fairport Convention.

Album: *Fotheringay* (1970).

Further reading: *Meet On The Ledge*, Patrick Humphries.

4 Yn Y Bar

This Welsh folk group includes Iwan Roberts (b. 24 October 1953, Carmarthen, Dyfed, South Wales; mandolin/mandola), Tudur Huws Jones (b. 29 October 1955, Bangor, Gwynedd, North Wales; banjo/mandolin/whistle/bouzouki), Tudur Morgan (b. 8 May 1958, Bangor, Gwynedd, North Wales; guitar/bass/vocals), and Huw Roberts (b. 1 September 1957, Bangor, Gwynedd, North Wales; fiddle/vocals). Fiercely nationalistic, they make a point of using only Welsh traditional and contemporary songs and tunes in their repertoire. They first performed in 1983, and followed up with the release of *Byth Adra* (*We're Never At Home*), on Sain Records. *Byth Adra* features 'Nos Galan', a traditional Welsh tune which the Americans 'borrowed' and turned into 'Deck The Halls'. The independent Christmas release, *Seren Nadolig,* was followed by a tour of Scotland, in April 1986, and the group's second Sain release, *Newid Cynefin*, in October of the same year. In 1987, on St David's Day, the group appeared at London's Royal Albert Hall, and their second independent production *Ffiwsio*, saw them experimenting with bluegrass and reggae. In 1988, Morgan produced the first solo release by Plethyn's Linda Healy, with all of the members of 4 Yn Y Bar playing on some of the tracks. In 1989, the group were invited to play at the Orkney Islands Folk Festival, in May, and in November the same year the group recorded their first television special. Since then, 4 Yn Y Bar have given up live performances, but Tudur Morgan released *Branwen* in November 1991, an album based on an Irish/Welsh mythological character, and containing mostly original material. 4 Yn Y Bar also have a new album, tentatively called *Stryd America*, (America Atreet), released on St David's Day (1 March) 1992.

Albums: *Byth Adra* (1984), *Seren Nadolig* (1985), *Newid Cynefin* (1986), *Ffiwsio* (1987), *Stryd America* (1992). Tudur Morgan: *Branwen* (1991).

Frank, Jackson C.

b. 1943, Buffalo, New York, USA. Frank was one of several American folk performers, including Shawn Phillips and Paul Simon, who temporarily lived in Britain during the mid-60s. Indeed, Simon produced *Jackson C. Frank*, the artist's lone album, which showcased his gift for melody and a lyrical perception. Released in 1965, several of its songs, including 'Blues Run The Game' and 'You Never Wanted Me', have since been recognized as standards. Folksinger Sandy Denny befriended Frank and regularly performed his compositions both as a solo act and on joining Fairport Convention. Jackson's final British appearance of note came in September 1968 at the Royal Festival Hall. Billed as 'An Evening Of Contemporary Song', he shared the stage with Joni Mitchell, Al Stewart and the Fairports, but returned to the United States without consolidating his undoubted early promise.

Album: *Jackson C. Frank* (1965 - re-issued in 1978 as *Jackson Frank Again*). Compilation: *Blues Run The Game* (1987).

Fuller, Blind Boy

b. Fulton Allen, 1908, Wadesboro, North Carolina, USA, d. 13 February 1941. One of a large family, Fuller learned to play the guitar as a child and had begun a life as a transient singer when he was blinded, either through disease or when lye water was thrown in his face. By the late 20s he was well-known throughout North Carolina and Virginia, playing and singing at county fairs, tobacco farms and on street corners. At one time he worked with two other blind singers, Sonny Terry and Gary Davis. Amongst his most popular numbers were 'Rattlesnakin' Daddy', 'Jitterbug Rag' (on which he demonstrated his guitar technique) and the bawdy 'What's That Smells Like Fish?' (later adapted by Hot Tuna as 'Keep On Truckin'') and 'Get Your Yas Yas Out'. At one point in his career he was teamed with Brownie McGhee. In 1940, in Chicago, Fuller's style had become gloomy as can be heard on 'When You Are Gone'. Hospitalized for a kidney operation, Fuller contracted blood poisoning and died on 13 February 1941. One of the foremost exponents of the Piedmont blues style, there was a strong folk element in Fuller's work. The manner in which he absorbed and re-created stylistic patterns of other blues forms made him an important link between the earlier classic country blues and the later urbanized forms. Among the singers he influenced were Buddy Moss, Floyd Council, Ralph Willis and Richard 'Little Boy Fuller' Trice. (Shortly after Fuller's death Brownie McGhee was recorded under the name Blind Boy Fuller No 2.)

Compilations: *East Coast Piedmont Style* (1935-39 recordings), *Blind Boy Fuller* (1935-40 recordings), *Blind Boy Fuller And Brownie McGhee* (1936-41 recordings), *On Down* (1937-40 recordings), *Truckin' My Blues Away* (1991).

Fuller, Jesse 'Lone Cat'

b. 12 March 1896, Jonesboro, Georgia, USA, d. 29 January 1976, Oakland, California, USA. A veteran of the tent shows, Fuller fashioned himself a unique one-man-band of six-string bass (played with his right foot), a combination of kazoo, harmonica, microphone fixed to a harness around his neck, a hi-hat cymbal (played with the left foot) and a 12-string guitar. His success came in the late 50s as a result of appearances on USA television following Ramblin' Jack Elliot's lionization via his recording of 'San Francisco Bay Blues'. In the 50s he made three albums of original and traditional material and by the mid-60s became the darling of the 'coffee house circuit' after Bob Dylan cited him as one of his influences. Similar success was to follow in Britain resulting from Donovan's performance of 'San Francisco Bay Blues' on UK Independent Television's *Ready Steady Go* music programme in 1965.

Selected albums: *'Frisco Bound* (1968), *San Francisco Bay Blues* (1988), *Railroad Worksong* (1993).

Fungus

Similar in style to Fairport Convention and Steeleye Span, the founder members of Fungus were Fred Piek (guitar, vocals), Sido Martens (guitars), Kees Maat (piano), and Koos Pakvis were joined later Louis Debij (drums). They mixed Dutch and British material, although *Lief Ende Leid*, their finest album, is devoted to the traditional music of their homeland - a thorough exercise in folk rock. After Martens had left to pursue a solo career, he released *Land And Water*, and developed a style similar to Richard Thompson. In 1977, Fungus released the impressive, ironically titled, *Mushrooms*, devoted to English songs and tunes. In the following year,

Debij and the lead guitarist Arie Graff, departed, leaving the remaining trio, Piek, Pakvis and Rens Van Der Zalm to cut their final album acoustically, before disbanding in 1980. Fungus is seen as having served as an example to other Dutch musicians on the local folk scene, and a small group of bands followed in their footsteps. Piek went on to a solo career, whilst the remainder of Fungus's personnel formed a comedy band, The Amazing Strompwa Fels. A Fungus reunion took place in October 1984.

Albums: *Fungus* (1974), *Lief Ende Leid* (1975), *Van Keil Naar Vlaring* (1976), *Mushrooms* (1977), *De Kaarten Zign Geschud* (1979).

Fureys

This musical family group from Ballyfermont, Dublin, Eire, featured George Furey (b. 11 June 1951, Dublin, Eire; vocals, guitar, accordion, mandola, autoharp, whistles), Finbar Furey (b. 28 September 1946, Dublin, Eire; vocals, uillean pipes, banjo, whistles, flute), Eddie Furey (b. 23 December 1944, Dublin, Eire; guitar, mandola, mandolin, harmonica, fiddle, bodhran, vocals) and Paul Furey (b. 6 May 1948, Dublin, Eire; accordion, melodeon, concertina, whistles, bones, spoons, vocals). During the 60s Finbar and Eddie Furey had performed as a duo, playing clubs and doing radio work. Despite the offer of a recording contract, they turned it down, and went to Scotland to play. Having established a reputation for themselves, they later signed to Transatlantic, and joined the Clancy Brothers on the latter group's American tour in 1969. In 1972, the duo toured most of Europe, but while they were away, Paul and George had formed a group called the Buskers, with Davey Arthur (b. 24 September 1954, Edinburgh, Scotland; multi-instrumentalist, vocals). This group were involved in a road crash, bringing Finbar and Eddie back home, where they formed Tam Linn with Davey and Paul, and played the Cambridge Folk Festival. George later joined the line-up, and they became the Fureys and Davey Arthur. The following year, 1981, the group, credited as the Fureys And Davey Arthur, reached the UK Top 20 with 'When You Were Sweet Sixteen'. By contrast, the album, having the same title, only just made the Top 100 in Britain in 1982. A follow-up single, 'I Will Love You (Every Time When We Are Gone)' failed to make the Top 50 in Britain. *Golden Days*, released on K-Tel, made the UK Top 20 in 1984, selling in excess of 250,000 copies, while *At The End Of A Perfect Day*, also on K-Tel, made the UK Top 40 in 1985. Numerous compilations abound, but *The Sound Of The Fureys And Davey Arthur*, on PolyGram, was released only in Ireland. *Golden Days* and *At The End Of A Perfect*

Day were re-packaged, in 1991, as *The Very Best Of The Fureys And Davey Arthur.* The group have successfully followed the middle-of-the-road folk musical path, by producing melodic and popular music. Folk purists argue that this detracts from 'real' folk music, whilst others say that the group have encouraged people, to listen to folk music. Either way, their concerts are popular worldwide, and while not a hugely successful chart act domestically, their records still sell extremely well.

Albums: *The Cisco Special* (1960), *Songs Of Woody Guthrie* (1961), *I Ain't Got No Home* (1962), *When You Were Sweet Sixteen* (1982), *Steal Away* (1983), *In Concert* (1984), *Golden Days* (1984), *At The End Of A Perfect Day* (1985), *The First Leaves Of Autumn* (1986), *The Scattering* (1989). Compilations: *The Sound Of The Fureys And Davey Arthur* (1981), *The Fureys Finest* (1987), *The Fureys Collection* (1989), *The Very Best Of The Fureys And Davey Arthur* (1991), *The Winds Of Change* (1992). Solo albums: Finbar And Eddie Furey *The Dawning Of The Day* (1972); Finbar Furey *Love Letters* (1990).

G

Garbutt, Vin

b. Vincent Paul Garbutt, 20 November 1947, South Bank, Middlesbrough, Cleveland, England. Having served a six-year apprenticeship with ICI, Vin decided to go to Europe in 1969. While there he managed to earn his living by singing and playing in bars. When he returned to England, he continued performing in a full-time capacity as a singer/songwriter, guitarist and whistle player. Garbutt has a distinctive voice and a small cult following on the folk circuit. His albums have been well-received but many feel that live performance show Garbutt at his best. His combination of jigs and hornpipes, played on tin whistle, are backed by songs of strong insight. One example of this is 'The Chemical Workers Song', from *The Young Tin Whistle Pest*, written by Ron Angel. *Little Innocents* caused considerable comment on release due to its uncompromising stance on abortion. All royalties from the sale of the album were directed to a number of pro-Life charities. *When The Tide Turns* remains Garbutt's best-selling album. The recording features a number of notable musicians from outside the folk arena including Robbie McIntosh (ex-Average White Band) from Paul McCartney's band. Garbutt completed a world tour in April 1991, having played venues in Canada, New Zealand, Hong Kong and Europe. A video, *The South Banker Show*, was released in 1991 featuring Garbutt singing and telling stories.

Albums: *The Valley Of Tees* (1972), *The Young Tin Whistle Pest* (1975), *King Gooden* (1976), *Eston California* (1977), *Tossin' A Wobbler* (1978), *Little Innocents* (1983), *Shy Tot Pommy - Live* (1985), *When The Tide Turns* (1990), *The Bypass Syndrome* (1991).

Gas Mark 5

This group formed following the demise of the UK folk dance band Flowers And Frolics. The line-up of Dan Quinn (b. 11 October 1949, Grimsby, South Humberside, England; melodeon), Nick Havell (b. Nicholas George Havell, 7 January 1951, Stratford, London, England; bass trombone/piano), Trevor Bennett (b. 4 August 1945, Grantham, Lincolnshire, England; tenor and alto trombones/wind synthesiser/keyboards), Rob Gifford (b. 1 March 1955, Wanstead, London, England; drums/percussion), and Chris Taylor (mouth organs/melodeon/guitar) got together in 1985. Taylor had formerly been with the Oyster Band. Quinn left in November 1989, and his place was taken by Terry Mann (b. 6 October 1963, Barking, London, England; guitar/soprano saxophone/melodeons/bass/wind synthesizer). Regularly seen at folk festivals, and essentially a dance band, the group draw their material from both the British Isles and elsewhere, unlike their predecessors, Flowers And Frolics, who specialized in English country dance.

Albums: *In The Kitchen* (1987), *Gas Mark V* (1988), *Jump!* (1991).

Gateway Singers

Like many groups formed during the popular commercial folk explosion of the late 50s, the Gateway Singers had a relatively short life. The line-up consisted of Jerry Walter (vocals/banjo), Elmerlee Thomas (vocals), Lou Gottleib (bass), and Travis Edmondson (guitar). Following a path started by others, such as the Almanac Singers and the Weavers, they became one of the better-known US groups in the field at the time. Gottleib left the group in 1959, after the group's two releases on Decca, and was replaced by Ernie Sheldon as lead guitar player. The group split up in 1961, at the height of the folk boom. For a time, the Gateway Trio, comprising Milt Chapman (bass/vocals), Betty Mann (guitar/vocals), and original founder Jerry Walter, continued performing. After releasing

Vin Garbutt

albums for Capitol Records, the trio broke up.
Albums: *The Gateway Singers At The Hungry i*
(1956), *The Gateway Singers In Hi Fi* (1958).

Gaughan, Dick

b. Leith, Scotland. A veteran of Scotland's thriving
folk circuit, Gaughan rose to national prominence
in the 70s as a member of the Boys Of The Lough.
From there he became a founder member of Five
Hand Reel, an electric folk group that enjoyed
considerable critical acclaim. Gaughan left them in
1978 following the release of their third album,
Bonnie Earl Of Moray, having already embarked on a
concurrent solo career. His early releases, *No More
Forever* and *Kist O' Gold*, concentrated on
traditional material, while *Coppers And Brass*
showcased guitar interpretations of Scottish and
Irish dance music. However, it was the release of
Handful Of Earth which established Gaughan as a
major force in contemporary folk. This politically-
charged album included the vitriolic 'Workers'
Song' and 'World Turned Upside Down' while at
the same time scotched notions of nationalism with
the reconciliatory 'Both Sides Of The Tweed'. This
exceptional set is rightly regarded as a landmark in
British traditional music, but its ever-restless creator
surprised many commentators with *A Different Kind
Of Love Song*, which included a version of Joe
South's 60s protest song, 'Games People Play'.
Gaughan has since enjoyed a fervent popularity
both at home and abroad while continuing to
pursue his uncompromising, idiosyncratic musical
path. Gaughan calls himself a 'hard-nosed
Communist' and is a passionate lover and supporter
of Scotland, while not tolerating any anti-English
feeling. Both his playing and singing come from the
heart in the 90s he is arguably Scotland's greatest
living troubadour.
Albums: *No More Forever* (1972), *Coppers And Brass*
(1977), *Kist O' Gold* (1977), *Gaughan* (1978), with
Tony Capstick, Dave Burland *Songs Of Ewan
McColl* (1978), *Handful Of Earth* (1981), with Andy
Irvine *Parallel Lines* (1982), *A Different Kind Of Love
Song* (1983), *Fanfare For Tomorrow* (1985), *Live In
Edinburgh* (1985), *True And Bold* (1986), *Songs For
Peace* (1988), *Woody Lives* (1988), *Call It Freedom*
(1989).

Geesin, Ron

One of Britain's leading *avant garde* composers and
performers, Geesin first attracted attention for his
radical mid-60s' recording, *A Raising Of The
Eyebrows*. This experimental sound collage blended
unusual vocal and instrumental effects with
synthesizer and banjo and proved influential on
Britain's progressive groups. Pink Floyd adapted
several of its ideas for the studio segments on

Ummagumma, and Geesin later collaborated with the
group on *Atom Heart Mother*. His spell within their
circle was more fully realized on the soundtrack to
the film *The Body*, which he recorded with bassist
Roger Waters. Such work introduced Geesin to a
wider audience, as did a stint as the support act to
Genesis in 1973, but subsequent solo releases on his
own Geesin label proved too uncompromising for
the public at large. A skilled studio technician, he
was later involved in the remastering of blues
recordings for the specialist Flywright label.
Albums: *A Raising Of The Eyebrows* (1968), with
Roger Waters *The Body* (1970), *Electrosound* (1979),
Patruns (1975), *Right Through* (1979), *As He Stands*
(1979).

Gibson, Bob

b. 16 November 1931, New York City, New
York, USA. Although commercial success would
prove illusive, Gibson was one of folk music's most
influential figures. His songs were recorded by the
Kingston Trio and Peter, Paul And Mary and he
was responsible for launching and/or furthering the
careers of Bob Camp, Judy Collins and Joan Baez.
Having recorded his debut single, "I'm Never To
Marry", in 1956, Gibson embarked on a series of
excellent albums including *Offbeat Folksongs* and
Carnegie Concert. Indifferent to marketplace
pressure, his novelty collection, *Ski Songs*, was
issued at the height of the hootenanny boom while
Yes I See, arguably the nadir of his recording career,
appeared as Bob Dylan began to attract peer group
acclaim. These disappointing releases were followed
by a duet with Bob (Hamilton) Camp, *At The Gate
Of Horn*, paradoxically one of American folk's
definitive works. Gibson was absent from music for
much of the 60s, but he re-emerged early in the 70s
with a melodic album which featured Roger
McGuinn, Spanky McFarland and Cyrus Faryar.
This respected artist has since pursued a more
public path. During the 80s he toured with Tom
Paxton and was a frequent performer at
international folk festivals.
Albums: *Folksongs Of Ohio* (1956), *Offbeat Folksongs*
(1956), *I Come For To Sing* (1957), *Carnegie Concert*
(1957), *Hootenannny At Carnegie* (c.50s), *There's A
Meeting Here Tonight* (1959), *Ski Songs* (1959), *Yes I
See* (1961), with Bob 'Hamilton' Camp *At The Gate
Of Horn* (1961), *Where I'm Bound* (1964), *Bob
Gibson* (c.70s), *Funky In The Country* (1974), with
Camp *Homemade Music* (1978).

Giltrap, Gordon

b. 6 April 1948, East Peckham, Tonbridge, Kent,
England. A renowned and innovative guitarist,
Giltrap came through the early days of the UK folk
revival, and established himself in rock music

Dick Gaughan

circles. His first guitar was a present, at the age of 12, from his mother. Leaving school aged 15, he wanted to pursue a career in art, but had insufficient qualifications, so spent time working on building sites. As his interest and ability, developed, he started playing regularly at Les Cousin's, in London's Greek Street. There he met a number of singers and musicians who were later to become household names in the folk and blues world. Names such as Bert Jansch, John Renbourn, John Martyn and Al Stewart were just a few such notables. Although still only semi-professional, Giltrap signed a deal with Transatlantic Records and released *Early Days* and *Portrait*. Playing the college, folk club and university circuit, and establishing a growing following, Giltrap had begun to write mainly instrumental pieces by the 70s. This change of direction led to *Visionary*, an album based on the work of William Blake, the 18th century English artist and poet. By now Giltrap was receiving favourable reviews for his style of blend classical and rock music, and this led to him being commissioned to write for a number of special events. 'Heartsong', from *Perilous Journey*, just failed to broach the Top 20 in the British singles charts in 1978. The tune, a Giltrap composition, was later used by BBC Television, as the theme tune to the *Holiday* programme during the 80s. The album from which it came reached the Top 30 in the British charts, while the following year, 1979, 'Fear Of The Dark' narrowly failed to make the Top 50 singles chart. In 1979, he composed, for London's Capital Radio, an orchestral piece to commemorate 'Operation Drake', a two-year round-the-world scientific expedition following in the footsteps of Sir Francis Drake. This resulted in the premiere, in 1980, of the 'Eyes Of The Wind Rhapsody' with the London Philharmonic Orchestra, conducted by Vernon Handley. Many of Giltrap's other compositions have been used for UK television work, on programmes such as ITV's *Wish You Were Here*, *The Open University*, and, in 1985, the television drama *Hold The Back Page*, and other subsequent television films. Giltrap now tours regularly with Ric Sanders in addition to solo work, and has also duetted with John Renbourn, and Juan Martin. *The Best Of Gordon Giltrap - All The Hits Plus More*, includes a previously unreleased track, 'Catwalk Blues', which was recorded live at Oxford Polytechnic. As well as performing and recording, Giltrap is a regular contributor to *Guitarist* magazine.

Albums: *Early Days* (1968), *Gordon Giltrap* (1968), *Portrait* (1969), *Testament Of Time* (1971), *Giltrap* (1973), *Visionary* (1976), *Perilous Journey* (1977), *Fear Of The Dark* (1978), *Performance* (1980), *The Peacock Party* (1981), *Live* (1981), *Airwaves* (1982), *Elegy* (1987), *A Midnight Clear* (1988), *Gordon Giltrap-Guitarist* (1988), *Mastercraftsmen* (1989), with Ric Sanders *One To One* (1989), with Martin Taylor *A Matter Of Time* (1991). Compilations: *The Very Best Of Gordon Giltrap* (1988), *The Best Of Gordon Giltrap - All The Hits Plus More* (1991).

Gods Little Monkeys

Based in York, England, this indie group plays a mixture of rock and folk. The founder members were Jo Swiss (vocals), Jon Townend (vocals, guitar), Dave Allen (drums), and Martin Appleby (bass), with the addition of various keyboard players. Initially named Malcolm's Mother, their own Eggs Will Walk label issued an excellent 12" EP in 1986, on which they reworked the traditional 'Cruel Mother'. When Appleby departed, the band recruited Dave Wall. Capturing the atmosphere of 80s urban bleakness, with Townend's oblique, witty political comments, they recorded an album for Special Delivery, and two more noise-folk releases for the modernist label Cooking Vinyl. After *Lip*, which was remixed against the band's wishes, they disbanded. Townend and Swiss retained the band's name, and continue to search for a US label. God's Little Monkeys were always more popular in Canada and Europe than in the UK, so a move abroad may be a sensible decision for this novel unit.

Albums: *Breakfast In Bedlam* (1987), *New Maps Of Hell* (1989), *Lip* (1991).

Goodman, Steve

b. 25 July 1948, Chicago, Illinois, USA, d. 20 September 1984. An engaging singer/songwriter from Chicago, Goodman was a favourite among critics, although his albums rarely achieved the commercial success which reviews suggested they deserved. His first appearance on record came in 1970 on *Gathering At The Earl Of Old Town* an album featuring artists who regularly performed at a Chicago folk club, the Earl Of Old Town, which was run by an enthusiast named Earl Plonk. Released initially on Dunwich Records and later by Mountain Railroad, the album included three tracks by Goodman, 'Right Ball', 'Chicago Bust Rag' (written by Diane Hildebrand) and his classic train song, 'City Of New Orleans'. By 1972, Goodman's talent had been spotted by Kris Kristofferson, who recommended him to Paul Anka. Anka, who was an admirer of Kris Kristofferson, convinced Buddah (the label to which Anka was signed at the time) to also sign Goodman, while Goodman in turn recommended his friend and fellow singer/songwriter, John Prine, to both Anka and Kristofferson, resulting in Atlantic signing Prine. Unfortunately for Goodman, Prine's career took off and Goodman remained a cult figure. He made two excellent albums for Buddah. *Steve Goodman* (which was produced by Kristofferson) included his two best known songs in commercial terms, 'You Never Even Call Me By My Name', which was David Allan Coe's breakthrough country hit in 1975, and 'City Of New Orleans', a 1972 US Top 20 hit for Arlo Guthrie which was also covered by dozens of artists. Recorded in Nashville, the album featured many Area Code 615 musicians including Charlie McCoy and Kenny Buttrey. It was followed by *Somebody Else's Troubles* (produced by Arif Mardin) which featured musicians including David Bromberg, Bob Dylan (under the alias Robert Milkwood Thomas) and members of the Rascals.

Although his album had failed thus far to chart, Goodman quickly secured a new deal with Asylum, a label which specialized in notable singer/songwriters. While his next two self-produced albums, *Jessie's Jig And Other Favourites* (1975) and *Words We Can Dance To* (1976), were minor US hits, 1977's *Say It In Private* (produced by Joel Dorn and including a cover of the Mary Wells classic written by Smokey Robinson, 'Two Lovers'), 1979's *High And Outside* and 1980's *Hot Spot* failed to chart, and his days on major labels ended at this point. By this time, Goodman, who had been suffering from leukemia since the early 70s, was often unwell, but by 1983, he had formed his own record label, Red Pajamas, with the help of his (and Prine's) manager, Al Bunetta. The first album to be released on the label was a live collection covering 10 years of performances by Goodman. *Artistic Hair*'s sleeve pictured him as almost bald, due to the chemotherapy he was receiving in a bid to cure his illness. Soon afterwards came *Affordable Art*, which also included some live tracks and at least one outtake from an Asylum album, and with John Prine guesting. Goodman's final album, *Santa Ana Winds*, on which Emmylou Harris and Kris Kristofferson guested, included two songs he co-wrote with Jim Ibbotson and Jeff Hanna of the Nitty Gritty Dirt Band, 'Face On The Cutting Room Floor' and 'Queen Of The Road', but in September, 1984, he died from kidney and liver failure following a bone marrow transplant operation. In 1985, Red Pajamas Records released a double album *Tribute To Steve Goodman*, on which many paid their musical respects to their late friend, including Prine, Bonnie Raitt, Arlo Guthrie, John Hartford, Bromberg, Richie Havens and the Nitty Gritty Dirt Band. It is highly likely that the largely excellent catalogue of this notable performer will be re-evaluated in the future - while he may not be aware of the posthumous praise he has received, few would regard it as less than well deserved.

Selected albums: *Gathering At The Earl Of Old Town* (1970), *Steve Goodman* (1972), *Somebody Else's Trouble* (1973), *Jessie's Jig And Other Favourites* (1975), *Words We Can Dance To* (1976), *Say It In Private* (1977), *High And Outside* (1979), *Hot Spot* (1980), *Artistic Hair* (1983), *Affordable Art* (80s), *Santa Ana Winds* (80s).

Goulder, Dave

b. John David Goulder 29 June 1939, Greenwich, London, England. Gouder was initially influenced by the steam songs from the American railroad tradition, and writers such as Ewan MacColl and Ralph Vaughan Williams. After a variety of jobs, Goulder started working for the railways in 1954, and a year or so later formed a group with workmates playing and singing in working men's clubs in the north of England. He left the railway in 1961 and moved to Scotland to live and spent the next 10 years running hostels for mountaineers, while occasionally playing folk clubs to supplement his income. Still writing songs, Goulder turned to dry stone walling for a living where he achieved a master craftsman certificate. His surroundings provided inspiration for songs and poems, an interest in nature started by his father, who had been a travelling farmworker for the War Agricultural Department. It was not until Goulder's first tour of the USA, with Gordon Bok, that he began writing seriously again, producing *The Man Who Put The Engine In The Chip Shop* , and a retrospective book of songs, *January Man*. 'January Man' is probably Goulder's most famous song, having been covered by countless performers. His lifelong passion for anything concerning railways continues, even to the extent of including the actual sounds of locomotives and engines on *The Man Who Put The Engine In The Chip Shop*.

Albums: *January Man* i (1969), with Liz Dyer *The Raven And The Crow* (1971), *Requiem For Steam-The Railway Songs Of Dave Goulder* (1973), with Miriam Backhouse, Irvine Hunt and Brian Miller *Fortuna* (1976), *January Man* ii (1986), *The Man Who Put The Engine In The Chip Shop* (1989), *Stone, Steam And Starlings* (1991).

Further reading: *Green All The Way (Songs Of The Steam Age)*, Robbins Music. *January Man*, Robbins Music. *January Man*, Machair Books, Stornoway.

Graham, Davey

b. 22 November 1940, Leicester, England, of Scottish and Guyanese parents. An influential guitarist in British folk circles, Graham's itinerant travels throughout Europe and North Africa resulted in a cosmopolitan and unorthodox repertoire. By the early 60s he was a fixture of the

Davey Graham

London fraternity and his 1961 recording with Alexis Korner, *3/4 A.D.*, showcased his exceptional talent. The EP included the much-feted 'Angie', an evocative instrumental which Paul Simon and Bert Jansch would later cover. *Folk, Blues & Beyond* showcased Graham's eclectic talent, with material drawn from Charles Mingus, Leadbelly, Bob Dylan and Blind Willie Johnson. The expressive instrumental, 'Maajun (A Taste Of Tangier)', emphasized the modal element of Graham's playing and although never more than adequate as a singer, his inspired guitar work was a revelation. *Folk Roots New Routes* was an unlikely collaboration with traditional vocalist Shirley Collins, and while the latter's purity was sometimes at odds with Graham's earthier approach, the album is rightly lauded as a milestone in British folk music. Graham maintained his idiosyncratic style throughout the 60s, experimenting with western and eastern musical styles, but although the respect of his peers was assured, commercial success proved elusive. Drug problems and ill health undermined the artist's progress, but he later re-emerged with two excellent albums for the specialist Kicking Mule outlet. During his latter years, he has resided in west Scotland where he has taught guitar, whilst continuing to perform on the folk club circuit, often performing on double bills with Bert Jansch, and demonstrating his credentials as one of Britain's finest folk-blues guitarists.

Albums: *Guitar Player* (1963), *Folk, Blues & Beyond* (1964), with Shirley Collins *Folk Roots New Routes* (1965), *Midnight Man* (1966), *Large As Life And Twice As Natural* (1968), *Hat* (1969), *Holly Kaleidoscope* (1970), *Godington Boundary* (1970), *Complete Guitarist* (1978), *Dance For Two People* (1979), *Playing In Traffic* (1993). Compilation: *Folk Blues And All Points In Between* (1990).

Grainger, Richard

b. 21 May 1949, Middlesbrough, Cleveland, England. Grainger first played in folk clubs in Teeside at 17 years of age, accompanying himself on guitar. Having worked with several groups, including the Teeside Fettlers, Grainger has written a number of songs that have become well-known on the folk circuit. His songs reflect many of the social problems that have beset the north-east of England. Based in Whitby, North Yorkshire, he travels the UK regularly, working at folk clubs and festivals alike, combining musical talent and dry north-east humour. His recording debut in 1984 was well-received, and he continues to produce quality songs. *Herbs On The Heart* contained a number of Grainger originals, including 'Whitby Whaler'. As a contemporary songwriter, Richard still has a strong feel for traditional song, and this is evident on 'Teeside And Yorkshire'. 'Give Me A Job', from *Darklands* deals with the problem of unemployment, especially prevalent in his region.

Albums: *Herbs On The Heart* (1984), *Darklands* (1989), with Dick Miles *Home Routes* (1990).

Greenbriar Boys

Formed in New York, USA in 1958, the Greenbriar Boys were one of the leading exponents of urban bluegrass. The original line-up comprised John Herald (guitar, lead vocals), Bob Yellin (banjo, tenor vocals) and Eric Weissberg (banjo, mandolin, dobro, fiddle), but in 1959 the latter was replaced by Ralph Rinzler (mandolin, baritone vocals). The following year the group won the top award at the annual Union Grove Fiddler's Convention, while Yellin secured the first of several hits as a solo artist. The Greenbriar Boys completed several excellent albums for the Vanguard label and became a highly popular attraction in the club, concert and festival circuits. Individually the members appeared as session musicians for, among others, Ramblin' Jack Elliott, Joan Baez and Patrick Sky. The trio was later augmented by vocalist Dian Edmondson; this reshaped unit recorded a lone release for Elektra Records. The group then underwent a radical change. Edmondson dropped out of the line-up, while Rinzler left for an administrative post with the Newport Folk Festival committee. Herald and Yellin added Frank Wakefield (mandolin) and Jim Buchanan (fiddle), but the Greenbriars' impetus was waning and the group was officially disbanded in 1966.

Albums: *The Greenbriar Boys* (1962), *Ragged But Right* (early 60s), *Better Late Than Never* (early 60s), *Dian And The Greenbriar Boys* (1964). Compilation: *The Best Of John Herald And The Greenbriar Boys* (1972).

Greenthal, Stanley

b. Stanley Scott Greenthal, 16 April 1949, New York City, New York, USA. Greenthal's family came from England around the time of the Mayflower. His father's family originate from Alsace Lorraine; this combination probably explains his passion for the various musical styles emanating from those areas. Receiving his first guitar at the age of 14, he moved west at the age of 17. He studied English Literature at the University of Colorado, achieving a B.A. By now he was married, but two years later his wife died, and the title track of *Songs For The Journey* was written about the experience. The album includes two exceptional instrumentals, 'January/After Midnight Polkas' and 'Still Untitled'. As well as Stanley on guitar and mandocello the album includes such respected musicians as Kevin Burke, of Patrick

Street (fiddle), and Michael O' Dhomhnaill, of the Bothy Band and Relativity, who also produced the album. In the early 70s, Greenthal was living in southern England, and listened to Irish music a great deal. He also spent time travelling round Scotland, Ireland, Greece and Brittany, and absorbed the many musical influences inherent in the different cultures. *All Roads* continues the Celtic and Balkan themes in the music. Greenthal has played both coasts of the USA, and has performed with Robin Williamson.

Albums: *Songs For The Journey* (1986), *All Roads* (1990).

Gregson And Collister

This UK duo comprised Clive Gregson (b. 4 January 1955, Ashton-Under-Lyne, Manchester, England; guitar/keyboards/vocals), and Christine Collister (b. 28 December 1961, Douglas, Isle Of Man; guitar/percussion/vocals), and were one of the most notable duos working in folk music. Gregson was already known as the writer and prominent front man of the group Any Trouble, with whom he recorded five albums before turning solo. He released *Strange Persuasions* in 1985, and then became a member of the Richard Thompson Band. In addition, he acquired the role of producer on albums by such artists as the Oyster Band, Stephen Fearing and Keith Hancock. Another solo album was released in 1990, *Welcome To The Workhouse*, comprising material that had hitherto been unreleased. Collister had made a living singing

and playing guitar in Italian bars, and as a session singer for Piccadilly Radio in Manchester. She was discovered performing in a local club by Gregson and this led to her place in the Richard Thompson Band, and subsequent position in the duo with Gregson himself. Collister has also provided backing vocals for Loudon Wainwright and Mark Germino. Her warm sensuous vocals were instantly recognizable as the soundtrack to the BBC television series *The Life And Loves Of A She Devil*. Gregson's lyrical ability and harmonies, together with Collister's unmistakable vocal style produced a number of critically acclaimed albums. The duo toured extensively throughout the UK, USA and Canada, and also played in Japan and Europe. In 1990 they completed their first tour of Australia. In March 1992 they began a farewell tour. Later that year, Collister worked with Barb Jungr (of Jungr And Parker) and Heather Joyce in a part-time unit, the Jailbirds.

Albums: *Home And Away* (1986), *Mischief* (1987), *A Change In The Weather* (1989), *Love Is A Strange Hotel* (1990), *The Last Word* (1992).

Grey, Sara

b. Sara Lee Grey, 22 March 1940, Boston, Massachussetts, USA. Playing banjo, dulcimer and autoharp, Grey is a well qualified performer and folklorist. Between 1958 and 1968, she studied theatre arts and music, achieving a B.F.A. Degree with honours in theatre arts and speech. She also studied for Masters degrees in theatre arts and

Gregson And Collister

folklore. Her career combined acting and teaching, but she spent the period between 1967 and 1970 travelling the USA, collecting and performing traditional North American and British ballads and songs. An exponent of 'Old Time Banjo', of frailing, Grey has toured many countries, and has featured on television and radio. She recorded a number of albums with Ellie Ellis - they also appeared on the Fellside Records sampler *Flash Company* (1987) - but personal plans and the desire to work on new material and projects meant that the partnership ended. Sara has a light, laid back vocal style which she accompanies with an equally gentle playing style on the banjo. She is also a member of the Lost Nation Band, which featured Roger Wilson and Brian Peters. Peters left in 1992 and was replaced by Dave Burland.
Albums: *Sara Grey With Ed Trickett* (1970), *Five Days Singing Vol. 1 & 2* (1971), with Ellie Ellis *A Breath Of Fresh Air* (1981), with Ellis *Making The Air Resound* (1984), with Ellis *You Gave Me A Song* (1987), *Promises To Keep* (1990).

Griffith, Nanci

b. 6 July, 1953, Seguin, Texas, USA. Singer and songwriter Griffiths straddles the boundary between folk and country music, with occasional nods to the mainstream rock audience. Her mother was an amateur actress and her father a member of a barbershop quartet. They passed on their interest in performance to Nanci, and although she majored in education at the University of Texas, she eventually chose a career in music in 1977, by which time she had been performing in public for 10 years. In 1978 her first album, *There's A Light Beyond These Woods*, was released by a local company, BF Deal Records. Recorded live in a studio in Austin, it included mainly her own compositions, along with 'Dollar Matinee', written by her erstwhile husband, Eric Taylor. The major song on the album was the title track, which Griffiths later re-recorded, concerning the dreams she shared with her childhood friend, Mary Margaret Graham, of the bigger world outside Texas. As a souvenir of her folk act of the time, this album was adequate, but it was not until 1982 that *Poet In My Window* was released by another local label, Featherbed Records. Like its predecessor, this album was re-released in 1986 by the nationally-distributed Philo/Rounder label. It displayed a pleasing maturity in composition, the only song included which she had not composed being 'Tonight I Think I'm Gonna Go Downtown' penned by Jimmie Gilmore and John Reed, (once again, Eric Taylor was involved as associated producer/bass player), while the barbershop quartet in which her father, Marlin Griffiths sang provided harmony vocals on 'Wheels'.

By 1984 she had met Jim Rooney, who produced her third album, *Once In A Very Blue Moon*, released in 1985 by Philo/Rounder. This album featured such notable backing musicians as lead guitarist Phillip Donnelly, banjo wizard Bela Fleck, Lloyd Green and Mark O'Connor. It was recorded at Jack Clement's Nashville studio. As well as more of her own songs, the album included her version of Lyle Lovett's 'If I Was The Woman You Wanted', Richard Dobson's 'Ballad Of Robin Wintersmith' and the superb title track written by Pat Alger - Griffiths named the backing band she formed in 1986 the Blue Moon Orchestra. Following on the heels of this artistic triumph came 1986's *Last Of The True Believers*. Released by Philo/Rounder with a similar recipe to that which set its predecessor apart from run of the mill albums by singer/songwriters, it included two songs which would later achieve US country chart celebrity as covered by Kathy Maltea, Griffith's own 'Love At The Five And Dime' and Pat Alger's 'Goin' Gone', as well as several other songs which would become Griffith classics, including the title track, 'The Wing And The Wheel' (after which Griffiths formed her music publishing company), 'More Than A Whisper' and 'Lookin' For The Time (Working Girl)', plus the fine Tom Russell song 'St. Olav's Gate'. This album became Griffith's first to be released in the UK when it was licensed by Demon Records around the time that Griffith was signed by MCA Records. Her debut album for her new label, *Lone Star State Of Mind*, was released in 1987, and was produced by MCA's golden-fingered Tony Brown, who had been the most active A&R person in Nashville in signing new talent, including Steve Earle and Lyle Lovett as well as Griffith herself, who co-produced it. The stunning title track again involved Alger as writer, while other notable tracks included the remake of 'There's A Light Beyond These Woods' from the first album, Robert Earl Keen Jnr.'s 'Sing One For Sister' and Griffith's own 'Ford Econoline' (about the independence of 60s folk singer Rosalie Sorrels). However, attracting most attention was Julie Gold's 'From A Distance', a song which had become a standard by the 90s as covered by Bette Midler, Cliff Richard and many others. Griffith herself published the song, and her version was the first major exposure given to the song. *Little Love Affairs*, released in 1988, was supposedly a concept album but major songs included 'Outbound Plane', which she co-wrote with Tom Russell, veteran hit writer Harlan Howard's '(My Best Pal's In Nashville) Never Mind' and John Stewart's 'Sweet Dreams Will Come', as well as a couple of collaborations with James Hooker (ex-Amazing Rhythm Aces), and keyboard player of the Blue Moon Orchestra. Later that year Griffith recorded and released a live album, *One Fair Summer Evening*, recorded at Houston's Anderson Fair Retail Restaurant. Although it only included a handful of songs which she had not previously recorded, it was at least as good as *Little Love Affairs*, and was accompanied by a live video. However, it seemed that Griffiths' talent was falling between the rock and country audiences, the latter apparently finding her voice insufficiently radio-friendly, while Kathy Mattea, who recorded many of the same song some time after Griffith, became a major star.

In 1989 came *Storms*, produced by the legendary Glyn Johns, who had worked with the Beatles, the Rolling Stones, the Eagles, Steve Miller, the Who, Joan Armatrading and many more. Johns made an album with a bias towards American radio, which became Griffiths' biggest seller at that point. The album featured as well as Hooker, Irish drummer Bran Breen (ex-Moving Hearts), Bernie Leadon (ex-Eagles), guitarist Albert Lee and Phil Everly of the Everly Brothers providing harmony vocals on 'You Made This Love A Teardrop'. Although it was a sales breakthrough for Griffiths, it failed to attract country audiences. although it reached the Top 40 of the pop albums chart in the UK, where she had regularly toured since 1987. But her major European market was Ireland, where she was regarded as virtually a superstar. 1991's *Late Night Grande Hotel* was produced by the British team of Rod Argent and Peter Van Hook, and again included a duet with Phil Everly on 'It's Just Another Morning Here', while English singer Tanita Tikaram provided a guest vocal on 'It's Too Late'. In 1991, singing 'The Wexford Carol', she was one of a number of artists who contributed tracks to the Chieftains *The Bells Of Dublin*.

In 1993, Nanci Griffiths is poised to either finally break into the big time as a Carly Simon-type figure, or to retreat to (substantial) cult status. It will be fascinating for her many European fans to discover which direction she will choose.

Albums: *There's A Light Beyond These Woods* (1978), *Poet In My Window* (1982), *Once In A Very Blue Moon* (1984), *Last Of The True Believers* (1986), *Lone Star State Of Mind* (1987), *Little Love Affairs* (1988), *One Fair Summer Evening* (1988), *Storms* (1989), *Late Night Grande Hotel* (1991), *Other Voices Other Rooms* (1993).

Grisman, David

An accomplished mandolinist, Grisman forged his reputation on the mid-60s US bluegrass circuit as a member of several New York-based attractions, including the Washington Square Ramblers, the Galaxy Mountain Boys and the Even Dozen Jug Band. In 1966 Grisman joined Red Allen and the Kentuckians, but the following year teamed with fellow enthusiast and songwriter Peter Rowan in the Boston rock act, Earth Opera. This fascinating unit completed two albums, after which Grisman moved to San Francisco where he renewed an acquaintance with Grateful Dead guitarist Jerry Garcia. The mandolinist contributed to the group's stellar *American Beauty* before participating in several informal aggregations, notably Muleskinner, Old And In The Way and the Great American String Band. Grisman then recorded as a solo act, and as leader of the David Grisman Quartet, which initially included Tony Rice (guitar), Darol Anger (fiddle) and Todd Phillips and/or Bill Amatneck (bass). The group pursued a hybrid of jazz and bluegrass, dubbed 'Dawg Music', and remained a highly inventive attraction despite a plethora of line-up changes. Grisman's reputation within America's traditional music fraternity increased throughout the 70s and 80s. He built a recording studio at his Mill Valley home and in 1990 founded the Acoustic Disc label. An early release, *Dawg 90*, received a Grammy nomination in the country instrumental category, and was followed in 1991 by a further collaboration with longtime associate Jerry Garcia.

Albums: *The David Grisman Album* (1976), *The David Grisman Quintet* (1977), *Hot Dawg* (1979), *David Grisman And John Sholle* (1979), *Quintet: 80* (1980), with Stéphane Grappelli *Live* (1980), *Mando Mondo* (1981), *Here Today* (1982), *Dawg Jazz - Dawg Grass* (1983), *Acoustic Christmas* (1983), with Andy Statman *Mandolin Abstractions* (1983), *Home Is Where The Heart Is* (1988), *Dawg 90* (1990). Compilations: *Early Dawg* (1980).

Grossman, Stefan

b. 16 April 1945, Brooklyn, New York, USA. Grossman discovered traditional music during his forays into Manhattan's Greenwich Village. He studied under Rev. Gary Davis and absorbed the country-blues technique of Son House, Mississippi John Hurt and Skip James before forming the influential Even Dozen Jug Band in 1963. Three years later Grossman recorded an instruction record, *How To Play Blues Guitar*, and was working with the Fugs, a radical East Side poet/bohemian group. Stefan also played with the Chicago Loop, which featured pianist Barry Goldberg, prior to leaving for Europe in 1967. He remained in Italy and Britain for many years, recording a succession of impressive, if clinical country blues albums. A superb guitarist, his work is best heard on *Yazoo Basin Boogie* and *Hot Dogs*, while further tuition albums provided valuable insights into the rudiments of different techniques. In the late 70s Grossman helped establish the

Kicking Mule label which acted as a channel for his own releases and those working in a similar vein.

Albums: *How To Play Blues Guitar* (1966), *Aunt Molly's Murray Farm* (1969), *Grammercy Park Sheik* (1969), with Danny Kalb *Crosscurrents* (1969), *Yazoo Basin Boogie* (1970), *Ragtime Cowboy Jew* (1970), *Those Pleasant Days* (1971), *Hot Dogs* (1972), *Stefan Grossman Live* (1973), *Memphis Jellyroll* (1974), *Bottleneck Seranade* (1975), *How To Play Ragtime Guitar* (1975), *My Creole Belle* (1976), *Country Blues Guitar* (1977), *Fingerpicking Guitar Techniques* (1977), *How To Play Blues Guitar, Volume 2* (1978), *Stefan Grossman And John Renbourn* (1978), with John Renbourn *Under The Volcano* (1980), *Thunder On The Run* (1980), *Shining Shadows* (1988).

Gryphon

Originally called Spellthorn, Gryphon were formed in 1971 by Royal College of Music students Richard Harvey (b. 25 September 1953, Enfield, Middlesex, England; keyboards, woodwinds, mandolin) and Brian Gulland (b. 30 April 1951, Maidstone, Kent, England; renaissance wind instruments, bassoon, keyboards, vocals). Harvey had eschewed an offer to join the London Philharmonia Orchestra in order to pursue his vision of a blend of medieval music and progressive rock. The group had also comprised Graeme Taylor (b. 2 February 1954, Stockwell, London, England; guitar, keyboards, recorder) and David Oberlé (b. 9 January 1953, Farnborough, Kent, England; drums, percussion, flageolet, vocals). Gryphon started their career playing folk clubs, moving on to the usual rock venues and colleges, in addition to performing at special events such as the Victoria & Albert Museum. Their style made the group unique on the UK rock scene in the early 70s, with Gulland's Crumhorn solos making a refreshing change from the usually guitar sound of the day. By 1973 they were performing a mixture of minstrel airs and Beatles songs, and even a version of 'Chattanooga Choo Choo'. With the addition of a bassist, Philip Nestor (b. 1952, Epsom, Surrey, England), Gryphon were, by the time of *Midnight Mushrumps*, performing a lengthy composition, commissioned by Peter Hall of the London National Theatre, and moving into a more traditional rock style. By 1975 the group had joined Yes on a tour of the USA and Gryphon's line-up began to suffered various personnel changes. Taylor had left the group that year (later to join Home Service) and was replaced by Bob Foster; Alex Baird, formally of Contraband, was added as a drummer; and Malcolm Bennett, who had replaced Nestor was, in turn supplanted by Jonathan Davie. Very soon the group had begun to lose its sense of originality, becoming just another rock band and subsequently broke up in the face of the emerging punk rock explosion.

Richard Harvey moved into the very lucrative field of commercial jingles and television soundtracks, most notably with the collaboration with Elvis Costello for Alan Bleasdale's *G.B.H.* television play

Albums: *Gryphon* (1973), *Midnight Mushrumps* (1974), *Red Queen To Gryphon Three* (1974), *Raindance* (1975), *Treason* (1977). Compilation: *The Collection* (1991). Solo album: Richard Harvey *Divisions On A Ground* (1975), with Stanley Myers *L'Amant De Lady Chatterley* (1981), with Elvis Costello *G.B.H.* (1991).

Guillory, Isaac

Born in Cuba c.1950, and later domiciled in the north east of England, Guillory is a seasoned session guitarist on both sides of the Atlantic. In 1974 he recorded his first solo instrumental album, *Isaac Guillory*, and subsequently became a member of the jazz influenced, Pacific Eardrum from 1977-78. *Solo*, recorded in the mid-70s, was initially issued by CBS in Holland, and released in the UK some five years later. In the studio he has worked with such artists as Al Stewart, Elkie Brooks, and John Renbourn, with whom he played a series of highly successful British concerts. A highly skilled musician, Guillory's recorded output remains disappointingly small.

Albums: *Isaac Guillory* (1974), *Solo* (1980).

Guthrie, Arlo

b. 10 July 1947, Coney Island, New York, USA. The eldest son of folksinger Woody Guthrie, Arlo was raised in the genre's thriving environment. His lengthy ballad, 'Alice's Restaurant Massacre', part humorous song, part narrative, achieved popularity following the artist's appearance at the 1967 Newport Folk Festival. The composition became the cornerstone of Arlo's debut album, and inspired a feature film, but the attendant publicity obscured the performer's gifts for melody. An early song, 'Highway In The Wind', was successfully covered by Hearts And Flowers as Arlo emerged from under the shadow of his father. *Running Down The Road*, produced by Van Dyke Parks, indicated a newfound maturity, but his talent truly flourished on a series of excellent 70s recordings, notably *Hobo's Lullaby*, *Last Of The Brooklyn Cowboys*, and *Amigo*. Although offering a distillation of traditional music - wedding folk and country to ragtime, blues and Latin - such recordings nonetheless addressed contemporary concerns. 'Presidential Rag' was a vitriolic commentary on Watergate and 'Children Of Abraham' addressed the Arab/Israeli conflict. The singer enjoyed a US Top 20 hit with a reading of Steve Goodman's 'City Of New Orleans' (1972) and, if now less prolific, Arlo Guthrie remains a popular figure on the folk circuit.

Albums: *Alice's Restaurant* (1967), *Arlo* (1968), *Running Down The Road* (1969), *Alice's Restaurant* (1969, film soundtrack), *Washington County* (1970), *Hobo's Lullaby* (1972), *Last Of The Brooklyn Cowboys* (1973), *Arlo Guthrie* (1974), with Pete Seeger *Together In Concert* (1975), *Amigo* (1976), *Outlasting The Blues* (1979), *Power Of Love* (1981). Compilations: *Arlo Guthrie* (1972), *The Best Of Arlo Guthrie* (1977).

Guthrie, Woody

b. Woodrow Wilson Guthrie, 14 July 1912, Okemah, Oklahoma, USA, d. 3 October 1967. A major figure of America's folk heritage, Guthrie was raised in a musical environment and achieved proficiency on harmonica as a child. By the age of 16 he had begun his itinerant lifestyle, performing in a Texas-based magic show where he learned to play guitar. In 1935 Guthrie moved to California where he became a regular attraction on Los Angeles' KFVD radio station. Having befriended singer Cisco Houston and actor Will Geer, Woody established his left wing-oriented credentials with joint appearances at union meetings and migrant labour camps. Already a prolific songwriter, reactions to the poverty he witnessed inspired several of his finest compositions, notably 'Pastures Of Plenty', 'Dust Bowl Refugees', 'Vigilante Man'

and 'This Land Is Your Land', regarded by many as America's 'alternative' national anthem. Guthrie was also an enthusiastic proponent of Roosevelt's 'New Deal', as demonstrated by 'Grand Coolie Dam' and 'Roll On Columbia', while his children's songs, including 'Car Car', were both simple and charming. At the end of the 30s Woody travelled to New York where he undertook a series of recordings for the folk song archive at the Library Of Congress. The 12 discs he completed were later released commercially by Elektra Records.

Guthrie continued to traverse the country and in 1940 met Pete Seeger at a folksong rally in California. Together they formed the Almanac Singers with Lee Hayes and Millard Lampell which in turn inspired the Almanac House, a co-operative apartment in New York's Greenwich Village which became the focus of the east coast folk movement. In 1942 Guthrie joined the short-lived Headline Singers with Leadbelly, Sonny Terry and Brownie McGhee, before beginning his autobiography, *Bound For Glory*, which was published the following year. He and Houston then enlisted in the merchant marines, where they remained until the end of World War II, after which Guthrie began a series of exemplary recordings for the newly-founded Folkways label. The artist eventually completed over 200 masters which provided the fledgling company with a secure foundation.

Arlo Guthrie

Woody Guthrie

Further sessions were undertaken for other outlets, while Woody retained his commitment to the union movement through columns for the *Daily Worker* and *People's World*. Guthrie's prolific output - he conscientiously composed each day - continued unabated until the end of the 40s when he succumbed to Huntington's Chorea, a hereditary, degenerative disease of the nerves. He was hospitalized in 1952, and was gradually immobilized by this wasting illness until he could barely talk or recognize friends and visitors. By the time of his death on 3 October 1967, Woody Guthrie was enshrined in America's folklore, not just because of his own achievements, but through his considerable influence on a new generation of artists. Bob Dylan, Ramblin' Jack Elliott, Roger McGuinn and Woody's son Arlo Guthrie were among his most obvious disciples, but the plethora of performers, including Judy Collins, Tom Paxton, Richie Havens and Country Joe McDonald, gathered at two subsequent tribute concerts, confirmed their debt to this pivotal figure.

Compilations: *Library Of Congress Recordings* (1964, released on CD in 1989 - 1940 recordings), *Dust Bowl Ballads* (1964, released CD issued in 1989 - 1940 recordings), *This Land Is Your Land* (1967), *Bound For Glory* (1958), *Sacco & Vanzetti* (1960), *Songs To Grow On* (1973), *Struggle* (1976), *A Legendary Performer* (1977), *Poor Boy* (1981), *Columbia River Collection* (1988), *Folkways: The Original Vision* (1989).

Further reading: *Bound For Glory*, Woody Guthrie. *Born To Win*, edited by Robert Shelton. *Woody Guthrie - A Life*, Joe Klein.

Gwendal

Formed in Brittany in 1973, this folk group recorded acoustic albums of Celtic material before *Gwendal 3*, and subsequently switched to an 'electric' lineup. The latter featured Bruno Barre (violin), Youenn Le Berre (flute), Jean Marie Renard (guitar), Roger Schaub (bass), Ricky Caust (guitar) and Armand Rogers (drums). For *Gwendal 4* they merged Celtic tunes with rock, jazz and reggae. In 1982, constant changes in personnel resulted in the recruitment Robert Le Gall (fiddle, guitar). He and Le Berre now form the core of the group; both write and decide on the musical direction. *Glen River* is a pleasing, swinging collection with the overtones of a pure folk jig. They made their British debut at Nottingham in May 1993.

Selected albums: *Gwendal 3* (1978), *Gwendal 4* (1979), *Glen River* (1990).

H

Hall, Robin, And Jimmie MacGregor

This well known folk duo from Scotland featured Hall (b. 27 June 1937, Edinburgh, Scotland; vocals/bodhran), and MacGregor (b. 10 March 1930, Springburn, Glasgow, Scotland; vocals/guitar). Hall had studied at the Royal Scottish Academy Of Music And Dramatic Art from 1955-58. There followed a brief spell as an actor in repertory theatres, plus some solo gigs and radio work. He met and teamed up with MacGregor at the World Youth Festival in Vienna. In contrast, MacGregor came from a working-class family, and was involved in the folk revival of the 50s. He learned a great number of songs at the famous house parties that took place at the time, with everyone singing and harmonizing. Jimmie's first influences were not Scottish at all, but Burl Ives and black American blues man Josh White. MacGregor built up a repertoire of Ives songs with the first guitar he bought. His next big influence was Ewan MacColl and 'Ballads And Blues'. Jimmie graduated after four years at art school, and worked as a studio potter and a teacher. He often hitch-hiked to London to visit what few folk clubs there were at the time. Eventually, he settled in London. He joined Chas McDevvitt's skiffle group, but left a few weeks before they had the hit record 'Freight Train'. Then followed a series of solo performances and membership of various groups, including the Steve Benbow Folk Four. After meeting Hall in Vienna, the two were given much encouragement by Paul Robeson who was playing at the same concert. Hall's solo album of child ballads from the Gavin Greig collection, *Last Leaves Of Traditional Ballads*, is now a collector's item. The duo were popular on television, making their first appearance on BBC's *Tonight*, and appeared five nights weekly for 14 years. In 1960, Decca released the single 'Football Crazy', which received a great deal of airplay and attendant publicity. Hall and MacGregor also appeared regularly on radio, and are remembered for the series *Hullabaloo*, which started on 28 September 1963, on ABC television. They went on to tour the world, and record more than 20 albums, and appear in countless radio and television programmes. One series they became known for was *The White Heather Club*, which they hosted for five years. After 21 years together, it was Hall who called a halt to the duo's career. He had always been nervous and had never really liked performing. After the split, Hall went into

Robin Hall And Jimmie MacGregor

broadcasting for the BBC World Service, as well as writing, arranging and producing records. In addition to scriptwriting, he also took up journalism as a music and drama critic. In 1977, he won two national radio awards, as best presenter and best documentary, for a documentary on Radio Clyde *The Sing Song Streets*, a programme about Glasgow told through songs, stories and children's games. The programme was written, produced and presented by Hall. MacGregor wrote three folk song books, did some solo work, and wrote a book on the West Highland Way, which became the basis of a successful television series. Subsequently,he has made six outdoor television series, and written five accompanying books. His own radio show for BBC Scotland, *MacGregor's Gathering*, has been running now for many years.

Selected albums: Robin Hall *Last Leaves Of Traditional Ballads* (1959), the Galliards *Scottish Choice* (1961), the Galliards *A Rovin'* (1961), *Scotch And Irish* (1962), *Tonight And Every Night* (1962), *Two Heids Are Better Than Yin* (1963), the Galliards *The Next Tonight Will Be-Robin Hall And Jimmie MacGregor* (1964), *By Public Demand* (1964), *The Red Yo-Yo* (1966), *Songs Of Grief And Glory* (1967), *One Over Eight* (1969), *We Belong To Glasgow* (1970), *Kids Stuff* (1974), *Scotland's Best* (1975), *Songs For Scotland* (1977).

Hallom, Gerry

b. 24 December 1950, Richmond, Surrey, England. Hallom has become known for his interpretations of traditional Autralian songs, as well as his own compositions. Spending some of his earlier years in Australia, Hallom began playing clubs, festivals and concerts in 1974. It was as a songwriter that he turned to re-workings of Australian themes from original tunes. He moved back to Britain in 1979. *Travellin' Down The Castlereagh* was well received by the popular press and the *Guardian* described it as the 'best debut album in years'. This was followed in 1982 by US and Canadian tours, culminating in appearances at the Philadelphia and Vancouver festivals. The follow-up, *A Run A Minute*, included the Ewan MacColl song 'My Old Man', and featured backing from Jez Lowe and Chris Coe among others. From 1984 to 1987, Hallom studied for a degree and apart from occasional club appearances, and continuing with songwriting, now lectures in sociology in York. For *Old Australian Ways*, Gerry coaxed Nic Jones back into the limelight, by getting him to provide backing vocals on the album. It also featured the work of a number of Australian writers set to tunes by Hallom.

Albums: *Travellin' Down The Castlereagh* (1981), *A Run A Minute* (1984), *Old Australian Ways* (1989).

Halpin, Kieran

b. Co. Louth, Eire. Halpin enjoyed a good deal of success during the early 80s. He had begun playing at the age of 15 and after an early apprenticeship in Europe and Britain, he teamed up with Tom McConville (b. Newcastle Upon Tyne, England; violin/vocals) in 1979. After two albums, and an appearance at the 1981 Cambridge Folk Festival, they split in 1982. McConville went on to join Dab Hand with Tom Napper (b. England; banjo/cittern/vocals), while Halpin went back to Dublin. Halpin has appeared at the Fairport Convention festival in Cropredy, Oxfordshire, and other folk festivals both at home and abroad. *The Man Who Lived In Bottles* was Halpin's first solo release after the split with McConville. Having kept a somewhat low profile during the late 80s, apparently due to contractual difficulties, Halpin re-emerged on a new label, Round Tower Music, for *Mission Street*. On this release he was backed by performers of the quality of Davy Spillane, and Martin Allcock of Fairport Convention. Always a writer of quality songs, *Mission Street* did not quite live up to the high standards set by earlier releases.

Albums: with Tom McConville *Port Of Call* (1981), *The Man Who Lived In Bottles* (1983), with Tom McConville *Streets Of Everywhere* (1983), *Live And Kicking* (c.1985), *Crystal Ball Gazing* (c.1987), *Mission Street* (1991).

Hamill, Claire

b. Josephine Clare Hamill, 4 August 1954, Port Clarence, Middlesbrough, Cleveland, England. This 70s singer songwriter played the folk circuit and recorded a number of relatively successful albums. Her first release, *One House Left Standing* (1971), on Island Records included John Martyn on guitar. Her 1973 album, *October*, was produced by Paul Samwell-Smith. Hamill toured the folk circuit extensively to promote the recordings, gradually moving into the rock arena. This included tours supporting King Crimson, Procol Harum and Jethro Tull. In 1975, she spent four months touring in the USA, only returning to the UK to fulfil contractual obligations. Between 1975 and 1984 she stopped recording and formed a series of bands, gradually moving into writing for groups such as Wishbone Ash, with whom she toured. She also played on sessions for Steve Howe and Jon And Vangelis. Her initial promise was not realized commercially, and she gradually disappeared from the folk scene. The highly original, *Voices* (1986), was made up entirely of Hamill's multi-tracked voice and was released on her husband's Coda record label. She has subsequently enjoyed considerable success as a new age artist.

Albums: *One House Left Standing* (1971), *October*

Kieran Halpin

Claire Hamill

(1973), *Stage Door Johnnies* (1974), *Abracadabra* (1975), *Touchpaper* (1984), *Voices* (1986), *Love In The Afternoon* (1988).

Hancock, Keith

b. 28 October 1953, Audenshaw, Lancashire, England. Hancock started his musical life playing for Morris Dance sides while his father was the lead banjo player with the Manchester Kentucky Minstrels. After moving from his native nort west to the east coast, Hancock joined the Grimsby Morris Men in 1975. He later returned to Manchester and played with various folk bands until forming a duo with his wife Janet. Hancock became a full-time performer in 1983. His debut, *This World We Live In* included 'Chase The Dragon', a Hancock original about drug addiction. The song was made popular by Clive Gregson who also produced the album. Hancock was able to combine a solo career with playing for the Electropathic Battery Band, later to become the Electropathics ,but left in 1987 after the band had recorded *Batteries Not Included*. In 1988, *Madhouse* was released, again produced by Gregson, who played on the record. The track 'Headline News' took a swipe at the UK gutter press, and the Gregson production style is evident. On record, Hancock borders on the edge of rock music in style without losing sight of his folk roots. In 1990, he assembled the Keith Hancock Band, consisting of Martin Carthy, Dave Swarbrick, and Ruari McFarlane (b. Rory McFarlane, 24 September 1959, Taplow, Slough, Buckinghamshire, England; bass).

Albums: *This World We Live In* (1986), with the Electropathics *Batteries Not Included* (1987), with the Triffids *Calenture* (1987), with various artists *The Children In Need Album* (1987), with various artists *Squires Fancy* (1988), *Madhouse* (1988), with various artists *Choices, Rights And Liberties* (1989), with various artists *Hard Cash* (1990), with various artists *The Circle Dance* (1990).

Handle, Johnny

b. John Alan Pandrich, 15 March 1935, Wallsend On Tyne, Newcastle, England. Handle specializes in music and song from the northeast of England. Having been evacuated during World War II, he returned to complete his education in Newcastle before leaving, in 1952, to work in coal mining. Having had piano lessons from the age of eight, Handle found himself with a wide-ranging taste in music. Following a meeting with Louis Killen in 1957, they teamed up for a while to play blues and skiffle.He started playing folk music in 1958, and started Newcastle's first folk club and in 1961 initiated a new venue at Stockton-on-Tees. Handle studied folk archives and started to introduce songs that he found into his performances and recorded a number of EPs for Topic Records in 1961. These were later released as the album *Along The Coaly Tyne*. In 1964, he formed the High Level Ranters with Colin Ross (b. England; fiddle) and Jim Hall (b. Gateshead, Tyne and Wear, England; Northumbrian small pipes), but continued to pursue his solo interests. *The Collier Lad* included the much covered 'The Old Pubs'. Handle has been involved with radio documentaries, as well as lecturing on folk music. He has played all the major folk festivals in the UK and has toured both Europe and the USA.

Albums: *Stottin' Doon The Wall* (c.60s), *Northumberland For Ever* (1968), *Ranting Lads* (c.60s), *The Bonnie Pit Laddie* (c.70s), *Four In A Bar* (c.70s), *Tommy Armstrong* (c.70s), *Along The Coaly Tyne* (c.70s), *Canny Newcassel* (c.70s), *The Collier Lad* (1975), *She's A Big Lass* (1979), *Border Spirit* (c.80s), with the High Level Ranters *Gateshead Revisited* (1990), *Handle With Care* (1990).

Hanly, Mick

An Irish singer-songwriter, raised in Limerick, Hanly was inspired by mid-50s rock 'n' roll before he became more interested in folk in the 60s. After performing Woody Guthrie songs in his spare time, in the late 60s and early 70s he turned to the Irish traditional music of his youth. Together with Michael O'Domhnaill, he formed Monroe, and supported Planxty on their 1973 tour, and released *Folk Weave*, before O'Domhnaill left for the Bothy Band in 1975. Hanly went to France for two years, and, on his return to Ireland, recorded two acclaimed solo albums with Donal Lunny, Andy Irvine and Declan Sinnott. He then toured Ireland and Europe with Irvine, who had recently left Planxty. In 1981, Hanly joined Moving Hearts as a vocalist, and contributed his own songs to *Live Hearts*. After the demise, in 1985, of one of Ireland's most successful and innovative traditional bands, he went solo again, and moved towards country music. His songs were covered by Christy Moore, Mary Black and a young American country singer, Hal Ketchum, who took Hanly's 'Past The Point Of Rescue' into the top 10 of the US country chart in 1993.

Selected albums: solo *A Kiss In The Morning Early* (1977), *As I Went Over Blackwater* (c70s), *Warts and All* (1993), as Monroe *Folk Weave* (1974), with Moving Hearts *Live Hearts* (1983).

Hardin, Tim

b. 23 December 1941, Eugene, Oregon, USA, d. 29 December 1980. Hardin arrived in New York following a tour of duty with the US Marines. He

Tim Hardin

initially studied acting, but dropped out of classes to develop his singing and songwriting talent. By 1964 he was appearing regularly in New York's Greenwich Village cafés, where he forged a unique blend of poetic folk/blues. Hardin's first recordings were made in 1964 although the results of this traditional-based session were shelved for several years and were only issued, as *This Is Tim Hardin*, in the wake of the singer's commercial success. His debut album, *Tim Hardin 1*, was a deeply poignant affair, wherein Tim's frail, weary intonation added intrigue to several magnificent compositions, including 'Don't Make Promises', 'Misty Roses' (sensitively covered by Colin Blunstone) and 'Hang On To A Dream' (which became a regular part of the Nice's live performances) as well as the much-covered 'Reason To Believe'. *Tim Hardin 2*, featured his original version of 'If I Were A Carpenter', an international hit in the hands of Bobby Darin and the Four Tops, which confirmed Hardin's position as a writer of note. However the artist was deeply disappointed with these releases and reportedly broke down upon hearing the finished master to his first selection. Tim's career then faltered on private and professional difficulties. As early as 1970 Hardin had alcohol and drug problems. A live album, *Tim Hardin 3*, was followed by a fourth set featuring lesser material recorded at the same performance. A conceptual work, *Suite For Susan Moore And Damion* reclaimed something of his former fire but his gifts seemed to desert him following its release. Hardin's high standing as a songwriter has resulted in his work being interpreted by a plethora of artists over the past four decades, including Wilson Phillips and Rod Stewart ('Reason to Believe') and Scott Walker ('Lady Came From Baltimore'). As Hardin's own songs grew less incisive, he began interpreting the work of other songwriters, including Leonard Cohen, but his resigned delivery, once so alluring, now seemed maudlin. Beset by heroin addiction, his remaining work is a ghost of that early excellence. Tim Hardin died, almost forgotten and totally underrated, in December 1980 of a heroin overdose.
Albums: *Tim Hardin 1* (1966), *Tim Hardin 2* (1967), *Tim Hardin 3 Live In Concert* (1968), *Tim Hardin 4* (1969), *Suite For Susan Moore And Damion/We Are - One, One, All In One* (1969), *Bird On A Wire* (1971), *Painted Head* (1973), *Nine* (1974), *The Shock Of Grace* (1981), *The Homecoming Concert* (1982). Compilations: *Best Of Tim Hardin* (1969), *Memorial Album* (1982).

Harding, Mike

b. 23 October 1946, Manchester, England. Harding started performing in skiffle groups and rock bands from the age of 14.including the Irk Valley Stompers and the Stylos. The latter group played all over the midlands and north of England. From there he moved into the folk arena, initially with the Edison Bell Spasm Band, and then solo. He had a natural ability for telling jokes and stories, and travelled the world entertaining British troops, before recording the spoof song 'Rochdale Cowboy', which made the UK Top 30 in 1975. As a result he appeared on BBC television's *Top Of The Pops*, sitting on a stuffed Alsatian dog. He subsequently hosted his own series *The Mike Harding Show* on BBC Television. *One Man Show*, on PhonoGram Records, achieved a silver disc. His humorous stage act proved to be as popular as ever, as evidenced by his sell-out date 'One Night Stand' tour of Britain, in 1987. Harding also showed his serious side with the release of *Bombers Moon,* and *Plutonium Alley.* Harding has also written soundtracks for film and television, such as the cartoon series *Dangermouse* and *Duckula.* He also provided a film score for *The Reluctant Dragon* which won a BAFTA award *,The Fool Of The World And His Flying Ship*, which, won awards in both Chicago and Los Angeles for the best children's film and was nominated for an Emmy . His book, *Walking The Dales*, was one of the best sellers of 1986. Among the many television series ,*The Harding Trail* saw him cycling along the Appalachian trail in the USA, meeting people and looking at the differing types of music from state to state. Harding has produced numerous books, often with a humorous slant, such as *When The Martian's Landed In Huddersfield*, which also topped the best seller lists. Although Harding continues to tour every two or three years, and record on his own Moonraker Music label, he is also very involved in conservation, having been president of the UK Ramblers Association for three years.
Albums: *A Lancashire Lad* (1972), *One Man Show* (1976), *Mrs 'Ardin's Kid* (1977), *Captain Paralytic And The Brown Ale Cowboys* (1978), *On The Touchline* (1979), *Komic Kutz* (1979), *Red Specs Album* (1981), *Mike Harding's Back* (1982), *Take Your Fingers Off It* (1982), *Rooted!* (1983), *Flat Dogs And Shaky Pudden* (1983), *Bombers Moon* (1984), *Roll Over Cecil Sharpe* (1985), *Foo Foo Shufflewick And Her Exotic Banana* (1987), *Plutonium Alley* (1989), *God's Own Drunk* (1989). Compilations: *Best Of Mike Harding* (1986), *Best Of Mike Harding 2* (1986), *Classic Tracks Vol. 1* (1992).
Further reading: *Napoleon's Retreat From Wigan* (1976), *The Unluckiest Man In The World* (1979), *The 14lb Budgie* (1980), *The Armchair Anarchist's Almanac* (1981), *Killer Budgies* (1983), *When The Martians Landed In Huddersfield* (1984), *You Can See The Angel's Bum, Miss Worswick* (1985), *Cooking*

One's Corgi (1988), *Walking The Dales* (1986), *Bomber's Moon*, Mike Harding. *Footloose In The Himalaya.*

Hardman, Rosie

b. Cecilia Rosemary Hardman, 26 February 1945, Manchester, England. Hardman began writing songs at the age of 13 and made her first folk club appearance in 1965, at the Manchester Sports Guild. She established herself as resident singer, and organizer of a number of folk clubs over the next three years. *Queen Of Hearts*, released on the Folk Heritage label, was a mixture of traditional and contemporary material. In December 1968, she turned fully professional, and six months later teamed up with south London guitarist Bob Axford, performing only original material. The first release as a duo, on the defunct Leader label, *Second Season Came*, contained the much lauded, and much covered, Hardman song 'Lady For Today'. The self-penned *Firebird* was a solo recording, and in 1974, Rosie played the Cambridge Folk Festival. In 1979, she was signed to the Plant Life label, with whom she made three albums. The backing musicians on these recordings included Dave Cousins of the Strawbs, Maddy Prior and Rick Kemp. From 1979, she toured briefly with a band which comprised of Nigel Pegrum (drums), Jon Gillaspie (keyboards), Pat Tate (guitar/vocals), and Rick Kemp (bass). She toured Europe regularly, and made her first visit to Hong Kong in 1981. That same year, she wrote and recorded 'The Man From Brooklyn'/'Just One Time'. Both songs were about Barry Manilow, always claimed by Rosie to be a major influence. Indeed, Hardman ran the Birmingham branch of the Barry Manilow Fan Club for a number of years. The release of *Weakness Of Eve* was an attempt to diversify her style, with musical influences ranging from Manilow to Whitesnake. She also ran the Whitesnake fan club for two years. In 1980, Hardman wrote the theme music for the children's television programme 'Talk Write And Read'. The programme went on to win the Royal Television Society award for the best primary school television programme of 1986/87. There followed a number of festival appearances, including Hong Kong in 1986, and Jersey in 1987. For a while, Hardman teamed up as a duo with ex-Whitesnake guitarist, Mel Galley. Owing to the smoking in many of the venues she played, and lack of sound systems, Rosie suffered a lot of throat problems during the mid-80s, resulting in a long course of hospital treatment. By 1990 Hardman had virtually retired, apart from two one-off 'farewell performances' in Germany and Jersey in 1991. There was always a strong romantic side to her songs, many of which have been covered by other folk singers. Her warm voice having a strong feel for both traditional and contemporary material. She now teaches swimming for Birmingham City Council.

Albums: *Queen Of Hearts* (1968), with Bob Axford *Second Season Came* (1970), *Firebird* (1971), *Jerseyburger* (1975), *For My Part* (1975), *Eagle Over Blue Mountain* (1978), *Stopped In My Tracks* (1980), *The Weakness Of Eve* (1983).

Harper, Roy

b. 12 June 1941, Manchester, England. Although introduced to music through his brother's skiffle group, Harper's adolescence was marked by a harrowing spell in the Royal Air Force. Having secured a discharge by feigning insanity, he drifted between mental institutions and jail, experiences which left an indelible mark on later compositions. Harper later began busking around Europe, and secured a residency at London's famed Les Cousins club on returning to Britain. His debut album, *The Sophisticated Beggar* (1966), was recorded in primitive conditions, but contained the rudiments of the artist's later, highly personal, style. *Come Out Fighting Genghis Smith* was released as the singer began attracting the emergent underground audience, but he was unhappy with producer Shel Talmy's rather fey arrangements. *Folkjokeopus* contained the first of Harper's extended compositions, 'McGoohan's Blues', but the set as a whole was considered patchy. *Flat, Baroque And Berserk* (1970) introduced the singer's long association with the Harvest label. Although he would later castigate the outlet, they allowed him considerable artistic licence and this excellent album, considered by Harper as his first 'real work', offered contrasting material, including the uncompromising 'I Hate The White Man' and 'Tom Tiddler's Ground', as well as the jocular 'Hell's Angels', which featured support from the Nice. *Stormcock*, arguably the performer's finest work, consists of four lengthy, memorable songs which feature sterling contributions from arranger David Bedford and guitarist Jimmy Page. The latter remained a close associate, acknowledged on 'Hats Off To Harper' from *Led Zeppelin III*, and he appeared on several succeeding releases, including *Lifemask* and *Valentine*. Although marred by self-indulgence, the former was another remarkable set, while the latter reaffirmed Harper's talent with shorter compositions. An in-concert album, *Flashes From The Archives Of Oblivion* completed what was arguably the artist's most rewarding period. *HQ* (1975) introduced Trigger, Harper's short-lived backing group consisting of Chris Spedding (guitar), Dave Cochran (bass) and Bill Bruford (drums). The album included 'When An Old Cricketer Leaves

Roy Harper

The Crease', in which a colliery brass band emphasized the melancholia apparent in the song's cricketing metaphor. A second set, *Commercial Break*, was left unreleased on the group's demise. The singer's next release, *Bullinamingvase*, centred on the ambitious 'One Of Those Days In England', but it is also recalled for the controversy surrounding the flippant 'Watford Gap' and its less-than-complimentary remarks about food offered at the subject's local service station. The song was later removed. It was also during this period that Harper made a memorable cameo appearance on Pink Floyd's *Wish You Were Here*, taking lead vocals on 'Have A Cigar'. Harper's subsequent work, while notable, has lacked the passion of this period and *The Unknown Soldier*, a bleak and rather depressing set, was the prelude to a series of less compulsive recordings, although his 1990 album, *Once*, was critically acclaimed as a return to form. Roy Harper remains a wayward, eccentric talent who has steadfastly refused to compromise his art. Commercial success has thus eluded him, but he retains the respect of many peers and a committed following.

Albums: *The Sophisticated Beggar* (1966), *Come Out Fighting Genghis Smith* (1967), *Folkjokeopus* (1969), *Flat, Baroque And Berserk* (1970), *Stormcock* (1971), *Lifemask* (1973), *Valentine* (1974), *Flashes From The Archives Of Oblivion* (1974), *HQ* (1975 - retitled *When An Old Cricketer Leaves The Crease*), *Bullinamingvase* (1977), *The Unknown Soldier* (1980), *Work Of Heart* (1981), with Jimmy Page *Whatever Happened To Jugula* (1985), *Born In Captivity* (1985), *Descendants Of Smith* (1988), *Loony On The Bus* (1988), *Once* (1990), *Death Or Glory?* (1992). Compilations: *Harper 1970-1975* (1978), *In Between Every Line* (1986).

Harris, Roy

b. 15 June 1933, Nottingham, England. While Harris is essentially a singer of largely traditional songs, he is also a collector of songs, specializing in east midlands material, and has acted on television and radio, worked as a journalist. Through the 50s, he was involved with amateur skiffle groups and, from 1960, became a singer and folk club organizer. He worked semi-professionally from 1961 then took up performing full time in 1964, specializing in English traditional and contemporary material. In 1962, Harris started the Cardiff Folk Song Club, the first folk club in Wales. It was in 1965 that Harris decided to give up playing guitar and concentrate on singing a cappella. In 1965 he produced the ballad *Landmarks*, and two years later secured his first festival bookings. That same year, Harris started the Nottingham Traditional Music Club. Surprisingly, it was not until 1972 that

he released an album, *The Bitter And The Sweet*, on Topic. He was appointed director of the Loughborough Folk Festival in 1976 , and continued in this capacity until 1979. He wrote 'Bone Lace Weaver', the theme tune to the 70s radio folk programme, *Folkweave*. He presented the folk programme for Radio Nottingham from 1980 to 1988. *Utter Simplicity*, was so-called because of Harris's belief that the song should be presented simply, and without undue, or unnecessary, arrangements.He is still busy, having founded the Traditions At The Tiger Folk Club, Long Eaton, Nottingham in 1991, although his career was interrupted when he suffered a stroke that same year.

Albums: *The Bitter And The Sweet* (1972), *Champions Of Folly* (1975), *Sea Shanties* (1976), *The Valiant Sailor* (1976), *By Sandbank Fields* (1977), with other artists *The Tale Of Ale* (1978), *The Rambling Soldier* (1979), *Utter Simplicity* (1981), *Songs From The Penguin Book Of English Folksongs* (1983), with other Fellside artists *Flash Company* (1983).

Harrold, Melanie, And Olly Blanchflower

Melanie Harrold (b. 5 May 1951, Cornwall, England; guitar/vocals) teamed up with Olly Blanchflower (b. 5 February 1952, Axminster, Devon, England; double bass), towards the end of the 80s. Both had come from differing backgrounds, Harrold having played the folk circuit during the 70s, while Blanchflower had been through a number of rock 'n' roll and R&B bands during the same period. Harrold, as Joanna Carlin, recorded *Fancy That* for DJM Records, employing the talents of a wealth of session musicians, including Jerry Donahue and Henry Spinetti. Melanie also appeared on *City To City*, by Gerry Rafferty in 1977, while Olly featured on recordings by Loudon Wainwright III. Shortly after, Harrold joined the Hank Wangford Band, as vocalist Irma Cetas and appeared on *Hank Wangford Live* in 1981. Meanwhile, Blanchflower had been on the London jazz scene for 10 years, playing double bass on everything from be-bop, to standards and free jazz. Together, their style encompasses elements of Blanchflower's jazz influences with Harrold's folk/rock background, capped by her powerful vocal style. As a duo, they have toured Ireland, Scotland and Europe, and continue to play folk clubs and festivals in the UK.

Albums: as Joanna Carlin *Fancy That* (1977), *Blue Angel* (1979), *Live In The City* (1988), *From The Heart* (1990), *The Last Leviathan* (1992).

Hart, Tim, And Maddy Prior

Apart from their work with Steeleye Span, singer

Melanie Harrold

and multi-instrumentalist Hart (b. 9 January 1948, Lincoln, Lincolnshire, England) and singer Prior (b. 14 August 1947, Blackpool, Lancashire, England; daughter of playwright Alan Prior), had also worked and recorded together outside of the confines of the group. Prior had started to visit folk clubs in her teens, and, having failed to get to university, took up singing full time. For a time, working as a 'roadie cum chauffeur', she was driving performers such as the Rev. Gary Davis around. Hart and Prior played their first booking as a duo in 1966. They quickly built up a repertoire of traditional songs, many of which remained uncovered by other performers at the time. Having made two albums, Hart and Prior were approached by Ashley Hutchings, in 1969, with a view to joining a band made up of himself, and Gay and Terry Woods. Thus Steeleye Span were born. Having recorded *Hark The Village Wait*, Gay and Terry Woods left, but Hart and Prior continued together until Steeleye Span was reformed, this time with Martin Carthy, and later Peter Knight. Hart now lives on La Gomera, in the Canary Islands, and has made one album, *Tim Hart*, in 1979. Hart however, continues to perform and record, with husband Rick Kemp (b. 15 November 1941, Little Handford, Dorset, England), June Tabor, and Steeleye Span.
Albums: *Folk Songs Of Olde England Vol.1* (1968), *Folk Songs Of Olde England Vol.2* (1968), *Summer Solstice* (1971). Tim Hart: *Tim Hart* (1979), with friends *Drunken Sailor And Other Kids' Songs* (1983). Maddy Prior: *Woman In The Wings* (1978), *Changing Winds* (1978), *Nyon Folk Festival* (1979), *Hooked On Winning* (1982), with the Answers *Going For Glory* (1983), with June Tabor *No More To The Dance* (1990), with the Carnival Band *Sing Lustily And With Good Courage* (1990), with Rick Kemp *Happy Families* (1990), with the Carnival Band *Carols And Capers* (1991).

Hartford, John

b. John Harford, 30 December 1937, New York City, New York, USA. Hartford was a multi-instrumentalist country performer whose most famous composition was 'Gentle On My Mind'. He grew up in St. Louis where his early influences included bluegrass music and he became adept on banjo and fiddle as a teenager. He later mastered dobro and guitar. After working as a sign-painter, commercial artist, Mississippi riverboat deckhand and disc jockey, Hartford moved to Nashville in the early 60s. There he became a session musician before signing a solo recording deal with RCA, for which he made eight albums between 1966 and 1972. In 1967, Glen Campbell recorded the million-selling version of the lyrical 'Gentle On My

Mind', which was subsequently covered by over 300 artists including Frank Sinatra, Elvis Presley and Max Bygraves. Presley's producer Felton Jarvis supervised Hartford's own recording of the song on his second album. During the late 60s, Hartford undertook selected session work, most notably on the Byrds' influential *Sweetheart Of The Rodeo*.
In 1971, he moved to Warner Brothers, where David Bromberg produced the highly-praised *Aereo Plain*. A year later, however, he left the music business to concentrate on renovating steamboats. He returned in 1976 with the Grammy-winning *Mark Twang* (on Flying Fish) which featured Hartford making all the percussion noises with his mouth. In 1977, Hartford teamed up with the Dillard brothers, Rodney and Doug, to record two country-rock flavoured albums which included quirky Hartford compositions like 'Two Hits And The Joint Turned Brown'. *Annual Waltz* was the first album under a new contract with MCA.
Albums: *Looks At Life* (1967), *Earthwords And Music* (1967), *The Love Album* (1968), *Housing Project* (1968), *John Hartford* (1969), *Iron Mountain Depot* (1970), *Aereo Plain* (1971), *Morning Bugle* (1972), *Tennessee Jubilee* (1975), *Mark Twang* (1976), *Nobody Knows What You Do* (1976), *All In The Name Of Love* (1977), *Heading Down Into The Mystery Below* (1978), *Slumbering On The Cumberland* (1979), *You And Me At Home* (1981), *Me Oh My, How Does Time Fly* (1982), *Mystery Below* (1983), *You And Me At Home* (1984), *Catalogue* (1985), *Annual Waltz* (1986), *Gum Tree Canoe* (1987), *John Hartford* (1988), *All In The Name Of Love* (1989). With Doug and Rodney Dillard *Dillard, Hartford, Dillard* (1977), *Permanent Wave* (1980).

Havalinas

The brainchild of vocalist-guitarist Tim McConnell, who released several solo records for Geffen in the early 80s, the Havalinas was formed from the remnents of several high energy Los Angeles guitar combo's, and included Smutty Smith (bass) and Charlie Quintana (drums). Disillusioned with rock, the trio fused traditional folk instruments such as banjo, mandolin, flute and dobro, with a belligerent street-wise approach, that also drew on influences as diverse as Woody Guthrie and Hank Williams. Released in 1990, their debut album, produced by Don Gehman (REM, John Mellencamp), was a shambolic, yet rivetting set that dealt with contemporary socio-political ills. Their Guns N'Roses persona won them few friends on the folk scene, and they have since disappeared from view.
Album: *The Havalinas* (1990).

Havens, Richie

b. Richard Pierce Havens, 21 January 1941, Bedford-Stuyvesant, Brooklyn, New York, USA. Havens' professional singing career began at the age of 14 as a member of the McCrea Gospel Singers. By 1962 he was a popular figure on the Greenwich Village folk circuit with regular appearances at the Cafe Wha?, Gerdes, and The Fat Black Pussycat. Havens quickly developed a distinctive playing style, tuning his guitar to the open E chord which in turn inspired an insistent percussive technique and a stunningly deft right hand technique. A black singer in a predominantly white idiom, Havens' early work combined folk material with New York-pop inspired compositions. His soft, yet gritty, voice adapted well to seemingly contrary material and two early releases, Mixed Bag and Something Else Again, revealed a blossoming talent. However, the artist established his reputation interpreting songs by other acts, including the Beatles and Bob Dylan, which he personalized through his individual technique. Havens opened the celebrated Woodstock Festival and his memorable appearance was a highlight of the film. A contemporaneous release, Richard P. Havens 1983, was arguably his artistic apogee, offering several empathic cover versions and some of the singer's finest compositions. He later established an independent label, Stormy Forest, and enjoyed a US Top 20 hit with 'Here Comes The Sun'. A respected painter, writer and sculptor, Havens currently pursues a lucrative career doing voice-overs for US television advertisements.
Albums: Richie Havens Record (1965), Electric Havens (1966), Mixed Bag (1967), Something Else Again (1968), Richard P. Havens 1983 (1969), Stonehenge (1970), Alarm Clock (1971), The Great Blind Degree (1971), Richie Havens On Stage (1972), Portfolio (1973), Mixed Bag II (1974), The End Of The Beginning (1976), Mirage (1977), Connections (1980), Common Ground (1984), Simple Things (1987). Compilations: A State Of Mind (1971), Richie Havens Sings The Beatles And Dylan (1990).

Hearts And Flowers

Formed in 1964 at the Troubador Club in Los Angeles, California, when Rick Cunha (guitar/vocals) and Dave Dawson (autoharp/vocals), then working as a duo, met Larry Murray (ex-Scotsville Squirrel Barkers; guitar/vocals). Together they formed an acoustic country/folk act which quickly became an integral part of the west coast circuit. Now Is The Time For Hearts And Flowers revealed a group of breathtaking confidence, whose three-part harmonies and gift for melody brought new perspectives to a range of material drawn from Donovan, Carole King, Tim Hardin and Kaleidoscope. Terry Paul and Dan Woody were then added to the line-up, but Hearts And Flowers were a trio again for Of Horses, Kids And Forgotten Women. Although Rick Cunha had been replaced by another former Barker, Bernie Leadon, the blend of styles remained the same, with Murray emerging as the unit's chief songwriter. Commercial success did not ensue, and the group split up soon after its release. Leadon and associate bassist David Jackon reappeared in Dillard And Clark and while Dawson dropped out of music altogether, both Murray and Cunha recorded as solo artists.
Albums: Now Is The Time For Hearts And Flowers (1967), Of Horses, Kids And Forgotten Women (1968).

Hedgehog Pie

The saying: 'Everyone south of the River Tyne has been in Hedgehog Pie', is generally attributed to the Lindisfarne drummer, Ray Laidlaw. The original 1969 line-up of this folk group from Newcastle Upon Tyne, that played blues, folk, ragtime, and much else besides, is unclear. However, in 1971, when they backed Tony Capstick on two albums, the personnel consisted of Mick Doonan (flute), Jed Grimes (guitar), Andy Seagroat (fiddle) and Phil Murray (bass). Confusion returned again in 1972, when Stu Luckley (guitar, bass), Margi Luckley (vocals) and Ian Fairburn (fiddle), amongst others, were recruited. Soon afterwards, Fairburn and Murray departed to Jack The Lad. When Martin Jenkins arrived from Dando Shaft, the group 'went electric', and recorded Hedgehog Pie. As a six piece unit, they toured in support with other folk rockers and singer-songwriters. In the summer of 1976, everyone left, with the exception of two of the originals, Doonan and Grimes. The addition of and Dave Burland (guitar, vocals), completed a scaled-down acoustic trio. Two years later, the group issued Just Act Normal, before disbanding in 1979. In 1990 they held an open reunion, and were surprised to find just exactly how many ex-members turned up.
Albums: Hedgehog Pie (1975), The Green Lady (1976), Just Act Normal (1978).

Hemphill, Sid

b. 1876, Como, Mississippi, USA, d. c.1963, Senatobia, Mississippi, USA. Hemphill played guitar, drums, mandolin, banjo and harmonica besides the fife, panpipes and fiddle that appear on the recordings his band made in 1942 for the Library of Congress. These are a vital documentation of two black traditions: string band music, and the fife and drum bands of northwestern Mississippi. The repertoire played by Hemphill and

Richie Havens

his musicians seems to have remained largely unchanged since around 1900, and included blues-ballads, religious music, popular songs and dance tunes. The latter owed much to white music and so, more generally, did their fife and drum music, which displayed little improvisation or syncopation, in contrast to more recent recordings. Hemphill, who was the father of Rosa Lee Hill, was recorded for the last time in 1959.

Albums: *Sounds Of The South* (1960), *Traveling Through The Jungle* (1974), *Afro-American Folk Music From Tate And Panola Counties, Mississippi* (1978).

Henderson, Dorris

Although best-known for her spell with the innovative Eclection, this American-born singer was a well-known attraction in Britain's folk clubs. She enjoyed a partnership with guitarist John Renbourn and completed two excellent albums, the second of which inferred a switch from traditional to contemporary styles. Henderson replaced Kerilee Male in Eclection in October 1968. A single, 'Please Mark 2', was the new singer's only creative involvement with this respected unit, and she resumed her solo career on the group's subsequent demise. Henderson did attempt to resurrect the Eclection name during the 70s, but this proved ill-advised.

Albums: *There You Go* (1965), *Watch The Stars* (1967).

Hennessys

Formed in 1966, this Welsh group was fronted by Frank Hennessy (b. 2 February 1947, Cardiff, Wales; guitar, vocals), the other two members were Dave Burns (b. 4 November 1946, Cardiff, Wales; mandolin, guitar, vocals), and Paul Powell (b. 1946, Cardiff, Wales; banjo, vocals). Initially they played folk clubs, and took up performing full time in 1968. During the following year, the trio lived and worked in Eire. On their return to Wales, the Hennessys began to broadcast with BBC Wales. Their first release, *Down The Road*, on the Cambrian label, appeared in 1969. Spending time researching Welsh traditional material, they released a number of singles and EPs and were given a residency on BBC television's folk programme *The Singin Barn*. In 1972, founder member Powell left the group. Tom Edwards (double bass) joined in 1979, and continued with the group until 1991, when he had to retire through ill health. The line-up was augmented by the addition of Iolo Jones (b. 12 February 1955, Plymouth, Devon, England; fiddle). The Hennessys still tour, mostly concerts and promotional work for the Welsh Tourist Board and British Tourist Authority. Dave Burns also runs Wobbly Records, which released his *Last Pit In The*

Rhondda. The group retained a great deal of popularity, despite their relatively sparse output. Edwards retired from performing in 1991. Iolo Jones also performs with folk group Ar Log.

Albums: *Down The Road* (1969), *Ar Lan Y Mor* (1970), *Yr Hen Dderwen Ddu* (1970), *Cardiff After Dark* (1984). Dave Burns: *Last Pit In The Rhondda* (1986). Frank Hennessy: *Thoughts And Memories* (1988).

Henske, Judy

b. c.1942, Chippewa Falls, Wisconsin, USA. Henske moved to the west coast of the USA, where she sang solo until 1961, when she joined the Whiskeyhill Singers. The latter featured former Kingston Trio member Dave Guard, David Buck Wheat, and Cyrus Faryar. The group recorded only one album, *Dave Guard And The Whiskeyhill Singers*, for Capitol, before splitting up. The following year, Henske was signed to Elektra, which released *Judy Henske* and *High Flying Bird*. She subsequently recorded for Reprise and Mercury. Despite her dramatic stage presence, commercial success eluded her. She later married former Lovin' Spoonful member Jerry Yester, with whom she also performed and recorded as a duo, Henske And Yester. *Farewell Alderbaran*, and *Rosebud* were recorded for Frank Zappa's Straight label.

Albums: *Judy Henske* (1963), *High Flying Bird* (1964), *Death Defying* (1965), *A Little Bit Of Sunshine* (1965). As Henske And Yester: *Farewell Alderbaran* (1969), *Rosebud* (1971).

Heron, Mike

b. 12 December 1942, Scotland. This multi-instrumentalist was a founder member of the Incredible String Band. Heron's first solo outing, on Island, included such names as the Who, and John Cale in the credits. After the band split, in 1974, Heron remained in the UK and formed Mike Heron's Reputation, following a more rock-orientated path. They released only *Mike Heron's Reputation*, this time on Neighbourhood Records. Although Heron recorded a number of albums, albeit on a different label every time, none of these achieved the degree of success that his former association with Robin Williamson had brought. *The Glenrow Tapes* was a set of remastered demo recordings that had not previously been released.

Albums: *Smiling Men With Bad Reputations* (1971), *Mike Heron's Reputation* (1975), *Diamond Of Dreams* (1977), *Mike Heron* (1980), *The Glenrow Tapes, Vol. 1* (1987), *The Glenrow Tapes, Vol. 2* (1987), *The Glenrow Tapes, Vol. 3* (1987).

Hester, Carolyn

b. 1936, Waco, Texas, USA. Hester spent her

childhood in Austin and Dallas (her grandparents had been folk singers) and then she relocated to New York in 1956 to study acting with the American Theater Wing. In 1958 Hester left to sing in clubs in Cleveland and Detroit. She first came to Britain to play at the Edinburgh Festival with Rory McEwen. After marrying Richard Farina, she became well-known both in the USA and the UK. Hester regularly appeared on British television, and in subsequent Edinburgh Festival shows. She was one of the organizers of the singer's boycott of ABC television's *Hootenanny* show, after its refusal to allow Pete Seeger to perform during the anti-communist McCarthy period in the 50s. Separation and divorce from Farina followed after what Hester described as financial problems. Her first CBS album, *Carolyn Hester*, included Bob Dylan on Harmonica, alongside Bruce Langhorne (guitar) and Bill Lee (bass). *Thursday's Child Has Far To Go* was produced by Tom Clancy of the Clancy Brothers, who owned the Tradition label on which it was released. At the time Hester had not long been married to Farina, who played a very supportive role to her career. Although Hester remained a popular live attraction, her position in folk's heirarchy was gradually over-run by Joan Baez and Judy Collins. In the late 60s she embraced a rock-oriented direction with a group, the Carolyn Hester Coalition, but it was a largely unremarkable flirtation. Carolyn then abandoned music for a short while before returning to the folk circuit in the 70s.
Albums: *Scarlet Ribbons* (late-50s), *Carolyn Hester* (1961), *Carolyn Hester* (1962) *This Is My Living* (1963), *That's My Song* (1964), *Carolyn Hester At The Town Hall* (1965), *The Carolyn Hester Coalition* (1969), *Thursday's Child Has Far To Go* (1971), *Carolyn Hester* (1974).

Hickey, Chris

Based in Los Angeles, Hickey was a member of the late 70s punk group, the Spoilers. In 1985 he released *Frames Of Mind, Boundaries Of Time*, an outstanding, semi-political acoustic album, which had been recorded at home. It recalled the sparse arrangements of Nick Drake and Suzanne Vega. Unfortunately, Hickey's melancholic neo-folk was out of step during this period, and little has been heard of him since.
Albums: *Frames Of Mind, Boundaries Of Time* (1985).

Higginbottom, Geoff

b. 13 February 1959, Stockport, Cheshire, England. During his early career Higginbottom played the circuit of folk clubs and pubs in his native northwest. In August 1985, he was placed third in a competition at the Warwick Folk Festival. In the November of the same year, he released *Songs From The Levenshulme Triangle*. The following year, he performed at the Sidmouth International Festival Of Folk Arts, and was subsequently re-booked for 1987 and 1988. This gave Higginbottom a wider profile, and brought club and festival bookings all over England. He has since ventured further afield, playing Scotland, Wales and the Channel Islands. In addition to his musical career, Higginbottom has also made numerous appearances on UK television in bit parts, turning up in such soaps as *Coronation Street*, *Brookside* and *Emmerdale*, as well as a number of other productions. *Flowers Tomorrow* received a good response and brought Higginbottom to wider attention. The title track has been sung by a number of other performers, and the album as a whole mixed contemporary and traditional styles, with his guitar and bodhran to the fore. *More Than Pounds And Pence*, released in December 1990 has helped to establish Higginbottom as a highly-regarded performer and writer.
Albums: *Songs From The Levenshulme Triangle* (1985), *Flowers Tomorrow* (1987), *More Than Pounds And Pence* (1990).

Highwaymen

This self-contained folk quintet comprised Dave Fisher (b. 1940, New Haven, Connecticut, USA); Steve Butts (b. 1940, New York, New York, USA); Chan Daniels (b. 1940, Buenos Aires, Brazil d. 2 August 1975); Bobby Burnett (b. 1940, Mystic, Connecticut, USA) and Steve Trott (b. 1940, Mexico City, Mexico). The group recorded their self-titled album for United Artists in 1961 whilst still students at the Wesleyan University in Middletown, Connecticut, where they had first met. Their haunting version of an old slave song 'Michael', arranged by Fisher, took them to the top on both sides of the Atlantic in 1961, despite a UK cover version by Lonnie Donegan. They followed their gold record with another 19th-century folk song 'Cotton Fields'. It too made the US Top 20 but it was to be their last major success. The group, whose repertoire included folk songs from around the world, sang in English, French, Spanish and Hebrew. For them, music was never much more than a hobby and they continued their studies rather than pursuing full-time musical careers. They unsuccessfully re-recorded 'Michael' in 1965 before recording for a brief time on ABC.
Albums: *The Highwaymen* (1961), *Standing Room Only!* (1962), *Hootenanny With The Highwaymen* (1963).

Hillside Singers

The Hillside Singers were brought together in 1972 by record US producer Al Ham and left their mark

with one chart hit, 'I'd Like To Teach The World To Sing (In Perfect Harmony)', that year. Ham, a music business veteran who once played bass and arranged for big band artists such as Glenn Miller and Artie Shaw, later worked as a staff producer for Columbia Records during the 50s and produced the original cast recordings of *West Side Story*, *My Fair Lady* and other Broadway shows. The members of the Hillside Singers were chosen by Ham for the express purpose of recording the single which Ham believed had potential beyond the Coca-Cola commercial it accompanied. The group consisted of Mary Mayo, Ham's daughter Lori, brothers Ron and Rick Shaw and members of another group called Good Life. The single was recorded for the Metromedia label and reached number 13. A rival version by the New Seekers from the UK climbed even higher at number 7, as well as topping the UK charts. The Hillside Singers recorded two albums and other singles, one of which was adapted from a McDonald's commercial, but did not chart after 1972, when Metromedia folded. The group, with personnel changes, still exists in the early 90s.
Album: *I'd Like To Teach The World To Sing* (1972).

Holland, Maggie

b. 19 December 1949, Alton, Hampshire, England. Holland plays guitar/banjo/vocals/bass guitar, and her early career was spent performing in the folk clubs of Surrey, Bristol and Hampshire from 1967-72. In 1973, she formed the duo Hot Vultures with her husband Ian A. Anderson. Recording a number of albums, she and Anderson then formed the English Country Blues Band in 1980 with Rod Stradling, formerly with Oak and the Old Swan Band, (melodeon), and either Sue Harris (formerly of the Richard Thompson Band - hammer dulcimer), or Chris Coe (formerly of the New Victory Band (hammer dulcimer). Despite the various group commitments, and also working in a solo capacity since 1982, Holland found time to record *Still Pause*, her first solo album. She then became a member of the roots dance band Tiger Moth from 1984-89. Holland also supplied vocals and bass guitar on the Ian A. Anderson and Mike Cooper release *The Continuous Preaching Blues* in 1984. *A Short Cut*, recorded with Jon Moore (guitar), led to the formation of the trio Maggie's Farm which toured both in the UK and Bangladesh. Also during the period 1984-86, Holland worked occasionally as a duo with Chris Coe, touring the UK, Nepal, Thailand, the Phillipines and Ghana. In 1985, Maggie had the role of lead singer in the National Theatre's production of *The Mysteries* at the Lyceum, London. Another solo release, simply called *The Cassette*, appeared in 1989. In 1992, she issued *Down To The Bone.*
Albums: *Still Pause* (1982), *The Cassette* (1989), *Down To The Bone* (1992). Hot Vultures: *Carrion On* (1975), *The East Street Shakes* (1977), *Up The Line* (1979). Compilation: *Vulturama* (1983). English Country Blues Band: *No Rules* (1982), *Home And Deranged* (1984). Tiger Moth: *Tiger Moth* (1984), *Howling Moth* (1988), Orchestre Super Moth *The World At Sixes And Sevens* (1989), *Down To The Bone* (1992).

Holy Modal Rounders

Peter Stampfel (b. 1938, Wauwautosa, Wisconsin, USA) and Steve Weber (b. 1942, Philadelphia, Pennsylvania, USA). This on-off partnership was first established in New York's Greenwich Village. The two musicians shared a passion for old-timey music and unconventional behaviour, and together they created some of the era's most distinctive records. The duo completed their debut album, *The Holy Modal Rounders* in 1963. It contained several of their finest moments, including the influential 'Blues In The Bottle', which the Lovin' Spoonful, among others, later recorded. The Rounders' second collection, although less satisfying, continued the same cross-section of 20s/30s-styled country and blues. Having accompanied the Fugs on their early releases, Stampfel and Weber broke up, the former began writing for 'alternative' publications. The musicians were reunited in 1967 to complete the experimental, but flawed, *Indian War Whoop*. This often incoherent collection also featured drummer Sam Shepard, an off-Broadway playwright from a parallel Stampfel venture, the Moray Eels. The amalgamation of the two groups led to another album, *The Moray Eels Eat The Holy Modal Rounders*, which was a marked improvement on its predecessor. It featured the sweeping 'Bird Song', later immortalized in the film *Easy Rider*. Shepard left the Rounders in 1970, from where he became a successful writer and actor. Three albums of varying quality were then completed until the group, which suffered a plethora of comings and goings, ground to a halt in 1977. Weber and Stampfel were reunited five years later. *Goin' Nowhere Fast* was an excellent set, evocative of the duo's first recordings together, but their revitalized relationship proved temporary. The latter later worked with an all-new group, Pete Stampfel And The Bottlecaps.
Albums: *The Holy Modal Rounders* (1964), *The Holy Modal Rounders 2* (1965), *Indian War Whoop* (1967), *The Moray Eels Eat The Holy Modal Rounders* (1968), *Good Taste Is Timeless* (1971), *Alleged In Their Own Time* (1975), *Last Round* (1978), *Goin' Nowhere Fast* (1982).

Maggie Holland

Home Service

Formed in 1980 as the First Eleven, this UK group evolved from the ever changing Albion Band, which at the time included John Kirkpatrick in the line-up. Led by John Tams (vocals), the group featured Bill Caddick (b. June 1944, Wolverhampton, England; vocals/guitar/dobro), Graeme Taylor (b. 2 February 1954, Stockwell, London, England; vocals/guitar), Michael Gregory (b. 16 November 1949, Gower, South Wales; drums/percussion), Roger Williams (b. 30 July 1954, Cottingham, Yorkshire, England; trombone), Howard Evans (b. 29 February 1944, Chard, Somerset, England; trumpet) and Jonathan Davie (b. 6 September 1954, Twickenham, Middlesex, England; bass). Both Evans and Williams were concurrently members of Brass Monkey, and Caddick had already released a number of solo albums. The group was involved with work for the National Theatre, for which they provided the music for the York Mystery Plays. The resultant album appeared in 1985. This release included Linda Thompson, and covered both traditional and contemporary material. By 1985, Caddick had left the group, unhappy with the lack of live concert work. This situation was caused by the many commitments the group had to theatre, television and film work. The following year, 1986, Andy Findon (saxophone) and Steve King (keyboards) were added to the line-up. It was 1991 before the line-up played together again, on the Hokey Pokey charity compilation *All Through The Year.*

Albums: *The Home Service* (1984), *The Mysteries* (1985), *Alright Jack* (1986). Compilation: *All Through The Year* (1991).

Hopkins, Lightnin'

b. Sam Hopkins, 15 March 1912, Centreville, Texas, USA, d. 30 January 1982. One of the last great country blues singers, Hopkins' lengthy career began in the Texas bars and juke joints of the 20s. Towards the end of the decade he formed a duo with a cousin, Texas Alexander, while his Lightnin' epithet was derived from a subsequent partnership with barrelhouse pianist Thunder Smith, with whom he made his first recordings. Hopkins' early work unveiled a masterly performer. His work first came to prominence when, after being discovered by Sam Charters at the age of 47, *The Roots Of Lightnin' Hopkins* was released in 1959 and numerous sessions followed. His sparse acoustic guitar and narrated prose quickly made him an important discovery, appealing to the audience of the American folk boom of the early 60s. His harsh, emotive voice and compulsive, if irregular guitar work, carried an intensity enhanced by the often personal nature of his lyrics. He became one of post-war blues most prolific talents, completing

Home Service

hundreds of sessions for scores of major and independent labels. This inevitably diluted his initial power but although Hopkins' popularity slumped in the face of Chicago's electric combos, by the early 60s he was re-established as a major force on the college and concert-hall circuit. In 1967 the artist was the subject of an autobiographical film, *The Blues Of Lightnin' Hopkins*, which subsequently won the Gold Hugo award at the Chicago Film Festival. Like many other bluesmen finding great success in the 60s (Muddy Waters and John Lee Hooker), he too recorded a 'progressive' electric album: *The Great Electric Show And Dance*. He maintained a compulsive work-rate during the 70s, touring the USA, Canada and, in 1977, Europe, until ill-health forced him to reduce such commitments. Hopkins was a true folk poet, embracing social comments into pure blues. Lightnin' died in 1982, his status as one of the major voices of the blues assured.

Selected albums: *The Roots Of Lightnin' Hopkins* (1959), *Down South Summit Meeting* (1960), *The Great Electric Show And Dance* (1968), *King Of Dowling Street* (1969), *Lightnin' Hopkins* (1991), *The Complete Prestige/Bluesville Recordings* (1992), *The Complete Aladdin Recordings* (1992), *Sittin' In With Lightnin' Hopkins* (1992), *Blues Is My Business* (1993, rec. 1971), *You're Gonna Miss Me* (1993), *It's A Sin To Be Rich* (1993, rec. 1973), *Coffee House Blues* (1993, rec 1960-62).

Horslips

This innovative and much imitated Irish folk-rock band comprised Barry Devlin (bass/vocals), Declan Sinnott (lead guitar/vocals), Eamonn Carr (drums/vocals), Charles O'Connor (violin), and Jim Lockhart (flute/violin/keyboards). Sinnott, later joined Moving Hearts and was replaced by Gus Gueist and John Fean in turn. Horslips, formed in 1970 and took the theme of Irish legends for many of their songs. The group toured as support to Steeleye Span and featured a complete performance of *The Tain*, a more rock-based recording than their previous recordings. Feans guitar work could switch from the melodic style of 'Aliens', to the much heavier 'Man Who Built America'. They maintained a strong cult following, but, only one album, *The Book Of Invasions - A Celtic Symphony*, reached the UK Top 40. *The Man Who Built America* received a lot of air-play when it was released in 1979, but wider acceptance evaded them, and the group split. Fean, O'Connor and Carr later formed Host, with Chris Page (bass), and Peter Keen (keyboards), in order to pursue the folk path still further.

Albums: *Happy To Meet Sorry To Part* (1973), *The Tain* (1974), *Dancehall Sweethearts* (1974), *Unfortunate Cup Of Tea* (1975), *Drive The Cold Winter Away* (1976), *Horslips Live* (1976), *The Book Of Invasions - A Celtic Symphony* (1977), *Aliens* (1977), *Tour A Loor A Loor* (1977), *Tracks From The Vaults* (1978), *The Man Who Built America* (1979), *Short Stories - Tall Tales* (1980), *The Belfast Gigs* (1980). Compilations: *The Best Of Horslips* (1982), *Folk Collection* (1984), *Horslips History 1972-75* (1983), *Horslips History 1976-80* (1984).

Houghton Weavers

This folk-based group from Lancashire, England was formed in 1975 by Tony Berry (b. Anthony Berry, 15 January 1950, Bolton, Lancashire, England; vocals), Norman Prince (b. Norman Anthony Prince, 26 April 1946, Eccles, Manchester, England; vocals/guitar), David Littler (b. David George Littler, 13 March 1949, Westhoughton, Lancashire, England; vocals/banjo/guitar/ukelele), and John Oliver (b. Appley Bridge, Wigan, Lancashire, England; vocals). They were the resident group at a number of venues in the north west of England, but within 12 months, Oliver left the group. He was replaced by Denis Littler (b. Westhoughton, Lancashire, England; bass/vocals), who himself left in February 1984. Jeff Hill (b. Jeffrey Martin Hill, 14 September 1958 Warrington, Lancashire, England; vocals/bass/guitar) joined the group the same month. A featured spot on a BBC television series, *We'll Call You*, in 1977, led to the group receiving their own television series, *Sit Thi Deawn*, which started in January 1978. In addition, the group's popularity on radio has enabled them to hold down five series of their own show on BBC Radio 2, with a new series being recorded early in 1992. As a result of success in pantomime, the Houghton Weavers now regularly tour at Christmas under the banner of the Christmas Cracker Tour, playing 20 dates in 24 nights. *Keep Folk Smiling* was released to coincide with the group's 10th anniversary. Given the depth of popularity that the group command, it is surprising that they are not better known nationally.

Albums: *Howfen Wakes* (1976), *Gone Are The Days* (1977), *Sit Thi Deawn* (1978), *In Concert* (1979), *Up Your Way* (1980), *Alive And Kicking* (1981), *In The Rare Old Times* (1983), *Keep Folk Smiling* (1985), *It's Good To See You* (1986), *Lancashire Lads* (1988), *When Granny Sang Me Songs* (1990), *Christmas Collection* (1991).

House Band

Comprising Ged Foley (b. Gerard Foley, 24 February 1955, Peterlee, Co. Durham, England; vocals, guitar, Northumbrian pipes), Chris Parkinson (b. 31 March 1950, Rawtenstall,

Lancashire, England; piano accordion, vocals, melodeon, synthesizer, harmonica) and John Skelton (b. 26 September 1954, Bromley, Kent, England; flute, whistle, bombarde, bodhran), the House Band have rapidly established themselves on the UK folk circuit, despite their relatively recent emergence. The group, formed in 1985, originally consisted of Parkinson and Foley with Iain MacLeod (mandolin), and Jimmy Young (flute, small pipes). With the departure of both MacLeod and Young, in February 1986, the House Band were joined, in the same month, by Skelton and Brian Brooks (bouzouki, keyboards, whistle, vocals). In January 1988, Brooks left the group due to family commitments. Combining traditional instruments, augmented by synthesizer and modern arrangements, the House Band have played to a wide range of audiences, and even supported Status Quo at a Swiss rock festival. The various members of the band have all been involved in performing in other capacities, in particular Foley in the Battlefield Band, and both Skelton and Brooks in Shegui. This has resulted in tours of the USA, Canada and New Zealand, in addition to Europe and the UK. Although Foley is now resident in the USA, the group are still performing at folk festivals and folk clubs in the UK.
Albums: *The House Band* (1986), *Pacific* (1987), *Word Of Mouth* (1988), *Stonetown* (1991).

Houston, Cisco

b. Gilbert Vandine Houston, 18 August 1918, Wilmington, Delaware, USA, d. 25 April 1961, San Bernadino, California, USA. Houston's family moved to California in 1919. Having spent his early years in a variety of simple jobs, he found himself, like many others in the 30s, unemployed. He wanted to become a comedian, but obtained only secondary roles in a few Hollywood movies. Houston subsequently became involved in a number of folk festivals and theatre work as well as union meetings and political gatherings. He then travelled with Woody Guthrie, and Will Geer. In 1940 Houston joined the USA merchant marine with Guthrie and performed for the benefit of fellow seamen. It was after the war that Houston and Guthrie returned to New York and Houston began touring and performing at concerts and recording. In 1959, the US State Department sent him, together with Sonny Terry and Brownie McGhee, to India on a cultural exchange. By this time Houston knew that cancer of the stomach was leaving him little time to live. Despite this fact, he still performed at the 1960 Newport Folk Festival and continued to record for Vanguard. He made his last appearance in Pasadena at a folk concert, in spite of his painful illness, and died in April 1961.

Tom Paxton commemorated his memory in the song 'Fare Thee Well Cisco'.
Albums: *American Folksongs* (c.50s), *Songs Of The Open Road* (c.50s), *The Cisco Special* (c.50s), *I Aint Got No Home* (c.60s), *The Legendary Cisco Houston* (c.60s), *Cisco Houston* (c.60s), *Songs Of Woody Guthrie* (c.60s), *Cisco Houston* (c.70s).
Further reading: *900 Miles - The Ballads, Blues And Folksongs Of Cisco Houston*.

Hugill, Stan

b. 19 November 1906, in the coastguard cottages at Hoylake, Cheshire, England, to a seafaring family, d. 13 May 1992. A veritable encyclopaedia of songs nautical and shanties from the last great days of sail, Hugill went to sea with the Merchant Service during the early 20s. He served in Sail (square riggers and fore 'n' afters), of ships from the USA, Germany, and Britain, for 10 years. He then moved into steam (Blue Funnel Line), to China and Japan; and Hugill then spent over four years as a prisoner of war. After the war, Hugill studied for three years at the London University Oriental and African school of languages, and obtained a diploma in Japanese in 1949. From 1950, Hugill joined the Outward Bound movement, as an instructor, and later as bosun. He married Bronwen Irene Benbow in 1952, and both his sons later became folk musicians. When *Shanties From The Seven Seas* was published, Hugill went to the BBC in London to be interviewed, later turning up at the famous Singer's Club', then run by Peggy Seeger and Stan Kelly. It was here that he sang in public for the first time. He was later introduced to the Bluecoat School, in Liverpool, and met both the Spinners and A.L. Lloyd. For the next few years, while still working, Hugill sang at clubs and colleges all over Britain. He later limited himself to singing at festivals worldwide, after he retired in 1975. In addition to his recordings and books, Hugill also painted marine oils, as well as illustrating his own books. Hugill lived in Wales, but continued to travel giving lectures on shanty singing, and old sailing ships. He also made two videos, *Jack Tar*, in Poland in 1987 and *Stan Hugill* in Holland in 1991. He was probably the last of the British Shantymen.
Albums: *Shanties From The Seven Seas* (1961), *Men And The Sea* (c.70s), *Reminisces* (1977), *Aboard The Cutty Sark* (1979), with others *Songs Of The Sea* (1979), *Ratcliffe Highway* (c.80s), with others *Sea Songs* (1980), with others *Sea Music Of Many Lands* (1980), *Shantyman* (1987), *Salty Foretopman* (1988).
Further reading: *Shanties From The Seven Seas*, Stan Hugill. *Sailortown*, Stan Hugill. *Shanties And Sailor Songs*, Stan Hugill. *Songs Of The Sea - The Tales And Tunes Of Sailors And Sailing Ships*, Stan Hugill.

Alan Hull (right) and Rod Clements

Hull, Alan

b. 20 February 1945, Newcastle-Upon-Tyne, England. Alan Hull's career began as a founder member of the Chosen Few, a Tyneside beat group which also included future Ian Dury pianist, Mickey Gallagher. Hull composed the four tracks constituting their output, before leaving to become a nurse and sometime folk-singer. In 1967 Alan founded Downtown Faction, which evolved into Lindisfarne. This popular folk-rock act scored hit singles with 'Meet Me On The Corner' and 'Lady Eleanor', both of which Hull wrote, while their first two albums were critical and commercial successes. *Pipedream*, Hull's debut album, was recorded with assistance from many members of Lindisfarne, in 1973. Its content was more introspective than that of his group and partly reflected on the singer's previous employment in a mental hospital. Although Hull continued to lead his colleagues throughout the 70s and 80s, he pursued a solo career with later releases *Squire* and *Phantoms*, plus a one-off release on the Rocket label as Radiator, a group formed with the assistance of Lindisfarne drummer Ray Laidlaw. None of these albums was able to achieve the same degree of success as *Pipedream*, the second decade proved more low-key, resulting in only one collection, *On The Other Side*.
Albums: *Pipedream* (1973), *Squire* (1975), *Phantoms* (1979), *On The Other Side* (1983), with Radiator *Isn't It Strange* (1977).

Humblebums

This Scottish folk-singing duo originally consisted of Tam Harvey (guitar/mandolin) and Billy Connolly (b. 1942, Anderston, Glasgow, Scotland; guitar/banjo). Their debut, *First Collection of Merrie Melodies*, showcased a quirky sense of humour, but it was not until Harvey was replaced by Gerry Rafferty (b. 16 April 1946, Paisley, Scotland), that the group forged an individuality. Rafferty, a former member of the beat group, Fifth Column, introduced a gift for melody and the first release with Connolly, *The New Humblebums*, featured several excellent compositions, including 'Please Sing A Song For Us' and 'Her Father Didn't Like Me Anyway'. A further collection, *Open Up The Door*, confirmed Rafferty's skills but the contrast between his Paul McCartney-influenced compositions ('My Singing Bird') and his partner's lighter, more whimsical offerings was too great to hold under one banner. Connolly returned to the folk circuit, where his between-songs banter quickly became the focal point of his act and introduced a newfound role as a successful comedian. Meanwhile his erstwhile partner began his solo career in 1971 with *Can I Have My Money*

Back, before forming a new group, Stealers Wheel. Albums: *First Collection Of Merrie Melodies* (1968), *The New Humblebums* (1969), *Open Up The Door* (1970). Compilations: *The Humblebums* (1981), *Early Collection* (1987 - includes Rafferty's early solo tracks).

Hurley, Michael

b. 20 December 1941, Buck County, Pennsylvania, USA. Hurley began playing guitar at the age of 13 and subsequently led an itinerant lifestyle until gravitating to the folk enclave at New York's Greenwich Village. An accomplished performer and songwriter, he was about to secure a major recording deal when a combination of hepatitis and mononucleosis led to a lengthy spell in hospital. Hurley made his delayed debut in 1964 on the traditional outlet, Folkways. *First Songs* featured support from longtime friend and associate Robin Remaily and revealed an artist of quirky imagination and vocal delivery. The set included the singer's first version of 'The Werewolf', later popularized by the Holy Modal Rounders, and the piece for which its creator is best remembered. The same group recorded several other Hurley compositions, including 'Radar Blues' and 'Morning Glory', while the Youngbloods acknowleged their respect by signing Hurley to their Raccoon label, thus ending a six-year hiatus. *Armchair Boogie* and *Hi-Fi Snock Uptown* maintained the singer's idiosyncratic style while offering muted instrumental support. During the 70s Hurley completed several releases for the traditional outlet Rounder, and was a major contributor to *Have Moicy*, a various artist's compendium declared 'best album of 1975' in the New York *Village Voice* and 'one of the Top 10 albums of the decade' in *Rolling Stone*. By this point the singer had repaired to rural Vermont and although opportunities to record lessened, the enchanting *Watchtower* showed Hurley's gifts and wit intact.
Albums: *First Songs* (1964), *Armchair Boogie* (1970), *Hi-Fi Snock Uptown* (1972), with others *Have Moicy* (1975), *Long Journey* (1977), *Snockgrass* (70s), *Blue Navigator* (1984), *The Watchtower* (1988).

Hurt, Mississippi John

b. John Smith Hurt, 3 July 1893, Teoc, Mississippi, USA, d. 2 November 1966. One of the major 'rediscoveries' during the 60s' folk blues revival, Mississippi John Hurt began playing at informal gatherings and parties at the turn of the century, when guitars were still relatively uncommon. Although he worked within the idiom, Hurt did not regard himself as a blues singer and his relaxed, almost sweet, intonation contrasted with the aggressive approach of many contemporaries. In

1928 he recorded two sessions for the OKeh label. These early masters included 'Candy Man Blues', 'Louis Collins' and 'Ain't No Tellin' (aka 'A Pallet On The Floor'), songs which were equally redolent of the ragtime tradition. For the ensuing three decades, Hurt worked as a farm-hand, reserving music for social occasions. His seclusion ended in 1963. Armed with those seminal OKeh recordings, a blues aficionado, Tom Hoskins, followed the autobiographical lyric of 'Avalon Blues' and travelled to the singer's hometown. He persuaded Hurt to undertake a series of concerts which in turn resulted in several new recordings. Appearances at the Newport Folk Festival ensued, before the artist completed several sessions for the Vanguard label, supervised by folksinger Patrick Sky. These included masterly reinterpretations of early compositions, as well as new, equally compelling pieces. Hurt's re-emergence was sadly brief. He died at Grenada County Hospital on 2 November 1966 following a heart attack, having inspired a new generation of country-blues performers.

Albums: *Mississippi John Hurt - Folk Songs And Blues* (1963), *Worried Blues* (1964), *Blues At Newport* (1965), *Best Of Mississippi John Hurt* (1965, live recording), *Last Sessions* (1966), *Mississippi John Hurt - Today* (1967), *Last Sessions* (1973). Compilations: *The Immortal Mississippi John Hurt* (1967), *Avalon Blues* (1982), *Shake That Thing* (1986), *Monday Morning Blues* (1987), *Mississippi John Hurt 1963* (1988).

Hutchings, Ashley

b. 26 January 1945, Southgate, Middlesex, England. Although largely remembered as the founder member of Fairport Convention, where he was often afforded the nickname 'Tyger', Hutchings also went on to form Steeleye Span, in 1970. He played on the first four Fairport Convention albums, ending with the classic *Liege And Lief*. Ashley had grown unhappy with the increase in original material that the group was playing, at the expense of more traditional works. While with Fairport Convention he contributed to their one hit record, 'Si Tu Dois Partir', in 1969. After three albums with Steeleye Span, Hutchings formed the Albion Country Band, in 1971, and has led a succession of Albion Band line-ups ever since. The first of these line-ups was on *No Roses*, which included a total of 26 musicians, including himself and his then wife Shirley Collins. Many of the personnel involved have worked with Hutchings on other occasions, such as John Kirkpatrick, Barry Dransfield, Nic Jones, and the late Royston Wood, formerly of Young Tradition. With Hutchings the Albion Band became the first electric group to appear in plays at the National Theatre, London.

The group also 'electrified' Morris dancing, exemplified in *Morris On*, and *Son Of Morris On*. Hutchings has also done much work with former Fairport Convention members, Richard Thompson, and the late Sandy Denny. Hutchings has written and presented programmes on folk music for the BBC, and both he and the Albion Band were the subject of their own BBC television documentary, in 1979. More recently, Hutchings wrote and acted in his own one-man show about, song collector Cecil Sharp. The show has been performed nationwide since 1984. The presentation resulted in *An Evening With Cecil Sharp And Ashley Hutchings*. Hutchins continues to tour and record. It is not undeserved that he has been called the Father of Folk Rock in Britain.

Albums: with others *Morris On* (1972), with John Kirkpatrick *The Compleat Dancing Master* (1974), *Kicking Up The Sawdust* (1977), *An Hour With Cecil Sharp And Ashley Hutchings* (1986), *By Gloucester Docks I Sat Down And Wept* (1987), the Ashley Hutchings All Stars *As You Like It* (1989), *A Word In Your Ear* (1991). Compilations: various artists *49 Greek Street* (1970), various artists *Clogs* (1971), with Shirley Collins *A Favourite Garland* (1974), with Richard Thompson *Guitar Vocal* (1976), various artists *Buttons And Bows* (1984), various artists *Buttons And Bows 2* (1985), with Sandy Denny *Who Knows Where The Time Goes?* (1985).

Ian And Sylvia

Ian Tyson (b. 25 September 1933, British Columbia, Canada) and Sylvia Fricker (b. 19 September 1940, Chatham, Ontario, Canada). One of Canada's leading folk attractions, Ian And Sylvia met in 1959 at a Toronto club, the Village Corner, but by the early 60's they had switched their attentions to the American circuit. Their debut album, *Ian And Sylvia*, showed a debt to traditional stylings, but a second collection, *Four Strong Winds*, saw them embrace a more contemporary direction. This release not only featured Tyson's evocative title song, which quickly became a standard, but also contained an early reading of Bob Dylan's 'Tomorrow Is A Long Time'. *Northern Journey*, released in 1964, opened with 'You Were On My Mind', a much-covered Fricker song which became a folk-rock hit in the hands of We Five and Crispian St. Peters. Ian And Sylvia, meanwhile, began using session musicians on their recordings. Rick Turner, later of Autosalvage, and bassist Felix Pappalardi, helped define the duo's new direction, while a trip to Nashville in 1968 resulted in their embracing country music. Henceforth that particular genre would be prevalent in the couple's work. In 1974 Ian And Sylvia decided to pursue their own, independent careers. Both have recorded solo albums and remain an integral part of the Canadian music circle.

Albums: *Ian And Sylvia* (1962), *Four Strong Winds* (1964), *Northern Journey* (1964), *Early Morning Rain* (1965), *Play One More* (1966), *So Much Dreaming* (1967), *Nashville* (1968), *Full Circle* (1968), *Lovin' Sound* (1969).

Ian, Janis

b. Janis Eddy Fink, 7 April 1951, New York City, New York, USA. A teenage prodigy, Ian first attracted attention when her early composition, 'Hair Of Spun Gold', was published in a 1964 issue of *Broadside* magazine. Performances at New York's Village Gate and Gaslight venues inspired a recording deal which began with the controversial 'Society's Child (Baby I've Been Thinking)'. Brought to national prominence following the singer's appearance on Leonard Bernstein's television show, this chronicle of a doomed, inter-racial romance was astonishingly mature and inspired a series of equally virulent recordings attacking the perceived hypocrisy of an older generation. Ian's dissonant, almost detached delivery, enhanced the lyricism offered on a series of superior folk-rock styles albums, notably *For All The Seasons Of Your Mind*. Later relocated in California, Janis began writing songs for other artists, but re-embraced recording in 1971 with *Present Company*. *Stars* re-established her standing, reflecting a still personal, yet less embittered, perception. The title song was the subject of numerous cover versions, while 'Jesse' provided a US Top 10 hit for Roberta Flack. *Between The Lines* contained the evocatively simple 'At Seventeen', Ian's sole US chart topper, and subsequent releases continued to reflect a growing sophistication. *Night Rains* featured two film theme songs, 'The Foxes' and 'The Bell Jar', although critics began pointing at an increasingly maudlin, self-pity. The artist's impetus noticeably waned during the 80s and Janis Ian seemed to have retired from music altogether. However, she re-emerged in 1991 giving live performances and appearing on a British concert stage for the first time in 10 years.

Albums: *Janis Ian* (1967), *For All The Seasons Of Your Mind* (1967), *The Secret Life Of J. Eddy Fink* (1968), *Present Company* (1971), *Stars* (1974), *Between The Lines* (1975), *Aftertones* (1975), *Miracle Row* (1977), *Janis Ian* (1978), *Night Rains* (1979), *Restless Eyes* (1981). Compilation: *The Best Of Janis Ian* (1980).

Incredible String Band

This UK folk group was formed in 1965 in Glasgow, Scotland, at 'Clive's Incredible Folk Club' by Mike Heron (b. 12 December 1942, Glasgow, Scotland), Robin Williamson (b. 24 November 1943, Edinburgh, Scotland) and Clive Palmer (b. Glasgow, Scotland). In 1966 the trio completed *The Incredible String Band*, a collection marked by an exceptional blend of traditional and original material, but they split up upon its completion. Heron and Williamson regrouped the following year to record the exceptional *5000 Spirits Or The Layers Of The Onion*. On this the duo emerged as a unique and versatile talent, employing a variety of exotic instruments to enhance their global folk palate. Its several highlights included Mike's 'Painting Box' and two of Robin's most evocative compositions, 'Way Back In The 1960s' and 'First Girl I Loved'. The latter was later recorded by Judy Collins. A *de rigueur* psychedelic cover encapsulated the era and the pair were adopted by the emergent underground. Two further releases, *The Hangman's Beautiful Daughter* and *Wee Tam And The Big Huge*, consolidated their position and saw Williamson, in particular, contribute several lengthy, memorable compositions. *Changing Horses*, as its title implies, reflected a growing restlessness with the acoustic format and the promotion of two previously auxiliary members, Licorice McKechnie (harp/violin/percussion) and Rose Simpson (bass/violin/percussion), indicated a move to a much fuller sound. The album polarized aficionados with many lamenting the loss of an erstwhile charm and idealism. *I Looked Up* continued the transformation to a rock-based perspective although *U*, the soundtrack to an ambitious ballet-cum-pantomime, reflected something of their earlier charm. 1971's *Liquid Acrobat As Regards The Air* was stylistically diverse and elegiac in tone. Dancer-turned-musician Malcolm Le Maistre was introduced to the group's circle and, with the departure of both Rose and Licorice, a keyboard player, Gerald Dott, joined the String Band for *Earthspan*. By this point the group owed little to the style of the previous decade although Williamson's solo, *Myrrh*, invoked the atmosphere of *Wee Tam* rather than the apologetic rock of *No Ruinous Feud*. The two founding members were becoming estranged both musically and socially and in 1974

Incredible String Band

they announced the formal end of their partnership. Albums: *The Incredible String Band* (1966), *5000 Spirits Or The Layers Of The Onion* (1967), *The Hangman's Beautiful Daughter* (1968), *Wee Tam And The Big Huge* (1968), *Changing Horses* (1969), *I Looked Up* (1970), *U* (1970), *Be Glad For The Song Has No Ending* (1970), *Liquid Acrobat As Regards The Air* (1971), *Earthspan* (1972), *No Ruinous Feud* (1973), *Hard Rope And Silken Twine* (1974), *On Air* (1991 - rare BBC recordings). Compilations: *Relics Of The Incredible String Band* (1970), *Seasons They Change* (1976).

Indigo Girls

This American duo comprised Amy Ray (vocals/guitar) and Emily Saliers (vocals/guitar). Saliers and Ray met while in school, in their home town of Decatur, Georgia, USA, and later started to perform together, initially as 'Saliers and Ray'. They changed their name to Indigo Girls while at university. The duo's early releases were on their own label, Indigo Records, and commenced with a single, 'Crazy Game' in 1985, followed by an EP the following year. The latter recording included 'Blood And Fire' and 'Land Of Canaan', both of which re-appeared on *Indigo Girls*. Ray and Saliers were signed to Epic in 1988, and the first release featured, among others, Michael Stipe of R.E.M., and the Irish group Hothouse Flowers. Indigo Girls toured heavily throughout the USA to promote the album, in addition to playing support to Neil Young and R.E.M. *Indigo Girls* went gold in September 1989, and the duo won a Grammy award as the 'Best Contemporary Folk Group' of 1989. *Strange Fire* was re-issued towards the end of 1989, but with an additional track, 'Get Together', made famous by the Youngbloods. In addition to playing an AIDS research benefit in Atlanta, Georgia, in 1989, the duo were also asked by Paul Simon to perform at a fundraising event, in 1990, for the Children's Health Fund, a New York based fund founded by the singer. *Nomads, Indians, Saints* included the excellent Emily Saliers song 'Hammer And A Nail' which features Mary Chapin Carpenter on backing vocals.

Albums: *Strange Fire* (1987), *Indigo Girls* (1989), *Nomads, Indians, Saints* (1990), *Rites Of Passage* (1993).

Insect Trust

One of the most engaging groups to emerge from New York's folk and blues enclaves, the Insect Trust - Luke Faust (banjo, guitar), Bill Barth (guitars), Bob Palmer (woodwind, saxophones), Trevor Koehler (saxophone, upright bass, piano) and Nancy Jeffries (vocals) - were steeped in Greenwich Village heritage. Their eponymous debut album included material from artists as diverse as Gabor Szabo and Skip James, while the quintet's own compositions offered glimpses of

Indigo Girls

traditional American music, which echoed the experimentation found in the early Fairport Convention. A second Insect Trust album, *Hoboken Saturday Night*, was less purposeful, yet offered its own share of excellent moments. The use of former John Coltrane drummer Elvin Jones provided an undeniable muscle, but overall the collection lacked the element of surprise which made the group's debut so spellbinding. The group broke up soon after its recording. Palmer subsequently became a respected journalist but although Faust reappeared in the Holy Modal Rounders' circle, the rest of this excellent group failed to maintain a significant career in music.
Albums: *The Insect Trust* (1969), *Hoboken Saturday Night* (1970).

Irvine, Andy

This highly-regarded Irish singer/songwriter, and guitarist has been involved in a number of highly influential groups. Having followed acting as a career in the late 50s, and learned classical guitar, Irvine then chanced upon the music of Woody Guthrie. Turning away from classical to folk guitar, and adding harmonica and mandolin, hurdy-gurdy, bouzouki and mandola, he moved into the Dublin folk scene, after travelling with Derroll Adams and Ramblin' Jack Elliott. Overseas trips widened his musical sphere and in 1966, he formed Sweeney's Men with Johnny Moynihan and Joe Dolan. After one album, a trip to the Balkans led him to discover new rhythms and musical styles to add to his acquisitive talent. In 1972, with Christy Moore, Donal Lunny and Liam O'Flynn, he formed Planxty. Drawing on the experiences of his Eastern trip, and adding to his earlier work with Sweeney's Men, Planxty, with Irvine, became one of the most innovative, and influential, groups to emerge from Ireland's folk scene. After the group split in 1975, Irvine teamed up with Paul Brady, and toured and recorded, receiving praise from the popular music press, and appearing at the Cambridge Folk Festival in 1977. He also performed and recorded with De Dannan. When Planxty reformed in 1979, Andy divided his time between the group and solo performances, travelling to Australia and New Zealand, in addition to the USA and Europe. *Rainy Sundays...Windy Dreams* saw Irvine accommodate many varied influences from his travels, such as jazz and Eastern European music. When Planxty disbanded in 1983, Irvine, formed Mosaic, a group featuring members from Ireland, Denmark, Hungary and Holland. Despite a successful British and European tour, the group split due to rehearsal problems. Irvine, continued to work solo, then formed Patrick Street in 1986 with Kevin Burke (fiddle), Jackie Daly (melodeon) and Gerry

O'Beirne. Arty McGlynn (guitar) joined, replacing O'Beirne who was unable to commit himself to the group. Despite the success of Patrick Street, Irvine continues working in a solo capacity and his enthusiasm shows no sign of abating.
Albums: with Sweeney's Men *Sweeney's Men* (1968), with Christy Moore *Prosperous* (1972), with Planxty *Planxty* (1972), with Planxty *The Well Below The Valley* (1973), with Planxty *Cold Blow And The Rainy Night* (1974), *Andy Irvine/Paul Brady* (1976), with Planxty *After The Break* (1979), *Rainy Sundays...Windy Dreams* (1980), with Planxty *The Woman I Loved So Well* (1980), with Dick Gaughan *Parallel Lines* (1982), with Planxty *Words And Music* (1983), *Rude Awakening* (1991), with Davy Spillane *East Wind* (1992). Compilations: *The Planxty Collection* (1976).

Ives, Burl

b. Burl Icle Ivanhoe Ives, 14 June 1909, Hunt Township, Jasper County, Illinois, USA. One of the world's most celebrated singers of folk ballads, with a gentle, intimate style. Ives was also an actor on the stage and screen, an anthologist and editor of folk music. A son of tenant farmers in the 'Bible Belt' of Illinois, Ives was singing in public for money with his brothers and sisters when he was four years old. Many of the songs they sang originated in the British Isles, and were taught to them by their tobacco-chewing grandmother. After graduating from high school in 1927 Ives went to college intending to become a professional football coach. Instead, he left college early, in 1930, and hitch-hiked throughout the USA, Canada and Mexico, supporting himself by doing odd jobs and singing to his own banjo accompaniment, picking up songs everywhere he went. After staying for awhile in Terre Haute, Indiana, attending the State Teachers College, he moved to New York, and studied with vocal coach, Ekka Toedt, before enrolling for formal music training at New York University. Despite this classical education, he was determined to devote himself to folk songs. In 1938, he played character roles in several plays, and in the same year had a non-singing role on Broadway, in George Abbott's musical comedy, *The Boys From Syracuse*, followed by a four-month singing engagement at New York's Village Vanguard nightclub. He then toured with the Richard Rodgers/Lorenz Hart musical, *I Married An Angel*. In 1940 Ives performed on radio, singing his folk ballads to his own guitar accompaniment on programmes such as *Back Where I Come From*, and was soon given his own series entitled *Wayfaring Stranger*. The introductory, 'Poor Wayfaring Stranger', one of America's favourite folk songs, and by then already over 100 years old, became his

Burl Ives

long-time theme. Drafted into the US Army in 1942, Ives sang in Irving Berlin's military musical revue, *This Is The Army*, both on Broadway and on tour. In 1944, after medical discharge from the Forces, Ives played a long stint at New York's Cafe Society Uptown nightclub, and also appeared on Broadway with Alfred Drake in *Sing Out Sweet Land*, a 'Salute To American Folk And Popular Music'. For his performance, Ives received the Donaldson Award as Best Supporting Actor. During the following year, he made his concert bow at New York's Town Hall, and played a return engagement in 1946. Also in that year he made his first film, *Smoky*, with Fred McMurray and Anne Baxter, and appeared with Josh White in a full-length feature about folk music. Ives's other movies, in which he played characters ranging from villainous to warmly sympathetic, included *So Dear To My Heart* (1948), *East Of Eden* (1955) and *Cat On A Hot Tin Roof* (1958), in which he played Big Daddy, re-creating his highly acclaimed Broadway performance in the Tennessee Williams play; *Wind Across The Everglades* (1958), *Desire Under The Elms* (1958), *The Big Country* (1958), for which he received an Oscar as the Best Supporting Actor; and *Our Man In Havana* (1960). In 1954, Ives played the role of Cap'n Andy Hawkes in a revival of Jerome Kern and Oscar Hammerstein II's *Show Boat* at the New York City Center. In the 60s and 70s he appeared regularly on US television, sometimes in his dramatic series, such as *O K Crackerby* and *The Bold Ones*, and several music specials. In the 80s, he was still continuing to contribute character roles to feature films and television, and perform in concerts around the world. Back in 1948, his first chart record, 'Blue Tail Fly', teamed him with the Andrews Sisters. The song, written by Dan Emmett in 1846, had been in the Ives repertoire for some years. Other US Top 30 hits, through to the early 60s, included 'Lavender Blue (Dilly Dilly)', 'Riders In The Sky (Cowboy Legend)', 'On Top Of Old Smokey', 'The Wild Side Of Life', 'True Love Goes On And On', 'A Little Bitty Tear', 'Funny Way Of Laughin'' and 'Call Me Mr In-Between'. Many other songs were associated with him, such as 'Foggy Foggy Dew', 'Woolie Boogie Bee', 'Turtle Dove', 'Ten Thousand Miles', 'Big Rock Candy Mountain', 'I Know An Old Lady (Who Swallowed A Fly)', 'Aunt Rhody' and 'Ballad Of Davy Crockett'. Ives published several collections of folk ballads and tales, including *America's Musical Heritage - Song Of America*, *Burl Ives Song Book*, *Tales Of America*, *Burl Ives Book Of Irish Songs*, and for children, *Sailing On A Very Fine Day*.
Albums: *The Wayfaring Stranger* (1959), *Burl Ives Sings Irving Berlin* (1961), *The Versatile Burl Ives!* (1962), *It's Just My Funny Way Of Laughin'* (1962),

Ballads And Folk Songs (early 60s), *Walt Disney Presents Burl Ives - Animal Folk* (1964), *Times They Are A-Changin'* (late 60s), *Chim Chim Cheree* (1974), with the Korean Children Choir *Faith And Joy* (1974), *Bright And Beautiful* (1979), *Burl Ives Live In Europe* (1979), *How Great Thou Art* (1974), *Songs I Sang At Sunday School* (1974), *I Do Believe* (1974), *Junior Choice* (1974), *Payin' My Dues Again* (mid-70s), *Little White Duck* (1977), *Shall We Gather At River* (1978), *Talented Man* (1978), *Live In Europe* (1979), *Stepping In The Light* (1984), *Love And Joy* (1984) and the series *Historical America In Song*, for Encyclopedia Britannica.
Further reading: *The Wayfaring Stranger*, Burl Ives.

Iwan, Dafydd

Singer and songwriter b. 24 August 1943, Brynaman, South Wales. One of four sons born to a Non-conformist preacher, who himself came from a family of Welsh poets. Dafydd sang in chapel, whilst very young, learning from his mother how to read music. When Iwan was 12, the family moved to the farming community of Llanuwchllyn, near Bala, in North Wales, a contrast to the mining village he had been brought up in. After trying to learn a variety of instruments, he finally settled for the guitar. Dafydd studied Architecture in Cardiff, and graduated in 1968. It was during this time that he started writing, and singing, his own songs. His main influences at the time were singer/songwriters such as Pete Seeger, and Bob Dylan. It was during the mid-60s that he started appearing on Welsh television, releasing his first EP, *Wrth Feddwl Am Fy Nghymru (When I Think Of My Wales)*, in 1966. This appeared on the Welsh Teldisc label. In all, between 1966 and 1969, he released 8 EP's and 2 singles. The 1969 release, 'Carlo' was a satire on the Investiture of Prince Charles as the Prince Of Wales. During the 60s and 70s, Dafydd became very active in the non-violent Welsh language campaigns, being imprisoned in 1970. In 1969, he set up Sain records with fellow singer Huw Jones, and Brian Morgan Edwards. In 1982, he collaborated for the first time with Ar Log to record *Rhwng Hwyl A Thaith*, an album combining traditional and new material. In 1988, a video was released, *Dafydd Iwan Yng Nghorwen*, of a concert held in Corwen, Wales, celebrating Iwan's 25 years of singing. He is Vice-President of Plaid Cymru in North Wales with an ambition "to see Wales free in a new Europe of the peoples, a world at peace, and to retire gracefully". A volume of 152 of his songs was published in 1992, another video was released entitled *Dafydd Iwan Yn Fyw O'r Cnapan*, recorded at the 1992 Cnapan Folk Festival, and he is listed in the "International Who's Who". He has been honoured with a Gold Disc for his services to

Welsh music, and he is an honorary member of the Gorsedd of Bards for his services to the Welsh language. Dafydd has sung, both at home and overseas, for over 30 years, and a strong feature of his songs is his reflection of the aspirations of the Welsh people, and the Welsh language, and his empathy with the struggles for human rights in other parts of the world.

Albums: *Mae'r Darnau Yn Disgyn I'w Lle* (1976), *Bod Yn Rhydd* (1979), *Dafydd Iwan Ar Dan* (1981), *Rhwng Hwyl A Thaith* (1982), *Yma O Hyd* (with Ar Log 1983), *Gwinllan A Roddwyd: I Gofio'r Tri* (1986), *Dal I Gredu* (1991).

Compilations: *Yma Mae 'Nghan* (1972), *Carlo A Chaneuon Eraill* (1977), *I'r Gad* (1977).

Further reading: *Dafydd Iwan* (Autobiography 1982).

J

Jack The Lad

This off-shoot of Lindisfarne, comprising Billy Mitchell (guitar, vocals), Simon Cowe (guitar, vocals), Ray Laidlaw (drums) and Rod Clements (bass), was formed in 1973. The quartet recorded some rock 'n' jig material with Maddy Prior's vocals, before Clements left for sesssion and production work. Ian Walter Fairburn (fiddle) and Phil Murray (bass) were recruited for The *Old Straight Track*, a song cycle of 'Geordie' electric folk songs. After the failure of this somewhat experimental project, the group returned to philosophical good time material, and, in 1976, signed for United Artists. Cowe assisted in the preparation of the *Jackpot*, but had left before the band recorded the dense, commercial album which was produced by Tom Allom. Despite having a loyal cult following on the college and club circuit, Jack The Lad disbanded shortly after Laidlaw's departure to Radiator, playing a few farewell gigs with Eric Green on drums. In 1993, after several CD releases, and Lindisfarne's impending 25th anniversary, Jack The Lad reformed in two forms: the original band, and as a festival act which included Mitchell, Fairburn and Murray.

Albums: *It's Jack The Lad* (1974), *The Old Straight Track* (1974), *Rough Diamonds* (1975), *Jackpot* (1976).

James, John

A highly talented Welsh guitarist, James's versatile style is usually that of ragtime and blues, but he is equally at home in a variety of musical genres. He has worked with numerous talented combinations, but is generally thought to be at his best as a solo artist, although on some of his recordings it is sometimes difficult to believe that one musician is providing the full range of sound. In person, he is much in demand as a performer in small, intimate clubs.

Selected albums: *Morning Brings Light* (1970), *John James* (1971).

James, Siân

b. 24 December 1961, Llanerfyl, Powys, Wales. James singing career began when she was put on the stage of a local musical competition at the age of four. She learned to play piano at six years old and, by 11, the harp. By the age of 16, James was touring with a harp trio, playing for music and Welsh societies in England and Wales. James then studied for a music degree at Bangor University, North Wales, and began to travel extensively, singing and playing harp. On 14 March 1981, the group Bwchadanas was formed, at Bangor University. The acoustic line-up featured, in addition to James; Geraint Cynan (b. 20 June 1961, Treorci, Rhondda, Mid-Glamorgan, Wales; piano), Rhys Harries (b. 6 January 1962, Newbridge, Gwent, Wales; guitar), Gareth Ioan, who left in 1986, (b. 19 September 1961, Aberynolwyn, Gwynedd, Wales; pipes), Lilio Rolant, who also left in 1986, (b. 3 May 1962, Cardiff, South Glamorgan, Wales; harp) and Rhodri Tomas (b. 15 April 1962, Llanelli, Dyfed, Wales; guitar). The group were gigging constantly, and were voted the Best Welsh Folk Band for 1983, 1984 and 1985. *Cariad Cywir*, released on Sain Records, gained the group a wider audience, but with the making of the album, a new electric line-up was formed. This included Marc Jones (bass), who was later replaced by Ray Jones (b. 11 October 1951, London, England; bass), Meredydd Morris (electric guitar), and Owen Huws (drums). Other musicians who have contributed to the band have included drummers Gwyn Jones, Graham Land, and Charlie Britten, as well as Dafydd Dafis (soprano and alto saxophone). The group represented Wales in the Pan-Celtic Festival in Killarney, Eire, in 1985, winning the folk song competition. Bwchadanas also supported Moving Hearts in 1985, and played one date with Runrig, in 1987. Owing to individual members' commitments, Bwchadanas now only play a handful of dates every year. Much television coverage has, however, enabled the group to become one of the most successful folk

John James

rock bands in Wales. Meanwhile, Siân James has continued to tour in her own right throughout Ireland, Scotland, Brittany and America, and *Cysgodion Karma*, released on Sain, attracted a good deal of interest in the artist. James is currently performing with Tich Gwilym (b. 10 September 1950, Pen y graig, Rhondda, South Wales; guitar, charango), and Geraint Cynan (keyboards), with herself on harp and vocals. She continues to sing traditional and contemporary Welsh folk songs, as well as fronting Bwchadanas as vocalist.

Albums: with Bwchadanas *Cariad Cywir* (1984), *Cysgodion Karma* (1990). Compilation: featuring 3 tracks from Bwchadanas *Cwlwm Pedwar* (1981).

Jansch, Bert

b. 3 November 1943, Glasgow, Scotland. This gifted and influential performer learned his craft in Edinburgh's folk circle before being absorbed into London's burgeoning circuit, where he established a formidable reputation as an inventive guitar player. His debut *Bert Jansch*, is a landmark in British folk music and includes 'Do You Hear Me Now', a Jansch original later covered by Donovan, the harrowing 'Needle Of Death', and an impressive version of Davey Graham's 'Angie'. The artist befriended John Renbourn who played supplementary guitar on Bert's second selection, *It Don't Bother Me*. The two musicians then recorded the exemplary *Bert And John*, which was released alongside *Jack Orion*, Jansch's third solo album. This adventurous collection featured a nine-minute title track and a haunting version of 'Nottamun Town', the blueprint for a subsequent reading by Fairport Convention. Bert continued to make exceptional records, but his own career was overshadowed by his participation in the Pentangle alongside Renbourn, Jacqui McShee (vocals), Danny Thompson (bass) and Terry Cox (drums). Between 1968 and 1973 this accomplished, if occasionally sterile, quintet was one of folk music's leading attractions, although the individual members continued to pursue their own direction during this time. *LA Turnaround*, released following the quintet's dissolution, was a promising collection and featured assistance from several American musicians including former member of the Monkees, Michael Nesmith. Although Jansch rightly remains a respected figure, his later work lacks the invention of those early releases. In the late 80s he took time out from solo folk club dates to join Jacqui McShee in a regenerated Pentangle line-up.

Albums: *Bert Jansch* (1965), *It Don't Bother Me* (1965), *Jack Orion* (1966), with John Renbourn *Bert And John* (1966), *Nicola* (1967), *Birthday Blues* (1968), *Lucky Thirteen* (1969), with Renbourn *Stepping Stones* (1969), *Rosemary Lane* (1971), *Moonshine* (1973), *LA Turnaround* (1974), *Santa Barbara Honeymoon* (1975), *A Rare Conundrum* (1978), *Avocet* (1979), *Thirteen Down* (1980), *Heartbreak* (1982), *From The Outside* (1985), *Leather Launderette* (1988), *Bert Jansch + Jack Orion* (1993).

Bert Jansch

Compilations: *The Essential Collection Vol. 1* (1987), *The Essential Collection Vol. 2* (1987), *The Gardener: Essential Bert Jansch 1965-71* (1992).

Jenkins, Martin

A solid, reliable character; an essential component of a successful folk scene. An important member of Whippersnapper, Jenkins became interested in acoustic instruments at an early age. Throughout the late 60s and 70s he worked in a number of bands, such as Dando Shaft, Hedgehog Pie, Bert Jansch's Conundrum, Five Hand Reel and Plainsong. In 1982 he formed an occasional unit, Quiet Riot. The mixture of ex-Dando Shaft personnel and other old friends, resulted in *Carry Your Smile*. Now married to a Bulgarian singer, his musical tastes have moved in an Eastern European direction, and he has become a successful record producer.
Album: *Carry Your Smile* (1983).

Jiminez, Flaco

b. Leonardo Jiminez, 11 March 1939, San Antonio, Texas, USA. Jiminez' grandfather, Patricio, learned the accordion from German neighbours and played in towns in southern Texas at the turn of the century. Jiminez' father, Santiago, was a noted accordionist and played lively dance music around San Antonio. His best-known composition is the polka 'Viva Seguin', named after a small town near San Antonio. Santiago, who started recording in 1936 and made some records for RCA, played the two-button accordion and made no attempt to integrate his music with other American forms. Jiminez, nicknamed El Flaco 'the skinny one', played bajo sexto with his father and made his recording debut in 1955 on 'Los Tecolotes'. He recorded with a group, Los Caminantes and often had regional successes by considering contemporary lifestyle such as 'El Pantalon Blue Jean' and 'El Bingo'. His albums for Arhoolie gathered a following outside Texas, and his appearance alongside Bob Dylan on *Doug Sahm And Band* in 1973, brought him to the attention of rock fans. Ry Cooder began touring and recording with him, and Jiminez can be heard on Cooder's *Chicken Skin Music, Show Time, The Border* and *Get Rhythm*. Their key collaborations are the free-flowing 'He'll Have To Go' and the sombre 'Dark End Of The Street'. Jiminez's album, *Tex-Mex Breakdown*, showed that he was thinking in terms of a wider audience. He has also worked with Peter Rowan and a key track is 'Free Mexican Airforce'. Jiminez tours in his own right and is popular at arts centres and folk venues throughout the UK. His father died in 1984 and his younger brother, Santiago Jnr., is also a professional accordionist.

Selected albums: *El Principe Del Acordeon* (1977), *Flaco Jiminez Y Su Conjunto* (1978), with Santiago Jiminez *El Sonido De San Antonio* (1980), *Mis Polkas Favorites* (UK *Viva Seguin*) (1983), *Tex-Mex Breakdown* (1983), *On The Move* (1984), *San Antonio Soul* (1985), *Homenaje A Don Santiago Jiminez* (1985), with Los Paisanos, Los Hnos Barron, Los Formales *Augie Meyers Presents San Antonio Saturday Night* (1986), *Ay Te Dejo En San Antonio* (1986), with Ry Cooder, Fred Ojeda, Peter Rowan *The Accordion Strikes Back* (1987), *Flaco's Amigos* (1988), with Freddy Fender, Augie Meyers, Doug Sahm *Texas Tornados* (1990), with Fender, Meyers, Sahm *Zone Of Our Own* (1991), *Ay Te Dejo En San Antonio* (1991), *Partners* (1992), *Un Mojada Sin Licencia* (1993).

Johnson, Robert

b. Robert Leroy Johnson, 8 May 1911 (this often varies), Hazlehurst, Mississippi, USA, d. 16 August 1938, Greenwood, Mississippi, USA. For a subject upon which it is dangerous to generalise, it hardly strains credulity to suggest that Johnson was the fulcrum upon which post-war Chicago blues turned. The techniques which he had distilled from others' examples, including Charley Patton, Son House and the unrecorded Ike Zinnerman, in turn became the template for influential musicians such as Muddy Waters, Elmore James and those that followed them. Endowed by some writers with more originality than was in fact the case, it was as an interpreter that Johnson excelled, raising a simple music form to the level of performance art at a time when others were content to iterate the conventions. He was one of the first of his generation to make creative use of others' recorded efforts, adapting and augmenting their ideas to such extent as to impart originality to the compositions they inspired. Tempering hindsight with perspective, it should be noted that only his first record, 'Terraplane Blues', sold in any quantity; even close friends and family remained unaware of his recorded work until decades later, when researchers such as Gayle Dean Wardlow and Mack McCormick contacted them. In all, Johnson recorded 29 compositions at five sessions held between 23 November 1936 and 20 June 1937; a further 'bawdy' song recorded at the engineers' request is as yet unlocated. It has never been established which, if any, of his recordings were specifically created for the studio and what proportion were regularly performed, although associate Johnny Shines attested to the effect that 'Come On In My Kitchen' had upon audiences. Similarly, the image of shy, retiring genius has been fabricated out of his habit of turning away from the engineers and singing into the corners of the room, which Ry Cooder identifies as 'corner loading', a means of enhancing vocal power. That power and the precision of his guitar playing are evident from the first take of 'Kind-hearted Women Blues', which like 'I Believe I'll Dust My Broom' and 'Sweet Home Chicago', is performed without bottle-neck embellishment. All eight titles from the first session in San Antonis, Texas, exhibit the attenuated rhythm patterns, adapted from a boogie pianist's left-hand 'walking basses', that became synonymous with post-war Chicago blues and Jimmy Reed in particular. Several alternate takes survive and reveal how refined Johnson's performances were, only 'Come On In My Kitchen' being played at two contrasting tempos. Eight more titles were recorded over two days, including 'Walkin Blues', learned from Son House, and 'Cross Road Blues', the song an echo of the legend that Johnson had sold his soul to the Devil to achieve his musical skill. 'Preachin' Blues' and 'If I Had Possessions Over Judgement Day' were both impassioned performances that show his ability was consummate. The balance of his repertoire was recorded over a weekend some seven months later in Dallas. These 11 songs run the gamut of emotions, self-pity, tenderness and frank sexual innuendo giving way to representations of demonic possession, paranoia and despair. Fanciful commentators have taken 'Hellhound On My Trail' and 'Me And The Devil' to be literal statements rather than the dramatic enactment of feeling expressed in the lyrics. Johnson's ability to project emotion, when combined with the considered way in which he lifted melodies and mannerisms from his contemporaries, gainsay a romantic view of his achievements. Nevertheless, the drama in his music surely reflected the drama in his lifestyle, that on an itinerant with a ready facility to impress his female audience. One such dalliance brought about his end a year after his last session, poisoned by a jealous husband while performing in a jook joint at Three Forks, outside Greenwood, Mississippi. At about that time, Columbia A&R man John Hammond was seeking Johnson represent country blues at a concert, entitled 'From Spirituals To Swing', that took place at New York's Carnegie Hall on 23 December 1938, with Big Bill Broonzy taking Johnson's place. Robert Johnson possessed unique abilities, unparalleled in his contemporaries and those that followed him. The importance of his effect on subsequent musical developments cannot be diminished but neither should it be seen in isolation.

Selected albums: *Robert Johnson: The Complete Recordings* (c.80s), *Gold Collection* (1993).

Further reading: *Searching For Robert Johnson*, Peter Guralnick.

Johnstons

This mid-60s Irish close harmony group enjoyed immense success in their homeland. The original line-up, which used to play in the family pub in Slane, consisted of Adrienne Johnston (vocals), her sister Luci (vocals), and brother Michael (guitar). Their debut single, a cover of Ewan MacColl's 'Travelling People', reached number 1 in the Irish charts. Michael left the trio, and the sisters were joined by traditionalist Mike Moloney (guitar/banjo/vocals), and shortly after by Paul Brady (b. 19 May 1947, Co. Tyrone, Northern Ireland; guitar/vocals). Brady and Moloney had earlier met while at University College Dublin, where the latter had gained an MA in Economics. While *The Barley Corn* was traditionally based, *Give A Damn* saw the group working with contemporary material, by such writers as Joni Mitchell, Leonard Cohen, Jacques Brel, and Dave Cousins. By the time of *Bitter Green*, Luci had left the group, which continued as a trio *If I Sang My Song* was Brady and Adrienne Johnston only, the others having left. The majority of the songs contained on the album came from the pen of Brady and Chris McLoud. The album boasted backing musicians such as Tim Hart, Royston Wood, and Rick Kemp. Adrienne recorded only one solo album completed in 1975, before her premature death. Her solo outing, *Adrienne Johnston Of The Johnstons*, had a number of notable musicians in attendance including Simon Nicol, Gerry Conway and Pat Donaldson. Brady went on to solo success, outside the limits of the folk arena, while Moloney, resident in the USA, had a hand in the television series about the history of Irish music, *Bringing It All Back Home*, in 1991.

Selected albums: *Travelling People* (1966), *The Johnstons* (1968), *Give A Damn* (1969), *The Barleycorn* (1969), *Both Sides Now* (1969), *Bitter Green* (1969), *The Johnstons Sampler* (1970), *Colours Of The Dawn* (1971), *If I Sang My Song* (1972), *Anthology* (c.70s), *Streets Of London - The Johnstons Sampler* (1978), *The Transatlantic Years Featuring Paul Brady* (1992).

Jones, Mazlyn

b. Nigel Maslyn Jones, 26 June 1950, Dudley, Warwickshire, England. Jones started playing guitar, as well as writing poetry and music, when only 14 years old. When he left school, in 1969, he moved to the Channel Islands to work for Gerald Durrell and returned to the mainland in 1971, where he started to teach guitar. It was after moving to Cornwall in 1973 that he bagan to concentrate on performing and writing, and in 1975 toured folk clubs and smaller festivals. Due to confusion, he changed the spelling of his name to Mazlyn, as it was often misspelt or incorrectly pronounced. Jones is a performer who encompasses elements of world music, new age and rock, with a sprinkling of folk, often with environmental themes. He has played with a variety of well-known performers, including Roy Harper. Jones toured as support act to Barclay James Harvest in 1981, playing every major venue in the UK and Europe. Following the 1981 tour, Mazlyn took a break from live touring to concentrate on the recording of *Breaking Cover*. Live, Mazlyn also presents a show featuring songs accompanied by back projections to highlight the theme of the material. He produced the debut album by new age band Solstice, in 1984. Johnny Coppin is featured on Jones's first two albums, while the fourth release, *Water From The Well*, has Nik Turner, of Hawkwind, on saxophones and flute on two songs, and Guy Evans, from Van Der Graff Generator, on percussion. In 1986, material from *Breaking Cover* was used by independent television for a documentary on the World Surfing Contest, which was held in the UK the same year. Nik Turner again appeared, playing flute, on the 1991 release *Mazlyn Jones*. Jones now performs and records as Mazlyn Jones, having dropped the name prefix.

Albums: *Ship To Shore* (1976), *Sentinel* (1979), *Breaking Cover* (1981), *Water From The Well* (1987), *Mazlyn Jones* (1991).

Jones, Nic

b. Nicholas Paul Jones, 9 January 1947, Orpington, Kent, England. The earlier work of this highly-respected guitarist and fiddle player showed great promise, but a tragic accident interrupted his career. On 26 February 1982, he was involved in a car crash which left him in a coma for six weeks. He then spent the next six months in hospital while his broken bones were repaired. As a result, Nic has had to try and re-learn his old highly-innovative instrumental technique. *Ballad And Song* contained the folk standards 'Sir Patrick Spens' and 'Little Musgrave'. Jones backed Maddy Prior and June Tabor on *Silly Sisters* in 1976, and in 1978 recorded *Bandoggs* for Transatlantic. The title was also the name of the short-lived titular group which included Pete and Chris Coe and Tony Rose, as well as Jones himself. *Penguin Eggs* became *Melody Maker* folk album of the year, and contained some excellent songs including 'The Humpback Whale'. Jones in the past has been critical of the folk purists who refuse to allow songs to evolve, and on one occasion sang a Chuck Berry song at the Nottingham Traditional Music Club, with the inevitable hostile reaction. Nic provided vocals on the 1989 Gerry Hallom release *Old Australian Ways*, proving that his voice is still resonant.

Albums: *Ballad And Song* (1970), *Nic Jones* (1971),

with Jon Raven, Tony Rose *Songs Of A Changing World* (1973), *The Noah's Ark Trap* (1977), *From The Devil To A Stranger* (1978), *Bandoggs* (1978), *Penguin Eggs* (1980).

Jones, Wizz

b. Raymond Ronald Jones, 25 April 1939, Croydon, Surrey, England. After seeing Big Bill Broonzy, Jack Elliot and Muddy Waters in 1957, at London's Roundhouse, Wizz Jones took up the guitar. Throughout the early 60s, he busked his way around Europe and Africa until returning to England. Together with Pete Stanley (banjo), Jones formed a bluegrass duo and worked on the folk circuit until 1967. In the 70s Jones was working with the group Lazy Farmer, which included his wife Sandy (b. 23 July 1945, London, England; banjo), John Bidwell (flute/guitar), Don Cogin (banjo) and Jake Walton (hurdy-gurdy/dulcimer). Still playing many of the blues numbers that inspired him, his style transcends the straight 'folk' tag, and he is currently performing, festivals and clubs with his son Simeon (b. 10 March 1964; saxophone/flute/harmonica).

Albums: with Pete Stanley *Sixteen Tons Of Bluegrass* (1965), with Pete Stanley, Mac Wiseman *Folkscene* (1966), *Wizz Jones* (1969), *The Legendary Me* (1970), *Solo Flight* (1971), *Right Now* (1971), *Winter Song* (1972), *When I Leave Berlin* (1974), with Lazy Farmer *Lazy Farmer* (1975), *Happiness Was Free* (1976), *Magical Flight* (1978), with Werner Lammerhirt *Roll On River* (1981), *The Grapes Of Life* (1987). Compilation: *The Village Thing Tapes* (1993).

Journeymen

This US folk trio comprising Scott McKenzie (guitar/vocals), Dick Weissman (b. Richard Weissman; banjo/guitar/vocals), and John Phillips (b. John Edmund Andrew Phillips, 30 August 1935, Parris Island, South Carolina, USA; guitar/vocals). The group were formed, like many others at the time, as a result of the folk revival of the late 50s and 60s, and featured strong harmonies and a commercial sound that made folk such a saleable commodity at the time. The Journeymen made their debut in 1961, at Gerde's Folk City, New York, and shortly after signed to Capitol Records, releasing *The Journeymen* later the same year. The group's popularity, and commerciality, waned after a relatively short life span, and the members went their separate ways. John attempted to revive the trio's fortunes with the New Journeymen, which featured his wife Michelle Phillips and Marshall Brickman. Phillips went on to form the Mamas And The Papas, while McKenzie found fame as the singer of the hit song 'San Francisco'. Weissman

Wizz Jones (left) and his son Sim

continued in the business, recording *The Things That Trouble My Mind* and *Dick Weissman Sings And Plays Songs Of Protest*.
Albums: *The Journeymen* (1961), *Coming Attraction-Live* (1962), *New Directions* (1963).

JSD Band
This Scottish folk-rock act was one of genre's leading attractions during the early 70s. Having made their debut with the low-key *Country Of The Blind*, the group - Des Coffield (guitar/keyboards/vocals), Sean O'Rouke (guitar), Chuck Fleming (violin), Jim Divers (bass) and Colin Finn (drums) - then opted for a more expressive style, echoing that of Fairport Convention and Steeleye Span, but based on Fleming's showmanship and dexterity. *JSD Band* encapsulated the quintet's live fire and remains their most popular release, whereas *Travelling Days* was viewed as a disappointment. The loss of several members, including Fleming, proved fatal and although Iain Lyon, formerly of My Dear Watson, bolstered a group latterly known as the New JSD Band, the unit split up in 1974.
Albums: *Country Of The Blind* (1971), *JSD Band* (1972), *Travelling Days* (1973).

Jumpleads
Formed in Oxford, England, the Jumpleads, with Caroline Ritson (vocals), Jon Moore (guitars), Dave Townend (melodeon) and Tracy (drums/bass), enjoyed a brief but notorious career. In 1982 they released *The Stag Must Die*, in a blood-splattered cover. The album was called 'loud, noisy, daring and appealing', but its new-wave sensibility, combined with folk songs, (termed 'rogue folk'), appalled and offended many people. Disenchanted with the response, the Jump Leads disbanded. Rogue records released a remix single of 'False Knight On The Road', but the band have only reunited for one-off festival performances. Of the ex-members, Jon Moore has the highest profile with E2.
Album: *The Stag Must Die* (1982).

Jungr And Parker
Formed in 1985, the duo of Barbara Jungr (vocals) and Michael Parker (guitar/piano/vocals), ex-members of the Three Courgettes, performed on the UK cabaret circuit, and specialized in songs of a very English, middle-class manner. At times their documentation of everyday life's trials and tribulations were occasionally reminiscent of the work of Flanders And Swann. They momentarily reached a mass national audience by their regular appearances on Julian Clary's *Sticky Moments* television programme. Album: *Off The Peg* (1989), *Canada* (1992).

K

Kahn, Si

b. 23 April 1944, Pennsylvania, USA. With an artist mother and Rabbi father, Si Kahn has been active in the field of civil rights, and labour and community organization in the Southern states for over 25 years. Initially, he was a volunteer with the Student Non-Violent Co-ordinating Committee, but since then, having graduated from Harvard in 1965, Kahn has gone on to become involved in both African-American and white Southern communities. He is also an activist in the Jewish community, and a founder of the Jewish Fund for Justice. Kahn started performing in 1979, at the age of 35, his first appearance being at the Chicago Folk Festival that year. Apart from his own recordings, Si has recorded with Pete Seeger and Jane Sapp, *Carry It On: Songs Of America's Working People*, a collection of civil rights, women's and labour songs. Aside from the USA, Kahn has toured Europe and Britain, playing at festivals, and regularly gives lecture tours to community groups. In 1989, Kahn provided both narration and songs for an accompanying cassette to two children's books, *Goodnight Moon* and *The Runaway Bunny*. A third children's project, this time a recording called *Goodtimes And Bedtimes*, was completed around 1986, but, held up due to a number of problems, is scheduled for release in 1992. More recently, Kahn's songs, in particular 'Aragon Mill', and 'What You Do With What You've Got', have been covered by other singers, resulting in an increasing interest in his work.

Albums: *New Wood* (1975), *Home* (1980), *Doing My Job* (1982), *Unfinished Portraits* (1985), with John McCutcheon *Signs Of The Times* (1986), with Jane Sapp and Pete Seeger *Carry It On: Songs Of America's Working People* (1986), *I'll Be There* (1989), *I Have Seen Freedom* (1992).

Further reading: *How People Get Power*, Si Kahn. *The Forest Service And Appalachia*, Si Kahn. *Rural Community Organizing: History And Models*, Si Kahn with Harry Boyte. *Organizing: A Guide For Grassroots Leaders*, Si Kahn. *Si Kahn Songbook*, Si Kahn.

Kashmir

This short-lived English folk duo featured Lesley Davies (b. Lesley Anne Davies, 23 March 1959, Stockport, Cheshire, England; vocals/guitar), and her brother Steve Davies (b. Stephen Glyn Davies, 17 February 1964, Romiley, Cheshire, England; piano/synthesizer/vocals). Kashmir was formed in 1985, and performed a combination of contemporary and traditional folk material, touring clubs and festivals. Shortly after the release of *Stay Calm*, which included the vocals of Fiona Simpson, Steve decided to quit performing full time, and Lesley continued, for only a short while longer as Kashmir, with guitarist Jon Gibbons. Lesley had, by now, also joined Les Barker's Mrs. Ackroyd Band, providing vocals for *Earwigo* in 1987, and for *Oranges And Lemmings* in 1990. She was also touring with the band, as well as playing solo. She can still be seen singing with singer-songwriter Mike Silver, and Paul Metser's band, Cave Canem, in addition to a number of local jazz bands. In 1988-89, Davies took the female lead in the Les Barker Folk Opera *The Stones Of Callenish*, performed live at the Sidmouth Folk Festival, and on the recorded work. In 1990, she studied at Leeds College of Music, for a three-year diploma in jazz, contemporary and popular music.

Album: *Stay Calm* (1986).

Kavana, Ron

Kavana spent the 70s and early 80s in an R&B band, Juice on the Loose, before moving in a more traditional direction, inspired by the Pogues, and Shane McGowan in particular. He was invited to join McGowan's band after Ciat O'Riordan left, but the move was blocked by the Pogue's management. After eschewing R&B, he spent several years gigging with his Alias Ron Kavana. The new outfit incorporated African and South American rhythms with Irish sounds, and eagerly sought out further influences. The debut *Think Like A Hero*, emphasied this approach, coupled with an unsuppressable pop energy. Songs such as 'This Is The Night' (a worthy tribute to Van Morrison), sit comfortably alongside instrumentals like 'Soweto Trembles'. In the *Folk Roots* readers' poll of 1991, Alias Ron Kavana featured at, or near the top of six of the eight categories. Kavana next assembled the LILT (London Irish Live Trust) album *For The Children*, to promote peace in Northern Ireland, gathering a host of Irish traditional greats. The solo *Home Fires* followed. Mostly Irish in style, the material has the timbre of the traditional, particularly 'Young Ned Of The Hill' (co-written with Pogue Terry Woods). Of the band album, *Coming Days* (1991), *Folk Roots* stated: 'The man has delivered'. Alias Ron Kavana has since added an Irish piper, and become the Alias Big Band, but the energy and live appeal endures.

Albums: Alias Ron Kavana *Think Like A Hero* (1989), *Coming Days* (1991), Ron Kavana (solo) *Home Fires* (1991), as LILT *For the Children* (1990).

Keane, Dolores

b. Caherlistrane, Co. Galway, Eire. Keane was a former member of Irish group folk De Dannan. Her first solo album, which received a gold disc, was produced by ex-Silly Wizard member Phil Cunningham, and included the Si Khan classic 'Aragon Mill', Kate And Anna McGarrigle's much covered 'Heart Like A Wheel' and, most surprisingly, Marlene Dietrich's 'Lili Marlene'. *Farewell To Eirinn*, which included John Faulkner and Eamonn Curran, featured songs describing the story of the Irish emigration to America from 1845 to 1855, when nearly two million people (or 25 per cent of the population), left Ireland. *Lion In A Cage* remained in the contemporary setting, with songs by Chris Rea, Paul Brady and Kieran Halpin. The title track was a reference to Nelson Mandela, who was still a political prisoner in South Africa at the time. As with many songs of social statement, political changes often render them out of date very quickly. However, despite the freeing of Mandela, 'Lion In A Cage' remains a powerful song, and one of the better of the genre. Dolores participated in the television series *Bringing It All Back Home*, in 1991, performing with Mary Black and Emmylou Harris.
Albums: *There Was A Maid* (1978), with John Faulkner *Broken Hearted I'll Wander* (1979), *Farewell To Eirinn* (1980), with Faulkner *Sail Og Rua* (1983), *Dolores Keane* (1988), *Lion In A Cage* (1990), *Solid Ground* (1993).

Keith, Bill

b. October 1939, Boston, Massachusetts, USA. Keith is known for his innovative banjo style, and is credited with helping the development of the progressive bluegrass mode of playing, partly attributed to his chromatic technique. Having started out learning the piano Keith moved on to tenor banjo. In 1957, after seeing Pete Seeger of the Weavers, Keith bought a five-string banjo and gradually worked his way round the folk clubs and bars of New England with his partner Jim Rooney. In September 1962, Keith won the Philadelphia Folk Festival banjo contest. His first professional job was playing with Red Allen and mandolin player Frank Wakefield from Tennessee, eventually joining Bill Monroe's Blue Grass Boys and also the Country Gentlemen. In 1964, Keith recorded with Wakefield and Allen for the Folkways label, and the same year, joined the Jim Kweskin Jug Band, which featured Geoff and Maria Muldaur, and Richard Greene. When the group split up in 1968, Keith joined Ian And Sylvia Tyson's Great Speckled Bird, a country rock outfit, where he also played steel guitar. After approximately a year, he went on tour with Jonathan Edwards, and later Judy Collins.

From his work with the Blue Velvet Band, he then formed Muleskinner with David Grisman, Clarence White, Richard Greene and Peter Rowan. Keith spent much of the following period in session work and touring with Rooney, both in Europe and the UK. For *Something Auld, Something Newgrass, Something Borrowed, Something Bluegrass* Keith is backed by Vassar Clements (fiddle), Tony Rice (guitar) and David Grisman (mandolin). The album includes covers of a Mick Jagger/Keith Richard composition 'No Expectations', as well as Duke Ellington's 'Caravan'. During the 80s, he toured a number of British clubs along with long time colleague Jim Rooney.
Albums: with Jim Rooney *Livin' On The Mountain* (1962), *Sweet Moments With The Blue Velvet Band* (1969), *Something Auld, Something Newgrass, Something Borrowed, Something Bluegrass* (1976), *Bill Keith And Jim Collier* (1979), *Banjoistics* (1984), with Rooney *Collection* (1984), as Rowan, Grisman, Keith, Greene And White *Muleskinner* (1987).

Killen, Louis

b. January 1934, Gateshead, County Durham, England. This English folk singer is known for his a cappella vocals and occasional use of whistle and concertina. Following his time in the Oxford University Folk Song Club, he concentrated on this style exclusively. He formed one of Britain's first folk clubs, the 'Folk Song & Ballad Club' in Newcastle, in 1958. Finding himself unemployed in 1961, he pursued a professional singing career thereafter. One of his major influences in the early 60s, was Ewan MacColl which led Killen to concentrate on British, rather than American material. In 1962, Killen recorded two EPs for Topic Records, *The Colliers Rant*, with Johnny Handle, and *Northumberland Garland*. *Along The Coaly Tyne* included the material from these recordings, as well as Handle's *Stottin' Doon The Waall* EP. Killen emigrated to the USA in 1967, where he performed solo on the college and coffee house circuit. A move to the west coast in 1968 as an unknown artist, left Killen looking for extra work, occasionally finding employment in the shipyards. The following year, Louis headed back east, joining the crew of the Clearwater, the Hudson River Sloop that had been built for an ecological and educational restoration project. The crew included such luminaries as Pete Seeger and Gordon Bok. In addition, for two years from late 1970 he joined the Clancy Brothers, taking the place of Tommy Makem. Killen also recorded and performed with Peter Bellamy and Robin Williamson. Killen's career continued with concerts and lecture tours, often in collaboration with his wife Sally. *The Rose In June* was Killen's first album

Dolores Keane

since *Gallant Lads Are We*. Still based in the USA, Killen set out, in 1991, on his first British tour for 10 years and recommenced recording in 1990.

Albums: *Ballads And Broadsides* (1965), *Sea Shanties* (1968), with Johnny Handle *Along The Coaly Tyne* (1971), *50 South To 50 South* (1972), with Sally Killen *Bright Shining Morning* (1975), *Old Songs, Old Friends* (1978), *Gallant Lads Are We* (1980), *The Rose In June* (1990).

Kingston Trio

An influential part of America's folk revival, the Kingston Trio was formed in San Francisco in 1957 and were popular in the late 50s. The group consisted of Bob Shane (b. 1 February 1934, Hilo, Hawaii), Nick Reynolds (b. 27 July 1933, Coronado, California, USA) and Dave Guard (b. 19 October 1934, San Francisco, California, USA, d. 22 March 1991). The Kingston Trio had limited singles successes and are most often remembered for 'Tom Dooley' which reached number 5 in the UK charts, and number 1 in the US chart in 1958. The song, written by Guard, was based on an old folk tune, from the 1800s called 'Tom Dula'. *The Kingston Trio*, from which 'Tom Dooley' came, also reached number 1 in the US. The group had a line of successful albums in 1959, with *From The Hungry i*, a live recording, reaching number 2, and *The Kingston Trio At Large*, and *Here We Go Again* both achieving top placings. Further chart-toppers followed with *Sold Out*, and *String Along*. Their fresh harmonies and boyish enthusiasm endeared the trio to an America suspicious of the genre's New Left sympathies, but in the process paved the way for a generation of more committed performers. Guard was replaced by John Stewart (b. 5 September 1939, San Diego, California, USA) in May 1961, having left to pursue a solo career and form the Whiskeyhill Singers. *Close-Up* was the first release featuring Stewart, who had previously been with the Cumberland Three, and it reached number 3 in the US charts. 'San Miguel', the follow-up to 'Tom Dooley', only just managed to reach the Top 30 in the UK the following year. 'The Reverend Mr Black' achieved a Top 10 placing in the US chart in 1963. The line-up with Stewart continued until 1967.

Shane later re-formed the group, as the New Kingston Trio, with Roger Gamble and George Grove. The group continued to enjoy widespread popularity and their output, if stylistically moribund, was certainly prolific. However, the success of more exciting folk and folk-rock acts rendered them increasingly old-fashioned, and the Trio was disbanded in 1968. A group reunion was hosted on television, by Tom Smothers in 1981, when all six members were brought together for the first time. Stewart went on to achieve a cult following as a soloist, and continues to record and perform. In 1987 the Trio was on the road again, with Shane, Grove, and new member, Bob Haworth.

Albums: *The Kingston Trio* (1958), *From The Hungry i* (1959), *The Kingston Trio At Large* (1959), *Stereo Concert* (1959), *Here We Go Again* (1959), *Sold Out* (1960), *String Along* (1960), *The Last Month Of The Year* (1960), *Make Way!* (1961), *Goin' Places* (1961), *Close-Up* (1961), *College Concert* (1962), *Something Special* (1962), *New Frontier* (1963), *The Kingston Trio No. 16* (1963), *Sunny Side* (1963), *Sing A Song With The Kingston Trio* (1963), *Time To Think* (1963), *Back In Town* (1964), *The Folk Era* (1964), *Nick-Bob-John* (1965), *Stay Awhile* (1965), *Somethin' Else* (1965), *Children Of The Morning* (1966), *Once Upon A Time* (1969), *American Gold* (1973), *The World Needs A Melody* (1973), *Aspen Gold* (1979). Compilations: *Encores* (1961), *The Best Of The Kingston Trio* (1962), *Folk Era* (1964), *The Best Of The Kingston Trio Vol. 2* (1965), *The Best Of The Kingston Trio Vol. 3* (1966), *Once Upon A Time* (1969), *The Kingston Trio* (1972), *Where Have All The Flowers Gone* (1972), *The Historic Recordings Of The Kingston Trio* (1975), *The Very Best Of The Kingston Trio* (1987).

Further reading: *The Kingston Trio On Record*, Kingston Korner.

Kinnaird, Alison And Christine Primrose

Kinnaird (b. 30 April 1949, Edinburgh, Scotland) and Primrose (b. 17 February 1952, Carloway, Isle Of Lewis, Scotland), were known for their Gaelic-influenced folk music. Kinnaird studied the cello from the age of seven, and the Scottish harp from the age of 14, and has since gone on to win numerous competitions and awards. These include the Clarsach Trophy at the National Mod and the Harp competition at the Pan Celtic festival in Killarney. Having studied archaeology and Celtic studies at university, Alison recorded *The Harp Key*, the first record of the Scottish harp, after researching old manuscripts. This came out when fiddle music was particularly popular in folk circles, and the harp was often employed more as an instrument purely for accompaniment. A meeting with Ann Heymann, exponent of the wire-strung harp, in 1982, led to the follow-up *The Harper's Land*. By comparison, Christine Primrose has been singing since early childhood, with Gaelic as her first language. She too won the National Mod in 1974, and the Pan Celtic Festival in Killarney in 1978. As a result of the success of *Aite Mo Ghaoil*, Primrose has toured both Canada and the USA, as well as Europe, taking her voice and Gaelic language to a wide audience. The two together

Bob Shane and the New Kingston Trio

complement one another perfectly, with the purity of Primrose's voice combining with the equally pure harp sound of Kinnaird.

Albums: *The Quiet Tradition* (1990). Solo albums: Alison Kinnaird *The Harp Key* (1978), *The Harper's Gallery* (1980), with Ann Heymann *The Harper's Land* (1983); Christine Primrose *Aite Mo Ghaoil* (1982), *S Tu Nam Chuimhne* (1987).

Kipper Family

Discovered in 1978 by Norfolk singers Chris Sugden and Dick Nudds, the Kipper Family were originally founded by Ephraim Kipper in 1837. After a number of personnel changes over the years, the remaining duo of Henry Kipper (b. 4 August 1914, St. Just-near-Trunch, Norfolk, England; vocals, tremelodeon) and Sid Kipper (b. 3 September 1939, St. Just-near-Trunch, Norfolk, England; vocals, accordion, Trunch blow-pipes, walnut shells) continued the family tradition of keeping alive the songs from their native village. It is interesting to note that while Henry was born on the day that World War I began, so Sid was brought into the world the day that the World War II commenced. *The Ever Decreasing Circle* featured classic songs such as 'Spencer The Wild Rover', 'The Wild Mountain Thyme' and 'Joan Sugarbeet'. Active on the British folk scene from 1982, Henry decided to retire in 1991, while Sid continued in a solo capacity. *Broadside*, a compilation album of various artists, featured two songs by the Kipper Family, 'When I'm Abroad On The Broads' and 'Dicky Riding'.

Albums: *Since Time Immoral* (1984), *Ever Decreasing Circle* (1985), *The Crab Wars* (1986), *Fresh Yesterday* (1988), *Arrest These Merry Gentlemen* (1989), *In The Family Way* (1991). Compilation: *Broadside* (1989).

Kirkpatrick, John

b. 8 August 1947, Chiswick, London, England. Kirkpatrick is often held to be the master player of the accordion, melodeon and the concertina. Having spent some time in the early Steeleye Span line-up, he went on to be involved with folk-rock recordings of the 70s. He has toured and recorded with a veritable who's who of the folk-rock establishment, in particular Ashley Hutchings, Richard Thompson and Martin Carthy. Kirkpatrick also performed with Brass Monkey. *A Really High Class Band* included 'The Cherry Tree Carol' and Sir John Betjeman's 'A Shropshire Lad'. Kirkpatrick regularly records and performs with Sue Harris (b. 17 May 1949, Coventry, Warwickshire, England), who is known for her hammer dulcimer and oboe playing. They first started working together in 1971. Harris was, for a time, a member of the English Country Blues Band, and has contributed

incidental music for television, theatre and radio, including *The Canterbury Tales* on BBC Radio 4. Kirkpatrick, Harris and Carthy were in one of the early line-ups of the Albion Band. Kirkpatrick also played on *Night Owl* by Gerry Rafferty in 1979, and, in 1988, on Pere Ubu's *The Tenement Year*. By complete contrast, and highlighting Kirkpatrick's wide diversity, he also formed the Shropshire Bedlams Morris Dance team. In recent years, Kirkpatrick has toured as a trio with the two fine melodeon players Riccardo Tesi from Italy and Marc Perrone from France. Harris and Kirkpatrick also performed and recorded with Umps And Dumps, which included Derek Pearce (percussion), Tufty Swift (melodeon) and Alan Harris (banjo). Other commitments, such as performing with the Richard Thompson Band and his involvement with the National Theatre production of *Lark Rise To Candleford* have reduced Kirkpatrick's solo touring. In 1991, he presented a six-week radio series for the BBC, *Squeezing Around The World*, which featured many of the world's leading squeezebox players. Harris and Kirkpatrick have now started working, as a trio with Dave Whetstone (melodeon/guitar).

Albums: *Jump At The Sun* (1972), with Sue Harris *The Rose Of Britain's Isle* (1974), with Ashley Hutchings *The Compleat Dancing Master* (1974), with Harris *Among The Many Attractions At The Show Will Be A Really High Class Band* (1976), *Plain Capers* (1976), with Harris *Shreds And Patches* (1977), *Going Spare* (1978), with Harris *Facing The Music* (1980), with Umps And Dumps *The Moon's In A Fit* (1980), *Three In A Row - The English Melodeon* (1984), *Blue Balloon* (1987), *Sheepskins* (1988), with Harris *Stolen Ground* (1989). Solo album: Sue Harris *Hammers And Tongues* (1978).

Kitsyke Will

This UK three-piece group included Peadar Long (clarinet, whistles, flute, saxophones, vocals), Patrick Gundry-White (French horn, harmonium, vocals), and John Burge (guitar, bouzouki, fiddle, banjo, vocals). *Devil's Ride*, their only release, was a crossover jazz and folk recording, combining original material with traditional numbers. Peadar Long has since performed and recorded with other artists.

Album: *Devil's Ride* (1982).

Koerner, 'Spider' John

b. 31 August 1938, Rochester, New York. USA. A contemporary of Bob Dylan at the University of Minnesota, Koerner subsequently formed an influential country-blues trio with Dave Ray and Tony Glover. Koerner, Ray And Glover completed two albums for Elektra before John recorded his first solo collection, *Spider's Blues*. The three musicians were then reunited at different intervals, although each has pursued an independent path. *Running, Jumping, Standing Still*, Koerner's refreshing collaboration with singer Willie Murphy, was released in 1968, and the artist has since completed two further solo albums.

Albums: with Koerner, Ray And Glover *Blues, Rags And Hollers* (1963), *More Blues, Rags And Hollers* (1964), *The Return Of Koerner, Ray And Glover* (1965), *Live At St. Olaf Festival* (c.60s/70s), *Some American Folk Songs Like They Used To Be* (1974). With Willie Murphy *Running, Jumping, Standing Still* (1968). Solo *Spider's Blues* (1965), *Music Is Just A Bunch Of Notes* (1972), *Nobody Knows The Trouble I've Seen* (1986).

Kottke, Leo

b. Athens, Georgia, USA. This inventive guitarist drew inspiration from the country-blues style of Mississippi John Hurt and having taken up the instrument as an adolescent, joined several aspiring mid-60s groups. Induction into the US Navy interrupted his progress, but the artist was discharged following an accident which permanently damaged his hearing. Kottke subsequently ventured to Minneapolis where a spell performing in the city's folk clubs led to a recording deal. *Circle Round The Sun* received limited exposure via two independent outlets, but his career did not fully flourish until 1971 when John Fahey invited Kottke to record for his company, Takoma. *Six And Twelve String Guitar* established the artist as an exciting new talent, with a style blending dazzling dexterity with moments of introspection. Kottke's desire to expand his repertoire led to a break with Fahey and a major deal with Capitol Records. *Mudlark* included instrumental and vocal tracks, notably a version of the Byrds' 'Eight Miles High', and while purists bore misgivings about Kottke's languid, sonorous voice, his talent as a guitarist remained unchallenged. Several excellent albums in a similar vein ensued, including *Greenhouse*, which boasted an interpretation of Fahey's 'Last Steam Engine Train', and the in-concert *My Feet Are Smiling*. Prodigious touring enhanced Kottke's reputation as one of America's finest acoustic 12-string guitarists, although he was unable to convert this standing into commercial success. He later switched labels to Chrysalis, but by the 80s had returned to independent outlets on which his crafted approach has continued to flourish.

Albums: *Circle Round The Sun* (1970), *Six And Twelve String Guitar* (1971), *Mudlark* (1971), *Greenhouse* (1972), *My Feet Are Smiling* (1973), *Ice Water* (1974), *Dreams And All That Stuff* (1974),

Chewing Pine (1975), *Leo Kottke* (1976), *Burnt Lips* (1978), *Balance* (1979), *Leo Kottke Live In Europe* (1980), *Guitar Music* (1981), *Time Step* (1983), *Regards From Chuck* (1980s), *My Father's Face* (1989), *Great Big Boy* (1991). Compilations: *Leo Kottke 1971-1976 - Did You Hear Me?* (1976), *The Best Of Leo Kottke* (1979).

Kristina, Sonja

b. 14 April 1949, Brentwood, Essex, England. Former Curved Air vocalist, Kristina, released a solo album in 1988 on the Chopper Records label. A few 1977 tracks were produced by Roy Thomas Baker but remain unreleased. Marriage to her old group's drummer Stewart Copeland, (who had since joined the Police) and the rearing of two children delayed a resumption of an acting career that had been suspended since she resigned from the London cast of *Hair* in 1970. A role in the *Curriculum Curricula* musical and the lead in *Romeo And Juliet* were followed in 1988 by a spell performing in Britain's arts centres and more adventurous folk clubs. Later, she was the brains behind a UK tour of acts from this circuit, before forming her own 'psychedelic acoustic acid folk' combo whose personnel included a violinist and cellist. Subsequent album and live reviews have indicated an upturn in this artist's fortunes in the 90s.

Albums: *Sonja Kristina* (1980), *Songs From The Acid Folk* (1991).

Kweskin, Jim, Jug Band

b. 18 July 1940, Stamford, Connecticut, USA. Kweskin began to forge a ragtime/jugband style in the New England folk haunts during the early 60s. His early groups were largely informal and it was not until 1963, when he secured a recording deal, that this singer and guitarist began piecing together a more stable line-up. Geoff Muldaur (guitar/washboard/kazoo/vocals), Bob Siggins, Bruno Wolf and Fritz Richmond (jug/washtub bass) joined Kweskin on his enthusiastic, infectious debut. Siggins dropped out of the group prior to a second album, *Jug Band Music*. Bill Keith (banjo/pedal steel guitar) and Maria D'Amato (vocals/kazoo/tambourine) were now enlisted, while Kweskin's extended family also included several other individuals, the most notorious of whom was Mel Lyman, who added harmonica on *Relax Your Mind*, the leader's 'solo' album. D'Amato married Geoff Muldaur and later became better known for her solo career as Maria Muldaur. *See Reverse Side For Title*, arguably the Jug band's finest album, featured versions of 'Blues In The Bottle' and 'Fishing Blues', both of which were recorded by the Lovin' Spoonful. 'Chevrolet', a magnificent duet between Muldaur and D'Amato, was another highlight and the entire selection balanced humour with a newfound purpose. Fiddler Richard Greene worked with the line-up for what was the group's final album, *Garden Of Joy*. He subsequently joined Keith on several projects, including the excellent bluegrass quintet, Muleskinner, while Geoff and Maria commenced work as a duo. Kweskin's own progress was rather overshadowed by his immersion in Lyman's dark, quasi-religious, Charles Manson-like commune, but he emerged as a solo performer in the early 70s and has since continued to forge an idiosyncratic, traditional musical-based path.

Albums: *Jim Kweskin And The Jug Band* i (1963), *Jug Band Music* (1965), *Relax Your Mind* (1966), *Jim Kewskin And The Jug Band* ii (1966), *See Reverse Side For Title* (1967), *Jump For Joy* (1967), *Garden Of Joy* (1967), *Whatever Happened To Those Good Old Days* (1968), *American Aviator* (1969), *Jim Kweskin's America* (1971), *Jim Kweskin* (1978), *Jim Kweskin Lives Again* (1978), *Side By Side* (1980), *Swing On A Star* (1980). Compilation: *Best Of Jim Kweskin And The Jug Band* (1968), *Greatest Hits* (1990).

L

LaFarge, Pete

b. 1931, Fountain, Colorado, USA, d. 27 October 1964, New York City, New York, USA. The son of a Pulitzer Prize-winning author, LaFarge was a noted dramatist and painter, and an accomplished performer. Folksinger Cisco Houston first guided the aspiring musician's skills, which flourished in the 50s following Peter's active service in the Korean War. Of Pima-Indian heritage, LaFarge became a tireless champion of the oppressed, although his most famous composition, 'The Ballad Of Ira Hayes', a forthright indictment of the plight of the native American, achieved popularity through a sympathetic cover version by Johnny Cash. Pete also acted as a contributing editor to the radical *Broadside* magazine, and recorded for the Folkways and Columbia labels. However, he grew increasingly unhappy with his performing role and planned to abandon music in favour of writing and painting. Pete LaFarge died officially from a stroke, despite persistent rumours of suicide.

Albums: *On The Warpath* (1961), *As Long As The Grass Shall Grow* (1962), *Songs Of The Cowboys* (1964), *Iron Mountain And Other Songs* (1965).

Laycock, Tim

b. 20 February 1952, Malmesbury, Wiltshire, England. At the age of four, Laycock's family moved to Fontwell Magna, Dorset, and he later became interested in folk music through learning guitar chords from school friends. Leaving school in 1970, Laycock went to the University of East Anglia in Norwich, and he met singers and musicians in folk clubs who converted him to British traditional music. He started playing regularly in 1971 as part of a folk group at university, which included Terry Fisher and Dave Bordeway, who later played with the Crows. In 1974, after moving to London, Tim became a resident at Dingle's Folk Club and the Engineer Folk Club. In 1976, he joined Magic Lantern for a Christmas tour, and was later asked to join full-time when Mike Frost (Major Mustard), left to get married. *Lydlinch Bells*, produced by Laycock, was a strong collection of dialect poems by William Barnes, read by Laycock, David Strawbridge, Ethel Gumbleton, Charlie Andrews and Frank Hilliar. Since then Laycock has worked continuously as a singer, concertina player and actor, collaborating for three years from, 1979, with Peter Bond and Bill Caddick. Dividing his time between the theatre, folk clubs and festivals, Laycock occasionally works with Taffy Thomas and appears in a local Dorset group, the Hambledon Hopstep Band.

Albums: *Lydlinch Bells* (1977), *Capers And Rhymes* (1980), with Peter Bond, Bill Caddick *A Duck On His Head* (1984), *Giant At Cerne* (1985), *Blackmore By The Stour* (1985), with Sneaks Noyse *Christmas Now Is Drawing Near* (1988), *Shillingstone Moss* (1989).

Le Mystère Des Voix Bulgares

The State Radio and Television choir from Bulgaria was founded in 1952, in Sofia, and included 15 singers and instrumentalists. This number has gradually increased as new voices ben selected from various folk festivals and song contests. As well as traditional pieces, the choir also performs the work of modern composers. The choir was brought to the attention of the British music press and public by the esoteric 4AD label who released their UK debut set in 1986. The ethereal nature of their singing drew some comparisons with that of 4AD's own Cocteau Twins - a connection with attracted a young audience. *A Cathedral Concert* (released on the Jaro label), was recorded in a church in Bremen, Germany, on 6 December 1987, during one of the choir's first trips to the West. Subsequent releases have shown the powerful vocals of the choir to good effect. The general interest shown in world music has opened up Eastern Europe and shown it to contain a wealth of musical heritage hitherto unheard. Choir member Eva Georgeiva appeared as one of the Trio Bulgarka's *The Forest Is Crying* (1988) on Hannibal Records.

Albums: *Le Mystère Des Voix Bulgares* (1986), *Le Mystère Des Voix Bulgares Vol. 2* (1988), *A Cathedral Concert* (1988) *Le Mystère Des Voix Bulgares Vol. 3* (1990), *From Bulgaria With Love* (1993).

Leadbelly

b. Hudson ('Huddie') Leadbetter, 29 January 1889, Mooringsport, Louisiana, USA, d. 6 December 1949, New York City, New York, USA. Leadbelly's music offers an incredible vista of American traditions, white as well as black, through his enormous repertoire of songs and tunes. He learned many of them in his youth when he lived and worked in western Louisiana and eastern Texas, but to which he added material from many different sources, including his own compositions, throughout the rest of his life. He played several instruments, including mandolin, accordion, piano and harmonica, but was best known for his mastery of the 12-string guitar. In his early 20s, he met and played with Blind Lemon Jefferson, but the encounter was to leave little if any lasting impression on his music. His sound remained distinctive and individual, with his powerful, yet deeply expressive vocals, and his 12-string guitar lines, which could be booming and blindingly fast or slow and delicate as appropriate. His style and approach to music developed as he played the red-light districts of towns like Shreveport and Dallas - a tough, often violent background that was reflected in songs like 'Fannin Street' and 'Mr Tom Hughes Town'.

Although he built up a substantial local reputation for his music as a young man, he served a number of prison sentences, including two stretches of hard labour, for murder and attempted murder respectively. While serving the last of these sentences, at the Louisiana State Penitentiary at Angola, he was discovered by the folklorist, John A. Lomax, then travelling throughout the south with his son Alan, recording traditional songs and music - frequently in prisons - for the Folk Song Archive of the Library of Congress. On his release (which he claimed was due to his having composed a song pleading with the governor to set him free), Leadbelly worked for Lomax as a chauffeur, assistant and guide, also recording prolifically for the Archive. His complete Library of Congress recordings, made over a period of several years, were issued in 1990 on 12 albums. Through Lomax, he was given the opportunity of a new life, as he moved to New York to continue to work for the folklorist. He also started a new musical career, with a new and very different audience, playing university concerts, clubs and political events, appearing on radio and even on film. He also made many records, mainly aimed at folk music enthusiasts. However, he did get the opportunity to make some 'race' recordings which were marketed to the black listener, but these enjoyed little commercial success, probably because Leadbelly's music would have seemed rather old-fashioned and rural to the increasingly sophisticated black record buyer of the 30s, and although 50 songs were recorded, only six were issued.

The New York folk scene, however, kept him active to some extent, and he played and recorded with people like Josh White, Woody Guthrie, Sonny Terry and Brownie McGhee. There were also a series of recordings in which he was accompanied by the voices of the Golden Gate Quartet, although this was an odd pairing and rather contrived. Some newly composed songs, such as 'New York City' and in particular the pointed 'Bourgeois Blues', which described the racial prejudice he encountered in Washington, DC, show how his perspectives were being altered by his new circumstances. It was his apparently inexhaustible collection of older songs and tunes, however, that most fascinated the northern audience, embracing as it did everything from versions of old European ballads ('Gallis Pole') through Cajun-influenced dance tunes ('Sukey Jump') and sentimental pop ('Daddy, I'm Coming Home') to dozens of black work songs and field hollers ('Whoa Back Buck'), southern ballads ('John Hardy'), gospel ('Mary Don't You Weep'), prison songs ('Shorty George'), many tough blues ('Pigmeat Papa') and even cowboy songs ('Out On The Western Plains'). His best-known and most frequently covered songs, however, are probably the gentle C&W-influenced 'Goodnight Irene', later to be a hit record for the Weavers (one of whose members was Pete Seeger, who was also to write an instruction book on Leadbelly's unique 12-string guitar style) and 'Rock Island Line' which was a hit for Lonnie Donegan in the UK a few years later. His classic 'Cottonfields' was a major success for the Beach Boys. In 1949, he travelled to Europe, appearing at jazz events in Paris, but the promise of wider appreciation of the man and his music was sadly curtailed when he died later that same year.

Compilations: *Alabama Bound* (1990), *Leadbelly Sings Folk Songs* (1990), *Complete Library Of Congress Sessions* (1990).

Legg, Adrian

b. 16 May 1948, Hackney, London, England. Although a highly respected guitarist, Legg actually played oboe as a child, both for the school orchestra and the Cheltenham Young People's Orchestra. He left home at the age of 15, and stopped playing oboe. Three or four years later he took up the guitar, joining a country band in Liverpool, and turning professional a year later. After a period of working with Irish and UK country bands, he turned solo during 1973. By 1974, Legg had won both the composition and performance categories in the folk guitar competition run by *Guitar* magazine. From 1978, he stopped all performing, moving instead, in 1979, into the musical instrument industry, working in research, development and repairs. He also held instrument clinics and demonstrations. Legg resumed his playing during 1982, having produced the book, *Customising Your Electric Guitar*, the previous year. After recording *Technopicker*, for Making Waves, he left the musical instrument industry. He then followed up with *Fretmelt* and *Lost For Words*, again for Making Waves, who, unfortunately, were soon to go out of business. *Guitar For Mortals*, released on Relativity Records, was recorded in May 1991, in Los Angeles, and produced by Bobby Cochran. Legg also recorded a teaching video, *Beyond Acoustic Guitar*, for Arlen Roth's Hot Licks series, which was released in the autumn of 1991. Legg is still involved with the industry, with the final research and development, and subsequent launch, of the Trace Elliot acoustic guitar amplifier, as well as work for Ovation guitars. In addition to this, he still holds regular teaching clinics in the USA for Kaman Corporation, Ovation's parent company. Legg regularly contributes to magazines, on matters legal and technical, and has also been doing shows and clinics for the Dean Markley String Corporation, as well as fitting in a UK tour at least once a year.

Albums: *Requiem For A Hick* (1977), *Technopicker* (1983), *Fretmelt* (1984), *Lost For Words* (1986), *Guitars And Other Cathedrals* (1990), *Guitar For Mortals* (1992), *Mrs Crowes's Blue Waltz* (1993).

Further reading: *The All Round Gigster*, Adrian Legg. *Acoustic Guitars-A Musician's Manual*, Adrian Legg with Paul Colbert.

Levellers

This five-piece unit from Brighton, Sussex, England combined folk instrumentation with rock and punk ethics: 'We draw on some Celtic influences because it's a powerful source, but we're a very English band - this country does have roots worth using'. They took their name, and much of their ideology from the Puritans active at the time of the English Civil War between 1647 and 1649, whose agenda advocated republicanism, a written constitution and abolition of the monarchy. Their original line-up featured Mark Chadwick (songwriter; lead vocals, guitar, banjo), Jon Sevink (fiddle), Alan Leveller (vocals, guitars, mandolin, harmonica), Jeremy Leveller (bass, bouzouki) and Charlie Heather (drums). Sevink's violin, like many of their instruments, was typically unconventional and ecologically pure, 'recycled' from three different broken violin bodies. Chadwick, meanwhile, used a guitar which had an old record player arm acting as pick-ups, as well as an amplifier acquired from the Revillos. The *Carry Me* EP was released on Brighton's Hag Records in May 1989, after label boss Phil Nelson had taken over their management. They signed to French label Musidisc in 1989, and Waterboys' producer Phil Tennant recorded their debut album. When their guitarist left during a tour of Belgium in April 1990, they recruited Simon Friend, a singer-songwriter and guitarist from the north of England, and set off on a typically extensive UK tour. After signing to China Records, they made a breakthrough into the national charts with minor UK hits in 1991 with 'One Way' and 'Far From Home'. Their second album, *Levelling The Land*, reached the UK Top 20. A mixture of English and Celtic folk with powerful guitar driven rock, it was acclaimed throughout Europe where the band toured before performing sell-out UK concerts. In May 1992, the *Fifteen Years* EP entered the UK chart at number 11. Signed to Elektra in the USA, the Levellers made their initial impact touring small venues there before returning to the UK to stage three *Christmas Freakshows*, which combined music and circus acts at the Brighton Centre and Birmingham NEC. They also continued to play benefits for the environmental and social causes that are the subject of many of their songs. In 1993 they again toured Europe, released a compilation of singles and live tracks, *See Nothing, Hear Nothing, Do Something*, and recorded songs for a new album at Peter Gabriel's Real World studios. In the summer of that year, 'Belaruse', registered high in the UK Top 20. Their popularity, particularly in live appearances, make them regulars in the music press, wherein they took to criticizing the Men They Couldn't Hang and New Model Army who, paradoxically, appear to be their biggest influences! The Levellers' affinity with the neo-hippie/new age travellers looks likely to prevent them from ever achieving mass appeal, but in the meantime they have no worries about playing to a large and appreciative audience.

Albums: *A Weapon Called The Word* (1990), *Levelling The Land* (1991), *See Nothing, Hear Nothing, Do Something* (1993).

Gordon Lightfoot

Life And Times

This English duo features Graeme Meek (b. 7 September 1954, Luton, Bedfordshire, England; guitar/vocals), and Barry Goodman (b. 3 December 1950, Sutton, Surrey, England; melodeon/vocals). Life And Times were formed in 1983, and originally included Gregg Lindsay (flute). Meek had earlier been working in various rock bands, including one from his schooldays which included singer Paul Young. Subsequently, Meek worked as one half of a duo called Midas with Debra Arthurs, from 1977-80, playing folk clubs and festivals. The duo only recorded one single, in 1977. Meanwhile, Goodman had spent four years in folk duo Mead, with Steve Rackstraw, then Vermin with Gadfan Edwards, and later Gregg Lindsay, as well as solo work. Luton Museum and Art Gallery published *Strawplait And Bonelace* in 1983, and the following year, the Eastern Arts Association agreed to help fund Life And Time's recording of the songbook. *Strawplait And Bonelace,* was eventually released on Fellside Records, and featured song and music of Bedfordshire life over the past 200 years. During 1986, *Shropshire Iron* was made into a radio documentary and broadcast by local radio stations around the UK, and during the following year the duo represented Bedfordshire at the English Folk Dance And Song Society National Gathering in London. *Shropshire Iron*, featuring songs and music of the early industrial revolution, was also released on Fellside. From 1985, until February 1991, Meek also presented *Three Counties Folk* on BBC Radio Bedfordshire. The duo continue to play festivals and clubs, sometimes in the guise of dance band Time Of Your Life, with Brian Scowcroft (caller/bass), but currently no recordings are imminent.

Albums: *Strawplait And Bonelace* (1985), *Shropshire Iron* (1989).

Lightfoot, Gordon

b. 17 November 1938, Orillia, Ontario, Canada. Lightfoot moved to Los Angeles during the 50s where he studied at Hollywood's Westlake College of Music. Having pursued a short-lived career composing jingles for television, the singer began recording demos of his own compositions which, by 1960, owed a considerable debt to folksingers Pete Seeger and Bob Gibson. Lightfoot then returned to Canada and began performing in Toronto's Yorktown coffee houses. His work was championed by several acts, notably Ian And Sylvia and Peter, Paul And Mary. Both recorded the enduring 'Early Morning Rain', which has since become a standard, while the latter group also enjoyed a hit with his 'For Lovin' Me'. Other successful compositions included 'Ribbon Of Darkness', which Marty Robbins took to the top of the US country chart, while such renowned artists as Bob Dylan, Johnny Cash, Elvis Presley and Jerry Lee Lewis have all covered Lightfoot's songs. Having joined the Albert Grossman management stable, the singer made his debut in 1966 with the promising *Lightfoot. The Way I Feel* and *Did She Mention My Name* consolidated the artist's undoubted promise, but it was not until 1970 that he made a significant commercial breakthrough with *Sit Down Young Stranger*. Producer Lenny Waronker added an edge to Lightfoot's approach which reaped an immediate benefit with a US Top 5 hit, 'If You Could Read My Mind'. The album also included the first recording of Kris Kristofferson's 'Me And Bobbie McGee'. A series of crafted albums enhanced his new-found position and in 1974 the singer secured a US number 1 with the excellent 'Sundown'. Two years later 'The Wreck Of The Edmund Fitzgerald' peaked at number 2, but although Lightfoot continued to record mature singer-songwriter-styled material, his increasing reliance on safer, easy-listening perspectives proved unattractive to a changing rock audience. Gordon Lightfoot nonetheless retains the respect of his contemporaries, although his profile lessened quite considerably during the 80s.

Albums: *Lightfoot* (1966), *The Way I Feel* (1967), *Did She Mention My Name* (1968), *Back Here On Earth* (1969), *Sunday Concert* (1969), *Sit Down Young Stranger* aka *If You Could Read My Mind* (1970), *Summer Side Of Life* (1971), *Don Quixote* (1972), *Old Dan's Records* (1972), *Sundown* (1974), *Cold On The Shoulder* (1975), *Summertime Dream* (1976), *Endless Wire* (1978), *Dream Street Rose* (1980), *Shadows* (1982), *Salute* (1983), *East Of Midnight* (1986). Compilations: *The Very Best Of Gordon Lightfoot* (1974), *Gord's Gold* (1975), *The Best Of Gordon Lightfoot* (1981).

Limeliters

The Limeliters were one of the popular forces behind the 50s folk revival in America. The group comprised Lou Gottlieb (b. 1923, Los Angeles, California, USA; bass), Alex Hassilev (b. 11 July 1932, Paris, France; guitar/banjo/vocals), and Glenn Yarbrough (b. 12 January 1930, Milwaukee, Wisconsin, USA; guitar/vocals). They formed in Los Angeles in 1959 and took their name from a club, run by Hassilev and Yarbrough, called The Limelite in Aspen, Colorado, USA. Gottlieb was a Doctor of Musicology, having studied under the Austrian composer Arnold Schoenberg. The group had a minor hit with 'A Dollar Down' in April 1961 on RCA, but their albums sold better than singles. Many of their albums were live recordings, including the popular *Tonight: In Person,* which

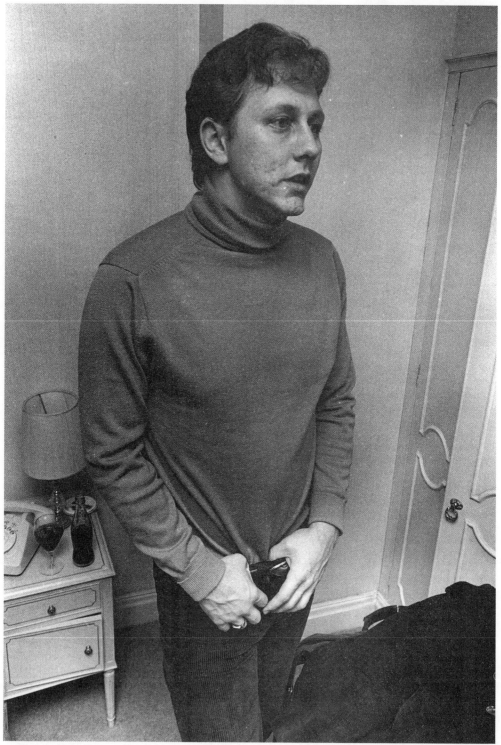

Bob Lind

reached number 5 in the US charts in 1961. The follow-up, *The Limeliters*, just reached the Top 40 the same year. A third release, *The Slightly Fabulous Limeliters* made the US Top 10, also in 1961. A series of albums followed with *Sing Out!* making the US Top 20 in 1962. Gradually their popularity waned, and when Yarbrough left in November 1963 to pursue a solo career, the group replaced him with Ernie Sheldon. In 1965, Yarbrough, also with RCA, reached the Top 40, in the US album charts, with 'Baby The Rain Must Fall'. The title track, taken from a film of the same title, made the Top 20 the same year.

Albums: *The Limeliters* (1960), *Tonight: In Person* (1961), *The Slightly Fabulous Limeliters* (1961), *Sing Out!* (1962), *Through Children's Eyes* (1962), *Folk Matinee* (1962), *Our Men In San Francisco* (1963), *Makin' A Joyful Noise* (1963), *Fourteen 14K Folk Songs* (1963), *More Of Everything!* (1964), *London Concert* (1965), *The Limeliters Look At Love In Depth* (1965), *The Original 'Those Were The Days'* (1968), *Time To Gather Seeds* (1970), *Their First Historic Album* (1986), *Alive In Concert* (1988). Compilation: *The Best Of The Limeliters* (1964).

Lind, Bob

b. 25 November 1942, Baltimore, Maryland, USA. Lind is best known for writing and recording the Top 5 folk-rock song 'Elusive Butterfly' in 1966. He moved around often with his family, and while settled in Denver, Colorado, he began singing folk music in clubs. He moved to the west coast and was signed to World Pacific Records, a division of the larger Liberty Records. Produced by Jack Nitzsche, Lind played guitar on his recordings for the label, while piano was handled by Leon Russell. His first single, 'Cheryl's Goin' Home', failed to catch on but was later covered by Cher and the Blues Project. 'Elusive Butterfly' was its b-side and became an international Top 10 hit. Lind was widely touted as 'the new Bob Dylan' and the latest spokesperson for youth during 1966. Despite his pop star looks and sensitive lyrics, however, his subsequent singles failed to reach the charts. *Don't Be Concerned* contained a number of sentimental, but attractive songs. His compositions continued to find interpreters, among them the Turtles, Noel Harrison, Nancy Sinatra and Bobby Sherman. Lind continued to record into the early 70s, switching to Capitol Records without a revival of his commercial fortunes. He was still performing in folk and country music circles in the early 80s.

Albums: *Don't Be Concerned* (1966), *The Elusive Bob Lind* (1966), *Photographs Of Feeling* (1966), *Since There Were Circles* (1971).

Lindisfarne

This Newcastle, UK-based quintet - Alan Hull (b. 20 February 1945, Newcastle-Upon-Tyne, Tyne And Wear, England; vocals/guitar/piano), Simon Cowe (b. 1 April 1948, Jesmond Dene, Tyne And Wear, England; guitar), Ray Jackson (b. 12 December 1948, Wallsend, Tyne And Wear, England; harmonica/mandolin), Rod Clements (b. 17 November 1947, North Shields, Tyne And Wear, England; bass/violin) and Ray Laidlaw (b. 28 May 1948, North Shields, Tyne And Wear, England; drums) - was originally known as the Downtown Faction, but took the name Lindisfarne in 1968. Their debut *Nicely Out Of Tune*, was issued the following year and this brash mixture of folk-rock and optimistic harmonies is arguably the group's most satisfying set. The album contained the wistful and lyrically complex 'Lady Eleanor'. Their popularity flourished with the release of *Fog On The Tyne* the humorous title track celebrating life in Newcastle and containing such verses as; 'Sitting in a sleazy snack-bar sucking sickly sausage rolls'. The number 1 album's attendant single, 'Meet Me On The Corner' reached the UK Top 5 in 1972 where it was followed by a re-released 'Lady Eleanor'. *Fog On The Tyne* was produced by Bob Johnston, and although they pursued this relationship on a third selection, *Dingly Dell*, the group was unhappy with his work and remixed the set prior to release. The final results were still disappointing, creatively and commercially, and tensions within the line-up were exposed during an ill-fated tour of the USA. In 1973, Laidlaw, Cowe and Clements left for a new venture, Jack The Lad. Kenny Craddock (keyboards), Charlie Harcourt (guitar), Tommy Duffy (bass) and Paul Nichols (drums) were brought in as replacements but this reconstituted line-up lacked the charm of its predecessor and was overshadowed by Alan Hull's concurrent solo career. A 1974 release, *Happy Daze*, offered some promise, but Lindisfarne was disbanded the following year. The break, however, was temporary and the original quintet later resumed working together. They secured a recording deal with Mercury Records and in 1978 enjoyed a UK Top 10 single with 'Run For Home'. Despite further releases, Lindisfarne was unable to repeat this success and subsequently reached an artistic nadir with *C'mon Everybody*, a medley of rock 'n' roll party favourites with six of the group's own best-known songs saved for the finale. In November 1990, Lindisfarne were back in the UK charts, joined together with the England international footballer, and fellow Geordie, Paul Gascoigne. Their re-worked, and inferior, version of 'Fog On The Tyne' reached number 2. Although they are now restricted to only the occasional chart success, the group's following remains strong, particularly in the north-east of England, and is manifested in their annual Christmas concerts.

Albums: *Nicely Out Of Tune* (1970), *Fog On The Tyne* (1971), *Dingly Dell* (1972), *Lindisfarne Live* (1973), *Roll On Ruby* (1973), *Happy Daze* (1974), *Back And Fourth* (1978), *Magic In The Air* (1978), *The News* (1979), *Sleepless Nights* (1982), *Lindisfarne Tastic Live* (1984), *Lindisfarne Tastic Volume 2* (1984), *Dance Your Life Away* (1984), *C'mon Everybody* (1987), *Amigos* (1989). Compilations: *Take Off Your Head* (1974), *Finest Hour* (1975), *Singles Album* (1981), *Buried Treasures Vol. 1* (1993), *Buried Treasures Vol. 2* (1993).

Liverpool Scene

The name 'Liverpool Scene' was derived from a poetry anthology which featured Roger McGough, Adrian Henri and Brian Patten. The writers subsequently appeared on UK television's *Look Of The Week*, where their readings were accompanied by guitarist Andy Roberts. McGough and Henri then recorded *The Incredible New Liverpool Scene*, which included definitive performances of their best-known work, including 'Let Me Die A Young Man's Death' (McGough) and 'Tonight At Noon' (Henri). While McGough pursued a career within Scaffold, Henri and Roberts added Mike Hart (guitar/vocals), Mike Evans (saxophone/vocals) Percy Jones (bass) and Brian Dodson (drums) to create an explicitly rock-based ensemble. UK disc jockey John Peel was an early patron and the group quickly found itself an integral part of music's underground circuit, culminating in their impressive appearance at the 1969 Isle Of Wight Festival. *The Amazing Adventures Of . . .* captured the sextet at their most potent, but successive albums, although worthwhile, failed to match the crucial balance between musical and lyrical content and the group broke up in 1970. Hart embarked on a solo career, but while Roberts initially found fame in Plainsong, he was later reunited with both Henri and McGough in Grimms.

Albums: *The Incredible New Liverpool Scene* (1967), *The Amazing Adventures Of . . .* (1968), *Bread On The Night* (1969), *Saint Adrian Co. Broadway And 3rd* (1970), *Heirloom* (1970). Compilation: *Recollections* (1972).

Lloyd, A.L

b. February 1908, London, England. Bert Lloyd was one of the prime movers of the 50s folk song revival in Britain. He returned to England in 1935 with a collection of some 500 songs and a determination to study and research into folk music. In 1937, he sailed to Antarctica with a whaling fleet, adding further songs to his repertoire. On his return he joined BBC radio as a scriptwriter. During the 40s he wrote *The Singing Englishman*, the first general book on folk song since Cecil Sharp's in 1909. He also compiled the *Penguin Book Of English Folk Song* with the composer Ralph Vaughan Williams. By the 50s, Lloyd was a full-time folklorist, making several field trips to record material in Bulgaria and Albania as well as publishing a selection of coalfield ballads which provided repertoire for young singers in the growing number of folk song clubs. At this time he met Ewan MacColl, with whom he made his own first recordings, as part of the *Radio Ballads* series. During the 60s he made a series of solo albums for Topic Records, with accompanists including singers Anne Briggs and Frankie Armstrong, Alf Edwards (accordion), Martin Carthy (guitar/mandolin), Dave Swarbrick (fiddle) and actor/singer Harry H. Corbett. They covered drinking songs, industrial songs and selections from his sheep-shearing and whaling exploits. Lloyd also arranged compilation albums of sea shanties, industrial songs (*The Iron Muse*) and recordings from the Balkan field trips.

Albums: *Selections From The Penguin Book Of English Folk Songs* (1960), *The Iron Muse* (1963), *All For Me Grog* (1964), *The Bird In The Bush* (1965), *First Person* (1966), *Leviathan* (1968), *The Great Australian Legend* (1969), with Ewan MacColl *English And Scottish Popular Ballads* (1974), *Sea Songs And Shanties* (1981).

Lomax, Alan And John A.

A well-known and well-read folklorist, Alan Lomax (b. 15 January 1915, Austin, Texas, USA), travelled with his father, John A. Lomax (b. John Avery Lomax, 23 September 1875, Goodman, Mississippi, USA, d. 26 January 1948, Greenville, Mississippi, USA), on field recording trips during the 30s, collecting folk songs and tunes from various States in the USA. They collected songs for the Library of Congress Archive for which Woody Guthrie was later recorded. Until that time, John Lomax had been an administrator at college, who had collected cowboy songs, including 'Home On The Range', as a hobby. As a result of the Depression and crash of the 30s, John Lomax, now jobless, started collecting folk songs and material on a full-time basis. By the time Alan was 23 years old he was assistant director of the Archive of Folk Song at the Library of Congress. The Lomaxes met a number of singers, who were later to become almost household names, including Huddie 'Leadbelly' Ledbetter, and Muddy Waters. Leadbelly was discovered in a Louisiana prison, but John Lomax managed to obtain his release, employing him as a chauffeur. Lomax later took him to New York where he performed to college audiences. In 1934, John Lomax became honorary consultant and head of the Library of Congress archive of folk song. Alan Lomax travelled to Britain during the 50s and collaborated with Ewan MacColl on the radio series *Ballads And Blues*. Lomax later returned to the USA to conduct field recordings in the southern States. The results were subsequently released on Atlantic Records as part of a series called 'Southern Folk Heritage'. John and Alan Lomax were also responsible for collecting a number of the songs of the Ritchie Family of Kentucky. In addition to his many other activities, Alan Lomax was still a fine performer in his own right, as can be heard on *Texas Folk Songs*, which contains the standards 'Ain't No More Cane On The Brazo's' and 'Billy Barlow'. *Alan Lomax Sings Great American Ballads*, on HMV, included Guy Carawan (banjo), and Nick Wheatstraw (guitar). It featured such classics as 'Frankie', 'Darlin' Corey' and 'Git Along Little Doggies'. The latter song had been recorded by John Lomax in 1908, and originates from an Irish ballad, converted and adapted by cowboys. After World War II, Alan was the Director of Folk Music for Decca, and then he worked for the Office of War Information from 1943-44 and then for the Army's Special Services Section until 1945. As a singer, Alan had performed both in the USA and Britain. Twelve years of research culminated in *Cantometrics*, a set of seven cassettes with a book.

Albums: John A. Lomax *The Ballad Hunter, Lectures On American Folk Music* (date unavailable, 10 record set). Alan Lomax *Alan Sings Great American Ballads* (1958), *Texas Folk Songs* (1958), *Folk Song Saturday Night* (60s), *Murderer Is Home* (1976).

Further reading: Alan Lomax: *Amercian Folk Song And Folk Lore*, with Sidney Robertson Cowell. *Mister Jelly Roll - The Fortunes Of Jelly Roll Morton, New Orleans, Creole And Inventor Of Jazz, The Folksongs Of North America*. Editor of: *Folk Songs Of North America In The English Language, Folk Song Style And Culture, Cantometrics - An Approach To The Anthropology Of Music*. John A. Lomax: *Cowboy Songs, Adventures Of A Ballad Hunter, Cowboy Songs And Other Frontier Ballads, Songs Of The Cattle Trail And Cow Camp*, John and Alan Lomax: *American Ballads And Folk Songs, Cowboy Songs And Other Frontier Ballads, Negro Folk Songs As Sung By Leadbelly, Folksong USA, Our Singing Country, The Penguin Book Of American Folk Songs*.

Longdancer

A short-lived English folk-rock band, Longdancer were best remembered as the first professional band to feature David A. Stewart (b. 9 September 1952, Sunderland, England). The group grew out of a folk duo comprising Stewart and Brian Harrison, formerly with the London-based band Ball Of Yarn. The pair played clubs and support gigs in the north east of England and in 1971 recorded an EP for the local Multichord label. Soon afterwards they added further singer/guitarists Steve Sproxton and Kai Olsson and became Longdancer. In 1973, they became the first artists to sign to Elton John's Rocket label, touring with Elton before Olsson left to be replaced by Matt Irving (keyboards) and Charlie Smith (drums). The new line-up made a second album and released an unsuccessful single, 'Puppet Man' in 1974. Shortly afterwards, Longdancer split up. Kai Olsson made a 1979 solo album for Chrysalis (*Crazy Love*) while Harrison and Smith later played with folk singers Robin and Barry Dransfield before Smith joined Blue. Irving recorded with Phil Rambow before joining the Lords Of The New Church in the 80s. In 1977, Stewart would form the Tourists and in 1981, with Annie Lennox, the Eurythmics.

Albums: *If It Was So Simple* (1973), *Trailer For A Good Life* (1974).

Lovin' Spoonful

Few American pop groups have gathered as much universal affection over the years as the brilliant and underrated Lovin' Spoonful. Their back catalogue of hits is constantly repackaged and reissued, as their stature increases. They were formed in 1965 by John Sebastian (b. 17 March 1944, New York, USA; vocal/guitar/harmonica/autoharp) and Zalman Yanovsky (b. 19 December 1944, Toronto, Canada; guitar/vocals) following their time together in the Mugwumps (as eulogized in the Mamas And The Papas hit 'Creeque Alley'). The band were completed by Steve Boone (b. 23 September 1943, Camp Lejeune, North Carolina, USA; bass) and Joe Butler (b. 19 January 1943, Long Island, New York, USA; drums/vocals). Their unique blend of jug-band, folk, blues and rock 'n' roll synthesized into what was termed as 'electric good-time music' kept them apart from every other American pop group at that time. In two years they notched up 10 US Top 20 hits, all composed by John Sebastian. From the opening strum of Sebastian's autoharp on 'Do You Believe In Magic?' the party began; from the evocative 'You Didn't Have To Be So Nice', to the languid singalong 'Daydream'. From the punchy and lyrically outstanding 'Summer In The City'; 'Hot town summer in the city, back of my neck getting dirt and gritty', to the gentle romanticism of 'Rain On The Roof'; 'You and me and the rain on the roof, caught up in a summer shower, drying while it soaks the flowers, maybe we'll be caught for hours'. Their four regular albums were crammed full of other gems in addition to the hits. Additionally Sebastian wrote the music for two films; Woody Allen's *What's Up Tiger Lily* and Francis Ford Coppola's *You're A Big Boy Now*, the latter featuring the beautiful 'Darling Be Home Soon'. Sadly the non-stop party came to an end in 1968 following the departure of Yanovsky and the arrival, albeit briefly, of Jerry Yester. The quality of Sebastian's lyrics and melodies makes him one of the finest American songwriters. In 1991, Steve Boone, Joe Butler and the Yester brothers announced the reformation of the band for a tour - however, without Yanovsky and Sebastian, the 'magic' will not be there.

Albums: *Do You Believe In Magic* (1965), *Daydream* (1966), *What's Shakin'* (1966), *What's Up Tiger Lily* (1966, film soundtrack), *Hums Of The Lovin' Spoonful* (1966), *You're A Big Boy Now* (1967, film soundtrack), *Everything Playing* (1968), *Revelation: Revolution* (1968). Compilations: *The EP Collection* (1988), *Collection: Lovin' Spoonful, 20 Hits* (1988), *The Very Best Of The Lovin' Spoonful* (1988), *Go To The Movies* (1991).

Lowe, Jez

b. 14 July 1955, County Durham, England. Having played on the folk circuit, with various groups from 1973, Lowe also worked for a time with Ged Foley, who was later to join the House Band. In 1979, Jez, performing mainly traditional songs, turned professional. His first release, in 1980, was on Fellside Records, and included three Lowe originals. He was supported on *Jez Lowe* by Jim Barnes (cittern/guitar) and Sylvia Barnes (whistle/vocals). Both had previously been members of the Battlefield Band. From 1981, Lowe pursued a largely solo career, but performed at festivals and concerts, both at home and in the USA and Europe, with Jake Walton (hurdy gurdy). However, Jez continued to record with Fellside, releasing *Old Durham Road* and the highly acclaimed *Galloways*, which contains the much covered Lowe composition 'Old Bones'. Subsequent releases contained more Lowe originals, and, following the release of *Bad Penny*, Jez formed Jez Lowe And The Bad Pennies, taking on Bev Sanders (vocals/percussion/whistle) and Rob Kay (vocals/keyboards/melodeon/recorder/percussion) who was in turn replaced in 1991 by Bob Surgeoner (bass/accordian/banjo/keyboards). They recorded *Briefly On The Street*, which contained the excellent 'The Famous Working Man' and 'Davis And Golightly'. Lowe has had songs recorded by artists such as Gordon Bok and Mary Black among others, and he continues to be a popular figure on the folk circuit. Billy Surgeoner (fiddle/whistle/keyboards/bass) joined in 1991.

Albums: *Jez Lowe* (1980), *The Old Durham Road* (1983), *Galloways* (1985), with Martin Carthy and

Roy Harris *The Penguin Book Of English Folk Songs* (1985), with Jake Walton *Two A Roue* (1986), *Bad Penny* (1988), with the Bad Pennies *Briefly On The Street* (1990). Compilation: *Back Shift* (1992).

Lucas, Trevor

b. 25 December 1943, Bungaree, Victoria, Australia, d. 4 February 1989. Lucas began as a singer-songwriter, performing contemporary folk songs, in the cafes and clubs of Melbourne, Australia. He recorded one obscure album before moving to the UK in 1964, where he established himself on the folk circuit, as a duo with fellow Australian Kerilee Male. They formed one of the first electric folk groups, Eclection, in 1967 and later formed Fotheringay with Sandy Denny, who he married. Lucas then became a producer at Island Records for 18 months until he joined Fairport Convention in 1972. He left the band in early 1976 to take up production work again. He returned to Australia in 1978, after Sandy Denny's death. His time fully engaged in the production of such bands as Paul Kelly, Bushwackers, Goanna, and Redgum, plus film documentaries and children's dramas. He died in Sydney, Australia of a suspected heart attack.

Albums: *See That My Grave Is Kept Clean* (mid-60s), *Overlander* (1966).

M

Mabsant

This Welsh trio took their name from the Patron Saint of festivals in Wales. The current line-up includes Siwsann George b. Suzanne George, 2 April 1956, East Glamorgan Hospital, Church Village, Wales, (guitar, harp, concertina, spoons, vocals), Stuart Brown b. 7 May 1956, Springburn, Glasgow, Scotland, (recorder, bouzouki, whistle, keyboards); and Steve Whitehead b. 10 March 1960, Coventry, Warwickshire, England, (clarinet/saxophone). The group was formed in mid-1978, playing Welsh and Irish songs and tunes in Cardiff pubs. The line-up at the time was Siwsann George, together with Pete Meazey (mandolin, banjo, mouth organ, dulcimer, vocals), Alun Roberts (mandolin) and Chris Jones. Following the departure of Jones, and Roberts

falling ill, Stuart Brown joined the group, this was to be the first of a number of personnel changes. After a three-week tour of Brittany in 1980, Meazey stayed behind, making way for Duncan Brown (Stuart's older brother) to join on double bass. Later the same year, Gareth Westacott (mandolin) and Non Harris (vocals) were added. Their debut album was followed by television work and touring. The following year, Siwsann won the Pan-Celtic traditional singing competition (solo category) with a song called 'Aberfan'. Mabsant were the first Welsh group to appear at the Inverness Folk Festival in Scotland in 1982. The group turned fully professional in 1984 and toured extensively. In November 1986, Robin Huw Bowen (b. 7 June 1957, Liverpool, England; harp), joined the group, and in 1987 Mabsant toured the Far East for the British Council. In 1988, they appeared at London's Royal Albert Hall and toured Hungary, Ireland, Denmark and Brittany. Bowen left in 1989 to pursue a solo career and continue his research work of Welsh folk tunes. Peter Stacey (pipes/saxophone/flute) joined temporarily, but family commitments forced him to play less and less and Steve Whitehead was recruited. In December 1989, Mabsant toured Germany for the first time, and by 1990 they were recording music for television. Despite the changes in personnel, Mabsant's sound has continued to develop with each change, without losing sight of the original feel for the music. *Cofeb* was almost folk/jazz, but still had the unmistakable Mabsant touch. Owing to Mabsant's success, the folk world at alrge now acknowledges that (good) folk music exists outside Scotland and Ireland; the group has paved the way for a number of other highly talented Welsh artists.
Albums: *Cwlwm Pedwar* (1982), *Trip I Forgannwg* (1983), *Gwyl Mabsant* (1984), *Chware Chwyldro* (1986), *Valley Lights* (1986), *Trwy'r Weiar* (1987), *Chwedlau Cymru I Ddysgwyr* (1989), *Cofeb* (1989), *Ton Gron* (1990).

Magna Carta

Magna Carta were renowned for their gentle ballad style and, often, mythical subject matter. Although they were never purely a folk group, they successfully bridged the gap between folk and folk-rock. They originally formed as a duo, in London, in 1969, with Chris Simpson (b. 13 July 1942, Harrogate, North Yorkshire, England; guitar/vocals), and Lyell Tranter (guitar/vocals). They obtained a deal with Fontana, and then Glen Stuart (vocals) joined them. In August 1970, *Seasons* made 55 in the UK album charts. *Times Of Change* was released on Fontana, and the highly regarded *Seasons* appeared on the Vertigo label. Tranter then returned to Australia. The group played the Royal

Albert Hall in 1971, with the Royal Philharmonic Orchestra, but the tapes of the recording were lost by Phonogram. Texts from *Seasons* and *Lord Of The Ages*, have been used as part of the English syllabus in several European countries. Davy Johnstone (guitar/vocals) then joined the line-up, recording, *In Concert* and *Songs From Wasties Orchard*, with them before leaving to work with Elton John and Kiki Dee. The latter album was regarded by many as the group's finest work. Simpson and Stuart were then joined by Stan Gordon (guitar), recording and releasing the much-lauded *Lord Of The Ages*. Graham Smith (bass), who had been on the sessions for this album, then joined the group. Shortly afterwards both he and Stan Gordon left, so by 1974, it was back to square one as a duo. There followed a period of much change and upheaval, as, in following more of a rock path, they added Mohammed Amin (bass), and a drummer, but Glen Stuart did not feel comfortable with the new direction. This short-lived set-up soon gave way to Simpson and Stuart being joined by Tom Hoy (b. 5 February 1950, Glasgow, Scotland; guitar/vocals). Stuart then left to run a pet shop in Richmond, Surrey.
In 1977, former Natural Acoustic Band member Robin Thyne (b. 1 November 1950, Newcastle Upon Tyne, England; guitar/vocals), joined the group, along with Lee Abbott (b. 21 January 1950, Gravesend, Kent, England; fretless bass/vocals). Soon afterwards, Pick Withers (drums) was added. Withers stayed only briefly, leaving to join Dire Straits. There followed upheavals in 1979, when Thyne and Hoy left to form Nova Carta. There had been much acrimony leading to the split. Tom McConville appeared on the *Live In Bergen* release, before the line-up changed again to include Al Fenn (b. Alastair Fenn, 9 March 1947, Chingford, Essex, England; guitar/vocals), and George Norris (b. 30 December 1945, Cowes, Isle Of Wight, England; guitar/vocals). Between 1980 and 1982, Doug Morter (electric and acoustic guitar) was added, together with a variety of drummers, one of whom was Paul Burgess (b. 28 September 1958, Stockport, Cheshire, England), who had formerly been with 10cc. The 1981 release, *Midnight Blue*, contained 'Highway To Spain', a track consistently on radio station playlists around the world. Subsequently, despite much touring and recording, Simpson pursued a solo career, while Norris and Burgess both left.
Eventually, Morter left to join the Albion Band. Simpson's solo release, *Listen To The Man* came out with Magna Carta now including, in addition to Simpson and Abbott, Linda Taylor (b. 28 June 1953, Halifax, West Yorkshire, England; guitar/vocals), and Willie Jackson (b. 18 February

1954, York, England; guitars). Between 1984 and 1986, Chris and Linda went to the Middle East, running a music club, eventually deciding to return home and re-form Magna Carta. In 1986, the extremely fluid line-up now included, in addition to Simpson, Taylor and Abbott, Glyn Jones (keyboards), John Carey (fiddle), Paul Burgess, again, (drums), and Simon Carlton (lead guitar). In 1987, *One To One* was finished, for the Tembo record label. The same year, Jones left the group, and the band played the Cambridge Festival, and the album was released in 1988. In 1990, Simpson and Taylor married, and with the semi-retirement of Lee Abbott, they continued as a duo touring worldwide. Phonogram then released the compilation *Old Masters/New Horizons*, in Europe only. *Heartlands* followed soon after, released in Holland, followed by a sell-out tour of Holland, with Will Jackson (keyboards/guitars) and Paul Burgess (drums) returning, together with Jonathan Barrett (b. 16 August 1962, Leeds, West Yorkshire, England; bass). Will's brother Eddie Jackson (b. 23 April 1957, York, England; bass), played on the *Heartlands* album, and on their January 1992 tour. Chris and Linda still work as a duo, as well as with the larger line-up for extensive touring. Over the years, the group has toured over 151 countries.

Albums: *Magna Carta* (1969), *Times Of Change* (1969), *Seasons* (1970), *Songs From Wasties Orchard* (1971), *Magna Carta In Concert* (1972), *Lord Of The Ages* (1974), *Martin's Cafe* (1974), *Putting It Back Together* (1975), *Prisoner's On The Line* (1978), *Live In Bergen* (1978), *Midnight Blue* (1981), *Sweet Deceiver* (1981), *No Truth In The Rumour* (1979), *One To One* (1988), *Heartlands* (1992). Compilations: *Greatest Hits 1* (1975), *Greatest Hits 2* (1977), *Spotlight On Magna Carta* (1977), *Old Masters/New Horizons* (1992). Solo: Chris Simpson *Listen To The Man* (1983).

Makeba, Miriam

b. 4 March 1932, Johannesburg, South Africa. The vocalist who first put African music on the international map in the 60s, Makeba began her professional career in 1950, when she joined Johannesburg group the Cuban Brothers. She came to national prominence during the mid-50s as a member of leading touring group the Manhattan Brothers, an 11-piece close harmony group modelled on African-American line-ups such as the Mills Brothers. She performed widely with the outfit in South Africa, Rhodesia and the Congo until 1957, when she was recruited as a star attraction in the touring package show African Jazz And Variety. She remained with the troupe for two years, again touring South Africa and neighbouring countries, before leaving to join the cast of the 'township musical' *King Kong,* which also featured such future international stars as Hugh Masekela and Jonas Gwangwa.

By now one of South Africa's most successful performers, Makeba was nonetheless receiving just a a few dollars for each recording session, with no additional provision for royalties, and was increasingly keen to settle in the USA. The opportunity came following her starring role in American film-maker Lionel Rogosin's semi-documentary *Come Back Africa,* shot - in defiance of the Pretorian government - in South Africa. When the Italian government invited Makeba to attend the film's premiere at the Venice Film Festival in spring 1959, she privately decided not to return home. Shortly afterwards, furious at the international furore created by the film's powerful exposé of apartheid, her South African passport was withdrawn. In London after the Venice Festival, Makeba met Harry Belafonte, who offered to help her gain an entry visa and work permit to the USA. Arriving in New York in autumn 1959, Belafonte further assisted Makeba by securing her a guest spot on the popular *Steve Allen Show* and an engagement at the prestigious Manhattan jazz club the Village Vanguard. As a consequence of these exposures, Makeba became a nationally-feted performer within a few months of arriving in the USA, combining her musical activities - such as major chart hits like 'Patha Patha', 'The Click Song' and 'Malaika' - with outspoken denunciations of apartheid. In 1963, after an impassioned testimony before the United Nations Committee Against Apartheid, all her records were banned from South Africa.

Married for a few years to fellow South African emigre Masekela, in 1968 Makeba divorced him in order to marry the Black Panther activist Stokeley Carmichael - a liaison which severely damaged her following amongst older white American record buyers. Promoters were no longer interested, and tours and record contracts were cancelled. Consequently, she and Carmichael, from whom she is now divorced, moved to Guinea in West Africa. Fortunately, Makeba continued to find work outside the USA, and during the 70s and 80s spent most of her time on the international club circuit, primarily in Europe, South America and black Africa. She has also been a regular attraction at world jazz events such as the Montreux Jazz Festival, the Berlin Jazz Festival and the Northsea Jazz Festival. In 1977, she was the unofficial South African representative at the pan-African festival of arts and culture, Festac, in Lagos, Nigeria. In 1982, she was reunited with Masekela at an historic concert in Botswana. As previously in the USA, Makeba combined her professional commitments with political activity, and served as a Guinean delegate to the United Nations. In 1986, she was awarded the Dag Hammarskjold Peace Prize in recognition of this work. In 1987, Makeba was invited to appear as a guest artist on Paul Simon's Graceland tour, which included emotional returns to the USA and Zimbabwe (she had been banned from the then Rhodesia in 1960). While some anti-apartheid activists, mostly white Westerners, criticized her for allegedly breaking the African National Congress' cultural boycott by working with Simon (whose Graceland album had been part-recorded in South Africa), Makeba convincingly maintained that the Graceland package was substantially helping the anti-apartheid movement by drawing attention to the culture and plight of black South Africans.

Selected albums: *The World Of Miriam Makeba* (1962), *Makeba* (1963), *The Click Song* (1965), *Pata Pata* (1972), *Live At Conakry* (1975), *Festac 77* (1978), *Greatest Hits From Africa* (1985), *Sangoma* (1989). Compilation: *The Best Of Miriam Makeba And The Sklarks* (1993).

Further reading: *Makeba, My Story* (1989).

Mákvirág

Formed in 1973, this trio from Hungary and Romania, have reached a wider audience due to the increasing interest shown in European and world music during the late 80s. The group won first prize in 1974 in a folk-jazz competition in Gyor, Hungary. They were subsequently afforded the accolade Young Master Of Folk Art in 1976. Then, in 1978, they won the Lászl Lajtha Award at Szombathely, Hungary. They appeared in Britain in 1988, while undertaking their first major UK and Irish tour. All multi-instrumentalists, Csaba Szijjártó (b. Budapest, Hungary), Zoltán Kátai, and Károly Horváth (b. Romania) have recorded a number of albums, each combining music from their own backgrounds as well as from other Eastern European countries. Instrumentation is supplemented by recorders, ocarina and pan pipes. All three members have spent time in various orchestras and choirs and music conservatories. Mákvirág have since played the UK again on a number of occasions, largely at festivals.

Albums: *Trifa* (1978), *Palóc Lakodalmas* (1978), *Mákvirág 1* (1979), *Mákvárig 2* (1981), *Mákávirag In Brazil* (1988), *Mákvirágék* (1988), *Népszokások-Jeles Napok* (1988), *Békesség-Peacefulness* (1991).

Malicorne

The brainchild of French music genius Gabriel Yacoub, Malicorne was formed after he and his then wife, Marie, spent some time in Alan Stivell's pioneering Breton unit. The original, innovative line-up, used antique instruments to play peasant songs, haunting harmonies and integrated rock rhythms. *Pierre De Gre Noble* (1973), although recorded before Malicorne came into being, set the style and manner of the band. Initially a four piece, the Yacoubs were joined by Laurent Vercambe (violin) and Hugh De Courson (bass, woodwinds). Their finest set in this form was *Almanach*, a song cycle based on the turning year, and based on rustic folklore. A commercially successful tour of France was followed, in 1978, by the recuitment of a fifth member, Oliver Zdrzalik (bass). Subsequently, an excellent live recording, *En Public A Mont Real*, preceded further fundamental personnel changes, and the birth of a new seven piece unit, which included ex-Gryphon bassoonist Brian Gulland. Following *Le Bestiare*, which proved to be an 'animalistic album, a story of French country folk', the band cut one final set before splitting up, but came together again in 1986 when an intended Gabriel Yacoub solo session was reorganized as a Malicorne piece. The Yacoubs, with Oliver Kowalski (bass), Jean Pierre Arnoux (drums) and Michel Le Cam (fiddle), recorded the industrial sounding *Les Cathedrales De L'industrie*. This line-up became Gabriel Yacoub's own band, and, with the addition of Nikki Matheson (keyboards), played both Malicorne and Yacoub material. Yacoub's own albums are all distinct; ranging from traditional folk and chamber music, to bizarre electronic pieces. Yacoub married Matheson in the late 80s, and they toured as an acoustic duo.

Selected Albums: *Almanach* (1976), *Le Extraordinaire Tour De France D' Adeland Rousseau* (1978), *En Public A Montreal* (1979), *Le Best Iare* (1980), *Cathedrales De L'industrie* (1986). Gabriel & Marie Yacoub: *Pierre De Grenoble* (1973). Gabriel Yacoub: *Elementary Level Of Faith* (1987), *Bel* (1990).

Martyn, Beverly

b. Beverly Kutner, Coventry, England. This underrated artist first attracted attention in 1966 when her anonymous demo tape solicited an inquiry by Decca employee Tony Hall in his *Record Mirror* column. She was subsequently signed to the label and, as Beverly, launched its Deram Records subsidiary with 'Happy New Year', an excellent Randy Newman composition. The singer appeared at the famed Monterey Pop Festival, and enjoyed an uncredited cameo part on Simon And Garfunkel's 'Fakin' It', prior to forming a duo with her husband, folksinger John Martyn. The couple recorded two superb albums, *Stormbringer* and *The Road To Ruin*, the latter of which featured Beverly's evocative song, 'Primrose Hill'. Their professional relationship was severed in 1971, and the couple were divorced later in the decade. Sadly, Beverly has subsequently failed to fulfil the promise shown in her early work.

Albums: with John Martyn *Stormbringer* (1970), *The Road To Ruin* (1970).

Martyn, John

b. Iain McGeachy, 11 September 1948, New Malden, Surrey, England, to musically-minded parents. At the age of 17, he started his professional career under the guidance of folk artist Hamish Imlach. The long, often bumpy journey through Martyn's career began when he arrived in London, where he was signed instantly by the astute Chris Blackwell, whose fledgling Island Records was just finding major success. Martyn became the first white solo artist on the label. His first album, the jazz/blues tinged *London Conversation* (1968), was released amidst a growing folk scene which was beginning to shake off its traditionalist image. The jazz influence was confirmed when, only nine months later, *The Tumbler* was released. A bold yet understated album, it broke many conventions of folk music, featuring the flute and saxophone of jazz artist Harold MacNair. The critics began the predictable Bob Dylan comparisons, especially as the young Martyn was not yet 20. Soon afterwards, Martyn married singer Beverly Kutner, and as John and Beverly Martyn they produced two well-received albums, *Stormbringer* and *Road To Ruin*. The former was recorded in Woodstock, USA, with a talented group of American musicians, including Levon Helm of the Band and keyboard player Paul Harris. Both albums were relaxed in approach and echoed the simple peace and love attitudes of the day, with their gently naive sentiments. Martyn the romantic also became Martyn the drunkard, and so began his conflict. The meeting with jazz bassist Danny Thompson, who became a regular drinking companion, led to some serious boozing and Martyn becoming a 'Jack the Lad'. Hard work in the clubs, however, was building his reputation, but it was the release of *Bless The Weather* and *Solid Air* that established him as a concert hall attraction. Martyn delivered a unique combination of beautifully slurred vocals and a breathtaking technique using his battered acoustic guitar played through an echoplex unit, together with sensitive and mature jazz arrangements. The track 'Solid Air' was written as a eulogy to his friend singer/songwriter Nick Drake who had committed suicide in 1974. Martyn was able to pour out his feelings in the opening two lines of the song: 'You've been taking your time and you've been living on solid air. You've been walking the line, you've been living on solid air'. Martyn continued to mature with subsequent albums, each time taking a step further away from folk music. *Inside Out* and the mellow *Sunday's*

Child both confirmed his important musical standing, although commercial success still eluded him. Frustrated by the music business in general, he made and produced *Live At Leeds* himself. The album could be purchased only by writing to John and Beverly at their home in Hastings; they personally signed every copy of the plain record sleeve upon despatch. Martyn's dark side was beginning to get the better of him, and his alcohol and drug intake put a strain on his marriage. *One World*, in 1977, has subtle references to these problems in the lyrics, and, with Steve Winwood guesting on most tracks, the album was warmly received. Martyn, however, was going through serious problems and would not produce a new work until three years later when, following the break up of his marriage, he delivered the stunning *Grace And Danger* produced by Phil Collins. This was the album in which Martyn bared all to his listeners, a painfully emotional work, which put the artist in a class of his own. Following this collection Martyn ended his association with Chris Blackwell. Martyn changed labels to WEA and delivered *Glorious Fool* and *Well Kept Secret*, also touring regularly with a full-time band including the experienced Max Middleton on keyboards and the talented fretless bassist, Alan Thompson. These two albums had now moved him firmly into the rock category and, in live performance, his much-revered acoustic guitar playing was relegated to only a few numbers, such as his now-classic song 'May You Never', subsequently recorded by Eric Clapton. Martyn's gift as a lyricist, however, had never been sharper, and he injected a fierce yet honest seam into his songs.

On the title track to *Glorious Fool* he wrote a powerful criticism of the former American president, Ronald Reagan (in just one carefully repeated line Martyn states, 'Half the lies he tells you are not true'). Following another home-made live album *Philentropy*, Martyn returned to Island Records and went on to deliver more quality albums. *Sapphire*, with his evocative version of 'Somewhere Over The Rainbow', reflected a happier man, now re-married. The world's first commercially released CD single was Martyn's 'Angeline', a superbly crafted love song to his wife, which preceded the album *Piece By Piece* in 1986. With commercial success still eluding him, Martyn slid into another alcoholic trough until 1988, when he was given a doctor's ultimatum. He chose to dry out, returning in 1990 with *The Apprentice*. *Cooltide* was a fine album, expertly produced but contained songs that tended to last too long, this was also the case with *Couldn't Love You More*. The latter was a bonus for loyal fans as it was an album of re-recorded versions from Martyn's exquisite back

John Martyn

catalogue. Martyn has retained his cult following for over 20 years. It is difficult to react indifferently to his important work as a major artist; although he has yet to receive major commercial success.

Albums: *London Conversation* (1968), *The Tumbler* (1968), *Stormbringer* (1970), *The Road To Ruin* (1970), *Bless The Weather* (1971), *Solid Air* (1973), *Inside Out* (1973), *Sunday's Child* (1975), *Live At Leeds* (1975), *One World* (1977), *Grace And Danger* (1980), *Glorious Fool* (1981), *Well Kept Secret* (1982), *Philentrophy* (1983), *Sapphire* (1984), *Piece By Piece* (1986), *Foundations* (1987), *The Apprentice* (1990), *Cooltide* (1991), *BBC Radio 1 Live In Concert* (1992), *Couldn't Love You More* (1992), *No Little Boy* (1993). Compilations: *So Far So Good* (1977), *The Electric John Martyn* (1982).

Matthews Southern Comfort

Formed in 1969 by former Fairport Convention singer/guitarist Iain Matthews, the group comprised Mark Griffiths (guitar), Carl Barnwell (guitar), Gordon Huntley (pedal steel guitar), Andy Leigh (bass) and Ray Duffy (drums). After signing to EMI Records, they recorded their self-titled debut album in late 1969. Country-tinged rather than folk, it nevertheless displayed Matthews' songwriting talents. In the summer of 1970, their next album, *Second Spring* reached the UK Top 40 and was followed by a winter chart-topper, 'Woodstock'. The single had been written by Joni Mitchell as a tribute to the famous festival that she had been unable to attend. Already issued as a single in a harde -rocking vein by Crosby, Stills, Nash & Young, it was a surprise UK number 1 for Matthews Southern Comfort. Unfortunately, success was followed by friction within the group and, two months later, Matthews announced his intention to pursue a solo career. One more album by the group followed, after which they truncated their name to Southern Comfort. After two further albums, they disbanded in the summer of 1972.

Albums: *Matthews Southern Comfort* (1969), *Second Spring* (1970), *Later That Same Year* (1970). As Southern Comfort: *Southern Comfort* (1971), *Frog City* (1971), *Stir Don't Shake* (1972).

Matthews, Al

b. Brooklyn, New York, USA. An all-round entertainer, Matthews began singing in New York street groups before progressing to the folk scene. He was a member of bands who supported artists including Bob Dylan, Tom Paxton and Peter, Paul And Mary, before moving to France where as a leading member of Petit Conservatoire de Chanson, he became a familiar voice on radio and television. Between 1965 and 1971, he served in Vietnam becoming the first black to be promoted to sergeant while still in the field. He returned to Europe and became successful on the English folk scene, and he later was signed by CBS Records. A UK Top 20 hit followed with 'Fool'. It also reached the Top 10 in 15 European countries. Although he continued to record, Matthews never matched his initial chart entry. In 1979, he became the first black disc jockey on BBC Radio 1. Throughout the 80s he turned his career entirely towards acting, starring in movies including *Aliens*, *Superman 3* and *Yanks*.

Albums: *Al Matthews* (1975), *It's Only Love* (1977).

Matthews, Iain

b. Ian Matthews McDonald, 16 June 1946, Scunthorpe, Lincolnshire, England. Matthews sang with small-time Lincolnshire bands, the Classics, the Rebels and the Imps, before moving to London in 1966, as one of the vocalists in a British surfing band Pyramid, who recorded a few tracks for Deram Records. To supplement his income, Iain worked in a shoe shop in London's famous Carnaby Street. He learnt of a vacancy for a vocalist in Fairport Convention, which he joined in 1967 before they had recorded (and before Sandy Denny joined them). He appeared on the group's first single 'If I Had A Ribbon Bow', released on Track and produced by Joe Boyd, and on their debut album on Polydor. Fairport then moved to Island Records in 1968, and Matthews appeared on their early breakthrough album, *What We Did On Our Holidays*, but left the group during the recording of mid-1969's *Unhalfbricking*, because it had become obvious to him that the group's new-found traditional folk/rock direction would involve him far less than its previous contemporary 'underground' work.

Matthews (who had changed his surname to avoid confusion with saxophonist Ian McDonald of King Crimson) then signed with starmakers Howard And Blaikley, who had been involved in the success story of Dave Dee, Dozy, Beaky, Mick And Tich. After making a solo album *Matthews Southern Comfort*, for MCA in 1970, a group, also called Matthews Southern Comfort, was formed around him, and released two more country/rock albums, *Second Spring* and *Later That Same Year*. The group also topped the UK singles chart with their version of Joni Mitchell's 'Woodstock'. By 1971, Matthews had left the band, which continued with little success as Southern Comfort. Matthews, meanwhile, signed a solo deal with Vertigo, releasing two excellent but underrated solo albums, *If You Saw Through My Eyes* and *Tigers Will Survive*, both featuring many of his ex-colleagues from Fairport, before forming Plainsong, an ambitious quartet which included Andy Roberts (ex-Liverpool Scene), Dave Richards and Bob Ronga.

Iain Matthews

Matthews was still obligated to make another album for Vertigo, but was unwilling to commit Plainsong to the label. As a result, he was given a small budget to make a contractual commitment album, *Journeys From Gospel Oak*, which Vertigo did not release but instead sold to Mooncrest, a label with which the album's producer Sandy Robertson was connected. Originally released in 1974, it became one of the earliest compact disc releases to feature Matthews' post-Fairport work. Plainsong then signed with Elektra, and released the magnificent *In Search Of Amelia Earhart* in 1972, before Bob Ronga left the band. During the recording of a second album (still unreleased, but supposedly titled *Plainsong III*, referring to the membership of the band rather than a third album), Matthews and Richards apparently fell out. To continue would have been difficult, and Matthews accepted an invitation to work with ex-Monkee Michael Nesmith in Los Angeles. An excellent solo album (organized and encouraged by Nesmith), *Valley Hi*, was followed by *Some Days You Eat The Bear*, which included the Tom Waits song, 'Ol' 55', which Matthews recorded a month earlier than label-mates the Eagles. He then signed with CBS for *Go For Broke* and *Hit And Run*, which were neither commercially successful nor artistically satisfactory. By 1978, Matthews was again 'available for hire', at which point Rockburgh (which was owned by Sandy Robertson) offered to re-sign him. The first fruit of this reunion was *Stealing Home*, on which the backing musicians included Bryn Haworth and Phil Palmer on guitar, and Pete Wingfield on piano. Robertson licensed the album for North America to a small Canadian label, Mushroom, which had been financed by the discovery of the group Heart. 'Shake It' was excerpted as a US single and reached the Top 10, but the founder and owner of Mushroom died suddenly, and the company virtually collapsed. A follow-up by Matthews, *Siamese Friends*, was already contracted to Mushroom, but swiftly vanished with little trace in the UK.

In 1980 came a third album for Rockfield, *A Spot Of Interference*, which was an ill-judged attempt to climb aboard the new wave. This also disappeared, and later that same year came *Discreet Repeat*, a reasonably selected double album 'Best Of' featuring post-Southern Comfort material, but this marked the parting of the waves between Matthews and Robertson. The former formed an unlikely band called Hi-Fi in Seattle, where he lived with ex-Pavlov's Dog vocalist David Surkamp. Two more contrasting vocal styles than those of Surkamp and Matthews could hardly be imagined, but the group made a live mini-album, *Demonstration Records*, in 1982, and followed it with a full- length studio album, *Moods For The Mallards* - both were released in the UK on the small independent label, Butt Records.

In 1983, Matthews signed with Polydor in Germany for a new album, *Shook*, which surprisingly remains unreleased in Britain, and more importantly from the artistic point of view, the USA. Matthews threw in the towel and took a job as an A&R man for Island Music in Los Angeles, but was made redundant in 1985. An appearance at the 1986 Fairport Convention Cropredy Festival in Oxfordshire convinced Matthews that he should return to singing, even though he had just ended a period of unemployment by starting to work for the noted new age label, Windham Hill. After a frustrating year during which it became clear that Matthews and the label were creatively at odds, Matthews left, but only after recording a vocal album for the predominantly instrumental label, *Walking A Changing Line* released in 1988, on which he interpreted a number of songs written by Jules Shear (ex-Funky Kings and Jules And The Polar Bears). While this was his best album to date according to Matthews, it sold little better than anything since *Stealing Home*.

In 1989, Matthews relocated to Austin, Texas, where he linked up with Mark Hallman, a guitarist and producer who had worked on 'Changing Line'. A cassette-only album by the duo, *Iain Matthews Live*, was made for sale at gigs, and Matthews signed in 1990 with US independent label Goldcastle, to which several comparative veterans, including Joan Baez and Karla Bonoff, were also contracted. *Pure And Crooked* was released in 1990, and later that same year, Matthews reunited with his Plainsong-era colleague, Andy Roberts, for a very popular appearance at Cambridge Folk Festival. By 1992, Goldcastle had gone out of business, leaving Matthews, an exceptional vocalist with excellent taste in both self-composed material and especially in cover versions, once again without a recording contract. In 1993 Matthews and Roberts released *Dark Side Of The Room* under the Plainsong monicker, which was funded by a German record-maker and supporter.

Albums: *If You Saw Through My Eyes* (1970), *Tigers Will Survive* (1971), *Journeys From Gospel Oak* (1972), *Valley Hi* (1973), *Somedays You Eat The Bear* (1974), *Go For Broke* (1975), *Hit And Run* (1976), *Stealing Home* (1978), *Siamese Friends* (1979), *A Spot Of Interference* (1980), *Shook* (1983), *Walking A Changing Line* (1988), *Pure And Crooked* (1990), *Nights In Manhattan - Live* (1991), *Orphans And Outcasts Vol. 1* (1991). Compilation: *Discreet Repeat* (1980). With Plainsong *In Search Of Amelia Earhart* (1972), *Dark Side Of The Room* (1993).

Mayor, Simon

b. 5 October 1953, Sheffield, England. Mayor taught himself guitar at the age of 10, and in his teens he added the whistle, mandolin and fiddle. He met Hilary James (b. 4 August 1952, Stoke On Trent, England; vocals/guitar/double bass), at the Reading University folk club, and began to work with her in various line-ups. After university, they formed Spredthick, a folk/blues/ragtime band. The group underwent many personnel changes at different times and featured musicians such as Andrew Mathewson (b. 1952; guitar) who was with them from 1973-76, Peter Jagger (b. 1954; guitar) from 1976-77, Andy McGhee (banjo) during 1978, and Phil Fentimen (b. 10 August 1954; guitar/double bass), from 1977-80. Spredthick released one album then disbanded.

Aside from working as a duo, Simon and Hilary make occasional outings fronting Slim Panatella And The Mellow Virginians, a bluegrass/western swing trio. For this they recruit the services of Andy Baum (b. 1953; vocals/guitar/mandolin). With Hilary, Simon has written topical songs for television programmes such as Newsnight, Kilroy, and children's songs for Play School, Listening Corner, and Green Claws. As a duo, they have played throughout Europe, and Singapore. Simon has also presented The Song Tree on BBC Radio 5 for six years. He has done much to revive interest in the much under-rated mandolin, via his mandolin album project, encompassing classical, bnaroque, and folk themes. The project featured Simon's own compositions alongside non-folk elements by composers including Vivaldi, Berlioz, and Handel. This series of albums received excellent reviews and a great deal of airplay.

Albums: Spredthick (1979), Craving The Dew (1981), Musical Mystery Tour (1985), Slim Panatella And The Mellow Virginians (1988), Musical Mystery Tour 2 - Up In A Big Balloon (1988), Musical Mystery Tour 3 - A Big Surprise (1989), Musical Mystery Tour 4 - Snowmen And Kings (1990), The Mandolin Album (1990), The Second Mandolin Album (1991), Winter With Mandolins (1992). Compilations: Children's Favourites From The Musical Mystery Tour (1990).

McCalmans

Formed on 6 October 1964, the original line-up of this Scottish trio was Hamish Bayne (b. Nairobi, Kenya), Ian McCalman (b. 1 September 1946, Edinburgh, Scotland; vocals/guitar/bodhran), and Derek Moffat (b. near Dundee, Fife, Scotland; vocals/guitar/mandolin/bodhran). All three met, in 1964, at the Edinburgh School of Architecture, where they called themselves the Ian McCalman Folk Group. Within the year the trio was regularly playing clubs and concerts, and signed a recording

deal with EMI in 1967. The group secured its first television series in 1970, on BBC Scotland, and worked in Europe. In 1982, Bayne left the group, to be replaced by Nick Keir (b. Edinburgh, Scotland; vocals/guitar/mandolin/tenor banjo/whistles/recorder). Throughout their career, the group have continued to base their style around three-part vocal harmony, both with and without instruments, performing traditional and contemporary material. Flames On The Water, featuring contemporary Scottish songs, was highly regarded, and in 1991 the group were given their own series on BBC Radio 2.

Albums: All In One Mind (1967), McCalmans Folk (1968), Singers Three (1969), Turn Again (1970), No Strings Attached (1971), An Audience With The McCalmans (1973), Side By Side By Side (1977), Burn The Witch (1978), Smuggler (1975), House Full (1976), McCalmans Live (1980), The Ettrick Shepherd (1980), Bonnie Bands Again (1982), Ancestral Manoeuvres (1984), Peace And Plenty (1986), Scottish Songs (1986), Listen To The Heat (1988), Flames On The Water (1990). Compilation: The Best Of The McCalmans (1979).

MacColl, Ewan

b. Jimmie Miller, 25 January 1915, Auchterader, Perthshire, Scotland, d. 22 October 1989. Having parents who sang enabled MacColl to learn many of their songs while he was still young. He subsequently wrote many classic and regularly covered songs of his own, including 'Dirty Old Town' which was inspired by his own home town of Salford. The song was later made popular by the Dubliners, among others. Having left school at the age of 14, MacColl joined the Salford Clarion Players, and by the age of 16 he was already actively involved in street theatre. His lifelong allegiance to the Communist Party was influenced by what he experienced first-hand during the Depression years, and by seeing what it had done to his own father and others around him. As a result of his early involvement in political theatre, MacColl, as playwright, actor, director and singer, co-founded the Theatre Workshop at Stratford, London, with Joan Littlewood, who became his first wife. A meeting with folklorist and collector Alan Lomax in the 50s persuaded MacColl to become involved in the revival of British folk songs, which at the time took a back seat to the wealth of American folk material that had arrived via the skiffle boom. The Critics Group was formed by MacColl in 1964, in an effort to analyze folk song and folk singing technique. This had its critics, who felt that MacColl and the group were setting themselves up as an elitist authority on folk music. It was in the Critics Group that he met Jean Newlove, who was to be his second wife. They had two children, Hamish and Kirsty MacColl. In 1965, a series of programmes called *The Song Carriers* was broadcast on Midlands Radio. Later, the innovative *Radio Ballads* was formulated, combining the voice of the ordinary working man with songs and music relevant to their work. The first series, *The Ballad Of John Axon,* was broadcast in 1958. This brought together Peggy Seeger and radio producer Charles Parker. Despite the success of these programmes, no more were commissioned by the BBC on the grounds of expense. It is more likely, however, that the views and opinions of the working man did not conform to the Establishment's idea of what was suitable for broadcast. Unlike many, MacColl believed that it was not sufficient to only perform old songs, but that new material should be aired and 'The Travelling People' emerged from these ideas. Both Seeger and MacColl continued to perform professionally throughout the 70s and 80s, having wed following the break-up of his second marriage. Together they set up Blackthorne Records. They were particularly noticeable during the UK miners' strike of 1984, recording and appearing at benefits.

Outside folk music circles, MacColl is probably best remembered for the beautiful 'The First Time Ever I Saw Your Face' which he wrote in 1957 for Peggy Seeger. Roberta Flack reached the top of the US charts with the song in 1972, as well as the UK Top 20. MacColl received an Ivor Novello Award for the song in 1973. He died in October 1989, having only recently completed an autobiography. *Black And White* is a compilation of live and studio recordings from 1972-86 and was compiled by his sons, Calum and Neill. In addition to the three children born to him and Peggy, songs such as 'My Old Man' and 'The Joy Of Living', and a pride in British traditional song are just part of the considerable legacy he left behind.

Selected albums: with Dominic Behan *Streets Of Song* (1959), with Peggy Seeger *Chorus From The Gallows* (1960), *Haul On The Bowlin'* (1962), with Peggy Seeger *Jacobite Songs* (1962), *Off To Sea Once More* (1963), *Fourpence A Day-British Industrial Folk Songs* (1963), with A.L. Lloyd *English And Scottish Folk Ballads* (1964), *The Ballad Of John Axon* (1965), *The Long Harvest 1* (1966), with Seeger *The Amorous Muse* (1966), *A Sailor's Garland* (1966), with Seeger *The Manchester Angel* (1966), *The Long Harvest 2* (1967), *Blow Boys Blow* (1967), *Singing The Fishing* (1967), *The Big Hewer* (1967), *The Fight Game* (1967), *The Long Harvest 3* (1968), *The Wanton Muse* (1968), with Seeger *The Angry Muse* (1968), *Paper Stage 1* (1969), *Paper Stage 2* (1969), *The Long Harvest 4* (1969), *The Travelling People* (1969), *The Long Harvest 5* (1970), *On The Edge* (1970), *The World Of Ewan MacColl And Peggy Seeger 1* (1970), *The Long Harvest 6* (1971), *The Long Harvest 7* (1972), *The World Of Ewan MacColl And Peggy Seeger 2* (1972), *Solo Flight* (1972), *The Long Harvest 8* (1973), *The Long Harvest 9* (1974), *The Long Harvest 10* (1975), with Seeger *Saturday Night At The Bull And Mouth* (1977), *Cold Snap* (1977), *Hot Blast* (1978), *Blood And Roses* (1979), with Seeger *Kilroy Was Here* (1980), *Blood And Roses Vol.2* (1981), *Blood And Roses Vol.3* (1982), *Blood And Roses Vol.4* (1982), *Blood And Roses Vol.5* (1983), *Daddy, What Did You Do In The Strike?* (1985), *Items Of News* (1986), with Seeger *Naming Of Names* (1990). Compilations: *Black And White - The Definitive Collection* (1990), *The Real MacColl* (1993). Further reading: *Journeyman*, Ewan MacColl.

McConville, Tom

b. 6 November 1950, Newcastle-Upon-Tyne, England, to a Scottish mother, and an Irish father. During the 70s, this fiddle player toured with comedian Mike Elliott, then teamed up with Bob Fox (guitar/vocals) to form a duo. McConville then worked briefly with Magna Carta in 1977. During 1979, he got together with songwriter Kieran Halpin to play clubs and festivals. Apart from the domestic circuit, they often performed on the Continent, particularly in Germany. They released two albums before reverting to solo work. In 1983, McConville formed Dab Hand with Jez Lowe and Tom Napper (b. England; tenor banjo). With only the one album to this line-up's credit, and insufficient work as a three-piece, McConville left in 1987, again returning to solo performances. In 1988, he released *Straight From The Shoulder*. The excellent follow-up *Cross The River* saw the fiddler establishing himself on the club and festival circuit. The album was produced, arranged and recorded by Chris Newman.

Albums: with Kieran Halpin *Port Of Call* (1981), with Halpin *Streets Of Everywhere* (1983), *Straight From The Shoulder* (1988), *Cross The River* (1990). With Dab Hand *High Rock And Low Glen* (1987).

McCormack, Count John

b. 14 June 1884, Athlone, Eire, d. 16 September 1945. McCormack was one of the most renowned tenors of the first part of the 20th century, as well as an early recording star. After winning a singing competition in Dublin, he made his first records in London in 1904. He studied opera singing in Milan, and regularly appeared at Covent Garden in London after 1909. From 1907 he had a dual recording career, releasing both operatic arias and popular songs. Among those most associated with McCormack were 'The Minstrel Boy', 'The Irish Immigrant' and 'The Sunshine Of Your Smile'. He made hundreds of records, covering virtually the

whole repertoire of Victorian parlour ballads and Irish folk songs and ballads. During World War I, he enjoyed tremendous success with his version of 'It's A Long, Long Way To Tipperary' and Ivor Novello's 'Keep The Home Fires Burning'. He also gave numerous fundraising concerts in the USA. In 1928, McCormack became a Papal Count and the following year made his film debut in *Song O'My Heart*. During the 30s he gave numerous radio broadcasts and continued to record and give recitals. During his lifetime, over 200 million copies of McCormack's recordings were sold and his continuing popularity is proven by the 15 reissued albums of his work released during the 80s.
Compilations: *John McCormack In Irish Song* (1974), *John McCormack Sings Ballads* (1974), *Golden Voice Of John McCormack* (1978), *John McCormack Sings Of Old Scotland* (1980), *20 Golden Pieces* (1982), *Popular Songs & Irish Ballads* (1984), *Art Of John McCormack* (1984), *Golden Age Of John McCormack* (1985), *Golden Songs* (1988), *John McCormack in Opera* (1988), *Rarities* (1988), *Turn Ye To Me* (1988).

McCurdy, Ed

b. 11 January 1919, Willow Hill, Pennsylvania, USA. McCurdy started out as a gospel singer on radio station WKY in Oklahoma City, and went on to work as a night-club and theatre performer, and radio announcer. Married in 1945, it was in 1946 that McCurdy began singing folk-songs on Canadian radio, and later recorded his first album for the Whitehall label. In 1952, he started writing and performing, for children's programmes, both on radio and on television, and, in 1954, moved to New York City. For *A Ballad Singer's Choice*, he was accompanied by Erik Darling on guitar and banjo. The album included folk standards such as 'Barbara Allen' and 'Pretty Saro'. McCurdy performed at the 1959 Newport Folk Festival, and appeared on four tracks on *Folk Festival At Newport Vol.3*. The album was recorded on 11-12 July 1959, and released the following year. McCurdy also played the festival in 1960 and 1963. He wrote the song 'Last Night I Had The Strangest Dream' in 1950. The song has been covered by many singers, including Simon And Garfunkel, and was especially popular with the peace movements of the 60s. Despite health problems during the 60s, McCurdy was able to undertake a European tour in 1976.
Albums: *Sings Songs Of The Canadian Maritimes* (c.50s), *The Ballad Record* (1955), *Bar Room Ballads* (c.50s), *A Ballad Singer's Choice* (1956), *The Folk Singer* (c.50s), *Frankie And Johnnie* (c.50s), *Sin Songs* (c.50s), *Children's Songs* (1958), *When Dalliance Was In Flower* (c.50s), *When Dalliance Was In Flower Vol. 2* (1958), *Son Of Dalliance* (1959), with Michael Kane *The Legend Of Robin Hood* (c.50s), with other

artists *Folk Festival At Newport Vol.3* (1960), *Last Night I Had The Strangest Dream* (1967). Compilations: *Best Of Ed McCurdy* (1967).

McCutcheon, John

b. 14 August 1952, Wisconsin, USA. McCutcheon, whose family background encompasses farmers and shoemakers, started playing guitar in the early 60s. He picked up a great number of traditional American songs and tunes from the Appalachians, and learned a wealth of instruments, including fiddle, banjo, autoharp, dulcimer. He is especially regarded for his songwriting and hammer-dulcimer playing, as can be heard on *Step By Step*. His dulcimer playing encompasses folk, classical, jazz and many other elements. *Fine Times At Our House* received a Grammy nomination on release, while *Step By Step* received the NAIRD Award, in 1987, for string music album of the year. In 1986, *Frets* magazine readers poll named McCutcheon the String Instrumentalist of the Year. 'Christmas In The Trenches', from *Winter Solstice*, tells the story from a soldier's point of view of the day when opposing troops got together in no-man's land during World War I, to celebrate Christmas. *Mail Myself To You*, and *Howjadoo*, in contrast, consisted of children's songs, both traditional and contemporary. In 1984, McCutcheon co-produced, co-wrote and arranged *Watch Out* by Holly Near. Occasionally, he tours the UK. He has also recorded with songwriter Si Khan, including *Signs Of The Times*. John also collected and recorded a good deal of Nicaraguan music, which was released on Rounder as a double album *Nicaragua Presente!* in 1989. Since 1989, he has been co-editor for 'Folk Blues And Bayond', a regular piece in *International Musician* magazine.
Albums: *How Can I Keep From Singing* (1974), *The Wind That Shakes The Barley* (1977), *Barefoot Boy With Boots On* (1980), *Fine Times At Our House* (1982), *Winter Solstice* (1984), *Howjadoo!* (1985), *Signs Of The Times* (1986), *Step By Step* (1986), *Gonna Rise Again* (1987), *Grandma's Patchwork Quilt* (1987), *Mail Myself To You* (1988), *Water From Another Time* (1989), *What It's Like* (1990), *Live At Wolf Trap* (1991).
Further reading: *Water From Another Time*, John McCutcheon.

McDevitt, Chas

b. 1935, Glasgow, Scotland. McDevitt was the banjo player with the Crane River Jazz Band in 1955 before forming a skiffle group which won a talent contest organised by Radio Luxembourg. Another contestant, vocalist Nancy Whiskey (b. 1936, Glasgow, Scotland) joined the McDevitt group which included guitarists Tony Kohn and

Chas McDevitt

Bill Branwell (from the Cotton Pickers skiffle group), Marc Sharratt (d. May 1991; washboard) and Lennie Hanson (bass). The group appeared in the film *The Tommy Steele Story* in 1957, performing 'Freight Train', a song introduced to Britain by Peggy Seeger who had learned it from its composer, black American folk singer Elizabeth Cotten. Issued by Oriole, the McDevitt/Whiskey version was a Top 10 hit in the UK and reached the US charts, although McDevitt did receive a lawsuit from America over the ownership of the copyright. After the release of a version of 'Greenback Dollar' and an EP as follow-ups, Whiskey left the group. With a studio group, the Skifflers, she made a series of singles for Oriole from 1957-59, including 'He's Solid Gone' and the folk song 'I Know Where I'm Going' and also released *The Intoxicating Miss Whiskey*. Having opened a Freight Train coffee bar in London, McDevitt continued to perform and record with new vocalist Shirley Douglas, (b. 1936, Belfast, Northern Ireland) whom he later married. He briefly followed the rock 'n' roll trend with conspicuous lack of success and later performed duets with Douglas after the manner of Nina And Frederik. Among his later efforts were 'It Takes A Worried Man' (Oriole 1957), 'Teenage Letter' (1959) and 'One Love' (HMV 1961). Both McDevitt and Douglas recorded for Joy Records in the 70s enlisting session support from Joe Brown and Wizz Jones.
Albums: *The Intoxicating Miss Whiskey* (1957), *The Six-Five Special* (50s), *Sing Something Old, New, Borrowed & Blue* (1972), *Takes Ya Back Don't It* (1976).

McGarrigle, Kate And Anna

Kate (b. 1944, Montreal, Canada; keyboards, guitar, vocals), and her sister Anna (b. 1946, Montreal, Canada; keyboards, banjo, vocals), were brought up in the French quarter of Quebec. As a result they learned to sing and perform in both French and English. While in Montreal the sisters were members of the Mountain City Four. As a duo, Kate and Anna came to public notice after other artists including Linda Ronstadt and Maria Muldaur, recorded and performed their songs. Kate McGarrigle met Muldaur after moving to New York, and Muldaur recorded 'Work Song', among others. As a result, Muldaur's label, Warner Brothers, asked the McGarrigle sisters to record an album. *Kate And Anna McGarrigle*, their first release, was produced by Joe Boyd, and contained the excellent, and much covered, 'Heart Like A Wheel'. Apart from *Dancer With Bruised Knees*, which made the Top 40 in the UK, none of their subsequent releases has had any significant impact in

the charts in either the USA or Britain. However, they have attracted a strong following and their concerts consistently sell out. They first came to the UK to perform in 1976, with Kate then married to Loudon Wainwright III. The McGarrigle sisters have an instantly recognizable sound, with a distinctive harmonic blend. Their early promise has not been realized on more recent albums, but they still command respect, and a loyal following.
Albums: *Kate And Anna McGarrigle* (1975), *Dancer With Bruised Knees* (1977), *Pronto Monto* (1978), *French Record* (1980), *Love Over And Over* (1983), *Heartbeats Accelerating* (1990).

McGuire, Barry

b. 15 October 1935, Oklahoma City, Oklahoma, USA. McGuire first came to prominence as a minor actor in *Route 66* before teaming up with singer Barry Kane as Barry And Barry. In 1962, he joined the New Christy Minstrels and appeared as lead singer on several of their hits, most notably, 'Green Green' and 'Saturday Night'. He also sang the lead on their comic but catchy 'Three Wheels On My Wagon'. While still a Minstrel, he composed the hit 'Greenback Dollar' for the Kingston Trio. After leaving the New Christy Minstrels, McGuire signed to Lou Adler's Dunhill Records and was assigned to staff writers P.F. Sloan and Steve Barri. At the peak of the folk-rock boom, they wrote the rabble-rousing protest 'Eve Of Destruction', which McGuire took to number 1 in the USA, surviving a blanket radio ban in the process. The anti-establishment nature of the lyric even provoked an answer record, 'Dawn Of Correction', written by John Madara and Dave White under the pseudonym the Spokesmen. Ironically, 'Eve Of Destruction' had originally been conceived as a flip-side and at one stage was offered to the Byrds, who turned it down. Coincidentally, both Barry McGuire and Byrds leader Jim (later Roger) McGuinn received a flattering namecheck on the Mamas And The Papas' hit 'Creeque Alley' ('McGuinn and McGuire were just a-getting higher in LA, you know where that's at'). McGuire, in fact, played a significant part in bringing the million-selling vocal quartet to Adler and they later offered their services as his backing singers.
McGuire attempted unsuccessfully to follow-up his worldwide hit with other Sloan material, including the excellent 'Upon A Painted Ocean'. He continued to pursue the protest route on the albums *Eve Of Destruction* and *This Precious Time*, but by 1967 he was branching out into acting. A part in *The President's Analyst* led to a Broadway appearance in the musical *Hair*. After the meagre sales of *The World's Last Private Citizen*, McGuire ceased recording until 1971, when he returned with

Barry McGuire

former Mamas And The Papas sideman Eric Hord on *Barry McGuire And The Doctor*. The work featured backing from the cream of the 1965 school of folk-rock, including the Byrds' Chris Hillman and Michael Clarke. Soon afterwards, McGuire became a Christian evangelist and thereafter specialized in gospel albums.

Albums: *Eve Of Destruction* (1965), *This Precious Time* (1966), *The World's Last Private Citizen* (1967), *Barry McGuire And The Doctor* (1971), *Seeds* (1973), *Finer Than Gold* (1981), *Inside Out* (1982), *To The Bride* (1982), *Best Of Barry* (1982).

McKenzie, Scott

b. Philip Blondheim, 1 October 1944, Arlington, Virginia, USA. McKenzie began his professional career in the Journeymen, a clean-cut folk group. He later recorded some undistinguished solo material before fellow ex-member John Phillips, currently enjoying success with the Mamas And The Papas, invited the singer to join him in Los Angeles. Although the folk/rock-inspired 'No No No No No' failed to sell, the pairing flourished spectacularly on 'San Francisco (Be Sure To Wear Some Flowers In Your Hair)'. This altruistic hippie anthem, penned by Phillips, encapsulated the innocent wonderment felt by many onlookers of the era and the single, buoyed by an irresistible melody, reached number 4 in the US chart, but climbed to the dizzy heights of number 1 in the UK and throughout Europe. Follow-ups, 'Like An Old Time Movie' and 'Holy Man', failed to emulate such success, and although McKenzie briefly re-emerged with the low-key, country-influenced *Stained Glass Morning*, he remained out of the public eye until the 80s, when he joined Phillips in a rejuvenated Mamas And The Papas.

Albums: *The Voice Of Scott McKenzie* (1967), *Stained Glass Morning* (1970).

McKuen, Rod

b. Canada. One of the revered poets of the late 60s love generation, Rod McKuen took a slow route to the top. He performed various manual jobs as a young man and embarked on both a pop career ('Happy Is A Boy Named Me' was released in the UK in 1957) and an attempted acting career, combining both by appearing as a musician in the rock 'n' roll exploitation movie *Rock Pretty Baby* in 1957. He also spent a spell as a disc jockey before heading to Paris in the 60s. It was here, in the company of Jacques Brel and Charles Aznavour, that he began writing poetry in a free verse form very typical of the times. Described by *Newsweek* as 'the king of kitsch', McKuen became one of the few poets able to sell his work in large volumes, and he became a wealthy man. His 60s books included

Lonesome Cities, Stanyan Street And Other Sorrows and *Listen To The Warm*. His musical career continued when he wrote the score for the movie *The Prime Of Miss Jean Brodie* including the title song 'Jean' and contributed six songs to the soundtrack of *A Boy Named Charlie Brown*. The most interesting of his albums is *McKuen Country*, on which he enlists the aid of Glenn Campbell, Big Jim Sullivan and Barry McGuire in a perfectly acceptable stab at country rock. Among his best remembered compositions are 'Seasons In The Sun' (music by Brel and a hit for Terry Jacks), 'If You Go Away', 'Love's Been Good To Me' (recorded by Frank Sinatra on an album of McKuen songs, *A Man Alone*), 'I Think Of You (music by Francis Lai and a hit for Perry Como), 'Soldiers Who Want To Be Heros', 'Doesn't Anybody Know My Name', and 'The Importance Of The Rose'.

Selected albums: *Greatest Hits* (1973), *At Carnegie Hall* (1974), *McKuen Country* (1976), *Rod McKuen 77* (1977), *McKuen* (1982). Compilation: *Greatest Hits* (1973).

MacLean, Dougie

b. 27 September 1954, Dunblane, Scotland. Before he was two years old, MacLean moved to Butterstone, near Dunkeld, Perthshire, and now lives in the old schoolhouse there. He was formerly a member of both the Tannahill Weavers and Silly Wizard, and an early Euro-band, Mosaic, in the mid-80s. The latter band included Andy Irvine, Donal Lunny and Márta Sebestyén. MacLean went solo in 1979 and released the excellent *Caledonia*. He formed Dunkeld Records in 1983, with the aim of promoting other Scottish performers. MacLean had one of his own compositions recorded by Kathy Mattea in 1990, for release on her album. Mattea also appears on backing vocals on *Whitewash*, in what is perhaps a classic parting song, 'Until We Meet Again'. *The Search* came out of a commission to write and record music for the official Loch Ness Monster Exhibition. In some ways a departure for MacLean, the album is highly atmospheric. MacLean has also completed music for a BBC television series, *MacGregor Across Scotland*, and his album *Real Estate* won a silver disc in 1988. Whether playing guitar, fiddle, bouzouki or didgeridoo, Dougie MacLean's songs combine a love of tradition with the contemporary. He enjoys playing as far afield as New Zealand, Canada, Australia and the USA.

Albums: with Alex Campbell and Alan Roberts *CRM* (1979), *Caledonia* (1979), *Snaigow* (1980), *On A Wing And A Prayer* (1981), *Craigie Dhu* (1982), *Butterstone* (1983), *Fiddle* (1984), *Singing Land* (1985), *Real Estate* (1988), *Whitewash* (1990), *The Search* (1990), *Indigenous* (1991).

Dougie MacLean

Don McLean

McLean, Don

b. 2 October, 1945, New Rochelle, New York,
USA. McLean began his recording career
performing in New York clubs during the early
60s. A peripatetic singer for much of his career, he
was singing at elementary schools in Massachusettts
when he wrote a musical tribute to Van Gogh in
1970. After receiving rejection slips from countless
labels, his debut *Tapestry* was issued by Mediarts
that same year, but failed to sell. United Artists next
picked up his contract and issued an eight-minutes
plus version of 'American Pie'. A paean to Buddy
Holly, full of symbolic references to other
performers such as Elvis Presley and Bob Dylan, the
song topped the US chart and reached number 2 in
the UK. The album of the same name was also an
enormous success. In the UK, 'Vincent' fared even
better than in his home country, reaching number
1. By 1971, McLean was acclaimed as one of the
most talented and commercial of the burgeoning
singer-songwriter school emerging from the USA.
According to music business legend, the song
'Killing Me Softly With His Song' was written as a
tribute to McLean, and was subsequently recorded
by Lori Lieberman and Roberta Flack. McLean's
affection for Buddy Holly was reiterated in 1973,
with a successful cover of 'Everyday'. Meanwhile,
his song catalogue was attracting attention, and
Perry Como registered a surprise international hit
with a cover of McLean's 'And I Love You So'.

Despite his promising start, McLean's career
foundered during the mid-70s, but his penchant as
a strong cover artist held him in good stead. In
1980, he returned to the charts with a revival of
Roy Orbison's 'Crying' (UK number 1/US
number 2). Thereafter, his old hits were repackaged
and he toured extensively. As the 80s progressed, he
moved into the country market, but remained
popular in the pop mainstream. In 1991, his 20-
year-old version of 'American Pie' unexpectedly
returned to the UK Top 20, once again reviving
interest in his back catalogue.
Albums: *Tapestry* (1970), *American Pie* (1971), *Don
McLean* (1973), *Playin' Favorites* (1974), *Homeless
Brother* (1974), *Solo* (1976), *Prime Time* (1977),
Chain Lightning (1980), *Believers* (1982), *Love Tracks*
(1987). Compilations: *The Very Best Of Don McLean*
(1980), *Don McLean's Greatest Hits - Then And Now*
(1987), *The Best Of Don McLean* (1991).

McMorland, Alison

b. 12 November 1940, Clarkston, Renfrewshire,
Scotland. When McMorland was aged four, her
family moved to Strathaven, where she spent most
of her school days. Later, when living in Helston,
Cornwall, during the 60s, she became involved in
the folk revival. In 1967, McMorland produced a
teaching manual for the Smithsonian Institute in
Washington DC, USA, to accompany a video made
a year earlier, *British Traditional Singing Games*. It

was not until 1970, however, that she first performed at a Scottish festival in Irvine. The following year, she won the women's traditional singing trophy at the Kinross folk festival. During the early 70s, McMorland worked on a project for the York Museum, producing a sound tape of songs and memories of old York called *These Times Be Good Times*. She also spent a great deal of time researching Scottish folk song tradition, as well as collecting songs on children's games and stories. In 1974, McMorland made a film on this particular subject, *Pass It On*, and was later invited by the Smithsonian Institute to appear in the Festival of American Folk Life. She also initiated workshops for children at festivals, specializing in songs and games. With Frankie Armstrong, she ran voice workshops, very innovative in the 70s, but now regarded as normal. For seven years, until the series ended, she presented *Listen With Mother* for BBC radio. For the series, she chose all the music, and always made a point of including folk material in the programme. Alison sang with the Albion Band at the National Theatre debut of *Lark Rise To Candleford*, and later went on a European tour with *The Passion And Creation*, produced by Bill Bryden. *Belt Wi' Colours Three*, an album of Scottish traditional songs, included Aly Bain on fiddle, and Rab Wallace on pipes. *My Song Is My Own* featured songs from a women's perspective, ranging from the traditional 'John Anderson, My Jo' to the 1977 composition 'Lady Bus Driver'. Both Alison and Peta Webb were the subject of one of a series of a films, made in 1980, by Phillip Donnelly, called *Pioneers Of The Folk Revival*. Others featured in the series were Martin Carthy, Peggy Seeger, Leon Rosselson and Roy Bailey, Frankie Armstrong and Ewan MacColl. McMorland also contributed to *That'd Be Telling-Tales Of Britain*, in 1985, a multi-cultural collection compiled by Mike Rosen and John Griffiths for the Cambridge University Press. One of McMorland's more recent projects, resulted in the book *Memories*, a reminiscence project on Humberside of old people's musical memories, which were also recorded. In 1986, sheheaded another project called *Threads*, featuring Grand Union, a group of exiled musicians from different ethnic communities, who fused Scottish and Asian musical styles. The project told the story of the cotton trade and slavery in music. In 1990, Alison took up the post of Traditional Folk Arts Lecturer for the Strathclyde Region.
Albums: with various artists *Scots Songs And Music-Live From Kinross* (1975), *Songs And Rhymes From Listen With Mother* (1977), *Belt Wi' Clours Three* (1977), *Alison McMorland Presents The Funny Family* (songs, rhymes and games for children 1977), with various artists *Freedom Come All Ye-Poems And Songs Of Hamish Henderson* (1977), with various artists *The Good Old Way-The Best Of British Folk* (1980), *Alison McMorland And Peta Webb* (1980), with Frankie Armstrong, Kathy Henderson, Sandra Kerr *My Song Is My Own-Songs From Women* (1980), with various artists *Nuclear Power No Thanks!* (1981), with various artists *Glasgow Horizons* (1990). Further reading: *British Traditional Singing Games* (1967), *The Funny Family* (1978), *Brown Bread And Butter* (1982), *Memories* (1987), *The Herd Laddie O' The Glen-Songs And Stories Of Willie Scott, A Border Shepherd* (1988).

McNeil, Rita

b. Big Pond, Cape Breton Island, Nova Scotia, Canada. McNeil appeared on the music scene in Britain almost overnight, and has had a degree of success in the field of country and folk music. In 1985, she went to Tokyo to perform at the Canada Expo pavilion, and in 1987, *Flying On Your Own* was released. The title track was also recorded by fellow Canadian Anne Murray. That same year, McNeil sang at the Edinburgh Folk Festival, and won a Canadian Juno award as Most Promising Female Vocalist. She first appeared in London, England, in September 1990, and Polydor released three of her albums, *Flying On Your Own*, *Reason To Believe* and *Rita*. In the same year, McNeil's *Reason To Believe* toppled Madonna from the top of the Australian album charts. Mixing country, folk and elements of Gaelic drawn from the fact that her family originally came from Scotland, Rita has had less success in Britain than on her home ground, but still charted with 'Working Man', which reached the UK Top 20. Her albums have achieved platinum sales and she was the subject of a 1991 documentary, *Home I'll Be*.
Albums: *Flying On Your Own* (1987), *Reason To Believe* (1990), *Home I'll Be* (1991).

McTell, 'Blind' Willie

b. probably May 1898, McDuffie County, Georgia, USA, d. 19 August 1959, Almon, Georgia, USA. Blind from birth, McTell began to learn guitar in his early years, under the influence of relatives and neighbours in Statesboro, Georgia, where he grew up. In his late teens, he attended a school for the blind. By 1927, when he made his first records, he was already a very accomplished guitarist, with a warm and beautiful vocal style, and his early sessions produced classics such as 'Statesboro Blues', 'Mama Tain't Long Fo Day' and 'Georgia Rag'. During the 20s and 30s, he travelled extensively from a base in Atlanta, making his living from music and recording, on a regular basis, for three different record companies, sometimes using pseudonyms which included Blind Sammie and

Georgia Bill. Most of his records feature a 12-string guitar, popular among Atlanta musicians, but particularly useful to McTell for the extra volume it provided for singing on the streets. Few, if any, blues guitarists could equal his mastery of the 12-string. He exploited its resonance and percussive qualities on his dance tunes, yet managed a remarkable delicacy of touch on his slow blues. In 1934, he married, and the following year recorded some duets with his wife, Kate, covering sacred as well as secular material. In 1940, John Lomax recorded McTell for the Folk Song Archive of the Library of Congress, and the sessions, which have since been issued in full, feature him discussing his life and his music, as well as playing a variety of material. These offer an invaluable insight into the art of one of the true blues greats. In the 40s, he moved more in the direction of religious music, and when he recorded again in 1949 and 1950, a significant proportion of his songs were spiritual. Only a few tracks from these sessions were issued at the time, but most have appeared in later years. They reveal McTell as commanding as ever. Indeed, some of these recordings rank amongst his best work. In 1956, he recorded for the last time at a session arranged by a record shop manager, unissued until the 60s. Soon after this, he turned away from the blues to perform exclusively religious material. His importance was eloquently summed up in Bob Dylan's strikingly moving elegy, 'Blind Willie McTell'.

Albums: *Last Session* (1960), *Complete Library Of Congress Recordings* (1969), *Complete Recorded Works 1927-1935* (1990, three CD vols.).

McTell, Ralph

b. 3 December 1944, Farnborough, Kent, England. Having followed the requisite bohemian path, busking in Europe and living in Cornwall, McTell emerged in the late 60s as one of Britain's leading folksingers with his first two albums, *Eight Frames A Second* and *Spiral Staircase*. The latter collection was notable for the inclusion of 'Streets Of London', the artist's best-known composition. He re-recorded this simple, but evocative, song in 1974, and was rewarded with a surprise number 2 UK hit. Its popularity obscured McTell's artistic development from acoustic troubadour to thoughtful singer/songwriter, exemplified on *You Well-Meaning Brought Me Here*, in which the singer tackled militarism and its attendant political geography in an erudite, compulsive manner. During live performances McTell demonstrated considerable dexterity on acoustic guitar. He was particularly proficient when playing ragtime blues. Subsequent releases included the excellent *Not Until Tomorrow*, which featured the infamous 'Zimmerman Blues', and *Easy*, but McTell was unable to escape the cosy image bestowed by his most successful song. During the 80s he pursued a career in children's television, and his later releases have featured songs from such work, as well as interpretations of other artist's compositions. Touring occasionally, McTell is still able to comfortably fill concert halls.

Albums: *Eight Frames A Second* (1968), *Spiral Staircase* (1969), *My Side Of Your Window* (1970), *You Well-Meaning Brought Me Here* (1971), *Not Till Tomorrow* (1972), *Easy* (1973), *Streets* (1975), *Right Side Up* (1976), *Ralph, Albert And Sydney* (1977), *Slide Away The Screen* (1979), *Love Grows* (1982), *Water Of Dreams* (1982), *Weather The Storm* (1982), *Songs From Alphabet Zoo* (1983), *The Best Of Alphabet Zoo* (1984), *At The End Of A Perfect Day* (1985), *Tickle On The Tum* (1986), *Bridge Of Sighs* (1987), *The Ferryman* (1987), *Blue Skies, Black Heroes* (1988), *Stealin' Back.* (1990), *The Boy With The Note* (1992). Compilations: *Ralph McTell Revisited* (1970), *The Ralph McTell Collection* (1978), *Streets Of London* (1981), *71/72* (1982), *At His Best* (1985).

McWilliams, David

b. 4 July 1945, Cregagh, Belfast, Northern Ireland. The subject of an overpowering publicity campaign engineered by his manager Phil Solomon, McWilliams was featured on the front, inside and back covers of several consecutive issues of the *New Musical Express*, which extolled the virtues of a new talent. He was incessantly plugged on the pirate Radio Caroline. Much was made of his rebellious youth and affinity with Irish music, yet the singer's debut release, 'Days Of Pearly Spencer'/'Harlem Lady', revealed a grasp of pop's dynamics rather than those of folk. The former song was both impressive and memorable, as was the pulsating follow-up, '3 O'Clock Flamingo Street', but McWilliams was unable to shake the 'hype' tag which accompanied his launch. His manager believed that Williams was a more promising protege than his other star artist, Van Morrison of Them, but his faith was unrewarded. Williams disliked live performance and failed to show his true talent in front of an audience. Neither single charted and a period of reassessment followed before the artist re-emerged the following decade with a series of charming, folk-influenced collections. In April 1992 Marc Almond took 'Days Of Pearly Spencer' back into the UK charts.

Albums: *David McWilliams Sings* (1967), *David McWilliams Volume 2* (1967), *Days Of Pearly Spencer* (1971), *Lord Offaly* (1972), *The Beggar And The Priest* (1973), *Living Is Just A State Of Mind* (1974), *David McWilliams* (1977), *Don't Do It For Love*

(1978), *Wounded* (1982). Compilation: *Days Of Pearly Spencer* (1971).

Melanie

b. Melanie Safka, 3 February 1947, New York, USA. One of the surprise discoveries of the 1969 Woodstock Festival with her moving rendition of 'Beautiful People', Melanie briefly emerged as a force during the singer/songwriter boom of the early 70s. Although often stereotyped as a winsome 'earth-mother', much of her work had a sharp edge with a raging vocal style very different from her peers. Her first US hit, the powerful 'Lay Down' (1970), benefitted from the glorious backing of the Edwin Hawkins Singers. In Britain, she broke through that same year with a passionate and strikingly original version of the Rolling Stones' 'Ruby Tuesday'. *Candles In The Rain*, was a best seller on both sides of the Atlantic, with an effective mixture of originals and inspired cover versions. 'What Have They Done To My Song, Ma?' gave her another minor hit, narrowly outselling a rival version from the singalong New Seekers. Her last major success came in 1971 with 'Brand New Key', which reached number 1 in the USA and also proved her biggest hit in Britain. In 1972, Melanie founded Neighbourhood Records, and its parochial title seemed to define her career thereafter. Marginalized as a stylized singer/songwriter, she found it difficult to retrieve past glories. Sporadic releases continued, however, and she has often been seen playing charity shows and benefit concerts all over the world.

Selected albums: *Born To Me* (1969), *Affectionately Melanie* (1969), *Candles In The Rain* (1970), *Leftover Wine* (1970), *The Good Book* (1971), *Gather Me* (1971), *Garden In The City* (1972), *Stoneground Words* (1972), *Melanie At Carnegie Hall* (1973), *Madrugada* (1974), *As I See It Now* (1975), *From The Beginning* (1975), *Sunset And Other Beginnings* (1975), *Photogenic - Not Just Another Pretty Face* (1978), *Ballroom Streets* (1979), *Arabesque* (1982), *Seventh Wave* (1983), *Cowabonga - Never Turn Your Back On A Wave* (1989).

Men They Couldn't Hang, The

In their seven-year span, The Men They Couldn't Hang combined folk, punk and roots music to create an essential live act alongside a wealth of recorded talent. The band emerged as the Pogues' sparring partners but, despite a blaze of early publicity and praise, they failed to follow them upwards, dogged as they were by numerous label changes. Their first gig at the Alternative Country Festival featured ex-Pogues Andrew Ranken and James Fearnley. Busking in Shepherds Bush, Welsh singer Stephen Cush met up with bassist Shanne

Bradley (who had been in the Nips with the Pogues' Shane McGowan), songwriter/guitarist Paul Simmonds, Scottish guitarist/singer Phil ('Swill') and his brother John Odgers on drums, in time for a ramshackle folk performance at London's alternative country music festival in Easter 1984. Labelled as part of some 'cowpunk' scene, the band were quickly signed by Elvis Costello to his Demon label, Imp. Their assured debut was a cover of Eric Bogle's 'Green Fields Of France' in October 1984 became a runaway indie success, and a favourite on BBC disc jockey John Peel's show. While playing live, the Men matched their own incisive compositions with entertaining covers. June 1985's 'Iron Masters' was just as strong, if more manic, and was accompanied by an impressive and accomplished debut, *The Night Of A Thousand Candles*.

Produced by Nick Lowe, 'Greenback was less immediate, but its success swayed MCA sign the group, resulting in 'Gold Rush' in June 1986. The group's second album, *How Green Is The Valley* continued their marriage of musical styles and a political sensibility drawn from an historical perspective. 'The Ghosts Of Cable Street' exemplified these ingredients. A move to Magnet Records catalyzed perhaps their finest work, with the commercial 'Island In The Rain' and the listenable *Waiting For Bonaparte*. By this time Rickey McGuire had replaced Bradley. 'The Colours' received airplay, but only skirted the charts. Fledgling label Silvertone's Andrew Lauder (who had worked with the group at Demon) signed the group in time for 'Rain, Steam And Speed' in February 1989. Hot on its heels came *Silvertown*. Two further singles followed: 'A Place In The Sun' and 'A Map Of Morocco'.

In 1990 they recorded their final studio album *The Domino Club*, for which the personnel was increased to six, with the addition of Nick Muir. On the strength of it, they supported David Bowie at Milton Keynes. Shortly afterwards they disbanded, following a long farewell tour, and a live album, *Alive, Alive - O.*

Albums: *Night Of A Thousand Candles* (1985), *How Green Is The Valley* (1986), *Waiting For Bonaparte* (1987, reissued 1988), *Silvertown* (1989), *The Domino Club* (1990), *Well Hung* (1991), *Alive, Alive - O* (1991).

Metsers, Paul

b. 27 November 1945, Noordwijk, Holland. In 1952, Metsers emigrated to New Zealand and was influenced by the American folk music that was available on record during the 60s. He bought his first guitar in 1963, and soon started writing songs. Paul arrived in the UK in 1980, and spent almost

Paul Metsers

two years touring round in a Volkswagen camper playing 'floor spots' in folk clubs to get himself noticed. He was rewarded with club and festival bookings the length and breadth of the country. The environment and 'green issues' have always figured largely in his songwriting, even before it became fashionable, and his first anti-pollution song, 'Now Is The Time', was written in 1969. By the time that *Caution To The Wind* was available, Metsers, was already established as an artist and performer of note. *In The Hurricane's Eye* contained the excellent 'Peace Must Come', and 'River Song'. The *Paul Metsers Songbook*, published in 1986, contained many of the songs from Paul's first four albums, but only one that would appear on *Fifth Quarter*. He was able to combine a busy touring schedule with campaigning for environmental pressure groups, but in November 1989, he decided to devote more time to his family. Now living in Cumbria, and working as a joiner as well as keeping bees, Metsers still performs occasionally.

Albums: *Caution To The Wind* (1981), *Momentum* (1982), *In The Hurricane's Eye* (1984), *Pacific Pilgrim* (1986), *Fifth Quarter* (1987).

Miles, Dick

b. 31 January 1951, Blackheath, London, England. From early days on the folk circuit, singer and concertina player, Miles turned professional in 1976. From 1977-85 he also played with the Suffolk Bell and Horseshoe Band, and was a founder member of the New Mexborough English Concertina Quartet from 1984-88. From 1988 until 1992, he toured occasionally, both at home and abroad, with songwriter Richard Grainger, in addition to pursuing his solo career. *The Dunmow Flitch*, recorded with his then wife Sue Miles, was an album of traditional English music, released on the now defunct Sweet Folk All label, and featured Jez Lowe. *Home Routes* includes 'The Alimony Run', a bitter song by Peter Bond about marital seperation and some of it's consequences. *Playing For Time* included a variety of songs such as Lennon and McCartney's 'Yesterday'/'All My Loving', and 'From Four Until Late' by blues guitarist Robert Johnson, as well as more traditional material, showing the range of the English concertina. Dick has established respect for himself on the folk circuit, where he is still much in demand as a soloist. In 1990, he recorded *On Muintavara* with the Irish group Suifinn, and then performed with them from 1991-92.

During his career Miles has appeared on *Folk On Two* on BBC radio, on numerous occasions, and has performed at both the Festival Hall, and Purcell Rooms on London's South Bank. Miles now lives in Ireland and tours regularly in Ireland, England and Holland. Apart from still working occasionally with Richard Grainger, he also plays with Ril-Gan-Anim, in addition to his solo work.

Albums: with Sue Miles *The Dunmow Flitch* (1981), *Cheating The Tide* (1984), *Playing For Time* (1987), *The New Mexborough English Concertina Quartet* (1987), *On My Little Concertina* (1989), with Richard Grainger *Home Routes* (1990), with Suifinn *On Muintavara* (1990).

Mitchell, Chad, Trio

Chad Mitchell, Mike Kobluk and Mike Pugh were students at Gonzaga University in Spokane, Washington, USA, when they formed this influential folk group in 1958. They then crossed America, performing when able, before arriving in New York to secure a recording deal. The following year, Mike Pugh dropped out in favour of Joe Frazier, while the Trio's accompanist, Dennis Collins, was replaced by guitarist (Jim) Roger McGuinn, who later found fame with the Byrds. The group then embarked on their most successful era, when they became renowned for songs of a satiric or socially-conscious nature. Chad Mitchell left for a solo career in 1965. He was replaced by aspiring songwriter John Denver, but the restructured act, now known as the Mitchell Trio, found it difficult to sustain momentum. Frazier and Kobluk also left the group, which was then sued by its former leader for continuing to use the 'original' name. The trio then became known as Denver, Boise And Johnson, but split up in 1969 when first Johnson, then Denver, left to pursue independent projects.

Selected albums: *The Chad Mitchell Trio Arrives* (1960), *Mighty Day On Campus* (1961), *The Chad Mitchell Trio At The Bitter End* (1962), *The Chad Mitchell Trio In Action* aka *Blowin' In The Wind* (1962), *Singin' Our Minds* (1963), *Reflecting* (1964), *The Slightly Irreverent Mitchell Trio* (1964), *Typical American Boys* (1965), *That's The Way It's Gotta Be* (1965), *Violets Of Dawn* (1966), *Alive* (1967). Compilations: *The Best Of The Chad Mitchell Trio* (1963), *The Chad Mitchell Trio And The Gatemen In Concert* (1964), *Beginnings: The Chad Mitchell Trio Featuring John Denver* (1973).

Mitchell, Joni

b. Roberta Joan Anderson, 7 November 1943, Fort McLeod, Alberta, Canada. After studying art in Calgary, this singer-songwriter moved to Toronto in 1964, where she married Chuck Mitchell in 1965. The two performed together at coffee houses and folk clubs, playing several Mitchell originals including 'The Circle Game'. The latter inspired fellow Canadian Neil Young to write the reply

'Sugar Mountain', a paean to lost innocence that Mitchell herself included in her sets during this period. While in Detroit, the Mitchells met folk singer Tom Rush, who unsuccessfully attempted to persuade Judy Collins to cover Joni's 'Urge For Going'. He later recorded the song himself, along with the title track of his next album, *The Circle Game*. The previously reluctant Collins also brought Mitchell's name to prominence by covering 'Michael From Mountains' and 'Both Sides Now' on her 1967 album *Wildflowers*.

Following her divorce in 1967, Mitchell moved to New York and for a time planned a career in design and clothing, selling Art Nouveau work. Her success on the New York folk circuit paid her bills, however, and she became known as a strong songwriter and engaging live performer, backed only by her acoustic guitar and dulcimer. After appearing at the Gaslight South folk club in Coconut Grove, Florida, the astute producer Joe Boyd took her to England, where she played some low-key venues. Her trip produced several songs, including the comical tribute to 'London Bridge', based on the traditional nursery rhyme. The song included such lines as 'London Bridge is falling up/Save the tea leaves in my cup . . .' Other early material included the plaintive 'Eastern Rain', 'Just Like Me' and 'Brandy Eyes', which displayed Mitchell's love of sharp description and internal rhyme. Mitchell was initially discovered by budding manager Elliot Roberts at New York's Cafe Au Go-Go, and shortly afterwards in Coconut Grove by former Byrds member, David Crosby. She and Crosby became lovers, and he went on to produce her startling debut album *Songs To A Seagull*. Divided into two sections, 'I Came To The City' and 'Out Of The City And Down To The Seaside', the work showed her early folk influence which was equally strong on the 1969 follow-up *Clouds*, which featured several songs joyously proclaiming the possibilities offered by life, as well as its melancholic side. 'Chelsea Morning' presented a feeling of wonder in its almost childlike appreciation of everyday observations. The title of the album was borrowed from a line in 'Both Sides Now', which had since become a massive worldwide hit for Judy Collins. The chorus ('It's love's illusions I recall/I really don't know love at all') became something of a statement of policy from Mitchell, whose analyses of love - real or illusory - dominated her work. With *Clouds*, Mitchell paused for reflection, drawing material from her past ('Tin Angel', 'Both Sides Now', 'Chelsea Morning') and blending them with songs devoted to new-found perplexities. If 'I Don't Know Where I Stand' recreates the tentative expectancy of an embryonic relationship, 'The

Gallery' chronicles its decline, with the artist as the injured party. The singer, however, was unsatisfied with the final collection, and later termed it her artistic nadir.

Apart from her skills as a writer, Mitchell was a fine singer and imaginative guitarist with a love of open tuning. Although some critics still chose to see her primarily as a songwriter rather than a vocalist, there were already signs of important development on her third album, *Ladies Of The Canyon*. Its title track, with visions of antique chintz and wampum beads, mirrored the era's innocent naivety, a feature also prevailing on 'Willy', the gauche portrait of her relationship with singer Graham Nash. Mitchell is nonetheless aware of the period's fragility, and her rendition of 'Woodstock' (which she never visited), a celebration of the hippie dream in the hands of Crosby, Stills, Nash And Young, becomes a eulogy herein. With piano now in evidence, the music sounded less sparse and the lyrics more ambitious, portraying the hippie audience as searchers for some lost Edenic bliss ('We are stardust, we are golden . . . and we've got to get ourselves back to the garden'). With 'For Free' (later covered by the Byrds), Mitchell presented another one of her hobbyhorses - the clash between commercial acceptance and artistic integrity. Within the song, Mitchell contrasts her professional success with the uncomplicated pleasure that a street performer enjoys. The extent of Mitchell's commercial acceptance was demonstrated on the humorous 'Big Yellow Taxi', a sardonic comment on the urban disregard for ecology. The single was a surprise Top 20 hit and was even more surprisingly covered by Bob Dylan.

Following a sabbatical, Mitchell returned with her most introspective work to date, *Blue*. Less melodic than her previous albums, the arrangements were also more challenging and the material self-analytical to an almost alarming degree. Void of sentimentality, the work also saw her commenting on the American Dream in 'California' ('That was a dream some of us had'). Austere and at times anti-romantic, *Blue* was an essential product of the singer/songwriter era. On *Blue*, the artist moved from a purely folk-based perspective to that of rock, as the piano, rather than guitar, became the natural outlet for her compositions. Stephen Stills (guitar/bass), James Taylor (guitar), 'Sneaky' Pete Kleinow (pedal steel) and Russ Kunkel (drums) embellished material inspired by an extended sojourn travelling in Europe, and if its sense of loss and longing echoed previous works, a new maturity instilled a lasting resonance to the stellar inclusions, 'Carey', 'River' and the desolate title track. Any lingering sense of musical restraint was thrown off with *For The Roses*, in which elaborate horn and woodwind sections buoyed material on which personal themes mixed with third-person narratives. The dilemmas attached to fame and performing, first aired on 'For Free', reappeared on the title song and 'Blonde In The Bleachers' while 'Woman Of Heart And Mind' charted the reasons for dispute within a relationship in hitherto unexplored depths. 'You Turn Me On, I'm A Radio' gave Mitchell a US Top 30 entry, but a lengthy two-year gap ensued before *Court And Spark* appeared. Supported by the subtle, jazz-based LA Express, Mitchell offered a rich, luxuriant collection, marked by an increased sophistication and dazzling use of melody. The sweeping 'Help Me' climbed to number 7 in the US in 1974, bringing its creator a hitherto unparalleled commercial success. The emergence of Mitchell as a well-rounded rock artist was clearly underlined on *Court And Spark* with its familiar commentary on the trials and tribulations of stardom ('Free Man In Paris'). The strength of the album lay in the powerful arrangements courtesy of Tom Scott, and guitarist Robben Ford, plus Mitchell's own love of jazz rhythms, most notably on her amusing version of Annie Ross' 'Twisted'.

The quality of Mitchell's live performances, which included stadia gigs during 1974, was captured on the live album *Miles Of Aisles*.

In 1975, Mitchell produced the startling *The Hissing Of Summer Lawns*, which not only displayed her increasing interest in jazz, but also world music. Her most sophisticated work to date, the album was less concerned with introspection than a more generalized commentary on American mores. In 'Harry's House', the obsessive envy of personal possessions is described against a swirling musical backdrop that captures an almost anomic feeling of derangement. The Burundi drummers feature on 'The Jungle Line' in which African primitivism is juxtaposed alongside the swimming pools of the Hollywood aristocracy. 'Edith And The Kingpin' offers a startling evocation of mutual dependency and the complex nature of such a relationship ('His right hand holds Edith, his left hand holds his right/what does that hand desire that he grips it so tight?'). Finally, there was the exuberance of the opening 'In France They Kiss On Main Street' and a return to the theme of 'For Free' on 'The Boho Dance'. The album deserved the highest acclaim, but was greeted with a mixed reception on its release, which emphasized how difficult it was for Mitchell to break free from her 'acoustic folk singer' persona. *The Hissing Of Summer Lawns* confirmed this newfound means of expression. Bereft of an accustomed introspective tenor, its comments on suburban values were surprising, yet were the natural accompaniment to an ever-growing desire to expand stylistic perimeters.

However, although *Hejira* was equally adventurous, it was noticeably less ornate, echoing the stark simplicity of early releases. The fretless bass of Jaco Pastorius wrought an ever-present poignancy to a series of confessional compositions reflecting the aching restlessness encapsulated in 'Song For Sharon', an open letter to a childhood friend. The same sense of ambition marked with *Hejira*, Mitchell produced another in-depth work which, though less melodic and texturous than its predecessory, was still a major work. The dark humour of 'Coyote', the sharp observation of 'Amelia' and the lovingly cynical portrait of Furry Lewis, 'Furry Sings The Blues', were all memorable. The move into jazz territory continued throughout 1978-79, first with the double album, *Don Juan's Reckless Daughter,* and culminating in her collaboration with Charlie Mingus. The latter was probably Mitchell's bravest work to date, although its invention was not rewarded with sales and was greeted with suspicion by the jazz community. On *Mingus,* she adapted several of the master musician's best-known compositions. It was an admirable, but flawed, ambition, as her often-reverential lyrics failed to convey the music's erstwhile sense of spontaneity. 'God Must Be A Boogie Man' and 'The Wolf That Lives In Lindsay', for which Joni wrote words and music, succeeded simply because they were better matched.

A live double album, *Shadows And Light* featured Pat Metheny and Jaco Pastorius among the guest musicians. Following her marriage to bassist Larry Klein, Mitchell appeared to wind down her activities. Finally, she signed a long-term contract with Geffen Records and the first fruits of this deal were revealed on *Wild Things Run Fast* in 1972. A more accessible work than her recent efforts, it also lacked the depth and exploratory commitment of its predecessors. The opening song, 'Chinese Cafe', remains one of her finest compositions, blending nostalgia to shattered hopes, but the remainder of the set was musically ill-focussed, relying on unadventurous, largely leaden arrangements. Its lighter moments were well-chosen, however, particularly on the humorous reading of Leiber And Stoller's 'Baby, I Don't Care'. The Thomas Dolby produced *Dog Eat Dog* was critically underrated and represented the best of her 80s work. Despite such hi-tech trappings, the shape of the material remained constant with 'Impossible Dreamer' echoing the atmosphere of *Court And Spark.* Elsewhere, 'Good Friends', an uptempo duet with Michael McDonald, and 'Lucky Girl', confirmed Mitchell's newfound satisfaction and contentment. In interviews, Mitchell indicated her intention to pursue a career in painting, a comment which some took as evidence of the loss of her musical muse.

Joni Mitchell

Chalk Mark In A Rain Storm continued in a similar vein, while including two notable reworkings of popular tunes, 'Cool Water', which also featured Willie Nelson, and 'Corrina Corrina', herein retitled 'A Bird That Whistles'. Their appearance inferred the change of perspective contained on *Night Flight Home*, issued in 1991 following a three-year gap. Largely stripped of contemporaneous clutter, this acoustic-based collection invoked the intimacy of *Hejira*, thus allowing full rein to Mitchell's vocal and lyrical flair. Its release coincided with the artist's avowed wish to pursue her painting talents - exhibitions of her 80s canvases were held in London and Edinburgh - and future musical directions remain, as always, open to question. Her remarkable body of work encompasses the changing emotions and concerns of a generation: from idealism to adulthood responsibilities, while baring her soul on the traumas of already public relationships. That she does so with insight and melodic flair accounts for a deserved longevity. With *Chalk Mark In A Rainstorm* and *Night Ride Home*, Mitchell reiterated the old themes in a more relaxed style without ever threatening a new direction. Still regarded as one of the finest singer/songwriters of her generation, Mitchell has displayed more artistic depth and consistency than most of her illustrious contemporaries from the 70s. The creatively quiet

decade that followed has done little to detract from her importance and she remains one of popular music's most articulate and keen voices.

Albums: *Songs To A Seagull* (1968), *Clouds* (1969), *Ladies Of The Canyon* (1970), *Blue* (1970), *For The Roses* (1972), *Court And Spark* (1974), *Miles Of Aisles* (1975), *The Hissing Of Summer Lawns* (1975), *Hejira* (1976), *Don Juan's Reckless Daughter* (1978), *Mingus* (1979), *Shadows And Light* (1980), *Wild Things Run Fast* (1982), *Dog Eat Dog* (1985), *Chalk Mark In A Rainstorm* (1988), *Night Ride Home* (1991).

Moffatt, Katy

A Texan singer-songwriter whose country-based folk has won a limited, yet loyal following. Originally from Fort Worth, her early influences included Leonard Cohen and Tracy Nelson. She spent the early 70s playing folk clubs and small rock venues, mainly in Colorado, before signing to CBS, and releasing two commercially slanted records in the mid to late 70s. Disillusioned with the music business, Moffatt kept a low profile during the early 80s, but her appearance on the semi-legendary compilation, *A Town South Of Bakersfield* (1985), was a key career move. Her performance at the Kerrville Folk Festival a year later was another important step; she met the respected songwriter, Tom Russell, and they began a fruitful collaboration. In 1989, Moffatt gained favourable reviews for *Walkin' On The Moon*, her first album for 11 years. She has since recorded regularly for a variety of independent labels.

Selected albums: *Walkin' On the Moon* (1989), *Child Bride* (1990), *The Greatest Show On Earth* (1993).

Monroe, Bill

b. William Smith Monroe, 13 September 1911, on a farm near Rosine, Ohio County, Kentucky, USA. The Monroes were a musical family; his father, known affectionately as Buck, was a noted step-dancer, his mother played fiddle, accordion and harmonica, and was respected locally as a singer of old time songs. Among the siblings, elder brothers Harry and Birch both played fiddle, and brother Charlie and sister Bertha, guitar. They were all influenced by their uncle, Pendleton Vanderver, who was a fiddler of considerable talent, and noted for his playing at local events. (Monroe later immortalized him in one of his best-known numbers, 'Uncle Pen', with tribute lines such as 'Late in the evening about sundown; high on the hill above the town, Uncle Pen played the fiddle, oh, how it would ring. You can hear it talk, you can hear it sing'). At the age of nine, Monroe began to concentrate on the mandolin; his first choice had been the guitar or fiddle, but his brothers pointed out that no family member played mandolin, and as the baby, he was given little choice, although he still kept up his guitar playing. His mother died when he was 10, followed soon after by his father. He moved in to live with Uncle Pen and they were soon playing guitar together at local dances. Bill also played with a black blues musician, Arnold Schultz, who was to become a major influence on the future Monroe music. After the death of his father, most of the family moved away in their search for work. Birch and Charlie headed north, working for a time in the car industry in Detroit, before moving to Whiting and East Chicago, Indiana, where they were employed in the oil refineries. When he was 18, Bill joined them, and for four years, worked at the Sinclair refinery. At one time, in the Depression, Bill was the only one with work, and the three began to play for local dances to raise money to live on.

In 1932, the three Monroe brothers and their girlfriends became part of a team of dancers and toured with a show organised by WLS Chicago, the radio station responsible for the *National Barn Dance* programme. They also played on local radio stations, including WAE Hammond and WJKS Gary, Indiana. In 1934, Bill, finding the touring conflicted with his work, decided to become a full time musician. Soon after, they received an offer to tour for Texas Crystals (the makers of a patent purgative medicine), which sponsored radio programmes in several states. Birch, back in employment at Sinclair and also looking after a sister, decided against a musical career. Bill married in 1935, and between then and 1936, he and Charlie (appearing as the Monroe Brothers) had stays at various stations, including Shenandoah, Columbia, Greenville and Charlotte. In 1936, they moved to the rival and much larger Crazy Water Crystals and, until 1938, they worked on the noted *Crazy Barn Dance* at WBT Charlotte for that company. They became a very popular act and sang mainly traditional material, often with a blues influence. Charlie always provided the lead vocal, and Bill added tenor harmonies.

In February 1936, they made their first recordings on the Bluebird label of RCA-Victor, which proved popular. Further sessions followed, and in total they cut some 60 tracks for the label. Early in 1938, the brothers decided that they should follow their own careers. Charlie kept the RCA recording contract and formed his own band, the Kentucky Pardners. Since he had always handled all lead vocals, he found things easier and soon established himself in his own right. Prior to the split, Bill had never recorded an instrumental or a vocal solo, but he had ideas that he wished to put into practice. He moved to KARK Little Rock, where he formed his first band, the Kentuckians. This failed to satisfy him, and he soon moved to Atlanta, where he worked on the noted *Crossroad Follies*, at this time, he formed the first of the bands he would call the BlueGrass Boys. In 1939, he made his first appearance on the *Grand Ole Opry*, singing his version of 'New Muleskinner Blues', after which George D. Hay (the Solemn Old Judge) told him, 'Bill, if you ever leave the Opry, it'll be because you fire yourself'. (Over 50 years later, he was still there.)

During the early 40s, Monroe's band was similar to other string bands such as Mainer's Mountaineers, but by the mid-40s, the leading influence of Monroe's driving mandolin and his high (some would say shrill) tenor singing became the dominant factor, which set the Blue Grass Boys of Bill Monroe apart from the other bands. This period gave birth to a new genre of music, and led to Bill Monroe becoming known affectionately as the Father of Bluegrass Music. He began to tour with the *Opry* road shows, and his weekly network WSM radio work soon made him a national name. In 1940 and 1941, he recorded a variety of material for RCA-Victor, including gospel songs, old-time numbers and instrumentals such as the 'Orange Blossom Special' (the second known recording of the number). War-time restrictions prevented him from recording between 1941 and early 1945, but later that year, he recorded for Columbia. In 1946, he gained his first country chart hits when his own song, 'Kentucky Waltz', reached number 3, and his now-immortal recording of 'Footprints In The Snow' reached number 5 in the US country charts. By 1945, several fiddle players had made their impact on the band's overall sound, including Chubby Wise, Art Wooten, Tommy Magness, Howdy Forrester and in 1945, guitarist/vocalist Lester Flatt and banjo player Earl Scruggs joined. David 'Stringbean' Akeman had provided the comedy and the banjo playing since 1942, although it was generally reckoned later that his playing contributed little to the overall sound that Monroe sought. Scruggs' style of playing was very different, and it quickly became responsible for not only establishing his own name as one of the greatest exponents of the instrument, but also for making bluegrass music an internationally identifiable sound. It was while Flatt and Scruggs were with the band that Monroe first recorded his now-immortal song 'Blue Moon Of Kentucky'.

By 1948, other bands such as the Stanley Brothers were beginning to show the influence of Monroe, and bluegrass music was firmly established. During the 40s, Monroe toured with his tent show, which included his famous baseball team (the reason for Stringbean's first connections with Monroe), which played against local teams as an attraction before the musical show began. In 1951, he bought some land at Bean Blossom, Brown County, Indiana, and established a country park, which became the home for bluegrass music shows. He was involved in a very serious car accident in January 1953, and was unable to perform for several months. In 1954, Elvis Presley recorded Monroe's 'Blue Moon Of Kentucky' in a 4/4 rock tempo and sang it at his solitary appearance on the *Opry*. A dejected Presley found the performance made no impact with the *Opry* audience, but the song became a hit. It also led to Monroe re-recording it in a style that, like the original, started as a waltz but after a verse and chorus featuring three fiddles, it changed to 4/4 tempo: Monroe repeated the vocal in the new style. (Paul McCartney's 1991 album, *Unplugged,* contains a version in both styles). Monroe toured extensively throughout the 50s, and had chart success in 1958 with his own instrumental number, 'Scotland'. He used the twin fiddles of Kenny Baker and Bobby Hicks to produce the sound of bagpipes behind his own mandolin - no doubt his tribute to his family's Scottish ancestry. By the end of the decade, the impact of rock 'n' roll was affecting his record sales and music generally. By this time, (the long departed) Flatt and Scruggs were firmly established with their own band and finding success on television and at folk festivals. Monroe was a strong-willed person and it was not always easy for those who worked with him, or for him, to achieve the perfect arrangement. He had stubborn ideas and, in 1959, he refused to play a major concert in Carnegie Hall, because he believed that Alan Lomax, the organiser, was a communist. He was also suspicious of the Press and rarely, if ever, gave interviews. In 1962, however, he became friendly with Ralph Rinzler, a writer and member of the Greenbriar Boys, who became his manager.

In 1963, Monroe played his first folk festival at the University of Chicago. He soon created a great interest among students generally and, with Rinzler's planning, he was soon busily connected with festivals solely devoted to bluegrass music. In 1965, he was involved with the major Roanoke, Virginia, festival and in 1967, he started his own at Bean Blossom. During the 60s, many young musicians benefitted from their time as a member of Monroe's band, including Bill Keith, Peter Rowan, Byron Berline, Roland White and Del McCoury. In 1969, he was made an honorary Kentucky Colonel, and in 1970, was elected to the *Country Music Hall Of Fame* in Nashville. The plaque stated 'The Father of Bluegrass Music. Bill Monroe developed and perfected this music form and taught it to a great many names in the industry'. Monroe has written many songs, including 'Memories Of Mother And Dad', 'When The Golden Leaves Begin To Fall', 'My Little Georgia Rose' and 'Blue Moon Of Kentucky' (the latter a much-recorded country standard) and countless others. Many have been written using pseudonyms such as Albert Price, James B. Smith and James W. Smith. In 1971, his talent as a songwriter saw him elected to the Nashville Songwriters Association International Hall Of Fame. He kept up a hectic touring schedule throughout the 70s, but in 1981, he suffered with cancer. He survived after treatment and, during the 80s, maintained a schedule that would have daunted much younger men. In 1984, he recorded the album *Bill Monroe And Friends,* which contains some of his songs sung as duets with other artists, including the Oak Ridge Boys ('Blue Moon Of Kentucky'), Emmylou Harris ('Kentucky Waltz'), Barbara Mandrell ('My Rose Of Old Kentucky'), Ricky Skaggs ('My Sweet Darling') and Willie Nelson ('The Sunset Trail'). Johnny Cash, who also appears on the album, presumably did not know any Monroe songs because they sang Cash's own 'I Still Miss Someone'.

Over the years since Monroe first formed his bluegrass band, some of the biggest names in country music have played as members before progressing to their own careers. These include Clyde Moody, Flatt And Scruggs, Jim Eanes, Carter Stanley, Mac Wiseman, Jimmy Martin, Sonny

Osborne, Vassar Clements, Kenny Baker and son James Monroe. Amazingly, bearing in mind his popularity, Monroe's last chart entry was 'Gotta Travel On', a Top 20 country hit in March 1959. However, his records are still collected and the German Bear Family label has released boxed sets on compact disc of his Decca recordings. (Between 1950, when he first recorded for Decca and 1969, he made almost 250 recordings for the label) He continued to play the *Opry* and, in 1989, he celebrated his 50th year as a member, the occasion being marked by MCA (by then the owners of Decca) recording a live concert from the *Opry* stage, which became his first-ever release on CD format. He first visited the UK in 1966, did an extended tour in 1975, and has always been a very popular personality on the several occasions he has played the UK's Wembley Festival. He underwent surgery for a double coronary bypass on 9 August 1991, but by October, he was back performing and once again hosting his normal *Opry* show.

Albums: *Knee Deep In Bluegrass* (1958), *I Saw The Light* (1959), *Mr. Bluegrass* (1960), *The Great Bill Monroe & The BlueGrass Boys* (1961), *Bluegrass Ramble* (1962), *The Father Of Bluegrass Music* (1962), *My All-Time Country Favorites* (1962), *Early Bluegrass Music* (1963), *Bluegrass Special* (1963), *Sings Country Songs* (1964), *I'll Meet You In Church Sunday Morning* (1964), *Original Bluegrass Sound* (1965), *Bluegrass Instrumentals* (1965), *The High Lonesome Sound* (1966), *Bluegrass Time* (1967), *A Voice From On High* (1969), *Bill Monroe & His Blue GrassBoys (16 Hits)* (1970), *Bluegrass Style* (1970), *Kentucky Bluegrass* (1970), *Country Music Hall Of Fame* (1971), *Uncle Pen* (1972), *Bean Blossom* (1973, double album), *The Road Of Life* (1974), *Weary Traveller* (1976), *Bill Monroe & His Bluegrass Boys 1950-1972* (c1976), *Sings Bluegrass, Body And Soul* (1977), *Bluegrass Memories* (1977), *Bill Monroe With Lester Flatt & Earl Scruggs:The Original Bluegrass Band* (1978), *Bean Blossom 1979* (1980), *Bluegrass Classic (Radio Shows 1946-1948)* (1980), *The Classic Bluegrass Recordings Volume 1* (1980), *The Classic Bluegrass Recordings Volume 2* (1980), *Orange Blossom Special (Recorded Live At Melody Ranch)* (1981), *Master Of Bluegrass* (1981), *Live Radio* (1982), *MCA Singles Collection Volumes 1, 2 & 3* (1983), *Bill Monroe & Friends* (1984), *Bluegrass '87* (1987), *Southern Flavor* (1988), *Muleskinner Blues* (1991). Bear Family CD Boxed Sets: *Bill Monroe BlueGrass 1950-1958* (1989), *Bill Monroe BlueGrass 1959-1969* (1991). As The Monroe Brothers *Early Bluegrass Music* (1963), *The Monroe Brothers, Bill & Charlie* (1969), *Feast Here Tonight* (1975). With Birch Monroe *Brother Birch Monroe Plays Old-Time Fiddle Favorites* (1975). With James Monroe *Father And Son* (1973), *Together Again* (1978). With Kenny

Baker *Kenny Baker Plays Bill Monroe* (1976). With Lester Flatt *Bill Monroe And Lester Flatt* (1967). With Rose Maddox *Rose Maddox Sings Bluegrass* (1962). With Doc Watson *Bill & Doc Sing Country Songs* (1975).

Moore, Christy

b. 7 May 1945, Dublin, Eire. Moore's beginnings were fairly typical for a solo folk performer in the 60s: playing the club circuit in Eire, subsequently doing likewise in England while in between working on building sites and road gangs. Influenced by the American styles of Woody Guthrie, Bob Dylan and the British folk giant, Ewan MacColl, Moore performed in the UK folk clubs alongside the rising stars of the period. It was in England, in 1969, that he recorded his first album, a collaboration with Dominic Behan, *Paddy On The Road*. His first solo album led to the forming of Planxty, where he stayed until 1975. Having once again embarked on a solo career, he became involved in the mid-70s with the Anti-Nuclear Roadshow which featured performers, environmental activists and politicians. The 'Roadshow' established Moore's reputation as a campaigning and political performer and the ensemble's success made a heavy contribution to undermining the plans for a Irish nuclear power programme.

After a brief reunion with Planxty in the late 70s, Moore and fellow Planxty member Donal Lunny split in 1981 to form Moving Hearts. This progression from the former group fused folk with rock. Despite the group taking a similar ideologically agit-prop stance, Moore eventually felt uncomfortable within a group set-up and once again returned to solo work in 1982. Since that time, Moore's mixture of traditional songs with contemporary observations of Irish life, social and political, has also tackled the political problems of Central America and South Africa as well as the problems in his homeland and Ulster. His songs are notable not only for their spiky commentary but also an engaging humour. Christy Moore's standing in Irish folk music is of a stature unparalleled and his influence spills over into the field of pop and rock, winning critical favour, respect and debt, from such contemporary pop performers as the Pogues, Elvis Costello, Billy Bragg and U2.

Albums: with Dominic Behan *Paddy On The Road* (1969), *Prosperous* (1971), *Whatever Tickles Your Fancy* (1975), *Christy Moore* (1976), *The Iron Behind The Velvet* (1978), *Live In Dublin* (1978), *The Spirit Of Freedom* (1983), *The Time Has Come* (1983), *Ride On* (1984), *Ordinary Man* (1985), *Nice 'N' Easy* (1986), *Unfinished Revolution* (1987), *Voyage* (1989), *Smoke And Strong Whiskey* (1991). Compilation:

The Christy Moore Collection '81-'91 (1991).

Morgan, Elaine
Singer b. 11 February 1960, Wales, who has started to secure a place for her talent. She started out by working in a Cardiff recording studio, supplying voice overs and vocals for jingles. Additionally, she supplied backing vocals for many of the recording artists using the studio, with the result that Robin Williamson recruited her to sing on his *Ten Of Songs* album. Elaine's next break came, in 1985, when she was asked to play support, with her new band Rose Among Thorns, to Fairport Convention. Since then, Elaine has worked with Ashley Hutchings and the Albion Band, and has toured the UK, as support to Ralph McTell, on a number of occasions. Morgan's first solo release, *First Blush*, was produced by Ashley Hutchings and Phil Beer. The recording also featured other members of the Albion Band. Elaine has also appeared, in an acting capacity, in numerous television series. Despite one or two changes of personnel, the current line-up of Rose Among Thorns is husband Derek Morgan (b. 14 October 1953, Cardiff, Wales; bass), John Turner (b. 30 January 1949, Cardiff, Wales; drums), and Tim Gray (b. 2 August 1961, Abercynon, Mid-Glamorgan, Wales; lead guitar). Dave Dutfield (electric and acoustic guitar), who had earlier been with the group, left in January 1993, to return to teaching. With Elaine's strong vocals, the sound has taken the group outside of the confines of the purely folk spectrum, into the more mainstream, and commercial, market.
Albums: *Masquerade-On The Wings Of Change* (1988), *First Blush* (1989), *Changing Moods* (1989), *Rose Among Thorns* (1991), *This Time It's Real* (1992).

Morton, Pete
b. 30 July 1964, Leicester, England. Morton is one of the newer group of folk singer/songwriters to emerge in recent years who have gained a growing acceptance and respectability. During school days, he played in a punk band redolent of the Ramones, and subsequently moved into the folk scene. Having already 'discovered' Bob Dylan, Morton found a good deal of interest in the talent available on the circuit. He moved to Manchester in 1987, and was signed by Harbourtown Records, which released the highly acclaimed *Frivolous Love*. This brought Morton to the attention of a wider audience, and he began touring the UK. With the follow-up *One Big Joke* appearing a year later to good reviews, Morton undertook his first tour of the USA in 1989. His style is generally rock-orientated, but still based on traditional styles. 1992 saw the release of his third album, *Mad World Blues* and tours of the USA and Canada.
Albums: *Frivolous Love* (1987), *One Big Joke* (1988), with Roger Wilson, Simon Edwards *Urban Folk Volume One* (1990), *Mad World Blues* (1992).

Mouth Music
Formed by Martin Swan, a Sheffield born Scot, and an American, Talitha MacKenzie, Mouth Music made an impressive debut in 1990 with a fusion of Gaelic vocals, African percussion and synthesisers. An EP, *Blue Door, Green Sea*, released in 1992, confirmed their direction, and a constant stream of influences made their live shows exciting as well as experimental. One of the EP's tracks, a dance mix of their earlier, 'Sienn O', revealed a further advance. On *Mo-di* (1993), there were more apparent moves into the dance area, and it seems that the band's apparent folk origin is now only one aspect of its work, which includes samba and hip-hop. When Talitha MacKenzie departed, she was replaced by vocalist, Jackie Joyce. The group's live performances are usually augmented by a seven piece band.
Albums: *Mouth Music* (1990), *Mo-Di* (1993).

Moving Hearts
This Irish group was formed in 1981, by former Planxty members Christy Moore and Donal Lunny and was notable for its innovative use in Irish folk of traditional music of an eclectic array of instruments, which at times included saxophones, pipes, bouzoukis and synthesizers. All the original members had a history in Irish folk scene. The original line-up with Moore and Lunny comprised: Eoghan O'Neill (bass/vocals), Davy Spillane (uileann pipes/whistles), Brian Calnan (percussion/drums) and Keith Donald (saxophone). This exciting blend of folk music, jazz and electric rock challenged the popular pre-conceptions of Irish - indeed, British - folk music, although the group never gained the recognition it fully deserved. The song subject matter ranged from the traditional to the more contemporary, chronicling the internment of terrorist suspects ('On The Blanket') and nuclear weapons ('Hiroshima'). Moore ultimately found the group format uncomfortable and returned to solo work in 1982. He was replaced by Mick Hanly, who in turn was supplanted by Florence McSweeney in 1984. The costs of running such a large line-up led to the eventually demise of the group in 1985, although they have since reformed for special concerts as in 1986's Self-Aid benefit.
Albums: *Moving Hearts* (1981), *Dark End Of The Street* (1982), *Live Hearts* (1983), *The Storm* (1985).

Moving Hearts

Mr. Fox

One of the genre's forgotten acts, Mr. Fox's
pioneering influence in folk/rock was equal to that
of Steeleye Span and Fairport Convention.
Concerned at the lack of a band that could play
atmospheric English music, Ashley Hutchings and
traditionalist Bob Pegg, recruited Pegg's wife,
Carole (fiddle), Alun Eden (drums), Barry Lyons
(bass), Andrew Massey (cello) and John Myatt
(woodwinds). They recorded a powerful, haunting
album for Transatlantic, for which Pegg wrote
mature, gothic songs, inspired by his Yorkshire
homeland. Economically unfeasible, the band was
reduced to a rock four piece unit, and released the
excellent *The Gypsy*. In 1971 they toured the
festival circuit, but various aspects of their
perfomance at Loughborough were heavily
criticized. In the following year Alan Edun and
Barry Lyons left the group, to join Trees, and were
replaced by Nick Strutt (guitar) and Ritchie Bull
(bass). This drastic move changed the band's
character, and Carol Pegg's departure reduced Mr.
Fox to a trio, after which they disbanded. Carole
Pegg later worked with Graham Bond, and issued a
solo record influenced by 'magic'. Bob Pegg
continued to perform with Nick Strutt, and, in the
late 70s, released a series of characteristically black
folk albums. He has since remarried, and moved
into theatrical education, although he still has a
number of unreleased concept albums.

Albums: *Mr. Fox* (1970), *The Gypsy* (1971).
Compilation: *The Complete Mr. Fox* (1975). As Bob
& Carole Pegg *He Came From The Mountains*
(1971), as Carole Pegg *Carolanne* (1973), as Bob
Pegg & Nick Strutt *Bob Pegg & Nick Strutt* (1973),
The Shipbuilder (1974), *Ancient Maps* (1975).

Muckram Wakes

This largely traditional UK group specialized in
songs, and later, dance music of the Midlands.
Formed in 1970, the original line-up comprised
Roger Watson (b. 6 February 1946, Mansfield,
Nottinghamshire, England; concertina, tuba,
melodeon), Helen Wainwright (b. 16 May 1951,
Marchington, Staffordshire, England; harmonium,
whistle, piano, bouzouki) - Helen and Roger
married in 1972 - and John Tams (fiddle, banjo,
concertina). This unit survived until October 1973,
when Tams left to join the Albion Band. Shortly
afterwards John Adams (fiddle, banjo, trombone),
and Suzie Adams (drum, percussion), were added.
In this format they continued until 1980, gaining
much respect on the folk circuit. They also
contributed to the short-lived 11-piece New
Victory Band, and their highly-regarded 1978
release *One More Dance And Then*. In 1980 a
complete change of line-up, brought about by
personal and professional break-ups, meant that the
group comprised of John Adams, Keith Kendrick
(concertina), Barry Coope (vocals) and Ian Carter.

This group only lasted for a short while before disbanding.

Roger Watson also performed and recorded with American banjo player and singer Debbie McClatchy, and he was also a member of the Robb Johnson Band. Watson is now director of TAPS (Traditional Arts Projects), in Berkshire.

Albums: *Muckram Wakes* (1976), *A Map Of Derbyshire* (1973), *Warble, Jangles And Reeds* (1980). Roger Watson: *The Pick And The Malt Shovel* (1974), *Mixed Traffic* (1981), *Chequered Roots* (1988), with Debbie McClatchy *Radioland* (1988). Suzie Adams And Helen Watson: *Songbird* (1983)

Muldaur, Geoff

b. c.1940, Pelham, New York, USA. Muldaur began performing at the folk haunts of Cambridge, Massachusetts while a student at Boston University. He worked as a soloist at the *Club 47*, as well as becoming a featured member of the Jim Kweskin Jug Band. Muldaur's debut, *Sleepy Man Blues*, boasted support from Dave Van Ronk and Eric Von Schmidt, and offered sterling interpretations of material drawn from country-blues singers Bukka White, Sleepy John Estes and Blind Willie Johnson. Despite this recording, the artist remained with Kweskin until the Jug Band splintered at the end of the 60s. He then completed two albums, *Pottery Pie* (1970) and *Sweet Potatoes* (1972) with his wife, Maria Muldaur, before joining Paul Butterfield's 70s venture, Better Days. The singer resumed his solo career upon the break-up of both the band and his marriage. The Joe Boyd-produced *Geoff Muldaur Is Having A Wonderful Time* showed the artist's unflinching eclecticism, a facet prevailing on all his releases. A longstanding professional relationship with guitarist and fellow Woodstock resident Amos Garrett resulted in *Geoff Muldaur And Amos Garrett*, on which the former's penchant for self-indulgence was pared to a minimum. Despite this trait, Muldaur's entire catalogue is worthy of investigation and deserves respect for its attention to music's ephemera.

Albums: *Sleepy Man Blues* (1963), *Geoff Muldaur Is Having A Wonderful Time* (1975), *Motion* (1976), *Geoff Muldaur And Amos Garrett* (1978), *Blues Boy* (1979).

Muldaur, Maria

b. Maria Grazia Rosa Domenica d'Amato, 12 September 1943, Greenwich Village, New York, USA. Her name was changed to Muldaur when she married Geoff Muldaur, with whom she performed in the Jim Kweskin Jug Band. Although her mother was fond of classical music, Muldaur grew up liking blues and big band sounds. The 60s scene in Greenwich Village thrived musically, and she first joined the Even Dozen Jug Band, playing alongside John Sebastian, Stefan Grossman, Joshua Rifkin and Steve Katz. After leaving them she teamed up with the Jim Kweskin Jug Band. After two albums together, they split up, and Geoff and Maria were divorced in 1972. *Maria Muldaur*, her first solo effort, went platinum in the USA. It contained the classic single 'Midnight At The Oasis', which featured an excellent guitar solo by Amos Garrett. The album reached number 3 in the US charts in 1974, with the single making the US Top 10. A follow-up, 'I'm A Woman', made the Top 20 in the US charts in 1975. Muldaur toured the USA in 1975, and shortly after played in Europe for the first time. The US Top 30 album, *Waitress In A Donut Shop*, featured the songs of contemporary writers such as Kate And Anna McGarrigle, and with the assistance of musicians including Amos Garrett and J.J.Cale, she created a stronger jazz influence on the album. With sales of her records in decline, she was dropped by WEA, and since then has concentrated on recording with smaller labels such as Takoma, Spindrift, Making Waves and the Christian label Myrrh with whom she released *There Is A Love*. Shortly after *Live In London* was released, the label, Making Waves, folded. *On The Sunny Side* appeared on the largely unknown Music For Little People label. She has never been able to completely match the success of 'Midnight At The Oasis', but her soulful style of blues, tinged with jazz is still in demand.

Albums: *Maria Muldaur* (1973), *Waitress In A Donut Shop* (1974), *Sweet Harmony* (1976), *Southern Winds* (1978), *Open Your Eyes* (1979), *Gospel Nights* (1980), *There Is A Love* (1982), *Sweet And Slow* (1984), *Transblucency* (1985), *Live In London* (1987), *On The Sunny Side* (1991), *Louisiana Love Call* (1992).

Murphey, Michael Martin

b. c.1946, Dallas, Texas, USA. Having been influenced by gospel music at an early age, Murphey aspired to become a Baptist minister. From 1965-70, as a staff songwriter for Screen Gems, Murphey was writing theme tunes and soundtrack material for television. He grew disillusioned with the poor financial rewards, and left. For a short while he was a member of the Lewis And Clark Expedition, which he formed, before going solo. *Geronimo's Cadillac* was produced in Nashville by Bob Johnston, who had originally got Murphey signed to A&M Records. The title track was released as a single, and achieved a Top 40 place in the USA. As well as folk, country and blues, Murphey's early gospel leanings are evident in the overall sound of what is an excellent album. He signed to Epic in 1973, after releasing *Cosmic*

Maria Muldaur

Cowboy Souvenir which continued the urban cowboy theme of his earlier work. His albums followed a more middle-of-the-road format after this, with occasional glimpses of his better work, as in *Peaks, Valleys, Honky-Tonks And Alleys*. However, he did reach number 3 in the US singles charts, achieving a gold disc, in 1975, with 'Wildfire'. Apart from *Blue Sky, Night Thunder* also achieved gold status. Murphey has never had the degree of commercial success his writing would indicate that he is capable of. However, as a writer, Murphey has had songs covered by John Denver, Cher, Claire Hamill, Hoyt Axton, Bobby Gentry and the Monkees, for whom he wrote 'What Am I Doin' Hangin' 'Round'.

He also wrote songs for Michael Nesmith after the latter's exit from the Monkees, including 'The Oklahoma Backroom Dance'. Murphey later played at Ronnie Scott's club in London, for a press presentation, and was supported on the occasion by J.D. Souther, Don Henley, Dave Jackson and Gary Nurm. *Geronimo's Cadillac* is probably his best remembered work. *Michael Martin Murphey* included a number of songs Murphey had co-written with Michael D'Abo. Murphey was featured in the film *Urban Cowboy* which included his song 'Cherokee Fiddle'. Much of the film was shot at Mickey Gilley's Bar. Murphey has continued recording easy listening country and, in 1987, had a number 1 country single with a wedding song, 'A Long Line Of Love'. He had US country hits with 'A Face In The Crowd', a duet with Holly Dunn, and 'Talkin' To The Wrong Man', which featured his son, Ryan. His 1990 album, *Cowboy Songs*, saw him return to his roots.

Albums: with the Lewis And Clark Expedition *I Feel Good, I Feel Bad, Geronimo's Cadillac* (1972), *Cosmic Cowboy Souvenir* (1973), *Michael Murphey* (1973), *Blue Sky Night Thunder* (1975), *Swans Against The Sun* (1976), *Flowing Free Forever* (1976), *Lone Wolf* (1977), *Peaks, Valleys, Honky-Tonks And Alleys* (1979), *Michael Martin Murphey* (1982), *The Heart Never Lies* (1983), *Tonight We Ride* (1986), *Americana* (1987), *River Of Time* (1988), *Land Of Enchantment* (1989), *Cowboy Songs* (1990), *Cowboy Christmas - Cowboy Songs II* (1991). Compilation: *The Best Of Michael Martin Murphey* (1982).

Murphy, Delia

b. 1903, Mount Jennings, Claremorris, County Mayo, Eire, d. 1971. The daughter of wealthy farming parents, Murphy was educated at University College, Galway, and supplemented her studies by assimilating a diverse repertoire of Irish ballads. Her knowledge of the genre, both in English and Gaelic, was impressive enough to encourage the famous Irish tenor John McCormack

to seek her assistance in enunciating the ballad 'Una Bhan'. Her rendition so struck a visiting A&R representative from HMV Records that she was duly signed to the label. One of her first recordings was the extraordinary 'The Spinning Wheel'. Written in 1899 by John Francis Waller, the song hauntingly evoked the courtship of young lovers measured by the inexorable winding of the spinner's wheel. Murphy's ethereal West Ireland brogue and Gaelic pronunciation was reinforced by a harp arrangement which was quite remarkable for the period. With songs such as 'If I Were A Blackbird', 'Coortin' In The Kitchen', 'Goodbye Mike And Goodbye Pat' and 'Nora Creina', Murphy established herself as a traditionalist with a tremendous sense of humour and pathos. She borrowed freely, not merely from standard Irish ballads, but from obscure songs that had their origin in tinker folklore. Other material such as 'The Moonshiner' and 'Boston Burglar' were American adaptations, expertly gaelicized by Murphy's distinctive brogue and unique diction. Her marriage to the Ambassador Dr. Thomas Kiernan (author of *British War Finances And Their Consequences*) took her to the Vatican in 1941, where she spent the War years. While there she translated her version of 'Three Lovely Lassies' into Italian. After touring the world with her ambassador husband, she retired to Eire's Liffey Valley, where she died at the age of 68. Compilation: *The Legendary Delia Murphy* (1977).

Murphy, Noel

b. 27 November 1943, Killerney, County Kerry, Eire. Singer, guitar player, and storyteller, Murphy first visited London in 1962 and decided to stay. He went to a wide number of folk clubs, then springing up under the banner of the folk revival. Shortly afterwards, Murphy started out doing the obligatory 'floor spots' in the clubs, and was rewarded with offers of bookings. The residency of the famous London club Les Cousins in Soho followed. He then began playing a large number of folk festivals, including Norwich, Cambridge and Trowbridge. In 1965, Murphy released an EP, *Noel Murphy*, for EMI. Subsequent releases turned up on a variety of labels, including Fontana, and RCA. Noel had by now been working abroad a great deal, in places as diverse as Saudi Arabia, Bermuda, Kenya, and Hungary. However, in 1983, his throat was damaged when he choked on a piece of glass which was found in his drink. His full-time singing career now over, he left the scene for four years. During this time he developed his abilities as an after dinner speaker. As a result, he is now much in demand in his capacity as a storyteller at golf and rugby functions. In 1987, he released the single 'Murphy And The Bricks' aka 'Why Paddy's Not

At Work Today', recounting the amusing excuse given for someone not turning up for work on the building site. Murphy's career spans over 25 years, and includes numerous radio and television appearances, with many in Eric Sykes' television shows and films. Noel now does very few folk club bookings since he began touring with his one man show - An Evening With Noel Murphy.

Albums: *Nyaah!* (1967), *A Touch Of The Blarney* (1968), *Another Round* (1969), *Murf* (1972), *Noel Murphy Performs* (1975), *Caught In The Act* (1978), *Homework* (1988).

Muzsikás

This Hungarian group features Márta Sebestyén (vocals, recorder), Sándor Csoóri (bagpipes/hurdy-gurdy, viola, vocals), Mihaly Sipos (violin, zither, vocals), Péter Eri (bouzouki, turkish horn, cello, viola, vocals) and Dániel Hamar (bass/hurdy-gurdy, vocals). The ensemble specializes in traditional music from the Transylvania region of their country. Prior to 1987 Sebestyén had performed in the UK with a band called Mosaic. While still young, Sebestyén had heard her mother singing folk songs, so the interest in folk music passed on. Having won a competition at the age of 13, she was awarded a record player, which enabled her to listen to a wider sphere of music. The style of music Muzsikas play is often patronizingly called 'gypsy music', but it is far more than just a tourist attraction. Changing from a high-speed dance one minute, to a slow and melancholy air, the music covers a whole range of emotions and tempos. Péter Eri had previously played with a group called Sebo, where he learned much about the background to folk music. The original Muzsikas was a trio consisting of Sipos, Hamar and Csoóri. Eri joined them in 1978 after leaving Sebo. They recorded *Muzsikas Ketto* in Holland, but were not satisfied with the singer who had joined on lead vocals, so they asked Sebestyén to join them in 1979. A number of earlier recordings, from 1976-82, for the state-run label Hungaroton, are no longer available, but with the growing interest in Eastern European folk music, the possibility of re-releases seems likely.

Albums: *Living Hungarian Folk Music Vol.1* (1978), *The Prisoner's Song* (1986), *Nem Arról Hajnallik, Amerröl Hajnallot* (1986), *Márta Sebestyén With Muzsikas* (1987), *Blues For Transylvania* (1990), *Maramaros - The Lost Jewish Music Of Transylvania* (1993).

N

Natural Acoustic Band

This trio was formed in 1969, in Milngavie, Glasgow, Scotland. There were a number of personnel changes but the essential line-up was Tom Hoy (b. 5 February 1950, Glasgow, Scotland; guitar/vocals), Robin Thyne (b. 1 November 1950, Newcastle Upon Tyne, England; guitar/vocals), and Krysia Kocjan pronounced Kotsyan (b. 10 August 1953, Craigendoran, Scotland; vocals). Krysia had a Polish father and a Flemish mother. The group played their first gig on 5 November 1969, at Alloa Working Men's Club. Eventually, the press picked up on Kocjan's vocal talent, and they were increasingly billed as the Natural Acoustic Band, featuring Krysia Kocjan. Occasionally, the group were augmented by a Chinese drummer and an Australian bass player, a truly international line-up. The two albums for RCA, were both released in 1972; *Learning To Live* in May, and *Branching In* in October. Krysia left in late 1972, and Robin and Tom continued to work with Joanna Carlin. She then left to pursue a solo career, and is now better known as Melanie Harrold. Robin and Tom continued as a duo, until Tom joined Magna Carta in 1975. Initially this was as a sound engineer, but eventually as a full-time member of the group. Robin also joined the Magan Carta, in 1977. In 1979, both Hoy and Thyne left and formed Nova Carta, recording the sole album, *Roadworks*, for CBS, in Holland. Kocjan released a solo album in 1974, and has since worked with Al Stewart, Ray Davies, Robin Williamson, Mike Heron, and Glenn Yarborough. Now living in the USA, Kocjan is still busy with session work, and voice teaching, and has plans to record again. Robin continues to work in a solo capacity, whilst Tom works as a duo with his wife Geraldine as Tom And Gerry.

Albums: *Learning To Live* (1972), *Branching In* (1972).

Near, Holly

b. 6 June 1949, Ukiah, California, USA. For Near's first 10 years, her family lived on a farm but her adolescence was spent in urban Ukiah where she matured from a child television actor to a performer with the confidence to accept a role in a Broadway run of *Hair*. She also participated in Jane Fonda's controversial *Free The Army* revue that toured Vietnam with a message demanding US withdrawal. However, Near was to leave the 70s as an artist in direct descent from the early 60s protest singers. Indeed, it was Ronnie Gilbert of the Weavers who helped encourage interest in her on the US folk club and campus circuit. As a yardstick of the respect that became hers in this sphere, Gilbert, Pete Seeger and Arlo Guthrie were guests on *Lifelines* which, like all of her country-tinged body of mostly self-composed material, was issued on her and Jeff Langley's own Ukiah-based Redwood label. Largely by word of mouth, Near's first four albums sold a collective 155,000 by 1979 when *Imagine My Surprise* was voted 'Album Of The Year' by the National Association of Independent Record Distributors. That spring found her in a Los Angeles theatre on the same bill as the premiere of the Labor movement film, *With Babies And Banners*. She also played a Women Against Violence Against Women benefit concert that shamed Warner Brothers into banning the use of brutal images on record sleeves.

Albums: *Hang In There* (1973), *Live* (1974), *You Can Know All I Am* (1976), *Imagine My Surprise* (1979), *Fire In The Rain* (80s), *Speed Of Light* (80s), *Journeys* (1984), *Watch Out* (80s), *Lifelines* (80s), *Don't Hold Back* (1987).

Neil, Fred

b. 1937, St. Petersburg, Florida, USA. An important figure in America's folk renaissance, Neil's talent first emerged in 1956 when he co-wrote an early Buddy Holly single, 'Modern Don Juan'. By the following decade he was a fixture of the Greenwich Village circuit, both as a solo act and in partnership with fellow singer Vince Martin. The duo embarked on separate careers following the release of *Tear Down The Walls*. Neil's subsequent solo *Bleecker And MacDougal* was an influential collection and contained the original version of 'The Other Side Of This Life', later covered by the Youngbloods, Lovin' Spoonful and the Jefferson Airplane. The singer's deep, resonant voice was equally effective, inspiring the languid tones of Tim Buckley and Tim Hardin. A reticent individual, Neil waited two years before completing *Fred Neil*, a compulsive selection which featured two of the artist's most famous compositions, 'The Dolphins' and 'Everybody's Talkin''. The latter was adopted as the theme song to *Midnight Cowboy*, a highly-successful film, although it was a version by Harry Nilsson which became the hit single. Such temporary trappings were of little note to Neil, who preferred the anonymity of his secluded Florida base, from where he rarely ventured. An appearance at the Los Angeles club, the Bitter End, provided the material for *The Other Side Of This Life*, Neil's last album to date and an effective

resume of his career. This informal performance also contained other favoured material, including 'You Don't Miss Your Water', which featured assistance from country singer Gram Parsons. A major, if self-effacing talent, Fred Neil has now withdrawn from music altogether.

Albums: *Hootenanny Live At The Bitter End* (1964), *World Of Folk Music* (1964), with Vince Martin *Tear Down The Walls* (1964), *Bleecker And MacDougal* aka *Little Bit Of Rain* (1964), *Fred Neil* aka *Everybody's Talkin'* (1966), *Sessions* (1968), *The Other Side Of This Life* (1971). Compilation: *The Very Best Of Fred Neil* (1986).

New Christy Minstrels

Randy Sparks (b. 29 July 1933, Leavenworth, Kansas, USA), formed this commercialized folk group in 1961. Determined to create a unit that was 'a compromise between the Norman Luboff Choir and the Kingston Trio', he added a popular Oregon quartet, the Fairmount Singers, to his own Randy Sparks Three. A third unit, the Inn Group, which featured Jerry Yester, was absorbed into the line-up, while other Los Angeles-based performers embellished these core acts. Fourteen singers made up the original New Christy Minstrels but although the ensemble was viewed as supplementary to the participants' other careers, interest in the unit's debut *Presenting The New Christy Minstrels*, led to it becoming a full-time venture. Most of these early recruits, including the entire Inn Group, abandoned Sparks' creation at this point, creating the need for further, wholescale changes. New enlistments, including Barry McGuire, Barry Kane and Larry Ramos, joined the Minstrels whose next release, *In Person*, documented a successful appearance at the famed Troubador club. The following year (1963) the group secured its first hit single with 'Green Green' which established the ensemble as a leading popular attraction. The group, however, remained volatile as members continued to come and go. Gene Clark disbanded his Kansas-based trio, the Surf Riders, in order to join the Minstrels, but left after a matter of months, frustrated at the rather conservative material the ensemble recorded. He later formed the Byrds with (Jim) Roger McGuinn and David Crosby. Randy Sparks ended his relationship with the Minstrels in the summer of 1964. Maligned for creating their MOR image, his departure did not result in the more daring direction several members wished to pursue. McGuire, who was increasingly unhappy with such material as 'Three Wheels On My Wagon' and 'Chim Chim Cheree', left the group after seeing several British groups perform during the Minstrels European tour that year. His gravelly rasp was soon heard on his solo international protest hit, 'Eve Of

New Christy Minstrels

Destruction'. In 1966 Larry Ramos accepted an invitation to join the Association and although several excellent new vocalists, including Kim Carnes and Kenny Rodgers, had been absorbed into the Minstrels, their influential days were over. Longstanding members Mike Settle and Terry Williams left when their new ideas were constantly rejected. They formed the First Edition with the equally ambitious Rodgers, and subsequently enjoyed the kind of success the parent group previously experienced. Although the New Christy Minstrels continued to exist in some form into the 80s, singing early hits, show tunes and standards, their halcyon days ended during the mid-60s.

Albums: *Presenting The New Christy Minstrels* (1962), *The New Christy Minstrels In Person* (1962), *The New Christy Minstrels Tell Tall Tales, Legends And Nonsense* (1963), *Ramblin' (Featuring Green, Green)* (1963), *Merry Christmas!* (1963), *Today* (1964), *Land Of Giants* (1964), *The Quiet Side Of The New Christy Minstrels* (1964), *The New Christy Minstrels Sing And Play Cowboys And Indians* (1965), *The Academy Award Winner - Chim Chim Cheree* (1965), *The Wandering Minstrels* (1965), *In Italy...In Italian* (1966), *New Kick!* (1966), *Christmas With The Christies* (1966), *On Tour Through Motortown* (1968), *Big Hits From Chitty Chitty Bang Bang* (1968), *You Need Someone To Love* (1970), *The Great Soap Opera Themes* (1976). Compilation: *Greatest Hits* (1966).

New Lost City Ramblers

Mike Seeger (b. 15 August 1933, New York City, New York, USA - brother of folksinger Pete Seeger), John Cohen (b. 1932, New York, USA) and Tom Paley (b. 19 March 1928, New York, USA) formed this influential old-time string band in 1958. Rather than ape their immediate predecessors who popularized the style, the trio preferred to invoke the music's original proponents, including Gid Tanner And His Skillet Lickers and the Carolina Tar Heels. Seeger undertook numerous field recordings to preserve authenticity and while their adherence to traditional values made commercial acceptance difficult, the group enjoyed the admiration of their peers and was crucial in the development of the urban folk revival. The original line-up remained together until 1962, when Paley left to resume his teaching career. Replacement Tracy Schwarz (b. 1938, New York, USA) primarily played fiddle, but his arrival coincided with a broadening of the Ramblers' repertoire. They began to incorporate unaccompanied ballads and modern bluegrass music but although the trio remained a popular attraction on the college and coffee-house circuit, they began to drift apart during the latter half of the 60s. *Remembrance Of*

Things To Come included British traditional, riverboat songs and even some early bluegrass. *American Moonshine And Prohibition* was more lighthearted, but not lightweight in its criticism of the government legislation on prohibition. Cohen initially pursued his interest in photography before producing a series of excellent documentary films. Schwartz and Seeger meanwhile performed with different musicians and together formed the short-lived Strange Creek Singers.

Albums: *New Lost City Ramblers* (1958), *New Lost City Ramblers Vol. 2* (1959), *Songs From The Depression* (1959), *Old Timey Songs For Children* (1959), *New Lost City Ramblers Vol. 3* (1961), *New Lost City Ramblers Vol. 4* (1961), *American Moonshine And Prohibition* (1962), *New Lost City Ramblers Vol. 5* (1963), *Gone To The Country* (1963), *String Band Instrumentals* (1964), *Old Timey Music* (1964), *Rural Delivery No. 1* (1965), *Remembrance Of Things To Come* (1966), *Modern Times-Rural Songs From An Industrial Society* (1968), *On The Great Divide* (1973), *20 Years-Concert Performances* (1978), *20th Anniversary Concert, Carnegie Hall* (1978). Compilations: *Tom Paley, John Cohen And Mike Seeger Sing Songs Of The New Lost City Ramblers* (1961), *Twenty Years* (1979), *The Early Years 1958-62* (1991).

New Seekers

Ex-Seeker Keith Potger's television appearances with the trendier New Edition, in 1970, left a peculiar aftertaste for the old quartet's fans. Wisely, he retreated to the less public role of manager, leaving the stage to Eve Graham (b. 19 April 1943, Perth, Scotland), Lyn Paul (b. 16 February 1949, Manchester, England) - both former Nocturnes - Peter Doyle (b. 28 July 1949, Melbourne, Australia), Paul Layton (b. 4 August 1947, Beaconsfield, England) and Marty Kristian (b. 27 May 1947, Leipzig, Germany), a Latvian who had been raised in Australia. The male contingent played guitars in concert but the act's main strengths were its interweaving vocal harmonies and a clean, winsome image. Their entertainments also embraced dance and comedy routines. Initially they appealed to US consumers who thrust a cover of Melanie's 'Look What They've Done To My Song Ma' and 'Beautiful People' - all unsuccessful in Britain - high up the *Billboard* Hot 100. A UK breakthrough came with 'Never Ending Song Of Love' which reached number 2, and, even better, a re-write of a Coca-Cola commercial, 'I'd Like To Teach The World To Sing', topping foreign charts too, and overtaking the Hillside Singers' original version in the States. Their Eurovision Song Contest entry, 'Beg Steal Or Borrow' and the title track of 1972's *Circles* were also hits, but revivals of

the Fleetwoods' 'Come Softly To Me' and Eclection's 'Nevertheless' were among 1973 singles whose modest Top 40 placings were hard-won, though the year ended well with another UK number 1 in 'You Won't Find Another Fool Like Me'. With its follow-up, 'I Get A Little Sentimental Over You' likewise hurtling upwards in spring 1974, the five disbanded with a farewell tour of Britain. Two years later, however, the lure of a CBS contract brought about a reformation - minus Lyn Paul who had had a minor solo hit in 1975 - but no subsequent single could reconjure a more glorious past and, not-so-New anymore, the group broke up for the last time in 1978.

Albums: *Beautiful People* (1971), *We'd Like To Teach The World To Sing* (1971, US issue), *New Colours* (1972), *We'd Like To Teach The World To Sing* (1972, UK issue), *Never Ending Song Of Love* (1972), *Circles* (1972), *Now* (1973), *Pinball Wizards* (1973), *Together* (1974). Compilations: *15 Great Hits* (1983), *The Best Of The New Seekers* (1985), *Greatest Hits* (1987).

Newbury, Mickey

b. Milton J. Newbury Jnr., 19 May 1940, Houston, Texas, USA. Newbury began by singing tenor in a harmony group, the Embers, who recorded for Mercury Records. He worked as an air traffic controller in the US Air Force and was stationed in England. He later wrote 'Swiss Cottage Place', which was recorded by Roger Miller. In 1963 he worked on shrimp boats in Galveston, Texas and started song-writing in earnest. In 1964 he was signed to Acuff-Rose Music in Nashville. Among his early compositions are 'Here Comes The Rain, Baby' (Eddy Arnold and Roy Orbison), 'Funny Familiar Forgotten Feelings' (Don Gibson and Tom Jones), 'How I Love Them Old Songs' (Carl Smith) and 'Sweet Memories' (Willie Nelson). In 1968 Kenny Rogers And The First Edition had a US pop hit with the psychedelic 'Just Dropped In (To See What Condition My Condition Was In)'. Newbury recorded low-key albums of his own but his voice was so mournful that even his happier songs sounded sad. After two albums for RCA, he moved to Mercury and wrote and recorded such sombre songs as 'She Even Woke Me Up To Say Goodbye' (later recorded by Jerry Lee Lewis), 'San Francisco Mabel Joy' (recorded by John Denver, Joan Baez, David Allan Coe and Kenny Rogers) and 'I Don't Think About Her (Him) No More', which has been recorded by Don Williams and Tammy Wynette, and also by Bobby Bare, under the title of 'Poison Red Berries'. Newbury, who by now lived on a houseboat, was intrigued by the way his wind chimes mingled with the rain, thus leading to the sound effects he used to link tracks with. This gave his albums of similar material a concept. His gentle and evocative 'American Trilogy' - in actuality a medley of three Civil War songs ('Dixie', 'The Battle Hymn Of The Republic' and 'All My Trials') - was a hit in a full-blooded version by Elvis Presley in 1972. Says Newbury, 'It was more a detriment than a help because it was not indicative of what I could do.' Nevertheless, his *Rusty Tracks* also features reworkings of American folk songs. Amongst his successful compositions are 'Makes Me Wonder If I Ever Said Goodbye' (Johnny Rodriguez) and 'Blue Sky Shinin'' (Marie Osmond). He has scarcely made a mark as a performer in the US country charts (his highest position is number 53 for 'Sunshine') but he was elected to the Nashville Songwriters International Hall of Fame in 1980. Ironically, he has released few new songs since and his 'new age' album in 1988 featured re-recordings of old material. Although he performs USA dates with violinist Marie Rhines, he makes a habit of cancelling UK tours.

Albums: *Harlequin Melodies* (1968), *Mickey Newbury Sings His Own* (1968), *Looks Like Rain* (1969), *'Frisco Mabel Joy* (1971), *Heaven Help The Child* (1973), *Live At Montezuma* (1973, also issued as a double-album with *Looks Like Rain*), *I Came To Hear The Music* (1974), *Lovers* (1975), *Rusty Tracks* (1977), *His Eye Is On The Sparrow* (1978), *The Sailor* (1979), *After All These Years* (1981), *In A New Age* (1988). Compilation: *Sweet Memories* (1988).

Newman, Chris

b. 30 October 1952, Stevenage, Hertfordshire, England. This highly-accomplished guitarist gave his first public performance at the age of five, and spent time as a teenager playing with Diz Disley. In 1974 Chris joined the Pigsty Hill Light Orchestra, but left within a couple of years. Newman became a sought-after session player during the 70s, and was also a very capable producer and arranger. This was demonstrated in 1981 when he co-wrote, produced and arranged 'The Oldest Swinger In Town' by Fred Wedlock. The single reached number 4 in the UK charts, and topped a number of overseas charts, including Ireland and Israel. Chris received a silver disc for the production. He was then commissioned to write music for a variety of television and radio shows. At the same time, he was pursuing a career as a performer, touring Europe, the USA, Australia and the Middle East, both in a solo capacity and with other artists. Newman later teamed up with virtuoso harpist Máire Ní Chatasaigh (b Eire), and together they have played worldwide to great acclaim. They performed in Australia in 1988 as part of Ireland's contribution to the Bicentennial celebrations, and again the following year, to take part in the Guinness Celebration of Irish Music. *The Living Wood* was voted Folk Album of the Year by the *Daily Telegraph*, and among the newspaper's top four albums of the decade. The album was used as background music and became a signature tune for the regional UK television series *Off The Hook*. Their recordings all exude refinement and explain why they are extremely popular as a live act.

Albums: solo *Chris Newman* (1981), *Chris Newman Two* (1983); as Chris And Máire: *The Living Wood* (1988), *The Carolan Album* (1991), *Out Of Court* (1991).

Ní Chathasaigh, Máire

b. Eire. Ní Chathasaigh is one of the British Isles' leading harp players. She learned the instrument during the 70s and also learnt to play piano, tin-whistle and fiddle. She later graduated from University College, Cork with a BA Honours degree in Celtic studies. She followed this by winning the All-Ireland and Pan-Celtic Harp Competitions on a number of occasions. She then gave concert performances, as well as master-classes, in Europe, the USA and Australia, and turned professional in 1981. In 1985 Máire became the first harpist to produce an album comprised mainly of Irish traditional dance music, *The New Strung Harp*. Teaming up with guitarist Chris Newman has added a new dimension to the playing, and taken it out of the purely folk tag, by including elements of rock, jazz, and bluegrass. As its title implies, *The Carolan Album* is devoted to the work of the blind Irish harpist and composer, Turlough O'Carolan. Chris and Máire are joined on the album by musicians of the calibre of Danny Thompson, and Liam O'Flynn. Having recorded three albums with Chris, and secured an international reputation for concert performances, Máire produced *The Irish Harper*, a book of her own arrangements, in 1991.

Albums: *The New Strung Harp* (1985). Máire and Chris: *The Living Wood* (1988), *The Carolan Album* (1991), *Out Of Court* (1991).

Further reading: *The Irish Harper*, Máire Ní Chathasaigh.

Nicol, Simon

b. 13 October 1950, Muswell Hill, London, England. Vocalist/guitarist Nicol was the sole surviving member of the original Fairport Convention line-up. He has toured and recorded with Dave Swarbrick, and been involved in session work on a number of albums. He has also recorded and toured with, among others, Al Stewart, John Martyn, Julie Covington and the Albion Country Band. Many felt that Simon was overshadowed as a guitarist by former Fairport Convention member Richard Thompson. It was not until 1986 that

Simon Nicol

Nicol's long-overdue solo *Before Your Time* was released, although the well-received record did not achieve the commercial success that it deserved. In 1990 Simon provided the music for a video *Singing Games For Children* and, the same year, was recruited for the recording of the debut album by Beverley Craven. Despite these other commitments, his recording and touring work with Fairport Convention continues. Although his solo career looks sparse Nicol remains one of the most experienced performers in the UK, playing sessions and touring with countless artists.

Albums: with Dave Swarbrick *Live At The White Bear* (1982), with Swarbrick *In The Club* (1983), with Swarbrick *Close To The Wind* (1984), *Before Your Time* (1987), *Consonant Please Carol* (1992).

Nitty Gritty Dirt Band

Formed in Long Beach, California in 1965, this enduring attraction evolved from the region's traditional circuit. Founder members Jeff Hanna (guitar/vocals) and Bruce Kunkel (guitar/vocals) had worked together as the New Coast Two, prior to joining the Illegitimate Jug Band. Glen Grosclose (drums), Dave Hanna (guitar/vocals), Ralph Barr (guitar) and Les Thompson (bass/vocals) completed the embryonic Dirt Band line-up, although Groslcose and Dave Hanna quickly made way for Jimmie Fadden (drums/guitar) and Jackson Browne (guitar/vocals). Although the last musician only remained for a matter of months - he was replaced by John McEuen - his songs remained in the group's repertoire throughout their early career. *Nitty Gritty Dirt Band* comprised of jugband, vaudeville and pop material, ranging from the quirky 'Candy Man' to the orchestrated folk/pop 'Buy For Me The Rain', a minor US hit. *Ricochet* maintained this balance, following which Chris Darrow, formerly of Kaleidoscope (US), replaced Kunkel. The Dirt Band completed two further albums, and enjoyed a brief role in the film *Paint Your Wagon*, before disbanding in 1969. The group reconvened the following year around Jeff Hanna, John McEuen, Jimmie Fadden, Les Thompson and newcomer Jim Ibbotson. Having abandoned the jokey elements of their earlier incarnation, they pursued a career as purveyors of superior country-rock. The acclaimed *Uncle Charlie And His Dog Teddy* included excellent versions of Mike Nesmith's 'Some Of Shelly's Blues', Kenny Loggins' 'House At Pooh Corner' and Jerry Jeff Walker's 'Mr. Bojangles', a US Top 10 hit in 1970. *Will The Circle Be Unbroken*, recorded in Nashville, was an expansive collaboration between the group and traditional music mentors Doc Watson, Roy Acuff, Merle Travis and Earl Scruggs. Its charming informality inspired several stellar performances and

the set played an important role in breaking down mistrust between country's establishment and the emergent 'long hair' practitioners. Les Thompson left the line-up following the album's completion, but the remaining quartet, buoyed by an enhanced reputation, continued their eclectic ambitions on *Stars And Stripes Forever* and *Dreams*. In 1976 the group dropped its 'Nitty Gritty' prefix and, as the Dirt Band, undertook a pioneering USSR tour the following year. Both Hanna and Ibbotson enjoyed brief sabbaticals, during which time supplementary musicians were introduced. By 1982 the prodigals had rejoined Fadden, McEuen and newcomer Bob Carpenter (keyboards) for *Let's Go*. The Dirt Band were, by then, an American institution with an enduring international popularity. 'Long Hard Road (Sharecropper Dreams)' and 'Modern Day Romance' topped the country charts in 1984 and 1985, respectively, but the following year a now-weary McEuen retired from the line-up. Former Eagles guitarist Bernie Leadon augmented the group for *Working Band*, but left again on its completion. He was, however, featured on *Will The Circle Be Unbroken Volume Two*, on which the Dirt Band rekindled the style of their greatest artistic triumph with the aid of several starring names, including Emmylou Harris, Chet Atkins, Johnny Cash, Ricky Skaggs, Roger McGuinn and Chris Hillman. The set deservedly drew plaudits for a group about to enter the 90s with its enthusiasm still intact.

Albums: *The Nitty Gritty Dirt Band* (1967), *Ricochet* (1967), *Rare Junk* (1968), *Alive* (1968), *Uncle Charlie And His Dog Teddy* (1970), *All The Good Times* (1971), *Will The Circle Be Unbroken* (1972), *Live* (1973), *Stars And Stripes Forever* (1974), *Dreams* (1975), *Dirt Band vs The Hollywood Time Machine* (1976), *Dirt Band* (1978), *An American Dream* (1979), *Make A Little Magic* (1980), *Jealousy* (1981), *Let's Go* (1982), *Plain Dirt Fashion* (1984), *Partners, Brothers And Friends* (1985), *Hold On* (1987), *Workin' Band* (1988), *Will The Circle Be Unbroken Volume II* (1989), *Rest Of The Dream* (1991), *Not Fade Away* (1992). Compilations: *Pure Dirt* (1968), *Dead And Alive* (1969), *Dirt, Silver And Gold* (1976), *Gold From Dirt* (1980), *Early Dirt 1967-1970* (1986), *Twenty Years Of Dirt* (1986), *Country Store: The Nitty Gritty Dirt Band* (1987), *The Best Of The Nitty Gritty Dirt Band* (1988), *More Great Dirt: The Best Of The Nitty Gritty Dirt Band, Volume 2* (1989).

Noakes, Rab

A veteran of Scotland's folk circuit, Noakes' debut *Do You See The Lights*, although heavily produced, announced the arrival of a gifted songwriter. He then briefly joined Gerry Rafferty in the original Stealer's Wheel, appearing on the latter's solo

Rab Noakes

debut, *Can I Have My Money Back*, but subsequently preferred to follow his own direction. Rafferty did, however, guest on Noakes' 1972 solo collection. Signed to Warner Brothers in 1974, the artist's two albums for the company showed an increasingly American slant. *Red Pump Special* featured the famed Memphis Horns brass section, but despite critical acclaim, Noakes was unable to secure a commercial breakthrough. Further albums also met public indifference, and although he still pursues a performing career, this under-rated singer is now a producer with BBC Scotland.

Albums: *Do You See The Lights* (1970), *Rab Noakes* i (1972), *Red Pump Special* (1974), *Never Too Late* (1975), *Restless* (1978), *Rab Noakes* ii (1980), *Under The Rain* (1984).

Notes From The Underground

Based in Berkeley, California, USA, the NFTU were one of the region's first electric-folk bands. Fred Sokolow (b. 1945, Los Angeles, California, USA), an accomplished bluegrass musician, formed the group in 1965 with Mark Mandell (guitar), Joe Luke (drums) and David Gale. Mike O'Connor (bass) and Peter Ostwald (drums) replaced Gale and Luke while a pianist, Jim Work, also joined the unit prior to their recording debut, a privately-pressed EP. Work then left the line-up and his place was ultimately filled by Skip Rose. The quintet released their only album in 1968. *Notes From The Underground* was a remarkably eclectic set, featuring good-time music, jazz and Bay Area-styled interplay, but its disparate nature robbed the NFTU of any cohesion. The subsequent loss of several key members undermined their progress. In 1970 Sokolow and Mandell disbanded the group and re-emerged the following year with a new ensemble, Prince Bakaradi.

Album: *Notes From The Underground* (1968).

O'Flynn, Liam

b. Kill, County Kildare, Eire. O'Flynn, an uillean piper, is acclaimed as being one of the most influential pipers on the scene today. His father, a schoolteacher, had been a fiddle player, and Liam was brought up into a world rich in folk tradition.

He first came into contact with the uillean pipes through Sergeant Tom Armstrong of the Garda in Co. Kildare. During the 60s, O'Flynn won prizes at the Oireachtas festival and the Fleadh Ceoil, but it was not until joining the influential Irish group Planxty, in 1972, that his name came to prominence. O'Flynn has worked with other well-known names, such as John Cage and Kate Bush. The film *Cal*, featured his piping in the soundtrack written by Mark Knopfler. Both Liam and classical guitarist John Williams performed the 'Brendan Voyage Suite' at the London's Royal Festival Hall, in London, as part of the South Bank Festival.

Albums: *David Balfour* (1978, film soundtrack), with Sean Davey *The Brendan Voyage* (1980), *Liam O'Flynn* (80s), *The Fine Art Of Piping* (1992), with Sean Keane, Matt Molloy *The Fire Aflame* (1993).

Ochs, Phil

b. 19 December 1940, El Paso, Texas, d. 7 April 1976. A superior singer/songwriter, particularly adept at the topical song, Phil Ochs began his career at Ohio State University. He initially performed in a folksinging duo, the Sundowners, before moving to New York, where he joined the radical Greenwich Village enclave. Ochs' early work was inspired by Woody Guthrie, Bob Gibson and Tom Paxton, and its political nature led to his involvement with the *Broadside* magazine movement. The singer was signed to the prestigious Elektra Records label, and through his initial work was hailed as a major new talent. He achieved popular acclaim when Joan Baez took one of his compositions, 'There But For Fortune', into the pop charts. Ochs' own version later appeared on his *In Concert*, the artist's best-selling set which also featured the evocative 'When I'm Gone' and the wry 'Love Me I'm A Liberal'. Ochs' move to A&M Records in 1967 signalled a new phase in his career. *Pleasures Of The Harbour*, which included the ambitious 'Crucifixion', emphasized a greater use of orchestration, as well as an increasingly rock-based perspective. He remained a lyrical songwriter; his sense of melody was undiminished, but as the decade's causes grew increasingly blurred, so the singer became disillusioned. Although *Rehearsals For Retirement* documented the political travails of a bitter 1968, the sardonically-titled *Phil Ochs Greatest Hits* showed an imaginative performer bereft of focus. He donned a gold-lamé suit in a misguided effort to 'wed Elvis Presley to the politics of Che Guevara', but his in-concert rock 'n' roll medleys were roundly booed by an audience expecting overt social comment. This period is documented on the controversial *Gunfight At Carnegie Hall*. Ochs' later years were marked by tragedy. He was attacked during a tour of Africa and an attempted

Liam O'Flynn

Phil Ochs

strangulation permanently impaired his singing voice. Beset by a chronic songwriting block, Phil sought solace in alcohol and although a rally/concert in aid of Chile, *An Evening With Salvador Allende*, succeeded through his considerable entreaties, he later succumbed to schizophrenia. Phil Ochs' was found hanged at his sister's home on 7 April 1976. One of the finest performers of his generation, he was considered, at least for a short time, Bob Dylan's greatest rival.

Albums: *All The News That's Fit To Sing* (1964), *I Ain't Marching Anymore* (1965), *Phil Ochs In Concert* (1966), *The Pleasures Of The Harbour* (1967), *Tape From California* (1968), *Rehearsals For Retirement* (1968), *Phil Ochs Greatest Hits* (1970), *Gunfight At Carnegie Hall* (1975). Compilations: *Phil Ochs - Chords Of Fame* (1976), *Phil Ochs - Songs For Broadside* (1976), *Broadside Tapes* (1976), *A Toast To Those Who Are Gone* (1987), *There But For Fortune* (1989).

Further reading: *Phil Ochs: Death Of A Rebel*, Marc Elliott.

Odetta

b. Odetta Holmes Felious Gorden, 31 December 1930, Birmingham, Alabama, USA. A classically-trained vocalist, Odetta sang in the chorus of a 1949 Broadway production of *Finian's Rainbow*, before opting for a career in folk music. Successful residencies in San Francisco clubs, the Hungry i and Tin Angel, inspired interest in New York circles although her early releases revealed a still maturing talent. Odetta had been brought up in the blues tradition, but moved increasingly towards folk during the late 50s. Odetta had sung jazz and blues for the RCA and Riverside labels, and, only occasionally, folk for the Tradition label. Her blues was sung in the Bessie Smith tradition, but without the same emotion. Nevertheless, she recorded standards including 'House Of The Rising Sun' and 'Make Me A Pallet On Your Floor'. In 1960 she took to the solo acoustic guitar and moved to Vanguard. Possessed of a powerful voice, her style embraced gospel, jazz and blues, but eventually Odetta fell foul of the changing trends and fashions in music, and much was forgotten of her earlier work from the 50s and 60s. The singer was championed by Pete Seeger and Harry Belafonte, the latter of whom Odetta accompanied on a 1961 UK hit, 'Hole In The Bucket', while her solo career flourished with a succession of albums for the Vanguard label. The artist's emotional mixture of spiritual, ethnic and jazz styles is best captured in person and thus *Odetta At Town Hall* and *Odetta At Carnegie Hall* remain her most representative sets by revealing the full extent of her varied repertoire.

Albums: *Odetta Sings Ballads And Blues* (1956), *Odetta At The Gate Of Horn* (1957), *My Eyes Have Seen* (1959), *Christmas Spirituals* (1960), *Odetta And The Blues* (1962), *Sometimes I Feel Like Crying* (1962), *Odetta At Town Hall* (1962), *Odetta* (1963), *Odetta Sings Folk Songs* (1963), *One Grain Of Sand* (1963), *It's A Mighty World* (1964), *Odetta Sings Of Many Things* (1964), *Odetta Sings Dylan* (1965), *Ballads For Americans* (1965), *Odetta In Japan* (1965), *Odetta* (1967), *Odetta At Carnegie Hall* (1967), *Odetta Sings The Blues* (1968), *Odetta Sings* (1971), *It's Impossible* (1978). Compilations: *Best Of Odetta* (1967), *The Essential Odetta* (1989).

Ohrlin, Glenn

b. 26 October 1926, Minneapolis, Minnesota, USA. Ohrlin's father was a Swedish immigrant, and his mother's parents were from Norway. Apart from learning basic tunes and songs, and guitar technique, Glenn wanted to be a horse rider. At the age of 14, Ohrlin's family moved to California, and two years later he left home to go to Nevada to work in rodeo. He also worked on ranches throughout the West, and served in the US Army from 1945-46. After World War II, Ohrlin continued to absorb musical influences, including Flamenco guitar style, and traditional songs, learned from Mexican cowboys. He continued riding, both bareback and saddle, and, in September 1954, he and his wife moved to Mountain View, Arkansas to raise cattle. Later still, in 1960, having realized that some of the songs he was singing were important from a historical perspective, he began to collect songs from his friends and relations. Many of these were recorded in the field during the mid-60s. In April 1963, Glenn played at a Mountain View Festival, organized by the Rackensack Folklore Society. In September of the same year, Ohrlin travelled to Memphis, Tennessee, to play on the coffee house circuit. This, however, did not inspire any great reaction on the part of the music listening public at the time. He made his last rodeo ride in October 1963, at Andalusia, Alabama, and in less than three months made his debut recording, *Glenn Ohrlin*, in Illinois, in December 1963. It appeared on the University of Illinois Campus Folk Song Club Records label. The recording featured some of the songs performed at the University Folk Song Club on 14 December 1963, with other tracks taken from recordings made between 13 December and 16 March 1964. Glenn had already been recorded by Bruce Jackson during the summer of 1964. Between 1965 and 1966, Ohrlin collected and recorded a number of performers throughout the states of Arkansas, Minnesota, and North Dakota. The material ranged from unaccompanied works (some with guitar and fiddle), to material sung in Swedish and Norwegian. *The Hell-Bound*

Odetta

Train contained tracks from the concert recorded in 1963-64, at the Campus Folksong Club.

Albums: *The Hell-Bound Train - Glenn Ohrlin At The Campus Folksong Club* (1964), with other artists *The Midwinter Festival Of Traditional Music* (1970), *The Wild Buckaroo* (1983), with other artists *Roots Of Country Music* (1988). Recorded works held in sound archives at Indiana University: *Glenn Ohrlin At The Indiana University Folksong Club* (1964), *Glenn Ohrlin At The Illinois Folksong Club* (1964), *Glenn Ohrlin At The Indiana Folksong Club* (1964), *Glenn Ohrlin At The Campus Folksong Club* (1968), *The Hell-Bound Train: A Cowboy Songbook* (1973).

Further reading: *Hell-Bound Train: A Cowboy Song*, Glenn Ohrlin.

Oisin

This Irish folk group featured Geraldine MacGowan (vocals/bodhran), and Anne Conroy (accordion). For *Winds Of Change*, on Tara Records, was largely credited to MacGowan and Conroy but were supplemented by Davy Spillane (uillean pipes/low whistle), Tom McDonagh (bouzouki), Brian O'Connor (flute/whistle), Maire Bhreathnach (fiddle), Gerry O'Connor (fiddle), Steve Cooney (bass/synthesiser), Noel Bridgeman (percussion), and Shay MacGowan (vocals/guitar).

Albums: *Oisin* (1976), *Bealoideas* (1979), *Over The Moor To Maggie* (1980), *The Jeannie C* (1983), *Winds Of Change* (1987).

Old Swan Band

Formed in 1974 by Rod And Danny Stradling, the band comprised Rod Stradling (b. London, England; melodeon), Danny Stradling (b. London, England; tambourine/drum), Martin Brinsford (b. 17 August 1944, Gloucester, England; mouth organ/skulls), Fi Fraser (b. Fiona Mildred Newmarch Fraser, 31 July 1959, Barnet, Hertfordshire, England; fiddle/clarinet/hammer dulcimer), Jo Fraser (b. Jo-Anne Rachel Newmarch Fraser, 4 December 1960, St. Albans, Hertfordshire, England; whistle) and Ron Field (autoharp/banjo). The group played what was described as Southern English Country Dance music. At a time when the vast majority of other dance groups were performing Irish and Scottish dance music, the Old Swan Band were researching and revitalizing many English dance tunes that had been almost forgotten. As with many groups of the time, they were relatively short-lived due to the commitments of the various group members, with Brinsford joining Brass Monkey in 1981. Their influence resulted in a growing interest in English dance music, and the formation of a number of other groups who followed their example.

Albums: *No Reels* (1976), *Old Swan Brand* (1978), *Gamesters, Pickpockets And Harlots* (1981), *The Old Swan Band* (1984).

Ossian

This Scottish revival group, formed in 1976, performed traditional songs and tunes in an authentic setting combining contemporary instruments. The original line-up of Billy Jackson (b. Glasgow, Scotland; harp, uillean pipes, whistle, vocals), George Jackson (b. Glasgow, Scotland; cittern, guitar, whistle, flute), John Martin (b. Glasgow, Scotland; fiddle, viola), and Billy Ross (b. Glasgow, Scotland; guitar, vocals) changed in 1980 with the departure of Ross. He was replaced by Tony Cuffe (vocals/guitar/whistle/tiple). In 1981, Iain MacDonald (highland pipes/flute/whistle) joined the group. George and Billy Jackson and John Martin had played on the 1974 self-titled album by Contraband, fronted by singer Mae McKenna. The group provided music for a theatre group in Jura in 1976, which led to other theatrical music work, including providing music and songs for a play called 'Clanna Cheo'. This was a play based around the legend of Rob Roy, and it toured widely including London. *Ossian* was released on Springthyme Records. The various members have continued with other commitments outside of the group, including Billy Jackson teaming up with former member Billy Ross to record *Misty Mountain*, and George Jackson and Maggie MacInnes recording *Cairistiona*. More recent recordings have featured less Gaelic songs than before. Both Billy and George Jackson were touring with the Tag Theatre Company in 1991.

Albums: *Ossian* (1977), *St. Kilda Wedding* (1978), *Seal Song* (1981), *Dove Across The Water* (1982), *Borders* (1984), *Light On A Distant Shore* (1986); Billy Ross and Billy Jackson *Misty Mountain* (1986); George Jackson and Maggie MacInnes *Cairistiona* (1986), with William Jackson *Heart Music* (1987), with William Jackson *St. Mungo: A Celtic Suite For Glasgow* (1991); Billy Ross And John Martin *Braes Of Lochiel* (1991).

Overlanders

This UK vocal trio - Paul Arnold (aka Paul Friswell), Laurie Mason and Peter Bartholemew - initially pursued a folk-based career, but scored a surprise, if minor, US hit in 1964 with their version of 'Yesterday's Gone'. Buoyed by the addition of Terry Widlake (bass) and David Walsh (drums), they enjoyed a UK number 1 the following year with an opportunistic version of the Beatles' 'Michelle', but the reshaped group was unable to shake off a somewhat anachronistic image. A strong follow-up to their chart-topper, 'My Life', unfortunately failed to chart. Arnold left for a solo

Oyster Band

career in 1966, but despite the arrival of Ian Griffiths, the Overlanders failed to reap reward from their early success.

Album: *The Overlanders* (1966).

Oyster Band

This group originally emerged as Fiddler's Dram who had a UK Top 3 hit with 'Day Trip To Bangor', in 1979. Shortly afterwards, when the band split-up, vocalist Cathy Lesurf joined the Albion Band. A new line-up featured Ian Telfer (b. 28 May 1948, Falkirk, Scotland; vocals, fiddle, concertina, whistle), John Jones (b. 19 October 1949, Aberystwyth, Wales; vocals, melodeon), Alan Prosser (b. 17 April 1951, Wolverhampton, England; vocals, guitar) and Ian Kearey (b. 14 October 1954, London, England; vocals, bass guitar, banjo). Drummer Russell Lax joined the group in 1986, but a year later, after *Wide Blue Yonder*, Kearey left. Shortly after this Ray 'Chopper' Cooper (b. 22 September 1954, Romford, Essex, England) joined the band. It was with releases such as *Liberty Hall* and *Wide Blue Yonder*, and their signing up with Cooking Vinyl Records, that the group's harder-edged style became apparent. *Wide Blue Yonder* included the Nick Lowe song 'Rose Of England', a driving version far removed from the group's earlier folk roots. Both *Wide Blue Yonder* and *Step Outside* were produced by Clive Gregson. In 1989, the Oyster Band released a 10-inch single version of New Order's 'Love Vigilantes'. *Freedom And Rain*, recorded with June Tabor, saw the Oyster Band continuing to follow more of a rock music path. A concert and ceilidh band, they have succeeded in lowering the average age of many a folk audience by bringing together some of the best elements of both folk and rock music.

Albums: *Jack's Alive* (1980), *English Rock 'N' Roll - The Early Years 1800-1850* (1982), *Lie Back And Think Of England* (1983), *20 Golden Tie-Slackeners* (1984), *Liberty Hall* (1985), *Step Outside* (1986), *Wide Blue Yonder* (1987), *Freedom And Rain* (1990), *Deserters* (1992).

P

Pacheco, Tom

Singer and songwriter, b. Massachusetts, USA. His father, Tony, had played guitar, in Europe, with Django Reinhardt. He later moving to a farm in Massachusetts, where he also owned a music store and taught guitar. Tom started playing guitar at the age of 10, studying both Flamenco and classical styles whilst in High school. Leaving home at the age of 16, and already writing his own songs, he moved into the Greenwich Village scene in New York during the 60s. Gradually he emerged into the non-traditional country field of music, his early albums for RCA and CBS not being too well received. During the late 70s, Pacheco turned towards rock'n'roll, his song 'All Fly Away' being recorded by Jefferson Starship as the title track of their *Dragonfly* album. Spending 1982 and 1983 playing, and living, in Austin, Texas, Tom continued to build a following for himself. He then spent two years in Woodstock, before moving to Nashville in 1986. In 1987, he moved to Oldcastle, County Meath, Ireland, and then to Dublin. It was whilst here that *Eagle In The Rain* was recorded, which contained the excellent 'You Will Not Be Forgotten', and 'Jesus In A Leather Jacket'. Apart from being produced by Arty McGlynn, of Patrick Street fame, the album brought Pacheco some overdue critical acclaim. Appearances at the Cambridge Folk Festival in 1990, and sharing the bill with Townes Van Zandt at the Berlin Independence Day celebrations in September 1990, and numerous UK appearances, have all helped to get his music across to a wider audience.
Albums: *Pacheco And Alexander* (1971), *Swallowed Up In The Great American Heartland* (1976), *The Outsider* (1977), *Eagle In The Rain* (1989), *Sunflowers And Scarecrows* (1991).

Palmer, Clive

The 'forgotten one' from the Incredible String Band, Palmer founded the the group as a duo with Robin Williamson, and featured on the debut album. Subsequently, he moved to India, and, on his return, formed the Famous Jug band with Jill Johnson (vocals), Pete Berryman (guitar) and Henry Bartlett (jug), and himself on banjo. After recording *Sunshine Possibilities* (1969), he worked with C.O.B. (Clive's Original Band), along with John Bidwell (banjo) and Mick Bennett (percussion), on *Spirit Of Love* (1971) and *Moyshe Mcstiff And The Tartan Lancers Of The Sacred Heart* (1972). Since then, he

has continued to work with a variety of units, and as a solo performer. A highly accomplished musician, the Original String Band would probably have sounded rather differently had he remained with them.
Selected album: *Just Me* (1978).

Papasov, Ivo

b. 1952, Kurdzhali, Thrace, Bulgaria. The most famous practitioner of Bulgaria's most favoured musical format; master clarinetist Ivo Papasov is the King Of Wedding Music. Though Western European eyebrows might be raised at such a title, it equates Papasov with the status of superstar in his native country. Papasov and his Orchestra tour the Balkans, playing several weddings a week (many couples will re-arrange the dates of their ceremonies to coincide with a blank entry in his diary). He descends from a long line of zurna (double-reed instrument) and clarinetists. After forming his first ensemble in 1974, he gradually evolved from a traditional Thracian repertoire into a jazz-inspired improvisational set. This new work nevertheless maintained the complex time-signatures required of traditional Bulgarian dance music. Papasov had stumbled over the incredibly popular formula which would see him become a national toast. Though he boasts many domestic releases, the two albums listed below were the first to be circulated internationally.
Selected albums: *Orpheus Ascending* (1989), *Balkanology* (1991).

Pappalardi, Felix

b. 1939, New York City, New York, USA, d. April 17 1983. A highly respected bass player and arranger, Pappalardi was present at countless sessions, when folk musicians started to employ electric instruments on a regular basis. Ian And Sylvia, Fred Neil, Tom Rush, and Richard and Mimi Farina were among those benefiting from his measured contributions. He later worked with the Mugwumps, a seminal New York folk-rock quartet which included Cass Elliott and Denny Doherty, later of the Mamas And The Papas, and future Lovin' Spoonful guitarist, Zalman Yanovsky. Pappalardi also oversaw sessions by the Vagrants and the Youngbloods, contributing several original songs, composed with his wife Gail Collins, to both groups' releases. An association with Cream established his international reputation. Felix produced the group's studio work from *Disraeli Gears* onwards, a position he maintained when bassist Jack Bruce embarked on a solo career in 1969. Cream's break-up left a vacuum which Pappalardi attempted to fill with Mountain, the brash rock group he formed with former Vagrant guitarist Leslie West. Partial deafness, attributed to exposure to the excessive volumes that Mountain performed at, ultimately forced the bassist to retire and subsequent work was confined to the recording studio. He recorded two albums in the late 70s, one of which, *Felix Pappalardi & Creation*, included the services of Paul Butterfield and Japanese musicians, Masayuki Higuchi (drums), Shigru Matsumoto (bass), Yoshiaki Iijima (guitar) and Kazuo Takeda (guitar). Pappalardi's life ended tragically in April 1983 when he was shot dead by his wife.

Albums: *Felix Pappalardi & Creation* (1976), *Don't Worry, Ma* (1979).

Partridge, Don

b. 1945, Bournemouth, Dorset, England. Self-styled 'King of the Street Singers', Partridge was discovered busking in London's Berwick Street market by former Viscount Don Paul, who in turn became his manager. 'Rosie', the singer's self-penned debut single, was reputedly recorded for the sum of £8, but became a surprise UK Top 5 hit in 1968. The artist's unconventional lifestyle and penchant for straight-talking resulted in good copy, and engendered greater publicity than his novelty status might otherwise suggest. 'Blue Eyes', Partridge's follow-up single, reached number 3, yet the song is less well recalled than its ebullient predecessor. The singer later supervised *The Buskers*, a various-artists compilation, and enjoyed one further chart entry with 'Breakfast On Pluto' in 1969. After this brief flirtation with fame, Partridge returned to busking roots and continued to perform into the 90s.

Album: *Don Partridge* (1968).

Patrick Street

After touring the USA in 1986, the musicians, Kevin Burke, Andy Irvine and Jackie Daly, returned to Ireland and formed a permanent group, adding the guitarist, Arty McGlynn. From 1987-1991, they issued three albums under the name of Patrick Street, and reunited for a further release and tour in 1993. Kevin Burke (fiddle) is of London Irish parents, although his playing is influenced by the Sligo style. Before joining Patrick Street he played an important role in the Bothy Band's success, and has recorded with Arlo Guthrie and Christy Moore. He released the solo albums, *If The Cap Fits* and *Up Close*. Andy Irvine (guitar, harmonica, mandolin and bouzuki), a founder member of both Sweeny's Men and Planxty, has worked with many other leading figures in Irish, Scottish and English folk. Jackie Daly (accordion) first came to international attention when he joined De Dannan. Like Daly, Arty McGlynn started out on the accordion, but switched to the guitar,

inspired by the late 50s rock 'n' roll greats. At the age of 15, McGlynn joined an Irish showband and spent 18 years touring Irish dance halls. Feeling stifled, he switched to traditional music, and sang solo in folk clubs. His European tours with Andy Irvine led to his participation in Patrick Street. More recently, he was an important element in the high flying Four Men And A Dog. A true Irish supergroup, Patrick Street's main success has been in the USA, but their four albums have also registered strongly in their home country, and in the UK folk charts. The group has proved to be equal to the sum of its parts, and has effectively mixed dance tunes with stirring songs and ballads sung by Irvine.

Albums: *Patrick Street* (1987), *No. 2 Patrick Street* (1989), *Irish Times* (1991), *All In Good Time* (1993).

Paxton, Tom

b. 31 October 1937, Chicago, Illinois, USA. Paxton's interest in folk music developed as a student at the University of Oklahoma. In 1960 he moved to New York and became one of several aspiring performers to frequent the city's Greenwich Village coffee-house circuit. Paxton made his professional debut at the Gaslight, the renowned folk haunt which also issued the singer's first album. Two topical song publications, *Sing Out!* and *Broadside*, began publishing his original compositions which bore a debt to the traditional approach of Pete Seeger and Bob Gibson. Tom also auditioned to join the Chad Mitchell Trio, but although he failed, the group enjoyed a 1963 hit with 'The Marvellous Toy', one of his early songs. The following year Paxton was signed to the Elektra label for whom he recorded his best known work. *Ramblin' Boy* indicated the diversity which marked his recorded career and contained several highly-popular performances including 'The Last Thing On My Mind', 'Goin' To The Zoo' and 'I Can't Help But Wonder Where I'm Bound'. Subsequent releases continued this mixture of romanticism, protest and children's songs, while 'Lyndon Johnson Told The Nation' (*Ain't That News*) and 'Talkin' Vietnam Pot Luck Blues' (*Morning Again*) revealed a talent for satire and social comment. *The Things I Notice Now* and *Tom Paxton 6* enhanced Paxton's reputation as a mature and complex songwriter, yet he remained better known for such simpler compositions as 'Jennifer's Rabbit' and 'Leaving London'. Paxton left Elektra during the early 70s and although subsequent recordings proved less popular, he commanded a loyal following, particularly in the UK, where he was briefly domiciled. *How Come The Sun* (1971) was the first of three albums recorded during this period and although his work became less prolific, Paxton

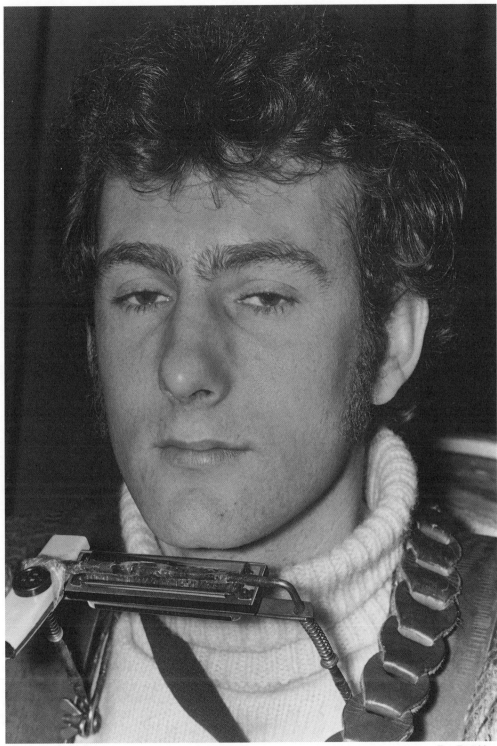

Don Partridge

Tom Paxton

was still capable of incisive, evocative songwriting, such as 'The Hostage', which chronicled the massacre at Attica State Prison. This powerful composition was also recorded by Judy Collins. Although Paxton was never fêted in the manner of his early contemporaries Bob Dylan, Phil Ochs and Eric Anderson, his work reveals a thoughtful, perceptive craftsmanship.

Albums: *Live At The Gaslight* (early 60s), *Ramblin' Boy* (1964), *Ain't That News* (1965), *Outward Bound* (1966), *Morning Again* (1968), *The Things I Notice Now* (1969), *Tom Paxton 6* (1970), *The Compleat Tom Paxton* (1971), *How Come The Sun* (1971), *Peace Will Come* (1972), *New Songs Old Friends* (1973), *Children's Song Book* (1974), *Something In My Life* (1975), *Saturday Night* (1976), *New Songs From The Briar Patch* (1977), *Heroes* (1978), *Up And Up* (1980), *The Paxton Report* (1981), *The Marvellous Toy And Other Gallimaufry* (1984), *In The Orchard* (1985), *One Million Lawyers And Other Disasters* (1985), *Even A Gray Day* (1986), *The Marvellous Toy* (1980), *And Loving You* (1988), *Politics-Live* (1989). Compilations: *The Very Best Of Tom Paxton* (1988), *Storyteller* (1989).

Pegg, Dave

b. Birmingham, England, 1947. After persuading his father to buy him a guitar, Pegg worked on the local rock scene with such as John Bonham (Led Zeppelin). He swapped bass guitar for a stand-up bass, and joined The Ian Campbell Folk Group, with whom he learnt to play the mandolin. More importantly, he was introduced to Dave Swarbrick, who, in 1969, enabled him to become the bass guitarist with Fairport Convention. It was the beginnning of a two-man partnership which steered Fairport through until 1979. Pegg then moved to Jethro Tull. In 1978, he bought an old Baptist chapel and converted it into Woodworm Studios, which became a recording Mecca for folk rock bands. Woodworm also acts as a label for various Fairport associates. In 1985, a reconvened Fairport Convention recorded for the first time for some years, and Pegg was firmly in control of both the band and the Cropredy reunion festivals - by then a regular August event. Three years previously he had released his only solo album, which, like Pegg himself, was jovial, none too serious, and filled with character. With his wife, Christine, Dave Pegg (Peggy) is now the acknowledged heart and soul of Fairport Convention.

Album: *The Cocktail Cowboy Goes It Alone* (1982).

Pentangle

Formed in 1967, the Pentangle was inspired by *Bert And John*, a collaborative album by folk musicians Bert Jansch (b. 3 November 1943, Glasgow, Scotland) and John Renbourn. Vocalist Jacqui McShee, an established figure on the traditional circuit, joined Danny Thompson (b. April 1939; bass) and Terry Cox (drums), both of Alexis Korner's Blues Incorporated, in a quintet which would also embrace blues and jazz forms. Their respective talents were expertly captured on *The Pentangle*, where the delicate acoustic interplay between Jansch and Renbourn was brilliantly underscored by Thompson's sympathetic support and McShee's soaring intonation. Stylish original material balanced songs pulled from folk's heritage ('Let No Man Steal Your Thyme', 'Brunton Town'), while the inclusion of the Staple Singers 'Hear My Call' confirmed the group's eclectism. This feature was expanded on the double-set *Sweet Child*, which included two compositions by jazz bassist Charles Mingus, 'Haitian Fight Song' and 'Goodbye Pork Pie Hat'. The unit enjoyed considerable commercial success with *Basket Of Light*, which included 'Light Flight', the theme song to the UK television series, *Take Three Girls*. However, despite an undoubted dexterity and the introduction of muted electric instruments, subsequent releases were marred by a sense of sterility, and lacked the passion of concurrent releases undertaken by the two guitarists. Pentangle was disbanded in 1972, following which Thompson began a partnership with John Martyn. Cox undertook a lucrative session career before backing French singer Charles Aznavour, and while Jansch continued his solo career, McShee fronted the John Renbourn Band between 1974-81. The original Pentangle reconvened the following year for a European tour and *Open The Door*, although defections owing to outside commitments led to considerable changes. McShee and Jansch were joined by Nigel Portman-Smith (bass) and Mike Piggott for *In The Round*, but by 1991 the latter had departed and Peter Kirtly (guitar) and Gerry Conway (drums) were now featured in the group. The future of this particular line-up was then jeopardized by plans to reunite the founding quintet, although by 1993 the band had continued to record.

Albums: *The Pentangle* (1968), *Sweet Child* (1968), *Basket Of Light* (1969), *Cruel Sister* (1970), *Solomon's Seal* (1972), *Open The Door* (1982), *In The Round* (1988), *So Early In The Spring* (1989), *One More Road* (1993). Compilations: *Reflections* (1971), *History Book* (1971), *Pentangling* (1973), *The Pentangle Collection* (1975), *Anthology* (1978), *The Essential Pentangle Volume 1* (1987), *The Essential Pentangle Volume 2* (1987), *People On The Highway 1968 - 1971* (1993), *One More Road* (1993).

Persen, Mari Boine

b. Gamehisnjarqa, Norway. Mari is a Sami, one of a small population of Arctic Europe. Spread across the northern extremes of Finland, Norway, Sweden and the former Soviet Union, the Sami are divided by politics but unified by culture and tradition. Having left teaching for music, Mari has for over a decade been writing, recording and performing material often based on traditional poetry. She has released two albums in Scandinavia although only *Gula Gula - Hear The Voices Of The Fore-Mothers* - is available elsewhere. Mari works with a variety of musicians, many playing traditional instruments such as the dozo n'koni, ganga and darboka, and through them has created a cross-cultural style whose roots remain with the Sami.

Album: *Gula Gula - Hear The Voices Of The Fore-Mothers* (1990).

Peter, Paul And Mary

Peter Yarrow (b. 31 May 1938, New York City, New York, USA), Noel Paul Stookey (b. Paul Stookey, 30 November 1937, Baltimore, Maryland, USA) and Mary Allin Travers (b. 7 November 1937, Louisville, Kentucky, USA) began performing together in the spring of 1961. They were brought together by Albert Grossman, one of folk music's successful entrepreneurs, in an attempt to create a contemporary Kingston Trio. The three singers were already acquainted through the close-knit coffee-house circuit, although Dave Van Ronk was briefly considered as a possible member. The group popularized several topical songs, including 'If I Had A Hammer' and were notable early interpreters of Bob Dylan compositions. In 1963 their version of 'Blowin' In The Wind' reached number 2 in the US chart while a follow-up reading of 'Don't Think Twice, It's Alright' also broached the Top 10. They were also renowned for singing children's songs, the most memorable of which was the timeless 'Puff The Magic Dragon'. The trio became synonymous with folk's liberal traditions, but were increasingly perceived as old-fashioned as the 60s progressed. Nonetheless a 1966 selection, *Album*, included material by Laura Nyro and featured assistance from Paul Butterfield, Mike Bloomfield and Al Kooper, while the following year's 'I Dig Rock 'N' Roll Music' became their fifth US Top 10 hit. Peter, Paul And Mary enjoyed their greatest success in 1969 with 'Leaving On A Jet Plane'. This melodramatic John Denver song reached number 1 in the US and number 2 in the UK, but by then the individual members were branching out in different directions. Yarrow had been the primary force behind *You Are What You Eat*, an eccentric hippie film which also featured Tiny Tim and John Simon, and in 1970 he, Travers and Stookey announced their formal dissolution. The three performers embarked on solo careers but were ultimately unable to escape the legacy of their

Peter, Paul And Mary

former group. They reunited briefly in 1972 for a George McGovern Democratic Party rally, and again in 1978. They have since continued to perform material reminiscent of their golden era. Although criticized for a smooth and wholesome delivery, Peter, Paul and Mary was one of the era's most distinctive acts and played a crucial bridging role between two contrasting generations of folk music.

Albums: *Peter, Paul And Mary* (1962), *Peter, Paul And Mary - Moving* (1963), *In The Wind* (1963), *Peter, Paul And Mary In Concert* (1964), *A Song Will Rise* (1965), *See What Tomorrow Brings* (1965), *Peter, Paul And Mary Album* (1966), *Album 1700* (1967), *Late Again* (1968), *Peter, Paul And Mommy* (1969), *Reunion* (1978), *Such Is Love* (1982), *No Easy Walk To Freedom* (1988), *Peter, Paul And Mommy Too* (1993). Compilations: *10 Years Together/The Best Of Peter, Paul And Mary* (1970), *Most Beautiful Songs* (1973), *Collection* (1982). Solo albums: Peter Yarrow *Peter* (1972), *That's Enough For Me* (1973), *Hard Times* (1975); Paul Stookey *Paul And* (1971), *Band And Body Works* (1980); Mary Travers *Mary* (1971), *Morning Glory* (1972), *All My Choices* (1973), *Circles* (1974), *It's In Everyone Of Us* (1978).

Peters, Brian

b. 15 December 1954, Stockport, Cheshire, England. Peters started playing guitar at the age of 15 and subsequently appeared in a college rock band. In 1978, he took up the concertina, to accompany his singing and started the round of folk club floor spots years later. His first professional booking was at the Unicorn Folk Club, Manchester, in September 1981. Combining a day job with club bookings, Brian started to learn to play the melodeon and was signed to Fellside Records in 1985. *Persistence Of Memory* was released to critical acclaim from the folk press. He appeared on BBC Radio's *Folk On 2* in 1988, and a year later signed to Harbourtown for his next release, *Fools Of Fortune*. This comprised largely of traditional tunes and songs arranged by Peters including 'Dallas Rag', a departure from the reels, jigs and hornpipes normally associated with concertina players. *Fools Of Fortune* was voted *Folk Roots* magazine's Album Of The Year, in the folk and country music category. In addition to touring clubs and festivals, Brian has also done session work for Mike Harding, and Hughie Jones, formerly of the Spinners. He has also performed with Sara Grey (b. 22 March 1940, Boston, Massachusetts, USA; banjo/vocals), and Roger Wilson (guitar/vocals), as the Lost Nation Band since 1990. *Seeds Of Time* was part funded by North West Arts. Peters continues to play folk clubs, both at home and abroad, and his following and popularity, continue to grow.

Albums: *Persistence Of Memory* (1986), *Fools Of Fortune* (1989), *Seeds Of Time* (1992).

Phillips, Bruce 'Utah'

b. 1935, Cleveland, Ohio, USA. Phillips's family were labour organizers and in 1947 they moved to Utah. Bruce subsequently worked at Yellowstone National Park, and, while there, he was nicknamed 'Utah'. When he left the Army, after serving in Korea, he became politically active, campaigning for a number of causes committed to peace. He ran for the Senate in 1968, but did not pursue a political career. After travelling to New York, he attempted unsuccessfully to sell some of his songs for publication. He recorded his first album for Prestige in 1960. In 1969 Phillips started travelling and singing, doing his first show in Norfolk, Virginia. In 1974, he took up truck farming. While based on a farm near Spokane, Washington, he wrote essays and poetry. Phillips earlier 'hoboed' around the USA, playing at free concerts and for trade unionists and, not surprisingly given his background, he specialized in union and railroad travelling songs. With the demise of the railroads, one song he sang was particularly poignant, 'Daddy, What's A Train?'. His first release for Philo Records, *Good Though!* includes the story with the subtle title of 'Moose Turd Pie'. The whole album is given over to songs and stories about hoboing and trains. The later *All Used Up: A Scrapbook* includes the classic 'Hallelujah! I'm A Bum'. *El Capitan* featured songs taken from the point of view of the working man and included the song 'Enola Gay', about the dropping of the first atomic bomb. Phillips's songs have been recorded by other artists including Joan Baez.

Albums: *Bruce 'Utah' Phillips* (1960), *Welcome To Caffe Lena* (60s), *Good Though!* (1968), *El Capitan* (1969), *All Used Up: A Scrapbook* (1975), *We Have Fed You All For A Thousand Years* (1984).

Further reading: *Starlight On The Rails And Other Songs*, Utah Phillips.

Phranc

b. 1958, Los Angeles, California, USA. Before her career as the self-styled 'Jewish-American lesbian folksinger' Phranc had served an apprenticeship, of sorts, by appearing in LA 'hardcore' groups (Gender, Catholic Discipline and Castration Squad). On her return to acoustic playing in 1980, Phranc's sets consisted of autobiographical, part-comic songs, at times performed to similar hardcore audiences from her recent past. These appearances led to the gay coffee-house/folk circuit. Her warmly received *Folksinger* set a standard with titles such as 'Female Mudwrestling', 'Amazons' and 'One O'The Girls'. Her willingness to tackle such subjects as her

Phranc

sexuality, left-wing politics and her own family problems have so far prevented her from achieving anything beyond cult status. Phranc's third album was highlighted by her role as support act on Morrissey's first full British tour of 1991.

Albums: *Folksinger* (1986), *I Enjoy Being A Girl* (1989), *Positively Phranc* (1991).

Pigsty Hill Light Orchestra

This group formed to play at Fred Wedlock's New Years Party in 1968. All the members came from various UK folk groups: Dave Creech (b. 4 March 1938, Bristol, England; trumpet/vocals/jug/trumpet mouthpiece) from the Elastic Band, Barry Back (b. 10 April 1944, Bristol, England, d. 2 April 1992; guitar/vocals/kazoo) and Andy Leggett (31 March 1942, Much Wenlock, Shropshire, England; vocals/guitar/brass) from the Alligator Jug Thumpers, and John Turner (b. 2 January 1947, Bristol, Avon, England; vocals/bass) from the Downsiders folk group. The party, held at the Troubadour club in Clifton, Bristol, England, became the birthplace of the Pigsty Hill Light Orchestra. The style of music was loosely based on jazz and blues from the 20s and 30s, and a variety of unorthodox instruments were employed to produce what became a highly original sound. Whether it be a paraffin funnel, ballcock sections from toilets, jugs and so on, they played it. In 1970, they released *Phlop!*, and *Melody Maker* voted them one of the bands most likely to succeed. The following year, they made their first Cambridge Folk Festival appearance. Fred Wedlock's *The Folker* and *Frollicks*, released in 1971 and 1973 respectively, featured members from the PHLO. Sadly, after a busy time playing the club and college circuit both at home and abroad, the group disbanded in May 1979. During that time, there had been various personnel changes, Turner had left in 1970, and Back departed in 1972. That same year the group were augmented by Dave Paskett (b. Dave Paskett Smith, 3 June 1944, Potters Bar, Hertfordshire, England; vocals/guitar), who remained for only two years, and John Hays (percussion/vocals), who stayed until 1979. In 1974, with the departure of both Leggett and Paskett, Chris Newman (b. 30 October 1952, Stevenage, Hertfordshire, England; guitar/bass) joined, as did Henry Davies (bass/brass). More changes occurred in 1975 with the departure of Davies, when Ricky Gold (bass) joined them. A year later, in 1976, Robert Greenfield (b. 14 May 1949, Norfolk, England; guitar) joined as Newman had now left the group. Finally, after Greenfield left in 1978, they were joined by Patrick Small (guitar/kazoo/vocals). Bill Cole (bass), joined the group for a short while, and appeared on *Piggery Joker*. He had also played with the Ken Colyer band. Despite the fairly frequent changes in their line-up, the group were still able to secure a strong and loyal following, and continued

recording. A chance telephone call came in 1988, asking Back to resurrect the line-up for a 'one-off' booking at the Village Pump Festival, Trowbridge, Wiltshire. The group, this time, included Hannah Wedlock, Fred's daughter, on vocals. In 1990, the band played the Sidmouth Folk Festival, and at the Tonder Festival, in Denmark, when they were on the bill with Peggy Seeger and Arlo Guthrie. The group are again playing clubs and festivals, and have reached a new audience, to add to those who knew them first time round. True to form, more changes occurred with the departure of both Small and Wedlock in December 1991. They were replaced by Jim Reynolds (b. 15 August 1950, Bristol, Avon, England; vocals/guitar) and Dave Griffiths (b. 23 August 1948, Leeds, West Yorkshire, England; mandolin/fiddle/bass/washboard), reverting the five-piece group to its early jug band sound.
Albums: *Phlop!* (1970), *Piggery Joker* (1972), *The Pigsty Hill Light Orchestra* (1976), *Back On The Road Again* (1991).

Planxty

This early 70s Irish group originally featured Christy Moore (b. 7 May 1945, Dublin, Eire; , Donal Lunny (guitar, bouzouki, synthesizer), Liam O'Flynn (uilleann pipes) and Andy Irvine (guitar, mandolin, bouzouki, vocals). After two albums, Lunny left, to be replaced by Johnny Moynihan (bouzouki). In 1974, Moore left and was replaced by Paul Brady (b. 19 May 1947, Co. Tyrone, Northern Ireland; vocals, guitar). The name Planxty is an Irish word for an air that is written to thank or honour a person. The group remained highly popular throughout its existence and their records sold well. Moynihan then left to join De Danann. After splitting up, the original group re-formed, this time with Matt Molloy (flute), who later joined the Chieftains in September 1979. Moore and Lunny departed once more in 1981 to form Moving Hearts. *Words And Music* featured the Bob Dylan song 'I Pity The Poor Immigrant'. The group were only ever formed as an extension of the various group members' solo commitments, and though they were always in demand at festivals, personal career moves saw an end to the line-up. By the time *The Best Of Planxty Live* emerged, they were pursuing solo projects.
Albums: *Planxty* (1972), *The Well Below The Valley* (1973), *Cold Blow And The Rainy Night* (1974), *After The Break* (1979), *The Woman I Loved So Well* (1980), *Timedance* (1981), *Words And Music* (1983), *The Best Of Planxty Live* (1987). Compilations: *The Planxty Collection* (1976), *The High Kings Of Tara* (1980), *Ansi!* (1984).

Plethyn

Plethyn were formed during the 70s and comprised Linda Healy (b. 11 May 1958, Welshpool, Powys, Wales), Roy Griffiths (b. 15 December 1952, Welshpool, Powys, Wales) and John Gittins (b. 30 November 1951, Welshpool, Powys, Wales). The name Plethyn is meant to convey the notion of three harmonic voices blending together to form one sound, like the three strands in a plait. Having started with local performances, the group extended their territory to cover the whole of Wales. From initial appearances on Welsh television, and playing at a festival in Brittany, they released *Blas Y Pridd*, which combined traditional and contemporary folk songs. They performed at the National Eisteddfod during the same year. The trio performed 'Can I Cymru' ('Song For Wales'), at the Pan Celtic Festival, in Killarney, Eire, in 1980, and two years later toured Sardinia. *Caneuon Gwerin I Blant* was an album of traditional children's songs. In 1985, the group toured California, USA, and in 1990, Vancouver, Canada. With numerous television appearances and regular airplay on Radio Cymru, they achieved sufficient fame to be given their own television series, *Blas Y Pridd*, on Channel S4C in 1991.
Albums: *Blas Y Pridd* (1979), *Golau Tan Gwmwl* (1980), *Rhown Garreg Ar Garreg* (1981), *Teulu'r Tir* (1983), *Caneuon Gwerin I Blant* (1984), *Byw A Bod* (1987), *Drws Agored* (1991). Solo album: Linda Healy *Amser* (1989).

Pogues

The London punk scene of the late 70s inspired some unusual intermingling of styles and the Pogues (then known as Pogue Mahone) performed punky versions of traditional Irish folk songs in pubs throughout the capital. They were fronted by singer Shane MacGowan (b. 25 December 1957, Kent, England) and also included Peter 'Spider' Stacy (tin whistle), Jem Finer (banjo/mandolin), James Fearnley (guitar/piano accordion), Cait O'Riordan (bass) and Andrew Ranken (drums). MacGowan had spent his late teen years singing in a punk group called the Nipple Erectors ('the Nips') which also contained Fearney. After several complaints the band changed their name (Pogue Mahone is 'kiss my arse' in Gaelic) and soon attracted the attention of the Clash who asked them to be their opening act. Record companies were perturbed by the band's occasionally chaotic live act where they would sometimes fight onstage and Stacy kept time by banging his head with a beer tray. In 1984 Stiff Records signed them and recorded *Red Roses For Me,* containing several traditional tunes as well as excellent originals like 'Streams Of Whiskey' and 'Dark Streets Of London'. Elvis Costello produced

Rum, Sodomy And The Lash on which Philip Chevron, formerly a guitarist with the Radiators From Space, replaced Finer who was on 'paternity leave'. The group was established as a formidable and unique live act and the record entered the UK Top 20. There were further changes when the multi-instrumentalist Terry Woods (a co-founder of Steeleye Span) joined and Cait O'Riordan was replaced by Darryl Hunt. She later married Elvis Costello. The group developed a strong political stance and their video to accompany the single 'A Pair Of Brown Eyes' had to be re-edited because the group were filmed spitting on a poster of Prime Minister, Margaret Thatcher. 'We represent the people who don't get the breaks. People can look at us and say, "My God, if that bunch of tumbledown wrecks can do it, so can I"', explained Chevron in a press interview.

If I Should Fall From Grace With God was produced by Steve Lillywhite and embraced Middle Eastern and Spanish sounds. It sold more than 200,000 copies in the USA and 'Fairytale Of New York', a rumbustious but poignant duet by MacGowan and Lillywhite's wife Kirsty MacColl, was a Christmas number 2 hit in the UK in 1987. In the autumn of 1989 there were fears for the future of the group when MacGowan's heavy drinking led to him pulling out of several shows. He was due to join the band in the USA for a prestigious tour with Bob Dylan when he collapsed at London's Heathrow Airport. He missed all the support spots with Dylan and the band played without him. 'Other groups in a situation like that would've either said, "Let's get rid of the guy" or "Let's split up", but we're not the sort to do that. We're all part of each other's problems whether we like it or not', said Chevron. *Peace And Love* featured songs written by nearly every member of the group and its eclectic nature saw them picking up the hurdy-gurdy, the cittern and the mandola. Its erratic nature drew criticism from some quarters, mainly from original fans who had enjoyed the early folk-punk rants. While the rest of the group are clearly strong players it is widely accepted that MacGowan is the most talented songwriter. His output has always been highly sporadic but there are fears that the drinking that fuelled his earlier creativity may have slowed him to a standstill. In an interview in 1989 he said he had not been 'dead-straight sober' since he was 14 and that he drank in quantity because 'it opened his mind to paradise'. It was announced in September 1991 that MacGowan had left the band and had been replaced by the former Clash singer, Joe Strummer. This relationship lasted until June the following year when Strummer stepped down and the lead vocalist job went to Spider Stacy.

Albums: *Red Roses For Me* (1984), *Rum, Sodomy And The Lash* (1985), *If I Should Fall From Grace With God* (1988), *Peace And Love* (1989). Compilation: *The Best Of The Pogues* (1991), *The Rest Of The Best* (1992).

Pokrovsky, Dmitri

b. Dmitri Pokrovsky, Russia. Pokrovsky's research into the traditional folk songs of his native Russia won him the Gorbachev award, the former Soviet government's highest artistic accolade. After initially studying conducting at the Gnessin Institute in Moscow, he took inspiration from ancient songs he heard women singing in a small remote village. He travelled all over Russia studying the music of the peasants and formed his own 'living laboratory', a study of village life where artists work closely with psychologists and scientists. *The Wild Field* by the Dmitri Pokrovsky Ensemble is the result of their research - a catalogue of communal, wedding and dance songs and other aspects of musical life of a remote part of southern Russia.

Selected album: *The Wild Field* (1991).

Poppy Family

This Canadian folk-rock quartet was fronted by Terry Jacks (b. Winnipeg, Manitoba, Canada) and Susan Jacks (b. Susan Peklevits, Vancouver, British Columbia, Canada). Vancouver-based Terry led local group the Chessmen before teaming with, and later marrying, singer Peklevits. They later added guitarist/organist Craig MacCaw and percussionist Satwan Singh (who had played tabla with Ravi Shankar). The group had a transatlantic Top 10 hit with Terry's song 'Which Way You Goin' Billy' in 1970, which they had recorded and originally released in the UK the previous year. They had four more US chart entries before Terry and Susan divorced and went separate ways professionally in 1973. Although Susan's voice was the main feature of the Poppy Family her later recordings on Mercury and Epic had little success. Terry however had further success with a plaintive version of a Jacques Brel and Rod McKuen song 'Seasons In The Sun'.

Albums: *Which Way You Goin' Billy* (1970), *Poppyseeds* (1971).

Previn, Dory

b Dory Langdon, 27 October 1937, Woodbridge, New Jersey, USA, she was the daughter of a musician who became a child singer and dancer in New Jersey, graduating to musical theatre as a chorus line member. Her abilities as a songwriter next brought Langdon work composing music for television programmes. After moving to Hollywood, she met and married André Previn in 1959, the year in which he composed the tune 'No

Words For Dory'. Now a lyricist for movie soundtracks, Dory Previn worked with Andre, Elmer Bernstein and others on songs for such films as *Pepe*, *Two For The Seesaw*, and *Valley Of The Dolls*, whose theme tune was a big hit for Dionne Warwick in 1967. By now the Previns had separated and in the late 60s Dory turned to more personal lyrics, publishing a book of poems before launching a recording career with United Artists. Produced by Nik Venet, her early albums were noted for angry, intimate and often despairing material like 'The Lady With The Braid' and 'Who Will Follow Norma Jean ?'. The title track of *Mary C. Brown & The Hollywood Sign* was based on a true story of a suicide attempt and was turned by Previn into a stage musical. In 1974, she left U.A. for Warner Brothers where Joel Dorn produced the 1976 album,. In that year she also published her memoirs, *Midnight Baby*.

Albums: *On My Way To Where* (1970), *Mythical Kings & Iguanas* (1971), *Reflections In A Mud Puddle* (1971), *Mary C. Brown & The Hollywood Sign* (1972), *Live At Carnegie Hall* (1973), *Dory Previn* (1975), *We Are Children Of Coincidence And Harpo Marx* (1976), *1 AM Phone Calls* (1977).
Further reading: *Midnight Baby*, Dory Previn.

Prine, John

b. 10 October 1946, Maywood, Illinois, USA. John came from a musical background in that his Grandfather had played with Merle Travis. Prine started playing guitar at the age of 14. He then spent time in College, worked as a postman for five years, and spent two years in the Army. He began, around 1970, by singing in clubs in the Chicago area. Prine signed to Atlantic in 1971, releasing the powerful *John Prine*. The album contained the excellent Vietnam veteran song 'Sam Stone' with the wonderfully evocative line 'There's a hole in daddy's arm where all the money goes, and Jesus Christ died for nothing I suppose'. Over the years Prine achieved cult status, his songs being increasingly covered by other artists. 'Angel From Montgomery', 'Speed Of The Sound Of Loneliness', and 'Paradise' being three in particular. He was inevitably given the unenviable tag 'the new Dylan' at one stage. His last album for Atlantic, *Common Sense* (produced by Steve Cropper) was his only album, to make the US Top 100. Whilst the quality and content of all his work has been quite excellant his other albums only scratched the US Top 200. His first release for Asylum, *Bruised Orange*, was well received, but the follow up, *Pink Cadillac*, was not so well accommodated by the public or the critics. However, *The Missing Years* changed everything with massive sales at home, and a Grammy nomination, making Prine almost a household name. His outstanding songs had been covered by the likes of Bonnie Raitt, and John Denver, over the years, and his career would appear to have taken on a new lease of life in the 90s. Prine presented *Town And Country* for Channel 4 Television in 1992, a series of music programmes featuring singers such as Nanci Griffith, and Rodney Crowell. In keeping with his career upswing *The Missing Years* is a faultless work containing some of his strongest songs in many years.

Albums: *John Prine* (1971), *Diamonds In The Rough* (1972), *Sweet Revenge* (1973), *Common Sense* (1975), *Bruised Orange* (1978), *Pink Cadillac* (1979), *Storm Windows* (1980), *Aimless Love* (1986), *German Afternoons* (1987), *John Prine Live* (1988), *The Missing Years* (1992).
Compilations: *Prime Prine* (1976).

Prior, Maddy

A dedicated and thoroughly professional performer who worked as a roadie for Rev. Gary Davis during the 60s folk scene, Prior went on to form a successful duo with the traditionalist, Tim Hart. Both were absorbed into Steeleye Span in 1969, and Prior quickly became the group's focal point and ambassador. When Steeleye Span disbanded in 1978, she signed to Chrysalis, and launched her solo career with *Woman In The Wings* and *Changing Winds*. Both albums contained several 'historical ballads' written by Prior herself. After an unsuccessful tour, for which she was backed by several prominent musicians, she worked with a basic four piece unit, which included her husband Rick Kemp (bass), and former Steeleye Span drummer, Nigel Pegrum. During the 80s, she also sang with the re-formed Steeleye Span. Her songs became more intimate and rootsy, and, with her backing group, the Answers, she recorded the poppy, *Going For Glory*, which included work with the Eurythmics, and Kemp's impressive 'Deep In The Darkest Night'. Prior's schedule involved television, a cappella folk concerts, world tours with Steeleye Span (she was the last original member), and smaller gigs with Kemp. In 1984, a broadcast with the early music specialists, the Carnival Band, led to three mutual albums of richly varied music, and annual tours. With Rick Kemp, she recorded *Happy Families*, a loose, swinging album, featuring his guitar playing. Just after its release, he was forced into temporary retirement because of an arm injury. Prior was subsequently accompanied by a 'jazz/shuffle' unit, and later toured with the sympathetic Nick Holland on keyboards, rediscovering much of her early influences. Of her own Radio 2 series *In Good Voice*, she says: 'I sit there and play all this wonderful music, and then tell people why I like it. Can you think of a better job?'. Prior remains one of the most diverse characters on the folk scene.

Albums: *Woman In The Wings* (1978), *Changing Winds* (1978), *Hooked On Winning* (1981), *Going For Glory* (1983), *Happy Families* (1990). With The Carnival Band: *Tapestry Of Carols* (1986), *Sing Lustily & With Good Courage* (1986), *Carols & Capers* (1991).

Proclaimers

This Scottish folk duo, who specialized in belligerent harmonies, consisted of identical twins Craig and Charlie Reid from Auchtermuchty. They had an early hit in 1987 with the Gerry Rafferty produced 'Letter From America'. Follow-ups included the typically boisterous 'Make My Heart Fly' and 'I'm Gonna Be'. Pete Wingfield was brought in to produce *Sunshine On Leith*, after which they took a two-year sabbatical. Writing for the third album was disrupted, however, when they spent much energy and money ensuring that their beloved, debt-ridden Hibernian Football Club did not close down. In common with many fans, they are now shareholders. They reappeared in 1990 with the *King Of The Road* EP. The title track, a cover of the old Roger Miller song, came from the film *The Crossing*. Other tracks on the EP, which reached the UK Top 10, included the folk/country classic 'Long Black Veil'.

Albums: *This Is The Story* (1987), *Sunshine On Leith* (1988).

Proffitt, Frank

b. Frank Noah Proffitt, 1913, Laurel Bloomery, Tennessee, USA, d. 24 November 1965. Proffitt was a tobacco farmer, part-time carpenter, singer, guitarist, banjo player, dulcimer player and song collector. He is mainly remembered for 'Tom Dooley' made popular by the Kingston Trio and Frank Warner. This song appears on *Frank Proffitt Of Reese, North Carolina*, and was 'collected' by Frank Warner from Proffitt in 1938. It was only one of over a hundred songs that the Warners collected from Proffitt. During lean times on the farm, he worked in a spark plug factory, in Toledo, Ohio, and even on road construction. He also made and sold mountain dulcimers and fretless banjos. Proffitt's acknowledged importance lies in his collection of the traditional material of America, in particular North Carolina. Many of the songs were picked up from his father, Wiley Proffitt, and his aunt Nancy Prather. Many were sung while working in the fields, and Frank absorbed all that he heard. His first public appearance was at the First Annual Folk Festival in Chicago. This had been brought about by the publicity that had accompanied the success of the Kingston Trio's recording of 'Tom Dooley'. *Frank Proffitt Of Reese, North Carolina*, was recorded at his home during the winter of 1961 by Sandy Paton. Considering his importance, it is surprising that Proffitt contributed only 11 songs to the *Frank C. Brown Collection Of North Carolina Folklore*. He died on Thanksgiving Day, 1965. In addition to his own recordings for Folk Legacy, Proffitt also contributed a number of tracks, in particular 'Cumberland Gap' and 'Satan, Your Kingdom Must Come Down', to a compilation album, *High Atmosphere - Ballads And Tunes From Virginia And North Carolina* (1974).

Albums: *Frank Proffitt Sings Folk Songs* (1961), *Frank Proffitt Of Reese, North Carolina* (1962), *North Carolina Songs And Ballads* (1962), *Memorial Album* (1969).

Purple Gang

Formed in Manchester, England, the original line-up comprised of Lucifer (b. Peter Walker; , Deejay Robinson (harmonica, mandolin), Ank Langley (jug), Geoff Bourjer (piano, washboard) and James 'Joe' Beard (guitar). All were students at Stockport College of Art. The Purple Gang achieved notoriety when 'Granny Takes A Trip', their debut single, was adopted by the English 'underground' as an unofficial anthem. Although a gentle, happy, jugband song, the 'trip' reference was taken to be about LSD, despite fervent claims by the group that this was not their intention. Joe Beard (12-string guitar), Gerry Robinson (mandolin), Geoff Bowyer (keyboards) and Lucifer completed an attendant album in the space of two days, but had split up by the time of its release. Continued interest in their anthemic single inspired a reformation in 1969, but with George Janken (bass) and Irish Alex (washboard/drums) replacing Lucifer. However, the heavy style embraced by the new unit lacked the charm of earlier acoustic, goodtime music and failed to generate interest.

Album: *The Purple Gang Strikes* (1968).

Pyewackett

This dance and concert outfit drew on John Playford's *English Dancing Master*, first published in 1651, for a good deal of their material. The group included vocalist Rosie Cross (b. 6 October 1954, Leeds, Yorkshire, England; bassoon, tambourine, hammer dulcimer), Ian Blake (b. 9 December 1955, Finchley, London, England; clarinet, recorder, saxophone, bass, keyboards, vocals), Mark Emerson (b. 15 August 1958, Ruislip, Middlesex, England; violin, viola, keyboards, drum, vocals), Laurie Harper (b. 22 November 1953, Lambeth, London, England; violin, mandolin, mandola, bass, vocals) and Bill Martin (b. 3 May 1955, Woolwich,

London, England; guitar, accordion, keyboards, vocals). The group formed in 1975, when Ian, Rosie and Bill were students together, and became the resident band at their university folk club. They played their first professional date in 1977, having already undergone numerous personnel changes. By 1977, both Emerson and Harper had joined the line-up. After the release of *Pyewackett*, on Dingle's Records in 1981, the group issued the single 'The Lambeth Walk'/'Poor Little Angelina', under the pseudonym of Des Dorchester And His Dance Orchestra. They employed the services of a number of drummers over the years, including session musician Ralph Salmins (b. 4 June 1964, Farnborough, Kent, England) but the first permanent drummer came in 1983, when Micky Barker joined them. He left the group around 1985, eventually joining Magnum. From then on the unit used drummers only on larger tours. Many of the tours were for the British Council, and took them the the Middle East, North Africa and Europe. Pyewackett mostly used Mike Barraclough as caller, and from the mid-80s, until 1991, they were the resident band for the BBC radio school programme *The Song Tree*. The group were very popular for their reworking of old dance tunes, utilizing a number of modern instruments supplemented by synthesizers. Owing to outside commitments Pyewackett ceased working regularly from 1989. Cross took up the post of Folk Development Worker for Humberside in 1987; Martin became involved in production work, and also arranged and recorded with the Firm for the hit single 'Star Trekkin'' and Emerson regularly tours with June Tabor. However, Pyewackett still get together for occasional appearances.

Albums: *Pyewackett* (1981), *The Man In The Moon Drinks Claret* (1983), *7 To Midnight* (1985), *This Crazy Paradise* (1987).

Q

Queen, Ida (Guillory)

b. Ida Lewis, 15 January 1930, Lake Charles, Louisiana, USA. Lewis grew up singing Louisiana French songs and began playing accordion shortly after the World War II. When the family moved to San Francisco and Ida married, she had little to do with music until 1976. Ida and her brother Al Rapone played at parties, and she was then invited to perform at a Mardi Gras celebration, which subsequently led to more bookings. She signed with GNP Records in 1976 and has made numerous albums since then, and has been a frequent visitor to Europe with her Bon Ton Zydeco Band. Ida's brand of zydeco is more accessible than that of many Louisiana artists, and she enjoys huge popularity among the non-Louisiana audience.

Albums: *Zydeco* (1976), *Cooking With Queen Ida* (1989).

R

Rafferty, Gerry

b. 16 April 1947, Paisley, Scotland. The lengthy career of the reclusive Rafferty started as a member of the Humblebums with Billy Connolly and Tam Harvey in 1968. After its demise through commercial indifference, Transatlantic Records offered him a solo contract. The result was *Can I Have My Money Back?*, a superb blend of folk and gentle pop music, featuring one of the earliest cover paintings from the well-known Scottish artist 'Patrick' (playwright John Byrne). Rafferty showed great promise as a songwriter with the rolling 'Steamboat Row' and the plaintive and observant, 'Her Father Didn't Like Me Anyway', but the album was a commercial failure. Rafferty's next solo project came after an interruption of seven years, four as a member of the brilliant but turbulent Stealers Wheel, and three through litigation over managerial problems. Much of this is documented in his lyrics both with Stealers Wheel and as a soloist. *City To City* in 1978 raised his profile and gave him a hit single that created a classic song with probably the most famous saxophone introduction in pop music, performed by Raphael Ravenscroft. 'Baker Street' became a multi-million seller and narrowly missed the top of the charts. The album sold similar numbers and Rafferty became a reluctant star. He declined to perform in the USA even though his album was number 1. *Night Owl* was almost as successful, containing a similar batch of strong songs with intriguing lyrics and haunting melodies. Rafferty's output has been sparse during the 80s and none of his recent work has matched his earlier songs. He made a single contribution to the film *Local Hero* and produced the Top 3 hit for the Proclaimers with 'Letter From America' in 1987. *North And South* continued the themes of his previous albums, although the lengthy introductions to each track made it unsuitable for radio play. During the early 90s Rafferty's marriage broke up, and, as is often the case this stimulates more songwriting creativity. *On A Wing And A Prayer* was a return to form, but although the reviews were favourable it made little impression on the charts.

Albums: *Can I Have My Money Back* (1971), *City To City* (1978), *Night Owl* (1979), *Snakes And Ladders* (1980), *Sleepwalking* (1982), *North And South* (1988), *On A Wing And A Prayer* (1992). Selected compilations: *Early Collection* (1986), *Blood And Glory* (1988).

Ray, Dave

As a member of Koerner, Ray And Glover, with John 'Spider' Koerner and Tony Glover, Dave 'Snaker' Ray was in the vanguard of the folk revival of the 60s. An accomplished six- and 12-string guitarist, the artist pursued a concurrent solo career with two compulsive country blues albums. The first included interpretations of material by, among others, Muddy Waters, Robert Johnson and Leadbelly, while the follow-up featured a greater emphasis on original material. The rise of electric styles obscured Ray's progress and it was 1969 before he re-emerged in Bamboo, a country-based duo he had formed with pianist Will Donight. Their eccentric album made little impression and Ray's subsequent profile was distinctly low-key. However, in 1990 Ray and Glover teamed up to record *Ashes In My Whiskey* for the Rough Trade label, winning critical acclaim.

Albums: Solo *Fine Soft Land* (1967). With Koerner, Ray And Glover *Blues, Rags And Hollers* (1963), *More Blues, Rags And Hollers* (1964), *The Return Of Koerner, Ray And Glover* (1965), *Live At St. Olaf Festival* (c.60/70s), *Some American Folk Songs Like They Used To Be* (1974). With Tony Glover *Ashes In My Whiskey* (1990).

Redgum

Formed in Adelaide, Australia in 1975, the success of Redgum's brand of folk/rock political satire has since been regarded as an anomaly, albeit thoroughly deserved. The core members comprised university students John Schumann (vocals/guitar), Verity Truman (vocals/tin whistle/saxophone), Michael Atkinson (vocals/guitar/mandolin), and have in the past included 15 other musicians. After going professional the band built up their support base by constant touring featuring an excellent live

show, with stage wit provided by Schumann, whose droll voice was the antithesis of the traditional rock hero. Their debut album provides some of their best material, comprising typically astute observations on the rich, the hypocritical, politicians and the plight of the under privileged, but it was only originally available on a small independent label. National mainstream success was not achieved until the release of 'I Was Only 19', in 1983, a song written about a survivor of the Vietnam war, which compares favourably with three other poignant anti-war songs by fellow Australians - 'Jungle Green' by Broderick Smith, 'The Band Played Waltzing Matilda' by Eric Bogle and 'Khe Sahn' by Cold Chisel. A second hit single, the reggae-flavoured 'I've Been To Bali Too' (1984) hit home with many Australian tourists. As the band lost more original members, they began to lack their characteristic bite even though their albums became better produced. A third Australian chart single in 1987, 'Roll It On Robbie', caused outrage amongst the conservative elements of the country because it encouraged the use of condoms to promote safe-sex. At their peak, Redgum were among the top five live acts in Australia despite not having a national hit for some time. Schumann has since recorded two solo albums, his collection of children's music is probably the more popular of the two. He has also worked in record production and children's television.

Albums: *If You Don't Fight You Lose* (1978), *Virgin Ground* (1978), *Brown Rice And Kerosene* (1983), *Caught In The Act* (1983), *Frontline* (1985), *Midnight Sun* (1987).

Redpath, Jean

b. 28 April 1937, Edinburgh, Scotland. This traditional singer and guitar player is well-known for her children's songs and her extensive collection of the works of Robert Burns. Redpath emigrated to the USA in 1961. After an indifferent start, she moved to New York, and within six weeks had played the renowned Gerde's Folk City. Although *Skipping Barefoot Through The Heather* was recorded on Prestige International before *Scottish Ballad Book*, on Elektra, the latter was released first. The Robert Burns project began in 1976, but was different from another series of Burns songs produced for Scottish Records. For *The Scottish Fiddle - The Music And The Songs*, Jean had wanted to combine the violin and cello as they have long been associated with Scottish traditional music. The blend was successful, giving a classic, almost mournful, feel to the music. During the latter part of the 70s, Jean was lecturing in the music department of the Wesleyan University. Always productive, Redpath continues to perform and record traditional folk music.

Albums: *Scottish Ballad Book* (c.1964), *Skipping Barefoot Through The Heather* (c.1965), *Songs Of Love, Lilt And Laughter* (1966), *Laddie Lie Near Me* (1967), *Frae My Ain Country* (1973), *Jean Redpath* (1975), with Lisa Neustadt *Shout For Joy* (1975), *There Were Minstrels* (1976), *The Songs Of Robert Burns Vol.1* (1976), *Jean Redpath With Guests* (1977), *Song Of The Seals* (1978), with Abby Newton *Father Adam* (1979), with Newton *Lowlands* (1980), *The Songs Of Robert Burns Vol.2* (1980), *The Songs Of Robert Burns Vol.3* (1982), *The Songs Of Robert Burns Vol.4* (1983), with the Angel Band *Anywhere Is Home* (1984), with Neustadt and the Angel Band *Angels Hovering Round* (c.1984), with Newton *Lady Nairne* (1986), *The Songs Of Robert Burns Vol.5* (1985), with Newton, Alistair Hardie *The Scottish Fiddle - The Music And The Songs* (1985), *The Songs Of Robert Burns Vol.6* (1987), with Abby *Lady Naime* (1987), with Newton *A Fine Song For Singing* (1987), *Leaving The Land* (1990), *The Songs Of Robert Burns Vol.7* (c.1990).

Relativity

An occasional Celtic folk group, formed in the 80s, the lineup consisted of the youngsters, Triona Ni Dhomhnaill (vocals, keyboards), Michael O Dhomhnaill (vocals, guitar) and Phil Cunningham (accordion), along with Johnny Cunningham (fiddle) from the Bothy Band and Silly Wizard. The members of the quartet each had flourishing solo careers, but cross-fertilised their Irish Scots heritage with absorbing results. A top line draw in the USA, where three of them lived, their British debut was a coup for the small salt-town of Northwich, Cheshire, who presented them in a packed marquee in the local park. Their music is an energetic Celtic force with some graceful rockist touches.
Albums: *Relativity* (1985), *Gathering Pace* (1987).

Renbourn, John

Having flirted with various part-time electric bands, Renbourn began his folk-singing career on London's club circuit. Startling guitarwork compensated for his less assured vocals and he quickly established a reputation as a leading traditionalist, whose interpretations of classic country blues and Elizabethan material provided a remarkable contrast to the freer styles of Davey Graham and Bert Jansch. Friendship with the latter resulted in Renbourn's debut album, but it was on the following collection, *Another Monday*, that the artist's talent truly flourished. The two guitarists were the inspiration behind the Pentangle, but Renbourn, like Jansch, continued to record as a solo act during the group's existence. When the individual musicians went their separate ways again in 1973, John maintained his unique, eclectic

approach and further excursions into medieval music contrasted with the eastern styles or country blues prevalent on later albums. His 1988 album was recorded with the assistance of Maggie Boyle and Steve Tilson under the collective title of 'John Renbourn's Ship Of Fools'. Although his studio releases are now less frequent, the guitarist remains a popular figure on the British and international folk circuit.
Albums: *John Renbourn* (1965), with Bert Jansch *Bert And John* (1966), *Another Monday* (1967), *Sir John A Lot Of Merrie Englandes Musik Thynge And Ye Grene Knyghte* (1968), *The Lady And The Unicorn* (1970), *Faro Annie* (1972), *The Hermit* (1977), *Maid In Bedlam* (1977), *John Renbourn And Stefan Grossman* (1978), *Black Balloon* (1979), *Enchanted Garden* (1980), *Live In Concert* (1985), *Three Kingdoms* (1987), *Nine Maidens* (1988), *Ship Of Fools* (1988). Compilations: *The John Renbourn Sampler* (1971), *Heads And Tails* (1973), *The Essential Collection Volume 1: The Soho Years* (1987) *The Essential Collection Volume 2: Moon Shines Bright* (1987), *The Folk Blues Of John Renbourn* (1988), *The Mediaeval Almanac* (1989), *The Essential John Renbourn (A Best Of)* (1992).

Reynolds, Malvina

b. 23 August 1900, San Francisco, California, USA, d. 17 March 1978, Berkeley, California, USA. Reynolds was primarily a songwriter who later took to performing her material on guitar. She did not begin writing until as late as the 50s. Prior to this she had worked in various jobs. In 1925, Malvina gained her BA in English Language and Literature, and, two years later, her MA. In 1939, she was awarded a PhD. During the Depression days, Reynolds had been able to findwork as a teacher. Such classic as 'Little Boxes' made popular by Pete Seeger, and 'What Have They Done To The Rain' brought Reynolds to public attention. The latter composition achieved hit status in 1965 when recorded by the Searchers. The following year the Seekers reached number 2, in the UK charts with their version of Reynolds' 'Morningtown Ride'. Reynolds' popularity increased when Joan Baez, Bob Dylan, and Judy Collins began to record her songs. Reynolds recorded two albums for children, *Artichokes, Griddle Cakes*, and *Funnybugs*, as well as writing for, and appearing on, television's *Sesame Street*. Reynolds died in March 1978. *Mama Lion* was a posthumous release.
Albums: *Another County Heard From* (1960), *Malvina Reynolds...Sings The Truth* (1968), *Malvina Reynolds* (1970), *Artichokes, Griddle Cakes* (1970), *Malvina* (1972), *Funnybugs* (1972), *Malvina..Held Over* (1975), *Magical Songs* (1978), *Mama Lion* (1980).
Further reading: *Tweedles And Foodles For Young*

Noodles, Malvina Reynolds. *Little Boxes And Other Handmade Songs*, Malvina Reynolds. *The Muse Of Parker Street*, Malvina Reynolds. *Cheerful Tunes For Lutes And Spoons*, Malvina Reynolds. *The Malvina Reynolds Songbook*, Malvina Reynolds. *There's Music In The Air*, Malvina Reynolds.

Rinzler, Ralph

b. 20 July 1934, New York, USA. A leading exponent of American folklore, Rinzler became acquainted with traditional music while in his teens. He studied in London under A.L. Lloyd and, in 1959, replaced Eric Weissberg in the Greenbriar Boys. An accomplished mandolin player, Rinzler performed with this influential bluegrass attraction until 1964. He then became director of field research for the Newport Folk Festival, and as such undertook several recording trips with archivist Alan Lomax. Three years later Rinzler became director of the Festival Of American Folklife at the Smithsonian Institution and embarked on a concurrent filming career. His documentaries have included two studies of traditional pottery, while he has published books about handicraft work and several folk artists, including Doc Watson and Uncle Dave Macon.

Ritchie, Jean

b. 8 December 1922, Viper, Kentucky, USA. Ritchie was the youngest of 14 children from a well-known family of traditional singers. Her parents, Balis and Abigail Ritchie were of Scottish-Irish descent. Jean's father taught her to play the mountain dulcimer. The family were visited by Cecil Sharp in 1917 during one of his song-collecting expeditions to the Appalachian Mountains. Jean was first recorded in 1948 when she was heard by Mitch Miller as she demonstrated a dulcimer in a store. Miller was impressed enough to produce *Round And Roundelays*. Later, having gained a degree in social work, she went to New York where she was introduced to Alan Lomax, the well-known, and equally well-respected, folklorist. Lomax recorded Ritchie's songs, both for his own collection and for the Library Of Congress Folksong Archives. She has performed all over the USA and given recitals at universities and colleges. In 1952 Ritchie travelled to the UK after winning a Fulbright scholarship. This also gave her the chance to trace the origins of her family's songs. While in the UK she appeared at the Royal Albert Hall and Cecil Sharp House, the headquarters of the English Folk Dance And Song Society. Jean's 1952 release, *Jean Ritchie Singing Traditional Songs Of Her Kentucky Mountain Family*, was the first folk recording to be issued on the Elektra label. In 1953 she attended the International Conference of Folk Music held in Biaritz-Pamplona, and appeared at many folk seminars countrywide. Numerous television and radio appearances, and a wealth of recorded material have ensured her place in her country's folk heritage. Her light voice and simple arrangements have gained the appeal of a wide audience. Many folk song collectors have sought the Ritchie family as a source of traditional tunes and songs. Ritchie's book, *The Singing Family Of The Cumberlands*, recounts the history of her family growing up in the Cumberland mountains. 'My Dear Companion' was recorded by Linda Ronstadt, Emmylou Harris and Dolly Parton on their album *Trio* in 1987. Ritchie's sister Edna also recorded on Jean's own Greenhays label.

Selected albums: *Round And Roundelays* (1948), *Jean Ritchie Singing Traditional Songs Of Her Kentucky Mountain Family* (1952), with Tony Kraber *Valleys In Colonial America* (1953), with Oscar Brand *Shivaree!* (1955), *Saturday Night And Sunday Too* (1956), *A Folk Concert* (1959), *Field Trip-England* (1960), *As I Roved Out-Field Trip Ireland* (1960), *Child Ballads Of The Southern Mountains Vol. 1* (1961), *Child Ballads Of The Southern Mountains Vol. 2* (1961), *Come On In, We're Pickin' And Singin'* (1962), with various artists *Folk Songs At The Limelight* (1962), *The Appalachian Dulcimer* (1963), *Marching Across The Green Grass And Other American Children's Game Songs* (1968), *None But One* (1977). Compilation: *Courtin's A Pleasure* (1957), *The Best Of Jean Ritchie* (1962).

Further reading: *Singing Family Of The Cumberlands*. *The Swapping Song Book*, Henry Z. Walck Inc. *A Garland Of Mountain Song*, Broadcast Music. *From Fair To Fair*, Henry Z. Walck Inc. *Loves Me Loves Me Not*, Henry Z. Walck Inc. *Jean Ritchie's Dulcimer People*, Oak Publications. *The Dulcimer Book*, Jean Ritchie Oak Publications.

Ritter, Tex

b. Woodward Maurice Ritter, 12 January 1905, Murvaul, Texas, USA, d. 2 January 1974. While studying political science at the University of Texas and during a later spell at law school, Ritter developed interests in the folklore and music of the southwestern states. He began singing folk songs and was soon a popular radio entertainer. He also appeared in concert and other stage performances, including a Broadway show in 1930. In the mid-30s he went to Hollywood, where he became one of the most popular singing cowboys in films, simultaneously making numerous recordings. Amongst his films were *Sing Cowboy Sing* (1937), *Song Over The Buckaroo* (1939), *Rainbow Over The Range* (1940) *Deep In The Heart Of Texas* (1942) and *Frontier Bullets* (1945). By the late 40s the type of film in which Ritter appeared had had its day,

Tex Ritter

and he subsequently toured extensively with his own stage show and also sang at the *Grand Ole Opry*. He continued to make records and in 1952 he had his biggest hit with the song 'High Noon (Do Not Forsake Me)', which he sang in the film *High Noon*. In the mid-50s and early 60s he made a handful of film appearances, mostly cameo roles. In the late 60s Ritter returned to his early interest in politics and tried unsuccessfully to gain nomination for the US Senate. He died in 1974.

Compilations: all various dates *The Streets Of Laredo*, *High Noon*, *Lady Killin' Cowboy*, *Singin' In The Saddle*, *Songs From The Western Screen*, *Collectors Series*.

Roaring Jelly

This UK comedy-folk trio comprised Clive Harvey (b. 27 November 1945, Watford, Hertfordshire, England; guitar/vocals/ukelele/harmonica), Derek Pearce (b. Birmingham, Warwickshire, England; vocals/multi-instrumentalist), and Mick Hennessey (b. Derby, Derbyshire, England; acoustic and electric bass/vocals). Harvey met Pearce in 1970 at Trent Polytechnic, Nottingham, where they played the college folk club and won a local talent contest. This led to folk club gigs in the Derby/Nottingham area. Hennessey joined the line-up soon after. The group took their name from a famous Irish jig. Even though their act was moving away from folk and increasingly towards comedy, the group continued playing folk clubs in and around the Midlands. They played the Sidmouth International Festival in 1975, which led to concerts and dates on a national scale. The the group split in 1985, while still at the height of their popularity. Harvey, along with Ian Carter, formed the short-lived Beverley Brothers, then joined R. Cajun And The Zydeco Brothers in December 1985. He also plays with another trio, the Back Seat Jivers. Pearce is now a furniture maker and sculptor. Roaring Jelly re-formed, briefly, in 1986 for a reunion tour/ titled 'Pay The Tax Bill Tour'. Still spoken of with affection, the group were considered pioneers of alternative comedy before the term became fashionable.

Albums: *Roaring Jelly's Golden Grates* (1977), *In The Roar* (1981).

Roberts, Andy

b. 12 June 1946, Harrow, Middlesex, England. Guitarist Roberts', solo achievements have been overshadowed by the work he has done for other artists. He first came to public attention after meeting BBC disc jockey John Peel in 1967. From 1966-67, Roberts had accompanied the Scaffold and later joined the Liverpool Scene from 1968-70. He recorded *Everyone* in 1971 with Everyone, and

then concentrated on session and solo work. In 1972, with Plainsong, he recorded the highly regarded *In Search Of Amelia Earhart*. He then joined Grimms from 1973-76, during which time he appeared on their final two albums. In 1974, he featured in his first stage musical *Mind Your Head*. Roberts then joined Roy Harper's, Band. In 1980, he performed with the Hank Wangford Band, with whom he recorded - *Hank Wangford* (1980) and *Live At The Pegasus* (1982) - and toured until 1984. He still continued with other session commitments, including playing guitar on Pink Floyd's *The Wall*, in 1981. Roberts also provided a singing voice for television's satirical puppet series *Spitting Image* from 1983-84. Since then he has released two solo albums, and has been heavily involved in composing music for the theatre, film and television. His flexibility is reflected in the diversity of the programmes he has composed for, ranging from television drama series such as *The Men's Room* to *Madhur Jaffrey's Far Eastern Cookery*. In his capacity as composer, Roberts has been involved with *Z Cars*, *Bergerac*, and more recently, the six-part television documentary series, *Where On Earth Are We Going*. He has also played on countless sessions by a wealth of artists.

Albums: *Homegrown* (1970), *Nina And The Dream Tree* (1971), *Urban Cowboy* (1971), *Andy Roberts And The Great Stampede* (1973), *Loose Connections* (1984, film soundtrack), *From Time To Time* (1985). Compilations: *Recollections* (1972). With Grimms: *Rockin' Duck* (1973), *Sleepers* (1976). With Roger McGough: *Summer With Monika* (1978).

Robertson, Jeannie

b. 1908, d. March 1975. This Scottish traditional singer learned a great deal of her repertoire from her mother, Marie Stewart of Ballater. Both parents came from travelling clans, the Stewart's and the Robertson's, who travelled the north-east of Scotland. Robertson was 'discovered' by Hamish Henderson during the 50s, when it was apparent that she possessed an outstanding voice and capacity for story-telling. She continued singing until her death, in 1975, having been awarded the MBE in 1968 for her services to traditional music.

Album: *Jeannie Robertson-The Great Scottish Traditional Ballad Singer* (1959).

Robeson, Paul

b. 9 April 1898, Princeton, New Jersey, USA, d. 23 January 1976. Robeson's father was born into slavery, but he escaped at the age of 15 and eventually studied theology and became a preacher. His mother was a teacher, but she died in 1904. Education was of paramount importance to the Robeson family, one son became a physician, and the daughter was a teacher. Of all the family, Paul Robeson was by far the most gifted. In 1911 he was one of only two black students at Somerville High School in New Jersey, yet maintained a potentially dangerous high profile. He played the title role in *Othello*, sang in the glee club and also played football. He graduated with honours and won a scholarship to Rutgers University. A formidable athlete, he played football at All-American level and achieved scholastic success. In the early 20s, while studying law at Columbia University, he took part in theatrical productions and sang. In 1922 he visited England where he toured in the play *Taboo* with the noted actress Mrs Patrick Campbell. During this visit he also met pianist Lawrence Brown, with whom he was to have a close professional relationship for the rest of Brown's life. In 1923 Robeson was in the chorus of Lew Leslie's *Plantation Revue*, which starred Florence Mills, and the following year made his first film, *Body And Soul*, for Oscar Micheaux, one of the earliest black film-makers. He appeared in prestigious stage productions, including *All God's Chillun Got Wings* (1924) and *The Emperor Jones* (1925).

In 1924 he had his first brush with the Ku Klux Klan over a scene in *All God's Chillun* in which he was required to kiss the hand of a white woman. In 1925 he made his first concert appearance as a singer. The impact of this concert, which awakened Americans to the beauty of his rich bass-baritone voice, was such that he was invited to tour Europe, appearing in London in 1928 in *Show Boat* with Alberta Hunter. Also in 1928 he played the title role of Porgy in the play by DuBose and Dorothy Heyward which formed the basis of George Gershwin's *Porgy And Bess*. In 1930 he was again in London, where he took the leading role in *Othello*, playing opposite Peggy Ashcroft and Sybil Thorndike. During the 30s he made a number of films including, *The Emperor Jones* (1933) and several in the UK, among them *Sanders Of The River* (1935) and *The Proud Valley* (1939) and in 1936 he made the screen version of *Show Boat*. As in the stage production, his part was small but his rendition of 'Ol' Man River' was one of the outstanding features. The 30s also saw his first visit to Russia and he travelled to Spain to sing for the loyalist troops. He also developed an amazing facility with languages, eventually becoming fluent in 25, including Chinese and Arabic. He incorporated folk songs of many nations in his repertoire, singing them in the appropriate language. This same period saw Robeson's political awareness develop and he extended his studies into political philosophy and wrote on many topics. In 1939 he again played Othello in England, this time at Stratford-upon-Avon, and also played the role in

Boston, Massachusetts, in 1942 and on Broadway in 1943. In the 40s Robeson's politicization developed, during another visit to Russia he embraced communism, although he was not blind to the regime's imperfections and spoke out against the anti-Semitism he found there. Reaction in his home country to his espousal of communism was hostile and a speech he delivered in Paris in 1949, in which he stated that although he loved America he loved Russia more than he loved those elements of America which discriminated against him because of his colour, was predictably misunderstood and widely misquoted. Also in 1949, Robeson led protests in London against the racist policies of the government of South Africa.

The FBI began to take an interest in Robeson's activities and conflict with right-wing elements and racists, especially during a rally at Peekskill in upstate New York, which drew the attention of the media away from his artistic work. An appearance before the Un-American Activities Committee drew even more attention to his already high political profile. In 1950 his passport was withdrawn because the State Department considered that his 'travel abroad at this time would be contrary to the best interests of the United States'. Ill health in the mid-50s allied to the withdrawal of his passport, severely damaged his career when he was in his vocal prime. He continued to address rallies, write extensively on political matters and make occasional concert performances by singing over telephone links to gatherings overseas. Repeated high-level efforts by other governments eventually caused the US State Department to reconsider and during his first New York concert in a decade, to a sell-out audience at Carnegie Hall, he was able to announce that his passport had been returned. This was in May 1958 and later that year he appeared on stage and television in the UK and in Russia. His comeback was triumphant and he made several successful tours of Europe and beyond. He was away for five years, returning to the USA in 1963 for more concerts and political rallies. However, pressures continued to build up and he suffered nervous exhaustion and depression. His wife of 44 years died in 1965.

Another comeback, in the late 60s, was greeted with considerable enthusiasm, but the power and quality of his voice had begun to fade. During the final years of his life Robeson toured, wrote and spoke, but his health was deteriorating rapidly and he died on 23 January 1976. Although Robeson possessed only a limited vocal range, the rich coloration of his tone and the unusual flexibility of his voice made his work especially moving. He brought to the 'Negro spiritual' an understanding and a tenderness that overcame their sometimes mawkish sentimentality, and the strength and integrity of his delivery gave them a quality no other male singer has equalled. His extensive repertoire of folk songs from many lands was remarkable and brought to his concert performances a much wider scope than that of almost any regular folk singer. Although beyond the scope of this work, Robeson's career as actor, writer and political activist cannot be ignored. His independence and outspokenness against discrimination and political injustice resulted in him suffering severely at the hands of his own government. Indeed, those close to him have intimated a belief that his final illness was brought about by the deliberate covert action of government agents. Perhaps as a side-effect of this, he is frequently omitted from reference works originating in his own country, even those which purport to be black histories. For all the dismissiveness of his own government, Robeson was highly regarded by his own people and by audiences in many lands. His massive intellect, his powerful personality and astonishing charisma, when added to his abilities as a singer and actor, helped to make him one of the outstanding Americans of the 20th century.

Albums: all various dates *Green Pastures*, *A Lonesome Road*, *Songs Of Free Men*, *Songs Of The Mississippi*, *The Essential Paul Robeson*.

Further reading: *Here I Stand*, Paul Robeson. *Paul Robeson Speaks: Writings Speeches Interviews 1918-1974*, Paul Robeson. *Paul Robeson*, Martin Bauml Duberman.

Roches

Sisters Maggie (b. 26 October 1951, Detroit, Michigan, USA) and Terre Roche (b. 10 April 1953, New York City, New York, USA) began singing a mixture of traditional, doo-wop and barbershop quartet songs in New York clubs in the late 60s. Their first recording was as backing singers on Paul Simon's 1972 album, *There Goes Rhymin' Simon*. Through Simon, the duo recorded an album for CBS in 1975 which attracted little attention. The following year, the Roches became a trio with the addition of the distinctive voice of younger sister Suzzy (b. New York City, New York, USA) to Terre's soprano and Maggie's deep alto. With Maggie's compositions, by turns whimsical and waspish, featuring strongly they became firm favourites on New York's folk club scene. A Warner Brothers recording deal followed and Robert Fripp produced the self-titled album, which included compositions by each of the sisters and remains their strongest recording. Among the many lyrical extravaganzas were Maggie's best-known song of infidelity 'The Married Men' (later covered by Phoebe Snow), Terre's poignant and autobiographical 'Runs In The Family' and 'We', the trio's a cappella opening number at live performances. The highly commercial 'Hammond Song' was arguably the star track (featuring a fine

Roches

Fripp solo). *Nurds* another Fripp production featured the extraordinary 'One Season' wherein the trio manage to sing harmony almost a cappella but totally (and deliberately) out of tune. (Harmony vocalists will appreciate that this is extremely difficult). *Keep On Doing*, maintained a high standard including a refreshing burst of Handel's 'Hallelujah Chorus' and Maggie's tragic love song 'Losing You'. If the Roches ever had strong desires on the charts *Another World* was potentially the album to do it. Featuring a full rock-based sound this remains an undiscovered gem including the glorious title track and a cover of the Fleetwoods' 'Come Softly To Me'. Throughout the 80s, the Roches continued to perform in New York and appeared occasionally at European folk festivals. They also wrote and performed music for theatre productions and the 1988 film *Crossing Delancy*. *Speak* went largely unnoticed in 1989. Their next album was a memorable Christmas gift, *Three Kings*. Containing traditional yuletide songs and carols it displayed clearly the Roches exceptional harmony. *A Dove* in 1992 featured the 'Ing' Song' a brilliant lyrical exercise with every word ending with ing. They remain a highly original unit with a loyal cult following.

Albums: *Seductive Reasoning* (1975), *The Roches* (1979), *Nurds* (1980), *Keep On Doing* (1982), *Another World* (1985), *Speak* (1989), *Three Kings* (1990), *A Dove* (1992).

Rockin' Dopsie

b. Alton Jay Rubin, 10 February 1932, Carencro, Louisiana, USA. Following the death of Clifton Chenier, Dopsie was acclaimed the new King Of Zydeco and crowned as such by the mayor of Lafayette in January 1988. He taught himself accordion at the age of 14, and in 1955 teamed up with scrubboard player Chester Zeno to work the local club circuit, adapting his name from that of 'Doopsie', a Chicagoan dancer. In 1969-70 he recorded for the Bon Temps and Blues Unlimited labels, and in 1973 began a successful collaboration with Sonet Records and producer Sam Charters. In 1986, Paul Simon featured Dopsie on his classic *Graceland*, and three years later, Bob Dylan hired him for another much-acclaimed set, *Oh Mercy*. In 1987, he made *Crowned Prince Of Zydeco* for Maison De Soul and in 1990 he was rewarded with a major three-year contract with Atlantic. The current line-up of his band, the Twisters, features his sons Alton and David Rubin, and legendary zydeco saxophone player John Hart.

Albums: *Clifton Chenier/Rockin' Dupsee* (1970), *Hold On* (1979), *Crowned Prince Of Zydeco* (1987), *Saturday Night Zydeco* (1988), *Zy-De-Co-In* (1989).

Rogers, Stan

b. 1949, Hamilton, Ontario, Canada, d. 2 June 1983. Singer-songwriter Rogers began as a bass player in a rock band before becoming a well-respected artist within the folk arena. In 1969, he turned professional and, the following year, released two singles for RCA. There followed a period of playing the coffee house circuit, with Nigel Russell (guitar), until Stan's brother, Garnet Rogers (violin/flute/vocals/guitar), joined them. Garnet worked with Stan for nearly 10 years. Stan Rogers' low-register voice exuded a warm sensitive sound, the perfect complement to his sensitive lyrics. Remembered for songs such as 'Northwest Passage' and 'The Lock-keeper', he is probably best known for 'The Mary Ellen Carter'. Writing for films and television, and having toured a number of countries, Rogers was poised for international success but was killed in an aeroplane fire in 1983. In 1976, Rogers composed 'Forty Five Years' for his wife, Diane and in fulfilment of his wishes, his ashes were scattered in Cole Harbour, Nova Scotia, the place where he had written the song. His recordings remain a testimony to his talent.

Albums: *From Fresh Water* (1975), *Fogarty's Cove* (1976), *Turnaround* (1978), *Between The Breaks-Live* (1979), *Northwest Passage* (1981), *For The Family* (1983), *The Great Lakes Project* (1983).

Further reading: *Songs From Fogarty's Cove*, Stan Rogers.

Rooftop Singers

Cashing in on the folk music revival of the early 60s, the Rooftop Singers were a trio specifically assembled for the purpose of recording a single song, 'Walk Right In', originally recorded in 1930 by Gus Cannon And The Jugstompers. The Rooftop Singers consisted of Erik Darling (b. 25 September 1933, Baltimore, Maryland, USA), Bill Svanoe and former Benny Goodman band vocalist, Lynne Taylor. Darling had played in folk groups, the Tune Tellers and the Tarriers, the latter including future actor Alan Arkin, and replaced Pete Seeger in the Weavers in 1958, remaining with them for four years. In 1962 he heard 'Walk Right In' and adapted the lyrics for a more modern sound, utilizing two 12-string guitars and an irresistible rhythm; he then assembled the trio and signed with Vanguard Records. 'Walk Right In' became that label's, and the group's, only number 1 record. The group placed one album and two other folk songs in the US charts: 'Tom Cat' and 'Mama Don't Allow'. They disbanded in 1967 and Taylor died the same year; Darling and Svanoe subsequently retired from the music business.

Albums: *Walk Right In!* (1963), *Goodtime* (1964), *Rainy River* (1965).

Tim Rose

Rose, Tim

b. September 1940. A one-time student priest and navigator for the USAF Strategic Air Command, Rose began his professional music career playing guitar with the Journeymen, a folk group active in the early 60s which featured John Phillips and Scott McKenzie. He subsequently joined Cass Elliott and James Hendricks in another formative attraction, the Big Three. Although initially based in Chicago, the trio later moved to New York, where Rose forged a career as a solo singer on the group's disintegration in 1964. A gruff stylist and individual, he was turned down by Elektra and Mercury before securing a deal with Columbia. A series of majestic singles then followed, including 'Hey Joe' (1966) and 'Morning Dew' (1967). Rose's slow, brooding version of the former was the inspiration for that of Jimi Hendrix, while the latter, written by Rose and folksinger Bonnie Dobson, was the subject of cover versions by, among others, Jeff Beck and the Grateful Dead.

Tim Rose was assembled from several different sessions, but the presence of several crack session musicians - Felix Pappalardi (bass/piano), Bernard Purdie (drums) and Hugh McCracken (guitar) - provided a continuity. The set included a dramatic reading of 'I'm Gonna Be Strong', previously associated with Gene Pitney, and the haunting anti-war anthem 'Come Away Melinda', already recorded by the Big Three, on which Rose's blues-soaked, gritty voice was particularly effective. The singer's next release, 'Long Haired Boys', was recorded in the UK under the aegis of producer Al Kooper, before Rose returned to the USA to complete *Through Rose Coloured Eyes* (1969). This disappointing album lacked the strength of its predecessor and the artist was never again to scale the heights of his early work. He switched outlets to Capitol for *Love, A Kind Of Hate Story*, before the disillusioned performer abandoned major outlets in favour of the Playboy label where his manager's brother was employed. The promise of artistic freedom was fulfilled when Gary Wright of Spooky Tooth, a group Rose revered, produced the ensuing sessions. The album, also entitled *Tim Rose*, contained a version of the Beatles' 'You've Got To Hide Your Love Away' performed at a snail's pace. It was not a commercial success and the singer again left for the UK where he believed audiences were more receptive. Resident in London, Rose undertook a series of live concerts with fellow exile Tim Hardin, but this ill-fated partnership quickly collapsed. *The Musician*, released in 1975, revealed a voice which retained its distinctive power, but an artist without definite direction. Little has been heard from Rose for many years.

Albums: *Tim Rose* (1967), *Through Rose Coloured Eyes* (1969), *Love, A Kind Of Hate Story* (1970), *Tim Rose* (1972), *The Musician* (1975).

Rose, Tony

b. Anthony Rose, 1 May 1941, Exeter, Devon, England. Rose specialises in songs of the west country of England. Performing on guitar and concertina, and often unaccompanied, Tony has established a reputation for quality translations of traditional songs. Rose found his interest in folk music through jazz, blues and skiffle via the American folk-song tradition. He started singing at the Oxford University Heritage Society in 1960 and was also a member of the resident group, the Journeymen. During the early 60s, he worked semi-professionally while still at Oxford, and from 1965-69 taught in London. He was a resident at a number of clubs during this time, including Cecil Sharp House, Karl Dallas's Goodge Street Centre, and the Mercury Theatre (along with Young Tradition, Andy Irvine, and Lou Killen). Tony finally turned professional in September 1969, and based himself in London. He was asked by Bill Leader to record for Leader's own Trailer label and *Young Hunting* resulted. The following year, *Under The Greenwood Tree*, featuring songs of the west country, was released to critical acclaim from the folk press. He joined Nic Jones, Pete Coe and Chris Coe, in the short-lived group Bandoggs who released just one album. Despite its short life span, the group is still fondly remembered. Tony changed labels to Dingles Records for his fourth solo release, *Poor Fellows*, which featured contemporary material. He has latterly turned to journalism in addition to still performing.

Albums: *Young Hunting* (1970), *Under The Greenwood Tree* (1971), with Jon Raven, Nic Jones *Songs Of A Changing World* (c.70s), *On Banks Of Green Willow* (1977), with Raven, Harry Boardman *Steam Ballads* (c.70s), with Nic Jones, Pete and Chris Coe *Bandoggs* (1978), *Poor Fellows* (1982).

Rosselson, Leon

b. 22 June 1934, Harrow, Middlesex, England. Rosselson is well-known in UK folk circles for his incisive satirical and political songwriting. 'The World Turned Upside Down', from *That's Not The Way It's Got To Be*, has been recorded by Billy Bragg and Dick Gaughan. Earlier in his career, Rosselson had been a member of the Galliards, and later the 3 City 4, which included Roy Bailey and Martin Carthy in the line-up. The 60s television series *That Was The Week That Was* included songs written by Rosselson and, in 1962, he recorded an EP *Songs For City Squares*. *Songs For Sceptical Circles* was Rosselson's first solo album release. As a part of the Campaign for Press and Broadcasting Freedom, he produced the popular 'Ballad Of A Spycatcher' in 1987. The record featured Billy Bragg and members of the Oyster Band. *I Didn't Mean It* included longstanding compatriots Carthy and Bailey and also Frankie Armstrong and John Kirkpatrick. Due to the obvious feminist leaning in the lyric, many thought that it had been written by a woman. Rosselson continues to produce songs strong on social comment and his satirical edge shows no sign of blunting.

Albums: with the Galliards *Scottish Choice* (1962), *A-Roving* (1962), *The Galliards* (1963). With the 3 City 4 *The Three City Four* (1965), *Smoke And Dust* (1966). Solo: *Songs For Sceptical Circles* (1967), *A Laugh, A Song And A Hand Grenade* (1968), *The Word Is Hugga Mugga Chugga Lugga Humbugga Boom Chit* (1971), *That's Not The Way It's Got To Be* (1973), *Palaces Of Gold* (1975), with Roy Bailey *Love, Loneliness, Laundry* (1977), *If I Knew Who The Enemy Was* (1979), *For The Good Of The Nation* (1981), *Temporary Loss Of Vision* (1983), *Bringing The News From Nowhere* (1986), *I Didn't Mean It* (1989), *Wo Sind Die Elefanten?* (1991). Compilation: *Rosselsongs* (1990), *Guess What They're Selling At The Happiness Counter* (1992).

Further reading: *For The Good Of The Nation*, Leon Rosselson with Jeff Perks. *Bringing The News From Nowhere*, Leon Rosselson.

Ruby Blue

A folk-pop group from Edinburgh, Scotland, Ruby Blue was formed in 1986 by drama student Rebecca Pidgeon (b Cambridge, Massachusetts, USA 1963 vocals) and Roger Fife (b 1963 guitar/bass). Adding Anthony Coote (bass) and Erika Spotswood (backing vocals), the group released 'Give Us Our Flag Back' on independent label Red Flame in 1987. The debut album was an enterprising mix of folk, blues, jazz and pop with Pidgeon's crystal-clear singing bringing comparisons with the late Sandy Denny. Adding a drummer (Chris Buck, replaced in 1990 by Karlos Edwards) Ruby Blue developed an electric sound for live shows and gained attention supporting John Martyn. Pidgeon also pursued a successful acting career, appearing at the National Theatre in London and in the film *The Dawning*. Both Anthony Coote and Rebecca Pidgeon departed at the end of 1990, following her marriage to the playwright David Mamet. Her replacement was Erika Woods (Spotswood); who took over lead vocals with a band that was still unable to find commercial success, which belies their considerable talent as writers and performers.

Albums: *Glance Askances* (1988), *Down from Above* (1990), *Broken Water* (early recordings)(1992), *Almost Naked* (1993).

Runrig

The phenomenon of Runrig is an extraordinary example of cultural differences. This premier Scottish group has emerged from the traditional folk background to a higher profile in the pop/rock field and is arguably the most popular band north of Carlisle. The group first played as a three piece, featuring Rory MacDonald (b. 27 July 1949, Dornoch, Sutherland, Scotland; guitar/bass/vocals), Calum MacDonald, ex-Skyvers (b. 12 November 1953, Lochmaddy, North Uist, Scotland; drums/percussion), and Blair Douglas (accordion), in the Kelvin Hall, Glasgow, in 1973. Donnie Munro (b. 2 August 1953, Uig, Isle Of Skye, Scotland; guitar/vocals), joined the following year. Eventually Douglas left the group, and was replaced by Robert MacDonald (accordion). Sadly, Robert died of cancer in 1986. Their first recording, *Play Gaelic*, appeared on the Scottish Lismor Records label. At this time they were still not performing in a full-time capacity. However, with the higher profile, and the extra credibility of an album behind them, Runrig took the step of setting up their own label, Ridge Records, and started to perform on a full-time basis. After the release of *Highland Connection*, the group then added Iain Bayne (b. 22 January 1960, St. Andrews, Fife, Scotland; drums/percussion/piano) to the line-up. By the release of *Recovery*, it was clear that the band were more than just another folk/rock act. The music still retained it's Gaelic feel and traditions, with many of the songs being sung in Gaelic, but the group's sound took them outside the narrow boundaries of the folk arena. Eventually, English keyboard player Richard Cherns joined the group although he left in 1986, and was replaced by former Big Country member Peter Wishart (b. 9 March 1962, Dunfermline, Scotland; keyboards).

After numerous changes of line-up, the current group of Donnie Munro, Rory and Calum MacDonald, Peter Wishart, Iain Bayne and Malcolm Jones (b. 12 July 1959, Inverness, Scotland; guitar/mandolin/accordion), performed successful concerts in Canada and East Berlin in 1987, and supported U2 at Murrayfield Stadium, Edinburgh, Scotland. After the release of *The Cutter And The Clan*, the group signed to Chrysalis the following year, who immediately re-released the album. In 1989 *Searchlight* almost made the UK Top 10. Much touring followed, and in 1990, their EP *Capture The Heart*, entered the Top 50 in the UK singles chart. A television broadcast of a live performance elicited huge response from viewers, to the extent that five concerts at Glasgow's Royal Concert Hall sold out, and their subsequent video, *City Of Lights* sold well, reaching the Top 10-selling videos in the UK. The highly-acclaimed *The*

Big Wheel reached number 4 in the UK charts and the open air concert at Loch Lomond, was attended by 45,000 people. The EP *Hearthammer* broached the UK Top 30 in September 1991, followed by 'Flower Of the West' (UK number 43) together with successful tours of Europe and the UK. The acceptance of Runrig outside Scotland now seems certain and with their national pride and political stance having been made, they are poised to awaken the world to Scottish popular and traditional music, without compromise.

Albums: *Play Gaelic* (1978), *Highland Connection* (1979), *Recovery* (1981), *Heartland* (1985), *The Cutter And The Clan* (1987), *Once In A Lifetime* (1988), *Searchlight* (1989), *The Big Wheel* (1991), *Amazing Things* (1993).

Further reading: *Going Home: The Runrig Story*, Tom Morton.

Rush, Tom

b. 8 February, 1941, Portsmouth, New Hampshire, USA. Tom Rush began performing in 1961 while a student at Harvard University. Although he appeared at clubs in New York and Philadelphia, he became a pivotal figure of the Boston/New England circuit and such haunts as the Cafe Yana and the Club 47. *Live At The Unicorn*, culled from two sets recorded at another of the region's fabled coffee houses, was poorly distributed but its competent mixture of traditional songs, blues and Woody Guthrie compositions was sufficient to interest the renowned Prestige label. *Got A Mind To Ramble* and *Blues Songs And Ballads*, completed over three days, showcased an intuitive interpreter. Rush's exemplary versions of 'Barb'ry Allen' and 'Alabama Bound' were enough to confirm his place alongside Dave Van Ronk and Eric Von Schmidt, the latter of whom was an important influence on the younger musician. *Tom Rush*, his first release on the Elektra label, was one of the era's finest folk/blues sets. The artist had developed an accomplished bottleneck guitar style which was portrayed to perfection on 'Panama Limited', an 8-minute compendium comprising several different songs by Bukka White. *Take A Little Walk With Me* contained the similarly excellent 'Galveston Flood', but its high points were six electric selections drawn from songs by Bo Diddley, Chuck Berry and Buddy Holly. Arranged by Al Kooper, these performances featured musicians from Bob Dylan's ground-breaking sessions and helped transform Rush from traditional to popular performer. This change culminated in *The Circle Game*, which contained material by Joni Mitchell, James Taylor and Jackson Browne, each of whom had yet to record in their own right. The recording also included the poignant 'No Regrets', the singer's own composition, which has since become a pop classic through hit versions by the Walker Brothers (1976) and Midge Ure (1982).

Tom Rush, the artist's first release for Columbia/CBS, introduced his long-standing partnership with guitarist Trevor Veitch. Once again material by Jackson Browne and James Taylor was to the fore, but the album also contained compositions by Fred Neil and Murray McLaughlin's beautiful song of leaving home, 'Child's Song', confirming Rush as having immaculate taste in choice of material. However two subsequent releases, *Wrong End Of The Rainbow* and *Merrimack County*, saw an increased emphasis on material Rush either wrote alone, or with Veitch. By contrast a new version of 'No Regrets' was the sole original on *Ladies Love Outlaws*, a collection which marked a pause in Rush's recording career. It was 1982 before a new set, *New Year*, was released. Recorded live, it celebrated the artist's 20th anniversary while a second live album, *Late Night Radio*, featured cameos from Steve Goodman and Mimi Farina. Both were issued on Rush's Night Light label on which he also repackaged his 1962 debut. In 1990 his New Hampshire home and recording studio were totally destroyed by fire, and this cultured artist has since moved to Wyoming.

Albums: *Live At The Unicorn* (1962), *Got A Mind To Ramble* (later known as *Mind Rambling*) (1963), *Blues Songs And Ballads* (1964), *Tom Rush* (1965), *Take A Little Walk With Me* aka *The New Album* (1966), *The Circle Game* (1968), *Tom Rush* (1970), *Wrong End Of The Rainbow* (1970), *Merrimack County* (1972), *Ladies Love Outlaws* (1974), *New Year* (1982), *Late Night Radio* (1984). Compilations: *Classic Rush* (1970), *The Best Of Tom Rush* (1975).

Russell, Janet

b. 11 January 1958, Buckhaven, Fife, Scotland. Russell is as well-known for her work with Sisters Unlimited as for her solo performances. Following an early career singing in the clubs of Edinburgh, she went on to support to a number of major artists at the Edinburgh Folk and Fringe Festivals from 1981-83. In addition, Russell worked with Christine Kydd, performing on *Folk On 2* for BBC Radio. The pair released *Janet Russell And Christine Kydd*, on Greentrax. Russell's first solo outing on record emerged with *Gathering The Fragments* on Harbourtown Records, a release that was well received and gained airplay on non-folk programmes on radio. She was one of a number of performers who took part in the Les Barker album, *The Stones Of Callanish*. Having taken some time out to have her first child she was inspired to write 'Breastfeeding Baby In The Park'. The following month saw the first broadcast, on BBC Radio, of a recording of a concert by Sisters Unlimited (*No Limits*) at the Purcell Room, on the South Bank, London. In March 1991, Janet appeared on the McCalman's television series on BBC Scotland, taking time out to have a second child in December of the same year. Although still performing solo, more of Russell's time is now given to Sisters Unlimited.

Albums: *Janet Russell And Christine Kydd* (1988), *Gathering The Fragments* (1988), with others *The Stones Of Callanish* (1989).

S

Sain (Recordiau) Cyf

Sain, Wales' leading record company, was founded in Cardiff, South Wales, in 1969, by Huw Jones, Dafydd Iwan and Brian Morgan Edwards. The company moved to Llandwrog, near Caernarfon, North Wales, in 1971, and a new studio was opened in 1980. A second studio was opened in 1987. With the resurgence in interest in Celtic folk music, it was apparent that Welsh folk music was under-represented, and extensive promotion was required. Responding to this market demand, Sain regularly issued approximately 40 albums a year in Welsh and English on their Sain/Cambrian label. Their Tryfan label handles private recordings of choirs, schools and clubs. Over the years, Sain has taken over the catalogues of Cambrian, Welsh Teledisc, and Ty ar y Graig, after those companies ceased trading. Sain have released a wide number of folk recordings from artists such as Ar Log, 4 Yn Y Bar, Plethyn, Calennig, and Mabsant. The label now has a catalogue of music covering the gamut from folk to rock, pop and choral work;it released two compilations of Welsh folk artists and now has international distribution.

Albums: *'Gorau Gwerin' The Best Of Welsh Folk* (1984), *'Gorau Gwerin' The Best Of Welsh Folk 2* (1985), *Valley Lights-Folk Songs Of Wales Today* (1987).

Sainte-Marie, Buffy

b. 20 February 1941, Piapot Reserve, Saskatchewan, Canada. An honours graduate from the University of Massachusetts, Buffy eschewed a teaching career in favour of a folksinger. She was signed to the Vanguard label in 1964, following her successful performances at Gerde's Folk City. Her debut *It's My Way*, introduced a remarkable compositional and performing talent. Sainte-Marie's impassioned plea for Indian rights, 'Now That The Buffalo's Gone', reflected her native- American parentage and was one of several standout tracks, along with 'Cod'ine' and 'The Universal Soldier'. The latter was recorded, successfully, by Donovan, which helped introduce Buffy to a wider audience. Her second selection included 'Until It's Time For You To Go', a haunting love song which was later recorded by Elvis Presley. However, Sainte-Marie was also a capable interpreter of other writer's material, as her versions of songs by Bukka White, Joni Mitchell and Leonard Cohen showed. Her versatility was also apparent on a superb C&W collection, *I'm Gonna Be A Country Girl Again*, and on *Illuminations*, which featured an electronic score on several tracks. A campaigner for Indian rights, Sainte-Marie secured an international hit in 1971 with the theme song to the film, *Soldier Blue*, but subsequent releases failed to capitalize on this success. Temporarily bereft of direction, Buffy returned to the Indian theme with *Sweet America*, but with the collapse of the ABC labels, she retired to raise her family and concentrate on her work for children's foundations. She composed the 1982 Joe Cocker/Jennifer Warnes' hit, 'Up Where We Belong' which featured in the film *An Officer And A Gentleman*. Her welcome return in 1991, following her signing with Chrysalis Records, produced the warmly-received *Coincidence And Likely Stories*, which displayed her current interest in computer technology.

Albums: *It's My Way* (1964), *Many A Mile* (1965), *Little Wheel Spin And Spin* (1966), *Fire, Fleet And Candlelight* (1967), *I'm Gonna Be A Country Girl Again* (1968), *Illuminations* (1970), *She Used To Wanna Be A Ballerina* (1971), *Moonshot* (1972), *Quiet Places* (1973), *Buffy* (1974), *Changing Woman* (1975), *Sweet America* (1976), *Coincidence And Likely Stories* (1992). Compilations: *The Best Of Buffy Sainte-Marie* (1970), *Native North American Child: An Odyssey* (1974), *The Best Of Buffy Sainte-Marie, Volume 2* (1974).

Sallyangie

This duo formed in 1968 featured Mike Oldfield (guitar/vocals) and his sister Sally Oldfield (vocals). Given the era it was recorded, there are definite shades of the Incredible String Band about the *Children Of The Sun*. Other musicians featured on the album were Terry Cox (drums), Ray Warleigh (flute) and John Collins (guitar). Sallyangie was a short-lived affair with Mike destined to progress further, and Sally later to have moderate chart

Buffy Sainte-Marie

success in her own right.
Album: *Children Of The Sun* (1968).

Sandburg, Carl

b. 6 January 1878, Galesburg, Illinois, USA, d. 22
July 1967. Sandburg has been an author, historian,
singer, poet, and folk song collector. He is
predominantly remembered for his collection of
American folk song and tradition. The son of
Swedish immigrant parents, Sandburg left home in
1897, travelling and working in various cities
throughout the USA   for a year. Enrolling at
Lombard College, he became Editor in Chief of the
Lombard Review, before leaving in 1902. Sandburg
later worked as a reporter, in New York, for the
Daily News, but returned to his native Mid-west
where he worked for the Social Democratic Party.
Still working in journalism, Carl then worked for
the *Daily Socialist* in Chicago, and later, from 1917-
27 for the *Chicago Daily News*. In 1914, Sandburg's
poem 'Chicago' received the Helen Haire Levinson
prize after appearing in *Poetry* magazine. Sandburg
wrote prolifically and his Pulitzer Prize winning
Abraham Lincoln: The War Years was just part of a
six- volume series on the past President. One of his
earlier books *The American Songbag*, which was
published in 1927, contains 280 songs. When his
novel, *Remembrance Rock* was published, it received
a lukewarm response. However, Sandburg received
a Pulitzer Prize for his *Complete Poems* in 1951.

Honey And Salt, another book of poems, was
published on Sandburg's 85th birthday in 1963. He
died on 22 July 1967 from a heart attack. A
commemorative stamp was issued by the US Postal
Service in 1973.
Albums: *Carl Sandburg Sings His American Songbag*
(50s).
Further reading: *Old Troubadour-Carl Sandburg With
His Guitar Friends*, Gregory d'Alessio.

Sanders, Ric

b. Richard Sanders, Birmingham, Warwickshire,
England. After appearing in local Birmingham
bands, violinist Sanders briefly joined Stomu
Yamashta's touring group. Having been influenced
by both folk and jazz, Sanders subsequently joined
both the Soft Machine and the Albion Band. While
with the latter he was involved heavily with theatre
work, Ric formed Second Vision, along with
former Soft Machine guitarist John Etheridge, Dave
Bristow (keyboards), Jonathan Davie (b. 6
September 1954, Twickenham, Middlesex,
England; bass), and Mickey Barker, later with
Magnum (drums). They released *First Steps,* for
Chrysalis Records, in 1980. Sanders returned to
session work and released his first solo *Whenever*. He
joined Fairport Convention in 1985, appearing on
Gladys' Leap, and other subsequent releases, as well
as touring with the group and taking part in the
now legendary Annual Festival at Cropredy in

Ric Sanders

Oxfordshire. Sanders has toured with Simon Nicol, as an acoustic duo, and with Gordon Giltrap. In addition, Ric regularly gives performance lectures in schools on playing violin. In 1991, he made a violin instruction video, and others are planned. He has contributed to many albums including those by June Tabor, Andrew Cronshaw, All About Eve and Jethro Tull.

Albums: with Soft Machine *Alive And Well* (1978), with Second Vision *First Steps* (1980), with the Albion Band *Rise Up Like The Sun* (1978), *Whenever* (1984), with Pete York and Steve Richardson *String Time* (mid-80s), with Gordon Giltrap *One To One* (1989), *Neither Time Nor Distance* (1991).

Sebastian, John

b. 17 March 1944, New York, USA. The son of the famous classical harmonica player John Sebastian. John Jnr. is best known for his seminal jug band/rock fusion with the much-loved Lovin' Spoonful in the 60s, which established him as one of the finest American songwriters of the century. When the Spoonful finally collapsed Sebastian started a solo career that was briefly threatened when he was asked to become the fourth member of Crosby, Stills And Nash, but he declined when it was found that Stephen Stills wanted him to play drums. In 1969 his performance was one of the highlights of the Woodstock Festival, singing his warm and friendly material to a deliriously happy audience. His tie-dye jacket and jeans appearance, warm rapport, and acoustic set (aided by copious amounts of LSD) elevated him to a star. Sebastian debuted in 1970 with an outstanding solo work *John B Sebastian*, containing much of the spirit of Woodstock. Notable tracks like the autobiographical 'Red Eye Express' and the evocative 'How Have You Been', were bound together with one of his finest songs, the painfully short 'She's A Lady'. Less than two minutes long, this love song was perfect for the times, and was a lyrical triumph with lines like 'She's a lady, and I chance to see her in my shuffling daze, she's a lady, hypnotised me there that day, I came to play in my usual way, hey'. Simply accompanied by Stills' and Crosby's mellow Gretsch guitar, it remains a modern classic. Sebastian faltered with the uneven *Four Of Us*, a travelogue of hippie ideology but followed a few months later with *Real Live*, an engaging record, recorded at four gigs in California. At that time Sebastian was performing at a punishing rate throughout Europe and America. *Tarzana Kid* in 1974 sold poorly, but has latterly grown in stature with critics.

At this time Sebastian was working with the late Lowell George, and a strong Little Feat influence is shown. The album's high point is a Sebastian/George classic, the beautiful 'Face Of Appalachia'. Two years later John was asked to write the theme song for a US comedy television series, *Welcome Back Kotter*. The result was a number 1 hit, 'Welcome Back'. Astonishingly, since then, no new album had appeared until 1992, when a Japanese label released his most recent songs. Throughout that time, however, Sebastian never stopped working. He accompanied Sha Na Na and NRBQ on many lengthy tours, appeared as a television presenter, wrote a children's book and among other commissions he composed the music for the *Care Bears* television series. Severe problems with his throat threatened his singing career at one point. He declined to be part of the 1992 reformed Lovin' Spoonful. Sebastian was, is and always will be the heart and soul of that band. He returned with the delightful Tar Beach in 1993. Although long-term fans noted that his voice was slightly weaker the album contained a varied mixture of rock, blues and country. Many songs he had written a decade earlier were included, the most notable being his uplifting tribute to Smokey Robinson; 'Smokey Don't Go.

Albums: *John B. Sebastian* (1970), *The Four Of Us* (1971), *Real Live* (1971), *Tarzana Kid* (1974), *Welcome Back* (1976), *Tar Beach* (1993).

Seeger, Mike

b. 15 August 1933, New York City, New York, USA. Mike is the son of well-known musicologist Charles Seeger, and Ruth Crawford Seeger, composer and author. From his youngest days he was surrounded by traditional music, and learned to play the autoharp at the age of 12. A few years later, he started to play guitar, mandolin, fiddle, dulcimer, mouth harp, and dobro. Together with his sister Peggy Seeger, he played with local square dance bands in the Washington area. His first involvement with country music came about while serving 'time' for conscientious objection, working in a hospital, when he teamed up with Hazel Dickens and Bob Baker. Mike formed the New Lost City Ramblers in 1958, with John Cohen and Tom Paley. That year, Seeger won the Galax Old Time Fiddlers Convention in Virginia for banjo work. It was during the late 50s that Mike started the first of his many recordings of other singers, including Elizabeth 'Libba' Cotten, and Dock Boggs. With changes in the personnel of the New Lost City Ramblers, Mike worked a great deal more in a solo capacity, but still recorded with the New Lost City Ramblers for the Folkways label. Among other projects, Mike was involved with the Newport Folk Festival in Rhode Island, and was a director of the Smithsonian Folklife Company from 1970. By the late 60s, he had formed the Strange Creek

Singers with Alice L. Gerrard, Lamar Grier and Hazel Dickens. On 16 August 1970 he married Gerrard, but they were later divorced. Mike has recorded numerous albums with the various line-ups, with sister Peggy, and solo, and has continued to perform at festivals in the same capacity at home and throughout the world. His earlier work as a collector has also helped to keep alive a great deal of Southern traditional music.

Albums: *Oldtime Country Music* (1962), *Mike Seeger* (1964), *Tipple, Loom And Rail: Songs Of The Industrialization Of The South* (1965), *Mike And Peggy Seeger* (1966), *Strange Creek Singers* (1968), with Peggy Seeger *American Folksongs For Children* (1970), *Mike And Alice Seeger In Concert* (1970), *Music From True Vine* (1971), *Second Annual Farewell Reunion* (1973), *Alice And Mike* (1980), as A. Roebic And The Exertions *Old Time Music Dance Party* (1986), *Fresh Old Time-String Band Music* (1988), with Peggy and Penny Seeger and members of their families *American Folksongs For Christmas* (1989), *Solo-Oldtime Country Music* (1990).

Seeger, Peggy

b. Margaret Seeger, 17 June 1935, New York City, New York, USA. Seeger was accomplished on guitar, banjo, Appalachian dulcimer, autoharp and concertina. Her parents, Ruth Crawford and Charles Seeger were both professional musicians and teachers. They insisted that their daughter receive a formal musical education from the age of seven years. At the same time they encouraged her interest in folk music and, at the age of 10 Peggy started to learn guitar. A few years later she began to play 5-string banjo. After majoring in music at college, she started singing folksongs professionally. In 1955, Seeger relocated to Holland and studied Russian at university. Peggy first came to the UK in 1956 as an actress, to take part in a television film, *Dark Side Of The Moon*, and also joined the Ramblers, a group which included Ewan MacColl, Alan Lomax and Shirley Collins. In 1957, together with MacColl and Charles Parker, she worked on a series of documentaries for the BBC which are now commonly known as *The Radio Ballads*. These programmes were highly innovative and, together with music, brought the thoughts and views of a whole range of workers to a large listening public. In 1959, Peggy became a British subject, since she has been in much demand at folk clubs and festivals. In addition, she holds workshops and seminars, both at home and abroad. Along with Frankie Armstrong, Seeger has long championed women's rights through many of her songs. One such song, 'Gonna Be An Engineer' is possibly her best-known on the subject of equal rights for women. Due to her knowledge of folk music, Peggy was a leading-

light in the English folk song revival. After Ewan died in 1989, Peggy again launched a solo career, touring both the USA and Australia. Her collaboration with MacColl, produced hundreds of songs and she has recorded a substantial number of albums in her own right, as well as with Mike and Penny Seeger. *The New Briton Gazette No.3* and *Fields Of Vietnam*, both recorded on Folkways in the USA, with Ewan MacColl and the Critics Group, were never released.

Selected albums: with Ewan MacColl *Two Way Trip* (1961), with MacColl *The Amorous Muse* (1966), with MacColl *The Long Harvest, Vol. 1* (1966), with MacColl *The Long Harvest, Vol. 2* (1967), with MacColl *The Long Harvest, Vol. 3* (1968), with MacColl *The Angry Muse* (1968), with Sandra Kerr and Frankie Armstrong *The Female Frolic* (1968), with MacColl *The Long Harvest, Vol. 4* (1969), with MacColl *The Long Harvest, Vol. 5* (1970), with Mike Seeger *American Folksongs For Children* (1970), with MacColl *The Long Harvest, Vol. 6* (1971), with MacColl *The Long Harvest, Vol. 7* (1972), with MacColl *The Long Harvest, Vol. 8* (1973), with MacColl *The Long Harvest, Vol. 9* (1974), with MacColl *The Long Harvest, Vol. 10* (1975), with MacColl *Penelope Isn't Waiting Anymore* (1977), with MacColl *Saturday Night At The Bull And Mouth* (1977), *Cold Snap* (1977), *Hot Blast* (1978), *Different Therefore Equal* (1979), with Ewan MacColl *Kilroy Was Here* (1980), *From Where I Stand* (1982), *Familiar Faces* (1988, with Seeger & MacColl families *American Folksongs For Christmas* (1989)), with Ewan MacColl *Naming Of Names* (1990). Compilations: *The Best Of Peggy Seeger* (1962), *The World Of Ewan MacColl And Peggy Seeger* (1970), *The World Of Ewan MacColl And Peggy Seeger, Vol. 2* (1972), *The Folkways Years 1955-92 - Songs Of Love And Politics* (1992).

Further reading: *Who's Going To Shoe Your Pretty Little Foot, Who's Going To Glove Your Hand?*, Peggy Seeger with Tom Paley. *Folk Songs Of Peggy Seeger*, Peggy Seeger. *Travellers Songs Of England And Scotland*, Peggy Seeger and Ewan MacColl. *Doomsday In The Afternoon*, Peggy Seeger and Ewan MacColl.

Seeger, Pete

b. 3 May 1919, New York City, New York, USA. Educated at Harvard University, he is the brother of Peggy Seeger and half brother of Mike Seeger. Pete Seeger's mother was a violin teacher, and his father a renowned musicologist. While still young Pete Seeger learned to play banjo and ukelele, and shortly afterwards he developed his interest in American folk music. Seeger took his banjo round the country, playing and learning songs from the workers and farmers. He served in the US Army

Pete Seeger

during World War II. In addition to being a member of the Weavers from 1949-58, he had earlier been in a group called the Almanac Singers. The group included Woody Guthrie, Lee Hays and Millard Lampell. The Almanac Singers had frequently given free performances to union meetings and strikers' demonstrations. Despite such apparent diversions, Seeger maintained a successfully high profile in his own solo career. The era of McCarthyism put a blight on many live performances, owing to the right-wing political paranoia that existed at the time. It was in 1948 that Seeger was blacklisted and had to appear before the House of Un-American Activities Committee for his alleged communist sympathies. This did not stop Seeger from performing sell-out concerts abroad and speaking out on a wide range of civil rights and environmental issues. He became known for popularizing songs such as 'Little Boxes', 'Where Have All The Flowers Gone' and, 'We Shall Overcome'. In more recent times Seeger also performed and recorded with Arlo Guthrie. Seeger was also involved with the Clearwater Sloop project on the Hudson River, attempting to publicize the threat of pollution. He has always worked and campaigned for civil rights, peace and equality, and has never compromised his ideals. By the mid-70s, Seeger had released in excess of 50 albums, several of which were instructional records for banjo playing. In addition to these albums Seeger has appeared on the work of many other artists providing either vocal or instrumental back-up. Seeger is one of the most important figures ever in the development of free speech and humanitarian causes through folk music.

Albums: *We Sing Vol.1* (1950), *Darling Corey* (1950), *Pete Seeger Concert* (1953), *Pete Seeger Sampler* (1954), *Goofing-Off Suite* (1954), *How To Play The Five String Banjo* (1954), *Frontier Ballads, Vol. 1* (1954), *Frontier Ballads, Vol. 2* (1954), *Birds, Beasts, Bugs And Little Fishes* (1954), *Birds, Beasts, Bugs And Bigger Fishes* (1955), *The Folksinger's Guitar Guide* (1955), *Bantu Choral Folk Songs* (1955), *Folksongs Of Our Continents* (1955), *With Voices Together We Sing* (1956), *American Industrial Ballads* (1956), *Love Songs For Friends And Foes* (1956), *American Ballads* (1957), *American Favorite Ballads* (1957), *Gazette With Pete Seeger, Vol. 1* (1958), *Sleep Time* (1958), *Pete Seeger And Sonny Terry* (1958), *We Shall Overcome* (1958), *Song And Play Time With Pete Seeger* (1958), *American Favorite Ballads, Vol. 2* (1959), *Hootenanny Tonight* (1959), *Folk Songs For Young People* (1959), *Folk Festival At Newport, Vol. 1* (1959), with Frank Hamilton *Nonesuch* (1959), *American Favorite Ballads, Vol. 3* (1960), *Songs Of The Civil War* (1960), *Champlain Valley Songs* (1960), *At Village Gate, Vol. 1* (1960), *The Rainbow Quest* (1960), *Sing Out With

Pete* (1961), *American Favorite Ballads, Vol. 4* (1961), *Gazette, Vol. 2* (1961), *Pete Seeger: Story Songs* (1961), *At Village Gate, Vol. 2* (1962), *American Favorite Ballads, Vol. 5* (1962), *In Person At The Bitter End* (1962), *American Game And Activity Songs For Children* (1962), *The Bitter And The Sweet* (1963), *Pete Seeger, Children's Concert At Town Hall* (1963), *We Shall Overcome* (1963), *Broadside Ballads, Vol. 2* (1963), *Little Boxes And Other Broadsides* (1963), *The Nativity* (1963), *In Concert, Vol. 2 (St. Pancras Town Hall)* (1964, rec. 1959), *Broadsides Songs And Ballads* (1964), *Broadsides 2* (1964), *Freight Train* (1964), *Little Boxes* (1964), *Pete Seeger And Big Bill Broonzy In Concert* (1964), *Strangers And Cousins* (1965), *The Pete Seeger Box* (1965), *Songs Of Struggle And Protest* (1965), *I Can See A New Day* (1965), *God Bless The Grass* (1966), *Dangerous Songs!?* (1966), *Pete Seeger Sings Woody Guthrie* (1967), *Waist Deep In The Big Muddy* (1967), *Traditional Christmas Carols* (1967), *Pete Seeger Sings Leadbelly* (1968), *American Folksongs For Children* (1968), *Pete Seeger Sings And Answers Questions At The Ford Hall Forum In Boston* (1968), *Where Have All The Flowers Gone* (1969), *Leadbelly* (1969), *Pete Seeger Now* (1969), *Pete Seeger Young Vs. Old* (1971), *Rainbow Race* (1973), *Banks Of Marble* (1974), *Pete Seeger And Brother Kirk Visit Sesame Street* (1974), *Pete Seeger And Arlo Guthrie Together In Concert* (1975), with Ed Renehan *Fifty Sail On Newburgh Bay* (1976), *Tribute To Leadbelly* (1977), *Circles And Seasons* (1979), *American Industrial Ballads* (1979), *Singalong-Sanders Theater 1980* (1980). Compilations: *The World Of Pete Seeger* (1974), *The Essential Pete Seeger* (1978), *Live At The Royal Festival Hall* (1986), *Can't You See This System's Rotten Through And Through* (1986).

Further reading: *How Can I Keep From Singing*, David King Dunaway. *Everybody Says Freedom*, Bob Reiser.

Seekers

Founded in Australia in 1963, the original Seekers comprised Athol Guy (b. 5 January 1940, Victoria, Australia, vocals/double bass), Keith Potger (b. 2 March 1941, Columbo, Sri Lanka, vocals/guitar), Bruce Woodley (b. 25 July 1942, Melbourne, Australia, vocals/guitar) and Ken Ray (lead vocals/guitar). After a year with the above line-up, Athol Guy recruited Judith Durham (b. 3 July 1943, Melbourne, Australia) as the new lead singer and it was this formation which won international success. Following a visit to London in 1964, the group were signed to the Grade Agency and secured a prestigious guest spot on the televised *Sunday Night At The London Palladium*. Tom Springfield, of the recently-defunct Springfields, soon realized that the Seekers could fill the gap left

Seekers

by his former group and offered his services as songwriter/producer. Although 1965 was one of the most competitive years in pop, the Seekers strongly challenged the Beatles and the Rolling Stones as the top chart act of the year. A trilogy of folk/pop smashes: 'I'll Never Find Another You', 'A World Of Our Own' and 'The Carnival Is Over' widened their appeal, leading to lucrative supper club dates and frequent television appearances. Apart from Tom Springfield's compositions, they also scored a massive chart hit with Malvina Reynolds' 'Mornington Ride' and gave Paul Simon his first UK success with a bouncy adaptation of 'Someday One Day'. Meanwhile, Bruce Woodley teamed up with Simon to write some songs, including the Cyrkle hit 'Red Rubber Ball'. In early 1967, the breezy 'Georgy Girl' (written by Tom Springfield and Jim Dale) was a transatlantic Top 10 hit but thereafter the group were no longer chart regulars. Two years later, they bowed out in a televised farewell performance. Judith Durham subsequently went solo, while Keith Potger oversaw the formation of the New Seekers. In 1975, the old Seekers briefly reformed with teenage Dutch singer Louisa Wisseling replacing Judith Durham. They enjoyed a final moment of chart glory when 'The Sparrow Song' topped the Australian charts.

Albums: *The Seekers* (1965), *A World Of Our Own* (1965), *The New Seekers* (1965, US release), *Come The Day* (1966), *Seen In Green* (1967), *Georgy Girl* (1967, US release), *Live At The Talk Of The Town* (1968), *Four And Only Seekers* (1969), *The Seekers* (1975). Compilations: *The Very Best Of The Seekers* (1974), *An Hour Of The Seekers* (1988), *The Seekers Greatest Hits* (1988).

Serendipity Singers

This nine piece group was formed at the University of Colorado in the wake of the success of the New Christy Minstrels. The line-up was based around Mike Brovsky (vocals), Brooks Hatch (vocals), and Bryan Sennett (vocals). To these were added Jon Arbenz (guitar), John Madden (guitar), Bob Young (bass), Diane Decker (vocals), Tommy Tieman (vocals) and Lynne Weintraub (vocals). Their material, though not strictly folk, encompassed a range of songs from traditional through to pop music. From performing on college campuses, they moved outside of the confines of university and sang at the Bitter End in New York. As a result, the group were offered a recording deal with Philips and a spot on the influential *Hottenanny* television show. *The Serendipity Singers* contained the group's one big hit, 'Don't Let The Rain Come Down (Crooked Little Man)', which reached the US Top 10 in 1964. The album scaled the US Top 20 the

same year. A follow-up 'Beans In My Ears' made the US Top 30, but despite regularly touring at home, mainly on the college circuit, and touring abroad, the group never repeated their earlier success.

Albums: *The Serendipity Singers* (1964), *The Many Sides Of The Serendipity Singers* (1964), *Take Your Shoes Off With The Serendipity Singers* (1965), *We Belong Together* (1966).

Shadowfax

Taking their name from Gandalf's horse in *The Lord Of The Rings*, this Windham Hill band pursued a path of new-age inspired folk, bringing in strong elements of jazz and medieval music. The unit was formed in near Chicago, Illinois, USA during the winter of 1972 by Chuck Greenberg (b. 1950, Chicago, Illinois, USA; saxophone/lyricon), Greg Stinson (b. August 1949, Oklahoma, USA; guitars) and Phil Maggini (b. March 1949, Chicago, Illinois, USA; bass), later adding Stuart Nevitt (b. March 1953, Elizabeth, New Jersey, USA; drums/percussion) in 1974. Their debut *Watercourse Way* made little impression upon release in 1976 and it was not until *Shadowfax* in 1982 that the group received both success and acclaim. This album reached a high placing on the Billboard jazz chart and won the top new jazz band award in *Cashbox*. The band added Jamii Szmadzinski (b. 1954, Michigan, USA; violin) and Jared Stewart (b. February 1956, Los Angeles, California, USA; piano/synthesizers) for *Shadowdance*. Additional personnel who have passed through this truly idealistic aggregation include Emil Richards, Michael Spiro, Mike Lehocky, Adam Rudolph, David Lewis and Charlie Bisharat

Albums: *Watercourse Way* (1976), *Shadowfax* (1982), *Shadowdance* (1983), *Dreams Of the Children* (1985), *Too Far To Whisper* (1986), *Folksongs For A Nuclear Village* (1988).

Shanty Crew

The Shanty Crew were formed in 1976 with the group specializing in both traditional and modern sea songs. They are the longest established group singing traditional sailor shanties, in Britain. Two of the founder members, Chris Roche and Gerry Milne, survived the changes to record *Let The Wind Blow Free*. The release included such standards as 'Rolling Down To Old Maui' and 'Haul Away For Rosie-O'. In 1986 the group appeared at the Liverpool and Douarnenez Sea Festivals. Inevitably, the line-up fluctuated again until Roche, teamed with Steve Belsey (the other founder member), Tony Goodenough, Phil Jarrett, Phil Money and Dominic Magog to record *Stand To Yer Ground*. With the addition of Goodenough, they have

Serendipity Singers

added French shanties to the group's repertoire, as Tony speaks fluent French. In addition to researching and performing, Roche is editor of the *Journal Of The Cape Horner Association*, and holds the largest private collection of books and records of shanties and sailors songs in the world.

Albums: *Let The Wind Blow Free* (1984), *Stand To Yer Ground* (1990).

Sharp, Cecil

b. Cecil James Sharp, 22 November 1859, Denmark Hill, London, England, d. 23 June 1924. Sharp is most commonly remembered for his collecting of folk songs and dance tunes in order to preserve the tradition of popular music. He collected a wealth of material, both in Britain and the USA, where he made regular trips to the Appalachian Mountains, often with his assistant Maud Karpeles (b. 12 November 1885, London, England). Sharp was the third child of nine, having four brothers and four sisters. Cecil, always a weak child, left school in 1874. His early hay-fever turned to asthma in later life. His interest in music was largely inherited from his mother, though both parents encouraged him. He entered Clare College, Cambridge, in October 1879, where he read Mathematics. Leaving in 1882, he went to Australia, where he took a job washing Hansom cabs in Adelaide. There followed various jobs as a bank clerk and violin teacher, and eventually he became assistant organist at St. Peter's Cathedral, Adelaide. During one trip to England, a bout of typhoid caused paralysis in Sharp's legs. In early 1891 he tried unsuccessfully to get his compositions published, and returned to England the following year. He taught in England until 1896, and was Principal of Hampstead Conservatory until 1905. In 1911 Sharp founded the English Folk Dance Society, which later became the English Folk Dance And Song Society (EFDSS), having amalgamated with the English Folk Song Society. The first song Sharp collected was 'The Seeds Of Love', which he heard his gardener, John England, singing. This song was the first to be included in his book *Folk Songs From Somerset*. Between 1916 and 1918, often accompanied by his long time assistant Karpeles, Sharp spent one year in the Southern Appalachian Mountains of America. He collected a wealth of material and produced numerous notes, books and articles on song and dance music. It is impossible to imagine what would have gone undiscovered, had it not been for his enthusiasm and knowledge of the subject. Sharp died on 23 June 1924, in Hampstead, London, and was cremated at Golders Green, London on 25 June. A memorial service was held at St. Martin-in-the-Fields, Trafalgar Square. A year earlier, his

university had conferred on him the degree of Master of Music. Maud Karpeles died on 1 October 1976 at the age of 91. Sharp left his manuscript collection of songs, tunes and dance notes to Clare College, and his library to the English Folk Dance Society. The foundation stone for Cecil Sharp House, the London Headquarters of the English Folk Dance And Song Society, was laid on 24 June 1929.

Further reading: *Folk Songs From Somerset*, with C.L. Marson. *Songs Of The West*, with S. Baring Gould. *English Folk Songs For Schools*, with S. Baring Gould. *English Folk Carols*, Cecil Sharp. *English Folk Chanterys*, Cecil Sharp. *English Folksongs From The Southern Appalachian Mountains*, Cecil Sharp, edited by Maud Karpeles. *Cecil Sharp*, A.H.Fox Strangeways with Maud Karpeles. *Cecil Sharp-His Life And Work*, Maud Karpeles. *The Crystal Spring: English Folk Songs Collected By Cecil Sharp*, edited by Maud Karpeles.

Shearston, Gary

b. 9 January 1939, Inverell, New South Wales, Australia. This singer/songwriter was also proficient on guitar and harmonica. Shearston moved with his family to Sydney at the age of 12, after his father's farm was destroyed by drought. By the time Gary was 19 he was a professional singer performing traditional Australian music in pubs, clubs and on radio and television. In the late 50s Gary made his first recording, for the Festival label, and this was followed by a number of albums for CBS in the early to mid-60s. Two of these albums were described as 'among the best records of traditional music ever made in Australia'. In 1965, Shearston received an award for the best composition of the year when 'Sometime Lovin'' was covered by a number of artists including Peter Paul And Mary. In the mid-60s, together with Martin Wyndham-Read, he recorded a live album on the Australian Score record label, although CBS would not let Shearston appear on the album. In addition, Shearston had his own folk music television programme. He then travelled to the US in 1968 and lived there for the next four years. During the mid-70s Gary travelled to Britain, where he recorded two albums for Charisma. Shearston's one major hit in the UK came in 1974, when 'I Get A Kick Out Of You' made the Top 10. This single made Shearston the first Australian artist to have a simultaneous hit in Britain and Australia. Despite the long gap between albums he carried on and worked the folk clubs of Europe. Returning to Australia from England in 1988, Shearston was made a Deacon of the Anglican Church in December 1991.

Albums: *Folk Songs And Ballads Of Australia* (1964),

Songs Of Our Time (1964), *Australian Broadside* (1965), *The Springtime It Brings On The The Shearing* (1965), *Bolters, Bushrangers And Duffers* (1966), *Gary Shearston Sings His Songs* (1966), *Abreaction* (1967), *Dingo* (1974), *The Greatest Stone On Earth And Other Two Bob Wonders* (1975), *Aussie Blue* (1989). Compilations: *Gary Shearston Revisited* (1975), *I Get A Kick Out Of You* (1976).

Shocked, Michelle

b. 1962, Dallas, Texas, USA. This roots singer/songwriter's music draws on frequently tough experiences of a nomadic lifestyle. Her childhood had been divided between a religiously inclined mother (Catholic then Mormon), and her estranged father, a some-time mandolin player. She originally came to prominence via a Walkman recorded gig, taped around a campfire, complete with crickets on backing vocals. *Short Sharp Shocked* highlighted more varied and less self-conscious stylings than the more mainstream Suzanne Vega/Tracy Chapman school. *Captain Swing* was her 'big band' record, where she was joined once more by Dwight Yoakam's producer/guitarist Pete Anderson, as well as a plethora of famous extras (Fats Domino, Bobby 'Blue' Bland, Randy Newman). Despite songs with titles like 'God Is A Real Estate Developer', its jazzy rhythms and swishing brass made it her most commercially accessible. The album's title was taken from the 19th Century leader of a farm labourer's revolt, the type of subject matter which put her in good company with touring companion Billy Bragg. The recording of *Arkansas Traveller* was completed by travelling across the US and further afield with a portable studio. Hence musicians like Taj Mahal, Doc Watson, Levon Helm (the Band), Clarence 'Gatemouth' Brown and Hothouse Flowers made their contributions in Ireland, Australia and elsewhere. Shocked had spent time researching the origins of American music and in particular the black-faced minstrel legacy, which she attacked with her own traditional songs. Shocked is one of the most interesting of the new generation of folk artists.
Albums: *The Texas Campfire Tapes* (1987), *Short Sharp Shocked* (1988), *Captain Swing* (1989), *Arkansas Traveller* (1992).

Shusha

b. Shusha Guppy, 7 January 1940, Teheran, Iran. This songwriter, singer and author emigrated to France at the age of 16, and was educated at the Sorbonne in Paris, studying Oriental Languages and Philosophy. Having married an English author during the 60s, she relocated to London. Although she had trained and studied as an opera singer, her interest lay in a range of musical styles from medieval folk through 16th century ballads, to the works of writers such as Jacques Brel and Joan Baez. Shusha garnered a good deal of critical praise for a number of her recordings during the 70s, and made a number of television and radio appearances. In 1973, she travelled with the nomadic Bakhtiari tribe in Iran, making two films. The first, *People Of The Wind*, a documentary about the migration of the tribe across the mountains, won an Oscar nomination for best documentary in 1977. A soundtrack album from the film was later released in the USA. The second film was a short of Shusha singing during the journey. Never predictable, her albums varied in content. *From East To West* saw a collaboration with arranger Paul Buckmaster, setting traditional Persian songs to a jazz/rock setting. *Here I Love You*, by comparison, was an album of her own songs, while. *Durable Fire* featured songs by English poets, including William Shakespeare and Ted Hughes.
Albums: *Song Of Long-Time Lovers* (1972), *Persian Love Songs And Mystic Chants* (1973), *Shusha* (1974), *This Is The Day* (1974), *Before The Deluge* (1975), *From East To West* (1978), *Here I Love You* (1980), with various artists *Lovely In The Dances-Songs Of Sydney Carter* (1981), *Durable Fire* (1983), *Strange Affair* (1987).
Further reading: *The Blindfold Horse-Memories Of A Persian Childhood*, Shusha Guppy, *A Girl In Paris*, Shusha Guppy, *Looking Back*, Shusha Guppy.

Siberry, Jane

This Canadian singer/composer stands outside the traditional boundaries of folk music, being compared to such artists as Laurie Anderson, Joni Mitchell and Suzanne Vega. Having graduated from the University of Guelph with a degree in Microbiology, Siberry began by performing on the local coffee house circuit in Canada. Her first, independently produced, album, in 1981, was followed by a Canadian tour. She financed the project by earning tips as a waitress. *No Borders Here* included 'Mimi On The Beach', an underground hit at home in Canada. *The Speckless Sky* went gold in Canada, and won two CASBYS, Canada's People Choice Award, for both album and producer of the year. Siberry made her first live appearance in Europe, following the release of *The Walking*, at the ICA in London. *The Walking* marked her recording debut for Reprise. Having recorded her earlier production demos in a 16-track studio located in an apple orchard near Toronto, she decided to record the whole of *Bound By The Beauty* at Orchard Studio. For the task, a 24-track unit was parachuted into the studio. The whole album was recorded in a matter of weeks, and included Teddy Borowiecki, who had played with k.d. lang (piano/accordion), Stich Winston (drums), John Switzer (bass), and Ken Myhr (guitar). The album was mixed by Kevin Killen, known for work with both Kate Bush and Peter Gabriel and was greeted with considerable critical acclaim.

Albums: *No Borders Here* (1984), *The Speckless Sky* (1985), *The Walking* (1988), *Bound By The Beauty* (1991).

Siebel, Paul

b. Buffalo, New York. For many years Paul Siebel was a popular performer in Greenwich Village clubs. His blend of country and folk music pre-dated its more widespread appeal following the release of Bob Dylan's *Nashville Skyline* album. Although actively pursuing a musical career thoughout most of the 60s, it was not until the following decade that the singer made his recording debut. *Woodsmoke And Oranges* was a critically acclaimed collection and featured 'Louise', Siebel's original composition which was later covered by several acts, including Linda Ronstadt and Iain Matthews. The artist's *Jack-Knife Gypsy* was equally meritorious and an excellent supporting group, including Richard Greene (fiddle) and David Grisman (mandolin), enhanced Siebel's evocative delivery. Public indifference sadly undermined his development although Paul has remained a popular live attraction.

Albums: *Woodsmoke And Oranges* (1970), *Jack-Knife Gypsy* (1971), *Paul Siebel Live* (1981).

Silber, Irwin

b. 17 October 1925, New York City, New York, USA. Silber has been involved in the music business as an editor, publisher, author and producer. His involvement in folk music started with the formation of the Folksay Group at Brooklyn College, from where he graduated with a BA in 1945. Soon afterwards, he formed People's Songs Inc, in an attempt to use the music to promote causes both social and political. Just a few years later, People's Songs Inc was declared bankrupt. Not to be outdone, Silber, along with a group which included Alan Lomax, Paul Robeson, and Pete Seeger, founded People's Artists Inc. The organization, acting as an agency, secured bookings for folk artists and performers who were regarded as 'political'. The following year, 1950, the publication of *Sing Out!* magazine started, and Silber remained its editor until 1967. In 1964, Silber published an open letter to Bob Dylan, criticizing Dylan's musical change of direction, away from political comment. The letter, naturally, brought forth complaints galore. Silber later teamed-up with Moses Asch, who founded both

Asch and Folkways Records. Together they formed Oak Publications, and published books about folk music, and folk music books. They produced books by such performers and writers as Tom Paxton, Jean Ritchie and many more. In 1967, Oak Publications was bought out by Music Sales Limited, London, at which point Silber resigned as editor, joining the *National Guardian* newspaper the following year. He continued to produce a number of albums, as well a numerous articles and books on the subject of folk music.

Further reading: *Lift Every Voice. Reprints From The People's Songs Bulletin. Songs Of The Civil War. Hootenanny Song Book. Songs Of The Great American West. Folksong Festival. Great Atlantic And Pacific Songbook. The Vietnam Songbook*, with Barbara Dane. *The Season Of The Year. Songs America Voted By. Songs Of Independence. The Folksinger's Wordbook*, with Fred Silber.

Sileas

This Celtic harp and vocal duo, pronounced Sheelis, comprises of Patsy Seddon (b. 12 January 1961, Edinburgh, Scotland) and Mary MacMaster (b. 22 November 1955, Glasgow, Scotland). The name Sileas is taken from a 17th century Gaelic poet, Sileas Na Ceapaich. Seddon learnt violin and Scottish harp as a child, studied music at school, and achieved an Honours Degree in Celtic Studies at university. MacMaster also learnt piano, recorder, cello, and guitar whilst young. Mary, however, spent time busking with the guitar and dulcimer, not taking up the harp until the age of 22. She studied Scottish History and Gaelic at Edinburgh University, receiving an Honours MA in 1985. Both were members of the all woman group Sprangeen from 1982-86, but it was in 1985, that the duo started playing professionally together. Sprangeen recorded only one album for Springthyme records in 1984.

In 1986, after leaving the group, they released their debut album as a duo, *Delighted With Harps*. Together they have toured Germany, Switzerland, and the USA, and have also played festivals in the UK, Europe and Scandinavia, in addition to travelling to the Sudan for the British Council. In Scotland they have been selected twice in the Top 10 folk albums category. In 1991, they formed the Poozies with Sally Barker and Karen Tweed. The same year Patsy and Mary were also asked by Dick Gaughan to join Clan Alba. The other members include Brian MacNeill, Davy Steele, Gary West, Mike Travis, and Dave Tulloch. In this outfit the two are featured on electric harps.

With Sileas, as with the other line-ups, they have successfully managed to span both traditional and contemporary music forms. Their imaginative and

Silkie

innovative playing has made them in demand on other artists recordings, including those of June Tabor and Maddy Prior (the Silly Sisters), and Sally Barker.

Albums: *Sprangeen* (1984), *Delighted With Harps* (1986), *Beating Harps* (1988), *Harpbreakers* (1990).

Silkie

Sylvia Tatler (vocals), Mike Ramsden (guitar, vocals), Ivor Aylesbury (guitar, vocals) and Kevin Cunningham (double bass) were students at Hull University, England, when they were 'discovered' by Beatles' manager Brian Epstein. The Silkie's folk credentials were established with their debut single, 'Blood Red River', but they achieved a commercial success with 'You've Got To Hide Your Love Away', which clipped the UK Top 30 in October 1965. This engaging release was produced by its composers - John Lennon and Paul McCartney - but the group was unable to repeat its charm and lost any prevailing pop/folk battle to the Seekers.

Albums: *The Silkie Sing The Songs Of Bob Dylan* (1965), *You've Got To Hide Your Love Away* (1965, US release).

Sill, Judee

b. c.1949, Los Angeles, USA, d. 1974. This Los Angeles-based artist first attracted attention for her work with the city's folk-rock fraternity. An early composition, 'Dead Time Bummer Blues', was recorded by the Leaves, whose bassist, Jim Pons, later joined the Turtles. He introduced Sill to Blimp, the group's publishing company, the fruit of which was 'Lady O', their finest late-period performance. The song also appeared on *Judee Sill*, the artist's poignant debut, which was largely produced by Pons in partnership with another ex-Leave, John Beck. Graham Nash supervised the sole exception, 'Jesus Was A Crossmaker', which drew considerable comment over its lyrical content and was one of the songs Sill featured on a rare UK television appearance. *Heart Food* continued this uncompromising individual's quest for excellence and deftly balanced upbeat, country-tinged compositions with dramatic emotional ballads. A gift for melody suggested a long, successful career, but Judee Sill subsequently abandoned full-time music and died in mysterious circumstances in 1974.

Albums: *Judee Sill* (1971), *Heart Food* (1973).

Silly Sisters

During the lull which followed the commercial high point of Steeleye Span's *All Around My Hat* album, vocalist Maddy Prior performed an abrupt volte face and plunged back into pure folk song recording with a traditional album recorded with June Tabor, a librarian in Swindon, England. Despite its 'awful' cover, *Silly Sisters* undoubtedly helped launch Tabor. It contained an all-star band of musicians, on the sometimes chaotic, though always jovial set. It has since become something of a legend, with Prior's high soaring voice, contrasted by Tabor's more earthy tones. The whole escapade attracted a great deal of media attention and quite naturally there was clamour for a follow up. In 1988 the Silly Sisters did reunite for *No More To The Dance* for the folkist Topic label. More touring followed, this time selective and considered, and whilst this set is still a fine record, backed by musicians of reputation and note, it hasn't the charm and innocence of the debut. However, neither singer has ruled out another collaboration

Albums: *Silly Sisters* (1976), *No More To The Dance* (1988).

Silly Wizard

This Scottish band was formed in 1972 by Gordon Jones (b. 21 November 1947, Birkenhead, Liverpool, England; guitar/mandolin), Bob Thomas (b. 28 July 1950, Robroyston, Glasgow, Scotland; guitar), and Chris Pritchard (b. Edinburgh, Scotland; vocals). Pritchard left within a matter of months and was replaced by John Cunningham (b. 27 August 1957, Edinburgh, Scotland; fiddle/mandolin), and Madelaine Taylor (b. Perth, Scotland; vocals/guitar/bodhran/spoons). This line-up recorded for Transatlantic Records, but with Taylor's departure, to join Witches Promise, the recording was never issued. Silly Wizard continued with this line-up until late 1974, when Neil Adams (b. England; bass) joined the group. Andy M. Stewart (vocals/banjo), then joined, and shortly afterwards, Adams left. The four were then augmented by Freeland Barbour (accordion), and Alasdair Donaldson (bass). By the time of *Silly Wizard*, Donaldson had left to join the Rezillos, while Barbour had taken up with the Wallochmore Ceilidh Band. Phil Cunningham (b. 27 January 1960, Edinburgh, Scotland; keyboards), and Martin 'Mame' Hadden (b. 23 May 1957, Aberdeen, Scotland; bass/vocals) arrived in late 1976, recording *Caledonia's Hardy Sons*. Following the release of *So Many Partings*, John Cunningham joined the US-based group Raindogs, but performed occasionally solo, and with brother Phil. Dougie MacLean (b. 27 September 1954, Dunblane, Scotland; guitar/fiddle/vocals), then joined the line-up temporarily, in 1979. He, along with Stewart and Hadden, had previously been with the group Puddock's Well. Phil had earlier won several Scottish accordion championships, and, in 1977, both he and John received the Heretic Award for services to Scottish Tradition. In 1980,

Judee Sill

Silly Wizard

the group recorded 'Take The High Road', the original theme from the Scottish television series. During the early 80s, a bootleg recording, tentatively titled *Live In Edinburgh*, was intercepted before it could be released, and the ensuing court case, being the first bootleg recording case in Scottish history, saw the group win the right for it to remain unreleased. The group helped to popularize Scottish traditional music among a wider audience, particularly in the USA. The final line-up saw all the various members involved in projects outside of the group.

Gordon Jones and Bob Thomas formed Harbourtown Records, Hadden teamed up with Allan Carr and Jane Rothfield to form Hadden Rothfield and Carr, while Stewart started working with Manus Lunny. Meanwhile, Phil went on to work and record with Relativity. Silly Wizard played their last date in 1988, in New York State.

Albums: *Silly Wizard* (1976), *Caledonia's Hardy Sons* (1978), *So Many Partings* (1979), *Wild And Beautiful* (1981), *Kiss The Tears Away* (1983), *Fair Warning* (1983), *Live In America* (1985), *Golden Golden* (1985), *A Glint Of Silver* (1987), *Live Wizardry - The Best Of Silly Wizard In Concert* (1988). Compilations: *The Best Of Silly Wizard* (1985). Solo albums: Phil Cunningham *Airs And Graces* (1984), *Relativity* (1987), *Palomino Waltz* (1989); John Cunningham *Fair Warning* (1988); Phil and John Cunningham: *Against The Storm* (1980).

Silver, Mike

b. 12 September 1945, Uffington, Berkshire, England. Silver began playing guitar at the age of 15. It was later during the 60s that he first wrote seriously and took an interest in acoustic music. He became a regular in the folk clubs of London and Cornwall during this period. In 1971, Silver formed Daylight, with Steve Hayton (guitar/mandolin/vocals) and Chrissie Quayle (guitar). They were signed to RCA the same year and produced one album. He then signed to Elton John's Rocket Records, and toured the USA, in 1973. At this time, Silver was in demand as a session guitarist, and recorded with Charles Aznavour, and Ray Thomas of the Moody Blues. In 1973, Silver recorded *Troubadour*, but this failed to bring him to a wider audience. However, that same year, he gained exposure when he supported Dory Previn and Ashford And Simpson at a number of concert appearances in the USA. Silver then appeared as guitarist for Brenda Wootton at the Norwich Folk Festival in 1976, in addition to playing a number of large festivals throughout the UK, Germany and Denmark. Justin Hayward recorded Mike's composition 'Maybe It's Just Love', on his solo *Night Flight*, in 1980. During the early part of the 80s, Mike appeared in concert on radio with Randy Newman and also worked on recordings with Allan Taylor, and Fiona Simpson. The number of other performers that he has worked with is considerable. In 1991, Silver formed Road Dog, which included Kit Morgan (guitar/guitar synthesizer), Paul Cleaver (drums/percussion) and Dave Goodier (bass guitar). Silver continues to play solo concerts in addition to working with the band.

Albums: *The Applicant* (1969), *Daylight* (1971), *Troubadour* (early 70s), *Come And Be My Lady* (1976), *Midnight Train* (1980), *Silver Songs* (1981), *Let's Talk About You* (1983), *Free* (1984), *No Machine* (1986), *Roadworks* (1990).

Silverstein, Shel

b. Shelby Silverstein, 1932, Chicago, Illinois, USA. A former artist with *Stars And Stripes* magazine, Silverstein joined the staff of *Playboy* at its inception during the early 50s and for almost two decades his cartoons were a regular feature of the publication. He later became a successful illustrator and author of children's books, including *Uncle Shelby's ABZ Book*, *Uncle Shelby's Zoo* and *Giraffe And A Half*. Silverstein was also drawn to the folk scene emanating from Chicago's Gate Of Horn and New York's Bitter End, latterly becoming a respected composer and performer of the genre. Early 60s collaborations with Bob Gibson were particularly memorable and in 1961 Silverstein completed *Inside Folk Songs* which included the original versions of 'The Unicorn' and '25 Minutes To Go', later popularized, respectively, by the Irish Rovers and Brothers Four. Silverstein provided 'novelty' hits for Johnny Cash ('A Boy Named Sue') and Loretta Lynn, ('One's On The Way'), but an association with Dr. Hook proved to be the most fruitful. A series of successful singles ensued, notably 'Sylvia's Mother' and 'The Cover Of *Rolling Stone*', and a grateful group reciprocated by supplying the backing on *Freakin' At The Freaker's Ball*. This ribald set included many of Silverstein's best-known compositions from this period, including 'Polly In A Porny', 'I Got Stoned And I Missed It' and 'Don't Give A Dose To The One You Love Most', the last-named of which was adopted in several anti-venereal disease campaigns. *The Great Conch Robbery*, released on the traditional music outlet Flying Fish, was less scatological in tone, since which Silverstein has adopted a less-public profile.

Albums: *Hairy Jazz* (1959), *Inside Folk Songs* (1961), *I'm So Good I Don't Have To Brag* (1965), *Drain My Brain* (1966), *A Boy Named Sue* (1968), *Freakin' At The Freaker's Ball* (1969), *Songs And Stories* (1972), *The Great Conch Train Robbery* (1979).

Simon And Garfunkel

Simon And Garfunkel

This highly successful vocal duo first played together during their early years in New York. Paul Simon (b. 5 November 1941, Newark, New Jersey, USA) and Art Garfunkel (b. Arthur Garfunkel, 13 October 1942, Forest Hills, New York, USA) were initially inspired by the Everly Brothers and under the name Tom And Jerry enjoyed a US hit with the rock 'n' roll styled 'Hey Schoolgirl'. They also completed an album which was later reissued after their rise to international prominence in the 60s. Garfunkel subsequently returned to college and Simon pursued a solo career before the duo reunited in 1964 for *Wednesday Morning 3AM*. A strong, harmonic work, which included an acoustic reading of 'The Sound Of Silence', the album did not sell well enough to encourage the group to stay together. While Simon was in England the folk rock-boom was in the ascendant and producer Tom Wilson made the presumptuous but prescient decision to overdub 'Sound Of Silence' with electric instrumentation. Within weeks, the song was number 1 in the US charts, and Simon and Garfunkel were hastily reunited. An album titled after their million-selling single was rush-released early in 1966 and proved highly commendable. Among its major achievements was 'Homeward Bound', an evocative and moving portrayal of life on the road, which went on to become a transatlantic hit. The solipsistic 'I Am A Rock' was another international success with such angst-ridden lines as, 'I have no need of friendship, friendship causes pain'. In keeping with the social commentary that permeated their mid-60s' work, the group included two songs whose theme was suicide: 'A Most Peculiar Man' and 'Richard Cory'. Embraced by a vast following, especially among the student population, the duo certainly looked the part with their college scarves, duffle coats and cerebral demeanour. Their next single, 'The Dangling Conversation', was their most ambitious lyric to date and far too esoteric for the Top 20. Nevertheless, the work testified to their artistic courage and boded well for the release of a second album within a year: *Parsley, Sage, Rosemary And Thyme*. The album took its title from a repeated line in 'Scarborough Fair', which was their excellent harmonic weaving of that traditional song and another, 'Canticle'. An accomplished work, the album had a varied mood from the grandly serious 'For Emily, Whenever I May Find Her' to the bouncy '59th Street Bridge Song (Feelin' Groovy)' (subsequently a hit for Harpers Bizarre). After two strong but uncommercial singles, 'At The Zoo' and 'Fakin' It', the duo contributed to the soundtrack of the 1968 film, *The Graduate*. The key song in the film was 'Mrs Robinson' which provided the group

with one of their biggest international sellers. That same year saw the release of *Bookends*, a superbly-crafted work, ranging from the serene 'Save The Life Of My Child' to the personal odyssey 'America' and the vivid imagery of 'Old Friends'. *Bookends* is still felt by many to be their finest work. In 1969 the duo released 'The Boxer', a long single that nevertheless found commercial success on both sides of the Atlantic. This classic single reappeared on the group's next album, the celebrated *Bridge Over Troubled Water*. One of the best-selling albums of all time (303 weeks on the UK chart), the work's title track became a standard with its lush, orchestral arrangement and contrasting tempo. Heavily gospel-influenced, the album included several well-covered songs such as 'Keep The Customer Satisfied', 'Cecilia' and 'El Condor Pasa'. While at the peak of their commercial success, with an album that dominated the top of the chart listings for months, the duo became irascible and their partnership abruptly ceased. The release of a *Greatest Hits* package in 1972 included four previously unissued live tracks and during the same year the duo performed together at a benefit concert for Senator George McGovern. The results were captured in 1981 on *The Concert In Central Park*. After a long break, a further duet occurred on the hit single 'My Little Town' in 1975. Although another studio album was undertaken, the sessions broke down and Simon transferred the planned material to his 1983 solo *Hearts And Bones*. Although the possibility of a Simon and Garfunkel reunion remains a lucrative proposition, neither artist has spoken favourably of a permanent reunion but plans were afoot in 1993 for an autumn series of 10 concerts at Madison Square Garden in New York.

Albums: *Wednesday Morning 3AM* (1968), *The Sound Of Silence* (1966), *Parsley, Sage, Rosemary And Thyme* (1966), *The Graduate* (1968, film soundtrack), *Bookends* (1968), *Bridge Over Troubled Water* (1970), *The Concert In Central Park* (1981). Compilations: *Simon And Garfunkel's Greatest Hits* (1972), *The Simon And Garfunkel Collection* (1981), *The Definitive Simon And Garfunkel* (1992).

Simon, Paul

b. Paul Frederic Simon, 13 October 1941, Newark, New Jersey, USA. Simon first entered the music business with partner Art Garfunkel in the duo Tom and Jerry. In 1957, they scored a US hit with the rock 'n' roll influenced 'Hey Schoolgirl'. After one album, they split up in order to return to college. Although Simon briefly worked with Carole King recording demonstration discs for minor acts, he did not record again until the early 60s. Employing various pseudonyms, Simon enjoyed a couple of minor US hits during 1962-63 as Tico And The Triumphs ('Motorcycle') and Jerry Landis ('The Lone Teen-Ranger'). After moving to Europe in 1964, Simon busked in Paris and appeared at various folk clubs in London. Upon returning to New York, he was signed to CBS Records by producer Tom Wilson and reunited with his erstwhile partner Garfunkel. Their 1964 recording *Wednesday Morning 3 AM*, which included 'The Sound Of Silence' initially failed to sell, prompting Simon to return to London. While there, he made *The Paul Simon Songbook*, a solo work, recorded on one microphone with the astonishingly low budget of £60. Among its contents were several of Simon's most well-known compositions, including 'I Am A Rock', 'A Most Peculiar Man' and 'Kathy's Song'. The album was virtually ignored until Tom Wilson altered Simon's artistic stature overnight. Back in the USA, the producer grafted electric instrumentation on to Simon And Garfunkel's acoustic recording of 'Sound Of Silence' and created a folk-rock classic that soared to the top of the US charts. Between 1965 and 70, Simon And Garfunkel became one of the most successful recording duos in the history of popular music. The partnership ended amid musical disagreements and a realization that they had grown apart.

After the break-up, Simon took songwriting classes in New York and prepared a stylistically diverse solo album, *Paul Simon* (1972). The work incorporated elements of latin, reggae and jazz and spawned the hit singles 'Mother And Child Reunion' and 'Me And Julio Down By The Schoolyard'. One year later, Simon returned with the much more commercial *There Goes Rhymin' Simon* which enjoyed massive chart success and included two major hits, 'Kodachrome' and 'Take Me To The Mardi Gras'. A highly successful tour resulted in *Live Rhymin'*, which featured several Simon And Garfunkel standards. This flurry of creativity in 1975 culminated in the chart-topping *Still Crazy After All These Years* which won several Grammy awards. The wry '50 Ways To Leave Your Lover', taken from the album, provided Simon with his first number 1 single as a soloist, while the hit 'My Little Town' featured a tantalizing duet with Garfunkel. A five-year hiatus followed during which Simon took stock of his career. He appeared briefly in Woody Allen's movie *Annie Hall*, recorded a hit single with Garfunkel and James Taylor ('Wonderful World'), released a *Greatest Hits* package featuring the catchy 'Slip Slidin' Away' and switched labels from CBS to Warner Brothers. In 1980, he released the ambitious *One Trick Pony*, from his film of the same name. The movie included cameo appearances by

the Lovin' Spoonful and Tiny Tim but was not particularly well-received even though it was far more literate than most 'rock-related' films. In the wake of that project, Simon suffered a long period of writer's block, which was to delay the recording of his next album.

Meanwhile, a double-album live reunion of Simon And Garfunkel recorded in Central Park was issued and sold extremely well. It was intended to preview a studio reunion, but the sessions were subsequently scrapped. Instead, Simon concentrated on his next album, which finally emerged in 1983 as *Hearts And Bones*. An intense and underrated effort, it sold poorly despite its evocative hit single 'The Late Great Johnny Ace' (dedicated to both the doomed 50s star and the assassinated John Lennon). Simon was dismayed by the album's lack of commercial success and critics felt that he was in a creative rut. That situation altered during 1984 when Simon was introduced to the enlivening music of the South African black townships. After an appearance at the celebrated USA For Africa recording of 'We Are The World', Simon immersed himself in the music of the Dark Continent. *Graceland* (1986) was one of the most intriguing and commercially successful albums of the decade with Simon utilizing musical contributions from Ladysmith Black Mambazo, Los Lobos, Linda Ronstadt and Rockie Dopsie And The Twisters. The project and subsequent tour was bathed in controversy due to accusations (misconceived according to the United Nations Anti-Apartheid Committee) that Simon had broken the cultural boycott against South Africa. The success of the album in combining contrasting cross-cultural musical heritages was typical of a performer who had already incorporated folk, R&B, calypso and blues into his earlier repertoire. The album spawned several notable hits, 'The Boy In The Bubble' (with its technological imagery), 'You Can Call Me Al' (inspired by an amusing case of mistaken identity) and 'Graceland' (an oblique homage to Elvis Presley's Memphis home). Although *Graceland* seemed a near impossible work to follow up, Simon continued his pan -cultural investigations with *The Rhythm Of The Saints*, which incorporated African and Brazilian musical elements.

Albums: *The Paul Simon Songbook* (1965), *Paul Simon* (1972), *There Goes Rhymin' Simon* (1973), *Live Rhymin'* (1974), *Still Crazy After All These Years* (1975), *One Trick Pony* (1980, film soundtrack), *Hearts And Bones* (1983), *Graceland* (1986), *The Rhythm Of The Saints* (1990). Compilation: *Greatest Hits, Etc.* (1977).

Further reading: *The Boy In The Bubble*, Patrick Humphries.

Martin Simpson

Simpson, Martin

b. 5 May 1953, Scunthorpe, South Humberside, England. Having started playing guitar at the age of 12, Simpson played the proverbial 'floor spots' at local folk clubs, and received his first paid booking at the age of 14. By the age of 18 Simpson had become a full-time professional on the folk club circuit. He came to the attention of a number of influential people, one of whom was Bill Leader who recorded Martin's debut *Golden Vanity* for his own Trailer label. The album mixed such folk standards as 'Pretty Polly' and 'Soldiers Joy', with contemporary works such as Bob Dylan's 'Love Minus Zero/No Limit'. That same year, Simpson opened for Steeleye Span on their UK tour, and, not long after became an accompanist for June Tabor. In 1979 he joined the Albion Band at the National Theatre and played with them on two subsequent tours. *A Cut Above*, recorded with Tabor on Topic, is still highly regarded. There followed a succession of fine albums, but without a great degree of commercial success. Since 1987, Simpson has lived in the USA with his American wife Jessica Radcliffe Simpson (b. 18 February 1952, Los Angeles, California, USA). The two also work as a duo, having released *True Dare Or Promise* in 1987. *The Pink Suede Bootleg* was released as a limited edition. Noted for his style of playing, Simpson is not as often in the limelight as he was in the 70s and 80s, but a tour of the UK in 1991 showed that he was still a talent of great merit. In addition to solo and duo work, Simpson played briefly with Metamora in the USA, and has also been working with Henry Gray, the Louisiana born blues pianist. Simpson also played on *Abbysinians* and *Aqaba* by June Tabor, and *Earthed In Cloud Valley* and *'Til The Beasts Returning* by Andrew Cronshaw. In 1991, Martin was made honorary guitarist of the American Association of Stringed Instrument Artisans (A.S.I.A). A new album from Martin and Jessica is in the pipeline, featuring their New York based band of Eric Aceto (violect), Hank Roberts (cello), Doug Robinson (bass), and Tom Beers (harmonica).
Albums: *Golden Vanity* (1976), with June Tabor *A Cut Above* (1981), *Special Agent* (1981), *Grinning In Your Face* (1983), *Sad Or High Kicking* (1985), *Nobody's Fault But Mine* (1986), with Jessica Radcliffe Simpson *True Dare Or Promise* (1987), *Leaves Of Life* (1989), *When I Was On Horseback* (1991).

Skin The Peeler

Based in Bristol, England, Skin the Peeler Bristol operated during 1984 as an excellent jazz/rock, Celtic slanted unit. Long time members, Terry Barter (mandolin) and Rod Salter (saxophone),

revived the unit in 1989, and joined with Rose Hull (cello) to become an acoustic world beat band. The recent esoteric *World Dance* album contains influences from Eire, Africa, and Java, amongst others.
Albums. *Skin The Peeler* (1984), *Facing The Sun* (1989), *World Dance* (1991).

Sky, Patrick

b. 2 October 1940, Live Oak Gardens, nr. Atlanta, Georgia. Sky's folksinging career flourished upon meeting fellow Native American Buffy Sainte-Marie. They toured together for three years, eventually arriving in New York's Greenwich Village during the early 60s. Sky's own recordings followed his appearance on Buffy's early work and one of his songs, 'Many A Mile', became the title track to her second album. Sky's debut featured both original songs and traditional material, a feature continued on his second collection. Pat was also actively involved in assisting the recently 'rediscovered' Mississippi John Hurt and his guitar work can be heard on several of the veteran bluesman's 60s sessions. It was not until 1968 that Sky released a third album, since when his recordings have been sporadic, partly through choice and partly because of the uncompromising nature of his later compositions. Unhappy with modern music, Sky has since restricted his performances to traditional and small-scale venues.
Albums: *Patrick Sky* (1965), *A Harvest Of Gentle Clang* (1966), *Reality Is Bad Enough* (1968), *Photographs* (1969), *Songs That Made America Famous* (1973), *Two Steps Forward One Step Back* (1976).

Smither, Chris

b. 11 November 1944, Miami, Florida, USA. Smither began his music career, during the 60s, by performing in the coffee houses and clubs in New Orleans. His first real blues influence came after listening to a Lightnin' Hopkins' recording, *Blues In My Bottle*, at the age of 17. He moved to Boston, Massachusetts in 1966, where he continued playing the lucrative coffee house/folk circuit. He also started associating with artists such as Bonnie Raitt, John Hammond, and Mississippi Fred MacDowell. After a promising start, with two albums on the Poppy label, the label folded. He recorded *Honeysuckle Dog*, for United Artists, which featured Raitt, but this was never released. Smither has had his songs covered by numerous performers, including Bonnie Raitt, who included his 'Love Me Like A Man', and 'I Feel The Same' on her *Collection* album. He has performed at various times with many musicians including Nanci Griffith, Jackson Browne, Van Morrison, and also at numerous major festivals throughout the US.

Smithers' smooth, lyrical guitar style encompasses elements of folk, blues, country and rock and his voice is capable of sounding soft one minute and gruff the next. The live *Another Way To Find You*, on Flying Fish records was recorded over two nights in a studio with an invited audience.

Albums: *I'm A Stranger Too* (1970), *Don't it Drag On* (1972), *It Ain't Easy* (1984, reissued 1990), *Another Way To Find You* (1991), *Happier Blue* (1993).

Sorrels, Rosalie

b. Rosalie Ann Stringfellow, 24 June 1933, Boise, Idaho, USA. Absorbing many of her influences at an early age via her parents, Nancy Kelly and Walter Pendleton Stringfellow, and her grandparents, Rosalie developed a taste for Anglo-American music. During the 50s, and by then living in Salt Lake City and raising a family of five children alone, she took a course in American folk music which eventually led to her becoming involved in collecting traditional song. Later, she took up the guitar, and this, coupled with the invaluable background she had been given, and the break-up of her marriage, encouraged her to take up singing professionally. Rosalie was taken on by Lena Spencer, to sing at the famous Caffe Lena, in 1966, and for a time Sorrels and her family lived with Spencer. Sorrels had never had an easy life, an abortion at the age of 16, a baby given up for adoption at 17, and then, in 1976, Sorrel's eldest son, David, took his own life.

Lonesome Roving Wolves, on Green Linnet, was produced by Patrick Sky who recorded for the Philo and Folkways labels. 'The Baby Tree', recorded by Sorrels on *Rosalie's Songbag*, was covered by Paul Kantner on *Blows Against The Empire* by Jefferson Starship. Known for her storytelling, as well as her songs, Sorrels has played virtually every major festival in the USA during her career, in addition to the many colleges and coffee houses on the circuit. *Then Came The Children* was recorded live, in 1984, at the East Cultural Center in Vancouver, Canada. In 1988, Sorrels was afflicted by a cerebral aneurysm which, fortunately, she recovered from. Thanks to Bruce 'Utah' Phillips, she was soon working again. *Be Careful, There's A Baby In The House* includes the Billie Holiday classic 'God Bless The Child', a song that Rosalie is well qualified to sing. She now lives on Grimes Creek, in the family cabin, near Boise, and continues to tour and record.

Albums: *Folksongs Of Utah And Idaho* (1959), *The Unfortunate Rake* (1960), *Rosalie's Songbag* (1963), *Songs Of The Mormon Pioneers* (1964), *Somewhere Between* (1964), *If I Could Be The Rain* (1967), *Travelling Lady* (1972), *Whatever Happened To The Girl That Was* (1973), *Always A Lady* (1976), *Moments Of Happiness* (1977), *Travelling Lady Rides Again* (1978), *The Lonesome Roving Wolves-Songs And Ballads Of The West* (1980), with Terry Garthwaite and Bobby Hawkins *Live At The Great American Music Hall* (1981), *Miscellaneous Abstract Record #1* (1982), live with Bruce Carver *Then Came The Children* (1984), *Be Careful, There's A Baby In The House* (1990), *Report From Grimes Creek* (1991).

Further reading: *Way Out In Idaho*, Rosalie Sorrels.

Spice Trade

Taking their musical starting point as 'Newgrass', an American term for the cross-fertilisation of folk and bluegrass styles in an improvisational, free-flowing hybrid, Spice Trade are built around former cajun swinger Chris Haigh (ex-Zumzeaux; fiddle). He has been joined in this new venture by several staples of the folk and jazz scene; Frank Kilkelly (also Companions Of The Rosy House; rhythm guitar), Rick Bolton (ex-Mike Westbrook and The Happy End; lead guitar), and Dudley Phillips (ex-June Tabor, Mary Coughlan, Womaks, John Etheridge; double bass). The band's first appearance outside of London came with the 1992 Shetland Folk Festival, and the heated critical reception afforded them there looks set to continue as they tour the mainland prior to their debut LP release.

Spillane, Davy

A founding member of Moving Hearts, Spillane has stamped his own identity onto the music he plays. *Atlantic Bridge* was an album of crossover material, in parts fusing folk and country themes. The musicians on the recording included Bela Fleck, Albert Lee, Jerry Douglas, and Christy Moore among others. For *Out Of The Air*, he had formed the Davy Spillane Band comprising Anthony Drennan (guitar), James Delaney (keyboards), Paul Moran (drums/percussion), and Tony Molloy (bass), as well as himself on Uilleann pipes and whistle. Rory Gallagher guested on a number of tracks on the album, including 'One For Phil', a tribute to Phil Lynott, written by Spillane and Gallagher. Currently, Spillane and the band are touring and the line-up now includes Greg Boland (guitar), Eoghan O'Neill (bass), as well as Delaney, Moran and Spillane, the others having left.

Albums: *Atlantic Bridge* (1987), *Out Of The Air* (1988), *Shadow Hunter* (1990), *Pipedreams* (1991), with Andy Irvine *East Wind* (1992).

Spinners (UK)

This popular folk group was formed in 1958 with the following line-up: Tony Davis (b. 24 August 1930, Blackburn Lancashire, England; banjo/tin

Davy Spillane

whistle/guitar/kazoo), Mick Groves (b. 29 September 1936, Salford. Lancashire, England; guitar), Hughie Jones (b. Hugh E. Jones 21 July 1936, Liverpool, England, guitar/harmonica/banjo) and Cliff Hall (b. 11 September 1925, Oriente Pourice, Cuba, guitar/harmonica). Hall was born to Jamaican parents who returned to Jamaica in 1939. He came to England after joining the Royal Air Force in 1942. The group was often augmented in concert by 'Count' John McCormick (double bass), who is generally regarded as the fifth 'Spinner'. Occasionally rebuked by folk 'purists' as bland and middle-of-the-road, the Spinners nevertheless brought many people into folk music. The regular sell-out attendances at their concerts are a testimony to this. Songs that are now covered by other performers and often mistakenly referred to as 'traditional' are in fact Hughie Jones originals: 'The Ellan Vannin Tragedy', 'The Marco Polo' and 'The Fairlie Duplex Engine'. In 1990, Hughie Jones produced *Hughie's Ditty-Bag*, a book of songs and stories. He is still performing occasionally as a soloist. After a 30 year career, the Spinners decided to call it a day, and released the double album *Final Fling*.

Spirit Of The West

Formed in 1983, this acoustic, but rock-minded trio, consisting of long-time Canadian friends, John Mann (vocals, guitar), Geoffrey Kelly (flute), J. Knutson (vocals, guitar), completely revived the Vancouver folk scene. In 1986, their *Tripping Upstairs* brilliantly demonstrated a use of airs and jigs to spice up their own protest compositions. Knutson left shortly afterwards, and the band recruited Hugh McMillan (bass) and Linda McRae (accordion). They toured Britain frequently during 1989-1990, and their association with the pop group, The Wonder Stuff, noticeably influenced *Go Figure*, which was more or less an indie rock album, featuring ethnic instruments.
Selected albums: *Tripping Upstairs* (1986), *Go Figure* (1991).

Spoelstra, Mark

b. 30 June 1940, Kansas City, Missouri, USA. Originally based in California, 12-string folk/blues guitarist Spoelstra's songwriting career burgeoned following a move to New York where he realized the potential of original material. A confirmed pacifist and a conscientious objector to military service, his songs often reflected such themes and he was a regular contributor to *Broadside*, a magazine founded as an outlet for topical and protest material. Having completed two albums for the Folkways label, Spoelstra joined Elektra Records. His debut *Five And Twenty Questions*, featured 12 original

songs and introduced his quiet, unassuming style. Mark later returned to California where he has continued to perform, but this committed individual has preferred to concentrate on social and community projects.
Albums: *The Songs Of Mark Spoelstra* (early-60s), *Mark Spoelstra At The Club 47, Inc.* (early 60s), *Five And Twenty Questions* (1964), *State Of Mind* (1965), *The Times I've Had* (mid-60s), *Mark Spoelstra At Club 47* (mid-60s), *The Songs Of Mark Spoelstra* (late-60s), *Mark Spoelstra* (1969), *Mark Spoelstra* (1972), *This House* (1972), *Mark Spoelstra* (1974).

Spriguns

Mike and Mandy Morton formed Spriguns Of Tolgus at their own folk club in Cambridge, England. On their first two, self-financed albums, the Mortons were joined by Rick Thomas (fiddle) and Chris Russon (electric guitar). Playing soft focus electric folk, the band signed with Decca, and were encouraged by Steeleye Span's Tim Hart, who produced *Revel, Weird & Wild* in 1976. By then known as the Spriguns, the group enlisted Dick Powell (keyboards), Tom Ling (fiddle), and Chris Woodcock (drums). Mandy Morton's songs reworked traditional ballads, making them difficult to distinguish from the original folk material. Powell was retained for *Time Will Pass*, and Australians Wayne Morrison (guitar) and Dennis Dunstan (drums) were recruited. Mandy Morton became the group's focus, and later releases were credited to her. *Magic Lady* involved several important folk guest artists, and when Morton signed for Polydor Scandinavia in 1979, she released her best work for some time. 'Scandinavia is great,' she said in 1980, 'they just turn up and listen to the music and don't think about categories or pigeon holes.' During the early 80s she toured with a straight rock band, and included a tribute on one of her albums to her all-time heroine Grace Slick (Jefferson Airplane etc.) - a paisley version of 'Somebody To Love'. The warm feyness of Morton's vocals fired the Spriguns, although they failed to break through despite a major recording deal. Mandy Morton was subsequently a presenter at BBC Radio Cambridge. The Spriguns releases later became the target of serious record collectors.
Albums: *Rowdy, Dowdy Day* (1974), *Jack With A Feather* (1975), *Revel, Weird & Wild* (1976), *Time Will Pass* (1977). as Mandy Morton *Magic Lady* (1978), *Sea Of Storms* (1979), *Valley Of Light* (1983).

Springfields

Formed in 1960, this popular UK folk-based attraction was based around singer/songwriter Tom O'Brien (b. 2 July 1934, Hampstead, London, England) and his sister Mary (b. 16 April 1939,

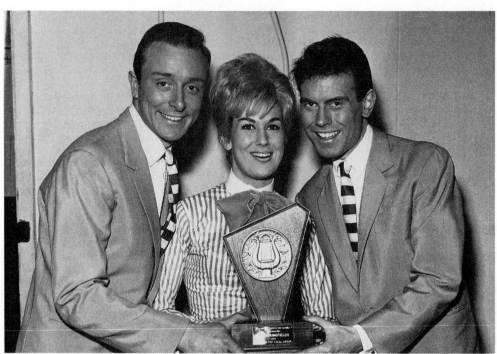

Springfields

Hampstead, London, England), who accompanied him on guitar. Better known as Tom and Dusty Springfield, the duo was later joined by the former's partner, Tim Field, and the following year the revitalized unit became one of Britain's top vocal groups. The trio enjoyed UK Top 5 singles with 'Island Of Dreams' (1962) and 'Say I Won't Be There' (1963), by which time Field had been replaced by Mike Longhurst-Pickworth, who took the less-cumbersome professional name Mike Hurst. The Springfields enjoyed success in America with 'Silver Threads And Golden Needles', a country standard which paradoxically failed to chart in Britain. However, although the single went on to sell in excess of one million copies, it was the group's only substantial US hit. The group split up in 1963 with each member then pursuing solo ventures. Dusty Springfield became one of the Britain's leading female singers, brother Tom continued his songwriting career while Hurst established himself as a leading pop producer through work with Cat Stevens.
Albums: *Silver Threads And Golden Needles* (1962), *Folk Songs From The Hills* (1963), *Kinda Folksy* (1963). Compilations: *The Springfields Story* (mid-60s).

Spud

A largely under-rated Irish electric group, who were active through the mid to late 70s. Their debut album was produced by the noted Irish fiddler, Donal Lunny, and the line-up consisted of Don Knox (fiddle), Michael Smith (bass), Austin Kenny (guitar) and Dermot O'Connor (guitar, vocals). By the time they recorded their most significant work, *Smoking On The Bog*, O'Connor had departed, to be replaced by multi-instrumentalist Ken Wilson and Dave Gaynor (drums). The album, recorded at Sawmills Studio in Cornwall, had a good time, boozy 'feel', and included an excellent cover of Richard Thompson's 'Shame Of Doing Wrong'. A further Irish-only single release signified the end of Spud, and its ex-members have been absent from the music scene for some time.
Albums: *A Silk Purse* (1975), *The Happy Handful* (1975), *Smoking On The Bog* (1977).

Staines, Bill

b. 6 February 1947, Medford, Massachussetts, USA. This singer/songwriter's early influences were Gordon Lightfoot, the Weavers, Woody Guthrie, Ian And Sylvia Tyson, and Peter La Farge. Bill grew up in the Boston area absorbing and listening to the music of the early 60s, and started playing professionally in 1965. Although largely playing guitar in concert, Staines also uses autoharp and banjo for recording work. In 1975, Bill won a National Yodelling contest at the Kerrville Folk Festival, Texas. The contest was built around the fact that Jimmie Rodgers, the singing and yodelling brakeman, was from Kerrville. Staines has successfully blended traditional and contemporary themes into a style that is highly original. His songs have been recorded by other artists, including Nanci Griffith, who included 'Roseville Fair' on her *The Last Of The True Believers*. In addition to touring regularly, Staines is currently working on a project to produce a complete book of all of his songs.

Albums: *Miles* (1976), *Old Wood And Winter Wine* (1977), *Just Play One More Tune* (1977), *Whistle Of The Jay* (1978), *Rodeo Rose* (1981), *Sandstone Cathedrals* (1983), *Bridges* (1984), *Wild, Wild Heart* (1985), *Redbird's Wing* (1988), *Tracks And Trails* (1991). Compilations: *The First Million Miles* (1989). Further reading: *If I Were A Word, Then I'd Be A Song*, Bill Staines, 1980. *Moving It Down The Line*, Bill Staines, 1987. *All God's Critters Got A Place In The Choir*, Bill Staines & Margot Zemach.

Stealers Wheel

The turbulent, acrimonious and comparatively brief career of Stealers Wheel enabled the two main members Gerry Rafferty and Joe Egan to produce some memorable and inventive, relaxed pop music. During the early 70s. Rafferty (b. 16 April 1946, Paisley, Scotland) and long-time friend Joe Egan (b. c.1946 Scotland) assembled in London to form a British Crosby, Stills And Nash, together with Rab Noakes, Ian Campbell and Roger Brown. After rehearsing and negotiating a record contract with A&M Records. The band had already fragmented, before they entered the studio to meet with legendary producers Leiber And Stoller. Paul Pilnick (guitar), Tony Williams (bass) and ex-Juicy Lucy member Rod Coombes (drums) bailed out Rafferty and Egan; the result was a surprising success, achieved by the sheer quality of their songs and the blend of the two leaders' voices. 'Stuck In The Middle With You' is an enduring song reminiscent of mid-period Beatles, and it found favour by reaching the Top 10 on both sides of the Atlantic. While the song was high on the charts Rafferty departed and was replaced by former Spooky Tooth lead guitarist Luther Grosvenor (aka Ariel Bender). Rafferty had returned by the time the second album was due to be recorded, but the musical chairs continued as all the remaining members left the band, leaving Rafferty and Egan holding the baby. Various session players completed *Ferguslie Park*, astonishingly another superb, melodic and cohesive album. The album was a failure commercially and the two leaders set about completing their contractual obligations and recording their final work *Right Or Wrong*. Even with similarly strong material, notably the evocative

'Benidictus' and the arresting 'Found My Way To You', the album failed. Rafferty and Egan, disillusioned, buried the name forever. Management problems plagued their career and lyrics of these troubled times continued to appear on both Egan and Rafferty's subsequent solo work.

Albums: *Stealers Wheel* (1973), *Ferguslie Park* (1974), *Right Or Wrong* (1975). Compilation: *The Best Of Stealers Wheel* (1978).

Steeleye Span

The roots of this pivotal English folk-rock group lay in several ill-fated rehearsals between Ashley 'Tyger' Hutchings (b. January 1945, London, England; bass, ex-Fairport Convention), Irish trio Sweeny's Men - Terry Woods (vocals, guitar, mandolin), Johnny Moynihan (vocals, fiddle) and Andy Irvine (vocals, mandolin) - and Woods' wife Gay (vocals, concertina, autoharp). When Moynihan and Irvine subsequently retracted, the remaining musicians were joined by Tim Hart (vocals, guitar, dulcimer, harmonium) and Maddy Prior (vocals), two well-known figures in folk circles. Taking their name from a Lincolnshire waggoner celebrated in song, Steeleye Span began extensive rehearsals before recording the excellent *Hark, The Village Wait*. The set comprised of traditional material, expertly arranged and performed to encompass the rock-based perspective Hutchings helped create on the Fairport's *Liege And Lief*, while retaining the purity of the songs. The Woods then left to pursue their own career and were replaced by Martin Carthy (vocals/guitar) and Peter Knight (vocals/fiddle) for *Please To See The King* and *Ten Man Mop*. This particular line-up toured extensively, but the departure of Hutchings for the purist Albion Country Band signalled a dramatic realignment in the Steeleye camp. Carthy resumed his solo career when conflict arose over the extent of change and two musicians of a rock-based persuasion - Bob Johnson (guitar) and Rick Kemp (bass) - were brought in. The quintet also left manager/producer Sandy Robertson for the higher-profile of Jo Lustig, who secured the group's new recording deal with Chrysalis Records. Both *Below The Salt* and *Parcel Of Rogues*, displayed an electric content and tight dynamics, while the punningly-entitled *Now We Are Six*, which was produced by Jethro Tull's Ian Anderson, emphasized the terse drumming of newcomer Nigel Pegrum. The group enjoyed two hit singles with 'Gaudete' (1973) and 'All Around My Hat' (1975), the latter of which reached the UK Top and was produced by Mike Batt. However, the charm of Steeleye's early work was gradually eroding and although their soaring harmonies remained as strong as ever, experiments with reggae and heavier rock

Steeleye Span

rhythms alienated rather than attracted prospective audiences. The group was 'rested' following the disappointing *Rocket Cottage* (1976), but reconvened the following year for *Storm Force Ten*. However, Knight and Johnson were otherwise employed and this line-up was completed by John Kirkpatrick (accordion) and the prodigal Martin Carthy. Although their formal disbanding was announced in March 1978, Steeleye Span has been resurrected on subsequent occasions. Hart, Prior and Carthy have also pursued successful solo careers.

Albums: *Hark, The Village Wait* (1970), *Please To See The King* (1971), *Ten Man Mop (Or Mr. Reservoir Strikes Again)* (1971), *Below The Salt* (1972), *Parcel Of Rogues* (1973), *Now We Are Six* (1974), *Commoners Crown* (1975), *All Around My Hat* (1975), *Rocket Cottage* (1976), *Storm Force Ten* (1977), *Live At Last* (1978), *Sails Of Silver* (1980), *Back In Line* (1986). Compilations: *Individually And Collectively* (1972), *Steeleye Span Almanac* (1973), *Original Masters* (1977). *Time Span* (1978), *Best Of Steeleye Span* (1984), *Steeleye Span* (1985), *Portfolio* (1988), *Tempted And Tried* (1989), *The Early Years* (1989).

Stewart, Al

b. 3 September 1945, Glasgow, Scotland. Stewart first came to prominence during the folk boom of the mid-60s. His musical career began in Bournemouth, where he playing guitar, backing Tony Blackburn in the Sabres. In 1965, he moved to London, played at various folk clubs and shared lodgings with Jackson C. Frank, Sandy Denny and Paul Simon. Stewart was signed to Decca in 1966 and released one unsuccessful single, 'The Elf', featuring Jimmy Page on lead guitar. The following year, he joined CBS and released the acoustic, string-accompanied, introspective *Bedsitter Images*. The succeeding *Love Chronicles*, a diary of Stewart's romantic life, was most notable for the lengthy title track and the fact that it used a contentious word ('fucking') in an allegedly artistic context. The singer's interest in acoustic folk continued on *Zero She Flies*, which featured the historical narrative 'Manuscript'. Stewart's interest in the confessional love song reached its conclusion on *Orange*, with the impressive 'Night Of The 4th Of May'. This was followed by his most ambitious work to date, *Past, Present And Future*. Pursuing his interest in historical themes, Stewart presented some of his best acoustic workouts in the impressive 'Roads To Moscow' and epic 'Nostradamus'. A considerable gap ensued before the release of *Modern Times*, which saw Stewart making inroads into the American market for the first time.

After leaving CBS and signing to RCA, he relocated to California and surprised many by the commercial power of his celebrated *Year Of The Cat*, which reached the US Top 10. The title track also gave Stewart his first US hit. Another switch of

Al Stewart

label to Arista preceded *Time Passages*, which suffered by comparison with its predecessor. The underrated *24 P Carrots* was succeeded by a part studio/part live album, which merely consolidated his position. With *Russians And Americans*, Stewart embraced a more noticeable political stance, but the sales were disappointing. Legal and contractual problems effectively deterred him from recording for four years until the welcome, if portentous, *The Last Days Of The Century*. During that time he had re-located to France and set about expanding his impressive cellar of vintage wines. Stewart remains one of the more underrated performers, despite his commercial breakthrough in the 70s.

Albums: *Bedsitter Images* (1967), *Love Chronicles* (1969), *Zero She Flies* (1970), *The First Album (Bedsitter Images)* (1970), *Orange* (1972), *Past, Present And Future* (1973), *Modern Times* (1975), *Year Of The Cat* (1976), *Time Passages* (1978), *24 P/Carrots* (1980), *Indian Summer/Live* (1981), *Russians And Americans* (1984), *Last Days Of The Century* (1988), *Rhymes In Rooms - Al Stewart Live Featuring Peter White* (1992). Compilations: *The Early Years* (1978), *Best Of Al Stewart* (1985), *Chronicles ... The Best Of Al Stewart* (1991).

Stewart, Andy M.

b. Andrew McGregor Stewart, 8 September 1952, Alyth, Perthshire, Scotland to a father who had a large collection of traditional songs, and a mother who wrote poetry and songs and music. He started playing in the early 70s, having previously sung at sessions and get togethers. In 1973, Stewart joined the already established duo of Dougie MacLean (b. 27 September 1954, Dunblane, Scotland; guitar, fiddle, vocals), and Ewan Sutherland (guitar, vocals). These three, together with Martin Hadden (b. 23 May 1957, Aberdeen, Scotland; bass, vocals), formed Puddock's Well. In 1974, Andy joined Silly Wizard, on tenor banjo and vocals, with whom he toured and recorded. It was with Silly Wizard, in 1980, that he recorded a single, 'Take The High Road' the original theme for the television series of the same name. *Take The High By The Hush* featured half traditional ballads and half original Stewart compositions. The album was well received, being voted *Melody Maker*'s Folk Album Of The Year. In 1984, Stewart teamed up with Manus Lunny (b. 8 February 1962, Dublin, Eire; bouzouki, guitar, vocals), regularly working as a duo, but adding Phil Cunningham (b. 27 January 1960, Edinburgh, Scotland; piano, accordion, whistles, vocals), to record *Fire In The Glen*. This album for Topic Records featured virtually all original material. As well as being featured on a number of compilation albums which include other artists, and having recorded with others, Andy still works with Lunny, and Gerry O'Byrne

John Stewart

(guitar/vocals), from the group, Patrick Street.

Albums: *By The Hush* (1982), with Manus Lunny and Phil Cunningham *Fire In The Glen* (1986), with Lunny *Dublin Lady* (1987), with Lunny *At It Again* (1990), *Andy M. Stewart Sings The Songs Of Robert Burns* (1990). Compilations: various artists *Flight Of The Green Linnet* (1988), with Lunny and various artists *The Celts Rise Again* (1990), various artists *The Irish Folk Festival-Back To The Future* (1990), various artists *The Irish Folk Festival Jubilee* (1991).

Stewart, John

b. 5 September 1939, San Diego, California, USA. Stewart's musical career began in the 50s when, as frontman of the Furies, he recorded 'Rocking Anna' for a tiny independent label. Having discovered folk music, Stewart began performing with college friend John Montgomery, but achieved wider success as a songwriter when several of his compositions, including 'Molly Dee' and 'Green Grasses', were recorded by the Kingston Trio. Indeed, the artist joined this prestigious group in 1961, following his spell in the like-sounding Cumberland Three. Stewart left the Kingston trio in 1967. His reputation was enhanced when a new composition, 'Daydream Believer', became a number 1 hit for the Monkees and this dalliance with pop continued when the artist contributed 'Never Goin' Back' to a disintegrating Lovin' Spoonful on their final album.

In 1968 Stewart was joined by singer Buffy Ford, whom he would marry in 1975. Together they completed *Signals Through The Glass*, before the former resumed his solo path with the excellent *California Bloodlines*. This country-inspired collection established Stewart's sonorous delivery and displayed a view of America which, if sometimes sentimental, was both optimistic and refreshing. It was a style the performer would continue over a series of albums which, despite critical approval, achieved only moderate success. Stewart's fortunes were upturned in 1979 when a duet with Stevie Nicks, 'Gold', became a US hit. The attendant *Bombs Away Dream Babies*, featured assistance from Fleetwood Mac guitarist, Lindsay Buckingham and although markedly different in tone to its predecessors, the set augured well for the future. However, despite contributions from Linda Ronstadt and Phil Everly, the follow-up, *Dream Babies Go To Hollywood*, proved an anti-climax. Stewart subsequently turned from commercial pursuits and resumed a more specialist direction with a series of low-key recordings for independent companies.

Albums: *Signals Through The Glass* (1968), *California Bloodlines* (1969), *Willard* (1970), *The Lonesome Picker Rides Again* (1971), *Sunstorm* (1972), *Cannons In The Rain* (1973), *The Phoenix Concerts - Live* (1974), *Wingless Angels* (1975), *Fire In The Wind* (1977), *Bombs Away Dream Babies* (1979), *Dream Babies Go Hollywood* (1980), *Blondes* (1982), *Trancas* (1984), *Centennial* (1984), *The Last Campaign* (1985), *Neon Beach* (1991), *Bullets In The Hour Glass* (1993). Compilation: *Forgotten Songs Of Some Old Yesterday* (1980), *California Bloodlines Plus...* (1987).

Stivell, Alan

b. Alan Cochevelou, 1943, Brittany, France. The son of a harp maker, Cochevelou was given his first harp at the age of nine. He later chose the professional name of Stivell, the Breton translation meaning fountain, spring or source. Having started out as a solo performer playing traditional Breton music on the wire strung Celtic harp, Stivell explored the music of Ireland, Scotland, Wales and the West country of England. In 1967, he formed a group comprising of himself on harp/bagpipes/Irish flute and Dan Ar Bras on electric guitar, as well as adding percussion, and bass. In 1976, Stivell left the group, and soon after released the solo *E. Langonned*. By integrating rock elements in traditional numbers such as 'She Moved Thro' The Fair', Stivell began to influence the growing folk rock movement. He put folk music in the UK charts for a while with a successful run of hits in the 70s. Stivell makes occasional appearances at festivals and continues to tour.

Albums: *Reflections* (1971), *A L'Olympia* (1972), *Renaissance Of The Celtic Harp* (1972), *Chemins De Terre* (1972), *Celtic Rock* (1972), *Alan Stivell Reflections* (1973), *From Celtic Roots* (1974), *A Longonnet* (1975), *In Dublin* (1975), *E. Langonned* (1976), *Trema'n Inis/Vers I'lle* (1976), *Before Landing* (1977), *Suzi MacGuire* (1978), *Journée A La Maison* (1978), *Tro Ar Bed* (1979), *Celtic Symphony/Symphonie Celtique* (1980), *Legend* (1984), *Harpes Du Nouvel Age* (1986).

Stockton's Wing

Formed in 1978, this rigid, traditionalist Irish band featured banjo, fiddles, whistles and mandolins, before they enlisted the didgeridoo player/bassist Steve Coone. Subsequently, whilst still jigging and reeling, they recruited a rhythm section and aimed for commercial acceptance. They even gained British radio play with the nagging 'Beautiful Affair'. *Light In The Western Sky* was a best seller, although their next album, *Take One, Live* is a more balanced and representative set. When it was recorded group's line-up was Paul Roche (whistle), Tony Molloy (bass), Mike Hanrahan (guitar), Keran Hanrahan (mandolin), Maurice Lennon (fiddle) and Fran Breen (drums). Breen later went on to play with Nanci Griffith. Through the 80s the band's

Alan Stivell

membership fluctuated, but they still released some pleasant albums. In 1992 they adopted a 'back to basics' acoustic line-up of Peter Keenan (keyboards) and Dave McNevin (banjo, mandolin) joining Roche, Mike Hanrahan and Lennon in a reduced five-piece unit.

Selected albums: *Light In The Western Sky* (1982), *Take One, Live* (1984), *Full Flight* (1986).

Storyteller

This UK folk-based quintet - Caroline Attard, Terry Durham, Mike Rogers (all vocals), Rodney Clark (bass/vocals) and Roger Moon (guitar/vocals) - released their debut album in 1970. The album was produced by two former members of the Herd, Peter Frampton and Andy Bown, the latter of whom maintained his association with the group as a songwriter and auxiliary member. Rogers was replaced by Chris Belshaw prior to the release of *Empty Pages*. A further acolyte from the Herd, drummer Henry Spinetti, contributed to this promising album, but Storyteller broke up soon after its completion. Attard, a former singer with pop duo the Other Two, later appeared, alongside Belshaw, on Bown's *Sweet William* collection.

Albums: *Storyteller* (1970), *Empty Pages* (1971).

Strange Creek Singers

This group was formed during the late 60s by Mike Seeger (b. 15 August 1933, New York City, New York, USA). The rest of the group were Lamar Grier (banjo), Tracy Schwartz, who had formerly been with Seeger's New Lost City Ramblers, (fiddle/guitar/banjo), Hazel Dickens (guitar), and Alice Gerrard (guitar). The name of the group is taken from Strange Creek, West Virginia, and the group played a mixture of bluegrass and old-time musical styles, both traditional and contemporary. It was very much a hobbyists affair, given the commitments outside of the group of all concerned. Nevertheless, they toured both Europe and the USA, playing a number of major festivals in the process. Seeger is still recording, while Schwartz performs and tours with the Tracy Schwartz Cajun Trio. Dickens, in the meantime, has recorded a number of albums in her own right.

Album: *Strange Creek Singers* (1968).

Strawbs

This versatile unit was formed in 1967 by guitarists Dave Cousins (b. 7 January 1945; guitar, banjo, piano, recorder) and Tony Hooper. They initially worked as a bluegrass group, the Strawberry Hill Boys, with mandolinist Arthur Phillips, but later pursued a folk-based direction. Truncating their name to the Strawbs, the founding duo added Ron Chesterman on bass prior to the arrival of singer Sandy Denny whose short spell in the line-up is documented in *All Our Own Work*. This endearing collection, released in the wake of Denny's success with Fairport Convention, features an early version of her exemplary composition, 'Who Knows Where The Time Goes'. Cousins, Hooper and Chesterman released their official debut, *Strawbs*, in

1968. This selection featured several of the group's finest compositions, including 'Oh How She Changed' and 'The Battle', and was acclaimed by both folk and rock audiences. *Dragonfly*, was less well-received, prompting a realignment in the band. The original duo was joined by former Velvet Opera members John Ford (b. 1 July 1948, Fulham, London, England; bass, acoustic guitar) and Richard Hudson (b. Richard William Stafford Hudson, 9 May 1948, London, England; drums, guitar, sitar), plus Rick Wakeman (keyboards), a graduate of the Royal Academy of Music. The Strawbs embraced electric rock with *Just A Collection Of Antiques And Curios*, although critical analysis concentrated on Wakeman's contribution. Such plaudits continued on *From The Witchwood* but the pianist grew frustrated within the group's framework and left to join Yes. He was replaced by Blue Weaver (b. 11 March 1947, Cardiff, South Glamorgan, Wales; guitar, autoharp, piano) from Amen Corner. Despite the commercial success generated by the outstanding *Grave New World*, tension within the Strawbs mounted, and in 1972, Hooper was replaced by Dave Lambert (b. 8 March 1949, Hounslow, Middlesex, England). Relations between Cousins and Hudson and Ford were also deteriorating and although 'Lay Down' gave the band its first UK Top 20 single, the jocular 'Part Of The Union', written by the bassist and drummer, became the Strawbs' most successful release. The group split following an acrimonious US tour. The departing rhythm section formed their own unit, Hudson-Ford while Cousins and Lambert brought in pianist John Hawken (ex-Nashville Teens and Renaissance), Chas Cronk (bass) and former Stealers Wheel drummer Rod Coombes. However, a series of poorly-received albums suggested the Strawbs had lost both direction and inspiration. Cousins nonetheless presided over several fluctuating line-ups and continued to record into the 80s despite a shrinking popularity. In 1989, the group reunited, including the trio of Cousins, Hooper And Hudson, for the *Don't Say Goodbye*.
Albums: *Strawbs* (1969), *Dragonfly* (1970), *Just A Collection Of Antiques And Curios* (1970), *From The Witchwood* (1971), *Grave New World* (1972), as Sandy Denny And The Strawbs *All Our Own Work* (1973), *Bursting At The Seams* (1973), *Hero And Heroine* (1974), *Ghosts* (1975), *Nomadness* (1976), *Deep Cuts* (1976), *Burning For You* (1977), *Dead Lines* (1978), *Don't Say Goodbye* (1988). Compilations: *Strawbs By Choice* (1974), *Best Of The Strawbs* (1978), *A Choice Collection* (1992), *Preserves Uncanned* (1993).

Strawhead

This UK folk group comprised of Chris Pollington (b. Christopher Harvey Pollington, 1948, Manchester, England; organ, vocals, recorder, guitar), Malcolm Gibbons (b. 1949, Chorley, Lancashire, England; bass drum, vocals, guitar), and Gregg G. Butler (b. 1946, Brixton, London, England; cornett, vocals, recorder, snare drum), evolved from a four piece, in 1974, who were all members of the Garstang Morris Men. They became a trio in 1976, the same year they played the Fylde Folk Festival. Strawhead represented Britain, for the BBC in an international folk festival in Belgium. They were involved in a project commemorating Preston Guild in 1992. It featured the history of Preston, Lancashire, in song up to 1900. The project also included a show, 'The Old Lamb And Flag', for which a book and album are planned. The group's sense of history is evident in most of their work, accentuated by their effective use of instrumentation. This was demonstrated on *Sedgemoor*, the story of Monmouth's rebellion in 1685.
Albums: *Farewell Musket, Pike And Drum* (1977), *Fortunes Of War* (1979), *Songs From The Book Of England* (1980), *Through Smoke And Fire* (1982), *Gentlemen Of Fortune* (1984), *Sedgemoor* (1985), *Law Lies Bleeding* (1988), *Tiffin* (1990). Compilations: *A New Vintage* (1987).

Stuart, Alice

b. 15 June 1942, Seattle, Washington, USA. Stuart began performing at the Pamir House, or P-House, a folk club based in her home city. She befriended several local performers, notably Don McAllister and Steve Lolar (both later of the Daily Flash), before securing a residency on the weekly KING-TV *Hootenany*. She moved to Los Angeles in 1963, and the following year was featured at the famed Berkeley Folk Festival, an appearance which inspired her solo debut. *All The Good Times*, issued on the specialist Arhoolie label, drew material from Charlie Poole, Mississippi John Hurt and Tom Paxton, and remained on catalogue for many years. Alice joined the Mothers Of Invention at the end of 1965, but finding their music too eclectic, quickly resumed her solo career. This blossomed with the accomplished *Full Time Woman*, the title track of which became a local 'standard' and was recorded by contemporaries Grootna. Stuart then formed Snake with Karl Sevareid (bass) and Bob Jones (drums), but *Believing* sadly failed to match the regional success of its predecessor. The singer later expanded her repertoire to include material from Boz Scaggs and Jimmy Cliff, but her popularity was confined to the Bay Area club circuit.
Albums: *All The Good Times* (1964), *Full Time Woman* (1970), *Believing* (1971).

Summerfield, Saffron

Singer/songwriter b. 29 August 1949, Weston Favel, Northamptonshire, England. Playing guitar and piano, Saffron enjoyed a good deal of popularity during the mid to late 70s. Having studied classical and modern guitar with Vic Jacques, in the early 70s, she went on to play support to Fairport Convention in Holland, Long John Baldry in the UK, Joan Armatrading in Holland, and Alquin in Holland and Germany, during the period 1976 to 1979. Despite working a great deal, and her style of combining blues/jazz influences, her career never took off, in England, as well as it should have done. However, she regularly toured in Holland and Belgium, where she was extrememly popular, and played Ireland and Scotland a great deal. Both her albums were released on her own Mother Earth label in the UK, but in Holland were released on Polydor. From 1984/85, she was the "musician in residence" at Battersea Arts Centre, in London, and in 1986/87, she was musical director for two documentaries, under the series title "Six Of Hearts", on Channel 4 television. From 1987, Saffron took a temporary lay-off from performing, but has now returned to live appearances, with a new album, for Brewhouse Records, being recorded for release in 1994.
Albums: *Salisbury Plain* (1975), *Fancy Meeting You Here* (1976).

Swan Arcade

Formed in Bradford, Yorkshire, England, in 1970, this group comprised Dave Brady (vocals), Heather Brady (vocals) and Jim Boyes (b. 14 November 1945, Bridlington, Yorkshire, England; vocals/guitar). The group take their name from a local landmark that was demolished during re-planning of the city. Renowned for their powerful unaccompanied vocals and strong harmonies, and their arrangements of both traditional and contemporary material, *Together Forever*, included songs such as the Beatle's 'Paperback Writer', and the Kinks' 'Lola'. In 1972, Boyes left the group, having moved to Sheffield, and his place was taken by Royston Wood from the Young Tradition, and later Brian Miller, who provided bass harmonies. They appeared at most of the major British festivals and on BBC disc jockey John Peel's radio show. By 1974, Boyes had returned and there followed tours of Europe and Britain, with a concert performance for Dutch television with Kate and Anna McGarrigle. *Matchless* stayed in the Belgian folk charts for three years, while later, in 1977, the group provided backing vocals on *We Are Like The Ocean* for Barry Melton of Country Joe And The Fish. Swan Arcade have also provided backing vocals for Richard And Linda Thompson, Ashley Hutchings and the Albion Band. Swan Arcade broke up in 1978, Jim joining Jiggery Polkary, and Dave and Heather running a hotel in the Lake District. Eventually, they were persuaded to get back together, and in 1985, the appropriately entitled *Together Forever* received good reviews from the folk music press, and radio and festival appearances followed. 1987 saw the formation of Blue Murder, comprising Swan Arcade with the Watersons (not to be confused with the heavy rock group of the same name). This line-up has proven successful at a number of festivals, but commitments for both groups prevent them from working together more often. 1988 saw further tours of Europe and Britain by Swan Arcade.
Albums: *Swan Arcade* (1973), *Matchless* (1977), *Together Forever* (1985), *Diving For Pearls* (1986), *Nothing Blue* (1988), *Full Circle* (1990). Compilations: (all with various artists) *Flash Company* (1987), *Square Roots* (1987), *Fellside Song Sample* (1987), *Circle Dance* (1990). Solo album: Jim Boyes *Out Of The Blue* (1991).

Swarbrick, Dave

b. 5 April 1941, New Malden, Surrey, England. Violinist and vocalist Swarbrick has played with many well-known groups and performers both in the folk and other areas of music. He is usually best remembered for his time with Fairport Convention which he joined in 1972. In his earlier days he played fiddle and mandola for the Ian Campbell Folk Group. Additionally, Swarbrick has recorded and toured with Simon Nicol and Martin Carthy. Swarbrick first teamed up with Carthy in 1966 and when he played on Carthy's debut album for Fontana in 1968, was fined by his own record company Transatlantic, for performing without their permission. Continual playing of the electric violin had a detrimental effect on Swarbrick's hearing, and is virtually deaf in one ear. This, however, has not stopped him working. Swarbrick left Fairport Convention in 1984, and shortly after formed Whippersnapper with Martin Jenkins, Chris Leslie and Kevin Dempsey. After two accomplished albums, Swarbrick left the band in the middle of a tour. In 1990, he once more teamed up with Martin Carthy to record the excellent *Life And Limb*. Swarbrick is now a member of the Keith Hancock Band, which includes long time associate Martin Carthy and Rauri McFarlane.
Albums: with Martin Carthy and Diz Disley *Rags, Reels And Airs* (1967), with Carthy *But Two Came By* (1968), with Carthy *Prince Heathen* (1969), *Selections* (1971), *Swarbrick* (1976), *Swarbrick 2* (1977), *Dave Swarbrick And Friends* (1978), *Lift The Lid And Listen* (1978), *The Ceilidh Album* (1978), *Smiddyburn* (1981), with Simon Nicol *Live At The*

Dave Swarbrick

White Bear (1982), *Flittin'* (1983), with Nicol *In The Club* (1983), with Nicol *Close To The Wind* (1984), with Carthy *Life And Limb* (1990), with Carthy *Skin & Bone* (1992).

Sweeney's Men

The forerunner of many bands to come out of Ireland, such as Planxty and Moving Hearts, and highly-influential in the field of electric folk, although they only lasted from 1966-69. The group, formed by Terry Woods (guitar, mandolin, vocals), included Andy Irvine (b. Eire; mandolin, guitar, bouzouki), and Johnny Moynihan (bouzouki). Eventually Irvine and Moynihan left and joined Planxty, while Irvine also ventured into solo work, occasionally with Paul Brady. Terry Woods was one of the original members of Steeleye Span, in 1969, replaced in 1971, and later joined the Pogues, in 1986, after working as a one half of a duo, with his wife Gay, as Gay and Terry Woods. Gay and Terry then had a two-year break from performing and recording, before supporting Ralph McTell in 1975.

Albums: *Sweeney's Men* (1968), *Rattlin' And Roarin' Willy* (1968), *Tracks Of Sweeney* (1969). Compilation: *Time Was Never Here 1968-9* (1993).

T

Tabor, June

b. 31 December 1947, Warwick, England. June is a singer of both contemporary and traditional songs and a fine interpreter of both. Her acclaimed debut *Airs And Graces* in 1976 immediately made her a favourite choice for numerous session appearances. She has collaborated with Martin Simpson on a number of occasions, resulting in *A Cut Above*, as well as with Maddy Prior from Steeleye Span with whom she has recorded as the Silly Sisters. *Freedom And Rain* was recorded with the Oyster Band, which saw Tabor departing into more of a rock format which many felt was long overdue. In addition, following a period of working with Huw Warren (piano), Tabor recorded *Some Other Time*, which included jazz standards such as 'Round Midnight'. Other collaborations utilizing her exceptional voice have been with Nic Jones, Martin Carthy, Peter Bellamy, the Albion Band and

Fairport Convention. A number of her earlier albums have recently been re-released, and the excellent Conifer compilation *Aspects* was well-received.

Albums: *Airs And Graces* (1976), *Ashes And Diamonds* (1977), *Bees On Horseback* (1977), with Martin Simpson *A Cut Above* (1980, *Abyssinians* (1983), *Theme From 'Spy Ship'* (1983), *The Peel Sessions* (1986), with Maddy Prior *Silly Sisters* (1986), *Aqaba* (1988), *Some Other Time* (1989), with Maddy Prior *No More To The Dance* (1990), *Angel Tiger* (1992). Compilation: *Aspects* (1990).

Tanega, Norma

b. 30 January 1939, Vallejo, California, USA. Her Filipino parents actively encouraged their daughter's interest in music and art, both of which she studied. Although classically-trained, Tanega quickly showed a preference for guitar. She moved to New York to work as a graphic artist, but quickly became immersed in the city's folk enclave. She drew encouragement from Bob Dylan and Tom Paxton and her prolific songwriting resulted in a recording deal. Tanega's debut single, 'Walkin' My Cat Named Dog' (1966), reached number 22 both in the US and UK charts, and she was optimistically categorized alongside other lyrical artists, including Janis Ian and Bob Lind. Sadly, Tanega's hit proved to be her strongest composition; further releases were unsuccessful and the first phase of the singer's career ended almost as quickly as it had begun. She briefly re-emerged in 1977 with an album recorded for RCA Records.

Albums: *Walkin' My Cat Named Dog* (1966), *I Don't Think It Will Hurt* (1977).

Tannahill Weavers

This group formed in Paisley, Scotland in 1968, and took their name from the town's weaving community. Over the years, the group have undergone numerous personnel changes, with John Cassidy (flute/guitar/whistles/vocals), Davie Shaw (bass/guitar), Stuart McKay (guitar/vocals) and Gordon Duncan (bagpipes), from the early line-ups, leaving before the group recorded. Initially, the group played mainly in Scotland, but in 1974 they set out on a short tour of Germany, followed by their first major tour of England. *Are Ye Sleeping Maggie*, their debut, was the first to be released on the Plant Life label. The line-up on this recording was Roy Gullane (b. Maryhill, Glasgow, Scotland; guitar/tenor banjo/vocals), who joined in 1969, Phil Smillie (b. 22 December 1955, Kelvin Hall, Glasgow, Scotland; flute/bodhran/vocals), who joined in 1975, Hudson Swan (b. 31 August 1954, Paisley, Renfrewshire, Scotland; fiddle/guitar/bouzouki), who joined in 1972, and

Dougie MacLean (b. 27 September 1954, Dunblane, Scotland; fiddle/guitar/vocals). Tours of Europe followed, and in 1978 the group played support to Steeleye Span on the latter's British tour. In complete contrast, later that same year the Tannahill Weavers played support to Dire Straits in Holland. The numerous personnel changes that have occurred over the years have included Willie Beaton (fiddle), Mike Ward (fiddle/mandolin), Alan McLeod (bagpipes/whistles), Bill Bourne (b. Red Deer, Alberta, Canada; bouzouki/vocals), Ross Kennedy (bouzouki/vocals), Iain MacInnes (bagpipes) and Stuart Morrison (fiddle). The current line-up includes Gullane and Smillie, plus John Martin (fiddle/cello/vocals), who joined in 1989 and was formerly with Ossian, Contraband, and the Easy Club and Kenny Forsythe (bagpipes), who joined in 1991. Les Wilson (bouzouki/keyboards), who originally joined in 1982, left within the year and returned in 1989. At one time the group changed their name, albeit briefly, to Faithless Nellie Grey. Most of the group's touring is done in the USA and Europe. 1991 saw the Tannahill Weavers' 10th annual tour of the USA, with further tours and recordings planned. Despite the various changes in the line-up, the strong Celtic flavour in the music, which combines bagpipes and electric instrumentation, remains consistent.
Albums: *Are Ye Sleeping Maggie* (1976), *The Old Woman's Dance* (1978), *The Tannahill Weavers* (1979), *Tannahill Weavers 4* (1982), *Passage* (1984), *Land Of Light* (1986), *Dancing Feet* (1987), *Cullen Bay* (1990), *The Mermaid's Song* (1992). Compilation: *The Best Of The Tannahill Weavers 1979-1989* (1989).

Tannen, Holly
b. New York City, New York, USA. Described as a singer, dulcimer and piano player, and writer, Tannen has become one of the better regarded exponents of the hammer, or hammered, dulcimer. From a well-educated background, having studied anthropology, zoology and psychology, Tannen learned to play the piano. After being given an Appalachian, or mountain, dulcimer, she fell in love with the instrument and set about teaching herself to play. Moving to Berkeley, California, she met up with singer Rita Weill and guitarist Janet Smith, and performed with them often. Later the idea of combining other instruments with the dulcimer took hold, and she set about putting this into practice. She had earlier worked with Pete Cooper in 1979, when they recorded *Frosty Morning*, and toured Britain, Europe and the USA. She returned to California from England, in 1981, releasing *Invocation* on Kicking Mule in 1983. She also appeared on two tracks on *All Around The World*, an album by Cooper in 1990. As well as performing, and recording the instrument, Holly has regularly written a column in the west coast magazine *Folkscene*, appropriately called 'Dulcimer Corner'. After moving to England she provided another column called 'Notes From England'.
Albums: with Pete Cooper *Frosty Morning* (1979), *Invocation* (1983), *Between The Worlds* (1985), with others *Berkeley Farms* (c.80s).

Tansads
Formed around the songwriting of guitarist John Kettle and members of his family, the Tansads dispense a mixture of English folk and pop influences, with a dash of funk. Coming together in the late 80s, Kettle, his long term partner Janet Anderton (vocals), and his brothers Robert, and Ed (bass) formed the nucleus of the band. When his youngest brother, Andrew, was recruited, the twin lead vocal sound reminded some of the 70s folk/rock giants. With Dominic Lowe on accordion and brass, 'Bug' (drums) and 'Cudo'(percussion), the band recorded *Shandyland* in 1991. Lyrically homespun, and tongue-in-cheek, *Folk North West* wrote: 'They are our future... and they are absolutely brilliant.' The album attracted the attention of producer Phil Tennant, and the group was signed to Musidisc (which had released the Levellers). Subsequent sessions resulted in the single 'Brian Kant' and *Up The Shirkers*, both of which gained national airplay, and featured in *Folk Roots* and the UK Independent Charts. By then the sound was harder, and the lyrics contemporary, but still humorous. Extensive touring followed, along with BBC Radio 1 sessions, and the release of *Up The Shirkers* in Europe and the USA.
Albums: *Shandyland* (1991), *Up The Shirkers* (1993).

Tarleton's Jig
Formed in 1979, Tarleton's Jig were an offshoot from two other groups, the City Waites and Common Ground. With a membership rich in classical training, this talented group utilized a vast array of exotic instruments, such as recorders, shawms, flutes, curtals, Danish, Flemish and English bagpipes, the Rauchespfeife, cornet, baroque violin, recorders, crumhorns, rebecs, lutes, uilleann pipes, theorbo and guitars. Tarleton's Jig comprises James Bisgood (b. 3 March 1959, Isleworth, Middlesex, England; also vocals), Jeremy West (b. 29 November 1953, Sussex, England), David Miller (b. 13 April 1953, Glamorgan, Wales) and Keith Thompson (b. 7 August 1951, Whitstable, Kent, England). The group has performed a wide spectrum of popular English music from the Middle Ages to the mid-18th Century, with particular emphasis on 16th and 17th centuries. They

regularly perform at stately homes and castles, and often in the presence of Royalty. *For King And Parliament* contained music from soldier's camps, taverns and street corners, as well as the battlefield. *A Fit Of Mirth For A Groat* was equally well-received. It was performed much as it would have been during the English Civil Wars. One of the musicians featured on this album, Sharon Lindo (b. 11 December 1959, Romford, Essex, England), left in 1989.

In 1990, Martin Pope (b. 22 June 1955, Kuala Lumpur, Malaysia) left the line-up, having joined in 1982. *Roaring Boys* was originally scheduled for release in 1990. With the departure of Lindo who had played on a substantial amount of the recordings, the release was shelved, but the tapes still exist, and subsequent release is not considered out of the question. Due to a large 'pool' of highly talented musicians, the group has managed to maintain its standards and continues to work, using authentic instruments of the period, and full costumes of the time. They have also provided soundtrack themes for a number of documentary television programmes, such as *The History Man*.

Other regular players in the now fluid line-up include, Nick Hayley (b. 5 April 1954, London, England), William Lyons (b. 13 May 1964, England), Jonathan Morgan (b. 21 April 1953, Birmingham, England), and Robert White (b. 10 March 1955, Lambeth, London, England).

Albums: *For King And Parliament* (1987), *A Fit Of Mirth For A Groat* (1989).

Tarriers

Formed c.1954, the Tarriers are remembered for two primary reasons: their 1957 US Top 5 recording of 'The Banana Boat Song' and the fact that one of its members was Alan Arkin, who went on to become a highly successful actor. The folk group was put together by Erik Darling (b. 25 September 1933, Baltimore, Maryland, USA), who was influenced by the folk revivalists of the day. After performing briefly with a large troupe of vocalists, Darling hooked up with Arkin (b. 26 March 1934, Brooklyn, New York) and Bob Carey as the Tunetellers. The group changed its name to the Tarriers and wrote and recorded 'The Banana Boat Song' to capitalize on the calypso music craze then sweeping the USA. Simultaneously they recorded a similar song called 'Cindy, Oh Cindy' with singer Vince Martin. Both singles were released on Glory Records, 'Cindy' reaching number 9 and 'The Banana Boat Song' number 4. The Tarriers never again made the charts, however, and the original trio dissolved two years later. Darling joined the Weavers and later went on to form the Rooftop Singers, Arkin began his acting

career and Carey kept a Tarriers group alive until 1964.

Albums: *The Tarriers* (1957), *Hard Travelin'* (1959), *Tell The World About This* (1960), *The Tarriers* (1962), *Gather 'Round* (1963), *The Original Tarriers* (1963).

Tawney, Cyril

b. 12 October 1930, Gosport, Hampshire, England. Most of this guitar-playing songwriter's work reflects his 12 years in the Royal Navy, during which time he started writing songs and singing. He took part in the English Folk Dance and Song Society's first National Folk Festival, in London, in October 1957. A fellow entrant was BBC producer Charles Parker, who booked Tawney for his Christmas broadcast *Sing Christmas*. Thus, with the attention of BBC West Region, Cyril started his radio and television career. Tawney is the only British career serviceman to have his own fully networked television programme, *Watch Aboard*, first broadcast in 1959. He made his recording debut in 1960, on *Rocket Along*, an anthology with other artists, on HMV Records. Turning to full-time singing in May 1959, he was initially employed solely by the BBC. He helped to pioneer the British folk revival in the 60s via the newly emerging folk clubs. His interest in west country and nautical songs, led him to found the Plymouth Folk Song Club in January 1962, and the West of England Folk Centre, in 1965. During the late 60s, Tawney presented *Folkspin*, a radio programme devoted solely to record requests for British traditional music. As time passed, his songwriting reflected more non-naval themes, and he maintained his singing career while gaining BA and MA degrees during the 70s.

A number of his earlier works, notably 'Sally Free And Easy', 'The Grey Funnel Line', 'The Oggie Man', and 'Sammy's Bar', have been recorded by numerous artists, and are performed regularly in folk clubs. It is a testament to their authenticity that they are often erroneously considered traditional, rather than self-penned. Tawney also appeared on a number of albums with other artists such as the *World Of Folk* series on Decca's Argo label. Tawney stopped touring British folk clubs in 1985, and now concentrates on concerts, festivals and special appearances. His book, *Grey Funnel Lines*, featuring traditional songs of the 20th Century Royal Navy, was the result of over 30 years research. Together with his wife, Rosemary, he founded Neptune Tapes, a label dealing with all aspects of maritime song. Tawney is now engaged in writing a series of tales with a Royal Navy background.

Albums: with others *Rocket Along* (1960), with others *A Pinch Of Salt* (1960), *Between Decks* (1963),

with others *Folksound Of Britain* (1965), *The Outlandish Knight* (1969), *Children's Songs From Devon And Cornwall* (1970), *A Mayflower Garland* (1970), *This Is A Man's World* (1970), with others *World Of Folk* (1971), *In Port* (1972), *I Will Give My Love* (1973), with others *World Of The Countryside* (1974), *Down Among The Barley Straw* (1976), with others *The Transports* (1977), with others *Reunion* (1984), *In The Naval Spirit* (1988), *Round The Buoy* (1989), *Sally Free And Easy* (1990), *Sailor's Delight* (1991), *In Every Port* (1991).
Further reading: *Grey Funnel Lines - Traditional Song And Verse Of The Royal Navy 1900-1970*, Cyril Tawney.

Taylor, Allan

b. 30 September 1945, Brighton, Sussex, England. This singer/songwriter/instrumentalist has achieved considerable acclaim on the UK folk circuit. After leaving school at the age of 16, he helped to organize local folk clubs, until turning professional five years later. Taylor attracted the interest of United Artists after supporting Fairport Convention on a national tour. *Sometimes* was released on the Liberty label, and aroused a degree of interest from the folk media. Backing musicians on the album were Fairport Convention members Dave Mattacks, Dave Pegg, and Dave Swarbrick. Following Taylor's move to New York from 1972-74, *The American Album* followed a different course, and included a wealth of respected Nashville and Los Angeles session musicians. In July 1975, Allan formed the group Cajun Moon in order to encompass traditional, Appalachian and cajun musical styles. The trio, which included Brian Golbey (fiddle), and Jon Gillaspie (keyboards), toured with Steeleye Span and Taylor signed a deal with Chrysalis resulting in *Cajun Moon* in May 1976. Due to overwork, Taylor damaged his vocal chords, and was forced to rest for three months. This more or less spelt the end of the group and, following an operation, Taylor recommenced solo work, signing a publishing deal with Chrysalis and a recording deal with Rubber Records. His first release, *The Traveller*, appeared in April 1978, and featured John Kirkpatrick on melodeon and accordion. Following an appearance at the Nylon Folk Festival in Switzerland, in July 1980, Allan was presented with the Grand Prix Du Disque De Montreux for the best European folk album of that year. Due to a greater influence of working on the continent, *Roll On The Day* presented a slightly different style of writing. *Circle Round Again* consisted of re-recordings of popular songs from previously deleted Taylor albums. Around the time of *Win Or Lose*, Allan received a BA from Leeds University, and was working on his MA at

Lancaster University, when he completed his first novel. Taylor then spent two years touring and working on material for *Lines*, which was released in March 1988. 'It's Good To See You', written by Taylor, was recorded by Don Williams, and other artists such as Frankie Miller, Françoise Hardy and Fairport Convention have recorded Allan Taylor songs.
He has now been included in the *Oxford Book Of Traditional Verse* as one of the writers who has best furthered the folk tradition. Taylor, more recently, gained a PhD in Ethnomusicology in addition to continuing to tour as well as writing music for television.
Albums: *Sometimes* (1971), *The Lady* (1972), *The American Album* (1973), *Cajun Moon* (1976), *The Traveller* (1978), *Roll On The Day* (1980), *Circle Round Again* (1983), *Win Or Lose* (1983), *Lines* (1988), *Out Of Time* (1990).

Taylor, Bram

b. Bramwell Taylor, 6 August 1951, Leigh, Lancashire, England. Both of Taylor's parents were musically-minded members of the Salvation Army. After initially learning to play cornet and tenor horn, he moved on to the guitar. Inspired by such artists as Harvey Andrews and Marie Little, he began playing at folk clubs. By 1975, in addition to playing to a wider audience, he was co-presenter/performer for BBC Manchester on the children's programme *Chatterbox*. Taylor released his *The Haymakers*, in 1975, more to sound out interest than anything else. Generally traditional in feel, it suffered in terms of production, but provided a good platform for Taylor and his clear vocal style. In 1979, together with Dave Dutton (b. 19 August 1947, Atherton, Lancashire, England; vocals, ukulele, banjo), and Eric White (b. 2 October 1946, Leigh, Lancashire, England; ukelele, banjo, lap organ, melodeon, penny whistle, accordion, concertina), he formed the comedy group, Inclognito. In 1985, White was replaced by Jackie Finney (b. 26 October 1960, Salford, Lancashire, England; penny whistle, accordion, keyboards, guitar, vocals). In 1989 the group split, due to Taylors solo commitments, and Dutton's acting involvement in the BBC situation comedy *Watching*. Taylor signed to Fellside Records, an independent label run by Paul and Linda Adams on 1 August 1984. His first release, *Bide A While*, was well received by the folk music press. *Dreams And Songs To Sing* reflected a slight departure in style by the use of more contemporary material, but kept the same formula and the same musicians, including the strong vocal harmonies of Fiona Simpson. The album received the 1987 British Music Retailers award for excellence in the Folk and Country

Allan Taylor

category. *Taylor Made* was evidence of his ability to take contemporary songs and record them with an underlying traditional feel, thus pleasing both sides of the folk music 'divide'.

Albums: *The Haymakers* (1982), *Bide A While* (1984), *Dreams And Songs To Sing* (1986), *Taylor Made* (1990). Compilations: with various artists *Flash Company* (1986), with various artists *Beyond The Seas* (1988).

Taylor, Eric

b. c.1947, USA. Taylor wrote stories as a child and later put his talent into narrative songs. He served in Vietnam, experiencing drug and alcohol problems, and then he befriended singer-songwriters, Guy Clark and Townes Van Zandt, in Houston, Texas in 1969. He and his ex-wife Nanci Griffith recorded albums for the small Featherbed label, *Shameless Love* and *Poet In My Window*, respectively. Each was featured on the other's album and Taylor's 'Only Lovers' is about their relationship. Despite his talents as a performer, Taylor decided to qualify as a psychologist and devote his time to helping addicts in Houston. He sang background vocals on Griffith's 1988 live album, *One Fair Summer Evening*, which included his song about the death of Crazy Horse, 'Deadwood, South Dakota', described by Griffith as 'one of the best pieces of writing I've ever heard'.

Album: *Shameless Love* (1981).

Taylor, James

b. 12 March 1948, Boston, Massachusetts, USA. The embodiment of the American singer-songwriter from the late 60s and early 70s was the frail and troubled James Taylor. He was born into a wealthy family. His mother was a classically trained soprano and encouraged James and his siblings to become musical. As a child he wanted for nothing and divided his time between two substantial homes. He befriended Danny 'Kootch' Kortchmar at the age of 15 and won a local talent contest. As is often the case, boarding school education often suits the parents more than the child, and James rebelled from Milton Academy at the age of 16 to join his brother Alex in a rock band, the Fabulous Corsairs. At only 17 he committed himself to the McLean Mental Institution in Massachusetts. Following his nine-month stay he re-united with 'Kootch' and together they formed the commercially disastrous Flying Machine. At 18, now being supported by his parents in his own apartment, the seemingly affluent James drew the predictable crowd of hangers-on and emotional parasites. He experimented and soon was addicted to heroin. He had the drive to move out, and after several months of travelling he arrived in London and found a flat

in Notting Hill (which in 1968 was hardly the place for someone trying to kick a drug habit!). Once again 'Kootch' came to the rescue, and suggested Taylor take a demo tape to Peter Asher. 'Kootch' had supported Peter And Gordon on an American tour, and Asher was now looking for talent as head of the new Apple Records. Both Asher and Paul McCartney liked the work and the thin, weak and by now world-weary teenager was given the opportunity to record. *James Taylor* was not a success when released, even though classic songs like 'Carolina On My Mind' and 'Something In The Way She Moves' appeared on it.

Depressed and still hooked on heroin, Taylor returned to America, this time to the Austin Riggs Mental Institution. Meanwhile Asher, frustrated at the disorganized Apple, moved to America, and persevering with Taylor, he secured a deal with Warner Brothers and rounded up a team of supportive musician friends; 'Kootch', Leland Sklar, Russ Kunkel and Carole King. Many of the songs written in the institution appeared on the superlative *Sweet Baby James*. The album eventually spent two years in the US charts and contained a jewel of a song: 'Fire And Rain'. In this, he encapsulated his entire life, problems and fears; it stands as one of the finest songs of the era. Taylor received rave notices from critics and he was quickly elevated to superstardom. The follow-up *Mud Slide Slim And The Blue Horizon* consolidated the previous success and contained the definitive reading of Carole King's 'You've Got a Friend'. In 1972, now free of drugs, Taylor worked with the Beach Boys' Dennis Wilson on the cult drag-race film *Two Lane Blacktop* and released *One Man Dog* which contained another hit 'Don't Let Me Be Lonely Tonight'. Fortunately Taylor was not lonely for long; he married Carly Simon in the biggest show business wedding since Burton and Taylor. They duetted on a version of the Charlie And Inez Foxx hit, 'Mockingbird' which made the US Top 5 in 1974.

Taylor's albums began to form a pattern of mostly original compositions, mixed with an immaculately chosen blend of R&B, soul and rock 'n' roll classics. Ironically most of his subsequent hits were non-originals. Holland Dozier And Holland's 'How Sweet It Is', Otis Blackwell's 'Handy Man', Goffin And King's 'Up On The Roof'. Taylor was also displaying confidence and sparkling onstage wit, having a superb rapport with his audiences, where once his shyness was excruciating. Simon filed for divorce a decade after their marriage, but Taylor accepted the breakdown and carried on with his profession. The assured Taylor is instrumentally captured by Pat Metheny's joyous composition 'James' recorded on Metheny's *Offramp* album in

James Taylor

1982. In 1985 Taylor released the immaculate *That's Why I'm Here*. The reason he is here, as the lyric explains is; 'fortune and fame is such a curious game, perfect strangers can call you by name, pay good money to hear "Fire And Rain", again and again and again'. This one song says as much about James Taylor today as 'Fire And Rain' did many years ago. He has survived, he is happy, he is still creative and above all his concerts show that he is genuinely grateful to be able to perform.
Albums: *James Taylor* (1968), *Sweet Baby James* (1970), *James Taylor And The Original Flying Machine - 1967* (1970), *Mud Slide Slim And The Blue Horizon* (1971), *One Man Dog* (1972), *Walking Man* (1974), *Gorilla* (1975), *In The Pocket* (1976), *JT* (1977), *Flag* (1979), *Dad Loves His Work* (1981), *That's Why I'm Here* (1985), *Never Die Young* (1988), *New Moon Shine* (1991). Compilations: *Greatest Hits* (1976), *Classic Songs* (1987), *The Best Of James Taylor - The Classic Years* (1990).

Taylor, Livingston
b. 1951, Chapel Hill, North Carolina, USA, d. 1993 Taylor was the youngest of four singing and guitar-playing brother and sisters. With a home background of folk music, he played coffee houses in Boston and attracted the interest of rock critic Jon Landau. His first two albums for Phil Walden's Capricorn label were produced by Landau and contained the minor hits 'Carolina Day', and 'Get Out Of Bed', both written by Taylor. His acoustic style was reminiscent of the work of his brother, James Taylor, but retained a bluesier edge. James Taylor and Carly Simon sang on *Over The Rainbow*, but after its release Livingston was dropped by Capricorn. He continued to tour regularly throughout the 70s and after signing to Epic, he had Top 40 hits with the Nick de Caro-produced 'I Will Be In Love With You' (1979) and 'First Time Love' (1980), produced by John Boylan and Jeff 'Skunk' Baxter, formerly of the Doobie Brothers. He continued to record sporadically during the 80s, scoring a minor hit with 'Loving Arms', a duet with Leah Kunkel and also performed at US colleges and folk clubs.
Albums: *Livingston Taylor* (1970), *Liv* (1971), *Over The Rainbow* (1973), *Three Way Mirror* (1978), *Man's Best Friend* (1980), *Life Is Good* (1988).

Tester, Scan
b. Lewis Tester, 1887, Chelwood Common, Sussex, England, d. 1972. Tester showed a penchant for music from a very young age, progressing quickly from tambourine to melodeon, concertina and fiddle. In addition to his early days busking in Brighton, Sussex, Scan played for dances in a number of local inns. After World War I, he continued playing for dances and formed Tester's Imperial Band which featured, in addition to Tester, his second wife Sarah on drums, and daughter Daisy on piano. Occasionally, Tester's brother Will would play on bandoneon. The band survived until 1931, after which Scan played at a pub called the Stone Quarry, until he died in 1972. In his lifetime, he had built an extensive repertoire of dance material. It was thanks to a collector, Mervyn Plunkett, that Tester's music, and the music of Sussex, came to the attention of a much wider audience in 1957. Plunkett recorded Tester and his music; *I Never Played Too Many Posh Dances*, is a double album featuring recordings from 1957-68.
Albums: *The Man In The Moon* (1975), *I Never Played Too Many Posh Dances* (1990); with other artists *Music Of The Sussex Weald* (1966), *Boscastle Breakdown* (1974), *Sussex Harvest* (1975).
Further reading: *I Never Played Too Many Posh Dances*, Reg Hall.

Thackray, Jake
b. 1938, Yorkshire, England. Thackray came to public attention after a prolonged residency on a UK television series, *Jake Thackray And Songs*. His distinctive, deep clipped intonation and hang dog expression enhanced his repertoire of comic, romantic, traditional and serious songs. He became a regular guest on numerous other television programmes, such as *The David Frost Show* and *On The Braden Beat*. Since his first paid job at the City Palace Of Varieties, in Leeds, Jake has toured the USA, Europe, Canada, Africa and many other points of the compass. Unlike many other folk performers who, having achieved a degree of commercial status, left the folk scene Thackray could still be seen playing small clubs, while filling engagements at the London Palladium, the Royal Albert Hall, and other large venues fulfiling the demand for old favourites such as 'Bantam Cock' and 'Sister Josephine'.
Albums: *The Last Will And Testament Of Jake Thackray* (1967), *Jake's Progress* (1969), *Live Performance - Jake Thackray* (1971), *Bantam Cock* (1972), *On Again, On Again* (1977), *Jake Thackray And His Songs* (1980), *Tramshed Forever* (1981). Compilations: *The Very Best Of Jake Thackray* (1975), *Lah-Di-Dah* (1991).

Therapy
This UK group formed in 1970, when Fiona Simpson (b. 8 May 1952, Farnborough, Hampshire, England; guitar/vocals), joined the existing duo of Dave Shannon (b. 7 February 1947, Belfast, Northern Ireland; keyboards/guitar/vocals), and Sam Bracken (guitar/vocals). While the former duo

Jake Thackray

had specialized in blues and ragtime, the addition of Fiona changed their repertoire to include songs by such writers as James Taylor, and Joni Mitchell. When Bracken left in 1971, Simpson and Shannon continued as a duo until 1983, touring Europe, playing venues as disparate as a folk club one night, and the Royal Albert Hall the next. One of the most requested songs at bookings was Joni Mitchell's 'Carey', which displayed Simpson's voice to startling effect. *Almanac*, released on CBS, featured all Dave Shannon originals. The album based a song around each sign of the Zodiac. The group undertook much television work during this period, and incorporated comedy into their act, opening shows for such acts as Max Boyce, Jasper Carrott, and the Barron Knights. *Bringing The House Down* included such diverse songs as 'Killing Me Softly With His Song', and the traditional 'Lord Franklyn'. Indeed, many of the songs featured in Therapy's live set came from outside the folk spectrum, much to the displeasure of some folk purists. 1977 saw the release of a single on DJM Records, 'The Most Important Part Of Me Is You', produced by Brian Bennett of the Shadows, followed by a remake of *Almanac*. Subsequent albums were released on their own label, Therapy Records. By financing and producing their own albums, largely for selling at gigs, they have encouraged other acts to pursue the same line in bypassing record companies, a practice that has now become commonplace on the folk scene. Shannon left to become a music producer for the BBC, while Fiona has continued to perform in a solo capacity, essentially in folk clubs and at festivals, both at home and abroad. She has also recorded in her own right and is a sought-after session singer on records and for BBC Radio.

Albums: *Almanac* (1971), *One Night Stand* (1973), *Bringing The House Down* (1975), *Supertrouper* (1980), *Schizophrenia* (1981), *Then There Was One* (1984), *Cold Hands* (1987), *Beneath The Rose* (1989).

Thompson, Danny

b. April 1939, London, England. An expressive, inventive double bass player, Thompson became established in British jazz circles through his work with Tubby Hayes. In 1964 he joined Alexis Korner's Blues Incorporated where he would forge an intuitive partnership with drummer Terry Cox. Three years later the duo formed the rhythm section in Pentangle, a folk 'supergroup' which featured singer Jacquie McShee and guitarists John Renbourn and Bert Jansch. Thompson remained with this seminal quintet until their demise in 1972 but had forged a concurrent career as a leading session musician. He appeared on releases by Donovan, Cliff Richard ('Congratulations') and Rod Stewart ('Maggie May'), but was acclaimed for peerless contributions to albums by folksingers Nick Drake and John Martyn. The bassist's collaborations with the latter were particularly of note (and their legendary drinking sessions) and their working

Danny Thompson (left) with Donovan

relationship spanned several excellent albums, including *Solid Air*, *Inside Out* and *Live At Leeds*. A notorious imbiber, Thompson then found his workload and confidence diminishing. He successfully conquered his alcohol problem and resumed session work with typically excellent contributions to releases by Kate Bush, David Sylvian and Talk Talk. In 1987 the bassist formed his own group, Whatever, and recorded new age and world music collections. He remains a leading instrumentalist, respected for his sympathetic and emotional style. Should his music ever desert him Thompson could carve a career as a stand-up comic.

Albums: *Whatever* (1987), *Whatever Next* (1989), with Toumani Diabate and Ketama *Songhai* (1989).

Thompson, Richard

b. 3 April 1949, Totteridge & Whetsone, London, England. The remarkably talented Thompson forged his reputation as guitarist, vocalist and composer with Fairport Convention which, although initially dubbed 'England's Jefferson Airplane', later evolved into the seminal folk-rock act through such acclaimed releases as *What We Did On Our Holidays* (1968), *Unhalfbricking* (1968), *Liege And Leif* (1969) and *Full House* (1970). Thompson's sensitive compositions graced all of the above but none have been applauded more than 'Meet On the Ledge'. This simple lilting song oozes with restraint, class and emotion and is one of the most evocative songs to come out of the late 60's 'underground' music scene. Thompson's innovative guitar style brought a distinctive edge to their work as he harnessed such diverse influences as Django Rheinhart, Charlie Christian, Otis Rush, James Burton and Mike Bloomfield. The guitarist left the group in 1971 and having contributed to two related projects, *The Bunch* and *Morris On*, completed an impressive solo debut, *Henry The Human Fly*. He then forged a professional partnership with his wife, Linda Peters and, as Richard And Linda Thompson, recorded a series of excellent albums, notably *I Want To See The Bright Lights Tonight* (1974), and *Hokey Pokey* which established the artist's reputation for incisive, descriptive compositions. Richard also collaborated with such disparate vocalists as Sandy Denny, John Martyn, Iain Matthews, Elvis Costello and Pere Ubu's David Thomas, which in turn enhanced his already considerable reputation.

The Thompsons separated in 1982, although the guitarist had completed his second solo album, *Strict Tempo*, a compendium of styles based on hornpipes, jigs and reels, the previous year. An in-concert set, *Small Town Romance* followed, before the artist recorded the acclaimed *Hand Of Kindness* and *Across*

The Crowded Room, the latter of which featured the embittered 'She Twists The Knife Again'. In 1986 Thompson undertook extensive US and UK tours to promote *Daring Adventures*, leading a group which included (Clive) Gregson And (Christine) Collister. He then completed the soundtrack to *The Marksman*, a BBC television series, before joining John French, Fred Frith and Henry Kaiser for the experimental *Live, Love, Larf And Loaf*. In 1988 Thompson switched outlets to Capitol. Thompson recorded with the Golden Palominos in 1991 and the same year performed with David Byrne. Thompson has for years been critically acclaimed; he is an outstanding guitarist and excellent songwriter. His recent albums have contained some of his finest ever compositions. *Watching The Dark* is a three CD set covering Thompson's career, it puts into perspective what an important figure was, is and will continue to be. Quite what this man has to do to receive commercial success appears to forever remain an astonishing mystery.

Albums: *Henry The Human Fly* (1972), *Strict Tempo* (1981), *Small Town Romance* (1982), *Hand Of Kindness* (1984), *Across A Crowded Room* (1985), *Daring Adventures* (1986), *The Marksman* (1987), *Amnesia* (1988), *Rumour And Sigh* (1990), *Sweet Talker* (1992). Compilation: *Watching The Dark* (3CD box set)(1993).

Further reading: *Meet On the Ledge*, Patrick Humphries.

Thompson, Richard And Linda

This husband-and-wife folk/rock duo began performing together officially in 1972 although their association dated from the previous year. When Richard Thompson (b. 3 April 1949, Totteridge & Whetsone, London, England; guitar/vocals) left Fairport Convention, he pursued a generally low-key path, performing in folk clubs and on various sessions, including *Rock On*, a collection of rock 'n' roll favourites which featured several Fairport acolytes. 'When Will I Be Loved?' was marked by a duet between Sandy Denny and Linda Peters, the latter of whom then provided vocals on Thompson's *Henry The Human Fly*. Richard and Linda then began a professional, and personal, relationship, introduced on *I Want To See The Bright Lights Tonight*. This excellent album contained several of Richard's best-known compositions, including the title track, 'Cavalry Cross' and the despondent 'End Of The Rainbow': 'Life seems so rosy in the cradle, but I'll be a friend, I'll tell you what's in store/There's nothing at the end of the rainbow/There's nothing to grow up for anymore'. The Thompsons toured with former-Fairport guitarist Simon Nicol as Hokey Pokey, which in turn evolved into a larger, more emphatic

Richard And Linda Thompson

unit, Sour Grapes. The former group inspired the title of a second enthralling album which blended humour with social comment. Its release was the prelude to a frenetic period which culminated in *Pour Down Like Silver*, the Thompson's second album within 12 months. It reflected the couple's growing interest in the Sufi faith, but despite a sombre reputation, the set included several excellent compositions.

A three year hiatus in the Thompson's career ensued, broken only in 1977 by a series of live performances accompanied by fellow converts Ian Whiteman, Roger Powell and Mick Evans, all previously with Mighty Baby. Now signed to the Chrysalis label, *First Light* provided a welcome return and many commentators rate this album as the duo's finest. The follow-up release, *Sunnyvista*, was in comparison, a disappointment, despite the inclusion of the satiric title track and the angry and passionate 'You're Going To Need Somebody'. However, it led to the duo's departure from their record label. This second, if enforced, break ended with the superb *Shoot Out The Lights*, nominated by *Rolling Stone* as the best album of 1982. Indeed such a response suggested the Thompsons would now secure widespread success and they embarked on a US tour to consolidate this newly-won recognition. Despite this, the couple's marriage was breaking up and in June 1982 the duo made their final appearance together at Sheffield's South Yorkshire Folk Festival. Richard Thompson then resumed his critically-acclaimed solo career, while Linda went

on to record *One Clear Moment* (1985).
Albums: *I Want To See The Bright Lights Tonight* (1974), *Hokey Pokey* (1975), *Pour Down Like Silver* (1975), *First Light* (1978), *Sunnyvista* (1979), *Shoot Out The Lights* (1982).

Tickell, Kathryn

b. 8 June 1967, Wark, North Tyne Valley, Northumberland, England. Tickell appeared like a breath of fresh air onto the folk scene, which was being criticized for its fuddy-duddy image. Playing the Northumbrian pipes and fiddle, Tickell had played piano from the age of six. Having learned the Shetland style of fiddle playing from Tom Anderson, she played at the first Shetland folk festival in 1981. Two years later, she was breaking new ground by appearing at the Edinburgh International Festival. In 1984 Kathryn was made official piper to the Lord Mayor of Newcastle-upon-Tyne, the same year as *On Kielderside* was released. As a result of the acclaim, she turned professional in 1985 and followed a busy touring schedule. Having been inspired by respected musicians such as Alistair Anderson, Joe Hutton, Willy Taylor and Will Atkinson, she recorded an album of Northumbrian music, *From Sewingshields To Glendale* that same year. Her Northumbrian pipe playing is highly regarded, especially when comparisons are made between age and proficiency. Tickell's musical development was chronicled in a television documentary, *The Long Tradition*, broadcast in 1987 and released on video the following year. Kathryn has broadened her horizons beyond that of pure folk, having played on Sting's *Soul Cages*. The new Kathryn Tickell Band which recorded *The Kathryn Tickell Band* included Lynn Tocker (accordion), Ian Carr (guitar) and Geoff Lincoln (bass guitar).

Albums: *On Kielderside* (1984), *From Sewingshields To Glendale* (1985), *Borderlands* (1987), *Common Ground* (1988), *The Kathryn Tickell Band* (1991).

Tikaram, Tanita

b. 12 August 1969, nr. Munster, Germany. Tikaram's intense lyrics brought her instant commercial success at the age of 19. She spent her early years in Germany where her Fijian-born father was serving with the British army. In 1982 the family moved to England, settling in Basingstoke, Hampshire. Tikaram began writing songs and in November 1987 played her first gig at London's Mean Fiddler, after sending a cassette of her songs to the venue. By the time of her fourth gig she was supporting Warren Zevon at the Hammersmith Odeon. Following an appearance on a local London television show, she was signed to Warner Brothers and recorded *Ancient Heart* in 1988. The producers were Rod Argent (ex-Zombies) and experienced session musician Peter Van Hooke. 'Good Tradition' and 'Twist In My Sobriety' were immediate hits in the UK and across Europe. The album was a huge success and Tikaram became a late 80s role model of late 60s bedsitter singer/songwriters. She spent most of 1989 on tour before releasing her second album which included 'We Almost Got It Together' and 'Thursday's Child'. Although not as consistent as her debut it reached the same position in the UK album chart, number 3. *Everybody's Angel*, at Bearsville Studio in Woodstock, was co-produced with Van Hooke and Argent. Former Emerald Express violinist Helen O'Hara was among the backing musicians. 'Only The Ones We Love' with harmony vocals by Jennifer Warners was issued in 1991, and in the same year she made her second world tour. In 1992 the self-produced *Eleven Kinds Of Loneliness* was released to a muted reaction.

Albums: *Ancient Heart* (1988), *The Sweet Keeper* (1990), *Everybody's Angel* (1991), *Eleven Kinds Of Loneliness* (1992).

Tilston, Steve

b. Stephen Tilston, 26 March 1950, Liverpool, England. Tilston has an almost 'classical' feel to his style of guitar playing, probably enhanced by his experience touring with the Ballet Rambert. He also works regularly with his wife, Maggie Boyle. Since his debut album in 1971, Tilston has continued to work in a solo capacity or with Maggie. In addition to this he has performed in partnership with Martin Jenkins of Whippersnapper. Both Steve and Maggie are members of John Renbourn's group Ship Of Fools, whose eponymous album received much acclaim from the folk press. Tilston also features the 19th century instrument the Arpeggione (or bowed guitar) in many of his performances. *Life By Misadventure* mixed a variety of styles and influences, but retains the almost laid-back Tilston vocal style. As a result of his different musical commitments, Steve has toured the USA, Europe, Canada and the Middle East, and continues to work the folk club circuit in Britain. Tilston is also involved with the running of the independent label Run River Records.

Albums: *An Acoustic Confusion* (1971), *Collection* (1973), *Songs From The Dress Rehearsal* (1977), *In For A Penny, In For A Pound* (1983), *Life By Misadventure* (1987), with Ship Of Fools *Ship Of Fools* (1989), *Swans At Coole* (1989), with Maggie Boyle *Of Moor & Mesa* (1992).

Tir nA nOg

Without drawing on traditional sources, there was, nevertheless, an indelible Celtic tincture in the mainly acoustic music of Dubliners Leo O'Kelly (guitar/violin/vocals) and Sonny Condell (guitar/percussion/ vocals). Condell had previously entered the Irish Top 10 with 'Tram Car 88' when a member of his cousin's group. With O'Kelly, his commercial prosperity was not as conspicuous but less transient. The duo's early 70s output for Chrysalis, including a *Melody Maker* Single Of The Week in 'The Lady I Love', gilded a cult reputation that remained strong enough to sustain a comeback on Britain's folk club circuit 17 years after a 1974 disbandment that had been prefaced by an experimental augmentation with a drummer, electric bass guitarist and the keyboards of Matthew Fisher. While the pair's repertoire in 1991 included items from obscure post-1974 solo projects, the loudest ovations were reserved for old Tir nA nOg favourites from albums still thought to be worthy of reissue.

Albums: *Tir nA nOg* (1971), *A Tear And A Smile* (1972), *Strong In The Sun* (1973).

To Hell With Burgundy

This acoustic group from Manchester, England, UK, made their recording debut on the local, cult Factory label in 1988 with an album based on a Latin gypsy sound. Two years later, with their own set up, they released two intimate, more structured EPs, with Kevin Metcheer (vocals, guitar), Karl Walsh (vocals, guitar), and Joanne Hensman (percussion, vocals), heading in a distinctly English,

arty direction. *Only The World* was the result of long, hard touring and much soul-searching over their future direction. It revealed a band capable of writing folksy pop melodies laced with aching harmonies, and able to adapt to smoky folk clubs, and stadium support duties. To Hell With Burgundy span different styles and barriers, and all three members are highly accomplished musicians who retain a fierce independence.
Albums: *Earthbound* (1988), *Only The World* (1992).

Toss The Feathers

Manchester based, but with strong Irish roots, Toss The Feathers built a loyal live fan base in the North West of England and London before delivering *Awakenings*. In a three year period up to 1993, they played an exhausting 650 live dates, including several in Europe. Their recorded songs have been constructed on-stage as much as in the studio, and, despite major record label interest, their work is released through an independent. In their live performances they have concentrated on a traditional-Celtic rock dance sound, while their studio output has more of the flavour of Moving Hearts.
Album: *Awakenings* (1993).

Toure, Ali Farka

b. 1948, Gao, Mali. Guitarist and vocalist Toure's intense, acoustic style shares striking resonances with the music of black American blues artists (notably Robert Johnson and John Lee Hooker), and proves beyond reasonable doubt that the blues did indeed mutate from traditional West African folk song. Carrying the cross-cultural fusion further, Toure's 1990 *The River*, recorded in London, features contributions from jazz saxophonist Steve Williamson and members of Irish folk band the Chieftains on fiddle and bodhran, and is a powerful argument in favour of Atlantis.
Albums: *Bandolobourou* (1980), *Ali Farka Toure* (1983), *Special* (1986), *Biennale* (1987), *Yer Sabou Yerkoy* (1989), *The River* (1990), *The Source* (1992).

Trader Horne

Trader Horne were a folk-based duo, consisting of Judy Dyble (b. 13 February 1949, London, England) and Jackie McCauley. Dyble had been the first female singer in Fairport Convention, but left following the completion of the group's debut album. She briefly appeared in the line-up of Giles, Giles And Fripp in 1968, dropping out after barely a month. McCauley was an early member of Them with brother Pat, who together formed the Belfast Gypsies in the wake of their erstwhile band's disintegration. Despite achieving some success in Scandinavia, the new group broke up in 1967.

Trader Horne's lone album was released in 1970 and features assistance from former Them flautist, Ray Elliot. The duo split up soon afterwards and while Dyble's later work was confined to occasional Fairport reunions, McCauley embarked on a solo career.
Album: *Morning Way* (1970).

Traum, Happy

b. 1939. Raised in the Bronx district of New York, Happy Traum became involved in folk music while studying at the High School Of Music And Art and took lessons from blues guitarist Brownie McGhee. He then formed a duo with younger brother Artie and together they performed extensively throughout the east coast circuit. The Traums later formed a rock group, Children Of Paradise, which also featured pianist Eric Kaz. Happy left the quintet in 1967 and moved to Woodstock, a renowned artistic enclave in upstate New York. In 1969 the brothers were reunited for their self-titled debut album, the first of several informal but enjoyable selections. Two years later Happy accompanied Bob Dylan on three songs specifically recorded for the artist's *Greatest Hits, Volume 2* selection. An accomplished musician on guitar and banjo, Happy Traum has written several instruction books and recorded tapes for a home music study course. He continues to pursue a sporadic solo career.
Albums: solo *Hard Times In The Country* (1975), *American Stranger* (1978); with Artie Traum *Happy And Artie Traum* (1969), *Doubleback* (1971), *Mud Acres* (1972), *Life On Earth* (1974), *Relax Your Mind* (1976), *Bright Morning Stars* (1980).

Travellers 3

One of the many groups inspired by the urban folk revival of the early 60s, the Travellers 3 was founded by Pete Apo, Charles Oyama and Dick Shirley while studying at the University of Oregon, USA. They quickly became a popular folk attraction through appearances at several influential venues, including the Troubador (Los Angeles), the Gate Of Horn (Chicago) and the Exodus (Denver). The Travellers 3 completed three albums for the renowned Elektra label before adding a drummer, Michael Gene Botta. They then switched outlets to Capitol, but despite this pioneering adoption of a folk-rock format, the group split up when unable to secure a new audience.
Albums: *The Travellers 3* (1962), *Open House* (1963), *Live! Live! Live!* (1963).

Trees

Formed in 1969, Celia Humphris (vocals), Bias Boshell (vocals/bass/acoustic guitar), Barry Clarke

(lead/acoustic guitars), David Costa (acoustic/12-string guitars) and Unwin Brown (drums) were signed to CBS Records the following year. The quintet's folk-rock albums drew favourable comparisons with Fairport Convention, particularly for their imaginative arrangements of traditional material. Trees displayed an even greater penchant for improvisation, evident on the extended versions of 'Lady Margaret' and 'She Moves Through The Fair' (*The Garden Of Jane Delawney*) and 'Streets Of Derry' and 'Sally Free And Easy' (*On The Shore*). Essentially a framework for Clarke's exhilarating guitarwork, the textured accompaniments bestowed on such excursions revealed a group of care and taste. Boshell and Brown left the line-up following the release of their second album. They were replaced by Barry Lyons and Alun Eden; although a violinist, Chuck Fleming, was also added, the group was unable to bridge the genres it pursued and broke up before a third release could be completed.
Albums: *The Garden Of Jane Delawney* (1970), *On The Shore* (1970).

Trio Bulgarka

This leading vocal trio from Bulgaria comprises Yanka Rupkina, discovered in 1959 at an amateur folk festival, (b. Strandja, Bulgaria), Stoyanka Boneva (b. Pirrin, Bulgaria), and Eva Georgieva (b. Dobroudja, Bulgaria). All three are soloists in their own right, and have all performed and recorded with the Sofia Radio Choir, featured on the Le Mystère Des Voix Bulgares albums. Their repertoire includes material from their respective regions of Bulgaria. *The Forest Is Crying*, co-produced by Joe Boyd, features such backing musicians as Roumen Sirakov (tambour), Ognyan 'Jimmy' Vassiliev (drums), Mihail Marinov (gadulka), Stoyan Velichkov (kaval), Hristofer Radanov (clarinet), and Pascal Pascalev (bass). The group impressed audiences in 1987 during their Balkana British Tour. Such is the power and quality of the group's singing that Kate Bush recruited their services on her 1989 release *The Sensual World*. With the increased popularity of world music in recent years the Trio Bulgarka have been assured of a large international audience.
Album: *The Forest Is Crying* (1988).

Tundra

Tundra was formed by Doug Hudson (b. 4 February, Surrey, England), while he was studying Russian at Bradford University. The original, short-lived line-up changed when Hudson moved back to Kent in 1971. Doug added Mike Peters and Peter Learmouth, followed by Sue Carroll, (b. 25 January 1952, Farnham, Surrey, England), a singer from Upchurch, Kent. Doug and Sue married in

October 1972 and six months later the group split. Learmouth subsequently formed Dr.Cosgill's Delight, later to become Blowzabella. Sue and Doug continued performing under the name Tundra, while researching and performing songs about Kent. In 1978, as a result of being offered both a recording deal with Sweet Folk All Records and an American tour, the duo turned professional. *A Kentish Garland*, the duos debut release, sold well, and television and radio coverage followed. *Songs From Greenwich* featured Alan Prosser of the Oyster Band on fiddle, guitar and synthesizer, and included songs about, and collected in, the Greenwich area of London. Their live act, which featured the guitar-playing Doug playing the fool to Sue's apparently more serious persona was highly popular, but after 12 years of solid work, they split. Doug continued solo, performing folk and comedy material, and toured Australia and New Zealand, where he topped the bill at the Auckland and Dunedin Folk Festivals in 1988. He has since toured Africa, the Middle-East and Hong Kong, and featured in his own radio show, *Hudson's Half Hour*, on BBC radio. He is currently working on a television series with former group member, Peter Learmouth, writer of the television show, *Surgical Spirit*. Sue now fronts Small Town Romance, a new country group, already featured on regional television.
Albums: *Folk In Sandwich* (1972), *Travelling Folk* (1976), *A Kentish Garland* (1978), *The Kentish Songster* (1980), *Songs From Greenwich* (1982); Solo albums: Doug Hudson *Tundra Live* (1984), *1987 And All The Rest Of It* (1987), *Shredded Wit* (1989), *Excuse Me, I'm Looking For Luxembourg* (1991).

Turner, Gil

b. Gilbert Strunk, 6 May 1933, Bridgeport, Connecticut, USA, d. 23 September 1974. Turner's early influences came via his father who was a machinist and a singer. Gil's mother sang in the church choir, and for a time Gil intended to become a lay preacher. Turner studied political science at the University of Bridgeport, and also attended the Columbia University School of Social Work. He later wrote papers on the management of autistic children through music, and the treatment of rheumatoid arthritis by the use of gold and cortisone. Turner was well placed to raise such issues since he suffered with the latter illness for most of his life. The illness eventually paralysed the left hand side of his body. His guitar and banjo-playing style was heavily influenced by the Rev. Gary Davis, but Turner later developed his own distinctive style. Gil worked as a master of ceremonies at Gerde's Folk City in Greenwich Village in 1961 and by the following year had founded *Broadside* magazine, together with Agnes 'Sis' Cunningham, Gordon Friesen, Toshi and Pete Seeger. In addition to arranging recordings of *Broadside* benefit albums, Turner toured on the college and school circuits, as well as concert halls, such as the Carnegie Hall.

Turner also recorded material for the Library of Congress, in addition to his own albums. He collected and wrote many folk songs which were covered by artists such as Joan Baez, Judy Collins and Carolyn Hester. One of his songs, 'Carry It On' became the title of a book by Pete Seeger and Bob Reiser. Turner joined the Student Non-Violent Co-ordinating Committee, and the War Resisters League. As well as this he helped to set up the New York Council of Performing Arts. One project he was involved with was the Mississippi Caravan of Music, for which a great many artists such as Phil Ochs, Judy Collins and Pete Seeger travelled and performed throughout Mississippi during 1964. Turner appeared in 1966 with the National Shakespeare Company in San Diego, California, taking part in a number of nationwide tours. With actor Will Geer, Gil worked on the Tribute To Woody Guthrie, which took place at the Hollywood Bowl on 12 September 1970. The following year, while involved in recording for Shel Silverstein, Turner contracted hepatitis. He subsequently moved to San Francisco while undergoing treatment. Sadly, while still actively involved in the folk movement on the west coast, and recording an album for Elektra, as well as working on playing the part of Lee Hays in a film about Woody Guthrie, he died in September 1974.
Albums: with Bob Cohen and Happy Traum *The New World Singers* (1963).

Turner, Steve

b. 18 March 1950, Manchester, England. Turner began his career in 1967 playing guitar, mandolin, tenor banjo, and singing. From 1971-79, he played with Canny Fettle, a group from Newcastle, which featured Bob Diehl (fiddle), Phil Bartlett (fiddle/concertina/mandolin/harmonium), Gerry Murphy (concertina/small pipes/whistle), Dave Hillery (concertina/vocals), Dave Howes (whistle/melodeon/vocals), and Bob Morton (guitar). Together they released *Varry Canny* and *A Trip To Harrogate*. Although Turner is known for his concertina playing, it was only in 1974 that he started to play the instrument. In 1980, Steve won a 'Stars Of The 80s' contest organized by Karl Dallas and the following year he turned professional. In addition to his solo work, Turner occasionally performs with the Steve Turner Band, which comprises George Faux (fiddle/guitar/vocals), Dave Walters (vocals/guitar), Bill Martin, previously with

Pyewackett (keyboards), and Steve Schwartek (bass). A fine interpreter of traditional song, Turner is held in esteem by others on the folk circuit. His albums, all on Fellside Records, include a number of noted folk personnel including Nic Jones, Paul Metsers, Martin Simpson and Jim Couza. Apart from the sleeve, which prompted some adverse comment, *Braiding* included the much-recorded Stephen Foster song 'Hard Times', plus two other Foster songs, 'Nelly Was A Lady' and 'Glendy Burk/Swanee River Hornpipe'. In club performances, Turner has often encored with the classic 'The Man On The Flying Trapeze'. Although not a prolific recording artist, Turner remains an important performer.
Albums: with Canny Fettle *Varry Canny* (1975), *Trip To Harrogate* (1977); solo *Out Stack* (1981), *Jigging One Now* (1982), *Eclogue* (1984), *Braiding* (1987).

Tyson, Ian And Sylvia

Ian Dawson Tyson, b. 25 September 1933, British Columbia, Canada. His father came to Canada in 1906 with dreams of being a cowboy and passed his love to his son who worked on a farm, entered amateur rodeos and worked as a lumberjack. He says, 'I'm always grateful for my logging and rodeo days because that's where the songs come from.' While recovering from a rodeo injury, Ian taught himself guitar and then played 'rockabilly in the chop-suey bars of Vancouver'. He says, 'I couldn't play very well as I only knew A, D and E. That's when I wrote 'Summer Wages'.' In 1959, he met Sylvia Fricker, (b. September 1940, Chatham, Ontario, Canada), the daughter of a music teacher. They formed a folk duo, Ian and Sylvia, and were married in 1964. They moved to Greenwich Village and were signed by Bob Dylan's manager, Albert Grossman. Ian says, 'I could never match Dylan's output. For every good song I wrote, he wrote eight.' They recorded folk-based albums and made popular the songs of fellow Canadian Gordon Lightfoot including 'Early Morning Rain' and 'For Lovin' Me'. Ian wrote about migrant workers in 'Four Strong Winds', later recorded by Neil Young, and about a rodeo from a girl's point of view in 'Someday Soon', beautifully recorded by Judy Collins. Fricker wrote 'You Were On My Mind', a US hit for We Five and a UK one for Crispian St Peters. By the end of the 60s, they went electric and formed a folk/rock group, the Great Speckled Bird, and the album of the same name was produced by Todd Rundgren. They then veered towards country music, and Sylvia wrote Crystal Gayle's US country hit, 'River Road'. They split up professionally in 1974 and were divorced in 1975, although Ian produced Sylvia's *Woman's*

World. Sylvia was featured on the Canadian Live Aid single, 'Tears Are Not Enough' by Northern Lights. Ian bought a 160-acre ranch in Longview, Alberta, Canada and reared cutting horses with his second wife, Twylla. His tributes to working cowboys, *Old Corrals And Sagebrush* and *Ian Tyson*, were made with the simplicity of albums by the Sons Of The Pioneers. The more high-tech *Cowboyography* sold 50,000 copies in Canada alone and Tyson had a hit with a song he wrote with his protege Tom Russell, 'Navajo Rug', since recorded by Jerry Jeff Walker. His songs show compassion and understanding for the cowboy's life and, when he has not written them himself, they have been immaculately chosen, for example, 'Night Rider's Lament' and 'Gallo De Cielo'. He comments, 'As the song says, my heroes have always been cowboys and still are it seems.'

Albums: by Ian And Sylvia: *Ian And Sylvia* (1962), *Four Strong Winds* (1964), *Northern Journey* (1964), *Early Morning Rain* (1965), *Play One More* (1966), *So Much For Dreaming* (1967), *Lovin' Sound* (1967), *Nashville* (1968), *Full Circle* (1968), *Great Speckled Bird* (1969), *Ian And Sylvia* (1971), *You Were On My Mind* (1972); by Ian Tyson *Ol' Eon* (1974), *One Jump Ahead Of The Devil* (1978), *Old Corrals And Sagebrush* (1983), *Ian Tyson* (1984), *Cowboyography* (1987), *I Outgrew The Wagon* (1989); by Sylvia Tyson *Woman's World* (1975), *Big Spotlight* (1986), *You Were On My Mind* (1990), *Gypsy Cadillac* (1992).

Wedding Present, Solowka also wrote and collected Ukrainian songs with Liggins and mandolin player Roman. In 1991, the break was made from the indie band, and the Ukrainians came into being. Their first album of original material was released on Cooking Vinyl. The second consisted of covers of songs by the Smiths, which revealed indie roots, but with definite Ukrainian delivery. The full band now featured Pete Solowka and Len Liggins, together with Stepan Pasicznyk (accordion), Paul Briggs (bass) and Dave Lee (drums). A second album of originals, varying from chants, to wild Cossack dance tunes, was released early in 1993.

Albums: *The Ukrainians* (1991), *Pisni Iz The Smiths* (1992), *Vorony* (1993).

Urban Folk

A sort of traditional based Travelling Wilburys, Pete Morton (vocals, guitar), Roger Wilson (fiddle) and Simon Edwards (accordion, vocals), decided to become an occasional unit after playing sessions on Morton's *One Big Joke*. Gigs were divided equally between Morton's acidic folk, Wilson's old time fiddling and Edward's pumping, squeezebox love songs. *Urban Folk- Volume 1* (1991) had everything from Jimi Hendrix covers to traditional ballads, and gained favourable reviews in the folk press, but no increased demand for their services. Frustrated and wanting to concentrate on his fledgling K.Passa unit, Edwards left in 1992. His replacement was Mike Willoughby - late of Strange Folk - himself something of a maverick protest writer.

Album: *Urban Folk Volume 1* (1991).

U

Ukrainians

The Ukrainians was formed originally as an offshoot of the UK indie rock band, the Wedding Present, by guitarist Pete Solowka, who had been influenced by his father's Ukrainian heritage. The Wedding Present itself had recorded a number of traditional songs for a John Peel BBC Radio session in 1988, for which they were joined by Solowka's friend, vocalist and violinist, Len Liggins, who had been a student of Slavonic languages. The first session was followed by another, and they were both were later released as an album, *Ukrainski Vistupi v Ivana Peel*. Promoted by a short tour, it climbed to number 22 in the UK charts. Continuing to play with the

V

Van Ronk, Dave

b. 30 June 1936, Brooklyn, New York, USA. Van Ronk learned to play guitar and later played in jazz groups in New York. He also learned to play the banjo. His first love was New Orleans jazz, and his initial involvement with folk music did not come about until 1957, when he worked with Odetta. From this, his interest in blues grew, inspired by Josh White. Van Ronk's reputation for playing blues, together with his distinctive gruff voice, grew until he was signed by Folkways Records in 1959. His first album, however, appeared during the same year on the Lyrichord label. After a couple of releases he moved to Prestige in 1962, and from the mid-60s concentrated more on jazz and jugband music. He formed a band called the Ragtime Jug Stompers, and in 1964 signed to Mercury Records. He continued playing concerts both in the USA and abroad and in 1965 played the Carnegie Hall as part of the New York Folk Festival. Van Ronk worked a lot less during the 70s. However, many of his earlier works were still available well into the 80s. In 1974 Dave took the stage with Bob Dylan and Phil Ochs for *An Evening With Salvador Allende*, for a closing version of Dylan's 'Blowin' In The Wind'. *Dave Van Ronk*, on Fantasy Records, was a re-issue of his first two Prestige albums.

Albums: *Sings Ballads, Blues And Spirituals* (1959), *Fo'csle Songs And Shanties* (1959), *The Unfortunate Rake* (1960), *Inside* (1962), *Dave Van Ronk, Folksinger* (1963), with the Red Onion Jazz Band *In The Tradition* (1963), *The Genius Of Dave Van Ronk* (1964), *Ragtime Jug Stompers* (1964), *Just Dave Van Ronk* (1964), *Gambler's Blues* (1965), *No Dirty Names* (1966), *Dave Van Ronk And The Hudson Dusters* (1967), *Van Ronk* (1969), *Sunday Street* (1976), *Black Mountain Blues* (70s), *Dave Van Ronk Sings Earthy Ballads And Blues* (70s), *Statesboro Blues* (1992). Compilation: *Hesitation Blues* (1988).

Van Zandt, Townes

A country and folk-blues singer and guitarist, Van Zandt is a native Texan and great grandson of one of the original settlers who founded Fort Worth in the mid-19th Century. The son of a prominent oil family, Townes turned his back on financial security to pursue the beatnik life in Houston. First thumbing his way through cover versions, his acoustic sets later graced the Jester Lounge and other venues where his 'bawdy bar-room ballads' were first performed. Although little-known outside of a cult country rock following, many of his songs are better publicized by the covers afforded them by Merle Haggard, Emmylou Harris, Don Gibson and Willie Nelson. This gave songs such as 'Pancho And Lefty' and 'If I Needed You' the chance to rise to the top of the country charts. Much of Van Zandt's material was not released in the UK until the late 70s, though his recording career actually began with *For The Sake Of A Song*, released in the US in 1968. His media awareness belies the debt many artists, including the Cowboy Junkies and Go-Betweens, profess to owing him. Steve Earle went further: 'Townes Van Zandt is the best songwriter in the whole world, and I'll stand on Bob Dylan's coffee table in my cowboy boots and say that'. Interest is still alive as the recent re-issue of the *Live And Obscure* (albeit re-titled *Pancho And Lefty*) on Edsel proves. Van Zandt continues to

live a reclusive life in a cabin in Tennessee, recording occasionally purely for the chance to 'get the songs down for posterity'.

Albums: *For The Sake Of A Song* (1968), *Our Mother The Mountain* (1969), *Townes Van Zandt* (1969), *Delta Momma Blues* (1971), *High And Low And In Between* (1972), *The Late Great Townes Van Zandt* (1972), *Live At The Old Quarter* (1977), *Flyin' Shoes* (1978), *At My Window* (1987), *Live And Obscure* (1987), *Rain On A Conga Drum* (1991) *Pancho And Lefty* (1992).

Vega, Suzanne

b. 12 August 1959, New York City, New York, USA. Vega is a highly literate singer/songwriter who found international success in the late 80s. She studied dance at the High School For The Performing Arts (as featured in the *Fame* television series) and at Barnard College, singing her own material in New York folk clubs. Signed by A&M Records in 1984, she recorded her first album with Lenny Kaye, former guitarist with Patti Smith. From this, 'Marlene On The Wall', a tale of bedsitter angst, became a hit. In 1987 'Luka' grabbed even more attention with its evocation of the pain of child abuse told from the victim's point of view. Vega's 'Left Of Center' appeared on the soundtrack of the film *Pretty In Pink* and she also contributed lyrics for two tracks on *Songs From Liquid Days* by Philip Glass. On her third album, Vega collaborated with keyboard player and co-producer Anton Sanko, who brought a new tightness to the sound. Meanwhile, Vega's lyrics took on a more surreal and precise character, notably on 'Book Of Dreams' and 'Men In A War', which dealt with the plight of amputees. In 1990 the serendipitous 'Tom's Diner' from *Solitude Standing* became a hit in the UK after it had been sampled by the group DNA. The track was remixed by Alan Coulthard for Vega's label; its success led to the release of *Tom's Album* (1991), devoted entirely to reworkings of the song by artists such as R.E.M. and rapper Nikki D.

Albums: *Suzanne Vega* (1985), *Solitude Standing* (1987), *Days Of Open Hand* (1990).

Vipers Skiffle Group

Formed in 1956, the group consisted of various members, including Wally Whyton, Tommy Steele, Hank Marvin, Jet Harris and Bruce Welch. It grew out of the 'frothy coffee' scene, centred at the 2 I's coffee bar, in London's Soho district in the late 50s. Whyton was the musical brains, and with Bill Varley, wrote the group's first hit, 'Don't You Rock Me Daddy-O', which was even more successful for the 'King Of Skiffle', Lonnie Donegan. After having their 'cleaned up' version of

Vipers Skiffle Group with Jim Dale (left)

'Maggie May' banned by the BBC, the Vipers had two other UK chart entries in 1957: 'Cumberland Gap' and 'Streamline Train'. However, the whole skiffle craze was short-lived. Before long, Steele had become an 'all-round entertainer'. Marvin, Harris and Welch had formed the Shadows, via the Drifters; and Whyton had carved out a career as a singer and broadcaster on radio programmes such as *Country Meets Folk* and *Country Club*; and previously as a host of childrens' television shows, notably with the irritating glove-puppet, Pussy Cat Willum. In 1960 the Vipers sang 11 songs in the musical play, *Mr. Burke M.P.* at London's Mermaid Theatre. Whyton also played the part of 'The Commentator'.

Compilation: *Coffee Bar Sessions* (1986).

Virginia Squires

This modern US bluegrass group comprised Rickie Simpkins (fiddle, mandolin, vocals), Ronnie Simpkins (bass, vocals), Sammy Shelor (guitar, banjo, vocals) and Mark Newton (guitar, vocals). The Simpkins Brothers originate from a musical family from the hills just southwest of Roanoke, Virginia. They played together in a family group but eventually formed Upland Express, a bluegrass band that had an album release on Leather Records in the 70s. They separated in the early 80s, when Rickie worked with the McPeak Brothers and

Ronnie became a member of the Bluegrass Cardinals. In 1982 they reunited in Richmond, in a band called the Heights Of Grass, but early in 1983, with Mark Newton (previously a member of Knoxville Grass) and Sammy Shelor (one time member of the Country Boys) they became the Virginia Squires. Playing a variety of bluegrass, rock, old time and country, they became a very popular band in their native state and recorded for the Rebel label.

Albums: *Bluegrass With A Touch Of Class* (1984), *Mountains And Memories* (1985), *I'm Working My Way* (1986), *Hard Times And Heartaches* (1987), *Variations* (1988).

Vujicsics

This group took their name from the late Hungarian composer and collector Tihamer Vujicsics, who was killed in a plane crash in 1976. The line-up comprises Gabor Eredics (concertina/accordion/bass tambura), Kalman Eredics (bass/tarabuka), Mihaly Borbely (clarinet/flute/ocarina/sopile/tambura), Karoly Gyori (violin/tamburica), Ferenc Szendrodi (guitar/tambura) and Miroslav Brczan (tambura cello/bass). Vujicsics specialize in the music and song of the southern parts of Hungary, in particular Serbia and Croatia (formerly). During their existence, the group have played throughout eastern and western Europe. Marta Sebestyen, known for her vocal work with Muzsikas, has also recorded with Vujicsics. Other vocalists who have performed or recorded with Vujicsics include Erika Frei, Marica Greges and Katalin Gyenis. Since the late 80s, much of the music of Eastern Europe has been able to reach a wider audience, due to political and social changes and the growing interest in world music. *Vujicsics*, recorded in Hungary, was released under licence by Hannibal Records.

Album: *Serbian Music From Southern Hungary* (1988).

W

Wainwright, Loudon, III

b. 5 September 1946, Chapel Hill, North Carolina, USA. Loudon Wainwright I was in insurance while his son, Loudon Wainwright II, became a journalist for *Life* magazine. Wainwright's parents settled in Westchester Country, 60 miles outside of New York City although he went to a boarding school in Delaware ('School Days') and he was friends with an adolescent Liza Minnelli ('Liza'). He studied acting in Pittsburgh where singer George Gerdes encouraged his songwriting. By 1968, after a brief spell in an Oklahoma jail for a marijuana offence, Wainwright was playing folk clubs in New York and Boston and was signed to Atlantic Records. His first albums featured his high-pitched voice and guitar with few additions, and his intense, sardonic songs, described by him as 'reality with exaggeration', were about himself. He was hailed as the 'new Bob Dylan' for such songs as 'Glad To See You've Got Religion', 'Motel Blues' and 'Be Careful, There's A Baby In The House'. He later said: 'I wasn't the new anyone. Media people call you the new-something because it's the only way they know to describe what you do'. His UK debut, opening for the Everly Brothers, was disastrous as Teddy Boys barracked him, but he found his *métier* at the 1972 Cambridge Folk Festival.

Wainwright's third album, for Columbia Records, included a surprise US Top 20 pop hit in 'Dead Skunk'. 'I had run over a skunk that had been run over a few times already. It took 15 minutes to write. I remember being bowled over at how much people liked it when I had put so little into it. It's about a dead skunk but people thought it was about Nixon and that's all right by me.' Wainwright wrote 'A.M. World' about his success and, almost defiantly, he followed it with *Attempted Moustache*, that had indistinct vocals and was uncommercial even by his standards, although it did include the whimsical 'Swimming Song'. *Unrequited*, partly

Loudon Wainwright III

recorded live, was a return to form and included the hilarious, but controversial, 'Rufus Is A Tit Man' (which Wainwright described as 'a love song, not a dirty song'), one of many songs he was to record about his children ('Pretty Little Martha' and 'Five Years Old') His marriage to Kate McGarrigle (see Kate And Annie McGarrigle) ended in 1977 and Loudon then had a child with Suzzy Roche of the Roches. His album, *A Live One*, actually recorded in 1976 demonstrates his wit but this gawky, lanky, square-jawed singer with enormous tongue, grimaces and contortions needs to be seen in person to be fully appreciated.

Wainwright has appeared in a few episodes of the television series *M*A*S*H*, appeared on stage in *The Birthday Party* and *Pump Boys And Dinettes*, and he is most recently best known in the UK for his topical songs on the Jasper Carrott television series. His wit and neuroses surfaced in such songs as 'Fear Of Flying' and 'Watch Me Rock, I'm Over 30' (both from *T-Shirt*), but he reached top form on three albums for Demon - *Fame And Wealth*, *I'm Alright* and *More Love Songs*. The albums, sometimes co-produced with Richard Thompson, have included 'I Don't Think Your Wife Likes Me', 'Hard Day On The Planet' (written while watching Live Aid), 'Unhappy Anniversary', 'Not John' (a tribute to John Lennon) and 'This Song Don't Have A Video'. Many of his later compositions are about the music industry of which he later claimed, 'I wanna be in showbiz one way or another until I die, so it's a mixed blessing not to be a huge success. I've been successful on my own terms - by failing'.

Albums: *Loudon Wainwright III* (1969), *Album II* (1971), *Album III* (1972), *Attempted Moustache* (1974), *Unrequited* (1975), *T-Shirt* (1976), *Final Exam* (1978), *A Live One* (1979), *Fame And Wealth* (1983), *I'm Alright* (1984), *More Love Songs* (1986), *Therapy* (1989), *History* (1992).

Walker, Eddie

b. 31 October 1948, England. This singer, guitarist and songwriter specialized in ragtime and country blues. His work encompasses the styles of artists such as 'Big' Bill Broonzy, Mississippi John Hurt and Rev. Gary Davis. Between 1977 and 1982 Walker released four albums, the second of which was a compilation of residency appearances at the Cutty Wren Folk Club in Redcar, Cleveland. This included Walker's song 'Candy'. Another Walker original, 'Stolen My Heart Away', was joint winner of the Tyne Tees television programme *Songwriter* in 1982. Eddie has now teamed up with the highly-repsected guitarist John James in the duo Carolina Shout. James was earlier featured playing guitar on Walker's 1985 release *Picking My Way*. The album

included a tribute to songwriter Steve Goodman. Walker has played the Hong Kong Folk Music Festival, in addition to regular dates in Europe, and continues to play the folk circuit, though more often these days as part of Carolina Shout.

Albums: *Everyday Man* (1977), *Folk At The Wren* (1978), *Castle Cafe* (1981), *Red Shoes On My Feet* (1983), *Picking My Way* (1985), as Carolina Shout *Carolina Shout* (1989).

Walker, Ian

b. Ian James Walker, 27 April 1948, Govanhill, Glasgow, Scotland. Ian started playing and singing during the early 60s in the Glasgow Folk Centre, but took a break from playing until 1975. In the late 70s, Walker started writing and appearing at folk festivals, but it was 1985 before he released *Roses In December*. Nevertheless, from playing clubs and festivals he started to become more widely known, and the follow-up *Flying High*, released on Fellside, was voted winner in the Folk and Country Music category by the UK Music Retailers Association. The album contains some excellent songs, such as the title track, an anti-war song, which was inspired by the Falklands conflict. Other songs, including 'Hawks And Eagles Fly Like Doves', have been sung and recorded by the McCalmans and Dick Gaughan, and 'Sing Me A Song Mr Bloom' by the Yetties and Bram Taylor. Since 1988, in addition to solo appearances, Walker has worked with fellow Glaswegian songwriter, Ian Bruce. A talented songwriter, with a subtle line in social comment, Walker's talent deserves to be more widely known.

Albums: *Roses In December* (1985), *Flying High* (1987), *Shadows In Time* (1989).

Warner, Frank

b. 5 April 1903, Selma, Alabama, USA. This guitar and banjo player and his wife Anne, are known for their song collecting. Frank went to university in 1921, where he learned a large number of folk songs. Following his degree, he pursued a career with the YMCA, but continued his hobby of singing, and lecturing on folk music. In 1935, he and Anne were married, and together they travelled regularly to rural areas along the US Eastern seaboard, collecting songs and tunes from the area. The two eventually met Frank Proffitt, the son-in-law of musical instrument maker Nathan Hicks. The family lived in the mountains of North Carolina. It was on the first visit that Proffitt taught the Warner's 'Tom Dooley'. Later, in 1939, Frank and Anne travelled to the Adirondacks, and, in 1940 to New England, still collecting songs and regional stories. It was only on the later trips that they were able to record some of the material.

Proffitt's version of 'Tom Dooley' was included on *Frank Warner Sings American Folk Songs And Ballads*, along with 'He's Got The Whole World In His Hands', which was collected in 1935. Frank Warner has performed all over the USA, and in Britain at colleges and historical societies, singing a great number of the songs he has collected and thus keeping those traditions alive. Frank even had a featured part in the 1956 film, *Run Of The Arrow*, which starred Rod Steiger. Anne spent eight years compiling the *American Folk Songs From The Anne And Frank Warner Collection*, having started it when she was 70 years old. After a lifetime commitment to collecting, she died in 1991. Proffitt's albums, recorded for labels such as Elektra and Vanguard, have included sleeve notes written by Anne.
Selected albums: *Frank Warner Sings American Folk Songs And Ballads* (1952), *Our Singing Heritage Vol.3* (1958), *Come All You Good People* (1976), *Story Of A Folksong USA* (1979).
Further reading: *Folk Songs And Ballads Of The Eastern Seaboard: From A Collector's Notebook*, Frank Proffitt, Southern Press Inc. USA, 1963. *Traditional American Folk Songs From The Anne And Frank Warner Collection*, Anne Warner, Syracuse University Press, 1984.

Water Into Wine Band

This UK acoustic folk-rock ensemble comprised Ray Wright (b. 27 April 1949, London, England), Trevor Sandford (b. 30 June 1952, Cookstown, Northern Ireland), Peter McMum (b. 10 November 1951, Salford, Greater Manchester, England), and William Thorp (b. 30 April 1952, Huddersfield, Yorkshire, England). They were formed at Cambridge University in 1971, and turned professional in 1974, performing at various colleges, folk clubs and festivals. That same year *Hillclimbing For Beginners* was released, and *Harvest Time* followed in 1976. A five-week tour of east and mid-west USA preceded their demise in 1976. William Thorp, an exceptional violinist, has stayed in music, working first for the Welsh National Opera, then the Royal Philharmonic Orchestra, and more recently in numerous chamber groups with especial interest in baroque and early music.
Albums: *Hillclimbing For Beginners* (1974), *Harvest Time* (1976).

Watersons

This British unaccompanied band, is regarded as one of the most important and influential of the UK folk revival groups. They were originally called the Mariners, then the Folksons, before using their family name. The essential group, with occasional later variations, comprises of Mike Waterson (b. 16 January 1941, England), Norma Christine Waterson (b. 15 August 1939, England) and Lal Waterson (b. Elaine Waterson, 15 February 1943, England). The other original member, their cousin John Harrison, left in 1966, with the group splitting up two years later. In 1972, with the reformation of the quartet, Harrison's place was taken by Bernie Vickers, who was then replaced by Martin Carthy, who married Norma the same year. The group have been cited by numerous artists, such as Anne Briggs, as being responsible for the development of unaccompanied harmony singing. *Frost And Fire* was named *Melody Maker* folk album of the year on release. *Sound, Sound Your Instruments Of Joy*, was an album of traditional Victorian hymnals. In 1985, Mike's daughter, Rachel (b. 3 April 1966, England), joined the group.
The Watersons have the ability to perform traditional songs, while retaining the freshness in the arrangement of the individual vocal lines. In addition, the various members of the group have recorded works in their own right, but the Watersons still appear occasionally at festivals.
Albums: *New Voices* (1965), *Frost And Fire* (1965), *The Watersons* (1966), *A Yorkshire Garland* (1966), *For Pence And Spicy Ale* (1975), *Sound, Sound Your Instruments Of Joy* (1977), *Greenfields* (1981). Lal And Mike *Bright Phoebus* (1972). Lal And Norma *A True Hearted Girl* (1977). Mike Waterson *Mike Waterson* (1977).

Watson, Doc

b. Arthel Watson, 2 March 1923, Deep Gap, North Carolina, USA. This blind acoustic folk-guitarist's work found great success in the 60s and was rediscovered by country-rock fans following his appearance on the Nitty Gritty Dirt Band's *Will The Circle Be Unbroken* in 1972. He played harmonica and banjo as a child, later progressing to guitar. In the 50s he played pop and commercial country in local clubs. After being spotted on a traditional music bill alongside his neighbour Clarence Ashley, Watson was booked for the famous Gerde's Folk City in New York in 1960. Recordings followed, for premier folk labels Folkways and Vanguard, and his reputation was enhanced by a notable Newport Folk Festival appearance in 1963. Two years later, he began to work with his son Merle, another excellent flat-picking guitarist who, in later years, inspired his father to diversify from the folk ballads and blues which were his wont. They won Grammys for *Then & Now* and *Two Days In November*; by the late 70s, Doc had become a revered figure, receiving rapturous receptions wherever he played and guesting on records by Flatt And Scruggs and Chet Atkins. Watson went into semi-retirement following the tragic death of his son in a farming accident in 1985, but remains well represented on record, via latter-day recordings for the Flying Fish and Sugar Hill labels.

Albums: *Doc Watson And Family* (1963), *Doc Watson* (1964), with Merle Watson *Doc Watson And Son* (1965), *Southbound* (1966), *Home Again* (1966), *Good Deal* (1968), *The Elementary Doc Watson* (1972), *Then & Now* (1973), *Two Days In November* (1974), with Merle *Memories* (1975), *In The Pines* (1984), *Riding The Midnight Train* (1984), *On Praying Ground* (1990). Compilations: *The Essential Doc Watson* (1974, double set), *A Folk And Country Legend* (1982), *Portrait* (1988), *The Essential Doc Watson, Volume 1* (1989), with Merle *Remembering Merle* (1992).

We Five

Formed in 1965, this Los Angeles, California, USA quintet was viewed as a stepping-stone between the clean-cut folk of the Kingston Trio and the rock-based perspective offered by the Byrds. Michael Stewart (guitar/vocals), Beverley Bivens (vocals), Bob Jones (guitar/vocals), Jerry Burgan (guitar/vocals) and Pete Fullerton (bass/vocals) enjoyed a US Top 3 hit that year with 'You Were On My Mind', an exuberant song which was a British hit in the opportunistic hands of Crispian St. Peters. We Five's conservative approach obscured their more inventive moments. Songwriter John Stewart, Michael's brother, contributed several excellent originals, but the group lacked the charm of the Mamas And The Papas and Spanky And Our Gang, two acts sharing similar roots and styles. The quintet scored another US Top 40 hit with 'Let's Get Together', before breaking up in 1967. We Five have since reformed and split on several occasions, although several new arrivals replaced unwilling original members. Stewart and Jones subsequently formed country-folk group West, while the former later pursued an executive career with Capitol Records.

Albums: *You Were On My Mind* (1965), *Make Someone Happy* (1967), *The Return Of We Five* (1969), *Take Each Day As It Comes* (1977).

Weavers

This US folk group was formed in 1949, from artists with a background of traditional music and comprised Lee Hays (b. 1914, Little Rock, Arkansas, USA, d. 26 August 1981; vocals/guitar), Fred Hellerman (b. 13 May 1927, New York, USA; vocals/guitar), Ronnie Gilbert (b. vocals) and Pete Seeger (b. 3 May 1919, New York City, New York, USA; vocals/guitar/banjo). Previously Seeger and Hays had been members of the Almanac Singers with Woody Guthrie. Unlike many similar groups of the time, the Weavers were able to attain commercial acceptance and success, without having to compromise their folk heritage. Virtually all their record releases charted, a precedent for a folk

We Five

group. They have at times been credited with creating the climate for the post-war folk revival. Many songs became 'standards' as a result of the popularity achieved by the group, in particular 'Goodnight Irene', which sold one million copies in 1950. Other successful songs were, 'Kisses Sweeter Than Wine' and 'On Top Of Old Smokey', the latter remaining at number 1 for three months. Despite Seeger being blacklisted in 1952, and brought before the House of Un-American Activities Committee, the group still sold over four million records during that period. The Weavers disbanded the same year because of personal reasons as well as the pressures brought about by the McCarthy era. The group had lost bookings after being added to the blacklist of left-wing, or even suspected left-wing sympathizers at the time. In 1955, their manager Harold Leventhal, persuaded them to reunite for a Christmas concert at Carnegie Hall. Such was the success of the event that they continued to tour internationally for a few more years, while still recording for the Vanguard Records label. Despite the acclaim, Seeger was still able to combine a successful solo career but, by 1958, he had left the group. He was replaced in fairly quick succession by Erik Darling, then Frank Hamilton and finally Bernie Krause. The Weavers disbanded at the end of 1963, after 15 years together, and capped the event with an anniversary concert at Carnegie Hall. Travelling and personal ambitions were given as the reasons for the split. After the group left the music scene, there were many who tried to fill their space but none had the combination of enthusiasm and commitment that had made the Weavers such a popular act. Lee Hays, in his latter years confined to a wheelchair, died after many years of poor health in August 1981. In compliance with Hay's wishes, his ashes were mixed with his garden compost pile! Nine months earlier, the original line-up had joined together to film the documentary *Wasn't That A Time?* recalling the group's earlier successes.

Albums: *Folk Songs From Around The World* (c.50s), *Travelling On With The Weavers* (c.50s), *The Weavers At Home* (c.50s), *Almanac* (50s), *The Weavers At Carnegie Hall* (1956), *The Weavers At Carnegie Hall, Volume Two* (1960), *The Weavers Reunion At Carnegie Hall Volumes 1 & 2* (1963), *Songbook* (1965), *We Shall Overcome - Songs Of The Freedom Riders And The Sit-Ins* (c.60s), *Weavers On Tour* (1970), *Together Again* (1984). Compilations: *The Best Of The Weavers* (c.50s), *Greatest Hits* (1957), *Weavers Greatest Hits* (1970), *Best Of The Weavers* (1984).

Webb, Peta

b. 23 August 1946, Woodford Green, Essex, England. Webb is a singer in traditional Irish style, known for her ballad singing as well as her workings of Appalachian and women's songs. She started out performing at the Oxford University Heritage Folk Club from 1964-67, and started performing with the group Oak from 1970-73 on lead and harmony vocals. By contrast, Peta has also sung with a jazz group, the Al Ward Band, since 1971. Webb also played English dance band fiddle with Webb's Wonders from 1972-81. From 1973, having recorded *I Have Wandered In Exile*, Webb worked in a series of duos, first with John Harrison (formerly of the Watersons), then Alison McMorland and later, in 1981, fiddle player Pete Cooper. *Alison McMorland And Peta Webb* was voted among the UK Top 10 folk albums of the year, in *Melody Maker*, in 1980. Webb later joined Sisters Unlimited, an a cappella women's group featuring Janet Russell, Rosie Davis and Sandra Kerr. Webb has also provided tracks for a number of sampler albums on Topic Records. Peta continues to work as a solo performer, despite her other involvements, which have included bluegrass and country with the Armadillos, new country with the Crazy Hearts, and old time and bluegrass with the Marx Brothers and Rosa.

Albums: with Oak *Welcome To Our Fair* (1971), *I Have Wandered In Exile* (1973), *Alison McMorland And Peta Webb* (1980), with Pete Cooper *The Heart Is True* (1986), *The Magpie's Nest* (1989), with Sisters Unlimited *No Limits* (1991).

Wedlock, Fred

b. 23 May 1942, Bristol, England. Wedlock worked variously in a youth employment office, a department store and as a teacher before his growing popularity as a comic singer and raconteur prompted him to become a professional entertainer in the early 70s. The essence of his diverting evenings in Britain's folk clubs, arts centres and colleges was distilled on records issued mostly by independent companies such as Village Thing and Pilluck (sic). However, it was with Elton John's Rocket label in the 80s that gave him a yuletide hit with 'The Oldest Swinger In Town' - long a highlight of his stage act - and much airplay for its follow-up, 'Jobsworth'. This success however was a mere bonus in a career that has since embraced a Channel Four television showcase, *Wholly Wedlock*, and a BBC radio series with fellow west countryman Acker Bilk, as well as a 'day job' as a regional television presenter.

Albums: *The Folker* (1981), *Frollicks* (1981), *This Is (Out Of Wedlock)* (1981), *The Oldest Swinger In Town* (1981), *Fred Wedlock Live* (1982).

West

Formed in San Francisco in 1967, West revolved around guitarists Ron Cornelius and Michael Stewart, the latter of whom was previously a member of We Five. Lloyd Perata (guitar), Joe Davis (bass), Bob Claire and Jon Sagen (drums) completed the line-up featured on *West*, a gentle country, folk collection which contrasted the acid-rock preferred by many geographical contemporaries. *Bridges* offered a similar fare and having shed some of the MOR trappings prevalent on their debut, West emerged with a confident, contemporary sound. However, the members embarked on separate careers soon after its release. Michael, brother of singer/songwriter John Stewart, then resurrected We Five, while Cornelius found fame accompanying Leonard Cohen, and as a solo act.
Albums: *West* (1968), *Bridges* (1969).

West, Hedy

b. 6 April 1938, Cartersville, Georgia, USA. West's father was Don West, a trade union organizer during the 30s, and a well-known Southern poet. Her father's union activities gave her a wealth of songs to draw on, in particular the many mining songs that prevailed at the time. Although West played largely all-American traditional music, she did include contemporary pieces in her repertoire. She later recorded traditional songs, such as 'Barbara Allen', as well as folk standards like '500 Miles' and 'Shady Grove'. Many of the songs West knew had been handed down from previous generations of her family. She had learned to play piano while aged four, and turned to the banjo, the instrument she is best known for, when at school. She later took up the guitar. In 1959, after moving to New York City, she studied music at Mannes College. Like many others of the time, she found herself influenced by the folk movement. West sang at the Indian Neck Festival in 1961 and Manny Solomon of Vanguard Records was informed about her talent. *New Folks* included the Greenbriar Boys among others. Having experienced playing in the coffee houses, such as the famous Caffe Lena and Gerde's Folk City, West moved to Los Angeles and continued singing and eventually married there. She later emigrated to England, subsequently recording for Topic Records. She later relocated to Germany, recording *Getting Folk Out Of The Country* with Bill Clifton for Folk Variety Records.
Albums: with various artists *New Folks* (1961), *Hedy West Accompanying Herself On The 5-String Banjo* (60s), *Hedy West Vol.2* (60s), with Bill Clifton *Ballads* (1967), *Serves 'Em Fine* (1967), with Clifton *Getting Folk Out Of The Country* (1974), *Love, Hell And Biscuits* (1980), *Pretty Saro, And Other Songs*

From My Family (1981, reissue), *Old Times And Hard Times* (1981, reissue).

Wheeler, Billy Edd

b. 9 December 1932, Whitesville, West Virginia, USA. He grew up in coal-mining camps and his song, 'Coal Tattoo', which was recorded by Judy Collins, is based on what he saw around him. He collected folk songs himself and elements of both folk and country music can be heard in his songwriting. He performed with his guitar at school and college events, was in the US navy from 1957-58 and then became a schoolteacher. In 1958 a rock 'n' roll version of 'The Boll Weevil Song', which he called 'Rock Boll Weevil', was recorded by Pat Boone. He performed folk songs with the Lexington Symphony Orchestra in 1961. He then became a full-time professional performer. 'Rev. Mr Black', a narrative song about a travelling preacher, made the US Top 10 for the Kingston Trio in 1963, and they followed it with the story of 'Desert Pete'. Wheeler himself had a solo US hit with a song about an outside toilet, 'Ode To The Little Brown Shack Out Back'. His 1967 composition, 'Jackson', was successful for the duos, Johnny Cash and June Carter, and Nancy Sinatra and Lee Hazlewood. Other compositions include 'Blistered' (Johnny Cash), 'Blue Roses' and 'The Man Who Robbed The Bank At Santa Fe' (both Hank Snow). His *Nashville Zodiac* album was made with Doug Kershaw and includes three Kershaw's compositions. Wheeler continues to perform and says, 'I can't bear to think how empty my life would have been without my guitar.'
Albums: *Billy Edd: USA* (1961), with the Bluegrass Singers and the Berea Three *Billy Edd And Bluegrass Too* (1962), *Memories Of America* (1963), *The Wheeler Man* (1965), *Goin' Town And Country* (1966), *Paper Birds* (1967), *I Ain't The Worrying Kind* (1968), *Nashville Zodiac* (1969), with Shelly Manne *Young Billy Young* (1969, soundtrack), *Billy Edd Wheeler - Love* (1971), *The Music Of Billy Edd Wheeler* (1973), *Wild Mountain Flowers* (1979).

Whippersnapper

Formed in 1984, this group was fronted by Dave Swarbrick (b. 5 April 1941, London, England; fiddle, vocals). The rest of the group comprised Martin Jenkins (b. 17 July 1946, London, England; mandolin, flute, vocals), Chris Leslie (b. 15 December 1956, Oxford, England; violin, mandolin, mandola, vocals) and Kevin Dempsey (b. 29 May 1950, Coventry, West Midlands, England; guitar, vocals). Whippersnapper were not just a platform for Swarbrick's virtuosity on the fiddle, as was shown by the musicianship of the rest of the group. The albums contained a healthy mixture of

traditional tunes and original compositions. Jenkins, along with Dempsey, had formerly been a member of the group Dando Shaft, with whom he recorded five albums, and additionally he had recorded with Bert Jansch and the Geordie folk-rock group, Hedgehog Pie. Jenkins also recorded one solo album *Carry Your Smile*, released in 1984. Leslie had earlier recorded with Steve Ashley and Roy Bailey, and toured with All About Eve. Dempsey's career has seen him tour with Percy Sledge and the Marvelettes. *These Foolish Strings* contained outtakes and live material, and was released in cassette format only on the groups own WPS label, for selling at bookings. While they were on tour in 1989, Swarbrick left, but the group continued to perform, at home and abroad. Lesley and Dempsey recorded *Always With You* and Whippersnapper continue to tour as a three- piece outfit.
Albums: *Tsubo* (1984), *Promises* (1985), *These Foolish Strings* (1988), *Fortune* (1989), *Stories* (1991).

Whiskey Priests

Strongly influenced by the Pogues and the Men They Couldn't Hang, the Whiskey Priests evolved as a five piece in the late 80s around the nucleus of twins Gary and Glenn Miller, and Bill Bulmer. Their repertoire consisted of lively mixture of the traditional, and their own material, delivered in strong North East dialect. Two 1988 EPs, *No Chance* and *Grandfatha's Fatha*, indicated their future direction. The lyrics are based on their experience of growing up in County Durham. After the two EPs, they worked briefly as a trio, before expanding to include Pete French (Northumbrian pipes and fiddle), Mick Tyas (bass) and Steve Green (drums), and recorded their debut album, *Nee Gud Luck*, in 1989. The style remained uncompromising, and the power of the songs undiluted, but it was their last release for three years. A compilation of earlier recordings, and the new *Timeless Street*, heralded a resurgence in 1992, and this has been followed by extensive touring, and *Bloody Well Live*, a good example of their finely-honed punk-folk.
Albums: *Nee Gud Luck* (1989), *The First Few Drops* (1992), *Timeless Street* (1992), *Bloody Well Live*. (1993).

Whiskey, Nancy

b. c.1937, Glasgow, Scotland. Nancy started her career playing and singing traditional songs but later, during the skiffle music boom in the 50s, she moved south, with her repertoire of Scottish traditional songs. She was given the surname Whiskey having become associated with the song 'The Calton Weaver' whose chorus includes the line 'Whiskey, Whiskey, Nancy Whiskey'. An EP, recorded for Topic Records, *Nancy Whiskey Sings*, included the Irish rebel song 'The Bold Fenian Men' on the track listing, but this track did not appear on the record, having been substituted. Her major claim to fame came in 1957, when the Chas McDevitt Skiffle Group, featuring Nancy Whiskey, made the UK Top 5 with 'Freight Train'. They had a degree of success with a subsequent single, 'Greenback Dollar', which made the UK Top 30 the same year. In 1958, Nancy left the group to be replaced by Shirley Douglas, since when she has occasionally performed as a folk artist but appeared performing with McDevitt on UK television as recently as 1991.

Whiskeyhill Singers

This short-lived unit from the USA was formed in 1961 by Dave Guard ((b. 19 November 1934, Honolulu, Hawaii, USA, d. 22 March 1991), a former member of the Kingston Trio. The Whiskeyhill Singers also included Cyrus Faryar, Judy Henske and guitarist David 'Buck' Wheat, who had accompanied the Kingston Trio in concert. *Dave Guard And The Whiskeyhill Singers*, the group's only album, featured scholarly interpretations of such traditional material as 'Brady And Duncan', 'The Bonnie Ship The Diamond' and Woody Guthrie's 'Plane Wreck At Los Gatos'. Although the quartet contributed to the 1963 film score of *How The West Was Won*, they broke up barely a year after inception. Many critics and fans were unable to forgive Guard for his defection from the Trio, and the Whiskeyhill sound was somewhat uncommercial for the era. Faryar went on to form the Modern Folk Quartet, prior to beginning a solo career, while Henske recorded several albums before joining her husband Jerry Yester as a duo, and in the rock group Rosebud. Wheat joined Bud And Travis while Guard emigrated to Australia where he inaugurated several guitar workshops before returning to California to form a trio with Mike Settle (ex-Cumberland Three) and Alex Hassilev (ex-Limeliters). He also found time to write several children's fairy-tale books. Guard died in 1991.
Album: *Dave Guard And The Whiskeyhill Singers* (1962).

White, Bukka

b. Booker T. Washington White, 12 November 1906, Houston, Mississippi, USA, d. 26 February 1977, Memphis, Tennessee, USA. White learned guitar and piano in his teens, and hoboed from 1921, playing blues with artists such as George 'Bullet' Williams. In the mid-30s White was a boxer and baseball pitcher. White recorded for Victor in 1930, a largely unissued session including spirituals and the first of his breakneck train

imitations. Returning to Vocalion in 1937, he recorded his composition 'Shake 'Em On Down' and was given the misspelt billing which he always disliked. By the time 'Shake 'Em On Down' was a hit, White had been imprisoned in Parchman Farm for assault. There, he recorded two songs for the Library of Congress, and claimed to have had an easy time as a prison musician. However, when he recorded commercially again in 1940, he was clear that he had been traumatized by his experience. The result was a remarkable series of recordings, obsessed with prison, trains, drink, and death. The songs were poetic, complete and coherent, often with deep insights into their topics, their heavy vocal delivery perfectly complemented by fierce, percussive slide guitar. After his US Navy service during World War II, White settled in Memphis from 1944 onwards. In 1946, his second cousin B.B. King lived with him, learning perhaps less about music than about the blues singer's life. As white interest in blues increased, 'Fixin' To Die Blues' and 'Parchman Farm Blues' became cult songs. Rediscovered in 1963, White had retained most of his abilities, and was extensively recorded (including, for the first time, on piano). At his best, he could still produce stunningly inventive lyrics. White joined the folk club and festival circuit, performing across the USA, Canada, Mexico and Europe until the mid-70s, when illness enforced his retirement.
Album: *Big Daddy* (1974). Compilations: *The Complete Sessions 1930-1940* (1990), *Sky Songs* (1990), *The Legacy Of The Blues Vol. 1* (1991), *Aberdeen Mississippi Blues (1937-40)* (90s).

White, Josh

b. Joshua White, 11 February 1915, Greenville, South Carolina, USA, d. 5 September 1969, Manhasset, New York, USA. A grounding in church music stood Josh White in good stead, as it was something to which he returned at various points in a long career as blues singer and, later, folk entertainer. He learned guitar acting as a guide for blind street singers, and began his recording career at a young age. Between 1932-36, he recorded prolifically. The results often demonstrated a notable versatility, covering blues in local or more nationally popular idioms (sometimes under the pseudonym Pinewood Tom) or sacred material as the Singing Christian. In the mid-30s he moved to New York, where he found a new audience interested in radical politics and folk music. In retrospect, it seems as if he was diluting as well as tailoring his music for the consumption of white listeners who were at this time unused to hearing authentic black music. As the years went on, he learned a lot of new material, and turned his repertoire into an odd mixture, encompassing everything from traditional ballads like 'Lord Randall' to popular songs like 'Scarlet Ribbons', as well as protest songs and blues. He toured overseas in the post-war years and recorded extensively.
Selected albums: *The World Of Josh White* (1969), *Josh White With Molly Malone* (1974), with the Ronnie Sisters *Blues And Spirituals* (early 80s), *Joshua White 1936-41* (1989), *Joshua White (Pinewood Tom) Vol. 2* (1989).

Williams, Brooks

b. 10 November 1958, Statesboro, Georgia, USA. Williams began learning violin at three-years-old, moving on to guitar at the age of 10. It was not until his late teens that he started songwriting. He left his job as a teacher in 1986, and moved to Massachusetts, to take up music on a full-time basis. Beginning with appearances in colleges, bars and restaurants, he performed guest spots for such performers as Taj Mahal, David Bromberg, Maria Muldaur and the Band, especially in the north-eastern area of the USA. *North From Statesboro* produced a flood of good reviews, and national airplay, bringing Williams to a wider audience. His style combines a laid-back vocal alongside strong guitar patterns, occasionally using bottleneck. In August 1990, Williams was featured in an article on slide guitar players in *Acoustic Guitar* magazine. His follow-up, *How The Night-Time Sings*, released in 1991, has consolidated his position, and he now tours more extensively, having played at the Great Woods Folk Festival alongside Roger McGuinn and John Prine.
Albums: *North From Statesboro* (1990), *How The Night-Time Sings* (1991).

Williamson, Robin

b. 24 November 1943, Edinburgh, Scotland. After the Incredible String Band split in 1974, following almost 10 years of success, multi-instrumentalist Williamson departed for Los Angeles, USA. He has released a large number of albums, many with mystical subjects. In addition to his literary projects and solo offerings, Williamson still tours, both solo and with his Merry Band. He still has a strong feel for tradition, with some material almost akin to the fantasy writer, J.R.R. Tolkien. Williamson is involved in many aspects of the business, having provided soundtracks for television series, and music for theatre productions. In addition to his many album releases, Williamson has also produced a large number of books and story cassettes. He now divides his time between the USA and Britain.
Albums: *Myrrh* (1972), with the Merry Band *Journey's Edge* (1977), with the Merry Band *American Stonehenge* (1978), with the Merry Band

Glint At The Kindling (1979), Songs Of Love And Parting (1981), Music From The Mabinogi (1983), Legacy Of The Scottish Harpers (1984), Legacy Of The Scottish Harpers Vol.2 (1986), Winter's Turning (1986), Ten Of Songs (1988). Compilations: with the Merry Band Songs And Music 1977 (1986).

Further reading: English, Welsh, Scottish And Irish Fiddle Tunes, with flexi-disc 1976. Selected Writings 1980-83, with cassette 1984.

Story cassettes: The Fisherman's Son And The Gruagach Of Trick (1981), Prince Dougie And The Swan Maiden (1982), Rory Mor And The Gruagach Gair (1982), Music From The Mabinogi (1983), Five Humorous Tales Of Scotland (1983), Selected Writing 1980-83 (1984), Five Humorous Tales Of Scotland And Ireland (1984), Five Celtic Tales Of Enlightenment (1985), Five Bardic Mysteries (1985), Five Legendary Histories Of Britain (1985), Five Celtic Tales Of Prodigies And Marvels (1985), The Dragon Has Two Tongues (1985, film soundtrack), Five Tales Of Enchantment (1985), Songs For Children Of All Ages (1987), Music For The Newborn (1991).

Wilson, Roger

b. 22 July 1961, Leicester, England. Having studied graphic design at Wolverhampton Polytechnic, Wilson, playing guitar and fiddle, became a full-time musician in 1984. He played a wide variety of folk festivals and clubs, rapidly gaining a name for himself. Coupled with British Council tours of Pakistan and Malaysia, he has played extensively in Germany and Europe. Roger has also toured Scandinavia and the British Isles, with the Lost Nation Band, which includes himself, Sara Grey and Brian Peters. Wilson's debut release, on Harbourtown, The Palm Of Your Hand, was highly acclaimed in the folk music media. Since the initial impact of his appearance on the folk scene, he has continued with solo performing, session work, and working with his new band, Scam.

Albums: The Palm Of Your Hand (1988), with various artists Urban Folk Volume 1 (1991).

Winchester, Jesse

b. 17 May 1944, Shreveport, Louisiana, USA. After receiving his draft papers from the US Forces, Winchester moved to Canada where he settled. His self-titled debut album, produced by Robbie Robertson, was thematically reminiscent of the work of the Band with its evocation of life in the deep south of the USA. The moving, bittersweet memories described in 'Brand New Tennessee Waltz', plus its haunting melody line, persuaded a number of artistes to cover the song, including the Everly Brothers. Winchester's Third Down, 110 To Go was produced by Todd Rundgren, but in spite of its solid quality failed to sell. On Learn To Love

(1974), he commented on the Vietnam War in 'Pharoah's Army' and was assisted by several members of the Amazing Rhythm Aces. By 1976, Winchester was touring the USA, having received an amnesty from President Carter for his draft-dodging. He played low-key gigs abroad and continued to release albums, which veered slightly towards the burgeoning country rock market. His narrative love songs are effective and the quality of his writing is evinced by the number of important artists who have covered his songs, a list that includes Elvis Costello, Tim Hardin and Joan Baez.

Albums: Jesse Winchester (1970), Third Down, 110 To Go (1972), Learn To Love It (1974), Let The Rough Side Drag (1976), Nothin' But A Breeze (1977), A Touch On The Rainy Side (1978), Talk Memphis (1981), Humour Me (1988). Compilation: The Best Of Jesse Winchester (1988).

Wolf, Kate

b. 27 January 1942, Sonoma County, San Francisco, California, USA, d. 10 December 1986. Wolf was a songwriter-singer-guitarist who worked her home area and organized the Santa Rosa folk festivals. Her first albums, Back Roads and Lines On Paper, were recorded independently and released on her own Owl label. Those albums were made with a band named after a country song, Wildwood Flower, and although country and bluegrass feature in her work, Wolf is a contemporary folk artist. In 1979 she recorded Safe At Anchor for the Kaleidoscope label, which many claim to be her finest set. Wolf wrote and sang beautifully, clearly and perceptively about the preciousness of life and the precariousness of relationships. She was also a fine interpreter of others' material such as the slow version of Jack Tempchin's 'Peaceful Easy Feeling'(recorded by the Eagles), and John Stewart's 'Some Kind Of Love' on the live double-album Give Yourself To Love. In November 1985 she recorded a memorable television concert for Austin City Limits, which became An Evening In Austin. It was her last happy moment: she developed leukaemia and although she was not fit to record, she compiled the retrospective Gold In California. The title track of The Wind Blows Wild was recorded at her hospital bedside and she died in 1986. She had had no hits and her songs were largely unknown, but, gradually, the quality of her work has surfaced. Her husband, Terry Fowler - the subject of 'Green Eyes' - keeps her name alive. Her songs ironically include such titles as 'Love Still Remains' and 'Unfinished Life'.

Albums: Back Roads (1976), Lines On Paper (1977), Safe At Anchor (1979), Close To You (1981), Give Yourself To Love (1983), Poet's Heart (1985), The Wind Blows Wild (1988), An Evening In Austin

(1988). Compilation: *Gold In California* (1986).

Wolfstone

One of the hottest bands of the early 1990s, Wolfstone cheerfully blend Heavy Metal ideas with outright Highland jigging. Highly impressive, 'live', their transient studio membership evolved around a core of Duncan Chisholm (fiddle) and David Foster (bass). Chisholm totally reorganised their aims, emerging with the stable formation of Stuart Eaglesham (guitars), Struan Eaglesham (keyboards), Andrew Murray (guitars), and songwriter Ivan Drewer (vocals). *Unleashed* (1991), consisted of songs of tender simplicity and scorching reels. *The Chase* continued in similar vein and Wolfstone, now with Mop Youngson (drums) and Wayne MacKenzie (bass), looks ready to progress further.
Albums: *Wolfstone* (1988), *Wolfstone 2* (1989), *Unleashed* (1991), *The Chase* (1992).

Woods, Gay And Terry

Playing together in a duo during the late 60s, Gay and Terry Woods became pivotal figures in the Irish folk scene through their involvement with Sweeney's Men, Steeleye Span and Dr. Strangely Strange, whom they left at the end of 1970. Husband and wife, Gay and Terry, were ambitious mavericks at the adventurous end of folk rock. As the Woods Band, their debut album mixed traditional ballads and their own songs. They worked extensively in England and Europe, before disbanding and retiring to Eire. Subsequently, they signed with Polydor, and, with a familiar set of folk/rock musicians, recorded a series of increasingly experimental singer/songwriter albums. Gay's soft, tender vocal contrasted with Terry's lazy drawl and hypnotic Irish melodies. The finest of these is *The Time Is Right*, an appealing blend of acoustic/electric elements and intuitive compositions. *Tenderhooks* was cut for the small Mulligan label in Dublin, and was a much more upbeat piece of warm, rolling roots rock. Previously used to touring as an acoustic duo, the Woods once again assembled an electric band to promote it, and, although at the height of their creativity, decided to separate. Gay moved into prog ballad rock with Auto De Fe, and Terry temporarily revived the Woods Band before giving up music altogether. Some years later he emerged from retirement and joined the Pogues, where this enduring, rebellious musician continues to be influential.
Albums: *The Woods Band* (1971), *Backwoods* (1975), *The Time Is Right* (1976), *Renowned* (1976), *Tenderhooks* (1978).

Woolley, Shep

b. 15 October 1944, Birmingham, England. From an early age, Shep loved music, and played ukelele. His mother bought him a guitar in 1958 and he joined 15 others in a local skiffle group. In 1960, Woolley entered the Royal Navy, taking his guitar with him, and continued to play all over the world, at the same time organizing shows and groups. Woolley's first venture into a folk club came in 1969, when he was inspired by Bob Dylan and the songs of the American Depression. Writing his own songs, Shep found that he had a natural flair for humorous material, and jokes and monologues began to appear in his act. By 1973, he had essentially become a folk comedian, but he was also still a naval gunnery instructor, so, in 1975, Shep left the forces to concentrate on performing. In 1974, he appeared on *New Faces*, the television talent show. From 1975-85, Woolley presented the folk show on Radio Victory in Portsmouth, England. He has played all over the world and is regularly in demand for festivals. Woolley tends to play less folk clubs these days, concentrating on summer seasons and concerts. A naturally funny man, he deserves to become as widely known as others of the genre.
Albums: *Pipe Down* (1972), *Songs Of Oars And Scrubbers And Other Dirty Habits* (1973), *Goodbye Sailor* (1976), *First Take* (1980), with various artists *Reunion* (1984), *On The Button* (1986), *Delivering The Goods* (1990).

Wrigley, Bernard

b. 25 February 1948, Bolton, Lancashire, England. Wrigley never quite made the commercial breakthrough to the same degree as other comedian/folk artists, such as Billy Connolly, Richard Digance and Mike Harding. He was a self-taught guitar player who 'discovered' folk clubs as a result of the Bob Dylan boom during the 60s. As half of a duo called Dave And Bernard, he gave up being a Customs and Excise Officer and went professional in 1969 to provide a documentary, *The Bolton Massacre*, at the Octagon Theatre, Bolton. By 1970, the duo had split, so Wrigley joined the original Ken Campbell roadshow, during which time he wrote 'Knocking Nelly', 'Our Bill' and 'Concrete Mixer'. Actor Bob Hoskins was also a member of the roadshow at the time. Wrigley has sung and acted ever since, appearing on television and in a Royal Command Performance. In 1991, Wrigley appeared as Estragon in *Waiting For Godot* at the Octagon Theatre, alongside Mike Harding who played Vladimir. He has also done a great deal of television work, appearing in subject's as diverse as an Alan Bennett film and a Guinness advertisement. An example of his humour can be found in the popular 'Robin Hood And The Bogey Rolling Contest' which contains the lines 'There was Little John, who was not so small/in fact he was quite tall. If he had been small he'd have been called Big John/which makes no sense at all'.

Albums: *The Phenomenal Bernard Wrigley* (1971), *Rough And Wrigley* (1973), *Songs Stories And Elephants* (1976), *Ten Ton Special* (1977), *The Bolton Bull Frog* (Live-1981), *Rude Bits* (1985), *Instrumental Album* (1988), *Wanted-Live!* (1991). Compilation: *The Phenomenal Bernard Wrigley/Rough And Wrigley* (1988).

Wurzels

Originally Adge Cutler And The Wurzels, this English West Country group first scored a minor hit in 1967 with the comic 'Drink Up Thy Zider'. Following Cutler's tragic death in a car crash in 1974, Tommy Banner, Tony Baylis and Pete Budd soldiered on as the Wurzels. Producer Bob Barrett was impressed by their country yokel parodies of well-known hits and persuaded them to provide comic lyrics to Melanie's 'Brand New Key', which emerged as 'Combine Harvester', a surprise UK number 1 in the summer of 1976. The trio almost repeated that feat with their reworking of the continental hit 'Uno Paloma Blanca' retitled ' I Am A Cider Drinker'. Although they only achieved one more success with 'Farmer Bill's Cowman' (based on Whistling Jack Smith's 'I Was Kaiser Bill's Batman') they continued to appear occasionally on British television shows and maintain their popularity on the UK club circuit.

Albums: *Adge Cutler And The Wurzels* (1967), *Adge Cutler's Family Album* (1967), *Cutler Of The West* (1968), *The Wurzels Are Scrumptious* (1975), *The Combine Harvester* (1976), *Golden Delicious* (1977), *Give Me England* (1977), *I'll Never Get A Scrumpy Here* (1978), *I'm A Cider Drinker* (1979). Compilation: *The Very Best Of Adge Cutler And The Wurzels* (1977), *Greatest Hits* (1979), *Wurzels* (1981).

Wyndham-Read, Martin

b. 23 August 1942, Crawley, Sussex, England. This singer and guitarist compiled a number of recordings of British and Australian songs. Martin left England in 1960 to live in Australia. In 1961, he was already playing in coffee bars in Melbourne and Sydney. He built up a large repertoire of Australian songs during this time and also recorded a number of albums for the Score label, commencing with *Moreton Bay*, the title synonymous with the imprisonment of convicts in Australia in a place now called Brisbane. Martin also recorded a live album, during the mid-60s, with Gary Shearston. Returning to Britain in 1967, Wyndham-Read recorded *Leviathan* for Topic Records, with such luminaries as Bert Lloyd, Dave

Swarbrick, and Martin Carthy. *Ned Kelly And That Gang* on Trailer was Martin's first solo UK release. The album features two classics of the genre in 'The Wild Colonial Boy', and 'Moreton Bay'. On *The Valiant Sailor* and *Sea Shanties*, Martin was joined by Alistair Anderson, Frankie Armstrong, and Roy Harris. The later *Emu Plains* featured Nic Jones on fiddle, while *The Old Songs* included contributions from John Kirkpatrick and Sue Harris. *Maypoles To Mistletoe* features a cycle of seasonal songs and includes the much performed and recorded 'Dancing At Whitsun'. Martin regularly tours worldwide, appearing at festivals and clubs in the USA, New Zealand, Hong Kong, and India.

Albums: *Moreton Bay* (1963), *Will You Go Lassie Go?* (1964), *Australian Songs* (1964), *A Wench, A Whale, And A Pint Of Good Ale* (1966), *Bullockies, Bushwackers And Booze* (1967), *Leviathan* (1967), *Ned Kelly And That Gang* (1970), *Martin Wyndham-Read* (1971), *Great Australian Legend* (1971), *Songs And Music Of The Redcoats* (1971), *Harry The Hawker Is Dead* (1973), *The Valiant Sailor* (1973), *Sea Shanties* (1974), *Maypoles To Mistletoe* (1975), *Ballad Singer* (1976), *English Sporting Ballads* (1976), *Andy's Gone* (1979), *Emu Plains* (1981), *A Rose From The Bush* (1984), *The Old Songs* (1984), *Across The Line* (1987), *Yuletracks* (1986), *All Around Down Under* (1988), *Muscles On A Tree* (1991).

Y

Yarbrough, Glenn

b. 12 January 1930, in Milwaukee, Wisconsin, USA. Yarbrough was best known as lead vocalist of the 60s folk group the Limeliters. He also recorded numerous albums and scored a Top 20 single under his own name in 1965. Yarbrough sang in church as a child and became a folk singer in the mid-50s. He was discovered in Chicago and performed on the national folk circuit, eventually starting his own coffeehouse, the Limelite, in Colorado Springs, Colorado, with partner Alex Hassilev. Along with Lou Gottlieb, the two formed the Limeliters, who became very successful in the early 60s, placing 10 albums on the US top charts between 1961 and 1964. Yarbrough left the Limeliters in 1964 and recorded the theme song from the film *Baby The Rain Must Fall*, which reached US number 12 in

1965. Yarbrough eventually had 10 chart solo albums by the end of the 60s but only one further chart single. On three of his albums, *The Lonely Things*, *Each of Us* and *Glenn Yarbrough Sings The Rod McKuen Songbook*, the poet Rod McKuen wrote the lyrics. Yarbrough continued to record throughout the 70s and 80s, without repeating his commercial success of the 60s. In the late 80s Yarbrough re-formed the Limeliters with new members.

Albums: *Time To Move On* (1964), *One More Round* (1964), *Come Share My Life* (1965), *Baby The Rain Must Fall* (1965), *It's Gonna Be Fine* (1965), *The Lonely Things* (1966), *Live At The Hungry i* (1966), *For Emily, Wherever I May Find Her* (1967), *Honey & Wine* (1967), *Best* (1967), *The Bitter And The Sweet* (1968), *Let The World Go By* (1968), *We Survived The Madness* (1968), *Each Of Us Alone (The Words And Music Of Rod McKuen)* (1968), *Glenn Yarbrough Sings The Rod McKuen Songbook* (1969), *Somehow, Someway* (1969), *Jubilee* (1969), *Looking Back* (1970), *My Sweet Lady* (1974), *Reunion* (1974), *Marilyn Child And Glenn Yarbrough* (1978), *Glenn Yarbrough* (1978).

Yester, Jerry

b. Joshua Tree, California, USA. A producer, songwriter and performer, Yester first gained attention as a member of the Easy Riders. From there he joined a folk ensemble, the Inn Group, which was absorbed, wholly, into the original New Christy Minstrels. Objecting to their commercial approach, the singer left the group to found the Modern Folk Quartet. Initially a traditional act, the MFQ later embraced electricity to become a fully-fledged folk-rock attraction. Yester also produced material for the Association, a harmony group which featured his brother, Jim. Yester played guitar on Bob Lind's international hit, 'Elusive Butterfly' (1966). The artist then began a solo career with two imaginative singles, before joining the Lovin' Spoonful in 1967, in place of guitarist Zalman Yanovsky. Paradoxically, the two musicians remained close friends and together produced Tim Buckley's *Happy Sad* and Yanovsky's *Alive And Well In Argentina*. Yester then formed a duo with his wife, Judy Henske, the result of which was the atmospheric collection, *Farewell Alderbaran*. This in turn inspired their short-lived rock group, Rosebud, since when Yester has preferred production work, most notably with Tom Waits. However this talented individual has more recently resumed performing with a reformed MFQ.

Albums: with Judy Henske *Farewell Alderbaran* (1969), *Just Like The Big Time* (1990 - released only in Japan).

Yetties

The Yetties' original line-up comprised Bonny Sartin (b. Maurice John Sartin, 22 October 1943, near Sherborne, Dorset, England; percussion), Mac McCulloch (b. Malcolm McCulloch, 12 December 1945, London, England; guitar), Pete Shutler (b. Peter Cecil Shutler, 6 October 1945, Mudford, near Yeovil, Somerset, England; accordion/penny whistle/concertina/bowed psaltery) and Bob Common (b. 26 December 1940; vocals). The four eventually formed the Yetminster and Ryme Intrinseca Junior Folk Dance Display Team to play for dance evenings. Such was the problem with the name of the group, that one evening, for simplicity, they were introduced as the Yetties, and it stuck. They first performed in 1961 and shortly after this the group began Morris dancing with the Wessex Men, based in Yeovil, Somerset, and made their first appearance at the Sidmouth Folk Festival. The group also made subsequent regular appearances at the Yeovil Folk Dance club. They appeared on record in 1968, on an album recorded live at the Towersey Festival, along with other artists, but *Fifty Stones Of Loveliness* was their first proper release as a group. This was followed a year later by *Who's A-fear' d*. On some of the early Yetties recordings, a fiddle player, Oscar Burridge played, though he was essentially part-time. The group appeared on a Cyril Tawney album in 1972, *Cyril Tawney In Port*, providing background music and vocals. Another 1972 release, *Bob Arnold, Mornin' All* featured the group providing background music and vocals for Bob Arnold. The same year, the group's version of *The Archers* theme tune, 'Barwick Green', was first used for the Sunday omnibus editions of the series on BBC radio. Bob Common left the group in 1979 and the Yetties continued as a trio.

Roger Trim (fiddle), had played in various duos and trios before joining the Yetties. He joined as a full-time member of the group in 1984, but departed in 1991, leaving the group to continue once more as a trio. 1988 saw the start of the group's project, *The Musical Heritage Of Thomas Hardy*, incorporating the Hardy family manuscripts, and at one time using Hardy's own violin in the work. Originally recorded in 1985 as an album, the project continues to be performed at festivals and concerts and on radio and television, and as a result, a 1988 release materialized. Despite having played worldwide, the Yetties have never lost the almost boyish enthusiasm which pervades their music, and still retain a loyal following.

Albums: *Fifty Stones Of Loveliness* (1969), *Who's A-Fear' d* (1970), *Keep A-Runnin'* (1970), *Our Friends* (1971), *Dorset Is Beautiful* (1972), *All At Sea* (1973), *Up In Arms* (1974), *The Yetties Of Yetminster* (1975), *The World Of The Yetties* (1975), *Let's Have A Party*

(1975), *The Village Band* (1976), *Up Market* (1977), *Dorset Style* (1978), *Focus On The Yetties* (1978), *In Concert* (1979), *A Little Bit Of Dorset* (1981), *A Proper Job* (1981), *Roger Trim On The Fiddle* (1982), *Cider And Song* (1983), with John Arlott *The Sound Of Cricket* (1984), *The Banks Of Newfoundland* (1984), *Top Of The Crops* (1985), *The Yetties* (1986), *The Musical Heritage Of Thomas Hardy* (1988), *Rolling Home* (1991), *Looking For The Sunshine* (1992). Compilations: *Play It Again* (1989), *Singing All The Way* (1989).

Young Tradition

One of the leading practitioners of the English folk revival, the Young Tradition was formed in 1964 by Heather Wood (b. 1945; vocals), Royston Wood (b. 1935, d. 8 April 1990; vocals/tambourine) and Peter Bellamy (b. 8 September 1944, Bournemouth, Dorset, England, d. September 1991; guitar/concertina/vocals). The trio continued the oral harmony tradition of the influential Copper Family, while simultaneously enjoying the patronage of the Soho circuit and the emergent 'underground' audience. Their choice of material and powerful harmonies captured what was regarded as the essence of rural folk music. The group completed three albums during their brief sojourn. Their debut included guest performances from Dave Swarbrick and Dolly Collins and their much heralded *Galleries*, highlighted the divergent interests which eventually pulled them apart. Several selections featured support from David Munrow's Early Music Ensemble, a trend towards medieval perspectives which Bellamy felt unwelcome. Unable to make a commercial breakthrough, the Young Tradition split up in 1969, although Heather and Royston Wood remained together to record *No Relation*. The latter musician enjoyed a brief association with the Albion Country Band, before forming Swan Arcade. He died in April 1990, following a three-week coma after being run over by a car in the USA. Heather Wood teamed up with Andy Wallace to form the duo, Crossover. Pete Bellamy, meanwhile, enjoyed a successful solo career. This was abruptly cut short in 1991 when Bellamy committed suicide.

Albums: *The Young Tradition* (1966), *So Cheerfully Round* (1967), *Galleries* (1968). Compilations: *The Young Tradition Sampler* (1969), *The Young Tradition* (1989).

Young, Ed And Lonnie

Brothers Ed (b. c.1908, Como, Mississippi, USA, d. 17 July 1974, Como, Mississippi, USA) and Lonnie Young were discovered during folklore research in 1959. They were neither the first nor the finest of the Como fife and drum musicians to be recorded, but they were the first to show the increased Africanism (especially syncopation) and improvisation of the music played by the generation after Sid Hemphill, and the first to be brought to wider notice, playing the Newport Folk Festival and having their recordings issued on album.

Albums: *Sounds Of The South* (1960), *Roots Of The Blues* (1961), *Blues Roll On* (1961).

Z

Zumzeaux

This short-lived group, comprised Neti Vaandrager (b. 21 August 1957, Rotterdam, The Netherlands; fiddle/vocals), Chris Haigh (b. 17 August 1957, Huddersfield, West Yorkshire, England; fiddle/vocals/mandolin), Bernard O'Neill (b. 4 September 1961, Dublin, Eire; double bass/vocals) and Ashley Drees (b. 25 May 1956, Paddington, London, England; cittern). Formed in 1987, the various members came from a variety of musical backgrounds. Haigh had been heavily into western swing, while O'Neill had been playing jazz. Drees' earlier days of playing Irish traditional music in Dublin, had led to a teaming up with the Dutch born Texan Vaandrager. Playing a blend of cajun, swing, and folk music, the group impressed audiences from the start, and in 1988, they won the Ever Ready national busking competition at the BBC Radio Show. Their prize was a day in CBS Rooftop Studio which, with production help from Andrew Cronshaw, saw *Wolf At Your Door* emerge. Vaandrager has since joined cajun band the Companions Of The Rosy Hours as well as Vivando, and the Poozies. O'Neill has joined the trio George Bernard Shaw. Haigh performs occasionally with Jenny Beeching; while Drees is involved in various Irish music duos and record production.

Album: *Wolf At Your Door* (1989).

Add Ons
Additional entries deserving a brief mention.

Amazing Catsfield Steamers
Reputed to represent the biggest ever recorded 'crack', based on Sunday night revels at The United Friends pub, Ninfield, Sussex. Some 23 musicians cohabit in this semi-electric grouping.
Album: *United Friends* (1983).

Arizona Smoke Revue
A folk rock group, influenced by bluegrass music, with a constantly changing line-up. Regular members include, Pete Zorn (banjo/vocals), Phil Beer (fiddle) and Paul Downes (guitar). Their recording sessions are noted for the number of famous folk guest musicians sitting in.
Selected album: *Thundering On The Horizon* (1981).

Ancient Beatbox
In their spare time, two members of Blowzabella, Paul James and Nigel Eaton, applied electronics and mixers to French dance tunes, and produced a turntable dance hit, with 'My Eyes Are Filled With Clouds', which featured a vocal by ex-Monsoon singer Sheila Chandra.
Album: *Ancient Beatbox* (1989).

Avalon
A chunky Scottish folk/rock group, similar in style to Horslips. Their recordings are very boisterous, with the accent on stomping sing-alongs.
Selected album: *Rocky Roads* (1986).

Backroom Boys
A transient group of folk/rock veterans who play R&B and their own material. Doug Morter (guitar) and Jerry Donahue (guitar) are regular members, and other recruits have included Rick Kemp (bass) and Julian Dawson (harp/vocals).
Album: *Brief Encounters*.

Beggars Hill
A large, semi-electric band, comprised of several friends, that made one album of traditional and contemporary material. It now commands a high price from serious record collectors.
Album: *Beggars Hill* (1976).

Bwchadanas
Formed in Wales, this formative electric band has a nucleus of members from the students of Bangor University. Their music is flowing and breezy.

Bwchadanas was the proving ground for latent Welsh revivalists such as Sian James.
Album: *Cariad Cywir* (1984).

Cajun Moon
This trio of 70s musicians featured Brian Golbey (fiddle) and Jon Gillespie (keyboards), although its main focus was the songs of Alan Taylor (guitar), who was already an established artist. Their repertoire was a freewheeling, bouncy mix of originals, including 'Lady Of Pleasure', which has often been revived by others.
Album: *Cajun Moon* (1976).

Callies
A contemporary group of singer/songwriters from Newcastle, England, which is mainly noted for the presence of Billy Mitchell, who later led Jack The Lad.
Album: *On Your Side* (1971).

Caught On The Hop
A popular four-piece electronic group from Wigan, England, which is based around keyboards rather than bass and drums. The members' often quoted ambition is 'to be a cross between the Human League and the Bothy Band.'
Album: *Frozen Flames* (1986).

Chartists
A Welsh 'social conscience' folk/rock group, their material contains the recurring themes of industrial disputes and other social issues.
Selected album: *Cause For Complaint* (1987).

Clayton, Vikki
An ex-vocalist with Ragged Heroes, Clayton has since gone on to a successful solo career in the Midlands of England, with a band containing Home Service leader Graeme Taylor. Her voice has been compared to that of Sandy Denny, as a result of which she is often invited to sing with Fairport Convention.
Album: *Lady Found* (1988).

Cluster Of Nuts Band
A lively ceilidh derived rock music group, who enjoyed a reasonably high profile in the early 80s. Their motto was 'folk with a poke.'
Album: *Fridge In The Fast Lane* (1983).

Contraband
A formative Scots electric grouping responsible for nurturing members of Ossian, the Easy Club, Tannahill Weavers and vocalist Mae McKenna.
Album: *Contraband* (1973).

Corkscrew

A group from Bristol, England whose arrangements and approach, as captured on their only recording, indicated complex, commercial edged folk/rock. Sadly their promise remained unfulfilled.
Album: *For Openers* (1979).

Dr. Cosgill

A brilliant young band that held the torch for electric folk by playing medieval tunes as if they were the Stranglers. Their recorded highlight came with the 1981 single 'Benediction'/'Douce Dame'. Although they disbanded in the same year, their influence was felt a couple of years later with the 'rogue folk' movement. By then, leader Paul James had joined Blowzabella.

Dalriada

An electronic, boppy outfit that revitalise traditional Scottish material in a modern manner. Vocalist Colin Kennedy possesses a distinctive, grandiose voice which suits the epic ballads the band choose to play.
Album: *All Is Fair* (1991).

Den

A thumping folk/rock dance troupe from Brittany, based around veteran brothers Jacky and Patrick Molard. Their music is firey, pipe-driven and universally tuneful.
Album: *Just Around The Window* (1989).

Desperate Danz Band

An energetic Scots dance music group, with a free-wheeling approach to the trational Jimmy Shand type big band tunes.
Album: *Send Three And Fourpence We're Going To Dance* (1989).

Dingle Spike

A London Irish folk band, playing stock, second generation material. They have labelled themselves as 'folk/rock', but beyond an electric bass there is little evidence to support this.
Selected album: *Dingle Spike* (1978).

Douglas, Blair

Runrig founder who was actually in the band during two separate incarnations, and graduated quite naturally to keyboards from accordion. The music he now produces solo is atmospheric and Highland based, though his past still overshadows his current activities.
Selected album: *Celtology* (1984).

Eavesdropper

Early 80s electric band, much touted in certain quarters as the future of Celtic rock. The band's instrumentals moved along impressively, but matters were less convincing with the vocals.
Album: *The March Hare* (1984).

Elecampane

A strange, theatrical folk/rock unit, whose members dressed and acted as well as playing instruments. At one stage they furnished their audiences with an authentic Punch and Judy routine. Such gigs are remembered as odd, but appealing events.
Selected album: *When God's On The Water* (1975).

Electric Ceilidh Band

A promising Gaelic rock band that could have followed Runrig's success given better breaks. They were founded by Blair Douglas, athough he left before they recorded their album.
Album: *Electric Ceilidh Band* (1983).

Fastest Bat

Formed in Birmingham, England, in the mid-80s, this folk/rock band is in the tradition of Spud and Jack The Lad. Despite some good time, unpretentious drinking music, they have only released one promising album.
Album: *Cold, Haily, Windy Night* (1985).

Folk Och Rackare

A radical Swedish group, with stunning vocals from Carin Kjellman. The band began acoustically, later turning into a full-blown rock band and preceding the current new wave of Swedish roots acts. *Rackbag*, is a dark, brooding folk/rock effort, with a guest appearance by Richard Thompson.
Selected album: *Rackbag* (1985)

Folque

A Norwegian version of Steeleye Span, Folque had a strong, ringing sound, their music based on rich Norse folk legend. They disbanded in 1984, but reformed in 1992 as an acoustic four-piece unit, playing their old repertoire in a back-to-basics format.
Selected album: *Fredlos* (1980).

Frogmorton

A folk/rock band whose members wrote their own, characteristic material and distinguished themselves in the 70s by having no fiddle and not relying on juiced up jigs to create an atmosphere.
Album: *At Last* (1976).

Gone To Earth

Formed in Manchester, England, this 80s group of thrash folksters cut several rumbling singles (predominantly for Liverpool indie label Probe) and changed members constantly. One regular was fiddler and Christy Moore fan Dave Clarke, who wrote songs about Salford and drinking profusely.
Selected album: *Vegetarian Bullfighter* (1987).

Harvey, Richard

The ex-Gryphon keyboard genius who cut albums of classical recorder music whilst still in the band. He then started to compose jingles and television scores. His credits include the soundtrack to Channel 4's *GBH*. His album, *A New Way Of Seeing*, is the result of a commission from ICL. Despite working in a new area, it seems a logical extension of Gryphon's work.
Selected album: *A New Way Of Seeing* (1984).

Hickory Wind

A down-home, American bluegrass band who decided that they loved British folk rock so much they recorded a whole album of it. They even imported Dave Mattacks to play on half of the tracks.
Selected album: *Crossing Devils Bridge* (1978).

Hollandse Dance Band

A hoofing Dutch unit - a sort of continental Albion Dance Band - who played in towns and village squares or rural areas.
Album: *Spring Tig* (1982).

Hookey Band

An unconvincing electric band that grew out of many Oxfordshire folk and dance groups, claiming lineage to Dave Pegg (Fairport Convention) and Chris Leslie (Whippersnapper). One for completists only.
Album: *Making A Song & Dance About It* (1983).

Host

Eamon Carr, Johnny Fean, and Charles O'Connor regrouped with a couple of other friends post-Horslips to try to recapture the spirit of that band. It worked too; their sole album is dark and mystical, a rock concept written around the last witch burning in Eire. Sadly O 'Connor left and though the others briefly carried on, the group fell apart.
Album: *Tryal* (1982).

Hunter Muskett

A fine band of singer/songwriters, presenting a rich blend of pseudo ballads. The group was also notable for the inclusion of future Magna Carta/Albion guitarist Doug Morter.
Selected album: *Hunter Muskett* (1973).

Iona

Christian Celtic band with, of all things, ex-members of Kajagoogoo in their ranks. They produced moody, atmospheric recordings, but live they retained a rockier edge. Iona may yet prove capable of following Clannad and Capercaille on to bigger and better things.
Selected album: *Book Of Kells* (1990).

Islandica

A commercial folk/pop band from Iceland, supported as musical ambassadors for their country by Icelandair and the Icelandic Tourist Board. Their music is lightly electrified, featuring both the traditional, and their own folksy compositions.
Album: *Rammislensk* (1990).

Johnson, Robb

An excellent political protest singer from south London, who has been compared to a younger Leon Rosselson. He commands respect from fellow writers and singers who cover much of his material, although he still seeks a wider audience.
Selected album: *Overnight* (1992).

Kebnekaise

A Swedish communal 70s folk/rock band, characterised by ringing strings, spacey guitar and an ability to bring a fresh approach to old dance tunes. The music was pioneering, but the group remained little-known outside Sweden. Had they enjoyed greater exposure they could easily have been more widely influential.
Selected album: *Kebnekaise* (1990).

K-Passa

Simon Edward's voice, songs and accordion playing are the foundation for K-Passa's position as the favourite live folk-based act in Bristol, England, and for his work with Richard Thompson, Pete Morton and the Boothill Foot-Tappers. Local recognition led to their appearance on the main stage at the 1992 Glastonbury Festival. Their blend of folk, Cajun, dub and reggae are eminently displayed on the live cassette, *2 From The Front*.
Album: *2 From The Front* (1992).

Kormoran

A long-running Hungarian group that performs ancient folk tunes in a rock style. They had a hit single in their homeland, but very few of their releases can be obtained outside of Hungary.
Selected album: *Live In Holland* (1986).

Le Serf, Cathy

A vocalist on the Fiddler's Dram hit, 'Daytrip To Bangor', Le Serf went on to sing for nearly eight years with the Albion Band, and in 1985 with

Fairport Convention. Consequently, her solo album contained many well known electric folk musicians. She has since retired from music altogether.
Album: *Surface* (1985).

Lick The Tins
A well-crafted folk/pop group who became turntable favourites with a Celtified version of 'Can't Help Falling In Love'. Their excellent repertoire was characterised by a bustling energy. 'Accept no substitutes', ran their press blurb, but they disbanded soon afterwards.
Album: *Blind Man On A Flying Horse* (1987).

Little Big Band
A pseudonym for the talented blues musician, Rob Gray, from Manchester, England. Between high level gigs, he busks in city centre shopping arcades.
Album: *Little Big Band* (1989).

Loudest Whisper
A band of obscure Irish folk singer/songwriters, whose records now command unusually high prices.
Selected album: *Loudest Whisper* (1981).

McDermott's Two Hours
A thumping, jig along Celtic pub band, that began on the Levellers' label. They featured a high percentage of political protest songs in their repertoire, but have since disappeared from the music scene.
Album: *The Enemy Within* (1989).

McDonald, Shelagh
One of the leading females of the early 70s songwriter boom, McDonald signed to B&C where she cut a couple of coyly appealing, self-penned and traditional albums. She sang a particularly fine version of the traditional ballad 'Dowie Dens Of Yarrow', but has been absent from the music scene for some time.
Selected album: *Stargazer* (1971).

Mara (Tansey's Fancy)
This pleasingly diverse outfit took their later name, Tansey's Fancy, from their energetic front lady. Together they played folk tunes and jazz in an *avant garde*, irreverent manner. For a while the band included bass player Danny Thompson. Recordings throughout their career are wild and wilful.
Selected album: *On The Edge* (1987).

Miro
Leading lights of the late 80s acoustic music revival, Miro reflected pastoral traditions with a string section, guitars and Nick Drake-influenced songs,

composed by the leader, Roddy Harris. The press were fond of using phrases like 'Music for a Kensington bedsit' to describe their appeal.
Selected album: *Angel N.1.* (1990).

Mountain Ash Band
The Mountain Ash Band produced yet another of those 'old friends get it together' albums, forming a folk/rock band from Colin Cripps' musical about an old tramp, Job Senior. They made the album, did the show, and then vanished. The music was very gritty, and at times reminiscent of Bob Pegg.
Album: *The Hermit* (1975).

Mushroom
This group was an early, if somewhat Horslips-like attempt to marry hippie drug songs with Irish traditional dance tunes. Both the name of the band and the cover of the album reveal a good deal about the music they played.
Album: *Early One Morning* (1973).

N.R.T.
Formerly No Right Turn, N.R.T. are a hard working band from Derby, England, band who have an excellent repertoire of acidic roots rock. The focal point, Jayne Marsden, has a distinctive voice, put to effective use on a series of pacy releases which leave their folk prologues far behind. One of the best unsigned bands on the circuit.
Selected album: *New Rising Tide* (1992).

Na Fili
A band from Cork, playing straight Irish traditional music with depth and dedication. The name translates from old Irish as 'poets'. Certainly it is music with a rhythm and a rhyme.
Selected album: *Na Fili 3* (1973)

New Victory Band
A highly talented group of country dance musicians, New Victory Band comprise three pairs: Pete and Chris Coe, Roger and Helen Watson, John and Susie Adams. They are one of those legendary bands that did much to loosen the woolly pully and tweed skirts image of English dance.
Album: *One More Dance And Then* (1978).

Ophichus
A group from Wiltshire, England, with varying line-ups, who played 'rural English rock'. Often whimsical and certainly literate, they created music from rustic isolation and could well have earned the tag 'crusty' before the Levellers.
Album: *Pronounced Offeickus* (1989).

Oscar The Frog

A highly regarded band, surprisingly neglected. Oscar The Frog had far more energy than most of the competition of the time. Despite definite power pop overtones, they deserve consideration for adapting the Ian Dury hit to 'Hit Me With Your Morris Stick'.
Album: *Oscar The Frog* (1980).

Ougenweide

A punchy German electric outfit, who wrote in their national folk style and adapted Bohemian drinking songs and ancient harmonies in a series of very successful, endemic records.
Selected album: *Eulenspigel* (1976).

Peeping Tom

A well-established rocking ceilidh band from Coventry, England, who have sworn never to play anything but dances. They did however become involved in a lively adaptation of *Lark Rise To Candleford* (1990) with the Criterion Theatre.
Album: *A Sight For Sore Eyes* (1993).

Perry, Ray

Born in Lancashire, England, this writer and solo performer began drawing on traditional and 60s/70s songwriting influences after being a member of several failed rock bands. Increasingly prolific, his main release, *Common Knowledge* (Crow), amply displays his impressive ability.
Album: *Common Knowledge*.

Pisces

A contemporary trio of Plainsong-like guitar strummers, best known for delivering Richard Digance to the waiting world.
Album: *Pisces* (1971).

Piirpauke

A jazz/rock band from Finland that take tunes from anywhere in the world and adapts them to their own style. Arguably, they predated the whole world music movement, and, because of their locality, benefitted little from it. Sakari Kukko (saxophone), still leads this excellent, but obscure group.
Selected album: *Algazara* (1987).

Poormouth

A vehicle for the Irish-tinged rock songs of Jackie McAuley (ex-Them and Trader Horne). Their sound is a composite of heavy guitar and jigs and reels. The membership varies according to touring and recording demands.
Album: *Gaelforce* (1989).

Prelude

A light folk trio from Gateshead, England, chiefly covering contemporary material. They recorded a surprise hit single with their harmonious cover of Neil Young's 'After The Goldrush'.
Selected album: *After The Goldrush* (1974).

Pressgang

A noisy group of punk folksters from Reading, England, led by Damian Clarke, which change image with each successive release. A quote that sums up their musical ethos: 'We want to play it louder than Deep Purple'.
Selected album: *Rogues* (1989).

Radiator

Lindisfarne in everything but name. Led by Alan Hull, the band had two drummers, and operated directly before Lindisfarne reformed. Members were recruited from Lindisfarne and Snafu, and their music was rockier than much of Hull's work, revealing something of his thinking at the time.
Album: *Isn't It Strange?* (1977).

Ragged Heroes

An eight-piece electric folk band named after an Albion Band track. Vocalist Vikki Clayton went on to a solo career and guested with Fairport Attraction.
Album: *Annual* (1983).

Raindance

A reel 'n' reggae troupe from Oxford, England, they wrote their own material, but still played some jigs. Much more of a draw in France, the band were quite surprised to discover they had made a folk record. They just thought it was Raindance music.
Album: *Raindance* (1987).

Rattle 'n' Reel

A group formed of Irish ex-pats in Manchester, England, with Mike Harding's brother in charge. Their debut was melodic, and mainly featured their own songs, while many of their contemporaries were covering traditional material. A good, promising live act.
Album: *Not Just Anyone* (1992).

Red Jasper

Led by 'screaming' Davey Dodds, Red Jasper mix folkist sentiments with out and out heavy metal. A kind of Anthrax-go-rustic, they are restricted, but when 'live', it's all guitars, leather and thunder.
Selected album: *Sting In The Tale* (1990).

Rock, Salt & Nails

A product of the embryonic Shetland rock scene, Rock, Salt & Nails are a young, energetic group who smoothly reel and jig. They are currently building up a dedicated, folksy following north of the border. Their island heritage influence everything they write.
Album: *A Little Drop Of Red*.

Scafell Pike

An electric folk band with English and Swedish members. They displayed dubious taste by covering essential folk classics such as 'The Roast Beef Of Old England'. Despite this, they earned a contract with both Epic and Phonogram.
Selected album: *Lord's Rake* (1974).

Second Vision

After he left the Albion Band in 1979, Ric Sanders joined ex-Soft Machine colleague John Etheridge in the jazz fusion, Second Vision. Although they improvised, they were equally liable to end up reeling. Their sole album showed much promise, which sadly remained untapped. The band also included ex-Gryphon and future Home Service bassist Jon Davie and keyboardist Dave Bristow.
Album: *First Steps* (1980).

Skibberean

A Swiss folk/rock band, whose members sing British traditional material. Their accents lead to some confusing lyrical moments, especially when they tackle Geordie songs like 'Byker Hill'.
Album: *Get Up And Dance* (1980).

Spirogyra

Formed in Canterbury, England, Spirogya was one of a group of young bands signed to B&C Records at the same time as Steeleye Span. Writer Martin Cockerham and vocalist Barbara Gaskin - later to enjoy a hit with Dave Stewart - are the best known members. Their sound was similar to early Strawbs, and their records sounded whimsically English. Gaskin's voice gave them a pure, unsullied air.
Selected album: *Old Boot Wine* (1972).

Strange Folk

An eccentric, knockabout group, which included Mike Willoughby and Mike Gavin playing a mixture of skiffle environmental protest material. They discovered the folk scene for two summers, played the festivals, drove about in an old van, made music on anything available, recorded an album, and then split up.
Album: *Unhand Me You Bearded Loon* (1988).

Thursaflokkurim

An Icelandic rock band, in English, Thursaflokkurim means The Flock Of Giants. Heavily influenced by their national heritage, they created the first Icelandic folk/rock music. Their sound is distinctive and individual, if a little inaccessible at first. Further listening is rewarding.
Selected album: *Pursabit* (1988).

Tonight At Noon

The Human League of folk rock, Scots brothers Pete and Gavin Livingstone masterminded extreme Scottish sounds through sequencers and relays. Fiddler Pete has a thick burr of a vocal which ideally matches their stirring, patriotic sounds.
Selected album: *Down To The Devils* (1988).

Tower Struck Down

Rising from the debris of a punk outfit, Tower Struck Down, from Crewe, England, have gathered a loyal following for their live shows. A mixture of English, Celtic and Eastern European influences was displayed on their debut *Piggy In The Middle*.
Album: *Piggy In The Middle*.

Truss And Bucket Band

Despite an unhealthy name, this group had a lively commercial sound. Like many bands of the period they grew from dances and halls into a concert setting. Bass player Andrew King was an excellent songwriter, his numbers predominantly sombre and serious. His fellow members lightened the tone with a touch of good time, alcoholic bonhomie. Consequently they were one of the most complete folk groups of the early 80s.
Album: *Truss & Bucket Band* (1983).

Trunkles

A band from East Anglia, England, that electrified pure folk in a very respectful, but energetic manner. All very English and genteel.
Album: *Traditional* (1978).

Turasakis, Mark

Turasakis, aka Mark T., has worked solo, and with an esoteric backing band, the Brickbats. With the latter, tunes from Europe, Asia, and Africa reprocessed as eccentric, folk/jazz creations. In 1990, Mark T. returned to solo gigging, turning his attention to British material and attempting to present it in a radical format.
Selected album: *Johnny There* (1986).

TV Smith

A singer-songwriter, who was a member of the 70s punk band, the Adverts. In 1992 he released the solo album, *March Of the Giants*, on Cooking Vinyl.

It marked a return to form for his poignant writing and arrangements, and fused punk sensibility with gentle guitar, vocal and strings.

Album: *March Of The Giants* (1992).

Varda, James

This UK singer/songwriter released one album in 1990 and toured with Roy Harper before returning to teaching in 1992. *Hunger* (Murmur Records), gained good reviews, and was favourably compared to Roger McGuinn. Varda's songs are full of dark imagery and introspective observations. The album also included contributions from Roy's son, Nick Harper.

Album: *Hunger* (1990).

Webber, A.J.

A contemporary female, singer/guitarist, who performs in cabaret, as well as folk clubs. Webber has, however, earned the mainstream image of a folk singer, covering songs by Mike D'Abo and Jimmy Webb. Her albums are appealing despite the sometimes coy delivery.

Selected album: *A.J. Webber* (1976).

We Free Kings

A gleeful, raggle taggle acoustic Scottish group, politically active, their ideological stomping made them darlings for a while in certain sections of the pop press.

Album: *Hell On Earth & Rosy Cross* (1987).

We Saw The Wolf

A sonic, noisy folk band from New England, USA, who take equal inspiration from Siouxsie And The Banshees, the Adverts and Malicorne. Their eclectic music is highly individual and rewarding, although, as the comparisons suggest, not always comfortable to listen to.

Selected album: *Six Songs For Dirt Piggin'* (1991).

You Slosh

A powerful group dealing primarily in Celtic mood music. Piper Troy Donockley composed long, involved pieces for guitars and ethnic instruments (whistle/pipes/flute). The sound made by the other members of the band was big and exciting. An immensely popular college group, in late 1991 they mysteriously disbanded, just when they were starting to receive national attention.